Surrealist Women: An International Anthology

THE SURREALIST REVOLUTION SERIES
Franklin Rosemont, Editor

A renowned current in poetry and the arts, surrealism has also influenced psychoanalysis, anthropology, critical theory, politics, humor, popular culture, and everyday life. Illuminating its diversity and actuality, the Surrealist Revolution Series focuses on translations of original writings by participants in the international surrealist movement and on critical studies of unexamined aspects of its development.

Surrealist Women

AN INTERNATIONAL ANTHOLOGY

Edited with Introductions by
Penelope Rosemont

The Athlone Press London

First published in Great Britain 1998 by
THE ATHLONE PRESS
1 Park Drive, London NW11 7SG

British Library Cataloguing in Publication Data
A catalogue record for this book is available from the British Library

ISBN 0 485 30088 5

Printed and bound in the United States of America

To my mother, Mamie Krekule

Each part of Nature
accords with the whole of it.

—Spinoza

Contents

1. The First Women Surrealists, 1924–1929

2. In the Service of Revolution, 1930–1939

3. Neither Your War nor Your Peace:
THE SURREALIST INTERNATIONAL, 1940–1945

4. Surrealism versus the Cold War, 1946–1959

5. *The Making of "May '68" and Its Sequels*

6. Surrealism: A Challenge to the Twenty-First Century

Illustrations

Acknowledgments

Naturally my greatest debt is to the surrealist women whose writings and artwork make up this book, and most especially to those who—through correspondence and discussion—graciously provided me with information regarding their own and other women's participation in the Surrealist Movement: Eileen Agar, Hilary Booth, Elisa Breton, Emmy Bridgwater, Carmen Bruna, Leonora Carrington, Susanna Coggeshall (Susy Hare), Jayne Cortez, Rikki Ducornet, Aube Elléouët, Nicole Espagnol, Anne Ethuin, Alice Farley, Silvia Grénier, Marianne van Hirtum, Nelly Kaplan, Elisabeth Lenk, Mary Low, Joyce Mansour, Alena Nádvorníková, Ivanir de Oliveira, Mimi Parent, Elaine Parra, Nancy Joyce Peters, Katerina Piňosová, Nicole E. Reiss, Thérèse Renaud, Françoise Sullivan, Eva Švankmajerová, Toyen, Marie Wilson, and Haifa Zangana.

What I owe to André Breton can hardly be summed up in a few words, but I hope my gratitude will be evident throughout this book. His inspiration and thoughtful encouragement were decisive factors in shaping my life.

Special thanks to Rikki Ducornet, Guy Flandre, Edouard Jaguer, Mary Low, Michael Löwy, Conroy Maddox, Nancy Joyce Peters, Katerina Piňosová, Myrna Bell Rochester and my husband, Franklin Rosemont, all of whom supplied me with so much information and helped in so many other ways that they could almost be considered coeditors of this anthology.

Thanks to Richard Anders and Heribert Becker, for information on surrealism in Germany; Elisa Breton, for information on the contents of Nadja's letters in her possession; Carmen Bruna, for background on surrealism in Argentina; Leonora Carrington, for her recollections of Jacqueline Lamba and Remedios Varo; Eugenio Castro, J. F. Aranda, and Luis Garcia-Abrines, for material on surrealism in Spain; Her de Vries, for his biographical sketch of Gertrude Pape; Elie-Charles Flamand, Edouard Jaguer, Gérard Legrand, and

Michel Zimbacca, for their recollections of Jacqueline Senard and the proposed journal, *La Mante surréaliste*, in the early 1950s; Guy Flandre, for details on Elisa Breton, Marianne van Hirtum, and Toyen; David Gascoyne, for sharing his memories of Sheila Legge; Enrique Gomez-Correa, for information on the history of surrealism in Chile; Bruno Jacobs, for details on surrealism past and present in Sweden; Edouard Jaguer, for data on Anneliese Hager, Vera Hérold, Maruja Mallo, Jeanne Megnen, Drahomira Vandas, Hélène Vanel, and many others; Ted Joans, for interesting anecdotes about Elisa Breton and Joyce Mansour; Abdul Kader El Janabi, for data on Ikbal El Alailly and surrealism in Egypt and elsewhere in the Arab world; Susanna Coggeshall, Gerome Kamrowski, Philip Lamantia, and Clarence John Laughlin, for their recollections of surrealism in New York in the 1940s; Edith Smith, for her reminiscences of surrealist activity in Paris in 1948–1949; Sergio Lima, for details of the history of surrealism in Brazil (especially on Leila Ferraz and Maria Martins) and elsewhere in South America; Mary Low, for her reminiscences of Marcelle Ferry; Conroy Maddox, for a mass of information on surrealism in England from the 1930s on; Isabel Meyrelles, Mario Cesariny, and Artur do Cruzeiro Seixas, for information on surrealism in Portugal; Pierre Naville, for his recollections of Renée Gauthier and of surrealist interest in jazz in the 1920s; Henri Pastoureau, for data on Fanny Beznos, Vera Hérold, Simone Yoyotte and the *Légitime Défense* group, and Hélène Vanel; Katerina Piňosová, for information on women in surrealism in the Czech Republic; Antonia Rasicovici, for her letters on women in surrealism in Romania in the 1930s and '40s; Thérèse Renaud and Françoise Sullivan, for information on the automatist movement of Montreal; Gérard Rosenthal, for his recollections of Renée Gauthier; André Thirion, for responding at length to my queries about Simone Kahn, Denise Lévy, and Yolande Oliviero; Nanos Valaoritis, for details on surrealism in Greece; and Marie Wilson, for her reminiscences of Elisa Breton and surrealism in Paris in the early 1950s.

I am deeply grateful to Jayne Cortez, Guy Ducornet, Rikki Ducornet, Paul Garon, Michael Löwy, Nancy Joyce Peters, Myrna Bell Rochester, and my husband Franklin, for reading and commenting on various drafts of the introductions.

Several historians and other scholars generously made their work-in-progress available to me. Thanks to Nancy Deffebach, for sharing her important research on Alice Rahon; Hugh Ford, for information on Nancy Cunard; Daniel Guèrin, for his reminiscences of Simone Kahn Collinet; Libby Ginway, for details on Elsie Houston; Renée Riese Hubert, for details on Valentine Penrose, Alice Rahon and others; Michel Remy, for information on surrealism in England in the 1930s and '40s; Myrna Bell Rochester, for sending helpful

Toyen, *At a Certain Hour,* oil with collage, 1963. Photograph by J. Hyde, Paris. Courtesy of M. Guy Flandre and Maitre Louis Labadie.

articles and bibliographies, and for interviewing Dominique Desanti about her early interest in surrealism; Marie-Agnès Sourieau, for details on Suzanne Césaire and Lucie Thésée; Michael Stone-Richards, for documents on the early history of surrealism in Czechoslovakia; and Dale Tomich, for data on the *Légitime Défense* and *L'Etudiant noir* groups in 1930s Paris, and on the 1940s *Tropiques* group in Martinique.

Thanks also to Russell Maylone, Special Collections, Northwestern University Library; Christine Crowther, The Swiss Institute, New York; Eumie Imm Stroukoff, The Museum of Modern Art Library, New York; Cathy Henderson, Harry Ransom Humanities Center, University of Texas at Austin; Carey E. McDougall, Mattatuck Museum in Woodbury, Connecticut; and to the staffs of the Ryerson Library, The Art Institute of Chicago (which houses the important Mary Reynolds Collection), the Chicago Public Library, the University of Illinois Library in Urbana, and the Columbia University Oral History Project in New York.

To all the translators whose efforts appear in these pages, and especially those who did work specifically for this anthology—Gisela Baumhauer, Rachel Blackwell, Her de Vries, Guy Ducornet, Rikki Ducornet, Erin Gibson, Walter Gruen, Miriam Hansen, Natalie Kenvin, Nicole Knight, Jean R. Longland, Katerina Piňosová, Myrna Bell Rochester, Franklin Rosemont, Eloise Ryder, and Greta Wenziger—my warmest appreciation.

Many others contributed to this book in various ways, by facilitating communication with authors or their estates, passing on bits of information, answering questions, checking facts, and other acts of kindness. I am grateful to all of them. They include Gertrude Abercrombie, Branko Aleksič, Paul De Angelis, Enrico Baj, Mary Beach, Robert Benayoun, Jean Benoit, Rita Bischof, Vane Bor, Micheline and Vincent Bounoure, Paul and Mari Jo Buhle, Nicolas Calas, Jean-Claude Charbonel, Vèvè Clark, Tristan DeHarme, M. G. Devise, Eva Effenbergerová, Marcel Fliess (Galerie 1900–2000), Charles Henri Ford, Mrs. Simon Fraser, Laura Fronty, Paul and Beth Garon, Virginia Goldstein, Mel Gooding, Giovanna and Jean-Michel Goutier, Amparo and E. F. Granell, Walter Gruen, Jean-Pierre Guillon, Tom Gutt, Miriam Hansen, Jeremy Jenkinson, Alain Joubert, Konrad Klapheck, Djordje Kostič, Geoffrey Lawson, Dick Leutscher, Jean-Luc Majouret, Man Ray, Samir Mansour, Herbert Marcuse, Floriano Martins, Fabrice Maze, George Melly, John S. Monagan, Lygia and Gellu Naum, Guillermo de Osma, Euzhan Palecy, Antony Penrose, Dominique Rabourdin, David R. Roediger, Sylvie Sator, Georges Sebbag, Natalia Fernández Segarra, Louise Simons, Catherine Vasseur, Veronica Volkow, Susan Ware, ruth weiss, Pablo Weisz-Carrington, and Francis Wright.

At various stages of this project, indispensable technical assistance was provided by Paul Garon, Lisa Oppenheim, Constance Rosemont, Sally Kaye Rosemont, and Joel Williams: *Merci beaucoup!*

And finally, thanks to Ali Hossaini Jr., Sharon Casteel, Leslie Doyle Tingle, Madeleine Williams, Zora Molitor, and Laura Young Bost at the University of Texas Press, for their many good suggestions and great patience.

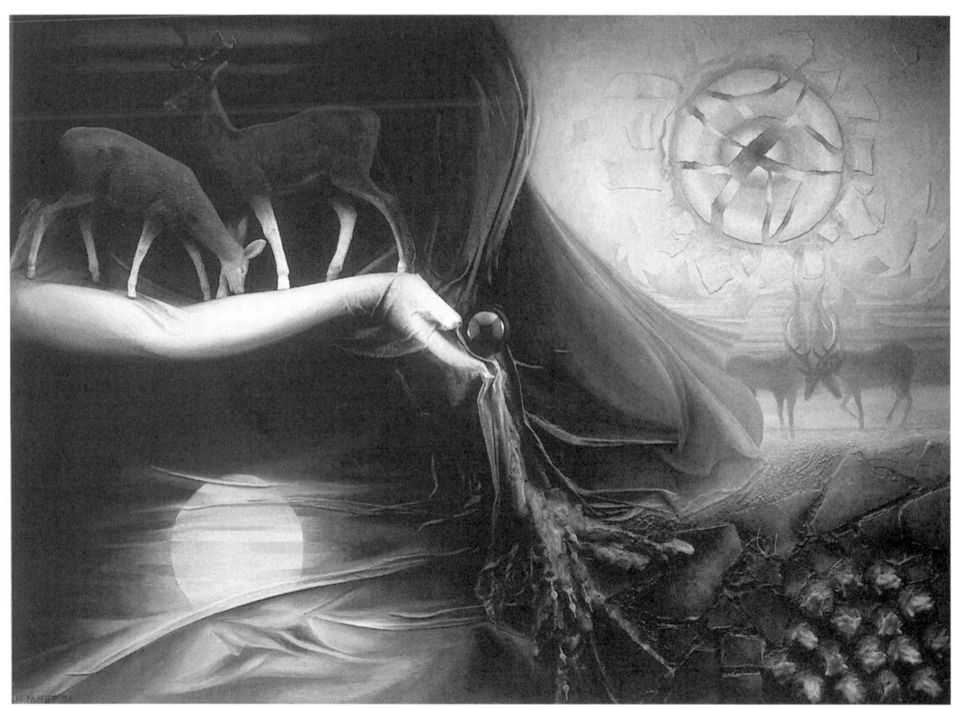

Mimi Parent, *Come,* 1978. Courtesy of the artist.

INTRODUCTION

All My Names Know Your Leap

Surrealist Women and Their Challenge

Knock hard. Life is deaf.
—Mimi Parent

Although the first women of surrealism have been almost entirely overlooked in the historical and critical literature, clearly they were a bold, imaginative, and remarkable lot. Even before surrealism's first *Manifesto* appeared in Paris in 1924, women were active in the movement, and they have been expanding and illuminating its universe ever since.[1] In all the arts and major genres of writing, women helped develop surrealism's radical poetic/critical outlook and thus helped make it what it was and is. To ignore their contributions is to ignore some of the best of surrealism.

This book seeks to bring to light as much as possible the quality, range, diversity, and vitality of women participants in the international Surrealist Movement. Although the contributions of women have been acknowledged and in some cases celebrated within the movement itself, they are hardly known outside it. In the United States, the few books devoted to the topic of women and surrealism are narrowly concerned with a dozen or so "stars"—mostly painters and photographers whose work has finally, and most often posthumously, attained some standing in the art market.[2] As a result, women surrealists whose principal vehicle of expression is the written word have been especially neglected. This neglect, in turn, has perpetuated old stereotypes and other misapprehensions of the surrealist project. Generalizations about surrealism based entirely on painters are bound to be misleading, because surrealism has never been primarily a movement of painters. Indeed, if the evidence of surrealism's numerous women poets and thinkers has been suppressed, how could the prevailing conceptions of surrealism be anything but false?

I hope that this gathering of poems, automatic texts, dreams, tales, theoretical articles, declarations, polemics, games, and responses to inquiries will help correct this distortion by revealing some of the many ways in which women have enriched surrealism as a ferment of ideas, an imaginative stimulus, a liberating critical force, and a practical inspiration to poetic, moral, and political insurgency.

Unlike most twentieth-century cultural and political currents, the Surrealist Movement has always opposed overt as well as *de facto* segregation along racial, ethnic, or gender lines. From the very first issue of *La Révolution surréaliste,* movement publications have featured writings by women alongside those of their male comrades. Works by women artists were regularly included in surrealist exhibitions. As one perceptive commentator has pointed out, "No comparable movement outside specifically feminist organizations has had such a high proportion of active women participants" (Short 1980, 56).[3] Moreover, until very recently most of the literature on women surrealists was written by other surrealists, male and female. If these women remain little known to the larger reading public it is because critics and scholars have been shirking their responsibilities.

Rebelling against the exclusion of women from patriarchal institutions, including art and the recounting of intellectual history, the women's liberation movement of the sixties and early seventies stimulated wider interest in the women of surrealism.[4] More recently, in the absence of mass-based radical social movements and in keeping with the rightward trend in U.S. and international politics, the focus on individual women artists has sometimes taken a conservative or reactionary turn. Certain critics and curators have attempted to isolate women surrealists from the Surrealist Movement as a whole, not only by reducing their work to the traditional aesthetic frameworks that surrealists have always resisted but worse yet by relegating them to a subbasement of the art world known as "Women's Art." Ironically, the old (mostly male) critics who ignored or minimized women in their studies of surrealism are not that different from these newer (often female) critics who ignore or minimize surrealism itself in their studies of women who took part in it. Each of these one-sided and erroneous views reinforces the other, and both prop up the insidious fiction that surrealism is yet another "Men Only" movement. Those who perpetuate such misunderstandings are missing much of what is most unique and momentous in surrealism.

Women who never renounced their youthful commitment to surrealist egalitarianism—Meret Oppenheim, Toyen, Anne Ethuin, and others—have strongly opposed this tendency toward segregation and have expressly refused to take part in books or exhibitions that sanction it. As Ethuin has written, declining to contribute to one such "No Men Allowed" collection, "I'm sorry, but not being a Moslem I have no taste for harems. Moreover, I have never thought that art and poetry could have a sex. On days when I feel the urge to write or create images, I do not decide before I begin that I am going to make 'a woman's work.' I have lived and worked for forty-seven years in a perfectly mixed milieu and I have no intention of changing now."[5]

The orientation of the present anthology has nothing in common with the divisive agendas that Ethuin rejects. My aim here has not been to separate the sexes or to exclude men, but rather to include more women than have ever been included before in an anthology of surrealism. The fact is, apart from the rare anthologies issued by the surrealists themselves, women have almost always been left out.[6] Well over two-thirds of the women included here have never been represented in any anthology; many of these writings have never been reprinted since their original publication. In all but a few of the hundreds of works on surrealism in English, women surrealists are barely even mentioned.[7] The exclusion of women from the existing compilations warrants—indeed, compels, if only for the sake of historical accuracy—an attempt to restore balance by emphasizing what so many others have denied.

It is essential, moreover, that the recovery of surrealism's lost voices not do violence to the ideas and inspirations that motivated them. Unfortunately, the few books that do acknowledge, to some extent, women's activity in surrealism tend to be less than scrupulous in their accounts of surrealism as a body of thought and an organized movement. My intention in putting together this mass of heretofore inaccessible material has not been to project fashionable new theories, much less to subject the recent literature on surrealism to a detailed critique, but simply to try to learn what the many women involved in surrealism have had to say for themselves.

What is different about this anthology is that here, for the first time, an unprecedentedly large number of surrealist women are allowed to speak *in their own voices* and in a specifically surrealist context—which is, after all, the context they chose for themselves. This anthology is thus the opposite of isolationist, for its guiding purpose is rather one of *reintegration*. By making these writings available at last, I hope to make it impossible—or at least inexcusable—for students of surrealism to continue to ignore them. I want first of all to call attention to an impressive number of important surrealist writers who for various reasons have not received the attention they deserve. The fact that they happen to be women helps explain why they have been ignored outside the movement, just as it also affects what surrealism has meant to them. I try to show not only what they took from surrealism but also what they gave to it; how they developed it, used it for their own purposes, played with it, strengthened it, and endowed it with a universality it could not have attained without them.

This anthology is arranged chronologically in six sections, covering (1) surrealism's beginnings as an organized movement, 1924–1929; (2) its rapid internationalization, 1930–1939; (3) its further internationalization, despite severe handicaps, during World War II, 1940–1945; (4) its postwar regroupment and survival as a radical "underground" during the Cold War, 1946–1959; (5) its worldwide resurgence, starting in the early 1960s; and (6) surrealism today. Each section includes a short introduction tracing the history of surrealism in that period, focused on the evolving role of women in the movement. Each individual represented in the book is in turn introduced by a brief biobibliographical headnote.

With this general introduction, I first attempt to provide some necessary background, beginning with a summary of surrealism's basic aspirations and principles—a summary which I hope will help clear up widespread misperceptions. Next, I set forth the criteria used in preparing this anthology, explaining who is included in it and why, as well as why others have not been included. A survey of surrealism's precursors—concentrating on women, who as usual have been slighted in the critical literature—is followed by a brief examination of the sexual politics of the first, largely male generation of surrealists in Paris in the 1920s. Finally, after considering some of the many ways in which the recovery of surrealism's lost voices profoundly challenges the "conventional wisdom" about surrealism—especially in the United States, where uncomprehending hostility to the movement has been entrenched for so long[8]—I conclude with some observations on the contemporary significance of these writings.

SURREALISM: WHAT IT IS AND WHAT IT IS NOT

> Can one explain the magic of life to someone who cannot perceive it in the smallest everyday things?
>
> —Rosa Luxemburg

All through this book women speak of surrealism in vibrant images: as natural process, great bear skin, voyage, tightrope of our hope, potlatch, and festival. Surrealism has never let itself be locked up in the dungeons of narrow definition. It has neither dogma nor catechism. Before one can grasp what is at stake in surrealism, one must first perceive that the many cages in which journalists, critics, and its other enemies keep trying to confine it are in fact empty and that surrealism is elsewhere.

To start at the beginning, with what is perhaps the single most common ments. All seem to have played "Exquisite Corpse" and other surrealist games. Most practiced automatic writing or recorded their dreams. Some also attended—how regularly does not appear to have been noted—the group's meetings, generally held twice a day: at noon (often at the Bretons' apartment at 42 rue Fontaine) and in the evening at a suitably disreputable café.[7]

Reports are scanty as to the degree to which women shared in the many surrealist demonstrations, disruptions, escapades, and other forms of "direct action." It is not clear, for example, whether they took part in the now-celebrated sabotage of the Saint-Pol-Roux banquet in 1925.[8] Cunard's article on the disruption of a Diaghilev ballet a year later seems to be the only published on-the-spot account of a surrealist protest written by a woman participant in the 1920s. It is certain, however, that all of surrealism's woman pioneers actively engaged in many other day-to-day surrealist activities, especially activities of refusal, such as not going to church, not saluting the flag, and not providing information to the police. As for not voting—a fixture of surrealist etiquette from the beginning—this was almost too easy for women, whose right to vote was in fact denied by French law until 1944. Significantly, in France in the twenties and thirties, the various parties of the extreme Left—Communists of all factions (Stalinist, Souvarinist, Trotskyist, etc.), the revolutionary syndicalists, and the Socialist Party as well—regarded women's suffrage as a probable disaster in a country which, like France, had an overwhelmingly peasant (and therefore uneducated and easily manipulated) population; in such conditions, these radicals argued, votes for women would benefit only the reactionary parties (Catholic, Royalist, Fascist). A prominent advocate of votes for French women was Pope Pius XI, a close associate of Mussolini (Anderson and Zinsser 1989).

Surrealists, for their part, shunned what they regarded as the hypocritical pseudo-democratic fraud of bourgeois elections long before becoming active in the revolutionary workers' movement. Even later, during the French Surrealist Group's prolonged involvement in Marxism-Leninism, their antiparliamentarianism remained intact. This basically anarchist orientation was evidently shared by the women in the group. In any case, no evidence has been found suggesting that any woman surrealist in France ever expressed even the slightest interest in women's suffrage, which undoubtedly seemed to them to be a meaningless reform in a period of war and revolution.[9] They did not want a mere vote, they wanted *life*—full, intense, and adventurous.

The first women surrealists certainly enjoyed an exciting freedom, intellectually and otherwise, that most women of their time and place scarcely even dared to dream about. As radical outsiders flouting the rules of a repressive society, they were probably models for many younger women and objects of envy for many more. At the same time, however, these women were somewhat less than full equals in the Surrealist Group itself and, strictly speaking, may not even have been considered—or considered themselves—full-fledged members. Although several had taken part in group activities prior to the publication of the first *Surrealist Manifesto* in 1924, none were included in that book's list of the nineteen who proclaimed their "absolute surrealism." With two exceptions—a letter to the anarchist paper *Le Libertaire,* signed by eleven surrealists, including Simone Kahn Breton and Gala Eluard; and a congratulatory note addressed to anarchist assassin Germaine Berton from Simone Breton, Louis Aragon, and Max Morise—the many surrealist collective declarations issued in those years appeared without women signatories.[10] The full-page homage to Germaine Berton in *La Révolution surréaliste* no. 1, which featured photographs of "all the collaborators," included such nonmembers as Freud and Giorgio de Chirico, but not Renée Gauthier or Simone Breton, who collaborated on the issue, or any other women. Twelve titles appeared under the Editions Surréalistes imprint in the twenties, but none by a woman. A "snowball" by Nadja—a liquid-filled glass ball, of the kind often used as a paperweight—titled "The Lovers' Soul," was announced in *La Révolution surréaliste* no. 8 in 1926, but for reasons that are not clear was not issued.[11] None of the shows at the Galerie Surréaliste in the 1920s featured work by a woman artist.[12]

The fact that women were only rarely in the forefront of surrealist activity in those early years does not mean that they played no role in the theoretical and practical development of the movement. The specific contributions of women during surrealism's first years is a topic demanding further research. So little is known of Gauthier, Beznos, and the near-phantom Suzanne that we can only guess at their impact. Mentions of these women by other surrealists, although not numerous, suggest that their influence was by no means negligible. Indeed, if we consider what Breton later called "the modern preoccupations that we regard as major"—love, dream, revolution, and knowledge—it is clear that the first women surrealists made important contributions in each of these areas (Breton 1967, 68). Suzanne Muzard's response to the group's 1929 inquiry on love so impressed Breton that he simply added a postscript to it, stating his complete agreement with her. It is no small thing that Renée Gauthier's dream was one of the first published in that journal which placed so much emphasis on the importance of oneiric activity. More than any other text by a woman surrealist in the twenties, Gauthier's flamboyantly erotic dream prefigures the assertive dynamism of such later women surrealist writers as Joyce Mansour, Nelly Kaplan, and Carmen Bruna.

Historians have ignored the politics of women in the Surrealist Movement, especially in its early years, but we have good reason to think that at least some women in the group did much to hasten surrealism's fruitful encounter with Marxism. It is true that no women took part in the 1925–1926 formal group discussions on the question of political action or the discussions later in 1926 on whether the surrealists should join the Communist Party.[13] The fact remains that four of the first women involved in surrealism—Beznos, Kahn, Lévy, and Penrose—distinguished themselves as revolutionary militants in working-class organizations, and a fifth, Cunard, became a celebrated publicist for far Left elements of the African diaspora. Beznos was a Communist activist when most male surrealists were still neophytes. According to one contemporary's account, Kahn was the only person in the surrealist milieu in those years who had actually read all of Marx's *Capital*.[14] Before the decade's end, Lévy enjoyed the esteem and friendship of Leon Trotsky and eventually translated some of his writings as well as works by Marx and Bukharin (Naville 1977, 479–481). Penrose went to Spain to join the workers' militia during the 1936 revolution. Cunard, who lived for a time at the surrealist phalanstery at 54 Rue du Chateau, is described by one of her roommates there, André Thirion, as "always ready for serious discussion" (Thirion 1975, 215) and was known to have been deeply interested in all forms of social radicalism. It is impossible to believe that such women did not take part in the political debates that engaged the whole group during the late twenties.

Revolutionary, too, though in a different sense, was the unorthodox behavior of the early women surrealists—Valentine Penrose, for instance. Her resolute cultivation of poetic insolence, a refusal to say and do the ordinary and expected, paralleled if not equaled the far better-known conduct of Benjamin Péret, celebrated in surrealism as the insulter of priests, and Antonin Artaud, whose outrageous provocations ultimately led to the madhouse. Cunard, too, excelled in the art of carrying nonconformity to daring extremes.

In the domain of knowledge, Denise Lévy—for some time the only one in the surrealist milieu who was fluent in German—played a key role: it was she, more than anyone else, who introduced her surrealist friends to the work of Hölderlin and other German romantics, writers immediately recognized by the group as major precursors of surrealist thought (Naville 1977, 479–481).

Above all, in matters of knowledge, there is the exemplary Nadja, the real-life heroine of Breton's most popular book. Most critics, accustomed to relegating women to the position of dispensable minor characters, have focused on Nadja's personal tragedy: her poverty, her precarious existence, her incarceration in a mental institution. All but a few seem to have missed the crucial fact that she was a vital, active force in surrealism and did much to shape its mature outlook. Breton's book can in fact be considered a chronicle of the enormous impact of a single nonconformist woman on the theory and practice of a group mostly made up of men. Like Alfred Jarry, Arthur Cravan, and Jacques Vaché, this young woman—whose name, the one she chose for herself, signified the beginning of hope—was recognized as a veritable model of surrealist behavior, worthy of emulation by men and women alike. Nadja's influence on the course of surrealism was more than noticeable—it was *decisive.*

In retrospect, and particularly in comparison with the burgeoning activity of women in surrealism in the thirties and later, the role of women in the movement in the twenties seems marginalized, circumscribed, a long way from smooth sailing. The surrealist life in the 1920s was crisis-strewn and tempestuous for all, but one suspects that it was doubly so for the women. The work produced by women surrealists in the period 1924–1929 is quantitatively small. Except for Cunard, whose 1925 book of poetry, *Parallax,* owes more to post-imagist English verse than to surrealism, none published a book in those years; most never did. Even Simone Kahn Breton, the woman most deeply and persistently involved in Surrealist Group activity throughout the decade—the only one, for example, to assume regular hours at the Bureau of Surrealist Research[15]—published only once in the first surrealist journal. To the best of our knowledge, several of the first women participants in surrealism never again published anything anywhere. It is possible that trunks may yet be found, full to overflowing with unknown writings by Gauthier, Beznos, or the surnameless Suzanne.[16] However, all we know now is that, of the seven women of *La Révolution surréaliste,* only Valentine Penrose continued to pursue creative activity as a poet and artist in later years. Penrose, Muzard, and Cunard were the only ones who still took an active part in surrealism in the thirties, though Kahn and Lévy maintained at least peripheral contact through "united fronts" such as the Federation International de l'Art Revolutionnaire Indépendant (FIARI) [International Federation for an Independent Revolutionary Art].

The few women (three out of eight) whose identification with surrealism survived into the next decade might seem to suggest that surrealism, for them, involved a relatively weak commitment—perhaps a mere "passing fancy"—or that they had become discouraged. We have no way of knowing what each of these women felt in her innermost heart. However, if brevity of involvement is taken as a sign of small interest or discouragement, then the fickleness of the first male surrealists was unquestionably greater, for out of nineteen who took the pledge of "absolute surrealism" in the autumn of 1924, three defected before the summer of 1925 and only five remained active in 1930.[17]

As it happens, one of the primary sources of information on the day-to-day life of the Surrealist Movement in its formative years leaves no doubt that the first women surrealists' devotion to the cause was equal to that of their male comrades. From 1920 through 1925, Simone Kahn carried on an extensive correspondence with her cousin Denise Lévy in Strasbourg. Often writing several times a week, she recounted in detail the activities, debates, and crises of the Surrealist Group as it took shape in those years. This rich correspondence was first brought to attention by historian Marguerite Bonnet, who drew on it amply in her unsurpassed study of the young Breton (1975).[18] Although the correspondence remains unpublished, the excerpts quoted and summarized by Bonnet and others demonstrate the depth and seriousness of Kahn's (and her cousin's) dedication to the surrealist project. These are not the letters of an indifferent spectator or bemused dilettante, but rather of a fierce partisan, for whom surrealism is the living embodiment of all that matters.

At the same time, Kahn's letters reveal an unmistakable deference to the leading men in the group. They reflect the writer's consciousness that her own role, and by inference that of other women, was, while not unimportant, nonetheless somehow secondary. Interestingly, there appears to be no suggestion in these letters that the role of women in the group was restricted by their male friends. Although masculine egotism surely existed in the Surrealist Group, what is known of Kahn's correspondence refutes the temptingly simple but shallow argument that the relatively small production of the first women surrealists can be blamed on male chauvinism alone. What held these women back, more than likely, was a complex of inhibitions and fears inherited from centuries of French and European patriarchal, capitalist, Christian culture: notions of "feminine reserve," "woman's place," and "biological destiny" that they had internalized more or less unconsciously as children and which continued to wreak havoc in their psyches in later years, despite themselves.

The fact that the first women surrealists actively rebelled against church, state, and the bourgeois family did not necessarily mean that they felt themselves ready to assume complete equality, much less leadership, as writers, thinkers, spokespersons, agitators. Whether they actually were or were not qualified to assume these roles is not the issue here. The point is that at that time they seem to have been unwilling to enter into competition with their male friends. Evidently they preferred—or at least resigned themselves to—a "behind-the-scenes" role, with occasional and tentative forays into the limelight. To belittle their admittedly modest contributions by viewing these women as unwitting dupes and victims would be absurdly ahistorical and wrong. What is important is that they helped initiate a revolution in consciousness and life that is still reverberating around the world today. The fact that they made a place for themselves in the most subversive and emancipatory movement of their time is itself an extraordinary achievement.

Notes

1. Although Renée Gauthier's name appears on the front cover of *La Révolution surréaliste* no. 1 and again in bold face on page 5, preceding her "Rêve," she and her surrealist sisters in the world's first surrealist journal have curiously escaped the attention of historians. See Chadwick 1985: "If the experiments in automatic writing . . . and the narrating of dreams . . . had female practitioners, they have gone unrecorded" (25); and Suleiman 1990: "No women were present as active participants in the early years of the movement. . . . Women were excluded before they even got started—and this was *especially* true of writers" (30).

2. According to Thévenin, *Bureau de recherches surréalistes: Cahier de permanence,* 1988, Roger Vitrac brought in "a surrealist page by Suzanne," presumably intended for *La Révolution surréaliste,* on 28 October 1925 (35). An editor's note describes Suzanne as "probablement l'amie de Vitrac à ce moment-là" (140). Suzanne is also mentioned in passing in Aragon 1924, 115, in Crevel 1925, 283, and in Thirion 1975, 125–126.

3. Others who had at least some involvement in surrealism in the 1920s include Jeannette Ducrocq Tanguy, Elsie Houston, Greta Knutson, Alice Prin (known as Kiki), Thérèse Cano de Castro (known as Thérèse Treize), Berenice Abbot, Mary Hubachek Reynolds, Lee Miller, Marie-Berthe Ernst, Valentine Hugo, Janine (sometimes spelled Jeanine) Kahn (Simone's sister), Toyen, Youki Foujita (later Desnos), Colette Jerameck Tual, Lise Deharme, Mick Soupault, Gabrielle Buffet, Germaine Everling, Alice Apfel, Odette Cabalé Masson, Ida Kar, and perhaps Jane Ascher, whose African/Oceanian art gallery on the Rue du Seine took out full-page advertisements in *La Révolution surréaliste.* Several of these women—notably Toyen, Hugo, Deharme, Ernst, and Kar—became active in surrealism a few years later. The Bureau of Surrealist Research daybook notes a number of other women who visited the bureau and indicated their interest in surrealism, including militant lesbian author Natalie Barney and the well-known translator of Russian- and English-language novels, Ludmila Savitzky, whose response to the inquiry on suicide is noted in *La Révolution surréaliste* no. 2 (15 January 1925), 9. Excerpts from Marie Bonaparte's translation of Freud's *The Question of Lay Analysis* appeared in *La Révolution surréaliste* no. 9–10 (1 October 1927), 25–32.

4. Renée Gauthier's participation in the surrealists' hypnotic trance research is noted by André Breton in his "Entrée des médiums" (Breton

1924, 130). An editor's note in the *Bureau de recherches surréalistes: Cahier de permanence* refers to her as "l'amie de Benjamin Péret" (139). See Péret's poem, "La Mort du cygne," dedicated to R.G., in his collection, *Le Grand jeu* (Péret 1969).

5. Henri Pastoureau, "André Breton et les femmes" (in Pastoureau 1992), suggests that Beznos and Breton may have had an affair, but evidence is lacking. Roland Penrose, husband of Valentine, helped cofound the Surrealist Group in England in 1936.

6. This characterization is based on photographs and scattered comments in memoirs as well as on correspondence with several members of surrealism's first generation: Pierre Naville, Gérard Rosenthal, and André Thirion.

7. Published accounts of attendance at Surrealist Group meetings in the 1920s are not common. In his memoirs Harold Loeb, editor of the literary magazine *Broom*, mentions that "wives and girl friends were present" at an early (summer 1923) meeting but typically does not tell us their names (Loeb 1959, 183). Crastre 1963 mentions Simone Kahn, Gala Eluard, and "Masson's wife" (*née* Odette Cabalé) as those who attended most frequently (68–69). At the first meeting attended by Youki Foujita (later Desnos), she noted the presence of twelve men and four women: Simone Breton, her sister Janine, Jeannette Tanguy, and Simone Prévert (Youki Desnos 1957, 84). Nancy Cunard attended Surrealist Group meetings at the Café Cyrano and elsewhere, and her own flat was the scene for many surrealist gatherings.

8. Poet Saint-Pol-Roux (1861–1940) was an important influence on the origins of surrealism; the Surrealist Group published an "Hommage" to him in *Les Nouvelles littéraires* (9 May 1925). It was not because of enmity to the poet, therefore, that the surrealists disrupted the banquet in his honor, but rather because of the event's official character, involving as it did the presence of many *littérateurs* that the surrealists regarded as reactionary. See Pierre, *Tracts surréalistes,* 1980, 389–391, 396–397.

   Youki Desnos recounts the disruption as told to her by Thérèse Treize, implying that the latter was a participant or at least an eyewitness and adding that she herself "always regretted" not having taken part in it. If Thérèse Treize was there, other women involved in surrealism may have been there as well (Desnos 1957, 86–87).

9. On this and many other matters, surrealists in different countries often had different ideas, no doubt resulting from different experiences. At least one participant in the Surrealist Group in England in the 1930s, Margaret Nash, was a veteran of the women's suffrage struggles of the 1910s, especially active in the women's direct-action Tax Resistance

League. See Paul Nash's autobiography (Nash, 1988), 151–156. How greatly the women's suffrage movement in France differed from its British and U.S. counterparts is suggested by the fact that the founder of the French movement, Hubertine Auclert (1848–1914), was a regular contributor to Edouard Drumont's rabidly anti-Semitic, xenophobic, protofascist paper, *La Libre parole,* in the 1890s. See Hause 1987, 156–159.

10. The letter to *Le Libertaire* appears in Pierre, ed., *Tracts surréalistes,* "Compléments au Tome I," 438. Curiously, the congratulatory note which accompanied a bouquet of roses is not included as a separate text in *Tracts surréalistes,* but is quoted in full in a footnote in (I: 384).

11. A notice for the "Collection de boules de neige" [Snowball Collection] on the inside front cover of *La Révolution surréaliste* no. 8 (1 December 1926) lists "L'âme des amants par N.D." as "en préparation." See Sebbag 1993, 28. *La Révolution surréaliste* no. 9–10 includes an excerpt from Breton's *Nadja.*

12. Because its invitation is headed "Le Cadavre Exquis a l'honneur de vous faire part" [The Exquisite Corpse has the honor of inviting you], the October 1927 Surrealist Gallery exhibition has frequently been mistaken for a show of "Exquisite Corpses." (See, for example, the catalog *André Breton: La Beauté convulsive* [Paris, 1991], 185–186.) Had that indeed been the case, work by women would surely have been included, for they were assiduous players of the game. Catherine Vasseur, the leading authority on the history of the *Exquisite Corpse,* informs me (in a letter dated 24 March 1997) that the October 1927 show in fact featured paintings by Picasso, Derain, and others, and that there is no hard evidence indicating that Exquisite Corpses were exhibited prior to the surrealist exhibition at the Galerie Pierre Colle in Paris in 1933. Moreover, since few "corpses" were signed in the 1920s, it is not always possible to identify the participants. According to Vasseur (letter dated 10 September 1996), the earliest surviving all-woman Exquisite Corpses, by Frida Kahlo and Lucienne Bloch, were made in New York in 1932.

13. See the following volumes in the "Archives du surréalisme," both edited, introduced, and annotated by Marguerite Bonnet: *Vers l'action politique: juillet 1925–avril 1926* (1988), and *Adhérer au Parti communiste?: Septembre–décembre 1926* (1992).

14. Youki Desnos 1957, 84. In a letter to the author dated 1 December 1996, André Thirion—who was active in the Surrealist Group in Paris (and in the Communist Party) between 1928 and 1934—notes that very few members of the Communist Party in France ever did more than leaf through Marx's *Capital.* Although he expresses doubts about

Youki Desnos's statement regarding Simone Kahn, he adds that Denise Lévy may well have read *Capital* in those years and that Kahn "without doubt" had studied Engels's *Anti-Duhring* and Lenin's *State and Revolution* as well as other Marxist works, although she tended to be more interested in Freud and psychoanalysis than in Marxism. According to Thirion, most of what the other women involved in surrealism in the 1920s knew of Marxist theory was derived from the Communist daily *L'Humanité*. However, they tended to support Trotsky against Stalin, judging Trotsky to be more radical as well as "a better writer than Stalin."

15. The *Bureau de recherches surréalistes: Cahier de permanence* contains numerous notes by Simone Kahn Breton as well as references to her by other surrealists (Thévenin 1988).

16. In recent years we have witnessed the discovery of a large number of heretofore unknown paintings by Jacqueline Lamba, a sizeable quantity of unknown photographs and unpublished correspondence by Claude Cahun, and an impressive number of photographs, previously thought to have been lost, by Dora Maar.

17. Paul Picon, Joseph Delteil, and Roger Vitrac left the Surrealist Group after a few months. The five still active in 1930 were Louis Aragon, André Breton, René Crevel, Paul Eluard, and Benjamin Péret.

18. These letters are also quoted at length in Naville 1977. The Simone Kahn/Denise Lévy correspondence is housed at the Bibliothèque littéraire Jacques Doucet in Paris.

Renée Gauthier

What may be the only sketch of Renée Gauthier appears in a letter to the author from Gérard Rosenthal (known in surrealism as Francis Gérard), the original director of the Bureau of Surrealist Research in Paris. He recalled Gauthier as "a fragile young woman, reserved, sober, working-class, neither fashionable nor theatrical." Although she "rarely put herself forward," he added, "her healthy presence was especially valued and admired" (letter dated 19 May 1990). Nothing is known of Gauthier's life apart from the fact that she was a close friend of Benjamin Péret. In the daybook of the Bureau of Surrealist Research, Paul Eluard noted that "When Renée is ill, Péret doesn't show up" (that is, he did not spend his regular hours at the bureau).

As one of the "sleepers" (trance-speakers) in what René Crevel called surrealism's "Period of Sleeping Fits" in the fall and winter of 1922–1923, Gauthier's role was acknowledged by Breton in his "Entrée des médiums" (Breton 1923), and by Louis Aragon in his manifesto, "A Wave of Dreams," published in the journal *Commerce* a few weeks before Breton's first *Manifesto* rolled off the presses in October 1924. To the best of our knowledge, this "Dream," published in *La Révolution surréaliste* no. 1 (1 December 1924), is her only published text.

DREAM: I AM IN A FIELD . . .

I am in a field with Jim. He wants to pick a fruit for me in the hedge along the field, a fruit that, to me, looks like a walnut. It isn't ripe yet, and I don't want it. He tries to reattach it to the branch he took it from, so that it will ripen. I don't have time to tell him that it's a crazy idea. He puts down the fruit; it falls on the other side of the hedge. A young man passing by—someone I think I recognize—seeing how sad Jim is, picks up a nut for him, but Jim tells him: "Not this one, no, that peach." The young man finds the peach and gives it to Jim who offers it to me. Then, gesticulating as he leaves, the young man announces that a walnut falling from a tree becomes a peach when it touches the ground.

Jim and I make our way through the wheat field. We follow the central path. At the end I glimpse some pots of multicolored China asters. They intrigue me, but I don't have time to look at them; my companion is so loving that his caresses make me forget everything else. All I can think of is finding a suitable place to make love. We stretch out in the hollow of a furrow; but my pleasure is spoiled when I notice the wet ground dirtying the beautiful white rabbit-skin cloak spread out on it. So I rise and go on farther to look for a drier spot. At the end of the furrow I find a nursery-grower's frame painted black. I read the following words all around it, written in black on the yellow ground and outlined in whitewash: "A thirsty, poisonous beast has sucked all the blood from my little six-month-old niece, who has died of it. This evening at seven o'clock wild camellias will surround the body of my dead niece." Most intrigued, I call Jim. He nods his head sadly when he reads it. Now I understand why I saw China asters. But suddenly I notice that Jim, standing before me, has his fly open like a tabernacle. I try to close the two little doors, because I see the young man who spoke to us a little while ago from the other side of the hedge—he's gleaning quite close by—but the hinges are rusted, and at that moment I'm certain that I must, that we absolutely must find a dry spot between two furrows. Suddenly, I hear cries and shouts. I look back in that direction, and I see at the end of the field the young man I saw a little while ago, slipping through an alley I knew in my youth. He has stolen something. Women in a neighboring field are shouting, "Stop, thief!", and a café waiter is pursuing him, running as fast as his legs can go. Jim and I make our way in that direction to see what will happen. When we arrive at the alley, we are repulsed. We are thrown to the ground, literally swept away by a "gods' hunt."* At the same time I see the young man cross the alley once again. An enormous dog is chasing him. I follow him with my eyes for a moment; then I see the man fly away and the dog make a mighty leap and fall back to earth where he remains motionless. I look for the man in the sky and see a great bird (Jim sees it at the same time as I do), but I immediately notice that it's the first of a flock that appears to be spread out like a fan. There are at least a hundred. They fly slowly like those flocks of birds you see over the ocean. In just a second, I've counted them off. There are eighty-five. They pass not far from us and lower their flight. We see then that they are beautiful, absolutely white birds, except for their necks and part of their feet; at the end of their legs they have extremely long, almost cylindrical feet: sugar-loaf feet. And the symmetry of the black feathers and the white feathers makes me think that these birds are wearing black suede shoes with bands on the shank and laces around the ankle, like

---

* This refers to a mystery from my childhood. My mother, who often frightened me, saying she'd heard the noise of the gods' hunt, was never able to explain exactly what it was. She'd say it was those enormous, deafening noises of men and monstrous beasts that pass over in the sky on a certain date of the year. When you hear them you must lie on the ground on your stomach and plug up your ears.

those worn by women. To me, these birds seem to be wearing black shoes and black ties. Their feet rock under them.

"You'd swear they were athletes doing air-skiing," said Jim.

I watch them descend slowly behind the hedge and the big oaks in the neighboring field. They all swoop down at once. Jim says to me:

"Come along. If they're sleeping, maybe you can steal a pair of shoes."

We run in their direction. There they are, pecking in the grass. We approach quietly. I take Jim's cane to kill one that's not moving, but as I get nearer he moves off. The others behave exactly the same way. Finally, the last one remaining is a very big one, and I spring upon him . . . I see myself standing, leaning on his breast. He has the head of a man now, but his arms are wings that close, open and close upon me again. I sing at the top of my lungs:

"It's a bird who flaps his wings . . ." (to the tune of: "It's a bird that comes from France . . .").

Suddenly I feel myself stretched out alongside him, my head on his breast. My heart and my temples are beating very hard. I've just become his mistress. With the tip of one big foot he raises my chin, forcing me to turn my head. Then I see Jim struggling desperately with one of the birds. The bird's trying to strangle the café waiter (the one who chased the thief), with its giant feet, and he's shouting:

"You're wearing our uniform, but you're not a member of our congregation."

The café waiter takes off his black vest and his shoes so that he's no longer in black and white. I turn toward my bird-man who keeps repeating:

"I'll stay here a week . . . I'll stay here a week . . . yes, yes, yes. . . ."

Translated from the French by Myrna Bell Rochester

Simone Kahn

Born in 1897 into a prosperous Alsatian-Jewish family residing in Iquitos, Peru, Simone Kahn grew up in Paris and later studied philosophy and literature at the Sorbonne. She married André Breton in 1921 and played a considerable role in convincing him to break with the stagnant Dada movement. She was a regular attendant at the nascent Surrealist Group's hypnotic sleep experiments (reported in detail in the letters she sent her cousin, Denise Lévy) and an enthusiastic player of surrealist games. At the same time, her critical intelligence and great culture (Youki Desnos called her "a living encyclopedia") made her an important contributor to the intellectual life of the first Surrealist Group. In his memoirs of his surrealist youth, Marcel Duhamel recalled that Simone Kahn took it upon herself to make newcomers to the group feel welcome (Duhamel 1972, 176). She was, in short, a militant—one of the core group who kept the Bureau of Surrealist Research open in 1924–1925.

Kahn's break-up with Breton in 1929 had unfortunate repercussions in the group (her friends Noll, Alexandre, the Navilles, Morise, and Queneau all left at that time), but she and Breton remained lifelong friends. Kahn later married Trotskyist Michel Collinet and shared his political activity. In 1939 she joined the FIARI. After the war she opened a gallery in Paris which featured the work of many surrealist painters.

Kahn's "Surrealist Text" appeared untitled in *La Révolution surréaliste* no. 1 (December 1924), in the section devoted to "Textes surréalistes." Her reminiscences of the "Exquisite Corpse" game were written for the exhibition catalog, *Le Cadavre exquis, son exaltation* [The Exquisite Corpse, Its Exaltation] (Milan, 1975).

SURREALIST TEXT: THIS TOOK PLACE IN SPRINGTIME . . .

This took place in springtime in a garden where the customary glowworms were replaced by black pearls with the virtue of emitting but one beam of light, which burns out the spot where it falls.

"You wish my breast to be a snowball," said the young woman. "Very well, I agree. But what will you do for me in return?"

"Make a wish, my divine! And I hope I can fulfill it!"

"I wish you to have, for seven days, as many sexes as you have fingers on your right hand."

And it happened that the young man was instantly transformed into a starfish. The girl leaned over to him, smiling contentedly.

She thought, "What am I to do? I did not know it was so easy to get rid of an overeager suitor. I am left with the trees and their majestic embraces." She had overlooked the ocean. Furious to see one of its children insulted by an earthling, it secretly invaded the land to take him back and seek revenge. The girl was soon nothing but a transparent veil on the calm waters, smartly governed by the wind, its movements following the capricious waves.

An event occurred then which no romantic imagining can justify: a seagull seized the veil and took it to the secret cabin of a ship captain. He was an austere and passionate man with two favorite occupations: to inflict upon the cheeks of his men an inflation which he called "hysterico-vernal" and to use poems specifically written for them in order to tame fishes caught in the bellies of sharks.

And so he was quite taken aback when, coming into the cabin where he kept the materials he needed for his experiments, he suddenly felt himself choking on a perfume similar to the sound of a violin dipped in holy oil which, due to a characteristic not found in other scents, imprinted on his eyes a slight weight. He knew right away that it could evolve into stupefying visions and, from that moment on, nothing could astonish him.

What is the captain of a vessel if not the whistling of danger and the subterranean confession of quicksand? That man, who so impressed others with his science, became the plaything of a silk veil brought to him by a bird. When he saw it, he had only one desire, and his ship sank gently into the sea.

An infernal din made this slow and crafty operation known to other earthlings.

Meanwhile, the captain had leaned out of the narrowest of his ship's portholes, feeling that his respiratory organs were finally finding an element in conformity with their constitution. The gilded buttons of his uniform, despite the anchors that adorned them, were like so many small balloons of a special kind that took him down to the depths.

• • •

He found old friends there: the chameleon he had once prevented from changing color; the weeping little girl he had stabbed; the tulip called parrot he had taught to pronounce the word "never." One day, a lifeboat found on the sea a flat and translucent seaweed with human veins: thus it was known that the captain had died.

Translated from the French by Guy Ducornet

THE EXQUISITE CORPSES

On one of those idle, weary nights which were quite numerous in the early days of surrealism—contrary to what is so often fancied in retrospect—the Exquisite Corpse was invented.

One of us said, "Let's play 'leaflets.' It's a lot of fun." So we played the traditional game of "leaflets": Mr. meets Mrs., he talks to her, and so forth. But that didn't last long. The game suddenly broadened. "Just write anything," said Prévert.

On the very next turn, the Exquisite Corpse was born—under the pen of Prévert, precisely, for it was he who wrote down the first words: *The Exquisite Corpse,* so well completed by *will drink the new wine.*

Once the imagination of these fellows was set loose, there was no stopping it. André shouted with joy, immediately recognizing in this game one of those natural wellsprings or waterfalls of inspiration that he loved so much to discover. It was an *unfettering*. Even more so than with automatic writing, we were sure of getting an astonishing amalgam. Violent surprise provoked our admiration and sparked an insatiable passion for new images: images unimaginable by one brain alone—images born of the involuntary, unconscious, and unpredictable combination of three or four heterogeneous minds. Some sentences assumed an aggressively subversive character. Others lapsed into excessive absurdity. And don't forget—the wastebasket had a role in all this.

Nonetheless, the suggestive power of those arbitrary meetings of words was so astounding, so dazzling, and verified surrealism's theses and outlook so strikingly, that the game became a system, a method of research, a means of exaltation as well as stimulation, and even, perhaps, a kind of drug.

One night someone suggested playing the same game with drawing instead of words. The technique of transmission was readily found: The sheet would be folded after the first player's drawing, three or four of its lines passing beyond the fold. The next player would start by prolonging those lines and giving them shape, without having seen the first.

From then on, it was delirium. All night long we put on a fantastic drama for ourselves. We were at once recipients of and contributors to the joy of witnessing the sudden appearance of creatures none of us had foreseen, but which we ourselves had nonetheless created.

This ingenuous collective creation called into question, once again, the very nature of artistic endeavor, as surrealism has done repeatedly over the years.

No doubt the participation of some of our great painters added a few jewels to the game. But real discovery was reserved for those who had no talent, for it offered them the possibility of creation and thereby opened, permanently, a door on the unknown.

Translated from the French by Franklin Rosemont

Denise Lévy

A first cousin of Simone Kahn, Denise Lévy was born and raised in Strasbourg. By 1920, still in her teens, she was a ringleader in the city's socialist intellectual life. Young men from Strasbourg who rallied to surrealism, such as Marcel Noll and Maxime Alexandre, looked to her for guidance and counsel. Her move to Paris had important ramifications for surrealism. Bilingual, she introduced her friends to presurrealist currents in German; her translations appeared in *Littérature, La Révolution surréaliste,* and *Commerce* (where Georg Büchner's "Leonce and Lena" appeared for the first time in French). Breton, Aragon, Char, and Eluard dedicated poems to her. Throughout surrealism's early years Denise Lévy was an active, stimulating presence.

In the mid-1920s Lévy married Pierre Naville, founding coeditor of *La Révolution surréaliste* and one of the movement's most important early figures. By late 1928 she and her husband had largely withdrawn from the Surrealist Movement to devote themselves to the Trotskyist struggle against the Stalinization of the Communist International. The exiled Natalia and Leon Trotsky became their close friends and correspondents. Denise Naville helped Trotsky translate several of his books into German, and she herself translated his 1928 book *Toward Socialism or Capitalism?* into French. In later years she translated Engels's *Dialectics of Nature,* Clausewitz's *On War,* and important works by Marx, Bukharin, Paul Celan, and above all Hölderlin. The Pleiadé edition of Hölderlin's works includes her complete translation of his correspondence, including the letters of Suzanne Gontard. Denise Naville died in 1970.

The examples of automatic writing translated here originally appeared, without titles, in *La Révolution surréaliste* no. 3 (April 1925) under the rubric, "Textes surréalistes."

SURREALIST TEXT: I WENT INTO A GREEN SONG . . .

I went into a green song which was turning blue with fieldparadise. And on the way offering me its arm, I found a vainglory hitting a wax squirrel. It had a hare's foot and gloriously juggled its front stage for the metaphor-monkey. As a fantasy circus the fieldparadise flowered its bathtub and went for a walk in furious contraband. On the way it was assaulted on the side of the road by an elephant image. After a struggle it went away, frenetically crossing itself. Then paradise left its terrestrial field and vaporized itself into what is—or could be known as—savage ridicule. From before, everything wears a leopard scarf, the elephant image ignored itself from morrow to morrow, always faster, so that finally all that was left was a one and only translucent and burlesque vigil, called "Field-beige." Cascades of kisses and phonograph cylinders were present; they came to kneel nobly before the strange window tale I just narrated.

SURREALIST TEXT: IVORY BLUE AND SHADY SATIN . . .

Ivory Blue and Shady Satin were two friends. They were both born on a Monday, which is not enough. They will soon flee together in order to better part, because Shady Satin loves vinegar while Ivory Blue loves mass. Way on its way, via vagabond and Montrouge, the old zigzag comes back again, and the innumerable devil's leaps bruise its thighs as it fastens a patch of cloud around its waist. But none of this is an excuse, and it'd be better to climb the sky—squarely and frankly. But too much malevolence, too many returns in all these countless nights, keep rocking my scaffolded brain, and as far as vanity goes, Shady Satin likes it so much that bats fight duels over it. Nevertheless, the worm-eaten cascades from another sphere reappeared ceaselessly at my isolated windows, and the faultless oblivion slammed them shut. So fast did the dismal destiny of those two beings, both born on a Monday, stick to mine, that I am still pulling each of them by the hand.

Translated from the French by Guy Ducornet

Nancy Cunard

Born in Leicestershire, England, in 1896 into a fabulously wealthy family (she was the granddaughter of Samuel Cunard, founder of Cunard Steamship Lines), Nancy Cunard as a teenager rebelled against all that her parents stood for. Passionately attracted to jazz, modern poetry, and painting as well as to radical politics, she moved to Paris in 1920, where she became friends with several Dadaists, including Man Ray and Tristan Tzara, who dedicated his 1925 play, *Mouchoir de nuages* [Cloud Handkerchief] to her.

In his chatty memoirs of 1920s Paris, Montparnasse bartender James Charters, known as "Jimmie the Barman," calls Nancy Cunard (1896–1965) one of the "leaders" of surrealism and suggests that she played more than a small part in the Surrealist Group's well-known disruption of the Diaghilev ballet in 1926. Exaggerated as his recollections may be, they do convey the sense that Cunard's identification with surrealism was vocal and unequivocal.

At least as notorious for her self-assurance and fierce determination as for her trademark excessive slimness and the quantity of African ivory bracelets she wore on each arm, Cunard was also in many ways modest and self-effacing. To what extent she considered herself a surrealist militant *per se,* or simply a friend and champion of surrealism, is hard to say. Clearly, however, from her first visit to the Bureau of Surrealist Research on 18 November 1924—five weeks after it opened—she manifested a stronger, more lasting commitment to surrealist revolution than many who cosigned tracts or exhibited in shows.

For several years she and Louis Aragon were companions and traveled all over France and to Spain, Italy, and England. It was during this period that Aragon wrote his greatest books: *Le Paysan de Paris* [Paris Peasant] (1926), *Iréne* (1928), and *Traité du style* [Treatise on Style] (1928). This long affair ended in 1928, when Cunard found a new lover (the African American jazz musician/composer Henry Crowder), but her involvement in surrealism persisted.

By all accounts Cunard in the 1920s was a living symbol of the "New Woman"—flamboyant, assertive, hard-drinking—and portrayed as such, under the name Iris March, in Michael Arlen's best-selling novel, *The Green Hat.* She also learned typesetting and letterpress printing and established one of the most celebrated "little presses" of the time: the Hours Press, which, among other titles, brought out Aragon's French translation of Lewis Carroll's *Hunting of the Snark.*

As a writer, Cunard's most important contributions to surrealist revolution—focused on the politics of the African diaspora—came later. The texts reprinted here show the centrality of surrealism in shaping her outlook and her life. The first is excerpted from a report on "Paris To-Day As I See It" in the July 1926 *Vogue,* the second from an article on France in the 7 May 1927 issue of *The Outlook.* The third—reminiscences written in the 1960s, shortly before her death—appeared in her posthumously published memoir, *Those Were the Hours* (1969), edited by Hugh Ford.

SURREALIST MANIFESTATION AT THE DIAGHILEV BALLET

That emotion about art is capable of being felt, worked up and very exactly organized into an energetic protest was obvious to (about a third of) the audience at *Romeo et Juliet* on the opening night of the Russian Ballet at the Théatre Sarah Bernhardt the end of last month. The other two-thirds were only agonizingly aware of a stupendous affray, the hub of which—might it not have been Communism?

Next morning the *Daily Mail* dramatic critic quoted Gautier: "A ballet is not a thing to be regarded lightly." This one certainly received a severe trouncing. The reason being that Max Ernst and Joan Miró, two members of the ever-vigilant *surréalistes,* had offended the art morality of that group by their collaboration with the Ballets Russes, and the *surréalistes* are intransigent in their denouncement of turncoats, who at one time (in this case very recently) professed the same tastes and opinions. When worthwhile they will protest and spare themselves neither the pains of a fracas with the *gendarmes* nor the possible *suites* of a *procés*. . . .

But the story—it had nothing to do with the music. With the first note barely out of the orchestra a salvo of whistles rose in unison as a leisurely fall of white leaves (the *Protestation* that explained, printed in scarlet) began to come down from the dome onto the bejeweled first-nighters. From a top box no finer scene for a flashlight memento. Pandemonium soon followed, but everything went on at the same time—the snowfall, the whistling, the counter-manifestation, threats and blows—the dancers courageously footing it, one hand up to their ears to catch any musical indications still audible. Some of the orchestra, slightly demoralized by the duration of the noise and the copious fall of handbills, dropped their instruments to read the *Protestation*. . . .

[Afterward] came a perfect harvest of misinformation as to the number (some two hundred, people thought, but in reality there were eighteen) and the fate of various manifestators, who were at that moment gathering together in a neighboring cafe . . .

THE BEGINNINGS OF THE SURREALIST REVOLUTION

The exact skeleton of the age is hard to get at. But the present time is an animated one, intellectually, in France. To compare it one way, it is far more intelligent than the just pre-war epoch (franker, better learned, with more to say, more advanced); to compare it to another, no one could deny the ascendance of the French writing (and of course painting) intellect over the English and the American creative sensibilities. Intelligence, intellect, is by no means the whole of the story, but it is the headpiece to the work. . . .

Many elements as diverse as numerous have been and are being drawn on. . . . At no other time surely has there been so much editing, fine editions, writing about writing, and France more than any other is the place of the young author. The impression of all this is confusing, but it is possible to say that the names of Benjamin Constant, Poe, Baudelaire, Rimbaud, Lautréamont, and more lately Apollinaire are fixed signs that have greatly affected what at present are the brains of France, the younger writers. After the academic *Parnassiens* and *Symbolistes* an important event was the reclassing of the values of the Romantic era, which established Gérard de Nerval and the less-known Pétrus Borel *le Lyncanthrope* as the true leaders of the movement. To Victor Hugo, so out of date with the general French mind, much is due from such poets as are now concerned with that (in France) out of date emotion, love. And much has come from the admirable passion, revolt and sweep of Lautréamont's *Chants de Maldoror*.

The first collective movement since the war was known as Le Cubisme Littéraire, with Apollinaire and Reverdy as moving spirits, and the review *Nord-Sud* [North-South, edited by Reverdy]. Founded by Breton, Aragon, and Soupault, another review, *Littérature* (1919–1922), combined such opposite personalities as Gide and Picabia, Valéry, Max Jacob, Reverdy. From this burst a few months later the bombshell of Dada, the paradox, whose noise was equal to that of Marinetti's clash of machines and general breaking up of concepts. But whereas Futurism was more of an anarchy, Dada's methods were more subtly contrived to startle and overthrow. Dada's being was the mystification of all those who take things seriously; integrally honest though often accompanied by all the attributes of a joke, it attacked everything academic, in life as much as in literature.

The first appearance of Dada (bred in Switzerland during the war) was regarded as a plot, the meaning of which could not be got at. Anti-literary, anti-art, a system against all systems (thus still a system), the writing-world and the public shuddered, laughed or raged as such dicta of its leader, Tristan Tzara, as this: To make a poem, take a newspaper article, cut out the words and mix together. Dada preached the absolute and utter negation of the absolute, spun like a top through all theories and classifications, vociferously denied the existence of everything, including its own existence. In conferences and in writings Tzara and the group denounced life *ex cathedra*. There was no setting up of new creeds, new morals, but an opening of doors to whatever might come in. The *Sept manifestes Dada* [Seven Dada Manifestoes] by Tristan Tzara is a brilliant formulation of this revolution, the violence of which split into two the group of *Littérature*, which continued to exist composed only of the young writers. Whatever the virtues of Dada (and it had great merit, being a revolution), much new beauty was born from it all. Tzara's own poems—*25 poèmes*, *De nos Oiseaux*, and *Cinéma-Calendrier du Coeur abstrait*—delicate, violent, intellectually new, would be sufficient attestation; and the poetry of that period by Eluard,

Breton, Soupault (to mention only the more important names) is corroborative of this.

After frequent manifestations (1919–1922) during which the public protested angrily that it was all a gross farce, lunacy, and even politically dangerous—Dada's empiricism being rhapsodic, high-flown, and a violent union of the abstract and the daily word—the movement broke up and was regrouped into what presently became the beginning of *surréalisme*. This term . . . was used already in the days of Dada by the future *Surréalistes* to designate such writings known as "automatic," obtained by the rapidest possible passage of pen over paper uncontrolled by the intellect and without preoccupation as to result—a sort of modern parallel of that "inspiration" so much decried at the beginning of the century. The beginning of *surréalisme* had its hypnotic seances, with particularly striking effects on René Crevel, and was an important factor in his prose writings, *Détours* and *Mon Corps et Moi*, as in the poems of Robert Desnos and Benjamin Péret.

Meanwhile, the sense of the word grew and stretched over a whole region as yet imperfectly defined (the subconscious, the dream, etc.) and was used in connection with an entire plan of researches, in themselves unliterary, inartistic, on the confines of the scientific and the philosophical. Apart from this small group of writers the word *surréaliste* was taken up by the newspapers, where it had no particular meaning beyond that of substituting itself for the word Dada, by then out of date. But those to whom it applied took it back formally, on the appearance of the first number of their review, *La Révolution surréaliste*, edited by Péret and Naville, and André Breton brought out his *Manifeste du Surréalisme*. An even greater curiosity and interest than Dada evoked immediately surrounded the new movement, with numerous criticisms, interviews, caricatures, and so on in the press. A sort of Bureau of researches into the subconscious was founded, to which the public was invited to contribute. Aragon's "Une vague de rêves" appeared in *Commerce*.

That the term Revolution should appear in the title of the *surréaliste* review shows at once that it is concerned only with what is new. But the spirit of the first numbers, a moral questioning of all that is in life, anarchically, poetically voiced, turns more and more toward the actual and an applied philosophy (the necessary development of Hegelism). And that its concepts should not remain purely rhetorical, from 1924 till today the *surréalistes* (with diverse modifications and schisms in their midst) identify the theories from which it sprang with the material consequences following these theories. The result is that the majority has joined the French Communist Party. The ideology of the group is to be found in *La Révolution et les Intellectuels* by Naville, André Breton's *Manifeste du Surréalisme* and his *Légitime Défense* [Self-Defense], in the *Lettre ouverte à Paul Claudel* [Open Letter to Paul Claudel, a collective tract], and *La Révolution d'abord et toujours!* [Revolution Now and Forever!, a collective tract, 1925].

Individually Breton, Eluard, Péret and Desnos are great if not widely understood poets. A new mythology is theirs. . . . They are, differently, difficult poets. That a thing must be understood to be enjoyed is not more than fifty percent true: It follows that appreciation does not *depend* on understanding, but is decided by the sudden sense of beauty, or excellence. Sudden because all fine poetry gives the reader surprise at the writer's invention, the writer's discovery. It surprises, even shocks, into enjoyment. In poetry such as Breton's the association of thought may be difficult to grasp whereas its quality is immediately sensed. It depends where the realities of your life are. Inspiration and integrity qualify the work of these four poets, as also the prose of Louis Aragon, which is now admittedly among the finest of its time. An immense vocabulary, firmness and suppleness of language, intellectual passion, lyricism sometimes mounting to *le délire poétique* invest *Anicet, Les Aventures de Télémaque, Le Libertinage,* and *Le Paysan de Paris* with a permanent beauty.

SURREALISM, ETHNOGRAPHY AND REVOLUTION

Personally, I think it is quite impossible to "explain" [surrealism] . . . What words [could] give the right idea of the aims and development of this far-more-than-a-movement revolution? . . .

An intellectual revolution it certainly was. . . . The most admired writings were revolutionary, not only in a social-political sense, but in the esthetic-iconoclastic one too. Writings on psychoanalysis and studies of the subconscious inspired as much as Bosch, Breughel, Arcimboldo, Rimbaud, Apollinaire and Lautréamont. . . . Anatole France's death and public funeral provoked a denunciatory sheet [titled *Un Cadavre*]. And true it was that on and off came waves of *le scandale pour le scandale* [scandal for scandal's sake]. And some artists of whom it was felt that they had betrayed their aesthetic integrity to box-office commercialism were castigated.

All the jingo values of *La Patrie* and *La Gloire,* the militarism so real to official France, were anathematized, and colonialism was consistently denounced. At one time all the group signed a protest against the continuation of the war against Abd-el Krim in the Spanish Moroccan Riff.

Ethnography, the study of sculpture, carving, and other handmade objects once thought of as the work of mere "savages" from ancient Africa, Oceania, and of the Indians of both the Americas, were greatly admired and prized, and several of the surrealists eventually became expert ethnographers from their sheer love of such things. . . .

La Révolution surréaliste, produced on astonishing little money, published a great variety of subject-matter, and all of it—from straight Marxism and political criticism of the way the country was run, to the latest "fortuitous encounter" of all sorts of material objects that had come together "on their own" (by medium of the artists)—was somehow grouped convincingly under the term surrealism. . . .

• • •

The new [Hours Press] printery was close to the Galerie Surréaliste in the Rue Jacques Callot, which the surrealists had started with almost no capital a year or so earlier, and which had already become the mecca of *avant-gardisme*, without exception, *the* mecca. Its character and prestige grew apace as the exhibitions of works by Picasso, Picabia, Arp, Chirico, Klee, Miró, Dalí, Tanguy, Masson, Gris, Man Ray and a score more succeeded each other. There was considerable *brio* to this gallery. . . .

In those days, ethnography was for specialists and but few others, although some artists had seen the beauty in the "works of the savages." It was Matisse who first bought, for almost nothing, a great painted Congo mask from a village cafe on the banks of the Seine—so the story goes—in 1909 or so, and this event has been quoted many a time as the entry of primitive art into the realm of advanced modern painting. Before then, it was usually referred to as "objets des colonies," or "the stuff the sailors bring back," or "native curios." Such carvings and sculptures from Africa, New Guinea, and Oceania, and work by the American Indians . . . were on sale at the gallery at the same time as the so moderately priced pictures (now worth how many times more than their 1930 prices). . . .

Breton, Aragon, Eluard, and most of the other surrealists had seen the affinity—and how strange it is—between such fetish figures and carvings from Africa and Oceania and avant-garde painting; the wonderful constructions from New Britain and New Ireland in the South Seas looked particularly fine in the gallery. The taste that went into its arrangement was remarkable and the ethnographical knowledge of its animators increased all the time. Much respect is due them for having been the first to create this juxtaposition between abstract painting and the often equally abstract or geometrical designs which sprang from the minds of the pre-Columbian and other tribal artificers. Many of the surrealists have written on this theme, and it was certainly thanks to them that such a vision—accepted everywhere nowadays where modern art is understood—was first presented to the public.

Aragon and I came several times to England in the mid-twenties before the Hours Press started to rake through the curio-shops and junk-dealers of several English ports. . . . Some of the best New Guinea and Oceanic art pieces in the gallery were bought there for very little. Sadly dirty or battered, such objects reacquired their primitive gloss once in the Galerie Surréaliste.

• • •

At one time Rue Guenégaud served as a refuge for a young French student of seventeen [Raymond Michelet] who had escaped from tyrannizing paternal authority. The father blamed the surrealists for having put subversive ideas into his head. This very brilliant young man (as he soon turned out to be) was then haunted by despair, almost to the point of suicide. His father was head of the police of a large provincial town and had treated his son to a taste of *la panier à salade*, or black maria, wherein, surrounded by gendarmes, he was taken to prison for disobedience. He had somehow escaped and Sadoul and Thirion brought him to me for hiding. I think of him with affection and admiration; he was one of my helpers in the often intricate ways of French commerce, and later became my main collaborator in the *Negro Anthology*.

Nadja

Born in 1902 near Lille, in France, the second daughter of five children, Léona Camille Ghislaine D. (her surname remains confidential) chose the name Nadja for herself "because in Russian it's the beginning of the word hope, and because it's only the beginning." In Paris she worked as a salesclerk, theatrical bit-player, and dancer. On 4 October 1926 she met André Breton; her impact on him, and on the entire Surrealist Group, was electrifying. Breton's most popular book, *Nadja* (1928), is devoted to this encounter.

La Révolution surréaliste no. 8 (1 December 1926) announced her "L'Âme des amants" [The Lovers' Soul]—perhaps based on her drawing, "The Lovers' Flower," reproduced in *Nadja*—as third in the group's "Snowball Collection." The first of these image-enclosing glass spheres was an "Hommage à Picasso," the second by Man Ray, but then the project fell through.

Nadja visited the Surrealist Gallery and met several others in the group, but her involvement in surrealism was brief. Arrested by police in March 1927, she was put in a mental institution and later, at her family's request, transferred to another institution in northern France, where she died in 1940 without ever regaining her freedom.

The more than twenty letters she wrote to Breton remain unpublished. The following statements are quoted in *Nadja,* except for the last, which was spoken over the phone to Denise Naville and quoted in Pierre Naville's memoir, *Le Temps du surréel* (1977).

THE BLUE WIND

I am the thought on the bath in the room without mirrors.

• • •

Time is a tease—because everything happens in its own time.

• • •

With the end of my breath, which is the beginning of yours.

• • •

The lion's claw embraces the vine's breast.

• • •

I want to touch serenity with a figure wet with tears.

• • •

Why this scale which wavered in the darkness of a hole full of coal pellets?

• • •

Not to weigh down one's thoughts with the weight of one's shoes.

• • •

A game: Say something. Close your eyes and say something. Anything, a number, a name. Like this: Two, two what? Two women. What do they look like? Where are they? In a park. . . . And then, what are they doing? Try it, it's so easy. . . . You know, that's how I talk to myself when I'm alone, I tell myself all kinds of stories. And not only silly stories: actually, I live this way altogether.*

• • •

The blue and the wind, the blue wind.

• • •

I cannot be reached.

Translated from the French by Richard Howard

Fanny Beznos

Born in 1907 in Vady Rachkoff in what was then known as Bessarabia (now Romania), Fanny Beznos was one of surrealism's many fascinating "shooting stars." Her initial encounter with members of the movement—at the Saint-Ouen flea market in Paris, where she kept a stall—was chronicled by André Breton himself, in *Nadja*: "Extremely cultivated, she has no objection to discussing her literary favorites which are: Shelley, Nietzsche, and Rimbaud. Quite spontaneously she even mentions the surrealists. . . . All her remarks indicate a great revolutionary faith."

An activist in the Communist Youth, Beznos was arrested in November 1927 and deported, as a politically undesirable foreigner, to Belgium. Soon, however, she returned secretly to France with the help of Paul Nougé and other Belgian surrealists, alerted by Breton.

To what extent she took part in surrealist activity is not known, but the poems included here, published without titles in *La Révolution surréaliste* no. 9–10 (1927), show that she was esteemed as a comrade. By

* This passage provoked Breton's footnote in *Nadja*: "Does this not approach the extreme limit of the surrealist aspiration, its *furthest determinant*?"

1930 she appears to have devoted herself exclusively to work as a Communist militant. Arrested and deported in 1939, she died in a concentration camp in Germany during World War II.

I GO, THE WIND PUSHING ME ALONG

I go, the wind pushing me along,
Where? . . . I don't know,
I laugh, I cry, and meditating,
Why? I don't know!

What is the best means of government,
says ARISTOTLE, Men, it's the one that
permits virtuous citizens everything and that
doubly possesses artisan-slaves.
Who are the virtuous citizens? First of all,
the well-off proprietors, the strong soldiers.
As for the slaves, the best compensation
is always to picture their emancipation,
(meaning, when they won't be good for work any more, vile and
 mercenary, and that doesn't lead to virtue!)
There you are, admire the worthy philosopher,
And woman? You must be joking, interrupter! Woman, but always busy
at the cradle, not entirely a slave, but . . .
woman? Half of a free being? Bad!

So ARISTOTLE never went near the proletariat,
the MEN OF WORK which alone leads to virtue,
the simple beings it would be sweet to liberate
from the yoke of those vile and mercenary PROPRIETORS
from MONEY! Those CITIZENS stiff with their GOALS,
ASSASSINS, be they democrats or demagogues,
ARISTOTLE, they are using you to make
THOUSANDS of FREE beings groan! Ha!
 Arise, misery!
Defend yourself! Unite! Those watchdogs,
we'll free them from their undeserved happiness,
We the PROLETARIAT, REVOLUTION! REVOLUTION!

PURITY! PURITY! PURITY!

Purity! Purity! Purity!
I am happy! Happy!
PASCAL AND NIETZSCHE! And their shouts
And their PRIDE! AND ABOVE ALL!
    Oh, above all
THEIR PURITY! AND BEETHOVEN . . .
    AND even MORE! AND THEIR IMMORALITY . . .
PURITY! PRIDE! PAIN!

AND ORIGINAL SIN AND DEATH!
AND THE SPIRIT AND LIFE!
AND ALL MEN, LIVING!
FANTASIA! CAVALRY! DUST!

AND THE FEMALE, AND INTELLIGENCE!
AND THE WILL TO POWER! HA! HA!
AND THE AFFIRMATION OF LIFE!
AND LAUGHTER! AND SCORN! HA! HA!

AND YOU, THE PROLETARIAT?
AND YOU, THE SLAVES, THE FAMISHED!
AND YOU, MY TORMENTS?
AND YOU, MY DOUBTS AND MY CERTAINTIES?
YOU AND I, WE SHALL PERISH!

Translated from the French by Myrna Bell Rochester

Suzanne Muzard

Suzanne Muzard (born 1900) met André Breton in November 1927, a collision dramatically reflected in the closing pages of *Nadja*. Many believe it was she who inspired Breton's famous poem, "Union libre" [Free Union] (1931). She was an avid participant in surrealist games (see "Dialogue in 1928" in *La Révolution surréaliste* no. 11, and "Surrealist Games" in *Variétès* [1929]), and a collage signed "S.M.," presumably her, was reproduced in *Le Surréalisme ASDLR* no. 1 (1930). Her active participation in surrealism ended with her marriage to novelist Emmanuel Berl. Interestingly, however, after a second marriage to Jacques Cordonnier, she sometimes showed up at Surrealist Group meetings in the 1950s. She died in 1992.

Published here are her response to the inquiry on love from the last issue of *La Révolution surréaliste* no. 12 (December 1929) and excerpts from a memoir dating from 1974, from Marcel Jean's *Autobiography of Surrealism* (1980).

ON LOVE: REPLY TO AN INQUIRY

I. What sort of hope do you place in love?

II. How do you envisage the passage from the idea of love *to the* act of loving? *Would you, willingly or not, sacrifice your freedom for it? Have you done so? Would you agree to sacrifice a cause which you had hitherto considered yourself obliged to defend, if it appeared necessary to do so in order to remain true to love? Would you be willing to forego becoming what you could have become if such was the price of your complete abandonment to the certainty of loving? How would you judge a man who went so far as to betray his convictions to please the woman he loved? Can such a condition be demanded? Can it be obtained?*

III. Would you grant yourself the right to deprive yourself for a certain time of the presence of the one you love, knowing how much absence can inflame love, yet recognizing the mediocrity of such a calculation?

IV. Do you believe in the victory of admirable love over sordid life, or in the victory of sordid life over admirable love?

I. The hope never to recognize (for myself) any *raison d'être* outside love.

II. The transition from the idea of love to the fact of loving? It's about the discovery of an object, the only one I deem indispensable. Such an object is hidden: as children do—one starts out "in the water," then one gets "hotter." There is a great mystery in the fact of *finding*. Nothing can be compared to the fact of loving. The idea of love is weak, and its representations lead to errors. To love is to be sure of oneself. I cannot accept nonreciprocal love, and therefore I reject that two lovers might be in contradiction on a topic as serious as love. I do not wish to be free, and there is no sacrifice on my part in this. Love as I conceive it has no barrier to cross, no cause to betray.

III. If I could manage to calculate, I would be too worried to dare pretend I am in love.

IV. I live. I believe in the victory of admirable love.*

Translated from the French by Guy Ducornet

MY PASSAGE IN SURREALISM

My walk backward, to remember my passage in surrealism in the years 1927–1932, may chance to be inconclusive. I cannot claim to have known André Breton as he really was, and other persons considered him from a different angle. I refer only to the fact that I was included in the Surrealist Group by means of a sentimental passion that was to upset my life for five years. . . .

Memories adorn themselves with many charms, and if I try to remember them, it is to give to that love the motives of its seductiveness, and particularly André Breton's; among others, the charming way he had of attaching as much importance to a wildflower as to a precious orchid grown in a hothouse; exactly as with women: thus Nadja, this strange castaway who lived on contingencies in sordid lodgings, or Lise Deharme, who placed her elegant existence in sumptuous settings—two opposite women whom Breton set in a frame more surrealist than concretely livable. It was after them that I came into his life, surprised by him and (because he wanted it so) surprising for him. Didn't I tell him that, as a very young girl, surely I had stood alongside him at a crossroads of that suburb where, when a student in Paris, he returned every evening to join his family . . . ? We gave that chance event the quality of a strange coincidence that was to lead us, inevitably, to meet later. . . . With Eluard, himself born in Saint Denis, we evoked the youth of these girls who grew up like myself at the gates of Paris, near wastelands and old battlements. Our suburban minds wore, like an aureole, a very special snobbism, and we linked our popular ideology to the Russian revolution, still freshly tinted with red.

Surrealism was also making, in its way, its revolution. André Breton took

---

* In *La Révolution surréaliste* Muzard's response was followed by this statement: "No answer, different from this one, could be called mine.—André Breton"

care that the movement should not be deprived of scandals. Hard blows had to be struck to impose new formulas, nonconformist and anticonventional. . . . There were many quarrels and expulsions in surrealism! André Breton showed a certain integrity regarding his self-imposed discipline of mind, and he never entered into a so-called evolution that, in fact, would have induced him to compromise himself. Even in politics he remained faithful to his admiration for Trotsky until the latter's death and his own, which came later.

André Breton is no more . . . and if memories fade away or are "arranged," his works remain, and biographers will refer to them. Surely love will be mentioned. Love casts a more humane light on a personage who could measure its strength as well as its weaknesses. . . . Two divorces, as well as charming adventures with charmed women, and the traces of that loving passion that was once his and mine, and that brought me a wealth of knowledge that I lacked and an experience that helped me to perfect my life. So I keep from that period many more tender feelings than accusing regrets. . . .

Valentine Penrose

Born in Mont-de-Marsan, France, in 1903, Valentine Boué rebelled against her parents and their values early on and never reconciled herself to any sort of conventional family life. Around 1923–1924 she met and married Roland Penrose, a young Englishman of Quaker background who, years later, fondly recalled her "incessant and sometimes embarrassing vituperations against banality, foolishness and stupid conventions." A close friend of Alexandra David-Neel, she was deeply interested in Eastern philosophy, studied Sanskrit, and lived for extended periods in India. In 1936 she joined the workers' militia in Spain, to defend the revolution, and during World War II she fought in the French Resistance. Valentine Penrose died in England in 1978.

After her first encounter with surrealism in the late 1920s, Penrose moved in its orbit for the rest of her life. Her first appearance in a surrealist publication was her response to the 1929 inquiry on love in *La Révolution surréaliste* no. 12, translated here. In later years she collaborated on *London Bulletin*, *VVV*, *Dyn*, and *Free Unions*. Her first book of poems, *Herbe à la lune* [Grass on the Moon] (1935), was prefaced by Paul Eluard.

Best known as a poet, she began making collages in the 1940s and published a memorable collage-novel, *Dons de feminins*, in 1951. Her most popular book was *The Bloody Countess,* a study of medieval Hungarian murderess Ersebet Bathory; it was first published in France in 1962, and an English translation by Alexander Trocchi appeared in 1970.

WHEN IT COMES TO LOVE: RESPONSE TO AN INQUIRY

Editor's note: For the questions, see preceding text by Suzanne Muzard.

I. No hope: proof of an irremediable malady, one of (according to life) always having to distinguish between the subject "I" and the object "you," especially when it comes to love.

II. Like a densifying of the preceding idea, along a vertical descending right to the point being accomplished in the world of facts. Even though the finish line suits our species better than the starting point, can we really be happy with a creation—that is, in spite of everything—with a descent?

Betray feelings, yes; but not ideas. I'd become the judge of the being that would ask me to fall. Love being truth, it tends to contain all that for me is truth. We therefore have not to ask for betrayals or retractions.

III. It's a petty game. It's certainly mediocre to surprise oneself with a personal truth.

IV. As long as we conduct love along the model of life, traced over its demands, so that it sometimes manages to transmit life, I don't see how it can be victorious. In reality, it's simple: one follows upon the other.

Translated from the French by Myrna Bell Rochester

Suzanne Muzard, Elsie Houston, and Jeannette Ducrocq Tanguy

Many surrealist games are variants of children's or parlor games, modified to give the subversive powers of chance and imagination full sway. Moreover, as Breton noted in the first *Surrealist Manifesto,* "The forms of surrealist language adapt themselves best to dialogue." In "If/When" one player writes the first half of a proposition; the second player, having no idea what the first has written, adds the conclusion. The maxims that result are always surprising, often exhilarating.

These examples appeared in the "Surrealism in 1929" issue of the Belgian journal, *Variétès*.

SURREALIST GAMES

Suzanne Muzard: When the capital letters make scenes before the small letters
Elsie Houston: The exclamation points won't have much to say.

Jeannette Ducrocq Tanguy: If there had been no guillotine
Suzanne Muzard: Wasps would remove their corsets.

Elsie Houston: If tigers could prove how grateful they are to us
Suzanne Muzard: Sharks would allow themselves to be used as canoes.

Elsie Houston: If bread crumbs turned liquid
Suzanne Muzard: The archer would serve a plate of water-spiders.

Suzanne Muzard: If bales of straw concealed their lust for burning
Elsie Houston: Harvests would indeed be beautiful.

Translated from the French by Franklin Rosemont

2. In the Service of Revolution, 1930–1939

LE SURREALISME
AU SERVICE DE LA REVOLUTION

5

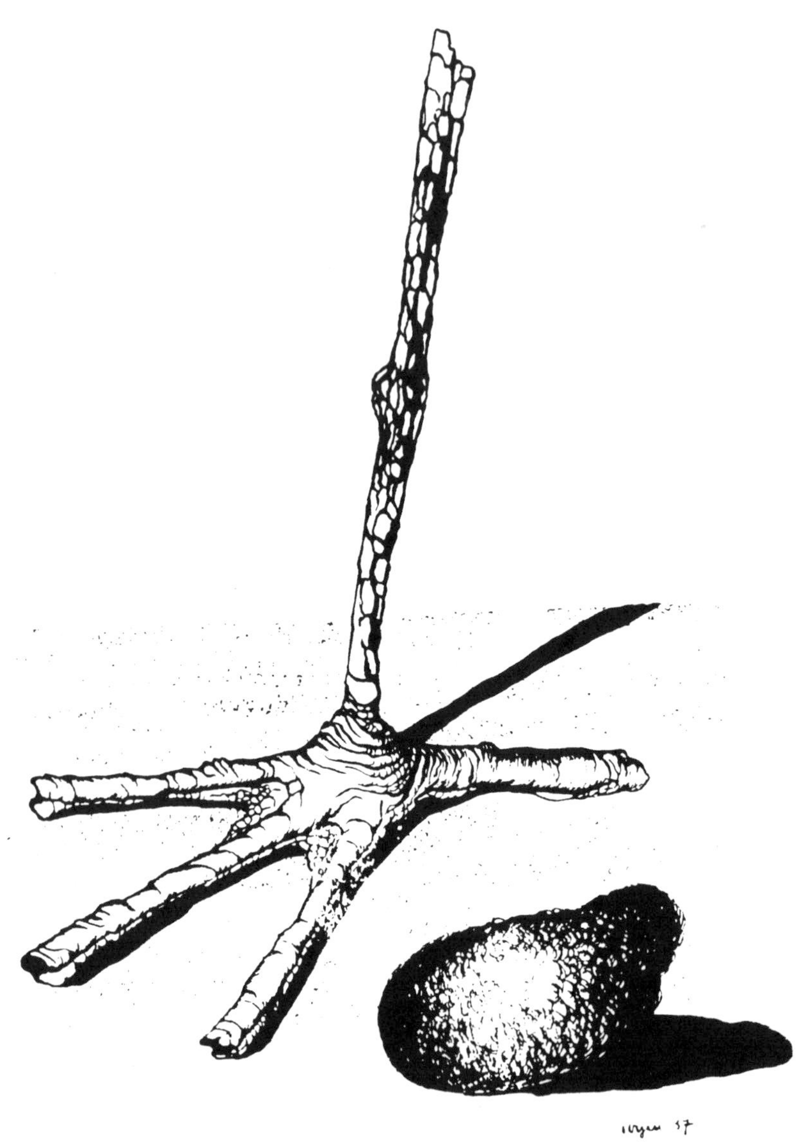

Toyen, ink drawing, 1937. From *Specters of the Desert*.

INTRODUCTION

Women and Surrealism in the Thirties

> She contemplated the past, and viewed the present, and when she compared them, the contrast struck her with astonishment. The whole appeared like one of those sudden transitions so frequent in dreams . . .
>
> —Ann Radcliffe

Surrealism in the 1930s started with a thoroughgoing critical self-examination and a broadening of perspectives, prompting an explosion of activity that extended all over Europe, to North and South America, the West Indies, Africa, and Japan. As surrealism grew, so did the role of women who took part in it.

After 1929 women's involvement in the movement began to expand on all levels and in all directions. Throughout the 1930s we find women surrealists writing books, illustrating books, formulating theory, cosigning collective tracts, participating in group demonstrations, taking a more active part in politics, innovating in diverse fields of plastic expression, and exhibiting their works individually, in group shows, and in major International Surrealist Exhibitions. No longer simply providing modest backup for a small circle of leading men, like most of the women involved in 1920s surrealism, a number of women in the thirties became spokespersons for the movement and initiators of collective activity. A few became well known internationally—as surrealists.

Interestingly, this worldwide expansion of surrealism, and of women's participation in it, accompanied the movement's most intense involvement with Marxism. Surrealism's concern with politics continues to confuse most critics, particularly in the English-speaking world where Marxism is widely assumed to be demonically restrictive. The historical record, however, suggests that the surrealists' involvement in politics had a salutary effect. Looking back from the Cold War era in 1952, Breton himself emphasized that the period in which surrealism was closest to the movement for world proletarian revolution was also when it flowered most splendidly in poetry and the arts (Breton 1969, 153–154).

The 1930s were years of economic depression, political collapse, the rise of fascism and Stalinism, and preparation for war. At the same time, revolution in

Spain, the French General Strike, and the wave of sit-downs in the U.S. awakened new hope in the workers' movement throughout the world. In the midst of such social turbulence, politics had become a life-and-death matter. Surrealists were among those who perceived that reformist solutions solved nothing. Although they desired and struggled for a revolution that would go far beyond politics—a revolution to actualize the Marvelous—they regarded the abolition of wage-slavery as a necessary first step. Convinced that they brought much that was new and vital to the revolutionary cause, the Surrealist Group titled its new journal *Le Surréalisme au service de la révolution* [Surrealism in the Service of Revolution] (1930–1933).

Breton and some of his comrades had joined the Communist Party in the mid-1920s, long before it became fashionable, and they were among the first revolutionary critics of Stalinism. In the thirties their political allies in France were among the comparatively small groups of the Far Left: Trotskyists, revolutionary syndicalists, and libertarian socialists. The group's revolutionary extremism, combined with its limited financial resources (no member of the Surrealist Group in France could be described as wealthy; many had incomes smaller than the average worker's), made the lively expansion of surrealism in those years especially remarkable.

As the 1929 depression deepened in the new decade, the always precarious position of women in French society was threatened with further perils. Women—along with racial minorities, immigrants, and revolutionary workers' groups—were made scapegoats for all the woes brought about by an unstable social system (Anderson and Zinsser 1989; Weber 1994). The plight of women wage-earners was demonstrably worse than that of men, but that did not stop politicians and journalists from blaming high unemployment on job-seeking women. The rise of the Far Right brought a frenzy of anti-birth-control propaganda; childless women were denounced as fomenters of "race suicide." Especially venomous was media hostility to the "new," "liberated," "independent" woman—the flapper and *garçonne* who flouted traditional values and attempted to live and love more adventurously than church, state, and parents permitted.

Antiwoman hysteria reached a crescendo in 1933, following two of the biggest scandals of the decade. In February two formerly docile maids, the Papin sisters, Christine and Léa, who had been brought up in a convent, massacred their officious *patronne* and her daughter with unprecedented ferocity. And in August teenager Violette Nozières was accused of poisoning her father and mother (the father died; the mother survived). The most sensational news stories of the period, both crimes made headlines for months.[1] With mass attention riveted on the Papin case, it proved impossible to conceal reports of the sisters' constant mistreatment at the hands of Madame and her daughter.

The Nozières case brought sordid revelations of its own. It was soon learned that the girl, at the age of twelve, had been raped by her father, who continued to abuse her thereafter. The father was a prosperous railroad engineer whose friends included prominent public officials, among them the president of France—for Monsieur Nozières drove the presidential train.

Of course, neither the inhumanly tormented servants nor the repeatedly raped daughter received any sympathy in the "free press" of France. Among respectable citizens these murders committed by young women unleashed an epidemic of fear and hate unmatched, perhaps, since the Dreyfus affair of the 1890s. The prosecution and the press did their utmost to stir up public hostility against the accused. The campaign against Nozières was especially vitriolic. She was portrayed as a demented flapper and prostitute whose main pleasures in life were dancing, listening to jazz bands, and drinking cocktails in cheap cafés. The popular weekly news magazine *Vu* [Seen] featured her on the cover and filled many pages with hair-raising stories on "The Demon of Sexuality and Crazed Youth" (VI:286, 6 September 1933). With such instigation from the Fourth Estate, it is no surprise that wrathful mobs attempted to lynch her. Typical of the tone and content of the firestorm of misogyny sparked by these sisters in crime is the vituperative article on Nozières by Janet Flanner, Paris correspondent for *The New Yorker*:

> Violette killed her father like a cannibal, because she wanted to eat and drink up the savings that were his French life and blood . . . In her brief career [she] had learned merely to drink bad cocktails with penniless collegiates . . . Violette was, one fears, not the last of the fake-silver-foxed, hard-toothed, modern young monsters of mediocre looks and without any sense of the business of life . . . [She was] a natural tart plus a born liar . . . Lust for money to spend on her lover in cafés (for bad Martinis) [was] accredited as her miserable motive. . . . (Flanner 1972, 158–164)

The Left press had little to say on these matters. At best, the Left attitude toward these women was somewhat less bloodthirsty than that of establishment and fascist journalists. No "Free the Papin Sisters!" or "Hands Off Violette Nozières!" defense committees were organized. For the Left, whose attention and efforts concentrated exclusively on a reified notion of the proletariat, these young women were too hot to handle—too "problematical." In all of France, only one group rose to the defense of the Papin sisters and Violette Nozières: the Surrealist Group. While everyone else was busy reviling these youthful female avengers as "monsters" and "cannibals," and demanding the severest penalties for their outrages, the surrealists recognized another dimension in their desperate deeds: a new variant of Hegel's radical master/slave dialectic expressed with Maldororian verve. As the surrealists saw it, these young women at the very bottom of the social heap had ripped the hypocritical façade off the so-called sanctity of the bourgeois family. Scandalously affirming their right to live without concessions, the Papin sisters and Violette Nozières hurled a red-hot monkey wrench into the moral machinery of a corrupt social order. In the fierce glare of their rage and violence, "respectability" stood exposed as a sham: brute force shielded by piety and the long arm of the law.

In May 1933, in *Le Surréalisme ASDLR,* Paul Eluard and Benjamin Péret saluted the two maids "marching out of one of the *Chants de Maldoror*" (Eluard and Péret 1933, 27–28). Under the sisters' direct inspiration, a young doctor who was also a surrealist sympathizer—Jacques Lacan—wrote one of his first articles, "Motives of Paranoiac Crime," a psychoanalytic study published in *Minotaure* in December (Lacan 1933, 25–28). In the same month appeared the pamphlet *Violette Nozières,* a collective homage to which most of the better-known surrealists contributed poems or drawings.[2]

I have discussed these two women-centered scandals at some length because it seems to me that the surrealists' response helps explain the ever-expanding influx of women in surrealism throughout the decade. The massive media coverage of these affairs and the hostile climate toward women that it fostered inevitably affected the female population, above all its younger, nonconformist element, some of whom doubtless sympathized at least secretly with the Papin sisters and Nozières. Few options were then available in France for women who rejected the "accepted" norms of female behavior. No radical women's movement existed at the time; the small suffrage groups were decidedly upper-class and the Left, afflicted with "workerism"—the sectarian notion that only labor issues are matters of concern—was utterly indifferent to women's special needs. Surrealism filled the breach in this particular configuration of circumstances. In a period of enormous social upheaval and dislocation, when the anarchist movement was pitifully small and when most of those who called themselves Marxists were either puritanical or cynical (and antifeminist in any case), the Surrealist Group provided an oasis for some rebellious, free-spirited women.

Surrealism's radical use of psychoanalysis was another factor that distinguished it from the repressive ideologies of the time, and it too attracted revolutionary-minded women to the movement. While elitist medical practitioners were reducing Freud's life work to an accommodative (and lucrative) therapy, surrealists put it in the service of poetry and revolution. What they found appealing in psychoanalysis was its revelation of unconscious life, the liberation of repressed desire, and the light it cast on the world of dreams, symbolic behavior, and "mental illness." They also realized that Freud's discoveries discredited the positivist rationalizations that make the world safe for capitalism and war. Surrealists, as Breton pointed out, rejected "by far the larger part of the Freudian system as *metaphysics*," but they recognized its central technique of free association as a critical and revolutionary method (Breton 1978, 147).[3] For Toyen, Mary Low, Simone Yoyotte, and Grace Pailthorpe—as for Suzanne Césaire, Nora Mitrani, and many others in later years—surrealism's use of psychoanalysis provided a crucial aid to self-awareness as well as a weapon against society's repressive machinery.

With its Hegelian-oriented Marxism, its passion for poetry, and its anarchist sensibility, surrealism was the most radical movement around. Anti-Eurocentric, antiracist, anti-imperialist, unafraid of the unconscious, critical of the myth of progress, distrustful of technology, surrealists were also friendly to wild nature and sympathetic to "primitive" cultures. As an international movement it embraced an incredible variety of "heterodox oppositions" to all forms of social domination.[4] No wonder women started seeking it out!

During the five-year period 1924–1929, as we have seen, only seven women made their presence felt in the twelve issues of *La Révolution surréaliste.* In the two and a half years from 1930 through May 1933, nine women contributed to the six issues of *Le Surréalisme ASDLR.* During the course of the decade others collaborated on *Minotaure, London Bulletin,* and other surrealist and surrealist-oriented publications. No fewer than nineteen women published texts—poems, tales, articles, and contributions to games—during the thirties. Ten of these women—Marcelle Ferry, Claude Cahun, Nancy Cunard, Valentine Penrose, Lise Deharme, Alice Rahon, Jeanne Megnen, Mary Low, Gisèle Prassinos, and Leonora Carrington—published books, three of them under the group's *Editions Surréalistes* imprint. Women surrealists brought out a total of twenty-six volumes between 1930 and the close of 1939. Seven of the women published at least two books each during that period. Penrose published four. Prassinos, prolific as well as precocious, brought out nine volumes in the five years, 1935–1939, two years before celebrating her twenty-first birthday.

Other women surrealists illustrated books—Toyen did Sade's *Justine,* and Valentine Hugo did Achim von Arnim's *Bizarre Tales,* prefaced by Breton. Lise Deharme's *Le Coeur de Pic* [The Woodpecker's Heart] (1937) included photographs by Claude Cahun.

Women's participation in surrealist exhibitions in the twenties was minimal, but they made up for it in the thirties, when thirty-two took part in the movement's many international exhibitions—in London, Paris, Amsterdam, Brussels, Tokyo, and other cities.[5] Nearly half were included in at least two shows. Several—Meret Oppenheim, Toyen, Valentine Hugo, Dora Maar, Eileen Agar, and Remedios Varo—exhibited in five or more. Work by many of these artists was reproduced in *Le Surréalisme ASDLR, Minotaure,* the *International Surrealist Bulletin,* and other movement publications. Works by Nusch Eluard, Jacqueline Lamba, Dora Maar, and Meret Oppenheim were featured in a set of surrealist postcards.

In all, at least fifty-three women took part in international surrealist activity in the years 1930–1939. Others who might seem peripheral to us now may at one time or another have played a more active role, unrecorded in periodicals and exhibition catalogs. Apart from Nancy Cunard, Valentine Penrose, Lise Deharme, and a very few others whose association with surrealism dates from the preceding decade, these women were all newcomers to the movement, and all but a handful were in their late teens or twenties when they began. Grace Pailthorpe, whose surrealist activity began in 1936 at age forty-six, was probably the oldest. Just over one-fourth of the fifty-three, and only four of the painters (Lamba, Marie-Berthe Ernst, Hugo, and Rahon), were French. Women's increased involvement in surrealism was a direct consequence of the movement's rapid internationalization.

Many of the newcomers came to Paris and lived there for extended periods. Often in flight from parents, family, and school, they came, as Meret Oppenheim put it, with "a conscious desire to be free" (Klüver and Martin 1989, 173). Oppenheim from Switzerland, Simone Yoyotte from Martinique (the first Black woman surrealist), Nusch Benz from Germany, Mary Low and Leonora Carrington from England, Lee Miller and Kay Sage from the United States, and Maruja Mallo and Remedios Varo from Spain are just a few of the many immigrants who added new energies and inspiration to surrealist activity in Paris in the thirties. Critic Whitney Chadwick, whose ambivalence toward surrealism often lapses into antipathy, admits that "almost without exception" the women artists she interviewed "spoke positively of the support and encouragement they received from Breton and other Surrealists. . . . Surrealism provided a sympathetic milieu. . . ." (Chadwick 1985, 11).

A good half of the women represented in this anthology lived for long periods in countries far from their homelands. Many have lived most of their lives abroad. Some voyagers from afar and others who did not come to Paris cofounded surrealist groups back home. In 1932, before collaborating on *Le Surréalisme ASDLR,* Simone Yoyotte was part of a group made up entirely of Black youth from Martinique studying in Paris. In 1934 Toyen and Katy King (the *nom de plume* of Libuše Jíchová) were charter members of the Surrealist Group in Czechoslovakia. Eileen Agar, Sheila Legge, and Grace Pailthorpe helped form the Surrealist Group in England in 1936. Ikbal El Alailly in Egypt, Maruja Mallo and Remedios Varo in Spain, and Rita Kerrn-Larsen and Elsa Thoresen in Denmark were among the inspirers and originators of surrealism in their own countries. Irène Hamoir did not cofound the Surrealist Group in Belgium, but she quickly became an important figure in it; at the opening of the 1935 surrealist exhibition in La Louvière, organized with the help of young trade unionists, she and E. L. T. Mesens were the featured speakers.

Women who joined the movement in the thirties were more numerous, more vocal, more assertive, more active, and more productive than their sisters in the twenties, and the surrealist work they left us is rich and many-faceted.

As painters and graphic artists, Agar, Carrington, Colquhoun, Hugo, Kahlo, Kerrn-Larsen, Lamba, Oppenheim, Rimmington, Toyen, and Varo opened whole castlesful of imaginative windows that have made life more thrilling for the dreamers of all countries ever since. For most of them, recognition by critics was slow in coming, but eventually—in a few cases, during the artist's lifetime—they came to be widely recognized as "masters."

Women were especially adept at such quintessentially surrealist activities as making collages and surrealist objects. Opening inexhaustible possibilities of genuine discovery to all, even to those without formal artistic training, these practices radically challenged the very foundations of the bourgeois, androcentric art establishment. Beyond art and aesthetics, such playful procedures opened the way to what Lautréamont had called "poetry made by all." Scissors in hand, Agar, Cahun, Nusch Eluard, Kahlo, and Toyen brought collage into realms unexplored by Kurt Schwitters and Max Ernst. Many of the most provocative "objects with a symbolic function" were signed Agar, Cahun, Hugo, Lamba, and Oppenheim.

Photography, in those years still disdained by the pooh-bahs of high culture, was yet another magnetic field which women surrealists made their own. Lola Alvarez Bravo, Denise Bellon, Ida Kar, Cahun, Maar, Mallo, and Miller (who, by the way, was a codiscoverer of the technique of solarization), were in the forefront of those who put the camera in the service of poetry.[6]

In the decorative arts, too, surrealist women excelled. Minneapolis-born Mary Hubachek Reynolds was the first to apply a surrealist approach to the art of bookbinding. Meret Oppenheim's jewelry and furniture were important parts of her rich and diverse oeuvre.

Like their male counterparts, women surrealist poets and writers tend to be less well-known than those who affirmed their surrealism in the visual arts. The reason is obvious: paintings, photographs, collages, and objects move around in the world unencumbered by language barriers. Nonetheless, the many marvelous tales by Prassinos and Carrington early on attracted wide notice and were soon awarded the status of "surrealist classics."[7]

Much less well known, even today, is the poetry of Marcelle Ferry, Alice

Rahon, Mary Low, and Valentine Penrose. Unforgivably omitted from anthologies—especially in the English-speaking world, where neglect of women surrealist poets has been particularly unrelenting—the work of these nomadic verbal alchemists will richly reward anyone willing to take the trouble to seek out their work.

Also rarely discussed is the world premiere of surrealism in dance, "The Unconsummated Act," choreographed and performed by Hélène Vanel at the opening of the International Surrealist Exhibition in Paris in 1938. Photographs and eyewitness accounts of the event suggest that Vanel's unique blend of dance in the style of Isadora Duncan and voodoo was an amazing performance.

Least known of all—invisible to such an extent that some critics have gone so far as to deny that it exists—are the incursions of women surrealists into what is often labeled the preeminently masculine domain of theory and polemic. In the twenties such participants as Simone Kahn and Denise Lévy, whose critical intelligence and philosophical erudition cannot be disputed, did not choose to develop their ideas in published writings. In the thirties a change occurred here, as in everything pertaining to women's activity in the movement. For the first time we find women in surrealism exploring questions of theory in a bold, rigorous, and systematic manner.

Claude Cahun is the principal pioneer in this area. Her prowess as a critical thinker and polemicist is formidable. Had she written more, she would have to be counted among the movement's leading theorists. Even so, her few published writings make up an invaluable body of work.

Nancy Cunard also expanded surrealist thought in this period. Her 1931 polemic, *Black Man, White Ladyship,* is a fierce denunciation of the kind that rolled so freely from the vitriol-filled pens of Aragon, Crevel, and Péret. Cunard's was the first of the genre written by a woman, and its invective, characteristically, is directed against her own racist, imperialist mother. Three years later, Cunard edited *Negro: An Anthology,* a formidable attack on white supremacist ideology and a powerful affirmation of the genius and promise of the Black peoples of the world. Along with a wide selection of writings by Black writers from Africa, the West Indies, and the U.S., the huge volume featured many surrealist and surrealist-inspired contributions, including the first-ever publication of the French group's anti-imperialist manifesto, "Murderous Humanitarianism" (incidentally the first surrealist tract to be cosigned by Black surrealists). Cunard's own essays for the book, at once painstakingly researched and full of passion, discuss racial injustice in the U.S. and the vibrancy of life in Harlem.

Remarkable, too, is the work of Mary Low, surrealist poet and organizer of the women's militia during the Spanish Revolution of 1936. Prefaced by West Indian Marxist C. L. R. James, Low's *Red Spanish Notebook* (1937), written with her companion, Cuban surrealist poet Juan Breá, was the first full-length English-language study of the revolution, in which she and Breá were active militants. Although it is basically a work of reportage, Low's insightful running commentary, notably in the chapter on women, reflects an inquiring spirit well-versed in critical theory.

Also interesting, though less ambitious, is Pailthorpe's attempt to define the scientific aspect of surrealist research, specifically in relation to psychoanalysis—her own field of expertise. Although Pailthorpe was not the first Freudian analyst associated with surrealism, she was the first to plunge into it head first and to put it into practice as a painter.

It should come as no surprise that the first women surrealist theorists were among those who were most aware of the movement's social implications—Cahun and Low as activists in Marxist organizations, Cunard as a living link between surrealism and Pan-Africanism, Pailthorpe as a psychoanalyst whose earlier work had proposed radical solutions to the problems of delinquency. Surrealists who were also active in revolutionary politics tended to be a minority. Throughout the history of the movement, however, they have also tended to be those who recognized most clearly how the various facets of surrealist activity form a coherent, dynamic whole. This perception of the "larger picture" is a major function of theory, and serious practical revolutionary activity is impossible without it.

Critics have often reduced women's role in surrealism to a voiceless passivity, as if they were pawns in someone else's game. I have emphasized their self-activity in surrealism—in the Hegelian sense of an *internally necessary* activity—because everything convinces me that their increasing involvement was no accident but was the result of their own doing, their own "rendezvous with history." Surely the influx of fifty-three women is one reason that surrealism in the thirties was a larger, stronger, more influential, and productive movement than it had been in the twenties.

Notes

1. A useful short account of the Violette Nozières case may be found in the notes to Pierre, ed., *Tracts surréalistes,* I, 1980, 483–486.

2. *Violette Nozières* (Brussels: Editions Nicolas Flamel, 1933). The volume was reprinted in 1991 by Terrain vague, with supplemental material and an introduction by José Pierre. The complete text and illustrations are also included in Pierre, ed., *Tracts surréalistes* I, 1980, 246–262.

Many years later other artists echoed the surrealists' enthusiasm for these rebellious women. The Papin sisters inspired Jean Genet's 1947 play, *The Maids,* and at least two feature films; and Nozières is the subject of Claude Chabrol's 1970s film, *Violette.*

3. The best critical study of surrealism and psychoanalysis remains Alexandrian 1974.

4. Marcel Duchamp used the chess term "heterodox opposition" in the title of an article (Duchamp 1930). In the context of surrealism, it would seem to have wider implications. See Franklin Rosemont 1989.

5. The first women to take part in a surrealist exhibition were Marie-Berthe Ernst and Valentine Hugo, in the "Exposition surréaliste" at the Galerie Pierre Colle in Paris in June 1933.

6. See Jaguer 1982; Krauss and Livingston 1985; Neusüss 1990.

7. Prassinos is represented in the "Double Surrealist Number" of the English journal *Contemporary Poetry and Prose* in 1936 and in Julien Levy's *Surrealism* (New York, 1936). Several of Carrington's stories were featured in *View* magazine in the early 1940s, and two were included in Ford 1945.

Claude Cahun

Born in 1894 in Nantes, Lucy Schwob—whose uncle, Marcel Schwob, author of *The Book of Monelle,* was a friend of Jarry's—grew up bilingual and studied in England before taking up philosophy at the Sorbonne in 1914. In 1917 she chose the name Claude Cahun in honor of her mother's brother, Léon Cahun, a distinguished orientalist and colleague of many symbolist poets. In the 1920s she frequented the group around the journal *Philosophies* (Henri Lefebvre and others) and later ex-dada Georges Ribemont-Dessaignes, editor of *Bifur.* Her 1930 book, *Aveux non avenus* [Absent Confessions]—an autobiographical mélange of maxims, poems, dreams, and excerpts from correspondence—reflected a surrealist spirit (Pierre MacOrlan, who prefaced it, compared it to the memoirs of Isabelle Eberhardt). By 1932, as a militant in the Association des Ecrivains et Artistes Révolutionnaires [Association of Revolutionary Writers], AEAR, Cahun was close to the Surrealist Group, which she soon joined.

She took part in the 1936 surrealist objects exhibition in Paris, illustrated Lise Deharme's book, *The Woodpecker's Heart,* in 1937, collaborated on the journals *Minotaure* and *Cahiers d'art,* and was also active in the "Contre-Attaque" [Counterattack] group organized by Breton and Georges Bataille in 1935. Four years later she joined the International Federation for an Independent Revolutionary Art (FIARI). Isolated on the Isle of Jersey during World War II, in 1946 she resumed contact with the Paris group, with whom she remained in sporadic communication until her death in 1954.

Thanks to the recent discovery of a large number of her photographs, Cahun is now well known as one of the greatest surrealist photographers, and the first photographer to specialize in self-portraits. But she was also an inspired theorist and pamphleteer. Her *Les Paris sont ouvert* [Bets Are On] (1934) remains one of the most luscious fruits of surrealism's early encounter with Marxism, and every one of her scattered articles is full of provocative ideas.

"Captive Balloon" is excerpted from "Carnaval en chambre" [An Armchair Carnival] in *La Ligne de coeur* [Life Line] no. 4 (March 1926). "The Invisible Adventure" prefaced her *Aveux non avenus.* "Poetry Keeps Its Secret" and the paragraphs titled "Surrealism and Working-Class Emancipation" are excerpted from Cahun's report prepared for the literary section of the AEAR in January–February 1933 and were first published in *Les Paris sont ouvert* (1934). "From Life I Still Expect . . . ," a response to an inquiry, was published in *Minotaure* no. 3–4 (December 1933). "Beware Domestic Objects!" first appeared in *Cahiers d'art* I–II, "L'Objet" (1936).

CAPTIVE BALLOON

The charm of the mask inspires petty romantic souls, but wearing the mask plays into the hands of those who, for material or psychological reasons, have an interest in not behaving in an open-faced way.

Masks are made of different quality materials: cardboard, velvet, flesh, the Word. The carnal mask and the verbal mask are worn in all seasons. I soon learned to prefer to all others these off-the-market stratagems. You study your self; you add a wrinkle, a fold at the corner of the mouth, a look, an intonation, a gesture, even a muscle. . . . You create for yourself several clearly defined vocabularies, several syntaxes, several ways of being, thinking, and even feeling—from which you'll choose a skin the color of time . . .

This game is so engaging that it'll soon rob you of the means to cause harm (or to live, as you please). A coin out of circulation. Devoid of social value. Disgusted with its ruts, the train car leaves its rails and falls over on its side. So, all it takes is for the flesh to make way for the spirit (that being the logical progress of evil). From now on, at the roll call you'll only be able to answer "absent," you'll be incapable of taking lessons, and you'll be able to make love only by correspondence. . . .

In front of the mirror, on a day full of enthusiasm, you put your mask on too heavily; it bites your skin. After the party, you lift up a corner to see . . . a failed decal. With horror you see that the flesh and its mask have become inseparable. Quickly, with a little saliva, you reglue the bandage on the wound.

"I remember, it was Carnival time. I had spent my solitary hours disguising my soul. Its masks were so perfect that when they happened to run into each other on the plaza of my consciousness, they didn't recognize one another. I adopted the most surly opinions, one after another: those that displeased me the most were the most certain of success. But the facepaints that I'd used seemed indelible. To clean them off, I rubbed so hard that I took off the skin. And my soul, like a face galled to the quick, no longer resembled human form."

Can they say "Well done!" when such suffering seems artificial? It isn't enough to be good for clumsy sparrows, you must be able to help mechanical birds take flight. More burdensome than pain, perhaps they'll traverse either time or space.

Translated from the French by Myrna Bell Rochester

THE INVISIBLE ADVENTURE

The invisible adventure.

The lens follows the eyes, the mouth, the wrinkles on the surface of the skin. . . . The face's expression is violent, sometimes tragic. And finally calm—the lucid, elaborate calm of acrobats. A professional smile—and *voilà!*

Then in the hand mirror the rouge and the eyeshadow reappear. A pause. A period. A new paragraph.

I start all over again.

But what a ridiculous game this is for those who have not seen—and I have shown nothing—obstacles, abysses, and steps, all cleared.

Shall I then load myself down with all the gear of facts, stones, tenderly cut ropes, precipices . . . ? This is not interesting. Guess, restore. Vertigo is understood, in the climb or the fall.

To please them must we follow the unknown woman step by step, to illuminate her up to the ankle? The worn-down heels, the mud, the bleeding foot—humble and precise evidence—would touch someone. While . . .

No. I shall follow the wake in the air, the trail in the water, the mirage in the pupils.

I try in vain to relax. The abstract, the world of dreams, are as limited for me as the concrete, the real. What can I do? Choose a narrow mirror and reflect only a part for the whole? Confuse a halo with some mud splatters? Refusing to smash myself against the walls, I instead banged myself against the windowpanes? All in the black night.

While waiting for clarity of sight, I want to track myself down, to wrestle. Sensing oneself armed against oneself, even if only with the most useless words, who would not make an effort, if only to fling oneself precisely into the void?

This is false. It is not much. But it exercises the eye.

I want to sew, to sting, to kill, and only with the sharpest point. The rest of the body, the continuation, what a waste of time! To sail ahead only in the direction of my own prow.

Translated from the French by Erin Gibson

POETRY KEEPS ITS SECRET

Some among us may think that poetry, devoid of practical utility, can henceforth tend only toward self-destruction and will play no role in future societies. In attempts at poetry, even those of the proletariat, they will see only vestiges of capitalist society and will decree that we must guide those confused comrades toward the more precise tasks of Marxist propaganda. To this I answer that poetry, having existed historically in all epochs and places, seems undeniably an inherent need of human, and even of animal, nature, a need undoubtedly linked to the sex instinct.[1] Obliged to witness the fact of poetry, we can only record and perhaps hurry along the transformations of its diverse manifestations.

On the other hand, many of us will admit that there exists today a type of poetry against which we must rebel with appropriate polemical and critical activity. To do so we would first need to determine which poetry we consider reactionary or counterrevolutionary. One difficulty, not specific to poetry, but that will bother poets in particular, is that we need to analyze each issue after the fact, from the outside as it were, and that our analysis is always prompted by external laws, rather than the intrinsic laws of poetry. Let us not forget that we are not studying two successive issues, but rather a moving network of links and the absence thereof, a constant bundle of changing relationships between poetic and social evolution—the latter, in our view, subordinate to the former.

A great number of the entries submitted to the Proletarian Literature Contest, are, at least in appearance, poems. We have been asked to guide the entrants and to give them advice. But watch out! There can be no ideological gimmicks, no technical recipes for writing revolutionary poetry. Poems cannot be called "revolutionary" or "not revolutionary" except insofar as, in their very inmost selves, they represent the people, the poets who created them. All poetry is poetry of circumstance. But I see a great difference between a poem whose subject the poet has imposed upon himself, that turns the poet into an actor, and the poem that imposes itself upon the poet by the force of *instantaneous* emotion from a given moment of his personal or collective life—a force that expresses itself through him and too often without his knowledge. That instant can be perfectly hateful to the conscious individual and may even commit a type of aggression upon him, but it is always aggression without the least premeditation. Here, we need to recall the distinction made by Tzara between the *manifest content* of a poem and its *latent content*. The manifest content of a poem, in my view, cannot be revolutionary, in the sense that we normally understand it here, except perhaps in the fleeting way of a song or a satirical poem.[2] That is why I think Communist propaganda should be entrusted only to the *directed thought* of *conscious prose* writers, journalists, orators (even they will need to be careful of lyricism). However, poets in their own way act upon people's sensibility. Their attack is more cunning; but even their most oblique blows can be fatal.

Poetry has already undergone considerable transformation. Criticism, even bourgeois criticism, is recording it; the same bourgeois criticism that earlier claimed to find value only in form, in the strict observance of precise rules, or in the invention of new rules, discounting all ideological content, has now brought content to the fore.[3] Liberation from formalism is precious because it prevents poetry from being reduced to games for the literate. On the other hand, the demand for ideological conformity would lead to the very suppression of all poetry. Let me point this out: Criticism that stresses the *manifest* ideological content of poems favors *charlatans,* all those who want to pass for what they are not and who, in this effort, devote themselves to a type of ideological outbidding. Such criticism is favorable to them as long as it isn't very searching, searching enough to notice at what point they are betraying themselves. For if it is impossible to keep consciousness completely out of the picture, it is impossible as well to avoid absences, a slackening of surveillance, and, consequently, latent content.

It would be interesting to take a *poem of average expression* and do an analysis of it that would uncover under the *manifest* revolutionary content, perhaps surprising to the author himself, all sorts of unconscious reticences. Several entries that were not accepted by the contest struck me as being particularly characteristic in this regard.

Moreover, may I reiterate, the *manifest content* cannot, even on its own territory, escape the critics, for it seems impossible to maintain a consistent ideology within a poem. All the poems that I know are, as far as their *manifest* ideology is concerned, full of fibs and heresies.[4]

It would further be useful to do an analysis of *poems engendered by an activity of the mind.* I am convinced that their translation would at times produce this type of revelation: A man believes he has photographed the hair of the woman he loves, mingled with bits of straw, as she sleeps in a field. But in the *developed* snapshot there appear a thousand divergent arms, shining fists, weapons; we see that it's the photo of a riot.

These analyses of poems could be envisaged as one of the numerous means of determining poetic directives, of laying down trails that can only be provisional. I must insist on their provisional status.

Having determined what factors allow us to reveal the ideological purity of a poem, it remains to be determined what factors allow us to measure and to become familiar with its action, its *propaganda* value.

The only concrete way to evaluate the propaganda quality of a poem would be to try to measure its action upon those whom it reaches. But that would be an impossible task, not only to accomplish but even to conceive of practically. We might imagine certain devices. However, they would never show us anything beyond the degree of intensity of the emotive impulses triggered by reading or hearing a text in variable, individual physiological conditions that would require us to take them into account in order to reduce the variability. In any event, information obtained in that fashion would naturally never deal with the nature nor the possible application of the emotion released, only the degree of its intensity. Perhaps it is only psychoanalysis that could shed some light on the nature of the feelings triggered by a reading. But in order to be able to draw directives from it, psychoanalysis would need to be more generally practiced. . . .

Notes

1. If poetic specialization tends toward its own ruination, it isn't that poetry itself needs to vanish. On the contrary, it's because it "needs to be made by all, not by one" (Lautréamont).
2. It will cease to be revolutionary, and it could even become counter-revolutionary (e.g., *La Marseillaise*) when the situation that inspired it changes.
3. However, in 1933 the author of the *Treatise on Style* (that is, Aragon) complacently insisted that technique decides everything (an industrial slogan ascribed to Stalin). This aberration in literary history connects Aragon—the regressive Aragon—to men of another age who never proclaimed themselves "traitors to their class": Oscar Wilde, Paul Valéry, Jean Cocteau. But Aragon provides more imperialism than his colleagues. He doesn't hesitate to supply the *rabcors* (worker-correspondents) with their shibboleth, his much-loved lesson of skepticism, or to have it transmitted, camouflaged by a "regeneration by the proletariat," to the writers he is trying to discipline: "to reach the height of their vocation, the *rabcors* must learn their métier well, starting with apprenticeship and technique, for it is a very difficult métier" (*Rabcor-Commune* no. 4). And the problem, marvels Aragon, is beyond the question (for whom and why do we write?); the problem—for him—is surely how to write.
4. Cf. these lines by Aragon (*Persécuté persécuteur* [1931]): "Long live the Guépéou, dialectical figure of heroism / that we may contrast with the imbecilic image of the aviators / who crash their mugs praised as heroes by imbeciles"; and these lines from *L'Humanité* (1–4 February 1934): "Workers in Moscow organize a grand state funeral for the three fallen heroes of Soviet aviation. Since yesterday, flags at half-mast . . . hundreds of thousands of workers have come to pay final homage to the three Soviet heroes who died in the fall of the Ossoviakhim. During the funeral the mourners' convocation was opened by . . . To the sound of a funeral march, the Molotov comrades, . . . Behind them, the families of the fallen, Stalin, Voroshilov, and other members of the C.C., members of the Revolutionary Military Council, and the repre-

Claude Cahun, *Coronation Carriage,* ca. 1938. Photograph courtesy of Edouard Jaguer.

> sentatives of other Moscow organizations. For their extraordinary courage and abnegation, the Central Executive Committee of the U.S.S.R. has decided to decorate the three aeronauts who died in the accident which befell the stratospheric balloon with the Order of Lenin . . . By decision of the Council of Commissars of the People of the U.S.S.R., a monthly pension of 500 rubles will be awarded to the families of the three heroes of the disaster."

Translated from the French by Myrna Bell Rochester

SURREALISM AND WORKING-CLASS EMANCIPATION

For France and probably for the rest of Europe as well, the experiment that began with dadaism and is now pursued by surrealism has shown itself to be, beyond all argument, the most revolutionary experiment in poetry. Its whole tendency has been to destroy the many myths about art—myths which for centuries permitted not only the ideological but also the economic exploitation of painting, sculpture, writing, etc. Consider, for example, Max Ernst's *frottages* which, among other things, have effectively overturned the scale of values long maintained by art critics and experts: values largely based on perfect technique, personal touch, and the durability of the artist's materials.

The dadaist-surrealist experiment, therefore, can and should serve the cause of working-class emancipation. Only when the proletariat has become conscious of the real meaning of the myths that uphold capitalist culture—indeed, only when the proletariat has destroyed these myths and revolutionized this culture—will working men and women be able, as a class, to proceed to their own self-development. The positive lesson of this experience in negation—that is, the dissemination of the surrealist experiment among the working class—is the only valid revolutionary poetic propaganda in our time.

Translated from the French by Franklin Rosemont

FROM LIFE I STILL EXPECT THAT OVERWHELMING EXPERIENCE: RESPONSE TO AN INQUIRY ON ENCOUNTERS

What has been the capital encounter of your life? To what extent does this seem to you to have been fortuitous? Necessary?—André Breton and Paul Eluard

From life I still expect that overwhelming experience which will serve as my criterion and which will allow me to give definitive preference to this or that encounter whose importance and meaning will never cease to brighten or grow dim in my eyes, to win or to lose.

The only encounter that has played a critical role during every moment of my life occurred before my birth. I might not have recalled such an ordinary fact (which goes without saying and can only be said rhetorically) except for this: as far back as I can remember, I have experienced the familiar but irritating feeling that my destiny was largely enacted outside of me and almost without my knowledge.

This irritation leads me to counterpose the two words "fortuitous" and "necessary." From a subjective and fragmentary point of view, everything seems ideally fortuitous, and I consider the countless possibilities which logically had to contradict the eruption of any coincidence, outside of its causes. But however little I may refer materially to the totality of objects and however little I attempt to connect them—and no matter how out of place, how disproportional and imponderable certain connections seem to me—the necessity of the most fortuitous encounter is indispensable. And what eludes me is nothing but ignorance.

So many fortuitous-necessary encounters occur for each one of us, and they are so precarious that the happiest day of our lives, or the dullest, might very well go unnoticed. I would therefore confess to having lived through that *all-important* encounter without noticing it, if referring to it in that way did not tell me that we cannot survive it.

Translated from the French by Guy Ducornet

BEWARE DOMESTIC OBJECTS!

Compared to humans, other animals seem quite reasonable. What differentiates the human animal, what constitutes its own peculiarity and best describes it is that it increasingly tends to surpass the rational field—that is, the field of synchronic adaptation of life to its environment. The human animal feels satisfied with a minimum of bodily adaptation, but it strives and succeeds in maintaining life despite circumstances that it worsens in order to reach, if only partially, ever more elusive and blindly pursued goals, while placing its fate in the hands of future generations. The human animal alone has the capacity to cause an upheaval of matter so great that its own organs are abloom with monstrosities and endless diseases. Only the civilized human possesses this ferocious power and the unbridled luxury of nursing it—that is, of preserving and cultivating such a variety of vain ornamentations, exhibiting leprosy and tumors—terrifying invented or found objects, irrational sproutings of flesh. Not only does such ornamentation display itself disdainfully against all *utility* (?) but also at its margins. The marvelous colors of the human iris defy the lovers' memory. The root structure of the small molars forces the dentist to conclude that "anatomy does not exist." Epileptic fits ceaselessly offer psychiatrists the most disconcerting heresies.

It is the same with so-called inanimate matter: it is wholly malleable for the irrational animal called human. Starting with the pink celluloid keys and green hammers the child uses as rattles, if he finds in them, beyond all pseudo-educational pretexts, the same satisfactions as those who (consciously or not) imagined or selected them; after the bread crumb pellets mechanically (?) rolled between the fingers, and after a tapered sugar needle in one's mouth, offered as a prize; after the sand castles on the beach, the charming lard palaces erected by pork butchers, the ignoble monuments honoring the dead, the revolutionaries and the carrier pigeons; after the fireworks displays where one last star lights up the sky when everything else has vanished—a pitiful and stillborn star that kindles nothing—there is nothing left of the awful feast where reason could show us only the enslavement of man by man, by matter, by systems. And it is for us to discover where reason stops, to seize matter and to hold onto it with the awareness of our liberation.

In today's society all of us are not always in a position to make ourselves ductile—good conductors of liberating forces—and we are often surprised to find ourselves resembling more the *little mimic* than the *great paranoiac*. But among other symptoms, the overproduction of stranger and stranger objects (such as microscopic tweezers, usable only under a microscope) assures us that all around us present-day reality is cracking at the seams: the assembly line of forced, mind-numbing labor and the golden bridle of passion will be broken again and again, before the photographs of perishable objects I am gazing upon at this very moment will have a chance to fade.

I could go on and on about those objects: they will speak to you better themselves, and they would speak still better if we could touch them in the dark. In contrast to the prodigiously liberated and liberating talents of those explorers and fabricators of the objects we see before us, thoughts of the oppressed come to me, and I mourn for their own beautiful talents, warped and lost. I am thinking of a child written up in an article—perhaps you read it too—that investigated these sad remnants: born deaf, mute, and blind, she was a bundle of "nerves and screams" surrendered to a religious education at age eight. You can guess what the cumulative effect of patience and resignation made of her. But you, she, and I could have touched upon the irrational object she might easily have created, mixing elements according to subtle clues, such as consistency or smells, thus playing, far beyond love, with what obscure superfluity. But today? In her and for her, infirmity and love are forever intertwined like pieces of a scarecrow around its pole. Catholicism did its work quite well, and proudly too. To familiarize the child with death, they had her touch and sniff corpses; on certain nights they put her to bed with her dying sister. They even managed to instill in her some vague notions about marriage and procreation, with the warning: "In her situation, could she even imagine it?"

I insist on this primordial truth: one must oneself discover, manipulate, *tame*, and construct irrational objects to be able to appreciate the particular or general value of those displayed here. That is why, in certain respects, *manual* laborers may be in a better position than intellectuals to understand them, were it not for the fact that the whole of capitalist society—communist propaganda included—diverts them from doing so. And that is why you are beginning to dig into your pockets, and perhaps to empty them out on the table.

Trim a sponge in the shape of a brain and staunch a bit of the blood that is spilled every day. Place it in a tub and see if it floats, if the water reddens, and if animal spirits do not squirt out of its pores: the *skinflower,* the *swiftwing,* the *turtlecat,* the *pink lirelie* (a tiny germinating potato), the *popegeon* (a kiss where eyelashes touch, a palpitating eyelid), the lascivious *civelle,* and all the lovable nameless ones. Muddy the water of the *animarium* with a glass stirring rod—the word *agitator* comes to mind and startles you. The long-awaited creature arrives at last, not knowing where to drop its tears.

Take a mirror. Scratch the silvering near your right eye. Behind the small clear spot, slip a strip on which small objects have been glued and look at your eyes as you walk by. This is called the Game of Cinders.

Find a small thatched house (the electrovox) at the back of which you discover a plate sensitive to certain sounds. You may make anything or anybody jump out of it, but *only if* you have previously put it or them inside: all you have to do is *speak loudly.* Your voice will cause the plate to vibrate. If there is more than one player in this not-so-innocent game, it may happen that the object inserted by one person and accidentally called by the other will respond to secret affinities. Did I say "*may* happen"? It's certain that it will. Be careful!

Moreover, act as though whatever I have said about it, in any case, is only to get you to construct (to destroy + x) with your own ideas and findings, which, however much they may have in common with ours, nonetheless remain—partly or entirely—*still* unknown.

Translated from the French by Guy Ducornet

Nancy Cunard

Notwithstanding her ultrapale complexion and eyes "bluer than any sapphires," as Kay Boyle put it, Nancy Cunard was a person who, in the words of her friend Marcus Garvey, "thinks sympathetically Black" (Garvey 1932, 314). Absorbed as a child by "extraordinary dreams about Africa," she was an early devotee of authentic jazz and African art. However, not until she met the African American jazz musician/composer Henry Crowder—in Venice in 1928, where he was playing piano with Eddie South's Alabamians—did her consciousness of Africa and the African diaspora really expand. They soon became lovers as well as coworkers at the Hours Press, which brought out a volume of Crowder's compositions with a cover by Man Ray.

Cunard's U.S.-born white supremacist mother, whom she always referred to ironically as "Her Ladyship," strongly objected to Nancy's relationship with Crowder and immediately cut off her allowance. What started as a family tiff became a national scandal when Nancy retaliated with an excoriating pamphlet, *Black Man and White Ladyship* (1931)—a militant polemic in the tradition of Surrealist Group diatribes such as *Permettez!* [Allow Us] (1927), denouncing a government commemoration of the poet Rimbaud.

In her excellent biography of Cunard, Ann Chisholm concludes a bit too hastily that "Nancy made little contribution to surrealist ideas" (Chisholm 1979, 106). Many surrealists later distinguished themselves as critics of racism, scholars of African culture, and defenders of Black struggles, but Cunard was the first to take up these matters in a systematic way. In 1931 she turned her Hours Press over to others in order to devote herself full-time to an unprecedented project: a monumental international compilation of scholarly articles, historical sketches, reportage, poetry, and revolutionary polemic representing the achievements and aspirations of the Black world. The book took years to put together, but when it was finally ready, no publisher would touch it—so Cunard had it printed at her own expense.

Negro: An Anthology (1934), dedicated to Henry Crowder, was by far the largest surrealist-related book up to that date: 864 large-format pages. For the first time, a solid contingent of surrealists—including René Crevel, Benjamin Péret, Raymond Michelet (whom Cunard acknowledged as her "chief collaborator" on the book), and John Banting, who was later active in the Surrealist Group in England—appeared together with such outstanding figures of the Black world as Sterling Brown, Zora Neale Hurston, W. E. B. DuBois, Langston Hughes, Nicolas Guillén, Jacques Roumain, and George Padmore.

Negro was a sensation, a landmark in public awareness of the wonders of Black culture. Exemplifying her generous nature, she sent numerous complimentary copies to libraries in Harlem and other Black communities. Unfortunately, actual sales of the book proved disappointing, and Cunard, who had sunk all her money into the project, made almost nothing in return. During the Spanish Civil War she made her living as a reporter for the Associated Negro Press of the U.S. and the *Manchester Guardian* in England.

In later years she lived mostly in isolation in the French countryside, where she wrote several book-length memoirs, most notably *Those Were the Hours*. After a long illness aggravated by drugs and heavy drinking, the formerly rich heiress, long since read out of the family fortune, died in poverty in a Paris hotel room in 1965.

Published here are the concluding paragraphs of *Black Man, White Ladyship* and two excerpts from Cunard's own essays in *Negro: An Anthology.* "The Scottsboro Case" reviews the background and significance of the notorious case in which nine young Black men were convicted, on trumped-up charges, of raping two white prostitutes. "A Trip to Harlem" (from a long essay titled "Harlem Reviewed") records Cunard's impressions of her extensive visits there while gathering material for her anthology. Like many other articles in *Negro,* this text reflects the surrealists' hope in world revolution under the banner of the Communist International. However, as Hugh Ford explains in the currently available (abridged) edition of *Negro,* Cunard never joined the Communist Party and indeed insisted that she was basically an anarchist.

HOW COME, WHITE MAN?

"In Africa," you [racists] say, "the Negro is a savage, he has produced nothing, he has no history." It is certainly true he has not got himself mixed up with machinery and science to fly the Atlantic, turn out engines, run up skyscrapers and contrive holocausts. There are no tribal presses emitting the day's lies and millions of useless volumes. There remain no written records; the wars, the kingdoms and the changes have sufficed unto themselves. It is not one country but many; well over four hundred separate languages and their dialects are known to exist.

Who tells you you are the better off for being "civilized" when you live in the shadow of the next war or revolution in constant terror of being ruined or killed? Things in Africa are on a different scale—but the European empire-builders have seen, are seeing to this hand over fist.

And what, against this triumph of organized villainy, had the Black man to show? His own example of *Homo Sapiens* is on better terms with life than are the conquering whites. Anthropology gives him priority in human descent. He had his life, highly organized, his logic, his customs, his laws rigidly adhered to. He made music and unparalleled rhythm and some of the finest sculpture in the world. Nature gave him the best body amongst all the races. Yet he is [in the opinion of racists] a "miserable savage" because there are no written records, no super-cities, no machines. But to prove the lack of these an insuperable loss, a sign of racial inferiority, you must attack the root of all things and see where—if anywhere—lies truth. There are many truths.

How come, white man, is the rest of the world to be re-formed in your dreary and decadent manner?

THE SCOTTSBORO CASE

To bring out the absolute fiendishness of the treatment of Negro workers by the governing white class in America, more specifically, but by no means restrictedly, in the Southern states, I am going to start with what may seem a fantastic statement—I am going to say that the Scottsboro case is not such an astounding and unbelievable thing as it must, as it certainly does, appear to the public at large.

What? Nine provenly innocent Negro boys, falsely accused of raping two white prostitutes, tried and re-tried, still held in death cells after two-and-a-half years. . . . It is unparalleled.

It is not *primarily* a case that can be called political, as is that of Tom Mooney, still held for eighteen years in San Quentin, a California jail, on an equally vicious frame-up because he was an active strike-leader; nor at first sight do the same elements predominate as in Meerut and the murder-by-law of Sacco and Vanzetti. But the same capitalist oppression and brutality are at the root—because every Negro worker is the potential victim of lynching, murder and legal lynching by the white ruling class, simply because he is a worker and Black.

No, this frame-up is not unparalleled, though the scale of it and its colossal development into what is now really a world-issue, are so. No previous Negro case has aroused such a universal outcry against the abomination of American "law."

• • •

One would like to engrave the entire [trial] report, the whole detail of these trial testimonies of both sides, the false along with the real, on some matter that would last as long as humanity; to record forever also the moment of this cutting open of the plague of hatred, the exposure of Southern courts' "justice." The whole of the American Negroes' misery tightens into one phrase, into two lines written by one of their own poets:

Oughta had mo' sense
Dan to evah git born.

That is by Sterling Brown. And if it rings agonizingly defeatist so often it rings as bitterly true. But it is going to change. Five years ago the Scottsboro boys would have been just another locally heard-of case of nine more dead victims.

• • •

It is only by fighting that anything of major issue is obtained. In the way of justice, of aid and of good the Black man in America until now has received from the white only what must be classed as the comparative crumbs of humanitarianism and philanthropy. We do not ask for our Negro comrades these tokens of guilty conscience, these palliative gestures. *We demand recognition and enforcement of the Negro's full rights, as an equal, as a brother, and an end to the oppression of colored peoples the world over.*

16 September 1933

A TRIP TO HARLEM

The snobbery around skin-color is terrifying. The light-skins and browns look down on the black. . . . All this, indeed, is Society with a vengeance! A bourgeois ideology with no horizon, no philosophical link with life. And out of all this, need it be said, such writers as Van Vechten[1] and Co. have made a revolting and cheap lithograph, so that Harlem, to a large idle-minded public, has come to mean nothing more whatsoever than a round of hooch-filled[2] nightclubs after a round of "snow"-filled[3] boudoirs. Van Vechten, the spirit of vulgarity, has depicted Harlem as a grimace. . . . The "Negro Renaissance" (the literary movement of about 1925, now said to be at a halt, and one wonders on whose authority this is said) produced many books and poems filled with this bitter-sweet of Harlem's glitter and heartbreak.

This is not the Harlem one sees. You don't see the Harlem of the romanticists; it is romantic in its own right. And it is *hard* and *strong*; its noise, heat, cold, cries and colors are so. And the nostalgia is violent, too; the eternal radio seeping through everything day and night, indoors and out, becomes somehow the personification of restlessness, desire, brooding. And then the gorgeous roughness, the gargle of Louis Armstrong's voice breaks through. As everywhere, the real people are in the street. I mean those young men on the corner, and the people all sitting on the steps throughout the breathless, leaden summer. I mean the young men in Pelham Park; the sports groups (and one sees many in their bright sweaters), the strength of a race, its beauty.

• • •

There is no color *problem*. The existence of the Negro race is not a problem; it is a *fact*. And in America, as in all other imperialist countries, this use of a wrong word is neither more nor less than a vicious lie on the part of the ruling class in urging the workers of each country into thinking that the Negro, the colored race, was created by nature as a *menace.* The growing volume of the Communist consciousness among the black workers, and in some of the Negro intellectuals, dates chiefly from five years ago, and has in that time made, and is making, rapid increase. It is something new, *more and more tangible. . . .*

One of the first things I was impressed by, the best thing that remains of Harlem, was the magnificent strength and lustiness of the Negro children. As I walked from end to end of it, down the length of Seventh Avenue, the schools were just out. The children rushed by in rough leather jackets in the cold wind, some of them playing ball on roller skates, shouting and free. May these gorgeous children in their leathers be the living symbol of the finally liberated Negro people.

Up with an all-Communist Harlem in an all-Communist United States!

Notes

1. Novelist Carl Van Vechten (1880–1964) was widely criticized by radicals for his stereotyped portrayal of African Americans. [Editor's note]
2. Drink. [Cunard's note]
3. Cocaine. [Cunard's note]

Simone Yoyotte

The first woman of African descent to take part in surrealism, Simone Yoyotte (ca. 1910–1933) was born and raised in Martinique. Nothing is known of her early life. The only woman in the *Légitime Défense* [Self-Defense] group formed by Martiniquan students in Paris in 1932, she published poems in that group's one-shot journal, and was soon frequenting the Paris Surrealist Group. She was probably also a member of the Communist-oriented Union Générale des Etudiants [General Union of Students]. According to surrealist poet Henri Pastoureau, Yoyotte married fellow *Légitime Défense* member Jules Monnerot in Paris and died, very young, a few months later.

Before Yoyotte, no woman of color in the Caribbean had written with such unrestrained verve. Surely she deserves recognition as one of the emancipators of language from colonialist inhibitions.

"Pale Blue Line" appeared in *Légitime Défense.* "Half-Season" was published by André Breton in *Le Surréalisme ASDLR* no. 5 (May 1933).

PALE BLUE LINE IN A FORCED EPISODE, I CUT A HOLE IN THE FLAG OF THE REPUBLIC

My beautiful bird in the eternal the downspouts call you but don't think about coming back. The feathers of a pleasant surname won't fail to admit fear fear of the wind in the glaciers. My beautiful bird the thunder of all my desires the satisfaction of the sun already set and of all my confused thorns in the undifferentiated anguish of a sojourn I did not wish to impose on you my bird my late bird blood my despair in short sleeves of shaded satin color of my recklessness your feathers your feathered wings on the back foot my bird counter-riddle let us dissipate the brightness of your light blue lines my white voracious gudgeon you are my beautiful bird my beautiful bird zephyr in the night and when all the lamps blow out in the leather of my little agony. I have flown into the embankments and into the poplars I have sold worry to the easygoing investor I have wandered through the temples of desolation by night by day at the setting of all the great sorrows and everywhere beautiful bird I saw you in the stones and you could not know that the mind does not cross the river for on the bridge that you tossed me it was in vain that I stoned all the ripples. The call of the rhombohedron at the edge of April resembles the music of your own shadow my useless bird who only knows how to people the revolt with all the great trees of the avenues and all the boulevards when the trumpet of the banquet halls resonate under the windows of the woman you do not yet love.

Translated from the French by Myrna Bell Rochester

HALF-SEASON

I.
Embarrassed cold
in that splendid time when I was naked
I think about saying

far from there
from feet to head
THE SONOROUS SHADOW

Cries
like the seagull
I'm afraid of those eyes

atonal desire
for the first roots

II.
To J.-M.
Living comet on the peak
such a one
who likewise plunges
does not possess the source of pleasure
I was
like the rocks
an extra immanent
truncated
evil-minded
but the murmuring makes me change
place and ink
to my own measure
like
a liquid
weight that obsesses me
finds its way in a dream
and turns

Translated from the French by Myrna Bell Rochester

Greta Knutson

Born in 1899 in Stockholm, Greta Knutson studied at the School of Fine Arts in that city, moving to Paris in the early 1920s where she became a student of the painter André Lhote. In 1925 she married Tristan Tzara, whose wife she remained until 1939. Philosophically inclined toward Husserl's phenomenology, Knutson participated in surrealism only for a few years in the early 1930s. Primarily a painter in the post-cubist abstract tradition, she also became a noted art critic. Knutson published no collection of her poetry. The poem translated here originally appeared in *Le Surréalisme ASDLR* no. 5 (1933).

FOREIGN LAND

Why interrupt
the conversation of sleepwalking clocks
to ask them the dangerous way

When they will have named
sailboats icebergs sugar and ebony
and the humble silk of the moon
that knows how to fasten the squall's seine to the dawn
among so many breaths
a woodland voice will flow
The story of the cliffside path
Will be a path between statues and doves
and the plant that licks the flagstone
will lift its hand toward the iron
Path to the broken porch shelter of the pursued
night came morning gone
toward the gentle flock and the boat sleeping
against the temple of the riverbank
to the bitter tree's bark
between the girl's teeth
road beneath blood under rock
Was it the stag throat slit by a thorn
but that would hunt at dark of night
that cried let us awake
where is the morning

Translated from the French by Penelope Rosemont

Lise Deharme

Paris-born Lise Meyer (née Hirtz), daughter of a famous doctor, visited the Paris Bureau of Surrealist Research in 1925 and, as a result of an incident recorded in Breton's *Nadja,* became known as "The Lady of the Glove." For the rest of her life she remained an ally of, and occasionally a participant in, the Surrealist Movement. As editor of a small paper in the Paris suburb of Neuilly, she regularly devoted space to surrealism and even reprinted surrealist tracts. Deharme was also a prolific author of surrealist tales, poems, and nursery rhymes as well as curious novels; her bibliography includes twenty-four volumes. In the 1950s she also contributed articles on such writers as Gérard de Nerval and

J.-K. Huysmans to the scholarly journal *La Tour Saint-Jacques* [The Saint-Jacques Tower], devoted to magic and hermetism. She died in Paris in 1979.

The two poems are from her *Cahier de curieuse personne* [Notebook of a Curious Person] (1933).

THE EMPTY CAGE

I missed
the book of my life
one night
when they forgot
to put a sharp pencil
next to my bed

THE LITTLE GIRL OF THE BLACK FOREST

Once there was a little girl
dressed in tatters
who had only one idea
in the depth of her despair
an idea of dying
in the Black Forest.

That's all for tonight.

Translated from the French by Franklin Rosemont

Denise Bellon, Gala Dalí, Nusch Eluard, Yolande Oliviero

EXPERIMENTAL RESEARCH: ON THE IRRATIONAL KNOWLEDGE OF THE OBJECT: THE CRYSTAL BALL OF THE SEERS

Editor's note: These questions and answers, part of a series of collective investigations into the possibilities of "irrational knowledge," appeared in Le Surréalisme ASDLR *no. 6 (May 1933).*

Questions:

1. Is it diurnal or nocturnal? 2. Is it favorable toward love? 3. Is it suitable for metamorphoses? 4. What is its spatial location with respect to the individual? 5. What epoch does it correspond to? 6. What happens if it is submerged in water? 7. in milk? 8. in vinegar? 9. in urine? 10. in alcohol? 11. in mercury? 12. What element does it correspond to? 13. What philosophical system does it belong to? 14. What disease does it remind you of? 15. What sex is it? 16. With which historical personage may it be identified? 17. How does it die? 18. What must it meet up with on a dissecting table for it to look beautiful? 19. With what two objects would one wish to see it in the desert? 20. On which spot of the nude body of a woman would you place it? 21. and if the woman were sleeping? 22. and if she were dead? 23. What sign of the Zodiac does it correspond to? 24. Where on an armchair would you place it? 25. Where on a bed would you place it? 26. What crime does it correspond to?

DENISE BELLON: 1. Diurnal. 2. Very favorable. 3. Yes. 5. The Middle Ages. 6. It lengthens and melts, and little fish come out of it. 9. It floats away like a child's balloon. 10. It becomes a prism that revolves endlessly. 11. It escapes from children's hands and rolls on the snow. 12. Water. 13. Physiocratic. 14. Tuberculosis. 15. Hermaphroditic. 16. Freud. 17. By infinite fissiparousness. 18. A nude woman's torso and a chronometer. 19. A pool of water and the sun. 20. In the hollow of her neck, half covered by her hair. 21. Under her legs. 22. On her belly, held by her open hand. 23. Libra. 24. Under one of the legs.

GALA (DALÍ): 1. Nocturnal. 2. Favorable, but at times threatening. 3. Yes, when exposed to artificial light. 4. Opposite the chest. 5. The Stone Age. 6. It becomes dazzling. 7. It warms toads. 8. It is transformed into a handful of straw. 9. It flattens out and opens like a book. 10. It bursts. 11. It contributes to a total eclipse. 12. Air. 13. Hegel. 14. Fever. 15. Feminine. 16. Freud.

NUSCH (ELUARD): 1. Diurnal. 2. Yes. 3. Yes. 4. Above him. 5. 1933. 6. It melts. 7. It grows. 8. It disappears. 10. I don't know. 11. It flattens out. 12. Air. 14. None. 15. Masculine. 16. Mars. 17. In water. 20. On her belly. 21. On her shoulder. 22. On her legs. 23. Libra. 24. On one of the arms. 25. On the pillow.

YOLANDE OLIVIERO: 1. Diurnal. 2. Extremely favorable. 3. Very suitable, since it's the seers' ball. 4. In both cupped hands. 5. The reign of Catherine de Medici. The Inquisition. 8. It changes the vinegar into innumerable pearls. 9. I don't want to. Impossible. 10. It multiplies infinitely, and each ball conceals an iceberg. 11. The end of the world; or perhaps it's Saturn itself. 12. Air.

13. *The Surrealist Manifesto. Letter to the Seers. Soluble Fish.* 14. Snow blindness. 15. Feminine. 16. Nostradamus. Cyclops. 17. It is eternal. 18. With a scalpel. 19. The cadaver of a man who dies of thirst and a black velvet neckband with a diamond cross. 21. On one of her eyes, like all her collected tears. 22. The ball cannot touch a dead woman. 23. Virgo. 25. On the pillow, so that it touches the left cheek.

Translated from the French by Myrna Bell Rochester

Maruja Mallo

Born in Lugo, Spain, in 1909, Maruja Mallo was by the late 1920s one of the strongest and strangest personalities in Spanish modernism, not only because of her highly original paintings and photomontages but also because of the virulence of her diatribes against religion, and her boundless nonconformism. A friend of Luis Buñuel, Salvador Dalí, and Federico García Lorca, she naturally encountered surrealism; her 1932 exhibition at the Galerie Pierre in Paris was enthusiastically hailed by André Breton. She collaborated regularly on the Spanish surrealists' journal, *Gaceta de arte,* published in the Canary Islands, took part in the "Exposicion Logicofobista" [Logicophobist Exhibition] in Barcelona in 1936, and in the International Surrealist Exhibition in London that same year. Her surrealist activity proved of short duration, however, largely for political reasons (she was married for a time to Rafael Alberti and was later closely associated with Pablo Neruda—top figures in Stalinism's cultural front).

Although she seems to have written little during the years of her active involvement in surrealism, the retrospective comments published here, written in 1981 and titled "El Surrealismo a través mi obra" [Surrealism as Manifest in My Work], provide a good summary of the outlook of this unusual woman who, as Edouard Jaguer has written, "played a determining role in the genesis of surrealism in Spain."

These excerpts were published in the catalog, *Maruja Mallo* (Guillermo de Osma Galeria, 1992).

SURREALISM AS MANIFEST IN MY WORK

My art is a dynamic process that constantly changes, an evolution of form and content . . . It comes from the incommensurate. What most surprises me in moments of creation is the vital explosion of the Fortunate Isles and the fascination of signs: verbenas, exactly measured magical creations; these are manifestations that rotate with the seasons of the year, pagan revelations that express their discord with ordinary existence.

• • •

The entire surrealist period of my work has been a conscious indictment of the cemetery of garbage that surrounds us. It emerged at that time in the series I called *Sewers and Belltowers*. In May 1932 my second exhibition was held at the Paris Galerie Pierre. It consisted of sixteen canvases containing *Sewers and Belltowers*, art that sprang from the slums and outskirts of Madrid.

At the time I was impressed by nature eliminating the rubble of the past, the earth aflame and bloated. Sewers clogged by winds and belfries toppled by storms, the world of things that pass often stumbles over seasons bristling with ramparts. This is the basis of the content of that work . . .

• • •

Nature is what began to attract me: I wanted to discover a new pattern. This pattern is the intimate architecture of nature and humankind, the living mathematics of the skeleton.

In nature—clairvoyant and mysterious, spontaneous and structured—devoid of anachronistic ghosts, I analyze the structure of minerals and vegetables, the diversity of crystalline and biological forms synthesized in numerical and geometric patterns, in a living and universal order.

To create as nature creates.

• • •

Surrealism always existed, like the original one-celled sea creature, like an anthropological secret.

Absent from physical vision, it must be viewed with eyes closed. And I, with my pencil ready under the pillow I never use, awaken with my brain in my hand.

Translated from the Spanish by Natalie Kenvin

Meret Oppenheim

The first woman to become well-known as a surrealist—as the maker of the surrealist object, "Dejeuner en fourrure" [Lunch in Fur] (1936), commonly called "Fur-Covered Cup, Saucer and Spoon"—Meret Oppenheim was born in Berlin in 1913 but grew up in Switzerland. A rebellious teenager, she left high school in 1931, and a year later, at eighteen, went to Paris, where she soon found her way to the Surrealist Group. Her involvement in surrealism proved to be deep and enduring, as evidenced by her participation in International Surrealist Exhibitions in Copenhagen and Tenerife, 1935; London, 1936; Paris, 1938; Mexico City, 1940; New York, 1942; Paris, 1959 (which opened with her scandalous banquet on a recumbent nude woman); New York, 1960; Milan, 1961; and in Lyons, 1981, in the "Permance du regard surréaliste" exhibition. She also took part in numerous smaller Surrealist Group exhibits, as well as solo shows (her first, in Basle, 1935, was prefaced by Max Ernst). A collaborator on *Documents 34* (1934); *Médium: Informations surréalistes* (1953); *Médium: Communication surréaliste* (1955); and *Le Surréalisme, même* (1956–1959), she also cosigned such tracts as "The Time the Surrealists Were Right" (1935) and "Coup de semonce" [Warning Shot] (1957).

Isolated from her surrealist friends during World War II, Oppenheim suffered a long crisis and painted little in that decade; she resumed her creative activity and participation in the Surrealist Group only in the 1950s. Like Breton, Péret, and others, she had her criticisms of much of what was done in the name of surrealism in the 1950s and 1960s, which did not, however, prevent her from taking part in surrealist activity. And even in her last years, when she pursued an independent course, she remained well within the surrealist trajectory. She died in 1985.

As her work becomes better known—her poetry and other writings, as well as her paintings, drawings, collages, objects, and furniture—it is increasingly conceded that Meret Oppenheim is indeed, as her comrades in the movement always maintained, a major figure in surrealism.

The texts published here, and in later sections of this anthology, are from the *catalogue raisonée* of Bice Curiger, *Meret Oppenheim* (1989).

WHERE IS THE WAGON GOING?

The wagon is going to the woods. The woods
belong to the winter blues

How do you find their address?
You turn the door around.
You read the paeans of migrant birds, of
water fishes, of damned and cursed
Puszta beetles.

There is no caste spirit here.
Here everyone may speak without restraint.
You may dine on an armful of hay if you have one.
Living or dead, you bow in reverence.
Age approaches, slowly. But it cannot
distinguish you.
You hide behind a night butterfly, doing its most beautiful
mimicry and sacrificing its sleep
for you.

(1933)
Translated from the German by Catherine Schelbert

IF YOU SAY THE RIGHT WORD, I CAN SING . . .

If you say the right word, I can sing
you the praises of the raven with its changeable
and shimmering feet.
I love these cold flowers of laughter
best and their nodding shadows that shine in
the dark.

Who will take the madness from the trees?
Who does heaven give steamviolets to?
How does one downfall advise the next?

There are answers to these and other questions:
You separate the scent from its path and
try to tuck in your ear while racing for a
mile. Now the air can narrow its limits
by two degrees and the result will not
be long in coming.

(ca. 1933)
Translated from the German by Catherine Schelbert

ANYONE THAT SEES HER WHITE FINGERS . . .

Anyone that sees her white fingers is ready to be transformed. They all climb out of their skins to surrender to the new world. They all know that no ship will bring them back, but the cornucopia beckons. It fans out and its fragrance streams forth. The green birds rip the sails, and the great sun falls into the water. But as long as someone beats the drum, night cannot sink.

The voyage has lasted more than a hundred years. People swim around their ship like sharks, and the sea is red with blood. Only the brown dogs stick their heads over the sides of the ship. They hold little knives in their jaws and drop them from time to time on the people below. The knives impale the sun which lies deep down at the bottom of the sea. The sun grows little fins.

(Between 1935–1940)
Translated from the German by Catherine Schelbert

Jacqueline Lamba

A much more important surrealist painter than is generally recognized, Jacqueline Lamba was born in Paris in 1910. In May 1934 she met André Breton—an encounter announced in Breton's premonitory poem, "La nuit de tournesol" [Night of the Sunflower] and recounted in detail in his book, *L'Amour fou* [Mad Love]. They married in August, and in December of the following year, their daughter Aube was born.

Lamba's paintings, especially the radiant psychological morphologies done in New York in the 1940s, are her chief contribution to surrealism, but she also made impressive drawings, objects, and collages. A vibrant presence in the Surrealist Group, she took part in several International Surrealist Exhibitions—London, 1936; Tokyo, 1937; Paris, 1947—and her work was reproduced in *Trajectoire du rêve* [Trajectory of the Dream], *VVV,* and other collective publications. Lamba separated from Breton in New York in 1943 and was for several years the wife of sculptor David Hare. After the International Surrealist Exhibition in Paris in 1947, her painting diverged from the surrealist field. She died in rural France in 1995.

These reminiscences are excerpted from a 1974 written interview based on her corrected transcripts of tape recordings she had made (with Arturo Schwarz) on André Breton's 1938 visit with Leon Trotsky in Mexico. Brief as they are, these few passages reflect Lamba's revolutionary spirit as a teenager in the 1920s and what the discovery of surrealism meant to her.

A REVOLUTIONARY APPROACH TO LIFE AND THE WORLD

I was fifteen years old in 1925. As was true of so many others at the time, my very nature, as well as my involvement in painting and poetry, had brought me to a state of mind of anarchistic revolt against the bourgeois society around me. Nonetheless, it was only in 1927 that I really became aware of the October Revolution in Russia. Despite my real desire, however, to somehow take part in this revolutionary ferment, I was unable to make up my mind to become a militant. The Leftist meetings I attended seemed to me utterly routine in character, elementary and gray; my expectations were usually deceived; they turned me off. And then, in 1929, I learned of the Surrealist Movement and particularly of the writings of André Breton, which were, for me and for many others at the time, a revelation.

These writings offered a definitive response to certain problems that are exceptionally difficult to resolve individually (as I have suggested above): problems regarding the relation between the poetic and artistic sensibility and a revolutionary consciousness, militant or otherwise, applied to all levels of existence. The thoroughgoing, exalting, unique spirit of Breton and his friends, their whole approach to life and the world, and the tone of certainty and supreme defiance that accompanied it: all this fulfilled me, liberated me, and instilled in me a joy such as I suspect young people today can scarcely grasp. . . .

Translated from the French by Franklin Rosemont

Gisèle Prassinos

Born in 1920 in Istanbul of a Greek father and an Italian mother, Gisèle Prassinos has lived in or near Paris since early childhood. Introduced to the Surrealist Group at age fourteen in 1934, she enchanted them all with her fantastic, witty poems and tales. Her first texts appeared in *Minotaure* (1934) and *Documents 34*; her first book, *La Sauterelle arthritique*

[The Arthritic Grasshopper], was published in 1935 and was followed by eight other volumes in the next four years. As Mariannne van Hirtum noted, Prassinos's surrealist friends recognized these early writings as a "veritable illustration of automatic language *par excellence.*" Two of her tales of dark laughter are included in Breton's *Anthology of Black Humor.*

After World War II Prassinos's association with organized surrealism was limited, but she has continued to publish widely.

ARROGANT HAIR

A child who was very hot entered the room which he smelled up with his moldy hair. He thought it appropriate to ask me the price of the jug which stood on a shelf in the entrance hall. But I told him his nephew would be very happy if he freed his head.

With a rather suspicious look he said, "Are they nasty, the swallows?"

Shortly after, another child appeared. From his bare stomach hung a hard, cylindrical thing, that gave him the appearance of a fugitive.

He sat next to the other one and said to him, "You have moldy hair." Then, while cleaning the tip of his red shoe, he threw me one of those little leather balls with which both had their hands filled.

I turned to look at the window. During that time undoubtedly some one came in. It must have been a little girl, for I heard her teeth cracking a nut shell. When I turned around I saw a little girl holding green nuts between her teeth. She looked at me, then, holding the first child tightly with her yellow hands, she said to me, "His hair must be moldy, for I found a tiny wood shaving on the landing." Soon after one heard a slight grating noise. It was the second child crying, while looking at his playmate's hair.

When I woke up there were no more children. But on the carpet lay a bandaged male foot, some moldy hair, and some nuts.

Children are afraid of idols.

Translated from the French by Fabienne Lloyd

THE GHOST OF CHATEAUBRIAND

A dog was walking up and down the left pavement of the rue de Seine. The ghost of Chateaubriand, shining with the fire of his entrails, was following him with his umbrella between his legs.

They went along like this for a considerable time. When they arrived on the plain that separates St. Martin's church from its steeple, the dog turned back, sniffed the misty air, and crossed himself. There soon appeared a certain number of lepers, who seemed feverish. But as everyone knows that people pray at the end of each month, the lepers were tiring their feet out in order to assuage their leader's anger. The leader, who seemed to be ill, directed his troop without much difficulty. In spite of this, the ghost of Chateaubriand, dignified and savage, watched over these easily mad creatures.

At last the dog got up. He ran nervously past the troop, which had become impregnated with his strength.

The lepers in front of him did not move. Each of them winked as he went by, and unrolled a cotton reel as though to be worthy of him. All of them, one after another, only in order to talk, stopped leading their predecessor. No one mocked him, knowing how easily annoyed he was.

Having passed into the ranks, he ran toward the ghost, who smiled and whispered a few words to him very softly. Then they went away together, leaving the fine army of simple, worthy lepers behind them.

They followed the pavement that leads to the Bastille. They did not stumble. Only once did the dog come to a standstill in order to say a single word; the mouth between his two nostrils gave a jerk as though to say "good day."

They walked all the time. At a given moment, the ghost sat down on the parapet. They began to talk about a certain innkeeper who used to put papier-mâché in place of the sugar.

At ten o'clock, the dog took a piece of silver lamé out of his waistcoat and shook it with a gesture that was almost old. Then he threw it into the river. The piece of cloth sank, then reappeared dragging a buffalo's skull along behind it. This was followed by a thread fastened to a picket that had just been staked by a miner.

On the sleeping bank where the sun had not yet penetrated, a buffalo's body was grazing the warm grass. The dog watched all this, both white and sleepy.

The ghost stole softly away, his feet in his heart, and was not seen again until the day of the lepers' inspection, which took place on November 22nd, 999.

Translated from the French by David Gascoyne

Toyen

Born Marie Čerminová in Prague in 1902, she chose the name Toyen in her late teens and never used her family name again. A cofounder of the eclectic but radical *Devětsil* group in 1920—a loose association open to constructivists, dadaists, and others—and also influenced by such heterodox natives as Kafka and Hasek, Toyen remained in the thick of everything vital in Czech and European intellectual life. Although she had some contact with surrealism in the 1920s—she lived in Paris between 1925 and 1929, and her first solo exhibit there was prefaced by Philippe Soupault—she did not take part in organized surrealist activity until 1934, when she helped cofound the Surrealist Group in Prague. Her work was included in the International Surrealist Exhibition in Tenerife the following year, and in every subsequent International Surrealist Exhibition except for those during World War II.

Inclined toward anarchism in her youth, Toyen evolved toward Marxism in the 1920s. Her longstanding revolutionary anti-Stalinism made it impossible for her to remain in her native land after 1948, so she fled to Paris where she quickly became one of the key figures in the French Surrealist Group.

Best known as a painter, Toyen was also an admirable graphic artist, as evidenced by her cycles of drawings: *The Specters of the Desert* (1939), *The Shooting* (1946), and *War, Hide Yourself!* (1946), all accompanied by poems by Jindrich Heisler; *Débris de rêves* [Wreckage of Dreams], published with Radovan Ivsic's *Le Puits dans la tour* [The Well in the Tower] (1967); and her drawings for Annie Le Brun's *Annulaire de lune* [Annular of the Moon] (1977). Her collages for Le Brun's *Sur-le-champ* [Right Now] (1967) reveal yet another facet of Toyen's rich and many-sided work.

One of the greatest painters of the twentieth century, a major contributor to the international avant-garde, Toyen was also, throughout her life, among the most outstanding exemplars of surrealism's revolutionary spirit. Surrealism has had many meteors, but Toyen—like her close friends André Breton and Benjamin Péret—is one of the movement's fixed stars.

The statement published here—part of her response to an inquiry on "The Situation of Painting" published in *Médium: communication surréaliste* no. 4 (1955)—is included in this section because it reflects on her experiences in the late 1920s and 1930s.

A COMMUNITY OF ETHICAL VIEWS

In nonfigurative art a tendency that was close to surrealism developed at the same time as surrealism itself and ran parallel to it. If it has attained its refined and mature form today, it is thanks to the very important influence exerted by surrealist theory.

To pursue a venture in common with a nonsurrealist painter is entirely possible if it is founded on the same basis as a common venture with a surrealist painter: the *moral* basis. I am convinced of this all the more resolutely as the term "lyrical abstraction" accurately describes the painting that Styrsky and I started doing in 1926. When the majority of the Czechoslovak group *Devětsil,* whose aesthetic conceptions were growing closer to those of the Surrealist Movement, joined it in 1933, it was precisely because they shared a community of ethical views.

Translated from the French by Franklin Rosemont

Alice Rahon

Of Breton origin, Alice Rahon was born Alice Marie Yvonne Phillippot in 1904 at her grandparents' home in the village of Chenecey-Buillon, Doubs, in eastern France. After an early divorce she adopted her mother's maiden name, Rahon. In 1931 she met Austrian painter Wolfgang Paalen and was soon living with him. A little over a year after their marriage in 1934, the couple joined the Surrealist Group in Paris.

Rahon's first book of poems, *A même la terre* [On the Bare Ground], illustrated by Yves Tanguy, was the first volume by a woman to appear under the group's *Editions Surréalistes* imprint (1936). Her *Sablier couché* [Hourglass Lying Down], illustrated by Picasso, was issued the same year by Librairie Tscharn.

In the early 1940s, with Paalen and photographer Eva Sulzer, Rahon moved to Mexico and shortly afterward traveled to Alaska and British Columbia, visiting many Native American tribes along the Pacific Coast. She helped Paalen organize the 1940 International Surrealist Exhibition in Mexico City; brought out another book of poems, *Noir animal* [Animal Black], with a frontispiece by Paalen (1941); and collaborated extensively on the journal *Dyn* (1942–1945). Although her husband publicly (and temporarily, as it turned out) broke with surrealism during World War II, Rahon did not; she continued to defend surrealism's fundamental perspectives till the end of her life.

After their marriage broke up in 1947, Wolfgang Paalen went to California and later to Paris for several years, but Alice Rahon remained in Mexico. One of her later paintings, "Man Crossed by a River" (1967), was painted in homage to André Breton, who had died the year before. Rahon died in 1987.

FOUR POEMS FROM *ON THE BARE GROUND*

Glances changed their source
A bell
made of stormy-blue bronze
chased off to the zenith of the wind
by the white wing
of the lost skyline

Sublime sulphur
foam of solitude
on my forehead
the reason of the wind

• • •

Cave of bronze amplifier of the storms
of two hemispheres
where shadows cannot die

the stone owl's head
watches over
the sailors' town
limbo of springs not born
to love suffocated
under pairs of false lovers
false presences
false windows
opening to the wall of the night
false virtue of the weak

our bones curling in the fire
desert burnt by waiting
where rules the madwoman in the mirror

• • •

In the night of the beginning
the fog left
his blood
between the salty lips
beyond the eyes of the sun

• • •

For those parallel destinies
there is no horizon line
where they meet where they rest
where they flee those cruel fish
of anguish and discord
They swim between the shores
of these dark rivers
which separate lovers

The shadow descends a staircase of sun
down to the bottom of my heart

I think about the chaste and thoughtful loves
of these animals that unite
as if holding hands

Translated from the French by Vanina Deler and Nancy Deffebach

DESPAIR

To Pablo Picasso

The fireworks have gone off. Gray is the absolute color of the present tense. I saw that nightingales imitate dead leaves well before autumn. Despair is a school for deaf-mutes taking their Sunday walk.

It would be better. I don't know what would be better. The thread breaks constantly; perhaps it's the same frustrating task as when a blind man tries to recall the memory of colors at his white window.

Beautiful women with silver waists always fly above cities—Patience—the signs on those roads where every mistake is irreparable end in a horsehead-shaped club.

We must cry out all our secrets before it's too late. It's previously too late if we've forgotten to leave the chair where despair will sit to join our conversation. Despair will never be reduced to begging even if they burn his arms.

Then he'll affect the silhouette of a poppy against a stormy sky. His pipe-like laughter will only become insulting.

For a while I've lived on a geography map on the wall. I think I'm at the wind's crossroads. I chat with him. The bouquet of larkspur takes flight at dusk and goes to spend the night on the ponds. The doll jumps rope with its shadow. I shall not tame that shadow that followed me during childhood.

I think that at the bottom of their graves the dead listen for a long time to see if their hearts will start beating again. For the noise, for the company of noise, let's greet the company tied by strings.

(29 May 1936)
Translated from the French by Myrna Bell Rochester

HOURGLASS LYING DOWN

No sleeping wind will bear my head
no handprint on my cheek no arm will hold me
at the open window your arm is alone
you could not exist
between this sun and this window at the spring's assault
here you are laced up and fastened
with no end of threads and knots
of your own mute web

the woman empty like the house just sold
trapped in a net without swaddling sounds
her mouth does not drink does not quench any language
long mouth in vain denied by the veins
each road lost before being born

the dove
whose dress is worn out by captivity
in a wicker cage at the window
your foliage is not born
the blackbird of nightfall
at dawn I cannot listen to your voice
which closes doors and eyes
after drinking my heart.

Translated from the French by Vanina Deler and Nancy Deffebach

Valentine Penrose

THERE IS THE FIRE

There is the fire it burns and I am the water I drown
o icy girl.
Earth is my friend
also the moon her servant
thus we meet at the end of our caverns
our repose our lassitudes lazed faraway
we spent long-drawn nights discovering ourselves
beside our three mysterious fraternal fires.
    I have the loveliest flowers
    I have the loveliest mirage
    I have the loveliest mirror
    I am water singing her being.

(From *Herbe à la Lune,* 1935)
Translated from the French by Roy Edwards

THE DATURA THE SERPENT

The datura the serpent
and life bandit of my blood
equator to this park only twenty years old.

Back into your angel's bark
my seven ogrish daughters
I am a beautiful cathedral
on the carpet of myself.

In the fiery ink of my eyes in a circle
are inscribed my games
even those from Adam

in a circle
it will touch the serpent touch the rock
    daughter of the earth
    at her zenith the Capricorn.

(From *Herbe à la Lune,* 1935)
Translated from the French by Myrna Bell Rochester

TO A WOMAN TO A PATH

This body here feminine that hangs like a distant drop
toward the other here this time feminine
where the hair equal across the smile
  wild shuttle
  angular bones
who will cross the plains with her hips
who will gather the straw not swathes it will sleep in barns
alone for the herbs
of whom the friend would never worry although green.
By fate by grain by way by satin
blades of leaves her flat eyes nails in the wood
to the forest all her teeth
rock soft skull of ferns
so big I have drawn her forth this born-one
like a herd of water hung down the cliffs
on the steppes when one believed her at the strawberries
with wild ribbons instead of asleep
on the total side green and red.

The beauty the chestnut lady
my brown mouse how far away you are under the bushes.

Caught by breasts by hands and by hair
never yielded herself whole
so mad of lichens lost
like a needle in moss
by all the ends urgent false
I have turned you you have woven me

Your cavern mattered as the mountains
where the slate makes its path
where it rains it shines the devil beats his daughters
where the gold splitting sickle dwells and hisses
Wounded indifferent lets her head cry
hands in tasks
and body rejected so soft although headless
caressed by her hands for other horizons.

Velvet song in the breastplate
herself stifled for a joke
tiny at the muzzles of the mountains was playing with the donkeys

At present let sleep on the arms of snow
at the end of time there you lie outstretched
if I think of you hot of desert length
tress to remake under the palms
forest on your fair days
elastic like the dream fox
hard like your fist
restored to your truest expression
    of being all

Great face of rock and grass
revealed so black that I no longer fear
with a wink seeing you you have lifted me from the well
fathomless from the lake where the sun was the same
same the black oak of winter's furniture
the dark corners of the house left at the crossroads
the arrows were false
blue with poison lied.
Bridge of earth
come to be broken
in the middle where they cross
Tower of earth where your king does not care for you
where the herd is swallowed up
whilst from out of its yellow skin obscure a road
wide like a woman feet foremost
warming itself at the world's end
the most uncertain
without velvet paws
leading to the panthers
whilst this path
without men's heads
carried itself like a head.

On a bank soft and russet the chamomile
in front of the drawing room full of maiden love
in the west of chestnut cup for chestnuts
where the cut wood shines alive lace like
the mule in the forest rings like a colony
the sweet lady for ever in the dahlia garden
    masked with mauve
    plant salved
your rabbit teeth you can do no more

On an Indian air
holding my apron
gathered my severed heads
Saint Germaine of Europe
upright in the little milkwort.
Like tiles rained from the north
like cow kisses everywhere
like a rosary round the neck
    now I am all
    now I am ended
    now I am knotted
    now I am joined
    necks severed I dance like a bird
the fountain out from the skull

Gambling with the sunbeams
it rolls at will this great furnished heart on the road
sweet like nothing
bordered with empty molds
frigate of the sun
on this one retrieved
whose marrow once bow-bent on the ceiling with its shadow augured
    the feastings of the white weasels
    of ecstasy.

Translated from the French by Roland Penrose and Valentine Penrose

Sheila Legge

As the "Surrealist Phantom" at the 1936 International Surrealist Exhibition in London, Sheila Legge was among the most photographed surrealists of all time. Photos of her standing in Trafalgar Square, her face covered with roses and her outstretched arms bedecked with pigeons, appeared in papers all over England and have been reproduced since in dozens of books. She also appeared (without roses or pigeons) in an oft-reprinted surrealist group photo taken at the exhibition.

Legge remains, however, a little-known figure. I have been unable to learn anything of her background or education. David Gascoyne recalls that she was in her mid-twenties when she first wrote to him in 1935, expressing her enthusiasm for his just-published *Short Survey of Surrealism* (the first book on the movement in English) and her readiness to help organize a Surrealist Group in England. Gascoyne describes her as "a warm, good-natured, intelligent, frustrated young woman" with an "eagerness for experience" and "a genuinely keen curiosity" about contemporary culture, "especially surrealism." He adds that she was fluent in French, "able to read Raymond Roussel in the original."

Legge exhibited a surrealist object at the 1936 international exhibition, cofounded the Surrealist Group in England, collaborated on the fourth issue of the *International Surrealist Bulletin* (the cover features her photo as the "Surrealist Phantom"), and took part in the 1937 surrealist objects show at the London Gallery. An active participant in group meetings and liked by all, she was especially close to Gascoyne, Roger Roughton, Margaret and Paul Nash, and E. L. T. Mesens, who wanted to hire her as secretary of his London Gallery in 1938. She is also known to have visited Paris, where she met Man Ray. Her reasons for leaving the Surrealist Group and data on her later life are not known. Gascoyne says he was later told that she married a farmer and moved to Cornwall.

The text reprinted here, the only one she is known to have written, appeared in *Contemporary Poetry & Prose* (December 1936).

I HAVE DONE MY BEST FOR YOU

And there appeared unto me a woman with chains upon her wrists, riding on a bicycle; and in her hand a banner bearing these words: THERE ARE NO MORE WHORES IN BABYLON.

"Look," she cried, "There is the Queen Mary setting out on her maiden voyage."

And indeed it was an impressive sight, out there in the desert, that tall ship built entirely of the most costly marble (for no expense had been spared) setting out on her maiden voyage with her cargo of candles and all her passengers climbing up the gangway, which was made out of *point de Venise* and had been lent by the Pope, with their clothes and their medicine bottles neatly packed in rooks' nests and a ham sandwich for the journey.

But I could not really give my full attention to the spectacle, diverting as it was, for I was already late so, bidding her farewell, I went on alone. Seeing that I was in earnest this time she pedaled away in the opposite direction, leaving me in total darkness. I took out the packet of needles which had never left my side since I waved goodbye to my mother only that morning at Liverpool Street station and, as I had expected, the largest needle of all gave out a phosphorescent glow sufficient to cast a beam of light on my path. (You can imagine how careful I was to keep an eye on it and the relief I felt when the sun rose six minutes later.)

Tea was over long ago when I arrived, but Mogador had left a note on the table to say he would be back shortly so I sat down to wait. But when the wax-figures who had left their showcases because it was halftime began to melt I realized that the house was on fire and there was nothing to be done. Everyone showed great signs of agitation and my calm was vastly envied.

"Oh dear," they moaned, "If only there had been a flood. We could easily have made ourselves boats out of all the chamois leather gloves in the garden and there would have been no danger."

However, it was only another FALSE ALARM. The ice creams on the table, who had been most undecided as to their chances of survival and would have hoisted the white flag long ago but for my sangfroid, quickly refroze themselves into even more spectacular shapes than before, and all was ready for the feast. All, that is, except myself for by now I was more than tired of so many interruptions; so, pushing my chair back, I lay down on the floor and fell asleep.

And on the third day I rose again and sold my wife for thirty pieces of camembert and my infant daughter for three francs fifty.

Eileen Agar

Painter, collagist and maker of surrealist objects, Eileen Forrester Agar was born in Buenos Aires in 1899 of a Scottish businessman father and an American mother. In 1911 the family moved to London where Agar lived her whole life, apart from lengthy visits to France. A cofounder of the Surrealist Group in England in 1936, she cosigned the group's inaugural declaration, collaborated on the *International Surrealist Bulletin* as well as the English group's chief organ, *London Bulletin*, and took part in several International Surrealist Exhibitions: London, 1936; Amsterdam, 1938; and Paris, 1947. During the 1960s surrealist resurgence she once again began to take part in movement-organized shows, such as "The Enchanted Domain" (Exeter, 1967) and "Surrealism Unlimited" (London, 1978).

Agar wrote little, and her autobiography, published shortly before her death in 1991, is—like most "as-told-to" books—not wholly reliable. In the excerpts reprinted here, however, Agar summarizes views she maintained consistently from her first encounter with organized surrealism in 1936.

AM I A SURREALIST?

Surrealism for me draws its inspiration from nature. I recall the account of Tanguy walking along the beach noting the tiny marine forms, studying the seaweed and the rocks. Then he would go back to his studio and create a painting which made references to what he had seen, yet nature would only be the starting point for his imagination. I adopt a similar approach, though at the same time, abstraction would also be exerting its influence upon me, giving me the benefit of geometry and design to match and balance and strengthen the imaginative elements of a composition. Outer eye and inner eye, backward and forward, inside out and upside down, sideways, as a metaphysical airplane might go, no longer classical or romantic, medieval or gothic, but surreal, transcendent, a revelation of what is concealed in the hide-and-seek of life, a mixture of laughter, play and perseverance.

You see the shape of a tree, the way a pebble falls or is formed, and you are astounded to discover that dumb nature makes an effort to speak to you, to give you a sign, to warn you, to symbolize your innermost thoughts. Chance is not a neutral but a distinctly positive force; the surrealists believe that you can get on good terms with chance by adopting a lyrical mode of behavior and an open attitude.

• • •

My own method is to put myself in a state of receptivity during the day. I sit about sometimes for a quarter of an hour or more, wondering what on earth I am doing, and then suddenly I get an idea for something. Either it is the beginning of a title or just the germ of a visual image. Later on, if I am stuck with a half-finished painting, I might take a snooze and after that it comes together quite simply. It may well be that we hunt too much when we are completely on the alert. Too much awareness can be as inhibiting as too little.

• • •

One must have a hunger for new color, new shapes and new possibilities of discovery. The twentieth century has begun to realize that most of life's meaning

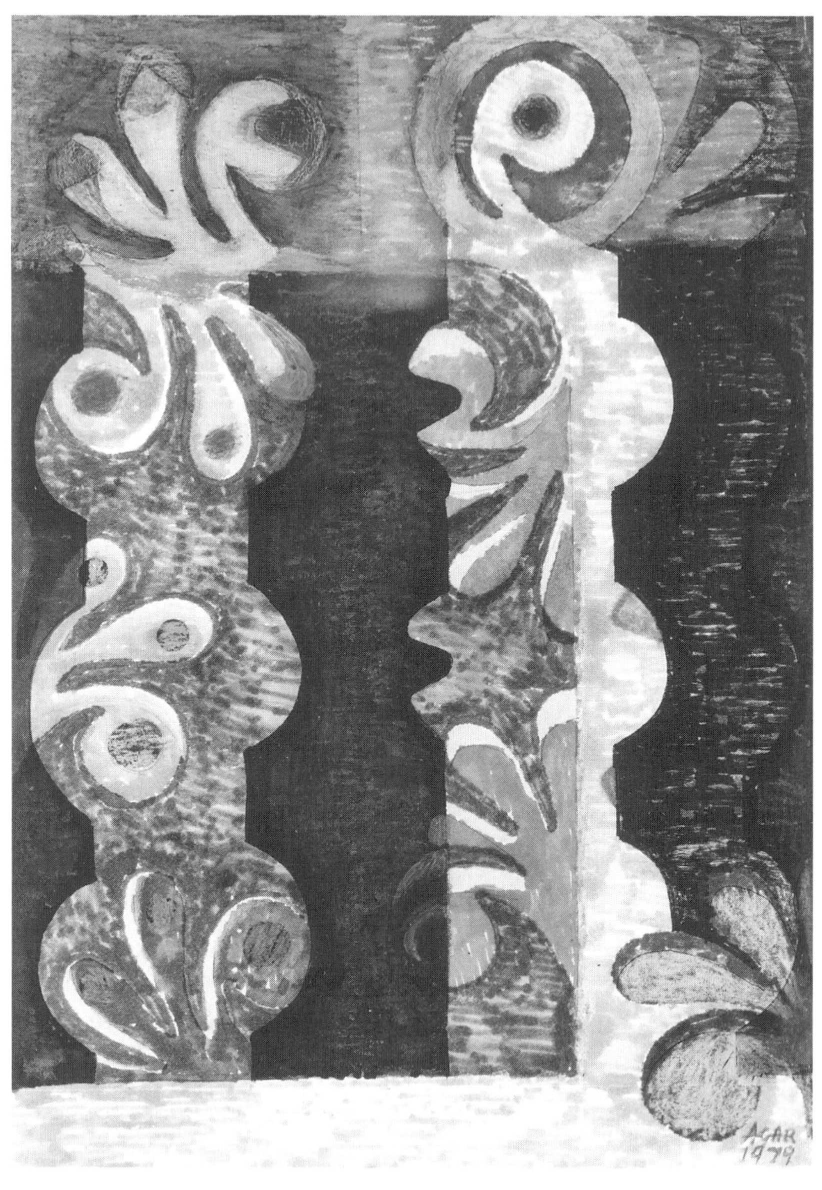

Eileen Agar, *Teacher and Pupil,* ink drawing, 1979. Courtesy of the artist's estate.

is lost without the spirit of play. In play, all that is lovely and soaring in the human spirit strives to find expression. To play is to yield oneself to a kind of magic, and to give the lie to the inconvenient world of fact, and the hideous edifice of unrelieved utility. In play the mind is prepared to accept the unimagined and incredible, to enter a world where different laws apply, to be free, unfettered.

The earliest anecdote told of me, at the age of four (when my stature was of little account), was of me looking up at the ornate ceiling lavishly painted with naked ladies and flying cupids in the large restaurant where my parents were lunching. I said: "I see something but I mustn't tell." Was this a shocked awareness of what went on in the clouds? The second anecdote is of my constant and pressing request to all and sundry to buy me a balloon. I was obviously intent on exploring those clouds for myself.

Mary Low

One of the stalwarts of surrealism for more than six decades, Mary Low was born in England of Australian parents and educated in England, Switzerland, and France. In 1933, in Paris, she met Cuban poet/revolutionist Juan Breá, cofounder of the "H-Group," Cuba's closest counterpart to surrealism in the 1920s, and also cofounder of Cuban Trotskyism. The nomadic couple joined the Paris Surrealist Group a few months later, and were also active in surrealism in Bucharest, Brussels, and Prague. Her closest friends in the Surrealist Movement in the 1930s were Benjamin Péret, Victor Brauner, Oscar Dominquez, Marcelle Ferry, and, "dearest of all," the Czechs Bohuslav Brouk, Jindrich Heisler, and Toyen.

In 1936–1937 Low and Breá were in Spain fighting for the revolution as members of the Partido Obrero de Unificacion Marxista [Workers' Party of Marxist Unification] (POUM). Low edited the POUM English-language paper, *Spanish Revolution,* and helped organize the women's militia. The Breá/Low *Red Spanish Notebook,* prefaced by C. L. R. James, was the first book-length account of that struggle to appear in English (1937) and was highly praised by George Orwell. In 1938 Low's and Breá's collection of poems, *La Saison des flutes* [The Season of Flutes], appeared under the Editions Surréalistes imprint (and was reissued by Editions Arabie-sur-Seine in Paris in 1987). At the outbreak of war Low and Breá went to Cuba, where Breá died in 1941, at the age of thirty-five. Their collection of essays, *La verdad contemporanea* [Contemporary Truth], prefaced by Benjamin Péret, was published in 1943 in Havana, where Low continued to live through the war and beyond.

Active in the revolution that overthrew Cuban dictator Batista in 1959, Low did not leave the island until 1964, when the Stalinization of the ruling party placed increasingly severe restrictions on intellectual life. After living for a time in Australia, she moved to the U.S. in 1974. A participant in the Surrealist Movement in the U.S. since 1983, Low has collaborated on *Arsenal* and *WHAT Are You Going to Do About It?* as well as the French journal *Ellebore* [Hellebore].

Low's many other books include *Alquimia del Recuerdo* [Alchemy of Memory], illustrated by Wifredo Lam (1946; reprinted, 1986), and *Where the Wolf Sings: New Poems and Collages* (1994). A Latin and classical scholar, she has also published a historical novel, *In Caesar's Shadow* (1975), and a collection of her own researches, *On Caesar's Trail* (1996). In recent years she has also made numerous collages, which she has exhibited in Paris, Chicago, Miami (where she now lives), and Montreal.

Although most of *Red Spanish Notebook* (1937) was written in collaboration with Juan Breá, the chapter published here, slightly abridged, was written entirely by Low.

WOMEN AND THE SPANISH REVOLUTION

The Anarchist trade unions had begun a group, "Free Women," which issued manifestos and edited a splendid paper. I knew one of the girls on the editorial committee. She was deep-bosomed and sweet, and talking to her you could see that she had realized more than the average woman what freedom could mean.

"They're so eager," she explained, "and so determined to be free. But most of them don't even know what freedom means. They're not stupid, only untrained to think, uneducated except in the art of pleasing. But they are awfully courageous, and full of determination. It's wonderful raw material."

She wrote clever things, and organized well. Later a French revolutionary fell in love with her, and she loved him, too. But when it came to bed, she refused with a comic and desperate virtue.

"Why not? Isn't it natural when one's in love?" she told me that he asked her. He had been hurt by her attitude.

"And why wouldn't you?" I asked.

"Oh, because one hasn't time for all that kind of thing during the revolution."

"It's not true," I said. "It's an excuse. You only say it to hide your prejudices."

She looked at me, and then shrugged.

"Well, after all, one can't really be expected to change over night, can one?"

The religious heritage was very hard to get rid of.

The family was another thing. Louise Gomez, Gorkin's wife, charming and energetic, decided to build a women's secretariat in the party, and form a women's regiment and women's classes and lectures and centers of education and child welfare. She received more than 500 adherents within the first week (it shows you something of their eagerness), but dozens of full-blown matrons, and young girls confided to me:

"Of course I wasn't able to tell my husband (or my father) that I was coming here, he would have had a fit. I just had to say I was joining a sewing-circle."

The regiment was composed in large part of these runaways. We used to meet at seven o'clock in front of the local, with the winter morning mist still rolling up the Ramblas and round the trunks of the trees, strapped into our new blue woolen uniforms with divided skirts and stand there blowing on our hands and most of us hoping that our families wouldn't catch us.

I have seldom seen such spirits. They were so glad and gay and seemed like children. While we waited for the members of the Directive Committee to come and lead us to the barracks they skipped on the hard pavement and played little girls' games, singing and holding hands and dancing in their pointed shoes. (It was a long time before we could make them all understand that they must go to drill in flat heels and leave their earrings at home.) In the excitement of being free, they were able to get up carelessly time after time in the rough morning air. They would wait endlessly on the drill-field in the wind. Even the weight of centuries of indolence did not deter them.

We used to go to the barracks, which were a long way out from the center of the town. On the way, in the tram or the metro, the militia-boys used to chaff us. We sang the "Internationale" very loudly and tried to convince them that our uniform was as serious as their own. Sometimes they ended by being impressed. They would stand whispering gravely together and looking at us seriously out of their thick-lashed eyes.

It was a long road from the tram-stop to the barracks. We swung along it in formation. The men leaned out of passing lorries and grinned at us and raised their fists and yelled:

"Comrades!"

"Comrades!" we yelled back in chorus and raised our fists too.

I remember the first day when we all lined up to file past the guards at the entrance to the barracks. How they stared, and afterwards laughed and cheered us, and all the regiments turned out to see us go by. We felt proud. A French boy ran down into the courtyard from one of the galleries, and demanded crossly: "Now what do you think you're all doing?" He looked as though he had a grievance. He had come back from the front.

"We're coming to learn to fight," I said, with some pride. "We're a battalion."

"Well, it's no use," he said, quickly. "I wouldn't have women at the front at all, if I had the choice. I've been there and I know."

"Why? Don't you think we're capable? Not brave enough?"

"It's not that," he said. "Far from it. There may have been something in that at the first, when crowds of untrained girls went there without knowing what they were going to, and so forth, but that was due to the confusion. Of course, everything has been organized since then. Oh, I haven't a word against the militia-women at the front for their courage, or what they can do, or any of that. Oh, no."

"Then what are you driving at? Why do you object?"

He gave a little, tired sigh.

"You see," he said, "it makes everything altogether too heroic. Especially for the Spaniards. They're conscious of being males every moment of the day and night, you know what I mean. They haven't got rid of their old-fashioned sense of chivalry yet, however silly they may think it is. If one of you girls get caught by the enemy, fifteen men immediately risk their lives to avenge her. All that kind of thing. It costs lives and it's too much effort."

"Then they must get over it," somebody said.

"And they never will unless we go on as we're doing."

"In any case," we explained for his greater comfort and joy, "you can rest yourself about this battalion. We don't put it up as a principle that women ought to go to the front, we don't think that, we only want to give a hand to all the individual cases who are good at that sort of thing. As for the rest of us here, we all have our own social or political work to attend to."

"Then why are you drilling?"

"How dense you are," Louise cried, while the early sun glinted on the polished shoes of the horses which were galloping riderless round and round the yard, "because human beings should be properly equipped for defense when they are liable to be attacked. Supposing Barcelona was shelled? It would be silly if we couldn't do anything—a bunch of sheep, like in bourgeois countries."

We went into an underground shooting gallery. It was stone paved, and the echo battered at one's ears, rebounding back endlessly from wall to wall.

The first day we were there the sergeant walked quietly to the back of the gallery while we stood facing the targets and let off a shot behind our backs

Mary Low, *Mermaid,* collage, 1994. Courtesy of the artist.

without warning. Everybody screamed. Louise Gomez came out firmly to the front and said:

"If that ever happens again, that is the end of the Women's Battalion."

It never did happen again.

We drilled for four hours without stopping, in every weather. The officers took us with full seriousness. They would not let the men come into the field and look on, and walked beside the leaders, patiently stamping the earth flat with their boots while giving us the beat. The drummers walked tirelessly in front of us to mark out the time. It was amazing that nobody ever complained, or fell out, or failed to come again. Some of their bodies were stiff and awkward, out of corsets for the first time. Yet they bore it all, and returned for more.

After the shooting and the drilling we used to have machine-gun practice. "Just supposing one of these things fell into your hands and you couldn't work it," as the instructor, with his cap lazily pushed over one eye, used to explain. It was the only thing which was really difficult. We had no mechanical turn, and spent a long time learning to take all the parts of the machine to pieces and put them correctly together again, and besides, the machine was so hard and heavy for us. But we did learn. In the end, I think that we could have assembled the parts of a machine-gun in the dark, without a clank to show the enemy where we were hidden, and fired it off as a surprise.

I remember we were very proud of this, and mentioned it in the next manifesto we issued.

The average woman in the street continued in most respects to look the same as before the revolution—that is to say that superfluous wealth and luxury had disappeared on the backs of the former ruling caste, but the women continued to have high heels and beautiful hair and to follow a dress style which is only ever in vogue in Spain. There was one marked difference, though. The mantillas, with their religious symbolism, had been torn to shreds and now everyone went bareheaded in sun and rain. The Anarchists had made a heavy campaign against hats.

Marcelle Ferry

Small (5′ 2″), with flame-red hair and deep blue eyes, Lila—as she preferred to be called—was flamboyant, adventurous, spontaneous, and always "full of vitality": such is the sketch of Marcelle Ferry provided by Mary Low, who knew her well in the surrealist milieux of Paris and Bucharest in the 1930s. Adds Low: "I never had such good times with any other woman friend."

According to André Thirion, Ferry was one of many new recruits to the Paris Surrealist Group in 1932. Still active fifteen years later, she cosigned the "Inaugural Break" manifesto in 1947.

At various times Ferry lived with Georges Hugnet, Breton, Oscar Dominguez, and other surrealists, but she married Jean Lévy, who later—during the Nazi occupation—took her surname and became well-known as Jean Ferry. His most popular books—*The Mechanic and Other Stories* (1953) and the *Study of Raymond Roussel* (1953), are both prefaced by Breton and both dedicated "to Lila." Marcelle Ferry died in 1992.

Illustrated by Yves Tanguy, her collection of poems, *L'Ile d'un jour* [The Daylong Island]—from which the selections here are taken—appeared under the Editions Surréalistes imprint in 1938.

YOU CAME DOWN FROM THE MOUNTAINS . . .

You came down from the mountains
red steps of the great temples
you traveled the world
with the haughty silhouette
of a Prometheus
chained standing
you went toward the island
hemmed with Brussels lace
and with clashing ermines
of flowing luxury.
The girl of Irish velvet
and of elsewhere
lying on skins of lions
tigers and boredom
killed by her father
listened on the wood of the islands

for the step of the one
who would make her life resonate
and would rig up the full sails
of the adventurers in gold and steel.
Once in a while the sea-green wind
bent the rushes
in the dark places.

Translated from the French by Myrna Bell Rochester

WHEN HE WENT AWAY . . .

When he went away
it was midnight at age twenty
He had his hands in Asia
and was following without understanding
the songs of winters for sleeping
the space to love you he said
with a quick blue motion
my hands are in Asia
and my heart is distant as shadow
I'll be back in the time it takes to love you
taking away the long countries
but when the mist had fallen
He became lost at the turn
then since the earth was round
He felt himself going mad

Translated from the French by Myrna Bell Rochester

THE ONE SEATED ON THE STONES OF CHEOPS . . .

To Joëlle

The One, seated on the stones of Cheops
creates butterflies
sings with the spider's thread
The Other, prisoner of movements
thinks guesses and chooses entwining with beauty
underground plants fruits of the abyss
birds of paradise.

The blue and red look of the One
drops onto the moss her curls of shooting stars fill space
the Other will see dawns again and Bathsheba the caterpillar
who was a sleeping cat at the heart of the lettuce
the Other sleeps in the mist . . .

Translated from the French by Myrna Bell Rochester

FRENZY, SWEET LITTLE CHILD, YOU SLEEP . . .

Frenzy, sweet little child, you sleep
your hand closed around a treasure of diamonds
that turn into hazelnuts.
Dawn's paths
lead you into the forest of a sobbing
night of rain and beautiful among the beauties.
Betelgeuse has stolen the heart of Charles II
that's the surprise inside which
you wakened will go forth
wearing about you your umbelliferous shadow
Undecided about gathering the crowned heads that will fall
Your little tooth is a dungeon
your uranium curls provide impunity for you alone
Frenzy, my Aventurine, my Peripatetic
my little million-dollar dream.
You wear emerald or green crystal sandals
And magnificently torn clothing
you name me you call me.
The night birds make your cradle
you can sleep anywhere my little spring of poison slow and clear
like your spring eyes my little poison;
in the shade of the vampires and while the fire keeps vigil
and precious stones fall from the sky in a silent spray.
The heart of Charles II is at your feet
He warms them and swells up to become mellow
He'll turn himself into an orange when you wake delicious and cold.
Butterfly on the heather little motherless cloud
don't you want to make the nasturtiums dance?
A pink spider is on your cheek
nothing is beautiful anymore, she looks at your lashes
like a single enemy

and measures the fight by their length
the enemy does not see her, he is sleeping
his wings tucked into a thin blue ray
you are blue gold, the devil's flower
the nostalgia of coral the first Daffodil in the world

Translated from the French by Myrna Bell Rochester

Leonora Carrington

In his *Prolegomena to a Third Manifesto of Surrealism or Not* (1942), André Breton named Leonora Carrington—along with such figures as Georges Bataille, Roger Caillois, Pierre Mabille, and Benjamin Péret—as one of "the boldest and most lucid" minds of our time. As painter, storyteller, and woman of ideas, Carrington has been a major force in surrealism for sixty years.

Born in 1917 into a wealthy family in Clayton Green, Lancashire, England, Leonora Carrington started drawing at age three. In her teens she persuaded her parents to let her study painting with Amédée Ozenfant. She was electrified by the 1936 International Surrealist Exhibition in London and by Herbert Read's anthology, *Surrealism,* published that same year and presented to her as a gift by her mother. In 1937 she met Max Ernst and went to live with him in Paris and later in the French countryside. The two were separated at the outbreak of war when Ernst was imprisoned in a concentration camp. Her subsequent travail, including a harrowing spell in a lunatic asylum in Spain, is recounted in her wonderful book *Down Below* (1944), excerpts from which appear in the following section.

Carrington took part in seven International Surrealist Exhibitions between 1938 and 1965–1966. Her most intense involvement in surrealism as a collective activity was in 1941–1942 as part of the Paris Surrealist Group in exile in New York. Most of her later years she has lived in Mexico, where no Surrealist Group existed, though her closest friends there included other surrealists in exile, notably Benjamin Péret (who returned to Paris after the war), Remedios Varo, and Luis Buñuel. For a few years in the 1980s Carrington lived in New York, and later in Chicago, where she took part in the activity of the Chicago Surrealist Group. Carrington returned to Mexico in 1992.

Carrington's first publication was a pamphlet, *La Maison de la peur* [The House of Fear] (1938), followed by a collection of stories, *La dame ovale* [The Oval Lady] (1939)—both illustrated by Ernst. *Down Below,* which appeared in English and French in the New York surrealist journal *VVV* in 1944, was issued in book form in *Radical America*'s Surrealist Research & Development monograph series in 1972 and has been kept in print by Black Swan Press in Chicago. Although written in the 1940s, her novel *The Stone Door* was published only in 1976. A suite of her drawings, paintings, and pastels, *El mundo magico de los Mayas* [The Magic World of the Mayans], appeared in Mexico in 1964. A second novel, *The Hearing Trumpet,* appeared in French in 1974 and in English two years later. Still uncollected are her plays, *Flannel Night-Shirt* and *Penelope.* In recent years many of her shorter writings have appeared under various titles in many languages.

"The Sand Camel" has not heretofore been published in English.

THE SAND CAMEL

Two boys, A and B, lived in the forest with the Old Grandmother. The Old Grandmother was always dressed in black like an umbrella and she had a little head round and red like an apple. Her soap and her pajamas were black too; it was her favorite color.

A and B went to the forest to play with white sand; they made a camel. When the camel was finished his look was so alive A and B said "the Camel is alive and he looks nasty."

It was true but it rained and the Camel went away in a stream of sand.

"Well done," says the Grandmother. "I didn't like that Camel because of his look."

But A and B mixed some butter into the next camel. This one's eyes were even nastier. This camel kept his shape in the rain.

"If we do something magical to him he'll stand up," said B. That would be useful; they had no dog. Then the Crow came down from the tree saying "Me, I know the magic thing you have to do." With his foot he scratched some letters on the camel's forehead. The Camel stood up with a sinister smile. He walked he went into the house. The Crow said, "it's because he is afraid of the rain."

A said, "Grandmother won't like it if the Camel goes inside, she's making chestnut jam."

The boys A and B hid behind the tree because they knew that the Grandmother would be angry when the Camel of Sand went into the kitchen; they were right, she was furious.

Soon they saw the Camel come back holding the Grandmother's head in his

Leonora Carrington, *Dog, come here into the dark house. Come here, black dog,* etching, 1995. © 1997 by Leonora Carrington/Artists Rights Society (ARS), New York.

mouth. Upside down she looked just like an umbrella. "It's because of the damp," said the Crow.

In the kitchen the jam burns, no one looks after it.

A and B went into the house to take care of the jam.

After eating chestnut jam for a week, A and B said, "we sure could eat some fries," but the Camel was walking slowly in the woods with the Grandmother, like an umbrella and he never put her down.

The Crow saw it all. "You owe me the Grandmother's jewelry," he said taking a big trunk of it from the house.

"We should do something with it." So he hung all the Grandmother's jewelry on the tree and you had to admit it looked nice.

Translated from the French by Rikki Ducornet

Grace W. Pailthorpe

Born in 1883 at St.-Edwards-on-the-Sea, Surrey, in England, Grace Winifred Pailthorpe studied medicine and served as a surgeon during World War I. During several years' travel abroad she worked as a physician in the wilds of western Australia. Back in England she took up the study of Freudian psychoanalysis, which she began to practice in 1922. For five years she concentrated on the psychoanalytic study of female prisoners; her pioneering *Studies in the Psychology of Delinquency* (1929) and *What We Put in Prison* (1932) attracted international notice. Her Institute for the Scientific Treatment of Delinquency (now the Portman Clinic) was the first of its kind in the world. Indicative of her stature in the field, its vice-presidents included Freud, Jung, Adler, Rank, and other analysts, as well as Havelock Ellis and H. G. Wells.

In 1935, with commercial artist Reuben Mednikoff, Pailthorpe began her research into automatic drawing and painting. In 1936 she took part in the International Surrealist Exhibition in London, where her three works were greatly admired by André Breton, and she helped found the Surrealist Group in London. Her 1939 joint exhibit with Mednikoff was enthusiastically reported in the group's journal, *London Bulletin*. Pailthorpe also contributed articles to the *International Journal of Psychoanalysis* as well as other psychoanalytic and medical journals. By 1941, however, disagreements with Mesens and others led to her and Mednikoff's departure from the Surrealist Group, though they continued their automatistic research throughout their lives. In later years they turned to Eastern mysticism; they left a large collection of their art to a yoga society, which burned it.

The first selection here, from *What We Put in Prison,* predates Pailthorpe's involvement in surrealism but reveals her radical psychoanalytic orientation. "The Scientific Aspect of Surrealism," published here slightly abridged, originally appeared in *London Bulletin* (December 1938/January 1939). "Surrealist Art" is excerpted from the "Foreword" to the catalog of the Pailthorpe/Mednikoff exhibition at the Guggenheim Jeune Gallery (London, 1939), and the text titled "On the Importance of Fantasy Life" is from a letter published in *London Bulletin* no. 17 (1939), responding to an anti-Freudian and antisurrealist critic.

WHAT WE PUT IN PRISON

This girl, aged twenty, was in prison for larceny. When I saw her she was recovering from revolver shot-wounds. She was in a highly excited state and unable to give me a coherent history of herself. She said she had always been a troublesome girl as far back as she could remember. She was sent to a convent school from which she ran away at the age of fourteen, refusing to go back. She then took up various employments, such as typing, mechanics and dressmaking, only to throw them over almost immediately. The longest time she stayed in any one place was for eighteen months as a mannequin in a shop. While she was there she "got in with" a lot of young men with whom she was very friendly. She does not know what it is to feel affectionate or to have any love for anyone. "That was knocked out of me between the ages of one and nine."

Although she has a mild fondness for her parents, she knows she would not grieve if they died. She looks down upon her mother and says of her that she is good, virtuous, religious, kind, generous and a very nervous little person. She speaks of her father as happy-go-lucky and irresponsible like herself. She makes platonic friendships with men and has no use for women. She has taken part in numerous escapades and glories in them. They seem to be mainly of a shady nature (business transactions), but strictly "non-sexual." On the present occasion, she went over to the Continent to see someone on business. She left her hotel here, where she had a suite of rooms, without paying for them; also she took several gowns from a person who was exhibiting them at the hotel. Her attitude to this theft is that "If people are foolish enough to trust they deserve all they get."

When she reached her destination abroad, the man she was to do business with failed her. She found herself in an hotel, without means to pay or to get away, so without apparently waiting to think things over, she said to herself, "I have had a good time and here is the end." She went up to her room, cleaned up her "gun" and went to bed. She thought it rather a cheerless way of "doing it," so rang the bell and ordered a cocktail. After this she felt more cheerful, thought she was being a coward, so put the pistol away in the drawer. She woke up three weeks later to find her head bandaged. She has no recollection of what had happened. From the position of the wounds I should judge they were self-inflicted. She poses as having an "Omar Khayyam" attitude toward the world, but nevertheless she gave me the impression that a terrific internal battle was being waged. This probably has to do with her references to something which happened between the ages of one and nine. Concerning the details of this she was markedly reticent although she frequently alluded to it. At subsequent interviews, she was in the same excited state. To herself she was a great person and was wonderful in what she had accomplished and could accomplish. She had a peculiar way of ending everything she was saying with a "ha! ha!"

There were moments when an expression of deep misery came into her face. At every interview she would interrupt her flow of conversation to interject at intervals in a tone of forced contempt that she loved no one—love meant nothing to her: all that was knocked out of her when she was a child.

She gave the impression that all the excitement and posing was a strong effort to shut out of consciousness a state of mind which was exactly the opposite of what she made it out to be. It was quite obvious that the girl was suffering acutely from severe mental conflict and that her abnormal behavior was *the only way* she could find of dealing with it.

THE SCIENTIFIC ASPECT OF SURREALISM

Surrealism is one of the outcomes of a demand, on the part of those dissatisfied with the world, for the complete liberation of mankind from all fetters which prevent full expression. Humankind demands full expression. It is a biological necessity.

In 1924, André Breton, one of the founders of surrealism and its present leader, defined surrealism as: "Pure psychic automatism, by which it is intended to express, verbally, in writing, or by other means, the real functioning of thought. The dictation of thought in the absence of all control exercised by reason and outside all aesthetic or moral preoccupations."

Psychoanalysis, although originally the outcome of a different aim, also strives to free the psychology of the individual from internal conflict so that she or he may function freely. Thus it can be assumed that the final goal of surrealism and psychoanalysis is the same—the liberation of man—but that the approach to this end is by different paths.

During the process of a research undertaken from the psychoanalytic point of view (by my colleague and myself), the results of certain experiments in painting and drawing led to surrealism. A considerable amount of interesting material was collected and in it some of the real values of surrealism became manifest. As a detailed description of the progress of this research is impossible in the limited space of this journal only a brief idea of some of the results, and the light these throw on the whole subject of art, will be practicable.

It is well known that unconscious fantasy is at work in all surrealist creations; but that the fantasy-story the unconscious is unfolding is intelligible is not such common knowledge. . . . Although the method by which the interpretations of drawings and paintings were obtained is complicated, the results are crystal clear. For instance, it can be clearly demonstrated that one unconscious meaning of traditional art (art that has become established and accepted) is painting according to parental wishes, or to please the parent. Such creations may display excellent craftsmanship but very little, if any, of the creator's basic personality—and vitality is restricted.

Art within the confines of any tradition is like an animal in a cage. An imprisoned creature will lose much of its inherent grandeur and vitality. A cramped freedom can only permit a mockery of life. There is little scope for fantasy within the cage of tradition-bound art. Art that is free from restriction becomes alive, colorful and vital.

When, however, such barriers to freedom are symbolically destroyed by an act of will and a surrealist career begun, the discovery that movement is still difficult is soon made. So early endeavors in surrealist art often are, to trained eyes, lacking in the essential qualities. This is due to the fact that firmly established inhibitions still maintain their hold no matter how much self-permission to be free is given. This is one reason why some give up their efforts, complaining that surrealism leads nowhere. But surrealism can lead to a greater understanding of the world around and within us, and it is a matter of time only before this will be recognized. It is impossible to create a well-organized external world unless at the same time the internal mental world is harmonized, since it is only through mental acquiescence on the part of the units that go to form the whole machinery of civilization that it can function smoothly. Further, the understanding of the world round us is reached by means of our sense organs, and if these are not functioning freely we are not capable of getting an accurate focus upon the happenings that affect us.

The unconscious is a master in its own form of art and its creations have qualities similar to those demanded of any form of art, whatever the media. It tells its story perfectly, with economy of language and with associations that convey the maximum effect. It gives only those details necessary for the complete understanding of its moods. It tells a perfect short story. Simplicity, directness and lucidity are its aims. It conforms to all that has vitality, perfection of rhythm and composition—and it cannot be ignored because it is truth expressed with vitality.

Every unconscious creation is not a work of art, but where complete freedom has been possible the results are perfect in balance, design, color, rhythm, and possess a vitality that is not to be found anywhere else than in surrealism. Because it is free from the limitations of traditionalism its movements have greater variation and infinitely greater daring.

Unfortunately, such paintings and drawings create a feeling of fear or distaste on the part of the public; but if they can bring themselves to look again and again they begin to feel an inexplicable attraction toward these pictures. They are being drawn toward a freedom which they, too, would like to experience. Eventually they admit that, although they do not understand surrealism, there is an indefinable attraction which excites them. And many artists, who still conform to the dictates of traditionalism, have admitted to being profoundly affected by the vitality of the color, movement and design of surrealist creations.

At present we are in the early stages of this form of art. The infantile unconscious can only become free gradually. Its stiffened limbs have to overcome the effects of previous binding. It has to overcome the fear of abandoning its cage, which is in large part of its own making in protection of itself from attacks from the external world. Until these bonds are broken and "limbs" are fully stretched, it will be impossible to get that perfection which is called "creation"—the conglomeration of qualities that make a thing "live," and by which it stands the test of time.

We are witnesses of the birth of a new form of art, of the transitional period during its progress from within to without. Surrealism is ushering into the world an art greater than has hitherto been known, for its potentialities are limitless. And this art of the future will arrive when completely freed fantasy evolves from uninhibited minds. It will be the dawn of a new art epoch.

As long as fantasy-life or the imaginative life is free, it learns by experience. The fantasies produced are richer in quality and content as a result of experience. But fantasy or imagination bound by early infantile inhibitions and fears remains infantile in what it creates. In the process of becoming free, surrealist

Grace Pailthorpe, *The Speckled Thrush,* oil on canvas, 1936. Photograph courtesy of Edouard Jaguer.

paintings, drawings and sculpture will necessarily be infantile in content. This does not preclude its right to be called art. The infantile fantasy, as it becomes freer and experiences more as a result of that freedom, will grow increasingly more adult in character, and its creations will show it.

Imagination travels well in harness with reason. The infant human comes into the world with a remarkable power to reason. It reasons through its senses. Its mistakes are not through lack of power to reason but through lack of experience. Hitherto humanity has stressed the value of reason and has restricted imagination. Imagination and reason are biological twins. They must grow up together. What affects the one will affect the other. If their development is such that one grows apace and the other remains stunted, the results are disastrous. The growth of our imagination and reason must, like our mental and physical development, be balanced. They are interdependent. The crippling of one or the other has its immediate effect on the living organism. The inhibition of fantasy-life, from whatever cause (internal or external), must result in a crippled creation. Equally, any loss of freedom in the use of one's reason results in a similar distortion. According to the degree we suffer from such mishandling, to that degree we are narrow, hidebound, mentally unhappy and limited individuals and, at worst, are among the many unfortunates who end their days in asylums, workhouses or prisons.

Surrealism is a serious project. If followed wholeheartedly to its final goal it has the power to bring happiness to all humanity. But it is a discipline, and one that must be persistently pursued if anything of value is to be the outcome, and if disaster is to be avoided. There are no half-way houses. There are many dangers in the achievement of this aim but these can be circumnavigated. The object of surrealism is to know the self. All the sages of the past have advocated self-knowledge but they have not shown us how to reach that ideal. Here is the opportunity.

SURREALIST ART

The paintings and drawings in this exhibition are works created during the progress of a psychological research. . . . [O]ur experiments have led both my colleague and myself to discover, among many things, the real meaning and value of surrealist art to the world. . . .

Surrealist art is a transitional art, or, to be more accurate, an art as yet in its infancy. . . . It is my belief, based on the scientific material amassed during these years of research, that surrealist art will surpass any previous form of art in the richness, quality and vitality of its creations when it reaches its more mature stage of development.

We humans are as yet out of tune with our inner selves. When the inner self is fully understood the conscious and unconscious sides of our personality merge to form a unity. When that stage is reached surrealist art will, I have no doubt, considerably alter the outlook of its critics and astound the world of art.

ON THE IMPORTANCE OF FANTASY LIFE

Without the imaginative side of life no scientific invention would have been possible. Fantasy, or vision, frequently has with it a wish to bring into being a world that would satisfy our unconscious and conscious needs, and this is the dynamic force which drives us to alter the external world. Without it there would be no progress. It is by reason of our visionary, or fantasy, life that we alter the reality world of today, creating an improved world for the future. It is only when fantasy life is anchored, through fear, to infantile misconceptions, that progress is slow, or halted. Freed fantasy will vitalize everything it touches in life, for fantasy is inherent in life itself; and when it is freed from an anchorage to repeat itself *ad infinitum,* it will enter into creative art and activity to a degree previously unknown.

• • •

One overhears many reactions to surrealist art, but the most pathetic of all is from those who ask, "What am I supposed to see and feel from this?" In other words, "What does papa say I may think and feel about this?"

Hélène Vanel

Only two names appear on the invitation to the 1938 International Surrealist Exhibition in Paris: André Breton and Hélène Vanel. In the catalog, Breton's and Eluard's *Abridged Surrealist Dictionary,* this "danseuse surréaliste" [surrealist dancer] was symbolically named "The Iris of Mists." Her performance at the opening, titled "L'Acte manqué" [The Unconsummated Act], was the first authentic example of surrealism in dance. The most detailed account of this extravaganza, in which she brandished a live rooster and jumped on and off one of the exhibition's several unmade beds, appears in Georges Hugnet's *Pleins et deliés* [Upstrokes and Downstrokes] (1972).

Biographical information on Vanel has proved elusive. A clipping in the New York Public Library's dance collection at the Lincoln Center shows that she was dancing on the Riviera in the mid-1930s. She evidently died in a Nazi concentration camp.

The following text, the only one she is known to have written, appeared in the *Cahiers G.L.M.* no. 9 in March 1939, as part of her response to an inquiry on "Indispensable Poetry."

POETRY AND DANCE

In the actual state of things, it is poetry that must save the world. Those who no longer see the Marvelous live in the desert—and death. Let the poets be read fervently each day! They alone reveal to us how precious, intimate, and astonishing the things around us are. They alone will reveal the secret of the ties that attach us to these things.

And let us know how to distinguish the false poets, who debase all that is human, from the true poets—those who "animate a world in recreating it."

Dance, joyous and powerful expression of the enthusiasm for life, must have the same mission as poetry. It creates forms in time and space. Dance is the vertigo of matter.

To communicate with life's forces by means of gesture and movement—the simplest and most direct expression. To rediscover the truth of being. To acquire, at the same time, the sense of the *invisible powers* that attract us even while repelling us: Is this not a means of surpassing ourselves, a way out of the marasmus and mediocrity—a method of attaining the *grandeur* that we so shamefully abandoned?

Translated from the French by Franklin Rosemont

Ithell Colquhoun

Ithell Colquhoun was born in 1906 in Shillong, Assam, India, and grew up in India and England in an atmosphere of alchemy, Kabbalah, and the Hermetic Order of the Golden Dawn. Although she attended the Slade School in London, she was basically self-taught as an artist. The 1936 International Surrealist Exhibition in London confirmed her interest in surrealism. For a time she lived in Athens and in Paris, where she met André Breton in 1939. She joined the Surrealist Group in England later that year and contributed many texts and images to its journal, *London Bulletin*. She broke with the group in 1940 after a dispute with E. L. T. Mesens regarding her occultist preoccupations. Two years later she joined Toni del Renzio in a short-lived dissident surrealist ferment around the one-shot magazine, *Arson*.

A devoted explorer of decalcomania, fumage, frottage, collage and other methods of pictorial automatism, Colquhoun invented several magic-inspired techniques of her own, including graphomania, stillomania, and parsemage. Of her many books, all of which are interesting, her *Goose of Hermogenes* (1960) is perhaps most important from the surrealist point of view. In her last years Colquhoun supported various efforts to reorganize a Surrealist Group in England and collaborated on the journal *Melmoth*. She died in 1988.

"What Do I Need to Paint a Picture?" appeared in *London Bulletin* no. 17 (June 1939).

WHAT DO I NEED TO PAINT A PICTURE?

Certainly not a canvas or an easel, because I need first a resistant surface (wall or panel) and a steady support (wall or table or bench). I like the surface on which I paint to be as near that of polished ivory as possible; sometimes this surface is so lovely that it seems a pity to paint it at all. Then I need a number, but not a large number, of opaque pigments and a small amount of medium. I am not going to say what is in the medium, but it smells very nice. Then a still smaller number of transparent pigments, and lastly a surfacing-wax which I put on when the paint is dry and which also smells very nice.

I need a line to work to (Blake's "bounding outline"); that means a full-sized detailed drawing afterwards traced. Then I put on the opaque colors very smooth and finally the glazes, if any, with the transparent colors. These are only the fixed and the cardinal qualities; what of the mutable? What of inspiration? What can one say of it except that it comes and goes, is helped and hindered, is unbiddable and unpredictable?

As to results, I aim for them to be sculptural: drawing and painting are branches of sculpture. For me, drawing is two-dimensional sculpture, painting is two-dimensional colored sculpture. If I do any sculpture, it is colored.

Mine is a very convenient way of painting, because it needs so many consecutive hours of work that it is almost impossible to do anything else.

Jeanne Megnen

The journal *Tropiques,* organ of a group in Fort-de-France, Martinique, during World War II, was also a prime vehicle of the international Surrealist Movement in those hard years. It published texts by surrealists Victor Brauner from Romania, Jorge Caceres from Chile, and, from France, André Breton, Charles Duits, Pierre Mabille, and Jeanne Megnen.

Although her 1938 collection of poems, *O rouge! O delivrée!,* bore the Paris imprint of Editions G.L.M., one of the principal publishers of surrealist works in those years, Megnen remains a little-known figure. Many know her only for her role in transcribing and editing Leonora Carrington's *Down Below* in Mexico in 1943. Initially married to French expressionist painter Marcel Gromaire, she later married Pierre Mabille, one of surrealism's outstanding theorists (and incidentally André Breton's personal physician). With Mabille, Megnen spent the war years primarily in Haiti.

The poem translated here appeared in *Tropiques* no. 3 (October 1941).

THE NOISE WILL START TOMORROW

The light screams, it backs me up.
The sunbeam perpetuates a steady ardor,
The strings are taut, ready to snap—
You say nothing—

I run into the bare tree trunk.
All is quiet and I can hear the air crackle—
I am patient.
Wings spread their shadows on the fields to protect us.
All the dogs are in.
Near the cliff, circles of small bells are on the move.

We'll take our rags in the flowered hangars of dawn
when everything goes dark in the light.

I am alone on a rock and smoke carries my hopes away
I walk on, bedecked with gold cloth
my boat, loaded with gems in the mineral waters, floats
away from the island of cork, lost and untouched by the plough.
In the distance, the air has cracked again in a leaden mist.
White hope whirls around vertiginously.
Nothing that is us can lose.

The water carries us
and screams in the door locks.
Our guts tighten on the crest of the foam.
Seized with terror I walk on sleepily.
The air rises and pierces the walls.

The woman has woven her glances like strands of wool
to plot the madness of one day.

I must bend heads in an empty kid glove.
A long-armed genie regulates the gear wheels of death.
On a stone mouth, lips annihilate a blood neutralized by an opaque poison.

Our boat has become heavier
Rocks are spitting on your chest
The sail whinnies in the fog
Water rolls on your impenetrable skin,
drop by drop, to fill an abyss of mercury.

Two of those pearls have nestled in my eyes
Two of those pearls have landed on a bird's wing.
I no longer see the overriding shiny domes.
Silence makes the ramparts desperately larger.

The noise will start tomorrow.

Translated from the French by Guy Ducornet

3. *Neither Your War nor Your Peace:*

THE SURREALIST INTERNATIONAL, 1940–1945

TROPIQUES

N° 3
OCTOBRE
1941

REVUE CULTURELLE — FORT-DE-FRANCE (MARTINIQUE)

Meret Oppenheim, *Paradise Is Under the Ground,* collage & gouache, 1940. © 1997 by Artists Rights Society (ARS), New York/Pro Litteris, Zurich.

Women in the Surrealist Diaspora

First Principles and New Beginnings

> In the gloom of a cloudy November,
> They uttered the music of May.
> —Emily Brontë

As history's worst depression turned into history's most devastating war, all groups concerned with human freedom and radical social and cultural transformation suffered. The Surrealist Movement was no exception. The high level of international organization and cohesion that surrealists had developed during the thirties was impossible to maintain in the police-state conditions that prevailed in Europe after 1939.

Nazi military occupation abruptly ended the public expression of surrealism in Czechoslovakia, Romania, Denmark, Holland, Belgium, and France. The advance of German troops drove most of the Paris group to Marseilles and then into exile: most went to New York, others to Mexico, some to the Caribbean. To one degree or another, surrealist activity persisted in most Nazi-occupied countries, but strictly underground. Its adherents, who circulated clandestine bulletins at the risk of their lives, had no way to communicate with surrealist comrades in other lands. In France several surrealists active in the Resistance were murdered by the Nazis. In Japan, which had an anti-surrealist law, surrealists were jailed or placed under house arrest. Four women involved in surrealism—Fanny Beznos, Hélène Vanel, Sonia Mossé, and Edith Hirschová, known as Tita—perished in Nazi concentration camps.[1]

Under dictatorships, fascist or Stalinist, surrealism was proscribed. Even in the democracies, its freedom of action was severely curtailed by the "war effort." Breton was granted asylum in the U.S. on the condition that he refrain from engaging in any radical political activity. He was under close FBI surveillance throughout his stay. There is reason to believe that the same conditions were imposed on other surrealist refugees.[2]

For women and men devoted to poetry, freedom, and love who had declared their attitude toward the war in the 1938 tract, "Neither Your War Nor Your Peace!," wartime restrictions were difficult to endure. However, one of the characteristics of revolutionary movements is that they thrive in conditions of adversity and persecution, and here too surrealism was no exception. Banned in one place, it always sprang forth somewhere else. If a few individuals dropped out, newcomers kept arriving. During World War II surrealist groups were publicly active in England, Egypt, Chile, Martinique, and New York, and some form of agitation was carried on in Mexico, Cuba, Haiti, and the Dominican Republic.

All through the war women's participation in the movement continued to expand. At least twenty-three women from ten countries made their first contributions to surrealism between 1940 and 1945. In addition to these newcomers, as many as twenty women who had joined the movement earlier remained active during the war. To pursue the surrealist adventure in the repressive intellectual climate of those years required courage and tenacity. "Once the war started," recalls Susanna Coggeshall—who as Susy Hare was a young surrealist recruit at the time—"internationalism was no longer 'in': quite the contrary, it was associated with Communism." Resentment against foreigners and radicals was especially rife in the highly competitive art world. Most New York artists and intellectuals greeted the surrealist refugees from Nazi Europe with nativist chauvinism; several openly feared what they called this "French invasion." Despite such provincial snobbism, however—or perhaps in conscious revolt against it—many women rallied to the reorganized Surrealist Group around Breton and his friends. The three issues of *VVV* published in New York from 1942 to 1944 not only include more texts and images by women than any earlier surrealist journal but they include more than all previous surrealist periodicals put together.[3]

The consciousness-raising effect of this influx of women in surrealism made itself felt in many ways. In the inquiry on mythical creatures in *VVV* no. 2–3 (1943), women's and men's responses for the first time were listed separately, with similarities and differences noted. The same year, at the urging of Marcel Duchamp, Peggy Guggenheim held an all-woman exhibition at her Art of This Century gallery in New York. Breton and Ernst were among the judges. Surrealism and the influence of surrealism were much in evidence in this show, which featured the work of thirty-one women, including Leonora Carrington, Frida Kahlo, Valentine Hugo, Jacqueline Lamba, Louise Nevelson, Meret Oppenheim, Kay Sage, Dorothea Tanning, and Julia Thecla. Contemporary critics responded to this surrealist initiative with typical sexist condescension and ridicule.[4]

The sheer number of women involved in surrealism in those years is itself remarkable. More impressive than their quantity, however, is the quality of the work some of these women produced. Toyen, Carrington, Lamba, Low, Agar, Penrose, Sage, Varo, and others whose participation in surrealism began earlier were now at the height of their creative activity. Among the newcomers Emmy Bridgwater, Sonia Sekula, Aline Gagnaire, and Dorothea Tanning enhanced surrealism's presence in the world of painting, while Maria Martins, Isabelle Waldberg, and Xenia Cage were on the cutting edge of surrealism in sculpture. Ida Kar and Hassia in Egypt, Eva Sulzer in Mexico, and Helen Levitt in New York showed that, in the hands of poets, the imaginative possibilities of the camera are limitless.

Women writers whose surrealist activity started in the World War II years have remained little known. Laurence Iché, a militant in the underground *La Main à plume* [Plumed Hand] group in France, Suzanne Césaire and Lucie Thésée in Martinique, and Gertrude Pape in the Netherlands are far from household names even in their homelands. An adequate study of the work of these and other women surrealist writers of those years runs up against onerous obstacles. In the years 1940–1945 at least five—Penrose, Carrington, Low, Ikbal El Alailly, and Laurence Iché—published books, but most were printed in small editions, and copies are not easy to find. The works of many more have never been collected in book form.

In the 1920s and 1930s women contributed more to surrealism than anyone outside the movement was willing to acknowledge. By the mid-1940s their contributions were so numerous and dazzling that even critics were finding it hard to ignore them. At the same time surrealism as a project of poetic and social liberation had entered a new phase of effervescence. Far from disintegrating during the war, it continued to extend its field of inquiry. Its critique of the repressive order, which in earlier years had relied mostly on psychology and philosophy, now drew increasingly on ethnography and history, which in turn illuminated surrealism's role in social and cultural change. As a radical poetic critique and an imaginative current of liberating ideas, surrealism in the war years achieved a qualitative growth as great as any in its history. What is more, the role of women surrealists in bringing all this about was a determining one.

It is not hard to trace the intellectual moments in this dialectical development. Just as Augusto Vera's pioneering French translations of Hegel had been instrumental in surrealism's evolution from what Breton called its "intuitive" period (1919–1925) to its "reasoning" period (starting in 1925), so too in 1940 Breton's study of Jean Hyppolite's just-published French translation of Hegel's *Phenomenology of Spirit* helped provide theoretical grounding for the advances to come.[5] In New York Breton immersed himself in the *Complete Works* of another great dialectician, Charles Fourier, which led him directly to Flora Tristan, the first incontestably feminist precursor recognized by the surrealists (Breton 1961). The "return to automatism" heralded by Breton in 1939 also opened the way for major surrealist breakthroughs (Breton 1972).

In the meantime, one of the crucial personal encounters in the history of the Surrealist Movement took place in 1941: Breton's meeting in Fort-de-France, Martinique, with Suzanne and Aimé Césaire and the group around the journal *Tropiques*, the brightest lighthouse of surrealist thought during the war years. Although her husband has monopolized the attention of critics, historians, and translators, Suzanne Césaire was a central figure not only in the *Tropiques* group, but in the international Surrealist Movement. As a woman, Black, West Indian, a scholar well-read in philosophy and ethnology as well as poetry, and a gifted theorist, she exemplified all that was most audaciously new in wartime surrealism. More specifically, she embodied the greatly expanded awareness of race, gender, precapitalist societies, popular culture, and the natural world which distinguished surrealism in the forties and provided its dialectical advance (Sourieau 1994; Franklin Rosemont 1996). The accent on surrealism as an "intervention in mythical life," as Breton put it in *VVV* in 1942, is a direct consequence of this marvelously heightened awareness (Breton 1978).

"Third World" and particularly Black inspirations had long figured in surrealist publications; surrealists from the beginning prided themselves on their treason to the so-called white race and—in collective tracts and such works as Nancy Cunard's *Negro: An Anthology*—added insights of their own to the struggle against racism and colonialism.[6] Suzanne Césaire's articles, however—most of which were in reality surrealist manifestoes—gave these inspirations and insights a dramatic new emphasis. Moreover, by situating them in a global anticolonialist revolutionary context, she also gave them a new concreteness and actuality. Thanks largely to Suzanne Césaire and the *Tropiques* group, the worldwide Black struggle for freedom was no longer regarded simply as a movement that surrealists supported: it became an organic part of surrealism itself. Significantly, the name *VVV*, or Triple V, chosen by André Breton and the Surrealist Group in exile for their New York journal, appears to have been inspired, at least in part, by the African American Double-V movement, which demanded Victory not only over fascism abroad but also over racism in the United States (Franklin Rosemont 1997). Meanwhile, in the Dominican Republic, Aída Cartegena Portalatín, a major proponent of Négritude in the Spanish-speaking world, was a frequent contributor to the journal *La Poesia Sorprendida* [Astonishing Poetry], coedited by exiled Spanish surrealist painter and poet E. F. Granell. Thus during the gloomiest days of the war, a new revolutionary hope was kindled.

Similarly, surrealists had questioned technology, "progress," and the dominant Euro-American attitude toward nature long before 1940. However, it was this young Black woman, Suzanne Césaire, and her surrealist friends on a tiny island in the Caribbean during a time of imperialist world war who, more than anyone else, made these issues paramount concerns of surrealists everywhere. In *Tropiques* the need for radical change in the relations between humankind and nature was presented with special urgency, as an inseparable component of poetic activity and revolutionary struggle. Interestingly, the first appearance of the word *ecology* in a surrealist publication turns up in this journal.[7]

Suzanne Césaire deserves a large share of the credit for precipitating some of the major developments in surrealism in the forties, but she was not alone. Mary Low, Leonora Carrington, Ikbal El Alailly, Jacqueline Johnson, Eva Sulzer, and Elisa Breton also contributed to the enlargement of surrealist perspectives in this difficult period. Oddly, although Césaire exemplified the new status of women in the Surrealist Movement, she was silent on women's issues in her published writings. This forbearance was not, however, shared by her women surrealist contemporaries.

In her 1943 collection of essays, *La Verdad contemporanea* [Contemporary Truth], mostly consisting of texts coauthored with Juan Breá, Mary Low surveyed "The Economic Reasons for Surrealism," "A Materialist Conception of Art," and "The Economic Causes of Humor," as well as "Woman and Love Through Private Property." This last, completed in 1941, is the first attempt by a woman surrealist to deal theoretically with woman in history. Prefaced by Benjamin Péret, this volume of slightly over a hundred pages is as notable for the wide range of problems it tackles as for its creative combination of surrealism, Marxism, and psychoanalysis.

Leonora Carrington's *Down Below* (1944) is a deeply moving, detailed account, suppressing nothing, of her harrowing adventures after being declared "incurably insane" in Spain in 1940. Admirably, Carrington's poetic lucidity and humor triumph over the sordidness of a nightmarish experience. In a perceptive study of the book, Pierre Mabille stressed its extraliterary value as "a human document prepared with the greatest possible rigor" and likened it to the classics of alchemy and Gérard de Nerval's *Aurélia* (Mabille 1981, 33–41). American readers will recognize its affinities with Charlotte Perkins Gilman's feminist classic, *The Yellow Wallpaper*. Widely reprinted and translated, *Down Below* has long been regarded as one of the most compelling surrealist texts.

In Cairo Ikbal El Alailly was compiling her anthology of poems and other writings by the German Romantics, *Vertu de l'Allemagne* [The Virtue of Germany] (1945). Her brilliant introduction explores the radical presurrealist currents in German poetry and relates them, historically as well as philosophically, to surrealism. El Alailly evidently foresaw the wave of Germanophobia that would overtake postwar France; her book, poetically and intellectually at the highest level, is also in the finest tradition of surrealist internationalism.

Meanwhile, in Wolfgang Paalen's *Dyn* magazine, produced in Mexico during the war, Jacqueline Johnson published texts prefiguring radical ecofeminism, and Eva Sulzer wrote insightfully on Native American art. Although the first issue of *Dyn* contained Paalen's editorial, "Farewell to Surrealism," it is clear today that Paalen and his cothinkers' disagreements with their surrealist friends occurred within the context of surrealism itself, and did not in fact represent a real break with it. By 1950 Paalen himself rejoined the Surrealist Group in Paris, and Breton praised his writings in *Dyn*. Like every other journal, *Dyn* published its share of less-than-wonderful texts, but the contributions by Johnson and Sulzer—as well as by Valentine Penrose and Alice Rahon—are alive, original, and authentically surrealist (Pierre 1970; Jaguer 1979, 54–56).

Chilean-born Elisa Bindhoff met Breton in New York in 1943 and married him a year and a half later. Although she is well-known as the inspirer of his *Arcanum 17*, her half-century of active participation in surrealism is rarely noted by critics. Multilingual and creative, a maker of enticing surrealist objects, Elisa Breton is a woman of vibrant imagination and a serious student of (among other things) the works of Hegel.[8] One cannot help wondering how much the feminist emphasis of *Arcanum 17* may owe to her influence. For example: how did André Breton, who disliked fiction, happen to read Thomas Hardy's *Jude the Obscure*, which he praises in *Arcanum 17*? Was it thanks to Elisa that he read this novel with powerful feminist themes?

It is often difficult and sometimes impossible to pinpoint particular influences by individuals. Here I simply suggest that major developments in surrealist thought during World War II—particularly concerning the emancipation of women, the relation of humankind and nature, the importance of popular culture, and a deeper appreciation of Black, native American, and other Third World cultures—were the result, in large part, of the cumulative and growing influence of women and Third World participants in the Surrealist Movement (Franklin Rosemont, ed., 1980).

These were highly promising developments, but the ravages of war and the ensuing Cold War impeded their fulfillment. Isolated by worldwide political reaction throughout the later forties and fifties, surrealism had to carry on as a radical underground. Many remarkable advances surrealists made during World War II would remain largely "theoretical" until the global renewal of radicalism in the sixties.

Notes

1. See René Passeron, "Répression du surréalisme," in Biro and Passeron, eds., *Dictionnaire Général du surréalisme*, 1982, 355–356; Jean and Mezei 1960, 294, *passim*; Jun Ebara, "Japon," in Biro and Passeron, eds., 1982, 222–223; Faure 1982, *passim*; and Cone 1992.

2. Documents obtained under the "Freedom of Information Act" confirm that Breton was under FBI scrutiny during his stay in the U.S.; according to FBI officials, the files of at least one of their investigations of Breton have been "lost," and others are not available to researchers because their contents might "endanger national security." See Franklin Rosemont 1997.

3. Ibid.

4. This achievement appears especially notable in view of Guggenheim's well-known misogyny, as evidenced in her autobiography: "I don't like women very much. . . . Women are so boring." Guggenheim 1979, 200.

5. André Breton's response to the inquiry, "Qui lisent les soldats?" in Pierre, ed., *Tracts surréalistes*, II, 1982, 3; Gérard Legrand, "Un non-anti-philosophe," in Saporta, ed., 1988, 184, 188.

6. Cunard herself, though long out of touch with her surrealist friends—as Conroy Maddox recalls, "she always seemed to be on the move" (letter to author, 7 May 1997)—articulated important themes of surrealism's postwar outlook in a small book she wrote in collaboration with Pan-Africanist George Padmore in 1942. "Never before in history," she observed in her preface, "has so much been said and insisted on for a total remaking of existence in the different countries of the Earth. At the cost of this, the Second World War, what transformation of the social and economic world situation is being envisaged? Are the white peoples to be the sole beneficiaries? British and United States leaders in clear terms tell us: 'No. This is to be for *all* peoples, for *all* races.' . . . Yet many of us, white as well as colored, are in doubt as to whether or not these sentiments and promises will materialize. We do not want to be cynical; but we remember. . . . We know that between the promises and their realization there is an immense No Man's Land" (Cunard 1942, 3–4).

7. The word *écologie* appears in E. Nonon, "La faune précolombienne des antilles françaises," *Tropiques* no. 10 (February 1944), 65. The complete run of *Tropiques* was reprinted by Editions Jean-Michel Place in 1978.

8. This paragraph is largely based on my own conversations and correspondence over the past thirty years with Elisa Breton and with many of her close friends, including Marie Wilson, Guy Flandre, and Ted Joans. Her study of Hegel is noted in a 14 August 1946 letter from André Breton to Enrico Donati, quoted in the exhibition catalog, *André Breton: La beauté convulsive* (1991), 394.

Suzanne Césaire

No important figure in the history of surrealism has been so overshadowed by a spouse as Suzanne Césaire, wife of poet/playwright Aimé Césaire. In view of her undeniably crucial role in the development of surrealism as well as of Négritude, it is astonishing how rarely she is mentioned in the voluminous critical literature on these movements.

Born Suzanne Roussy in 1913 in Trois-Islets, Martinique, she studied philosophy in Paris in the 1930s. It was there that she met and married (in 1937) fellow Martiniquan Aimé Césaire, in the milieu of the journal *L'Etudiant noir* [The Black Student], coedited by Léon-Gontran Damas from French Guiana and Léopold Senghor from Senegal. With her husband and René Ménil (a veteran of the earlier Martiniquan students' surrealist group, *Légitime Défense,* to which Simone Yoyotte had belonged), Suzanne Césaire welcomed André Breton to the island's capital, Fort-de-France, in 1941—truly a capital encounter for them all.

The journal *Tropiques* was an extraordinary crossroads of poetic and subversive thought; strongly influenced by Nietzsche, Frobenius, Victor Schoelcher, Marx, and Freud, it also published such poets of the Harlem Renaissance as Jean Toomer and Claude McKay. Above all, *Tropiques* was a major vehicle of surrealism during World War II, and Suzanne Césaire wrote some of the finest texts to appear in its pages. Far from being "converts" to "European" ideas, she and her cothinkers interacted critically and creatively with revolutionary and poetic theory and practice which, though initially set forth on the other side of the Atlantic, were themselves deeply influenced by non-European inspirations. The high esteem in which Breton regarded her is revealed in his lovely prose-poem, *For Madame Suzanne Césaire,* first published in *Tropiques* no. 5, and later in his book, *Martinique, charmeuse de serpents* [Martinique: Snake-Charmer] (1948), coauthored with André Masson.

After the last issue of *Tropiques* in 1945, Suzanne Césaire appears to have published nothing, although she did write plays which, unfortunately, have not yet found their way into print. I have been unable to learn anything of her later years apart from the fact that she and Aimé Césaire separated in the 1950s. One of surrealism's most brilliant and daringly original theorists, she has been disgracefully ignored by historians and critics. Perhaps the moments devoted to her in Euzhan Palcy's excellent 1994 film, *Aimé Césaire: A Voice for History,* will stimulate wider interest in the life and work of this extraordinary thinker.

"André Breton, Poet" (translated here, slightly abridged) appeared in *Tropiques* no. 3 (1941); "Discontent of a Civilization" in no. 5 (1942);

and "1943: Surrealism and Us" in no. 8–9 (1943). "Domain of the Marvelous" appeared (untitled) as a letter in the "Surrealist Number" of *View* magazine (1941).

ANDRÉ BRETON, POET

André Breton's poetry is a poetry of happiness. It ignores neither the anguish nor the maledictions that haunted the nightmares of Baudelaire and Rimbaud, but it goes beyond them and resolves them. Breton, like Rimbaud, is a "seer," but he does not allow himself to be hypnotized by the terrible visions of the Rimbaldian hell. Even in horror and despair, Breton knows how to discern the subterranean springs of joy. Despair? It "enchants" him! His own life? The most serious question! And yet, he knows how to attach no importance to it. For him, death is "pink," and all the mysterious aspects of existence are illuminated by his penetrating gaze—all contradictions, all mysteries.

Supreme reward of that supreme science: Poetry.

• • •

Breton inhabits a marvelous country where clouds and stars, winds and tides, trees and beasts, people and the whole universe yield to desire.

A fantastic and familiar land where all things beckon to him, and he answers their calls. He ushers us into the heart of a vaster, richer, truer, and more beautiful world, where our most troubling dreams flourish beyond ordinary consciousness. Monsters live here, sensitive and full of movement: the flowers that frightened and ravished our childhood, talking birds, winged devilfish, and sea-anemones. Here "coiled cats are chimneys on the rooftops"; here "giant cuckoo-pints whirl around their waist and the bleeding mannequin hops on three feet in the attic."

In this wonderland, telephone wires are enchanted, and grass is electric. And we are not surprised to hear "the sighs of the glass statue rising on its elbow when the sleeper is asleep, while bright gaps appears in his bed"—breaches through which we catch a glance of "deer with coral antlers in a clearing, naked women at the bottom of a mine." Who will doubt the reality of such visions? The most bewildering metamorphoses are stirring within us; the shapes of creatures and things have no limits, and time is abolished. And now, the marvel of marvels: Love. In *The Communicating Vessels* André Breton wrote that "Human love, like the rest, must be reconstructed. I mean that it must and *can* be re-established on its own true foundations." Love beyond all conventions takes its place again among the great elemental forces: Love, *mad* love—for here begins "the unutterable reign of the scorching, nameless woman / Who smashes the jewel of day into a thousand pieces."

For woman, that strange song, that convulsive call to the powers of the world and of desire, where love assumes its full meaning: to integrate the human into the cosmos through a direct link with the elements:

My woman with woodfire hair
with thoughts of heat lightning
with hourglass waist

• • •

[Breton's] poetic profusion unleashes the secret multitude of [his] desires, his true self, intoxicated with self-knowledge, astounded by personal freedom. . . .

The question, indeed, was to retrieve divine freedom, and the powers of dream and of childhood. Let's reread the first *Surrealist Manifesto*: "The mind which plunges into surrealism relives with exaltation the best part of its childhood . . . It is perhaps childhood that comes closest to 'real life' . . . Thanks to surrealism, it seems our luck is going to change."

And from the moment that space is abolished, when past, present, and future are fused, we live in this unique state which enables us to apprehend the meaning and plenitude and this sense of the instant which so ravishes us in small children when they are like puppies or kittens, calves or butterflies, flowers or sand—can't we then speak reasonably of freedom?

Freedom to do and to undo—the freedom defined by Breton [and Eluard]: "A poem must be a debacle of the intellect. . . . After the debacle, everything starts anew—sand, oxyhydric torches."

• • •

Abysses of the unconscious. Abysses of the Marvelous. Freedom—that other abyss. André Breton asks nothing more of life than their company. . . . And what magnificent riches the poet brings from the deep! The poet becomes a prophet.

Along these endless roads the mind acquires an ever-surer sense of its place in the world. Roads of yesteryear and tomorrow where the poet rediscovers forgotten links with the world's diversity.

Open roads where he is freed of the limits of time and space by poetry—he, the *seer* who reads a past that is also his future—who sees all the outer signs of his desire, all his dreams—which are also, at the same time, his waking acts of the day before: total knowledge.

"A prophet whose temples are purer than mirrors": Isn't this how Breton defines himself? And how can one deny his obvious poetic gift when *Mad Love* tells us of the marvelous encounter between the capital event of his life and a poem written ten years before—a poem "dictated" by the clairvoyant and unconscious self, suddenly luminous.

With no less emotion we read the troubling sentence written in 1925 in his *Letter to Seers*: "There are people who pretend that the War [of 1914–1918] taught them something; they are, all the same, less well off than I, who know what the year 1939 has in store for me."

• • •

The theorist should not let us forget the poet.

André Breton, initiator of the most extraordinary revolution (because it engages much more than art—indeed, our *whole life*) is, of today's French poets, the most authentic. Others—"prettier," more "pleasant," more traditional, and more cowardly, as it were—may be more popular. But who cares?

The least literary of our Men of Letters will remain the richest of all.

Supremely indifferent: "I am not on earth with all my heart."

Supremely knowledgeable and vigilant: "I touch only the heart of things / I hold the thread."

Within him, the exaltation of research, the dazzling discoveries, the smiling calm of one who knows, the assurance of one who sees.

André Breton: *richest* and *purest*.

Blocks of crystal piled high.

Translated from the French by Guy Ducornet and Franklin Rosemont

DISCONTENT OF A CIVILIZATION

In our legends we find a suffering, sensuous, occasionally mocking being who is our collective ego. But to search for the expression of this being, this ego, in the ordinary literary productions of Martinique is to search in vain.

Why have we been so uninterested in openly discussing this ancestral discontent?

The urgency of this cultural problem eludes only those who have decided that shutting their eyes, at any price, even the price of stupidity and death, is the way to avoid disturbing their artificial calm.

For our part, we feel that our troubled epoch is going to bring forth a ripe fruit, irresistibly summoned by the ardor of the sun which will spread its creative forces to the winds. On this peaceful and sunlit land we feel the formidable, inescapable force of destiny that has bloodied the entire world, but which tomorrow will give it a new visage.

Let's question life on this island of ours.

What do we find?

First, there is the geographical position of this parcel of land called "tropical." Indeed, the Tropics!

And so it was that an African population was able to adapt here. At the very beginning of slavery, the imported Blacks had to struggle against the severest mortality, against the most terrible working conditions imaginable, and against chronic malnutrition (which is still a problem today). And yet it is impossible to deny that, on the soil of Martinique, peoples of color have produced men who are strong, robust, supple, and women of natural grace and beauty.

But isn't it astonishing that this people, who in the course of time became adapted to this soil—these authentically Martiniquan people, have only recently begun to produce authentic works of art? How did it happen that, down through the centuries no living survivals of the original culture—for example, from those that so magnificently flourished on African soil: sculpture, printed fabrics, paintings, poetry—appeared here? Let the imbeciles blame the race and its so-called instinct for laziness, theft, and malice.

Let's speak seriously.

If this deficiency among the Blacks cannot be explained by the rigors of the tropical climate to which we have had to adapt, and even less by any sort of inferiority, we believe that it can nonetheless be explained:

1. By the atrocious conditions of the brutal transplantation to an alien soil. We have too quickly forgotten the slave traders and the suffering of our slave forebears. Here the act of forgetting amounts to sheer cowardice.

2. By the forced submission, under pain of whipping or death, to a system of "civilization" even more alien to the newcomer than the tropical earth itself.

3. And finally (after the emancipation of people of color from slavery) by a collective mistake: on the subject of our true nature, an error born of an idea anchored deeply in popular consciousness through centuries of suffering: "Since the colonizers owe their superiority to a certain life style, we in turn, can triumph over the colonizers only by mastering the technique of this 'style.'"

Let us pause a moment, and consider the scope of this gigantic misunderstanding.

What is a Martiniquan fundamentally, intimately, unalterably? And how does he live?

In response to this question, we shall see a profound contradiction between his deepest being, with all its desires, impulses, and unconscious forces, and life as it is lived, with its necessities, its emergencies, and its burdens. This is a phenomenon of decisive importance for the future of this country.

What is a Martiniquan?

He is the human plant.

Like a plant, he is ordered by the rhythm of universal life. He makes not the slightest effort to dominate nature. A mediocre farmer. Perhaps. I'm not saying that he makes plants grow, I'm simply saying that he grows—that he lives like a plant. His laziness? It is a vegetable laziness. Don't say, "he's lazy"; say "he vegetates," and you will be doubly on the mark. His favorite expression: "Take it easy." By this we understand that he lets life carry him along; likably, endearingly, he is docile, light, neither insistent nor rebellious.

A bit stubborn, but only as a plant can be. Independent, yes, but his autonomy is that of a plant. Given up to himself, to the seasons, to the moon, to the short days or the long ones. Harvesting. And always and everywhere, to the last example, preeminently a plant—trodden upon but still alive, dead but reborn, a free plant—silent and proud.

Open your eyes—a child is born. To which god should he be entrusted? To the Tree God. Coconut or Banana, among whose roots the placenta will be buried.

Open your ears. Here is a popular story from Martiniquan folklore. The grass that grows on the tomb is the living hair of the dead woman, who rebels against her death. It always comes down to the same symbol: the plant. A vital expression of a community both living and dead. In short, the Ethiopian concept of life.[1]

Thus the Martiniquan is typically Ethiopian.[2] In the depths of his consciousness, he is the plant-man, he identifies with the plant and wants to abandon himself completely to the rhythm of life.

Is this attitude sufficient to explain his failure in the world?

No. The Martiniquan has failed because he misunderstands his own deep nature and tries to live a life that is not right for him. Here we have an immense phenomenon of collective deceit, of pseudomorphosis. And the current state of civilization in the Caribbean demonstrates the consequences of this error: repression, suffering, sterility.

How and why did this fatal mistake occur among this formerly enslaved population? Through the most natural process, the play of the "instinct of survival."

Let us recall that the first rule of the slaveholders' regime was to completely prohibit assimilation of the Blacks into white society. Consider some laws: The law of 30 April 1764 forbade Blacks and people of color from practicing medicine; that of 9 May 1766 forbade them from being notaries, and the famous law of 9 February 1779 forbade Blacks from wearing clothes similar to those of whites and also compelled respect and submission on the part of Blacks "toward all whites in general," etc., etc.

Or consider the law of 3 January 1788 requiring free men of color "to obtain permits to work in any area other than agriculture." Citing these laws helps us understand why the main goal for people of color became *assimilation*. And how formidably, how powerfully their consciousness was affected by this disastrous confusion according to which liberation was supposed to equal assimilation.

At first 1848 was a good struggle. The mass of freed Blacks in a brief explosion of primitive ego refused all regular work, in spite of the danger of starvation. But then, subdued by economic necessity, the Blacks, no longer slaves but wage-workers, surrendered once more to the discipline of the hoe and cutlass.

It was during this period that the repression of the ancestral desire for free abandon was definitively carried out.

It was replaced especially among working-class people of color, by the alien notion of competition.

Herein lies the drama, plain to all who analyze in depth the collective ego of the Martiniquan people: the Ethiopian yearning for abandon continues to dwell in the very depths of their unconscious.

But their consciousness or rather preconsciousness now accepts the Hamitic desire for competition, struggle, chasing after riches and diplomas. Unscrupulous ambition, struggle toned down to suit the bourgeoisie. A race for mimicry. A vanity fair.

Most grievous is the fact that this desire to imitate, lately somewhat conscious—since it originated as a defensive reaction against an oppressive society—has by now joined the formidable and unknown forces of the unconscious.

The fact that not one cultured Martiniquan would admit that he is merely imitating indicates the extent to which this situation appears natural and spontaneous to him, born of the most legitimate aspirations. And he is sincere in this belief, for he really does not *know* that he is imitating. He does not know his true nature, which for all that has never ceased to live.

In the same way, hysterics do not know they are only imitating an illness, but the doctor who treats them and relieves their morbid symptoms knows.

Similarly, analysis shows that the Martiniquan effort to adapt to an alien style of existence can result only in a state of pseudocivilization which must be considered *abnormal*, monstrous.

Our problem now is to determine whether the Ethiopian attitude that we discovered was the very essence of our whole way of living can be the point of departure for a viable cultural style, however grandiose this may seem.

It is exalting to imagine on these tropical islands, restored finally to their inner truth, a lasting and fertile harmony between humankind and the earth—under the sign of the plant.

We are at last called on to know *who we are*. Splendors and hopes await us. Surrealism has restored to us some of our chances. Now it is up to us to find others. In its light.

Understand me well: It is not at all a question of going back, to resurrect an African past which we have learned to know and respect. It is rather a question of mobilizing all the mingled living forces on this soil where race is the result of an endless mixing, of becoming conscious of the formidable mass of diverse energies that we have heretofore locked up within ourselves. We must now put them to use in all their fullness, unswervingly, and without falsification. So much for those who think we are mere dreamers!

The most troubling reality is ours.

We shall *act*.

This land of ours can only become what we want it to be.

Notes

1. See Frobenius and *Tropiques* no. 1.
2. We may draw another argument from the realm of architecture: the typical Martiniquan hut is an exact reproduction (as opposed to the conical or saddle-shaped roof) of the huts of the Beni-Mai (from Congo Kassai) who display an "Ethiopian" sense of life. See Frobenius, *Histoire de la civilisation*, 198.

Translated from the French by Penelope Rosemont

1943: SURREALISM AND US

Many believe that surrealism is dead. Many have declared it so in writing. What childishness! Surrealism's activity today extends throughout the entire world, and it remains livelier and bolder than ever. André Breton may regard the period between the two wars with pride, and he can affirm that an increasingly immense, indeed boundless, "beyond" has opened up to the mode of expression he created more than twenty years ago.

If the entire world is struck by the radiance of French poetry just as the most terrible disaster in French history crushes France, it is in part because André Breton's powerful voice has not been silenced; it is also because everywhere—in New York, Brazil, Mexico, Argentina, Cuba, Canada, and Algiers—other voices also resound: voices that would not be what they are (either in timbre or resonance) without surrealism. In reality, today as twenty years ago, surrealism can claim the glory of being at the extreme point of life's super-taut bow.

Surrealism lives! And it is young, ardent, and revolutionary. In 1943 surrealism surely remains, as always, an activity whose aim is to explore and express systematically—and thus, neutralize—the forbidden zones of the human mind, an activity which desperately tries to give humankind the means of reducing the old antinomies, those "true alembics of suffering," and the only force enabling us to recover "this unique, original faculty, traces of which are retained by the primitive and the child, and which lifts the curse of the insurmountable barrier between inner and outer worlds."

But surrealism, further proving its vitality, has evolved—or, rather, *blossomed*. When Breton created surrealism, the most urgent task was to free the mind from the shackles of absurd logic and of so-called reason. But in 1943, when freedom herself is threatened throughout the world, surrealism, which has never for one instant ceased to remain in the service of the largest and most thoroughgoing human emancipation, can now be summed up completely in one single, magic word: *freedom*.

> The surrealist cause, in art as in life, is the cause of freedom itself. Today more than ever to speak abstractly in the name of freedom or to praise it in conventional terms is to serve it poorly. To light the world freedom must become flesh, and to this end must always be reflected and recreated in the *word*.

Thus speaks Breton. The demand for freedom. The necessity of total purity: that is the Saint-Just aspect of Breton—hence his "no thanks" refusals, so brutally condemned by those who side with compromise.

> To those who periodically ask why certain schisms have arisen in the Surrealist Movement, why certain interdictions have been brusquely issued, I believe I can reply in all honesty that those who were weeded out in the process had, in some more or less manifest way, broken faith with freedom. Since freedom is revered in its pure state by surrealists—that is to say, extolled in all its forms—there are, of course, many ways to break faith with it. In my opinion, it was for example breaking faith to return, as did certain former surrealists, to *fixed* forms in poetry, when it has been demonstrated, especially in the

> French language—the exceptional radiance of French poetry since romanticism permits a generalization of this viewpoint—that the quality of lyric expression has benefited from nothing so much as the will to be liberated from outmoded rules: Rimbaud, Lautréamont, the Mallarmé of *Un Coup de dés* [A Throw of the Dice], the most important symbolists (Maeterlinck, Saint-Pol-Roux), Apollinaire's "conversation-poems."
>
> And this would be just as true in the same epoch, true for painting. In place of the preceding names, it would suffice to cite those of Van Gogh, Seurat, Rousseau, Matisse, Picasso, Duchamp. It was also breaking faith with freedom to give up expressing oneself personally (and by that very fact dangerously, always) outside the strict framework in which a "party" wishes to contain you, even if it is thought to be the party of freedom (loss of the feeling of uniqueness). It was equally erroneous for some to believe that they would always be so much themselves that they could with impunity throw in their lot with anyone at all (loss of the feeling of dependence). Freedom is at once madly desirable and quite fragile, which gives her the right to be jealous.

Surrealism is thus as intransigent, as uncompromising as freedom itself, and this, moreover, is the very condition of its fruitfulness. And we see Breton, in his latest and most moving research, not hesitating to venture into the vast fields of the unknown that surrealism has presented to human audacity. What does Breton ask of the most clear-sighted spirits of our time? Nothing less than the courage to embark on an adventure which—who knows?—may well prove fatal, but from which one can hope—and that is what is essential—to attain the total conquest of the mind.

> An epoch such as ours justifies all journeys for the sake of the journey itself, after the fashion of Bergerac and Gulliver, particularly if these journeys constitute a challenge to conventional modes of thinking, the failure of which is only too obvious. And the journey to which I invite you today does not exclude every chance, after certain detours, of arriving somewhere, perhaps even in lands more reasonable than the one we leave behind.

Surrealism lives, intensely and magnificently, having found and perfected an effective method of knowledge. Therein lies surrealism's dynamism. And it is precisely this sense of movement that has always kept it in the forefront of cultural and intellectual life, infinitely sensitive to the upheavals and disruptions of an epoch which is the "scourge of balance."

"With all due respect to some impatient gravediggers," writes Breton,

> I think I understand a little better than they do what the demise of surrealism would mean. It would mean the birth of a new movement with an even greater power of emancipation. Moreover, because of that same dynamic force that we continue to place above all, my best friends and I would make it a point of honor to rally around such a movement immediately.

Such is surrealist activity, a total activity: the only one capable of liberating humankind by revealing the unconscious, an activity that will help free the peoples of the world as it illuminates the blind myths that have led them up till now.

• • •

And now let's return to us.

We know how things stand, here in Martinique. Dizzyingly, the arrow of history points to our human task. A society corrupted by crime at its foundations, currently propped up by injustice and hypocrisy, and, in consequence of its unhappy consciousness, terrified of its own becoming: such a society must perish morally, historically, and necessarily. And from the powerful bombs and other weaponry of war the modern world has placed at our disposal, our boldness has chosen surrealism, which in our times offers the surest chance of success.

One result is already evident. Not for one instant during these hard years of Vichy domination has the image of freedom been completely obliterated here—and this we owe to surrealism. We are glad to have sustained this image in the face of those who believed they had rubbed it out forever. Blinded by their ignorance, they could not see freedom laughing insolently, aggressively across our pages. When they did realize it, they succumbed to cowardice, timidity, and shame.

Thus, far from contradicting, diluting, or diverting our revolutionary attitude toward life, surrealism strengthens it. It nourishes an impatient strength within us, endlessly reinforcing the massive army of refusals.

And I am also thinking of tomorrow.

Millions of black hands will hoist their terror across the furious skies of world war. Freed from a long benumbing slumber, the most disinherited of all peoples will rise up from plains of ashes.

Our surrealism will supply this rising people with a punch from its very depths. Our surrealism will enable us to finally transcend the sordid antinomies of the present: whites/Blacks, Europeans/Africans, civilized/savages—at last rediscovering the magic power of the mahoulis, drawn directly from living sources. Colonial idiocy will be purified in the welder's blue flame. We shall recover our value as metal, our cutting edge of steel, our unprecedented communions.

• • •

Surrealism, tightrope of our hope.

Translated from the French by Erin Gibson

THE DOMAIN OF THE MARVELOUS

No longer is it a matter of the narrow roads where traditional beauty is offered in its clarity and obviousness to the admiration of the crowds. The crowds were taught the victory of intelligence over the world and the submission of the forces of nature to man.

Now it is a question of seizing and admiring a new art which leaves humankind in its true condition, fragile and dependent, and which nevertheless, in the very spectacle of things ignored or silenced, opens unsuspected possibilities to the artist.

And this is the domain of the strange, the Marvelous, and the fantastic, a domain scorned by people of certain inclinations. Here is the freed image, dazzling and beautiful, with a beauty that could not be more unexpected and overwhelming. Here are the poet, the painter, and the artist, presiding over the metamorphoses and the inversions of the world under the sign of hallucination and madness. . . . Here at last the world of nature and things makes direct contact with the human being who is again in the fullest sense spontaneous and natural. Here at last is the true communion and the true knowledge, chance mastered and recognized, the mystery now a friend and helpful.

Mary Low

PERCHANCE TO DREAM

He has taken flight through the tropic day and the night
Painting the far-off skyways with escape;
His deeds have crowned horizons with his thunder

And left a trail of flowers in his wake.
His crimson youth
His azure anguish
Stain the road
And dream-drops swell his heart and make him faint beneath its burden
Unknowing of the size of sleep he carries in his hands.

Open the four-dimensional door,
Light nonstop candles of vain return:
Out of the golden smoke of yesterday
Arises his turbulent, tender face,
His body of beauteous violence and turgid fire.
His leaden bed
Is gilded by his flesh,
His Byzantine kisses
Have planted gardens of joy and death
In the landscape of my mouth,
My body is sultry with stains
From the scattered violin-petals of his love.
The cardinal of kisses
Has left me faded from desire.

Lay him down between the easy legs of the palm trees,
Lay him against the grandiloquent breast of some high hill;
Give him for drink the slender hair of a wellspring
Daughter of the moonlight and a nightingale;
Clothe him with the sumptuous earth,
With the weight of her darkness and her jewels of living green,
With her floral eyes that suck up sleep;
Give him your kiss, you humble and haughty earth,
Touch his lips with the lascivious moistness of your own,
Then let him sleep to the deep rhythm of your womb.

Drops of his heart will leap up like banners
To swell the ancient sky with new delight;
Wherever flow the waters of his wake
Fresh wings will grow, and epic sails be set
To catch his silver breath,
While in the tranquil, pregnant, moon-wept countryside
Forever sings the subtle music of his mind.

Santiago de Cuba, 22 May 1941
(From *View* magazine, "Surrealist Number," 1941)

WOMEN AND LOVE THROUGH PRIVATE PROPERTY

Our aim is to cast a dialectical glance at the political and sexual situation of women.

It is not as a compliment, but as a necessity of our dialectical method that we shall go all the way back through history in order to show women in their best form. This form we shall find in matriarchy.

We all know what matriarchy was, and it is not necessary here to enter into details about the system it was based on. Let us simply remind ourselves that, in matriarchal days children were the offspring of the mother and not of the father and that sexual prejudice, in all its forms, was something unknown. In this "remote infancy of humankind," therefore, we shall linger only long enough to be present at the birth of the division of labor, a natural form of production that was brought about by difference in sex—not at all conducive to moral or economic discrimination or depreciation of either men or women.

In this golden age of the female sex, if "manna" did not really "fall from heaven," at least the concepts of superior and inferior were unknown, and "the demon of jealousy"—like all the other evils which today oppress humankind—had not yet appeared. A greater development of production was first necessary, in order that prisoners of war might be used as slaves in the gens, thus contributing to the increase of the clan's reserves. It was also first necessary that intertribal wars should frequently occur, creating the need for a species of permanent armed force. The physiological configuration of women, which disposes them unfavorably for this kind of activity, is the cause of their historical misfortune; for when war becomes one of the most productive occupations, their collaboration in this sort of work becomes almost useless. Men then begin by denying them their most natural rights—those of mothers and families—in order to demand for themselves the rights of fathers of families.

We are at the beginning of private property; or, as we might say, of family property. Up to this point, everything had belonged in common to the gens; but now we reach a stage which supposes, in practice, a transfer of the gens's property to its men. From now on, the properties of the gens must be the properties of its men, since, thanks to warfare, they have become the most active producers; therefore the properties should belong to them. Moreover, from the moment when it was no longer the gens itself that was to profit from all the benefits, but the men of the gens, paternity had to be assured. Men had to find a way of making certain that their children were not the children of others, because as soon as family property exists inheritance exists also. From this moment on, men refuse equal rights to women, inventing marriage, and thus proclaiming the first social injustice.

So the advent of private property surprises women on a level of military inferiority, because of which they are obliged to give up all their rights. No longer will sex determine the division of labor, but private property instead, a real Pandora's Box for the human race. We see that man, thanks to warfare and some advances in technology and general production, has managed so that woman—his companion until then—ceases to be his equal and is changed, through marriage, into his slave. The invention of marriage brings with it another rather absurd and strange invention: sexual prejudice.

In brief, the result of the arrival of private property in primitive society, is that women lose all their rights as men's companions. At first, men made no attempt to justify their position of force; they were content to enjoy it. The effort to justify it came only when class inequality, deepened by the development of production, rendered necessary a religious ethic or some other philosophy that would attenuate these social differences.

Then was invented the sexual prejudice of women's inferiority, just as racial prejudice was invented later. This invention has two aims. One of them is politico-religious: to make women resigned to their historical destiny as human types inferior to men; that is to say, to make them consider men as better gifted for the struggle for life and accept for themselves a secondary role in history. The other aspect reveals itself at the present time as a way of obtaining, thanks to this prejudice, the depreciation of women's work and lower wages for it. The same thing happens with racial prejudice. Women and Blacks, deprived (by this prejudice) of the chance of carrying out intellectual or technical work, find themselves taking refuge in unskilled labor. This vast army of the unemployed, a poorly paid reserve, is used to pressure other workers to accept starvation wages, since, thanks to such a reserve, demand is assured. Considered as productive forces, therefore, women and Blacks are nothing more—as a result of sexual and racial prejudices—than merchandise; worse still, depreciated merchandise.

After having rapidly surveyed women's social and economic path through history, let us now see how love has shown itself through its different stages. Love is the sexual reflection of the greater or lesser participation of women in social (not domestic) work in a country or an epoch; for women's sexual freedom depends on their economic freedom.

• • •

Ever since women, through a biological fatalism, ceased to take an active part in the principal work of men—warfare—the latter have, little by little, been denying them all participation in production, reserving domestic work for them. Men then talk about "the proper sphere of women" and keep them on a family-chore level. Ever since then, ever since women no longer work, they have been socially suppressed.

Their participation or nonparticipation in work has been, and is, the determining factor in all forms of love. The most irrefutable proof of this can be found in prehistory. In those times, since women worked on an equal footing with men and for that reason were really their equals, they had the right to sleep with all the men they wanted. So, in the consanguineous family, a woman slept with all the relatives of her husband—brothers, cousins, brothers-in-law, etc.—by family right and with others by choice. The feeling, or the so-called "instinct," of jealousy, is an instinct of civilized man. . . .

Love as we know it today—lyrical, romantic—is a relatively new invention. In this sense, the Greeks, for example, never loved. The advent of the Christian religion was necessary in order that occidental love might take on that form of erotic mysticism which has made it so celebrated throughout our era. . . . Through literature one may follow the development of this love-feeling, more easily than through any other art. We shall mention three well-known works: *The Divine Comedy,* in which Beatrice is something so divine and superhuman that we retain no memory of her face; next, the poems of Petrarch, in which, for the first time, in the person of Laura, the poet's muse possesses a human expression and is a woman of flesh and blood; finally, if you will, *The Lady of the Camellias*—for some strange reason generally known as "Camille" in English—of which the heroine, Marguerite Gautier, is a woman whose life is as uncelestial as that of a courtesan, and who dies of an illness as human as consumption. But if we look more closely at these personages, we shall notice the same religious sense of divinization, corresponding to religious concepts, and the diverse variations of private property throughout its different epochs.

In Dante's time, the reigning king or prince was more an idea than a man: that of respect and veneration for a superior being representing peace and order. Production, only slightly developed, offered no great contradictions to the concept of God and the king, and its inherent contradictions were not yet sufficiently visible to force the State to play a more effective role of oppression. The latter supposed, rather than an effective power, a principle of good order and justice which derived from the religious conception of God, but still very far removed from what we might call the human ideal.

It was something like the spiritual form of man. For this reason Beatrice, who is no more than the politico-religious expression of her epoch, is like God and the king: something so pure and intangible and remote from men that it would be profane to confuse her with anything human. She is nothing but this spiritual form of the love-ideal of her time.

With the next epoch it is no longer the same. Production, thanks to some technical discoveries, is developing craftsmen; and man has ceased, through the necessity of economy, to be a slave in order to become the owner of his product. This form of work reclaims the worker—that is to say, the slave—to the point of humanizing him. Hence humanist philosophy, on account of which Petrarch can do no less than humanize his ideal. This prestige of humanization reaches even God: the craftsman knows his lord and master; therefore his God can no longer be an idea, but a man. Without ceasing to be a divine expression, God now appears to us as a man with a beard. And Laura cannot be a goddess of indefinite form, like Beatrice, but must become a human woman who even goes to church. The State is naturally the determining factor of all these modifications, since, drawn out of its feudal lethargy by the increase in production, it must intervene in town and country in a more direct and repressive manner. If it has freed the slaves it is only to make them work more effectively, and therefore it has also to intervene more effectively in people's lives.

The Lady of the Camellias corresponds to another way of love-divinization: that of realism. God had ceased to be a principle in order to become a man; now, with realism, he will cease to be a man in order to become truth. With the arrival of the bourgeoisie, the development of bourgeois technique, in all senses, begins so openly to enter into contradiction with all the principles and concepts of the rest of the feudal world that these principles and concepts are called into question, and it is necessary to invent others that will adapt themselves to the new circumstances. Then, even God is judged, and the idea-concept of God as a man is lost, and instead of imagining God in their own likeness, people begin to see him as a force, an often contradictory power: that of production, which controls humankind. This is very difficult to represent as a human being, for if humanized it would cease to be that force or contradictory power. Rationalism, conveniently discovered, will fix everything: reason is human, humanity (human nature) is bourgeois, therefore truth is on our side.

The Lady of the Camellias answers to the religious concept in the manner in which all modern art identified itself with truth as the only positive value. That is to say, when, thanks to the influence of rationalism, God ceases to be a man in order to change into truth, and art ceases to be beauty in order also to change into truth, Beatrice and Laura cease being phantasmagoric and pure, changing instead into Marguerite Gautier, a human type no less real because impure. It is easy to note that Marguerite is just as deified as Beatrice or Laura, and it is precisely in this politico-religious conception of truth, as the one and only principle, that her divinization consists. In spite of being neither morally nor physically an ideal human type, she is deified because she is real. Marguerite's attacks of coughing, like Petrarchian melancholy, have drawn as many love sighs from their epoch as the tenuous shadow of Beatrice moving through *The Divine Comedy*. In the divinization of Marguerite we find her religious content, just as we do in the cases of Beatrice and Laura. If Marguerite is not a symbol of God, she is a symbolical way of loving God. Everything depends on and is explained by the way we must love and believe in God, that is to say, the way we must work.

Art does not express its conception of God until a little later, in the pretended dehumanization of the new art. In this fusion of the conscious and the unconscious, the conscious is represented by a yearning for liberation, for denial of the putrid canons of bourgeois morality, and the unconscious by an attempt to foretell a different sense. The new art appears to us today under a mysterious, contradictory, unknown aspect. This is the spiritual aspect of present-day society, with its production that controls us, with its wars and its contradictions. It is the aspect of a humanity moving toward another, unknown humanity: that of socialist society.

• • •

The love-ideal of the man of today consists in the feminine type of woman. We shall begin by analyzing this conception to discover its reason for being, since an ideal (like any concept) is only a lens that the epoch lends humankind to look at things. The first thing we notice is that femininity is not feminine. The feminine type is a type obtained by men at the price of making women all but useless, and as soon as the latter emerge from "the functions proper to their sex" to become doctors or chauffeurs, they cease to personify the feminine ideal. But the household duties "proper to their sex" are not such: they are merely secondary and restricted functions that have been determined, not by the sex of women, but by the political discrimination of which women are the objects. The feminine ideal does not correspond to the intellectual possibilities of women. It is a denial of them. The submissive housewife, resigned, obedient, monogamous, is not the ideal of a woman, but an ideal slave.

• • •

Women are different from men, but neither superior nor inferior to them on a human level. In order to reproach women for their inferiority, men accuse them for the slightness of the collaboration which, in comparison with themselves, they have brought to the culture of humanity. This same accusation might be brought against the proletariat that has suffered the same impossibility of being able to contribute to culture.

The feminine ideal—that of weakness—is the best trick for resigning women to their political inferiority. This is a prejudice so widespread that, with reason alone, it is impossible to struggle against it. We, men and women, have got this stupid conceit so deeply rooted in us that it is almost impossible to reach a serious understanding in love unless both sides do all they can to uphold the idea. . . . But let us not despair: women have begun to react against this unjust position of inferiority. . . .

• • •

Love has been, and continues to be, conditioned by the participation or nonparticipation of women in work. As this fact in its turn is brought about by private property, we can say that we see women and love through the successive deformations that private property has given to man and his civilization.

To state it briefly: as you work, so do you love.

Written in collaboration with Juan Breá (Barcelona, 1936, and Havana, 1941). First published in Juan Breá and Mary Low, *La Verdad contemporanea* (Havana, 1943). *Translated from the Spanish by Mary Low*

Frida Kahlo

"The art of Frida Kahlo," André Breton wrote in 1938, "is a ribbon around a bomb." Scarcely known outside surrealist circles for many years, Kahlo is today the most renowned of all the women who have been involved in the movement. Born in 1907 in Coyoacán, Mexico, of a Hungarian-Jewish father and a Spanish-Mexican mother, she was stricken with polio as a child; a later streetcar accident, and its attendant operations, left her an invalid for life. She took up painting in the mid-1920s, met Diego Rivera in 1928, and married him a year later. Her own course as an artist, however, was very different from that of her muralist husband.

In recent years, with the rise of a lucrative Frida Kahlo industry, it has become the fashion to belittle her association with surrealism. The facts remain: Not only did Breton arrange her first exhibition in Paris (1938) and write the first important (and often reprinted) text about her work, but Kahlo herself took part in the 1940 International Surrealist Exhibition in Mexico City, frequented the surrealist exiles' milieu (Carrington, Péret, Buñuel, et al.) in Mexico during the war, and for a time used the term surrealist as a self-description. The fact that she made some abrasive comments about Breton in letters counts for little, for it is well known that Kahlo made abrasive comments regarding practically everyone she knew.

However, well before her final capitulation to Stalinism in 1948, Kahlo had distanced herself from surrealism. Her last works include portraits of Stalin and other works "to serve the Party." After her death in 1954, her home in Coyoacán became the Museo Frida Kahlo.

I PAINT MY OWN REALITY

I adore surprise and the unexpected. I like to go beyond realism.

• • •

Surrealism is the magical surprise of finding a lion in a wardrobe, when you were "sure" of finding shirts.

• • •

I use surrealism as a means of poking fun at others without their realizing it and of making friends with those who do realize it.

• • •

I paint my own reality. The only thing I know is that I paint because I need to, and I paint always whatever passes through my head, without any other consideration.

FROM HER JOURNAL

Now he comes, my hand, my red vision. larger. more yours. martyr of glass. The great unreason. Columns and valleys. the fingers of the wind. bleeding children. the micron mica. I do not know what my joking dream thinks. The ink, the spot. the form. the color. I am a bird. I am everything, without more confusion. All the bells, the rules. The lands. the great grove. the greatest tenderness. the immense tide. garbage. bathtub. letters of cardboard. dice, fingers duets weak hope of making construction. the cloths. the kings. so stupid. my nails. the thread and the hair. the playful nerve I'm going now with myself.

An absent minute. You've been stolen from me and I'm leaving crying. He is a waverer.

• • •

Who would say that spots live and help one live? Ink, blood smell. I do not know what ink I would use that would want to leave its track in such forms. I respect its wishes and I will do what I can to flee from myself worlds, Inked worlds—land free and mine. Faraway suns that call me because I form a part of their nucleus. Foolishness . . . What would I do without the absurd and the fleeting?

Translated from the Spanish by Hayden Herrera

Lucie Thésée

Lucie Thésée was an integral part of the *Tropiques* group in Martinique, at least from its fifth issue (April 1942) when her name first appears in the journal. She contributed to four of the six subsequent issues and was one of six signers of the group's collective letter to a colonial officer (dated 12 May 1943, this letter was published in the 1978 Editions Jean-Michel Place reprint of *Tropiques*.)

Unlike Suzanne Césaire, who was a major theorist/polemicist of the group but published no poems, Thésée's contributions to the journal consisted entirely of poetry. Léon Damas in his *Poétes d'expression française, 1900–1945* praises Thésée's "abundance and excellence of images," and recognizes her as one of *Tropiques*'s core figures.

However, apart from the fact that she was a schoolteacher, I have been unable to locate any other biographical information about her. In the voluminous historical and critical literature on the Négritude movement and its progenitor, *Tropiques*, the name Lucie Thésée is almost never mentioned.

BEAUTIFUL AS . . .

Beautiful as a high foamy wave spurting in a crystal ball.
Beautiful as a light breeze in the tulle of life.
Beautiful as a tear on a perfectly immobile face at the peak of a radiant day.

Beautiful as flame.
Beautiful as an immense fathomless sky pierced by a star of the greatest
magnitude.

But beautiful as a sea sky and an Earth like the sea floor
But beautiful as sea sky, and earth like sea floor . . .
Fascinating to see what man could be in this tableau . . .

Beautiful as a sleeper under the open sky in the swarming activity of a vast
tropical night.
Beautiful as the fascinating decor of a great tropical midnight between two
fingers with feline nails . . .
Beautiful as the dazzling fireflight of a multitude of fireflies on a calm
horizonless sea on a marine night.
Beautiful as an iridescent soap bubble pierced by a fine pin and ceaselessly
grazing a black dress.
Beautiful as a heart pierced through by a rainbow arrow.

Beautiful as a giant shadow moving slowly on a half-tint partition
Beautiful as movement
Beautiful as life with life's poison
Beautiful as the sun's blood

Translated from the French by Myrna Bell Rochester

THE BUCKETS IN MY HEAD . . .

The buckets in my head stand open
Gone off in a great blue air here I am again for the fleeting minute
a length of gutter pipe
wide open under an open sky,
everything passes here, my parallel vision, a pipe's vision snapped up
everything.
Now who can question my eternity?
Myself whose prenatal eye is present
at the eternal bath of compact foliage in the surging river
in the river fecund with ferocious lives, colossal lives
in the river of crocodiles and hippopotamuses.
Who doubts my eternity I whose body
curled up when the greedy nails sank
cynically, ominously into my prenatal, uprooted flesh

and marked it indelibly, my virgin flesh
of a "makanguia" rich in silky noises of old and
retrospective perfumes of the equinoctial forest
my primitive possession,
my red-black flesh, still virgin of any name.
Calm yourself my frond of dynamited pink, vengeance is done:
my eternity is.
Why won't I now take my ease? I ask you this, I whose heart of filao swollen
with sap of the impossible, mooning about in her green plumes
makes the wind sing,
I whose antennae of filao burst forth to attack a sky of shivers.
Who wanted to steal my eternity
Oh Death, life doesn't sneer, she laughs and she loves
she loves laughing and it's she who kills laughing.
Who kills all her con men with vague and flaccid hearts
Oh you who couldn't yet even be a wretch.
And who says also that time doesn't belong to me? I who curry myself up to
the backbone of the sun
and embrace him and kiss him with my flame tongue.
The sovereign essence of my bow sailing the bunkered rage
upon the foam of the unjust and of crime
lights the 89, the 48, the 45
setting the horizon ablaze at the limits of fraternity and love.
And now you guffaw with your cheeks chubby with fat
pale paupers of the cloud
I am geysers, crater, the earth's belly deep below the earth
I throw the flame, now catch it on the wing of my laughter, on the wing of
my grief;
I inject song, I perpetuate shivers and trembling flowers of the eternal.
Eternity, I am Freedom.

Translated from the French by Myrna Bell Rochester

WHERE WILL THE EARTH FALL?

On the second story of an enormous gray house with a wooden balcony cut out in columns, covered and on a level with treetops clotted with green, with every kind of green, swelling up at the whim of the breeze. Opposite, in the background: a splendid, enigmatic view of Mt. Pelée, an eclipse-colored sky, the sea however of a violent blue running along the shore of a long opaque white fold. A little to the right, a wide, dark bluff leans into the big mountain; its aggressive head inhaled and retained all the light for itself—The surprise caused by this absolutely unexpected landscape forces me into anxious contemplation, incapable of attaching itself to an object.

Suddenly a block of live water rushes madly down from the side of the big mountain opposite the house. At the same time the big mountain brightens bit by bit with a light which in spite of its fragility puts all the crests into relief. However, the dark bluff, between the mountain and half of the house's façade, continues concealing all that it can of the white light powdering the sea, the sky, and the earth.

Imperceptibly the tableau's background draws nearer to the house. Suddenly, from a steep, rather wide, dazzling bright gray crack, an animal appears. It runs furiously down the path (from my vantage point, the direction of its run: right to left), now the dark bluff is directly behind it. Its run, felt mad with fear, makes it grow large terribly fast. I can make out a light-colored cow with particularly white glittering hooves, she passes watching me like a hunted beast. And soon before me an entire herd silently files by with a helpless look; each head dripping with silvery light appears, passes and disappears full size as in certain cinematographic effects. Dully, I ask myself: Might it be a volcanic eruption? A few minutes farther along, a great rustling of silk, I shiver "It's the sound of fire." Without turning around I see emerge at the foot of the dark bluff, in the orchard of the house, a pool of brilliant light where a mercury sun streaking the surrounding space with long white zigzags rises up and detaches itself. At this moment the great rustling of silk from a while back grown enormous and sinister dominates all the light. The luminously serene oranges in the garden watch the scene, impassive . . . Now the pool of light boils, the sun now detached from it is immobile glowing implacably . . . "But this second story with no ground floor is rocking!" Did you see? "The whole planet is collapsing with it!" . . . "the balcony is coming down!" Where will the earth fall? A great cry of sharp anguish as though from beyond the body: "The Earth is adrift" and I am awakened . . . .

Let the ice break, all the ice
And the overwhelming anguish will cease
And the Earth will drift entirely as it pleases.

Translated from the French by Myrna Bell Rochester

Leonora Carrington

DOWN BELOW

Exactly three years ago, I was interned in Dr Morales' sanatorium in Santander, Spain. Dr Pardo of Madrid, and the British Consul having pronounced me incurably insane. I fortuitously met you, whom I consider the most clear sighted of all, I began gathering a week ago the threads which might have led me across the initial border of Knowledge. I must live through the experience all over again, because, by doing so, I believe that I may be of use to you, just as I believe that you will be of help in my journey beyond that frontier by keeping me lucid and by enabling me to put on and to take off at will the mask which will be my shield against the hostility of Conformism. Before taking up the actual facts of my experience, I want to say that the sentence passed on me by society at that particular time was probably, surely even, a godsend, for I was not aware of the importance of health, I mean of the absolute necessity of a healthy body to avoid disaster in the liberation of the mind. More important yet, the necessity that others be with me that we may feed each other with our knowledge and thus constitute the Whole. I was not sufficiently conscious at the time of your philosophy to understand. *The time had not come for me to understand.* What I am going to endeavor to express here with the utmost fidelity was but an embryo of knowledge.

• • •

One day, I went to the mountain alone. At first I could not climb; I lay flat on my face on the slope with the sensation that I was being completely absorbed by the earth. When I took the first steps up the slope, I had the physical sensation of walking with tremendous effort in some matter as thick as mud. Gradually however, perceptibly and visibly, it all became easier, and in a few days I was able to negotiate jumps. I could climb vertical walls as easily as any goat. I very seldom got hurt, and I realized the possibility of a very subtle understanding which I had not perceived before. Finally, I managed to take no false steps and to wander around quite easily among the rocks.

It is obvious that, for the ordinary bourgeois, this must have taken a strange and crazy aspect: a well brought up young English woman jumping from one rock to another, amusing herself in so irrational a manner, this was wont to raise immediate suspicions as to my mental balance. I gave little thought to the effect my experiments might have on the humans by whom I was surrounded and, in the end, they won.

• • •

I am afraid I am going to drift into fiction, truthful but incomplete, for lack of some details which I cannot conjure up today and which might have enlightened us. This morning, the egg ideas came again into my mind and I thought that I could use it as a crystal to look at Madrid (July–August 1940), for why should it not enclose my own experiences as well as the past and future history of the Universe? The egg is the macrocosm and the microcosm, the dividing line between the Big and the Small which makes it impossible to see the whole. To possess a telescope without its essential half—the microscope—seems to me a symbol of the darkest incomprehension. The task of the right eye is to peer into the telescope, while the left eye peers into the microscope.

• • •

I ceased menstruating at the time, a function which was to reappear but three months later, in Santander. I was transforming my blood into comprehensive energy—masculine and feminine, microcosmic and macrocosmic—and also into a wine which was drunk by the moon and the sun.

I now must resume my story at the moment I came out of the anaesthesia (between the 19th and 25th of August, 1940). I came to in a tiny room with no windows on the outside, the only window being pierced in the wall to the right which separated me from the next room. In the left corner, facing my bed, stood a cheap wardrobe of varnished pine, to my right, a night table in the same style, with a marble top, a small drawer and, underneath, the empty stable of the chamber pot; besides, a chair; symmetrical with the night table, there was a door which, as I was to learn later, was the bathroom's; facing me, a glass door giving on a corridor and on another door paneled with opaque glass which I watched avidly because it was clear and luminous and I guessed that it opened into a room flooded with sunshine.

My first awakening to consciousness was painful: I thought that I was the victim of an automobile accident; the place was suggestive of a hospital and I was watched by a repulsive-looking nurse, who looked like an enormous bottle of Lysol. I was in pain and I realized that my hands and feet were bound by leather straps. I learned later that I had entered the place fighting like a tigress, that on the evening of my arrival there Don Mariano, the physician who was head of the sanitarium, had tried to induce me to eat and that I had clawed him. He had slapped and strapped me down and compelled me to absorb food through tubes inserted into my nostrils. I don't remember anything about it.

I tried to understand where I was and why I was there. Was it a hospital or a concentration camp? I asked the nurse questions, which probably were incoherent; and she gave me richly negative answers in English with a very disagreeable American accent. Later I learned her name was Asegurada ("Insured," in the commercial sense of the word), that she was German from Hamburg, and lived for a long time in New York.

I never was able to discover how long I had remained unconscious: days or weeks? When I became sadly reasonable, I was told that for several days I had acted like various animals—jumping up on the wardrobe with the agility of a monkey, scratching, roaring like a lion, whinnying, barking, etc.

• • •

It was, I am almost certain of it, the night before I was injected with Cardiazol that I had this vision:

The place looked like the Bois de Boulogne; I was on top of a small ridge bordered with trees; at a certain distance below me, on the road, stood an obstacle like those I had often seen at the Horse Show; next to me, two big horses were tied together; I was impatiently waiting for them to jump over that fence. After long hesitations, they jumped and galloped down the slope. Suddenly a small white horse detached itself from them; the two big horses disappeared, and nothing was left on the road but the colt who rolled all the way down and remained on his back, dying. *I myself was the white colt.*

The terrible downfall induced by Cardiazol was followed by a succession of rather silent days. Around eight in the morning, I would hear from a distance the siren of a factory, and I knew this was the signal for Morales and Van Ghent to call the *zombies* to work and also to wake me, who was entrusted with the task of liberating the day. Piadosa would enter then with a tray on which stood a glass of milk, a few cookies and some fruit. I ate that food according to a special ritual:

1st—Sitting bolt upright in my bed, I would drink the milk at one draught.

2nd—Half reclining, I would eat the cookies.

3rd—Lying down, I would swallow all the fruit.

4th—I put in a brief appearance in the bathroom where I would observe that my food went through without being digested.

5th—Back in my bed, I sat up again very straight and examined the remnants of my fruit: rinds and stones. I arranged them in the form of designs representing as many solutions to various cosmic problems. I believed that Don Luis and his father, seeing the problems solved on my plate, would allow me to go "Down Below," to Paradise.

• • •

On the way to Covadonga, followed by Asegurada, I met Don Mariano—God the Father—dressed as was his custom all in black with, at the level of his stomach, a crust of food dried up by time. He was spying on a very destitute child who wept as he picked up dry leaves. I asked what the child had done. Don Mariano answered: "He stole an apple in my orchard." I shouted to him indignantly: "You who possess so many apples! With such morality, no wonder the world is 'jammed' and miserable. But I have just broken your wicked spell in the tower and, now, the world is liberated from its anguish."

The grandson of Marquis da Silva went by at a run, and God the Father, reassured by the presence of a child who was so "well brought up," so decent, smiled at him kindly.

I returned to Egypt, rather disgusted with the Holy Family. . . . From the bathroom window, I gazed for a long time at a green and sad landscape: flat fields stretching down to the sea; near the coast, a cemetery: the Unknown and Death.

I learned from Asegurada that Covadonga (Don Mariano's daughter) was buried in that cemetery. Asegurada often spoke to me of Covadonga and surrounded her death with mystery; I thought that it was Don Luis who had killed her by torture to make her more perfect as he had tortured me. I thought that Don Luis was seeking in me another sister who, stronger than Covadonga, would withstand her ordeals and reach the *Summit* with him. I did not rely for this on my strength but on my skill. I thought that I had been mesmerized in Saint-Martin-de-l'Ardèche and drawn to Santander by some mysterious power. One day Don Luis tried to get me to sketch a map of that journey. As I was unable to do so, he took the pencil from my hand and began to draw the itinerary. In the center he put down an *M* representing Madrid. At that moment I had my first flash of lucidity, the *M* was "Me" and not the whole world, this affair concerned myself alone, and if I could make the journey all over again, by the time I reached Madrid, I would get hold of myself, I would reestablish contact between my mind and my Ego.

Soon after my visit to "Down Below," Don Luis decided to install me in

Amachu; this was a pavilion outside the walls of the garden; there I would be alone with my servants. Why did I find myself "jammed" once more and in great anguish? Why did I imagine that I had been deemed unworthy to live in the Garden of Eden?

Excerpts from *VVV* no. 4 (New York, 1944; Chicago: Black Swan Press, 1983)
Translated from the French by Victor Llona

Régine Raufast

With the poet Laurence Iché and the Czech artist Tita (Edith Hirschová), Régine Raufast was one of the most active women in the clandestine *La Main à plume* surrealist group in France during the Nazi occupation. Its first collective publication included one of her poems. I have not been able to locate any information about her except that she was, for a time, the companion of Belgian surrealist photographer Raoul Ubac, and later of poet Christian Dotremont, who evoked her movingly in a posthumous tribute published in the Belgian surrealist journal *Suractuel* in July 1946.

The following article, which originally appeared in *La Conquête du Monde par l'Image* [Conquest of the World by the Image] in June 1942, was reprinted in Edouard Jaguer's full-length survey of surrealism in photography, *Les Mystères de la chambre noire* [Mysteries of the Black Chamber] (1982).

PHOTOGRAPHY AND IMAGE

Strike "commercial" from the word photography and banish it to the family album and the fairground: Man Ray and Raoul Ubac propose a photography that is a far cry from the faithful reproduction of reality flattered by soft lights and facile tricks. In the relatively new activity of poetic photography, such ostracism poses no threat to the imagination whatsoever and, frankly, what does a practice that consists of fixing finished forms and immobilizing the immobile have to offer us anyway?

Man Ray and Raoul Ubac pose the problem of the imagination and its exigencies with increasing urgency. For example, works such as *Triomphe de la*

Sterilite [Triumph of Sterility], *Les Corps solarisés* [The Solarized Bodies], *La Nebuleuse* [The Nebulous], *L'Envers de la face humaine* [The Back of the Human Face], awaken an imagining emotivity in the viewer's mind: we are in the presence of an interaction, a *double imagination*—the image-making imagination of the operator and the imagination peculiar to the medium itself. This double action is objectified by the process of the operator, *alchemical* to the extent that it searches for new and pure elements in the putrefaction of formally elaborated substances which, deformed at the height of their development, conserve only what informs their future. Photographic acts such as *La Nebuleuse*[1] or *L'Envers de la face humaine* are examples of this analogous activity. The negative is exposed to fire which partially erodes the surface, precipitating a new form in the process of *becoming*. And because one form appears the instant another is destroyed, we assist at a veritable dialectic of matter: matter superseding itself. This tangible realization of a material future initiates a reverie at the heart of matter and engenders a chain of transformations influenced by the viewer's own *paranoiac-critical* activity.

Three elements enter into the composition of this poetic phenomenon: matter,[2] chance, operator. First we find ourselves in the presence of an evolution independent of the image making of the operator and assist at something like an objective marriage of matter and chance appearing like a veritable image making of matter: fertile, animated and drawn, despite itself, into the vortex of its own *élan vital*. At this point the operator decides the degree of the transformation and stops it the instant the visible image coincides with his own image-making mind. His imagination is nothing more than a will to power, not in the Nietzschean sense, but rather a will to transform a dead reality into one that allows itself to be eclipsed in order to be superseded. The image, produced from the encounter of the subjective preoccupation of the operator and the objective life of matter, is no more *sign*, but *act*.

Notes

1. *La Nebuleuse* was, at its origin, nothing more than a banal photograph of a woman.

2. By an image's "matter" we mean both matter properly speaking and literally the form it takes.

Translated from the French by Rikki Ducornet

Laurence Iché

Laurence Iché was active in the underground *La Main à plume* group in France during World War II and was the author of two booklets published under its auspices: a collection of poems, *Au fil du vent* [To Go with the Wind], illustrated by Oscar Dominguez (1942), and a series of surrealist texts, *Etagère en flamme* [Knick-Knack Shelf in Flames], with a drawing by Picasso (1943). Like most writings of the French surrealist underground during World War II, her work has largely been ignored by critics. The recorded details of her life are few indeed, beyond the facts that she was the companion of fellow *Main à plume* activist and poet Robert Rius and later of J. V. Manuel, better known as Manuel Viola, who was also active in *La Main à plume* and who later became one of the most prominent Spanish lyrical-abstractionist painters.

Several members of the *Main à plume* group continued to be active in surrealism after the war. However, Iché and J. V. Manuel moved to Spain and lost touch with the movement. She lives today in Madrid.

"Scissors Strokes by the Clock" and "I Prefer Your Uneasiness Like a Dark Lantern" appeared in *Au fil du vent* (1942); "Unpublished Correspondence" and "The Philosophers' Stone" in *Etagère en flamme* (1943).

SCISSORS STROKES BY THE CLOCK . . .

Scissors strokes by the clock
with harpsichord fingers
in your phosphorus breast
that opens out into a fan's breeze
The wind that great sculptor of unique erections
in the game of ninepins of tottered days
Under the bowler hat of habit
adventures sew themselves up again
into fountains to resew the air
so that the paper lanterns may tremble
like a false eye
so that the lamps may be moth-eaten like the cries of chimneys in the wind
all those rotting breaths of films
when mountains are clouds at rest
with nostalgic grasses
feather dusters of rolling inventions

Translated from the French by Myrna Bell Rochester

I PREFER YOUR UNEASINESS LIKE A DARK LANTERN . . .

I prefer your uneasiness like a dark lantern
without ever knowing that phantom that goes through me
when the lamp of battles burns all its thirst
Only the leaf
on a final point of life
will run into the hoop of knowledge.
The eagle-headed caterpillar
the wind-haired eagle
are engulfed by the bath of shredded mirrors
with nostalgic seals of lips
and glances that collide
Those are the shredded mirrors
that reptiles inhabit
for the smiles of the wind steal all the velvets of forgetfulness
with the same avidity that windows steal landscapes
underneath lines drawn from the sun
Like the meteor trail of a hope
they embraced
the nervous spurt of printer's blood
the cavalcade of inextricable branches of chance
in the ballet of days that shelter you
immobility cooked into table legs
and catacombs of the past in the shadow of the present
to make of me a drying umbrella

Translated from the French by Myrna Bell Rochester

UNPUBLISHED CORRESPONDENCE

One rainy day, a little mushroom emerged and immediately took himself to be an umbrella. He perched on a young woman's head, and his joy was boundless, until he caught a glimpse of the Eiffel Tower. "Goodness," he said to himself, "that's a really big mushroom!" And he set himself the task of climbing the Eiffel Tower. While he was climbing up, the Eiffel Tower felt tickled. She would have liked to scratch herself, but she didn't know how, and the mushroom kept on climbing and climbing. Then the Eiffel Tower, very flustered, lowered her head and started striding along. Daydreaming, she stepped on a house, and suddenly the house looked like a bread crust. All the starving birds ran up to the crust, but it was impossible to eat. They came in such great numbers that the sky turned black and soon after lost its balance and fell over backwards. It found itself in a puddle, on its back, feet in the air, and with its feet it tried to attach itself to a second sky it had just noticed. But the second sky, a very cold one, became extremely angry with these nasty proceedings. Slowly it turned over on its side and said to the sky in the puddle: "So, you're becoming a pickpocket now?"

Translated from the French by Myrna Bell Rochester

THE PHILOSOPHERS' STONE

Once there was a white stone in a wall. She was very unhappy because the wall constantly called her a bedsock. The stone didn't think she was a bedsock at all, but a beautiful shining stone.

One day she saw a donkey and called out to him, "Little donkey, please take me away on your back. I am a beautiful shining stone; all you need to do is pick me out with your teeth." The donkey said thank you without knowing why, and he put her in the hollow of his back.

And now the wall was unhappy because he didn't have his bedsock anymore, he said, and he couldn't grab the little slippers he saw under the bed in the bedroom.

Meanwhile, the stone, in the hollow of the donkey's back, was explaining that she was a beautiful shining stone and not a bedsock. She was, however, tiring of this trip and soon announced that she was sick of seeing things always from the same height. Now the donkey stayed angry until he came across a duck he wanted to eat. But the duck wanted to be eaten in the Spanish style, like a free man, and not with nettles as the donkey was suggesting. Then a great fight ensued, and the stone took advantage of the general confusion to let herself roll down into the ditch right near the duck. The duck disguised himself as a pigeon, and the donkey, who wasn't wearing his glasses, no longer recognized him and trotted away. The stone called over the duck and made him a proposal: "I am the one who gives many snails," said she to the pseudo-duck, "Take me along on your back. With that donkey I was really tired of seeing things always from the same height, and I'll be happy to fly a bit." The duck didn't dare refuse, and then and there he put her on his head.

But the stone wasn't satisfied, for she felt that a little pompom was growing on her peak and that she was simply turning into a nightcap. The duck was thrilled that his ears were no longer cold; but the stone felt her hair get mildewy as if she had had three noses, and yet she was too old to commit suicide.

Translated from the French by Myrna Bell Rochester

Gertrude Pape

Born in Leeuwarden in northern Holland in 1907, Gertrude Edith Pape spent most of her childhood in South Africa and London, returning to Holland in 1914. Fluent in English and French as well as Dutch, she wrote in all three. In Utrecht in 1929, she met Willem Wagenaar, whose Gallery Nord was *the* center for surrealism, jazz, and "primitive art" in the Netherlands; it was there, while listening to Louis Armstrong records, that Pape came to know *La Révolution surréaliste, Le Surréalisme ASDLR,* and *Minotaure*. In 1938 she attended the International Surrealist Exhibition in Amsterdam, and the following year met Dutch surrealist poet Theo van Baaren, whom she later married.

During World War II she and van Baaren produced twenty-two issues of *De Schone Zakdoek* [The Clean Handkerchief]; to avoid censorship under the Nazi occupation it was handmade in an edition of one copy, which they shared with friends at regular Monday evening meetings at their apartment. This unique publication was surrealist-oriented from the start, although it did publish some nonsurrealist work. Number 8–9 of the first volume was subtitled "Surrealist Number."

De Schone Zakdoek ceased publication in 1944. That same year Pape brought out a small edition of her *Verses by a Female Robinson Crusoe,* under the pen-name Evelyn Palmer. Utterly indifferent to the literary marketplace, she did not bother to publish anything in later years. When Her de Vries and others organized a Surrealist Group in Amsterdam in 1959, they recognized her as one of the true founders of surrealism in the Netherlands. She died in 1988. Selections from *De Schone Zakdoek* were published in book form in 1981.

"The Lake," written in English, is from *De Schone Zakdoek* no. 2 (1941). "Eardrops from Babylon" appeared (in Dutch) the same year in the "Surrealist Number," no. 8–9.

Gertrude Pape, *Be Sure,* collage, early 1940s. Courtesy of the artist's estate.

THE LAKE

Mirror of emptiness
called in the green
pallid in clearness
no clouds were seen

EARDROPS FROM BABYLON

The willow was ebbing. Freely the seedlings spun sand. In the barrack entered weeping the Nildo, windows and doors belonged to him; under his feet the boards uncracked: better beans! whispers the wood. Storm attacking! West on the run! Cloud around thunder trembles in the house. Strike the lightning, don't call me sinless! All my names know your leap. Silence felt. The bug took refuge in vain, light on the freezing hands. Just one beat of the heart the possibility, desire turns itself full. Lovable, relentless, lasting the sun turns.

• • •

Eliane, entangled in her own hair, wrests herself, sinks. End-rise. A blue toe, a white toe, embroidery of a bedspread getting longer and reaching farther and striking over the hedges, beyond. Non-pillar. Reedless. The stroke of the hour falls down every ten drops; coral-fungi dress the branches, many nests, remunerative plumes. Short blitzlightning jingles: the Walker! on all red roofs, in a synchronous undulatory movement, the tiles turn around.

With paint dates are skinned, but who recognized my climbing plant?

Translated from the Dutch by Her de Vries

Susy Hare

Born in New York in 1916, Susanna Winslow Wilson was the daughter of Frances Perkins, who later became Franklin Delano Roosevelt's Secretary of Labor. An art history major at Bryn Mawr, Susanna in 1938 met David Hare, whose mother was a friend of her mother's, and who also happens to have been a first cousin of surrealist Kay Sage. The couple soon married, and pursued their common interest in surrealism, which Sage had ignited. At that time the U.S. Immigration and Naturalization Service was under Department of Labor jurisdiction, and Susanna Hare enlisted her mother's aid in speeding up the bureaucratic process which eventually enabled André Breton and other surrealist refugees from Nazism to come to the U.S. during World War II. Susanna herself signed supportive affidavits in this regard—for Jacqueline and André Breton, as well as for Marcel Duchamp.

Susanna and her husband were "regulars" at the gatherings of the Surrealist Group in exile in New York, at the Larré French restaurant on 56th Street and at Breton's Greenwich Village apartment. David, a photographer and later sculptor, was chosen as editor of the group's journal, *VVV.* Vividly Susanna recalls the group's camaraderie and high level of discussion in those years, as well as its emphasis on play and games. The Exquisite Corpse was a favorite: "We played it *constantly!*" she reported (telephone interview, February 1997). Susanna had the unusual experience of helping Marcel Duchamp unwind five miles of string to create the complex network of webbing for the opening of the International Surrealist Exhibition in New York in 1942. Later she studied painting with Jack Tworkow. For a time she also ran a New York dress shop with Ann Clark Matta.

The Hares were divorced in 1945, and by the end of the decade organized surrealist activity in New York had ceased. Susanna, however, remained on good terms with André and Elisa Breton, whom she visited on her trips to France, and to this day she looks back on her participation in the movement as one of the brightest moments of her life. "The surrealist notion that poets could paint and painters could write poems," she says, "was admirable, and very fruitful—a far cry from today's so-called art and literary scene, when most poets can't write and most painters can't paint." Today, as Susanna Coggeshall, she lives in Maine where she is completing a critical study of Brancusi's sculpture.

The poem reprinted here, with the accompanying automatic drawing, appeared in the second issue of *VVV* (No. 2–3, March 1943).

COMPLAINT FOR A SORCERER

You've drawn 3 rings around me
And I make 4 around you
    Had it been another day of the week
    Our meeting would have been unremarkable

The number they make which is 7
Is quartered on the offside of thought
    If we can repeat this process once more
    There'll be a step sufficient to bear the
        weight of one man without offspring

I adjure you to make them with care
Allow but one egress one flaw
    The time hasn't come but it will
    You remember the unmistakable sign on the map

Susy Hare, drawing, 1943.
Courtesy of the artist.

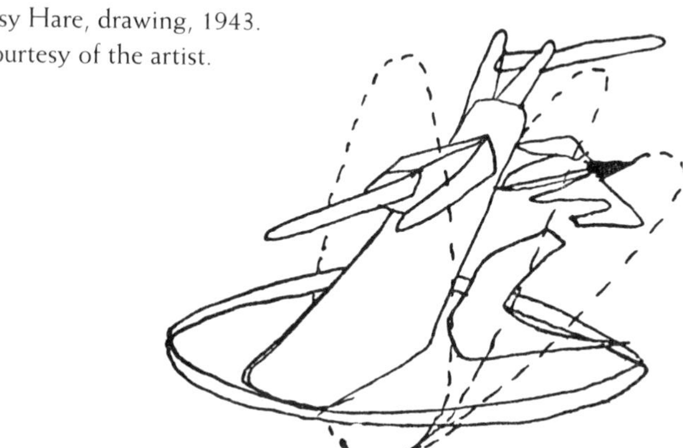

Heed well what you do as you forge them
Contrive them with skin and with hair
  Then we can read the writing on this pebble
  That you stowed in my brain

There is no time but be quick
The moon was red when I saw it
Will we know where to find among our effects
  The string that ties these moments together?

Sonia Sekula

Sonja Sekula was born in Lucerne, Switzerland, in 1918 of a Hungarian-Jewish father and a Swiss mother, and in 1936 moved to the U.S., where she always spelled her name Sonia. After studying philosophy, literature, and painting at Sarah Lawrence College for two years, in 1941 she joined the Art Students League in New York, where she studied with former dadaist George Grosz. Shortly afterward she met André Breton (whose studio she rented in 1943) and began frequenting the meetings of the Surrealist Group in exile. She was particularly close to Breton and his wife Jacqueline Lamba; her other surrealist friends included poet Charles Duits, sculptor David Hare, and Alice Rahon. In August 1944 Breton wrote to her, "I hope you will continue to speak to me in that scintillating voice which is all your own." She collaborated on *VVV,* had her first solo show at the Art of This Century gallery in 1946, took part in the International Surrealist Exhibition in Paris in 1947, and had a joint exhibit with Max Ernst at the London Gallery in England in 1950. After a nervous breakdown in 1952, Sekula returned to Switzerland where, except for a brief visit to New York in 1957, she remained. She committed suicide in Zurich in 1963.

Sekula was an inspiring and disturbing presence in the New York art scene for over two decades and produced an impressive number of dazzlingly original and disquieting paintings and drawings. Although she had many solo exhibitions in many countries and was represented in the U.S. by the powerful Betty Parsons Gallery, she has never been well-known as an artist and is usually ignored in histories of American art. Her diverse and widely scattered work, exemplifying a resolute automatism, awaits rediscovery. Her written work, too—only recently collected in book form—merits wider recognition. Let us hope that the 1996 Sonia Sekula retrospective at the New York Swiss Institute and its lavishly illustrated catalog will open the way to the wider appreciation of this heretofore neglected dreamer who, as she herself once put it, loved "to play football with words."

The poem reprinted here—the first and only work of hers published in her lifetime—appeared in *VVV* no. 2–3 (March, 1943), with her accompanying drawing.

WOMB

I am in the rain, with black writing,
I am in the night with strange hands
I swim in the heat in the humid fear
of day and hate, I close my ear. . . .
and the step the step of the stone that
falls is the space in the heart and
the man in the moon waving good-bye to
the boat that goes where the mouth
is red with a little word that parts
where the womb stands still beyond
speaking.

Sonia Sekula, drawing, 1943.

Meret Oppenheim

ROUND THE WORLD WITH THE RUMPUS GOD . . .

Round the world with the rumpus god
Fishes on his soles
Fins on his heels
The golden sun in the middle.

His heart wreathed in ivy
His face filled with berries
His nearest hands lie on the rocks.

When he loses the trail
He flees to the abyss
And drops all the spoons.

(1943)
Translated from the German by Catherine Schelbert

CONCERNING

THE PRESENT DAY RELATIVE ATTRACTIONS

OF VARIOUS CREATURES IN MYTHOLOGY & LEGEND

Having asked a few friends of both sexes to classify fifteen creatures of diverse mythological derivation in order of their attraction, we present the fellowing table. The results obtained give us some basis for judging their contemporary relative attraction.

The order of choice was as follows:

1. Sphinx;
2. Chimera;
3. Minotaur;
4. Gorgon;
5. Unicorn;
6. Vampire;
7. Succubus or Incubus;
8. Siren;
9. Bloody Nun;
10. Werewolf;
11. Narcissus;
12. Homonculus;
13. Dragon;
14. Circe;
14. Galatea.

The very definite preeminence of the Sphinx is evident, since not only does it come at the head of the general classification, but also at the head of the masculine as well as the feminine classification. Elsewhere the two viewpoints, masculine and feminine, have resulted in very different choices. For example the Vampire, the Werewolf, and the Siren were feminine preferences. The masculine antipathy to the Dragon should be noted in contrast to the feminine antipathy to the Bloody Nun and Circe, etc.

"Surrealist Inquiry on Mythological Creatures," from *VVV* No. 2–3, 1943.

WEREWOLF	VAMPIRE	UNICORN	SUCUBUS-INCUBUS	SPHINX	SIREN	NARCISSUS	MINOTAUR	GORGON	HOMONCULUS	GALATEA	DRAGON	CHIMERA	CIRCE	BLOODY NUN	
13	11	3	14	2	9	5	1	4	12	7	15	6	8	10	LIONEL ABEL
10	11	8	2	1	9	14	13	5	7	12	15	3	6	4	ANDRE' BRETON
13	4	8	11	1	9	6	2	5	14	10	7	15	12	3	NICOLAS CALAS
15	12	7	11	6	1	8	14	3	10	4	13	2	9	5	GEORGES DUTHUIT
11	10	13	9	5	6	15	3	2	12	8	7	1	4	14	MAX ERNST
11	4	6	10	1	2	7	3	5	15	12	14	8	9	13	BRION GYSIN
2	8	4	10	5	14	9	3	6	13	15	11	1	7	12	DAVID HARE
13	9	10	8	7	14	3	2	4	1	12	15	11	6	5	ANDRE' MASSON
7	8	12	1	6	3	14	10	9	13	15	11	2	15	4	MATTA
8	11	1	7	4	13	15	2	14	5	6	3	9	10	12	ROBERT MOTHERWELL
14	9	1	6	2	5	12	4	3	8	11	15	10	7	13	HAROLD ROSENBERG
1	4	10	6	7	15	9	12	5	3	13	11	8	14	2	KURT SELIGMANN
7	5	10	1	3	9	3	8	13	4	12	15	11	14	2	YVES TANGUY
14	7	11	8	2	5	6	3	4	15	13	10	1	12	9	PATRICK WALDBERG
139	113	104	104	52	114	126	80	82	132	140	162	88	133	108	♂ TOTAL
13	5	8	2	1	10	11	12	6	4	14	9	3	15	7	JACQUELINE BRETON
2	3	1	4	6	9	15	7	11	12	14	5	8	13	10	LEONORA CARRINGTON
9	7	2	6	1	5	14	8	4	12	13	11	12	15	10	SUSANNA HARE
15	5	12	1	2	3	11	7	12	6	13	8	4	10	14	ANN MATTA
2	5	3	13	6	1	15	9	10	14	9	11	4	12	7	ROSE MASSON
8	1	4	9	11	7	10	2	3	15	12	5	6	14	13	ARLETTE SELIGMANN
2	11	9	14	1	5	3	7	10	12	15	6	4	8	13	KAY TANGUY
51	37	39	49	28	40	79	52	56	75	90	66	41	97	74	♀ TOTAL
190	150	143	153	80	154	205	132	138	207	230	228	129	230	182	*GENERAL TOTAL*
10	6	5	7	1	8	11	3	4	12	15	13	2	14	9	*CLASSIFICATION*

Ithell Colquhoun

"EVERYTHING FOUND ON LAND IS FOUND IN THE SEA"

Isn't it time to break through that dismal convention of the scientific periodicals which orders, however suavely, that only the driest language be used? You'd hardly know that those people were making discoveries, the way they have to write them up. Their particular kind of good form decrees that every experiment, no matter how dramatically successful, should be tabulated with no more symptom of personal zest than the pages of a bus timetable. I can't imitate that style and don't want to; nevertheless, I have been able to observe some remarkable facts about plant life, hitherto unnoticed, particularly with regard to habitat; and I expect other biologists to give these investigations their due, despite their unusual guise and staging. Indeed I hope the more orthodox savants may even recognize here a certain justice, since the things I am going to describe seem like sports of nature; though who knows? Further research may prove them to be instances of some law previously unknown.

Experiment I.

As I was scrambling over the rocky ridges of a valley I came upon a wide fissure slanting down toward the center of the earth. I looked in and found that its distant floor was water. I began to climb down inside, taking hold of a natural banister here, stepping on an unhewn stair tread there, which the uneven surfaces provided. This descent was not easy, as the rock was green with damp and patched with a viscous wine-colored growth.

I had now penetrated to a vertiginous depth; if I looked upward, the walls rose above me in a cool shaft; turning downward, I could see a cave filled with water the color of chrysolite, illumined from some hidden source and darkened where a turn of wall or jutting rock threw a shadow. One such submerged projection hid the mouth of the cave, making it invisible from the surface of the ground.

I noticed that the water was not tideless, for it began to sink with gurgling sounds and in its retreat left the cave without light. The rhythm of this tide was very rapid, for scarcely had the cavern been emptied when the water came lapping back, bringing the light with it. I tasted the water and found it salt; and being unable to explore the cave further because of its swift return, I began to climb back toward the earth's surface. The going was still more difficult than before, as I now discovered fishlike flowers growing directly from the stone without leaves. I could hardly get foothold or handhold without crushing or gripping these cold petals, which spread their cherry and blue-gray all about the ascent, a salty deposit covering them with a dusty grapelike bloom.

Experiment II.

It is not generally known, and certainly I never before this realized, that scattered about even the most cancerously urban districts of London, there exist patches and stretches of wild marshy land or heath. Of course I don't mean the parks—they are as urban as the buildings. These stretches are different because you can't find them by looking for them—at least it seems to be so, as far as our present knowledge takes us.

The other day when I was with Orloff, I found a patch somewhere between Piccadilly and Oxford Street; a rough, tussocky piece of land, quite extensive, where flowers of a unique and curious species were growing. The petals were large and looked as if they were made of paper—more like sepals perhaps, rather stiff and pointed; the color was pale orange-pink at the edges, deepening further in and finally becoming a dusky reddish-brown at the center.

They grew in swampy places and we had to get a bit wet in order to come close to them; we had to climb over rocks, too, and I was annoyed by Orloff's lack of adventure in these matters—the way he jumped over the rock-pools you'd think a drop of water would kill him. But I didn't care; I made my way over the stones and streams to one of the biggest flowers.

I found that inside and below the petals was a kind of bowl made of the same stuff, but it must have been stronger, because when I lifted the petals I saw that it was full to the brim with dark water. In this water were strange living creatures, like sea anemones but larger and harder and without tentacles—more like scarabs perhaps. They were of various jewel-colors, ruby, sapphire, emerald, some of them spotted with white. They crawled and clung to the sides of the pool; I put my hand in and touched them, but Orloff seemed afraid to. Then we turned northwards across the moor and came out near Bond Street Station.

Experiment III.

Another day I was looking for somewhere to live and went in the direction of Maida Vale. From some dingy agent there I got the key of a house to let. Wandering along the streets I came to a road of peeling stucco houses with catwalks in front and moldering urns, which could hold nothing, surmounting the plastered gateposts.

My key fit the front door of one of these houses; I went in and up the stairs to the first floor. I entered a large room with three windows looking out upon the road; folding doors connected it with the room behind. These I pushed open and found myself in another room exactly like the first; I went over to the central one of its three windows and looked out. Instead of the characterless gardens and hinder facade of a parallel block, I saw a sloping strip of ground overgrown with brambles, then a pebbly shore, and beyond, the crash and smother of Atlantic waves, breaking ceaselessly and without side. This ocean stretched away to the horizon where it met a misty sky, but did not merge with it—the heaving water set up a melancholy distinction out there; and here within, a briny exultant smell penetrated the panes, cutting through the mustiness of a house long closed.

What extraordinary growths, I wondered, flowered in those wasteful depths? There must be a submerged garden whose silken green held curiosities far surpassing those I had come upon before. Idiots often visit such places and describe what they see; making idiots is one of the sea's favorite games. But when it tires of this from time to time, it casts up instead a supernatural being on an unwelcoming strand, who, ever afterward, spends his nights asleep at the bottom of some watery gulf.

(From *Goose of Hermogenes,* first published in the "Surrealist Section" of *New Road 1943*)

WATER-STONE OF THE WISE

Myth is a volcanic force, liberty a perpetual stream, an ambiance that results from eruption.

Myth must break through the crust, scatter a thousand new comets in the void, illuminate the black sky with bengal-lights, decorate the day sky with vaporous plumes. What superhuman shapes may not burst from the next eruption, august yet tender beings, who evolve themselves in the light of gold! They borrow a wisp of substance from the earth, but their color is from the purifying fire. We cannot have liberty without repeated explosions.

But we must have liberty. It is the clear stream, the embracing element without which we cannot move. Free air and free water! They are the interpenetrating silver-and-blue, they come from the gushing side of the mountain whose mouth yet steams. Freedom to move, to act, to speak, freedom to be still, to look, to be silent.

Myth comes from the region between sleeping and waking, the multitudinous abyss, the unceasing cauldron rimmed with pearls. If we let it pour out unhindered, we shall be free to plunge into its depths. What shall we find there, far from "lordship and bondage?"

> Un no rompida sueno—
> Un dia puro—allegre—libre
> Quiera—
> Libre de amor—de celo
> De odio—de esperanza—de recelo.
>
> [An unbroken dream
> A clear, joyous, free day
> I would love
> Free of love, zeal
> Hate, Hope and Suspicion]

No more tyrants and victims, no more the fevered alternations of that demon-star which sponsored the births of de Sade and von Sacher-Masoch; but the hermaphrodite whole, opposites bound together in mitigating embrace by a silkworm's thread. "And countenance once more beheld countenance." Oedipus will be king no longer but will return to Colonnus. The new myth, the myth of the Siamese Twins, will make of him a forgotten bogey.

In one of the planets' airy houses live the Twins, a boy and a girl, perpetually joined by an ectoplasmic substance which is warmed by the solar and lunar currents of their bodies. They cannot part, nor do anything apart. They eat and breathe each other day and night.

They are united face to face, having passed forward to the condition of the androgynous egg. Their faculty is dream, their body-of-fate the stream of images—sensual transpositions—induced by the incandescence of their own body and mind. They have no privacy from each other, and desire none, since theirs is a unity conscious of its own elements. They weigh down equally each scale of the Balance, and as the two Fishes, are held together in watery dance by a single cord.

(From the "Surrealist Section" of *New Road 1943*)

Emmy Bridgwater

Born in Birmingham, England, in 1906, Emmy Bridgwater studied art in her hometown as well as in Oxford and London, where the 1936 International Surrealist Exhibition proved to be "quite a revelation" for her and marked a turning point in her life. With Conroy Maddox and the Melville brothers, John and Robert, she took part in the surrealist-oriented Birmingham Group and in 1940 joined the Surrealist Group in England.

This "explorer of the sulfurous lavas and springtimes of the unconscious," as Michel Remy has called her, collaborated on *Arson* (1942) and *Free Unions* (1946), had her first one-artist show at Jack Bilbo's Modern Gallery in London, and in 1947 was invited by André Breton to take part in the International Surrealist Exhibition in Paris. After 1947 she all but gave up painting and writing to nurse her disabled older sister and invalid mother, but she resumed her automatistic research in later years.

An admirer of Emily Brontë, *King Kong,* and the Marx Brothers, Bridgwater is best known as a painter, collagist, and graphic artist; her poems have not yet been collected. In everything she does, as the poet Edouard Jaguer points out, "all is placed under the sign of metamorphosis," drenched in her "thoroughgoing humor."

The following poems are from the catalog, *Emmy Bridgwater* (1990), except for "The Birds," which is from *Free Unions* (1946).

ON THE LINE

Back to the Land
 To the grape-grown tree.
Red . . . Red . . . Full earth Red,
Grown Grass—Grass green growing.

There will be no spaces that were stars,
and signing in spaces on the line—signing.
Black death and watered down trees crying
Out shrieking with "It is time,
Now it is time,
And soon there will be no time."

No brushes and no colours and no inks running
No fingers and no hand holding.
The brush not moving in lines
Staying also staying so will Eyes looking at all.
Eyes always seeing
No rushing waterfall,
No flowering cherry tree.
NO.

(1940)

BACK TO THE FIRST BAR

After ten thousand years I will repeat my claim.
Repeat it in the grey garden in the morning when the clouds are swinging and the raindrops are singing and the ground is moist and the worms are turning, are turning the earth that is me.

Little brown bird you will hear

You will take no heed of the insistent whispers, again you will turn to pecking your insect with the striped black body and the blue eyes of a Mona Lisa.

Creeps the penetrating grass over the unvirgin soil, brown as the dried spilt blood.

And again, after the insect,
you will
You will sing.

(1941)

THE JOURNEY

Two battered at the Red Lamp Hitting the bars.
The shilling dropped darkness forced them up
And they lay sucking the corniced grape along the ceiling.
The corners of the room revolved and swayed
And tree trunks groaned.
Whole passages of time were sliced to pieces

As circling strands of snakes benibbled bits
While grey fish swimming in sawdust, glassy-eyed,
Carved sticky patterns, intricate as sin.
And slow—as the starfish crawls to meet the wave—
And slow, but moving as sand in quicksand,
The Chariot arrived . . .
        but they were gone.

(1942)

THE BIRDS

One

He pulled the blanket over and he drew up the blind. The yellow mice rushed into their corners. The spiders ran behind the pictures. The lecture began on Christ the Forerunner. Only the very young mice sat still to listen. The blackbirds flying near the window passed the word to each other. "Come on. Here we may find something. Something to put our beaks into." Snap went the window cord: down came the blind. The birds, disappointed, did the best they could. They flew nearer and nearer the windowpane. It was dangerous. It wasn't worth it. But they wanted to get the news—to be the first to know—to pass on the news. What had come to the lecture on Christ? Did one still lie under the blankets? The spiders laughed into their hands to think of the birds outside all twittering and over-anxious.

Two

As she walked into the garden the birds flew down to her pecking at her lips. "Don't do that," she cried. "It's mine. I'm alive you know." "Well, why don't you wear colors?" She heard them talking. "Dead people walk, but they don't wear colors. They scream and they talk too." The birds went on chattering about dead people. They all perched up on the holly bush but they didn't peck the soft berries. They just stared down at her. All of them stared with their little black beady eyes. They were looking at her red lips.

Three

"Sing a song for the King. Come on, now sing." The child was shy to start, but her mother, standing behind her gave her a little push which startled her into opening her mouth and she began, "Wasn't that a dirty dish to set before the

Emmy Bridgwater, *Daybreak,* collage, 1975. Courtesy of the artist.

king?" "Begin again dear," whispered her mother, "at the first line." "O.k. ma," and she chanted, "Four and twenty black . . . oooh," for a peacock had walked in front of her and spread out its tail and croaked "Frico. Frico." The little girl went very white. "Frico. Frico," she said. The birds, who had been sitting on the cornice as part of the decoration, flew down into the court and circled about the heads of the King and Courtiers, fluttering as close as possible. All the people flapped their hands helplessly. Suddenly the little girl pointed at the King. "You must get out of here," she said in a grown-up voice. "This is their Palace."

Edith Rimmington

Born in Leicester, England, in 1902, Edith Rimmington married Robert Baxter in the 1920s and moved to Manchester. She joined the Surrealist Group in England in 1937, took part in the London Gallery's surrealist objects exhibit that year and later in other group shows, and collaborated on *London Bulletin, Arson, Fulcrum, Message from Nowhere,* and *Free Unions*. Like her friends Emmy Bridgwater and Conroy Maddox, Rimmington was one of the mainstays of surrealism in England for decades. The original Surrealist Group in London disbanded in 1947, but her fidelity to the movement's basic aims and principles persisted to the end of her life in 1988.

Although she is chiefly known as a painter, Rimmington in later years concentrated on photography. Though far from numerous, her scattered poems and other writings have never been collected. The poems reprinted here first appeared in *Free Unions* (1946).

THE GROWTH AT THE BREAK

As fantasy in the claws of the poet is released by the broken arm it becomes imprisoned in the ossiferous callus wherein lice build themselves a tomb in which to escape the magic of the Marvelous. Instead of, with the blood of the wound, rushing like the river to the sea—oh life orgasm—the river is damned. The banks do not overflow and the lice choke as the arm stiffens. The wise eye sees the substitute running its poisonous imprisoned course in the cystic tomb. I see the dark sad face of the wounded man as the arm is amputated.

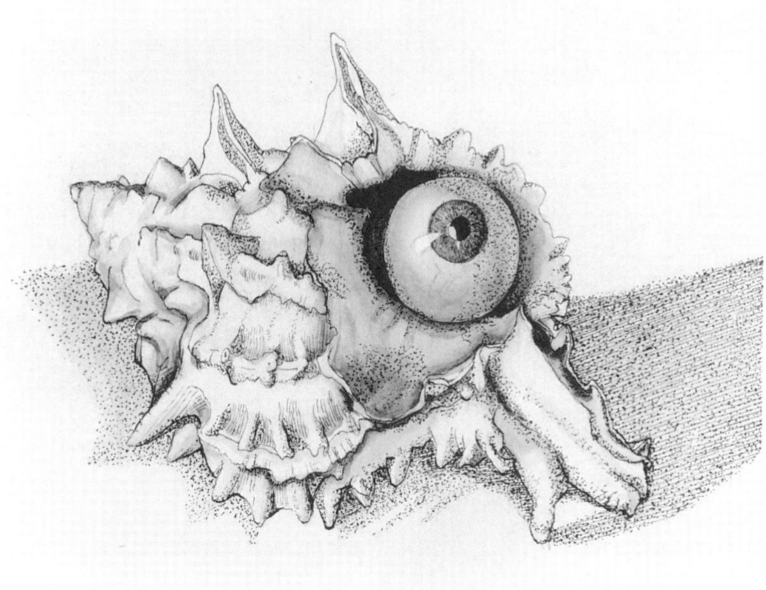

Edith Rimmington, *The Onlooker,* date unknown.

THE SEA-GULL

I try to catch the sea-gull with a silken cord but I find that the soft cord becomes a fagged iron chain which tears my hands. The gull flies out to sea where it sits brooding. I see it fly back to the beach to join a lazy crowd of gulls where it is fed on human flesh by tanks and guns. I am horrified by the greedy eagerness of the speckled young birds. I find I cannot escape from the chain unless I too offer my flesh to the gulls. I wait . . . thinking of death and living death. I decide that out of living death I may see the gull dive into the sea once more.

Alice Rahon

POINTED OUT LIKE THE STARS . . .

To Ixtaccihuatl

Pointed out like the stars
at the streaming boundaries of unlivable gold
at the top of trees flightless
when on the mountain slopes
men's houses warm their sides
I bore my life
like that sun carried from wall to wall
in this street
under the foreign woman's balcony
weeping in her hair
when the amaranth rocks the wind
and the roses erect
the highest towers of sense

from my fingers
crooked like the sparrow-hawk's wing
falls the frigate-bird
solitary
falls.

Translated from the French by Myrna Bell Rochester

LITTLE EPIDERMIS

Little epidermis of turquoise struck from all sides by claws of reddish cotton an arrow exposes the redhead for what he is he smells bad and always wears a backbone of black feathers for the backbone of spiny fish has windows for all the spokes of the king of Thule's wheel they don't come in by the window or by the door the stones they're the small defeats the reverse of the great victories or vice-versa as always the pianist has frozen hands the piano is an Eskimo who takes out his walrus bone knife the almanac that empties itself of dry losses of interplanetary speed isn't responsible for loves soon crossed that the reindeer's age congeals the cold on the ice-floe with the turquoise epidermis.

Translated from the French by Myrna Bell Rochester

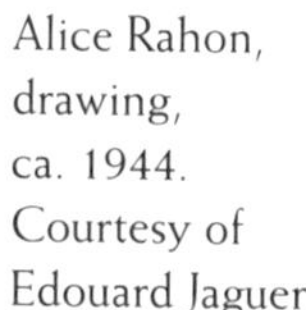

Alice Rahon, drawing, ca. 1944. Courtesy of Edouard Jaguer.

SUBLIMATED MERCURY

The rain's feet
beat upon the surface of the pond
the squall of the dazzling return

but you clutch my throat
thorny poppy
wild poppy
aborigine of despair

Translated from the French by Myrna Bell Rochester

THE APPELLANTS

Rendezvous of river
water gathering in clouds
and springs water that links me to your fate
water running free never consoled
by its source
sweet final dress promised to my fear
drawn toward you as by a nose ring
up to that death
like a drop of water the night
calling out until we arise
trap of fire to burn everything

Translated from the French by Myrna Bell Rochester

FERNS IN A HOLLOW OF ABSENCE . . .

To Valentine Penrose

Ferns in a hollow of absence
fine gold asters radiating toward blocks of nomadic amber
fossilized spirals where my blood
finds the axis to flow
born of the same wave I have carried
a green heart hanging like a mango
breaking all the spider's webs in the first gust
I've drawn from my half-closed and slovenly
hands fat with eternity like children's balloons
free days beyond the sickly weather

but soon
the black echoless sand
where my wide-open eye will have lost sight of the dawn's direction
tonight I left the nine stars of portent
hanging on Orion's shoulders

If tomorrow the crickets
from another night
raise their ladders of cries where I climbed
vertical thrown in all directions to oscillate
beating across skies of shadow or sun
if the sea slept me

horizontal like her
I existed
from an unfinished alphabet
to a game of knuckle-bones at the shore of a lagoon

mango of my heart
it's a friend coming in
it's the evening wind

Translated from the French by Myrna Bell Rochester

THE SLEEPING WOMAN

The sea held prisoner brown and grey sand with black stains in marching order. It was a carpet of possible adventures. The solitary young girl left the town and came to live near this beach.

One morning a great shark mouth appeared on the horizon with the smile of a stupid angel. Its body was a white and yellow colonnade representing human knowledge, human wisdom. A child's loud laugh shook the columns and a woman with one arm forming a wing approached the beach. She was the color of dead-leaf butterflies. Around her was a halo of glass which protected her from the ravages of time. She spoke:

I should have a great rock, flat smooth and warm where I could lean. The door would happen to be closed my heart would be warm and would sleep. I would be able to go up and down the length of the rock by sliding. The movement would make a quiet music. I don't in any event want a violent death. I wait for a friend who is very beautiful and a young man with the eyes of a wild animal surprised by man. He watches man appear among the leaves and questions him. If he turns his head away everything is obscured and the meaning half revealed for an instant is lost. Cities of scarlet under a dark blue sky slide on rails of copper toward a more stable equilibrium than that of this earth. This perpetual motion is tormenting like a fringe that is too long in front of the eyes. Oh truly what a lovely evening spent among those murmuring tins of preserves. The skulls were soon pierced by the light. All with one voice started to shout in chorus in an unknown language with the strength of soot. It was very cold on the right. A crane of white cotton refuses service to the sun which cannot rise alone.

Behind the grill the voices began again but that brought about a revolt of the fighting eagles who united in order to smell at once like caged eagles and like bucks. What means of escaping these odors these conjurations.

I was sent touching postal cards of frescoes where happily the heads were missing. They concerned nativity. These repugnant mysteries are only supportable as mysteries.

I beg you not to climb that column. It is 300 meters higher than the tops of the highest sequoias 2000 years old in the California forest. At the very top there is that platform made of all the blond heads of hair.

Rivers full of gold flowed from the woman and warmed the atmosphere a little. Full in the middle of the sky two clouds burst in each other's faces with the noise of dead fireplaces. Then taking hands they went away from the window of the handsome and sad young man with the eyes of an animal. Here are the rose-colored snakes fallen from the trees of repoussé leather who are losing their skins and every appearance of snakes. What a comfort for my friend to have escaped reconciliation.

(From *Dyn* no. 1, 1942)

Eva Sulzer

A close friend of surrealist painter Wolfgang Paalen, Swiss-born musician and photographer Eva Sulzer financed and accompanied Paalen and his wife Alice Rahon on an early 1940s voyage to Alaska and British Columbia in search of Native American house-poles, masks, and other art. Many of the photographs Sulzer took on this expedition later appeared in Paalen's journal, *Dyn*, published in Mexico, where she lived after 1940. She exhibited photographs at the International Surrealist Exhibition in Mexico City in 1940 and contributed poetry, articles, and reviews to *Dyn*. Although her later devotion to Gurdjieffian mysticism took her out of the surrealist orbit, Sulzer produced a documentary film on Remedios Varo in 1966.

"Butterfly Dreams" appeared in *Dyn* no. 1 (1942). "Amerindian Art" is excerpted from her review of Pal Kelemen, *Medieval American Art* (New York: Macmillan, 1944), from the "Amerindian Number" of *Dyn* no. 4–5 (1943).

BUTTERFLY DREAMS

I

I was sitting in my room. A butterfly comes in through the open window and lights on the wall opposite me. Its wings are painted with a nocturnal landscape: flanked by two ranges of hillsides, covered by those broad virgin

Alaskan forests, a solitary road plunges into the distance; there's a single deserted house near a crossroads whose signpost wears only the motto: Life for rent. To the North, a hesitant aurora borealis wraps the horizon in its phosphorescent gleam of glowworms; to the South, at the top of a hill, rises an immense star, an incendiary star, sparkling like the reassuring but equally troubling light from a lighthouse. At the zenith, the new moon, the night's comma.

Suddenly, I see the butterfly's body unhooked from its wings, go down that road and enter the house. I wait. The eternity of a drowning man. Then, the butterfly emerges, retraces its steps, settles back on its two wings, and takes off into the morning.

II

My sister and I, children, were strolling at the shore of Lake Sils, when a butterfly with fire-colored wings lit on the water near us. Drawing near it, we saw its wings transformed into sails and its whole body take on the aspect of a narrow pirogue whose whiteness and fragility reminded you of cuttlebone or fossil shells. With a gesture, it invited us to climb aboard. As we reached the opposite shore, it started to rain and we sought refuge in a little shepherd's hut. There, on the wall, in a glass box, were pinned several specimens of rare butterflies. My fascinated and terrified glance remained fixed on a Death's Head Sphinx. After a long moment of silence, my sister, who had seen me looking, said: "But aren't we far older than death?"

Translated from the French by Myrna Bell Rochester

AMERINDIAN ART

Amerindian art . . . until now has been appreciated above all for its archeological interest. Even the few private collectors have, in general, oriented their choice rather according to rarity, preciousness of the material, and technical perfection, than according to the purely artistic value of the objects. One might say with Oscar Wilde that one knew their price but not their value.

Until very recently contact with forms of exotic art has remained without influence upon European aesthetic. Although Dürer grasped the beauty of certain Aztec masterpieces, and Rembrandt was sufficiently interested in Persian miniatures to copy some of them, nevertheless, as Kelemen remarks, in those times Europe was still too much preoccupied with the discovery of her own forms of expression to experience any profound interest in the art of faraway peoples. The universalist tendencies of today and the facilities of modern communication were necessary in order to attain to an encyclopedic knowledge; but for this knowledge to become fertile the mediation of the artists was necessary. Art cannot be discovered except by artists. . . .

The work of Kelemen will open new horizons; the texts of his second volume in general complete his album very effectively, and thanks to his fusion of erudition and sensibility he is an excellent intermediary between the archeologist and the artist. . . .

The defect of Kelemen's book consists in the fact that the author, in order to impose his thesis of a "Medieval American Art" upon the reader, seeks at all costs to include the great pre-Columbian cultures in the Christian era—which confuses one's understanding of the amplitude and the development of these cultures. To say that all the objects and ruins gathered together in his volumes were created in a period synchronous with the European Middle Ages is an altogether untenable claim. . . .

According to the calculations of those best qualified, the very elaborate calendaric system of the Mayas, which still stirs the admiration of astronomers, was already fully developed at the beginning of the Christian era. Only a part of the works reproduced by Kelemen can be considered contemporary with Christianity, while a considerable number of them were without doubt created in epochs called in Europe "Antiquity" and "Prehistory." In any case, such parallels are not apt, as they artificially isolate art from the societies that produced it, and do not take account of the singularities characteristic of American developments.

The greatness of ancient Amerindian cultures becomes more and more resplendent with every new discovery; and they will finally be conceded the rank that they merit beside the great achievements of mankind. As these cultures have been irreparably destroyed, we must listen to the rare testimonies of the people who had the good fortune to see some of their glories intact. We are grateful to Kelemen for citing the enthusiastic lines written by one of the greatest artists of all time, Albrecht Dürer, when, some thirty years after the discovery of America, he saw the "things from the New Golden Land . . . fairer to see than marvels," of which he says: "I have never seen in all my days what so rejoiced my heart as these things." An enthusiasm shared by Las Casas, who speaks of this same gift sent by Cortés to Charles V, as a "present of such rich things, fabricated and made of such workmanship, that they appeared like a dream and not as if made by man's hands."

Jacqueline Johnson

Californian Jacqueline Johnson—poet, scholar, graduate of Stanford University—met and married English surrealist painter Gordon Onslow-Ford in New York in 1941 and frequented the surrealist exiles' milieu. Later that year the couple left for Mexico, where they encountered surrealist painter Wolfgang Paalen and his wife, surrealist poet/painter Alice Rahon. Jacqueline Johnson coedited the sixth and last issue of Paalen's *Dyn* magazine and wrote some of the most important texts ever published in that journal. In 1947 she and Onslow-Ford moved to San Francisco, where they coorganized a "Dynaton" exhibition at the San Francisco Museum of Art in 1951. Johnson contributed a major text to the catalog (see excerpts in the following section).

Although *Dyn* had evinced certain philosophical divergences from surrealism—most notably Paalen's superficial dismissal of Hegel and Marx and his odd (and evidently brief) infatuation with the work of John Dewey—much of the material it published was authentically surrealist, and it has come to be regarded as a mildly dissident surrealist publication. Paalen himself rejoined the Surrealist Group in Paris in 1951. In a preface to a Paalen exhibition that year, André Breton signaled the importance of his articles in *Dyn*. Also of exceptional interest are Jacqueline Johnson's texts, which can truly be said to be among the finest contributions to surrealist thought in those years.

Johnson and Onslow-Ford remained in California. The couple separated in the 1950s, and I have not been able to learn anything of her later years.

The following articles, published here somewhat abridged, are from *Dyn* No. 6 (1945).

THE PAINTINGS OF ALICE RAHON PAALEN

We no longer separate the work of men and women with taboos as in primitive society, and our effort in general is toward broadening the fields of understanding rather than restricting them. We are against feminine art as against other local picturesqueness. Yet as T. S. Eliot has said in a different connection, the damage of a life-time cannot be repaired at the moment of composition; there is a difference in the life and very often in the work of men and women. The work of Alice Paalen is not feminine in subject, as is for example that of Marie Laurencin; it is feminine because it expresses the plastic experience of an artist who happens to be a woman.

There have been few women painters of distinction, even in the time and circumstances in which they might reasonably be supposed to have had the opportunity and the materials to paint, perhaps in the last hundred and fifty years or so, in Europe, except for rare and hypothetical cases. Before that (as still today) one looks to costume, houses, weaving patterns, tapestries, embroidery, lace and such things for the plastic expression of women. Painting as a man's art has been taken over in the recent past with a self-conscious earnestness and technical virtuosity by women who did what men had done better and earlier. They sometimes added an artificial and sweet grace, a concentration on feminine interests (although here one remembers that the horses of the sturdy Rosa Bonheur hardly follow in the line of Le Brun, however heroic she may appear otherwise). One reason why Alice Paalen's work makes painting seem as natural for women as for children is that she is among the first to paint without having her eye on the subject as conceived by other painters.

The line varies as a voice varies; with such swelling, such shifts and stops, such innate artistry as a voice may have to move us. Probably the most striking characteristic is that a stroke of the brush takes on resonance, is the unit of structure: a square of color, scarcely more, is an invention of form as though it could be picked up and looked at like pebbles or twigs. . . . The wavering currents of the surface are to be followed in their fractures of reflecting depth and light; the focal points are local over the whole canvas in constantly improvised, constantly maintained balance.

In other paintings, done in a manner that has affinities with child and primitive drawings and with Klee, appear unknown hieroglyphics, pictographs of men and animals, symbols, marine and terrestrial vegetation that again cover the surface with many focal points. In making them and their interrelations will and hand seem to adventure, their impulse sprung both from the idea and from the act, naive and expert. In some paintings fine sand is sprinkled on the canvas and lines incised in cross hatching, in weaves and brick patterns, in prints of bird's feet to further fill the surface between larger patches of color. And the surface color or the sand may be scratched away over more color as though light were underneath, or under this layer other layers, the picture deep with notations of the casual exquisite creations of nature that are inhabited by the emotions of men who live among them and conceal in them hidden charges, like bears in hollow trees. . . .

Sometimes these canvases are windows holding windows on an outlook as fascinating and inexplicable, as desirable and unattainable as those in the luminous walls of Easter eggs held to the eye between two hands. They too spoke in their own equation of what we are and where.

These pictures are not pictures of anything, they are projections, they are things; the sensual center of awareness turns like a great lens that illuminates and extends outward the reflected wonder of tangential worlds; all that lies around and simultaneously lives in this habitat of space and light, caught in incidental lines that stand for the arbitrament of unknown destinies; though they lend their beauty and their forms to feeling, they are neither involved with the sufferings or projects of the ego, nor with its duration.

Tenderness is here seen to be the attitude within which mockery and wit and gaiety are natural and free. There appears in all this work a habit of feeling whose purity, justness and energy are fresh and one thinks it can never have refused any effort of readiness or response, in experience or in understanding, to have this color sense, incapable of insensitivity, to have this plastic poise on the tight-rope of any line.

THE EARTH

The earth we walk on, not the globe, not the subterranean nickel but what you have under your feet when you walk in the country, what I see in front of me in this cut in the hill, bare element that here dry secretes small circles of white lichen and straw stars, residual of time and tempestuous summer, frayed and dropped in silt fine layers in lakes now dry, blown up from sealed depths to cool in porous fragments, poured out molten in stone streams, this result and condition of existence, does it teach only of time and of process? What is there of meaning except to that which nourished on it fattens and increases it with rotting vein and excrement and bone, and although in this less important than the leaves, letting fall brain structure and cities into insect mouth and rain tunnel?

Here are harmonies, the thistle in its growing tower is blue-mauve like the sand it grows in; the madrone red-skinned, drops leaves of metallic ocher, sulphur and clear brown on yellow clay as though the tree extracted metals in this form from the dust of iron oxides; and this is the poor season when winter dries the hills.

Conic variations of a single form, the hills are flattened and rivuleted, modeled by earthquake and weather into irregular and melting shapes. Yet here and there is a long and perfect slope, while everywhere is scattered in the clay deposits of painted dust and rock, rose, violet, red and black. The gradual slope is the line and this the color left from explosions hidden in smoke by day, by night fountaining high geysers of terrible red rock to fall on a growing cone, pouring the even and increasing sides with glittering scarlet and vermilion from crown to base, a nightly fete and continual substance freshly falling and flowing, more splendid than sequins, for steadiness of display unimagined by Chinese releasing bouquets of colored comets over a summer field of upturned faces and dim white gowns.

The lake greater once, reached among the hills with secret springs and living creatures where wind and rain gathered mud that piled slow layers of such fertile dust as I hold now, letting it run out between my fingers until only the brown marks are left in the lines of my hand. Here in this finest sediment silent time compressed mountain and shell and forest with eons of plant curled in tepid shallow water. Hear this silence in the cobweb hand, in the dense present of a sunny morning when music for the bullfight comes up from a village, music in the open like music for a football game. Hear now how start in the earth the crackling seeds, when rain-sodden start the sand-small spheres cotyledons with color thick as jade, with roots to break the rocks, to fountain water to the peaceful beasts.

Product of fire, left by water, there is no word written within. Layer on layer in growth like the fine fibers of a tree, in detours and irregularities like watermark, like wind-mark, its kernel is not the inner unseen fundament, its kernel is outward to the light, uncentered, myriad: where the weeds are, where the women walk, where men have placed between themselves and such event guitar, plough, stone altar and cock fight.

There is no aspect of eternity where no one has cried alas for this short life. The long rhythmic cradling, the sporadic cataclysms, the early prismatic colors that were unseen exist for the imagination balancing a perspective of new knowledge in a little light now brilliant on the colored iris and the colored object. These fetes of the volcano, of the emergence and the end, sharpen the wish to be, to be more perfectly, as from the deep roots of the eye they widen the vision in which things are, or may come to be in an instant of love, as under the aspect of eternity, though immediate as the roped and runaway horse stopped at the lake-shore in sweat and high breathing, though secret as the trembling feather whose sight transfixes a child.

There are images buried in the fields. It is not possible to say why they are so many, standing, their small mask faces elaborated more than all the rest, as though in the long slanting eye the meaning or the mystery is centered of which the integral statement is the body. They are more than thousands, they are unnumbered; the same or almost the same, a hand's length high, a little more or less, the color of the clay. But the shoulders in each are rounded differently, the hips and breasts in various emphasis, the sex marked by a triangle, two strips of clay, the curving abdomen and the relations of all these differing as they differ in each woman; always the same statement, but the statement never the same.

In a sense all images are gods. Before Socrates conceived the world of moral absolutes in formless divine forms, the gods and goddesses had stood in stone and wood for generations, staring out from the enduring and thus awful beauty of their limbs, resistant as the carved figure-heads of ships that remained still and watching through uneven water and came home to port in many seasons and with many crews. And gods are a mirror of the mind, the will, or intuition where the image stays fixed as from that former instant, from that day when I knew or someone knew the god, where recoverable and ancient it repeats what was often lost, saying it as in the days of childhood, in the dimly remembered times, in the sunken unknown times before that were as real as this moment, extending as this space extends, stirring with light where no one is now or enters. The real image has this wonder of its very fixedness, and also of that which is felt in ritual and in all reflections, the wonder of the same thing charged with doubleness, as of reeds growing up and down, what you see and what you echo in recognition, the boat that sails below the boat that sails.

As in these images, turned up in the soil beside unglazed pots and water-jars, where are seen also the many who were alive and are dead. The many who, alive, equal and insistent in their being, made the image of their doubleness with high headdress and ornaments for love. They sat at their task, knees and thighs in this same dust, more polished than those crooks of living wood. Each was at a center point within the great circle of horizon holding crowded hill, tree and glassy air, as in her hands she held and shaped her likeness, that was the common image, or divine, subsuming destiny and power, as though to draw a greater ring within a small, a ring of fire within a ring of earth.

Ida Kar

Ida Karamanian was born of Armenian parents in Tanbov, Russia, in 1908 and grew up in Russia, Armenia, and Iran before moving with her family to Alexandria, Egypt, at the age of thirteen. In Paris in 1928, where she had been sent by her parents to study medicine and chemistry, she encountered the Surrealist Movement, attended the premiere of the Buñuel/Dalí film, *Un Chien anadalou,* began to consider herself a revolutionist, and became interested in photography.

After five years in Paris, she returned to Egypt, where she and her then-husband opened an experimental photography studio in Cairo.

Later in the decade she met Georges Henein, Ikbal El Alailly, and other members of the Surrealist Group in Cairo, and took part in the group's activities for several years, exhibiting in its "Art and Freedom" shows in 1942 and 1944. Tragically, none of her photographs from those early years appear to have survived.

In 1945 she moved to London, where her friends included E. L. T. Mesens, Paul Nash, and others who had taken part in the Surrealist Group in England. By the mid-1950s her camera work was well known. "If any one person might be said to have reestablished photography as a respected art form in post-war London," wrote Val Villiams in a monograph about her, "then that distinction must go to Ida Kar." One of her exhibitions was devoted to pictures she took in revolutionary Cuba. She was noted especially for her fine portraits (of Arp, André and Elisa Breton, Man Ray, Mesens, Miró, and many others). Militantly noncommercial—she consistently refused fashion and advertising work—her aim was to make one hundred portraits of people and then devote herself to photographing animals and, as an interviewer put it, "the life she sees in rocks and stones."

A major influence on photography, Ida Kar was in person a formidable presence; a reporter noted in 1965 that meeting her was "a little like turning a sharp corner and finding oneself staring down the barrel of a seventeenth-century cannon with a smoking fuse." A born agitator, she was a frequent soapboxer at London's Hyde Park, speaking in defense of prostitutes and other unfashionable causes.

Although Kar is known to have started an autobiography shortly before her death, she seems to have published almost nothing. Something of her rebelliousness, dynamism, and flamboyance is nonetheless evident in her interviews and in fugitive quotations that found their way into articles about her in British newspapers and magazines. The passages published here date primarily from the early 1960s, but the outlook they define was basically hers from the late 1930s on.

I CHOSE PHOTOGRAPHY

[In photography] I project my self-confidence and my overwhelming love of the subject.

• • •

I work rapidly and try to stimulate the subject so that we can have an affinity together, and after placing [the subject] in the best light and choosing the best position for composition, I take the photograph as quickly as I can—before I lose the mood or expression. If there is a doorknob or water pipe in the background that I couldn't have moved, or something else that I may have overlooked and which spoils the picture, I see nothing wrong with having it airbrushed from the print afterward.

• • •

Stick with one camera. Learn it backwards. So as you don't have to think of techniques and mechanics. I exploit my materials to their full limit. This doesn't mean falling for every brand of developer, every fresh batch of printing papers, which spill out from the manufacturers.

• • •

An artist is an individual who may be influenced by another artist but never copies him. For instance, I have been strongly influenced by Man Ray but I have never copied him. So if a pupil of mine works on his own imitating my work I would not worry, he could only be a copy of me. But if he carries on having learned from me but being an artist in his own right I would be very proud.

• • •

I do not understand why photography should be excluded from being an art just because there are so many bad photographers. There are many painters who could never be artists. Almost anything can be an art—the making of shoes, the planting of a garden, the designing of furniture, just so long as the person who does it is himself an artist.

• • •

My husband [in Cairo] became jealous of my success and asked me to choose between him and photography—so I chose photography.

• • •

I am a force! I am superhuman! That is why I must find myself through my work. I have no children, and no man is *big* enough for me.

• • •

Women are so silly to worry about their wrinkles—they can make a face so much more interesting.

• • •

I am fifty-five, but I have the vitality of a twenty-five-year-old. I am sure I shall never feel too old to do what I want.

Ikbal El Alailly

Ikbal El Alailly, known as Boula to her friends, was for many years a central figure in the Surrealist Movement in Egypt. A regular at the group's daily meetings at Tommy's Bar in Cairo, she helped organize group exhibitions and prepare its periodicals and other collective publications: *Don Quichotte, Al-Tattawor* [Evolution], *La Séance continue* [The Seance Continues], and *Le Part du sable* [The Sand's Share], to which she contributed her "Portrait of the Artist as a Young Rabbit."

Beyond the fact that she was the granddaughter of Egypt's "Prince of Poets," Ahmad Chawqi, and that her parents were Moslems, little seems to have been written about El Alailly's early life. In 1939 she met poet Georges Henein, who had been promoting surrealism in Egypt since 1935. It was love at first sight, and the two were inseparable thereafter, although both their families opposed the marriage (they did not in fact legally wed until 1954). After her husband's death in 1973, El Alailly, from her apartment in Paris, devoted her time and energy primarily to bringing out his unpublished writings and reprinting those that were out of print. In the 1970s she encouraged the youthful Arab Surrealist Movement in Exile. She died in 1984.

El Alailly's major contribution to surrealism was her large anthology of German presurrealist poetry and prose, *Vertu de l'Allemagne* [The Virtue of Germany] (1945), an inspired attempt to heighten public awareness of one of the wellsprings of surrealist thought. Her introduction to this volume is published here.

INTRODUCTION TO *VERTU DE L'ALLEMAGNE* [THE VIRTUE OF GERMANY]

German literature, and particularly its irreplaceable jewel—the romantic upheaval which truly had neither beginning nor end—seems to contain in an ever-shrinking space the whole metallic drama of German history since Frederick, not only the drama of its external destiny but also all that disavows that destiny. Ignoring the contingencies of victories and defeats, that disavowal prepares the only true lifeline for German thought.

These two aspects of German history—one, in which all light is lost in exercise of pure vanity, and the other, in those singing shadows where all who have dreamt of a better world still await their triumph—exist in varying degrees of intensity in the work of some of the most distinguished representatives of German thought. In Hegel the rights of poetry and those of the state appear reconciled only because a thousand ruses are drawn from an unstable dialectic which denies them the favor of confronting each other in broad daylight. In Nietzsche the antinomy enters the individual's heroic *vocation* as well as the social and national structure, in which heroism is loudly *professed,* only to be overtaken by a madness too brief or too late! As for Goethe's attempt to codify the admirable passional chaos in which German romanticism contemplated and strengthened its own image, it inevitably broke down from sheer excess of solemnity.

Night, so widely hailed, was for the romantic poets not only a great magic attic never before explored or imagined to such an extent. It was also the *rational refuge* of all those who, having hoped so much for the world to change, ended up detesting this change to the extent that it was identified with the tyrannical personality of Napoleon. In their rapture of hope for the century's material and social salvation, the German romantics let themselves glide to the extreme limit of their nocturnal delirium. Kleist's grandiose demise, Hölderlin's upheaval, Grabbe's slow alcoholic agony, Nietzsche's anguish and suffering—all testify to the depth of this evil or, more precisely, of this *virtue,* this supreme intransigence of desire in relation to all that pretends to substitute itself for its object, an object forever indisguisable because it is forever identified, pursued and beckoned to the storm's trembling light. Since 1918 such people as Jacques Vaché, Jacques Rigaut, and René Crevel have succumbed to this same form of intransigence, while others have recoiled, withdrawn, drifted off, and become mired in the renovated lies and deception into which our entire era has been tossed the way one tosses a dog into the pound.

From Lichtenberg's coriaceous humor to that of Jacques Vaché and Marcel Duchamp is a mere hop over a few trifling disasters. And when Karl-Philip Moritz speaks of "the divine voluptuousness of destruction," a mysterious agitation seizes the circles of cognoscenti as Alfred Jarry's calling card noiselessly falls on the fortune-teller's table. Remarkably, the romantics themselves sensed this immense "Stop dreaming"—this long and harrowing interim of thought—by which our epoch's law of conservation deprives romanticism's poetic legitimacy from enduring even one hour longer. The romantics responded in advance by rendering justice to the value—until then purely anecdotal—of the dream, and placing at its "doors of ivory or horn" the enriching sign of positive values. No longer would the dreamed experience be separated from the experience of real life. In Novalis, for example, what might at first seem to be a simple reaction against the harshness and weight of the real—or, in metaphysical terms, a denial of the existence of the sensible world—is rapidly transformed into a creative experience which, in turn, gives rise to the proliferation of whole new categories of the real. In Achim von Arnim's *Bizarre Tales,* the fields of action and reflection are continually confused, daybreak fails to dispel enchantment, and no one dreams of asking whether "Once upon a time, there was," because now the heretofore distinct domains of the so-called real and illusion share the same necessity and constitute a single phenomenon of interrelatedness and solidarity.

A new and fruitful familiarity is established with the unknown. Far from being on a first-name basis with mystery or breaking through the mist, the poet magnifies the majesty of the most insignificant aspects of reality. Arnim brilliantly anticipates Lautréamont's imperative: "Poetry must have practical truth for its goal." And these words are materialized in turn, irrefutably—along with many other confirmations—in the sparkling rediscovered desires known as *surrealist objects:* fur cups that one would love to offer the first woman-panther to enter one's life; chairs made of branches still thick with the forest's leaves; the unspeakable nostalgia for broken mirrors. Were it not for the intervention of André Breton and his decisive pages on Arnim, in which the latter's extraordinary importance is definitively recognized, all there is in German romanticism of driving forces, of the *will to poetry*—in a world that, if not yet clear, is at least potentially clarifiable, someday, by the words of poets—could all too easily again give rise to who knows what irritating weaknesses of judgment.

The contradiction running through all of German romanticism, and animating it with a "new tremor," is the contradiction between the flight from the real and the creative return to a reality at last regarded as conquerable and extensible to the scale of the poet's vision. This contradiction is not one of those which can be surmounted once and for all with a single flap of the wings. It is there, perhaps, where the conflict is most acute and the outcome most uncertain, that we find the exploding point of the most dramatic works (Kafka)—those which bind us, all criticism aside, to a long ordeal of shared vertigos. I know of nothing more overpowering, in this regard, than the story of a young man (a character in one of Kafka's novels) who is forced by sordid circumstances and against his liking to discover America; attempting to substitute an America of his own choosing for this forced discovery, he continually lapses into bitterness as a result of a never-ending series of unsuccessful efforts.

One can say what one likes of the slip-streams and fluctuating episodes of this exhausting struggle, to which the mouth of the poet returns again and again, and the taste of death and the hatred of possible servitudes in the poet's interaction with the everyday world. It remains to the credit of German romanticism that it traced, for the poetic and artistic inspiration of the nineteenth and the twentieth centuries, *our major ways of seeing*. In his immoderate ambition to transfigure all things or to perish, the romantic poet—albino voyager who, only yesterday, plunged into the night to become its fantastic chronicler—now learns, and not without delight, to taste light itself, like a long-forbidden fruit. Already it is *the poet's own light,* and its various reflections illuminate and touch all that is madly desirable in this world, thereby inciting people to liberate themselves from the *false night* that ignorance and tyranny have imposed on them in recent years. False night of war, false night of frenzied provocations that end up ruining all intelligence and all culture in a *volkish* and folkloric chauvinism. False night of slavery and flayed susceptibilities—oh, the time lost in "national hostilities"! False night for real and too numerous brigands at all points of the horizon. False night—the ultimate negation of poetry, of the *right* of poetry, of the *poetic sensibility* that humankind has evolved. False night that must be swept away once for all, so that we shall awaken one morning to find the very air we breathe flowering with *freedom,* this *other* ocean.

• • •

It is the intention of this anthology to render homage, today, to the generous German contribution to modern thought and to the orientation of all contemporary poetic activity. We do not pretend that this anthology is either complete or irreproachable. Inevitably it reflects our own preferences, and certain gaps are attributable to the fact that, in present-day circumstances, it has been impossible to secure all requisite references.

To this homage rendered to the contributions of German romanticism we must add here a tribute of gratitude to those who, with profoundest conviction, have done most to spread its message: above all, to Albert Béguin and to André Breton. We direct our readers to Béguin's essential study, *L'Âme romantique et la rêve* [The Romantic Soul and the Dream], and to Breton's numerous critical notices, written with such sensitivity and flawless firmness of mind.

Some readers may be surprised to discover at the end of this work an appendix featuring work by recent authors seemingly distinct from the romantic current. Our purpose in including this material is nevertheless clear. The romantic wave receded, but not before a new momentum had begun to gather force, developing at a distance its initial trajectory. The case of Kafka in particular demands to be appreciated in its relationship to the ensemble of revolts and despairs which constitute the course of German romanticism. It is important to insist on this poignant continuity, maintained most often at the cost of the poet's "viability" and sociability. Without this poignant continuity, the false night would have buried all, soiled all, muddled all.

Translated from the French by Erin Gibson

4. *Surrealism versus the Cold War, 1946–1959*

MEDIUM

Communication Surréaliste

Directeur : Jean SCHUSTER

Paraît tous les deux mois

Nouvelle Série N° 1 — NOVEMBRE 1953

★

SOMMAIRE :

Autres collaborations : Robert Benayoun, Nora Mitrani, José Pierre, Jean Schuster, François Valorbe, Michel Zimbacca.

et le problème

OUVREZ-VOUS?

Réponses de : Elisa Breton, Adrien Dax, Julien Gracq, Simon Hantaï, Wolfgang Paalen, Bernard Roger, Anne Seghers, Toyen, etc...

Le prochain numéro sera illustré par Wolfgang Paalen.

ADMINISTRATION : 201, Rue de Charenton, PARIS (12e)
RÉDACTION : 17, Rue Gramme, PARIS (15e).

Le No **120** fr.
Luxe **900** fr.

ABONNEMENT 6 N°

Édition ordinaire — France **700** fr.
— Étranger **800** fr.

Édition de luxe limitée à 50 exemplaires comportant une pointe-sèche, eau-forte ou lithographie. — France **5.000** fr. Étranger **5.500** fr.

Tout lecteur qui abonnera trois de ses amis à MEDIUM recevra un ouvrage à son choix paru aux éditions « Arcanes ».

SURRÉALISME n. m. Tendance d'une école (née vers 1924) à négliger toute préoccupation logique.

SURRÉALISTE n. et adj. Partisan du surréalisme.

(Petit Larousse illustré).

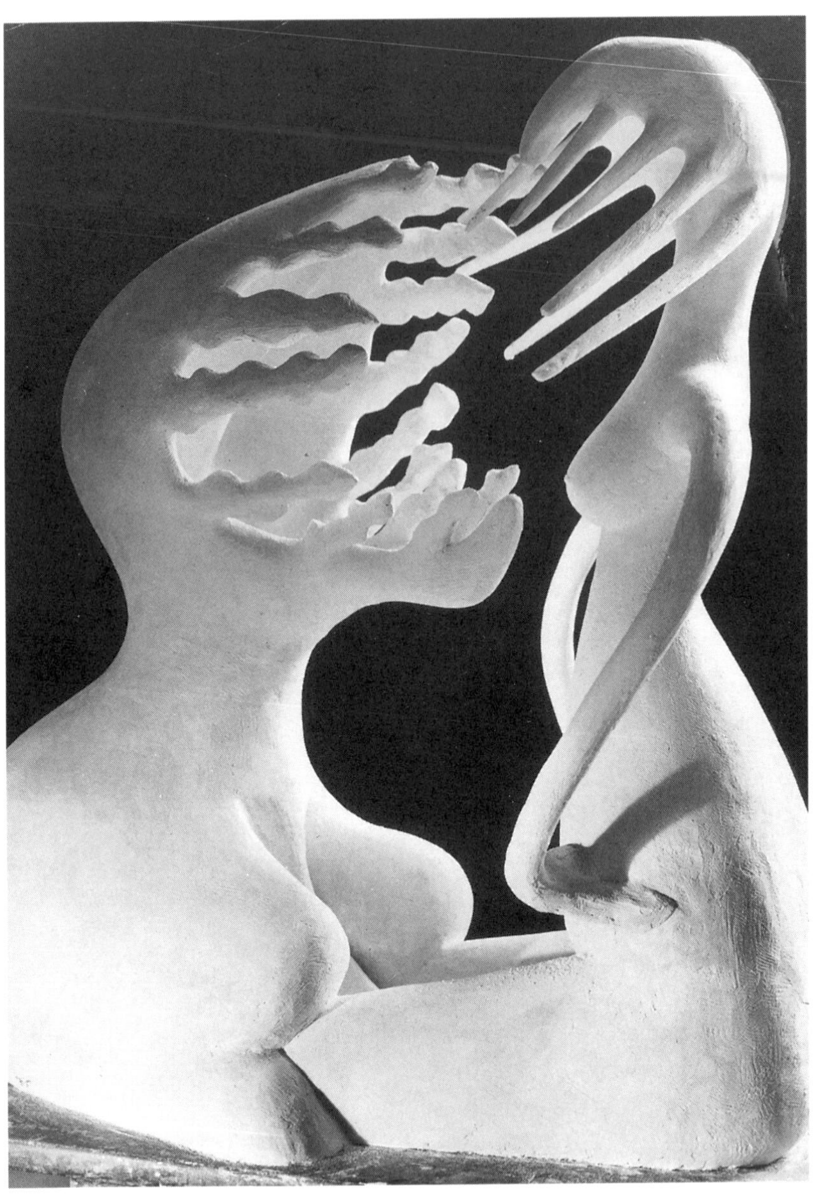

Maria Martins, sculpture, ca. 1947. Photograph courtesy of Edouard Jaguer.

Regroupment and Occultation

Women in the Surrealist Underground in the 1950s

> The winter has been dreadfully severe; but the spring promises well. . . .
> I am going to unexplored regions.
> —Mary Shelley

From the surrealist point of view, the postwar years in Europe and America added up to a long period of counterrevolution. In most of Europe and America, mass movements for radical social change had barely emerged at war's end before the whole world was divided into competing "camps" by the two giant power blocs. Fundamentally, the Ubuesque global social system that led to the Holocaust, the gulags, apartheid, and the atomic bombing of Hiroshima and Nagasaki remained in control.

Cynicism ruled, culturally and politically. Apathy was one of the watchwords of the age. In such conditions, surrealism was more than ever dismissed as utopian, silly, irrelevant, naive, childish, a remnant of romanticism, and, above all, out of fashion. In the U.S.S.R. surrealism was denounced as decadent and capitalistic, with close ties to American imperialism. In the U.S., it was decried as French, foreign, subversive, un-American. A lot has been written about U.S. anti-Communism, but the Cold War was also a period of rampant antisurrealism. In the vanguard of the antisurrealist crusade, of course, were the Stalinist usurpers of the cause of Communism.[1]

In France especially, leading ideologues of Left, Right, and Center—no matter how violently they disagreed about everything else—stood united in their efforts to marginalize what they regarded (not altogether incorrectly) as the surrealist threat to their power and privilege. The mood of hopelessness and ennui was reflected in the existentialist craze. Prosaic angst replaced the poetic Marvelous. *Mad Love* and *The Castle of Argol* were out; *Nausea* and *No Exit* were in.

Refusing to go along with the fashionable and reactionary trends, the reorganized Surrealist Group rallied considerable support. Breton returned to Paris in May 1946 to find the cafés he frequented jammed with standing-room-only crowds of young people eager to jump into the fray on the side of surrealism. U.S. artist Edith Smith, who attended many Surrealist Group meetings and demonstrations in Paris in 1948 and 1949 (often with African American writer James Baldwin), recalls surrealism's postwar years as a period of intense activity and excitement (telephone conversation, May 1997). The Paris group's first postwar tract, *Freedom Is a Vietnamese Word* (1947), protested France's war against a tiny country in southeast Asia that would loom large in the world in the 1960s. A year later, the tract *To Your Kennels, Curs of God!*, a critique of Catholic attempts to appropriate certain elements of surrealism, carried fifty-two signatures, more than had ever appeared on a surrealist declaration. The 1947 International Surrealist Exhibition in Paris showed work by eighty-seven surrealists (sixteen of them women) from twenty-four countries. Under the name "Surrealist Solution" a new Bureau of Surrealist Research was set up at the Nina Dausset Gallery to coordinate what showed every sign of becoming a worldwide renewal of surrealist activity.

Internationally, however, the situation of organized surrealism proved to be at least as precarious as it was in France and in many places much more so. As Stalinism took over eastern Europe, surrealists in those war-torn countries once again had to go underground or abroad. When the surrealist refugees in the U.S. returned to Paris, the New York Surrealist Group in Exile ceased to exist; its last collective manifestation was the exhibition *Bloodflames 1947*, organized by Nicolas Calas and featuring work by eight artists, including two women: sculptor Helen Phillips and mosaicist Jeanne Reynal. The *Tropiques* group in Martinique had broken up in 1945 when Aimé Césaire began a new life as Communist deputy in the French parliament.[2] Well before 1950 the Surrealist Groups of Copenhagen, London, Cairo, Stockholm, and Santiago, Chile, had folded their tents.

Surrealism in Romania and Portugal followed unusual trajectories of their own. With the advent of Stalinism, the Bucharest group had to disband; most members went into exile. Despite the geographical distance and differences that separated them, they maintained a fidelity to surrealism and even a collective identity. Antonia Rasicovici's participation in surrealism in Romania started in 1934 at the age of fifteen (she now lives in the U.S.). Sculptor Mirabelle Dors moved from Bucharest to Paris in 1950 and was active in the Paris group for a few years.[3] The most influential Romanian woman surrealist is surely Lygia Alexandrescu, for over fifty years the companion and coadventurer of poet Gellu Naum and the heroine of his fabulous androgynous chronicle, *Zenobia*. First published in 1985, this narrative which shares the climate and sensibility of *Nadja*, *Don Quixote*, and Jacques Vaché's *War Letters* has since been widely translated (Naum 1995).

Salazarist state repression quickly clamped down on the surrealist group which briefly flourished in Lisbon in the 1940s. Surrealist activity, however, although highly occulted and pursued with semiclandestine informality, persisted—and persists today. Unlike the U.S., England, Italy, Germany, Holland, Russia, and the Scandinavian countries, where surrealism has been an isolated radical undercurrent, surrealism in Portugal (as in Czechoslovakia, Serbia, Romania, France, Belgium, Spain, Greece, Japan, the French West Indies, Argentina, and Chile) has been a large force in the nation's cultural life. One of Portugal's major pioneers of modern art, Maria Helena Vieira da Silva, had strong links to surrealism. From postwar Portugal came painter Paula Rego and two important poets: Luiza Neto Jorge, also known for her translations of key surrealist works into Portuguese, and Isabel Meyrelles, who further manifests her surrealist spirit in sculpture.[4]

As always, new surrealist groups kept turning up. In 1948 the "Automatists" of Montreal, sixteen strong (including poet Thérèse Renaud, dancer Françoise Sullivan, and five other women), declared their solidarity with international surrealism in a stunning manifesto titled *Refus global* [Global Refusal]. A Surrealist Group formed in Argentina in 1952 and over the next four years brought out four issues of a lively journal, *A Partir de cero* [Starting from Zero]; among its collaborators were Olga Orozco and Peruvian poet Blanca Varela. A *Surrealistische Publikationem* [Surrealist Publication] issued in Austria in 1954 included texts by Anneliese Hager. A fascinating surrealist-oriented group—including Carol St. Julian (a.k.a. Beavy LeNora, the Nevermore Girl) and photographer Anne McKeever—burst onto the scene in New Orleans, Louisiana, in 1955.[5] The Surrealism Study Group, closely linked to the surrealists in Paris, was formed in Tokyo in 1958. Surrealists in Milan, Italy, brought out a journal, *Front unique*, in 1959. But the Cold War intellectual climate proved deadly, and none of these groups held out for long.

Meanwhile, a few seceding surrealists in Belgium, France, and other countries got embroiled in a bizarre effort to find a place for surrealism in the Stalinized Communist parties (which of course wanted none of it). Unfortunately, even after these politically naive would-be surrealists came to their senses a few months later, few of them resumed their participation in the international Surrealist Movement; mutual distrust was too great.[6] Many former "Revolutionary Surrealists," as they had pretentiously called themselves, later helped found the far more interesting "Cobra" movement (1948–1951), dedicated to the pursuit of automatism in the plastic arts. Cobra in turn was succeeded in 1954 by the international Phases movement, cofounded by Edouard Jaguer and Anne Ethuin, which embraced surrealism more fully. In the sixties, Phases carried out joint actions with the French Surrealist Group, as it has continued to do in later years with surrealist groups in the United States, Quebec, and other countries.[7]

The "Revolutionary Surrealists" and at least some members of Cobra thought of themselves as having superseded existing surrealism. Amusingly, some U.S. critics made the same claim for New York's abstract expressionists. Other 1950s would-be superseders of surrealism included the tiny French "Lettriste" movement and, more importantly, the Internationale situationniste [Situationist International], a small Paris-based group which was in fact well-grounded in pre–World War II surrealist political theory. Clearly, none of these groups succeeded in superseding surrealism; indeed, not one survived more than a few years as an organized force. However, the huge burst of creativity by Cobra especially, but also by some of the abstract expressionists and even the somewhat laughable "Lettristes," contributed something to the later development of surrealism. Situationists, for their part, helped elaborate surrealism's critique of advanced capitalism. Without exception, however, these groups included far fewer women than the Surrealist Movement; New York abstract expressionism and the Situationist International were basically men's clubs.[8] So it was in the late forties and fifties: declared nonexistent by the establishment, who feared them as blasphemous subversives, surrealists also had to contend with critics who mistook their own restlessness for the "supersession" of surrealism.

The first decade and a half of the Cold War were hard years indeed for the Surrealist Movement, especially for its women members. A depressing world political climate, factionalism, and splits led to extended periods of malaise. But there were also moments of joy, exciting discoveries, and splendid triumphs, and women had their share of all of them. Surrealism in painting and drawing was enhanced by the arrival of Marie Wilson, Judit Reigl, Mimi Parent, Paula Rego, Baya, Gundrun Åhlberg, Marcelle Loubchansky, Suzanne Besson, Marie Carlier, Henriette de Champrel, and Marianne van Hirtum. Isabel Meyrelles, Mirabelle Dors, and Helen Phillips made their mark in sculpture. Nelly Kaplan made her first films and thus became the first woman surrealist cinematographer. (Alice Rahon had earlier collaborated on a film with her second husband, Edward FitzGerald, but the project was never completed.) Kaplan's narratives published under the pen name Belen are some of the blackest black humor ever set loose on an unsuspecting public. Dark humor enriched with an aggressive sexuality is also the hallmark of the tales by Joyce Mansour and German-born Unica Zürn.

In Montreal, Françoise Sullivan explored the frontiers of kinetic automatism in a series of extraordinary dance performances and also wrote with passion and lucidity on the subject for the automatists' publication, *Refus global.* Around the same time in Paris André Breton wrote a moving tribute to the African American dancer Katherine Dunham—with whom he had worked closely on the Toussaint L'Ouverture Committee—for the program of her Paris debut. Meanwhile, in Dunham's hometown of Chicago, young Sybil Shearer amazed audiences with wildly magical dances of unmistakable surrealist inspiration.[9]

The late forties and fifties were especially fertile for surrealism in poetry, which blossomed in many languages. In 1945 eighteen-year-old Thérèse Renaud of Montreal published the first surrealist poems written in Canada. Although surrealism had not previously been active as an organized movement in Germany, the incandescent poems of Anneliese Hager—who also happens to be one of the masters of the photogram—and the meteorlike anagrams of Unica Zürn helped establish a postwar surrealist presence in the language of Lichtenberg and Annette von Droste-Hülshoff. In Portuguese the poetry of Isabel Meyrelles and Luiza Neto Jorge was a trumpet blast of dream and revolt, signaling a fresh look at the universe. Poets Olga Orozco in Buenos Aires and Blanca Varela in Peru fanned the flames of surrealist discontent and desire in Spanish.

In French the explosively unconventional work of Joyce Mansour and Marianne van Hirtum brought something new to surrealism. Asked by an interviewer in 1960 to name the three most important French-language surrealist poets of the postwar years, Breton replied: Malcolm de Chazal, Jean-Pierre Duprey, and Joyce Mansour.[10] The first two may be better known, at least in France, than any of the women poets mentioned above, but Mansour has become the best known of them all, not only in France but internationally. With her deep-sea insolence, mountain-high erotic rage, and bitter, insect-leggy laughter, Joyce Mansour gave the world an astonishing body of poetry such that no woman had ever written.

The poetry of Marianne van Hirtum is just as convention-shattering as the work of Mansour but very different. Van Hirtum's bold wilderness-restoring imagery startles us with her delightful sense of disaster and her desperate love of risk. Savage and shimmering, her lyrics are as androgynous and prehensile as sleep itself.

Several women whose involvement in surrealism began in the twenties or thirties were just as active in the fifties. Meret Oppenheim and Toyen were especially important in the Paris group. A significant monograph on Toyen—with texts by Breton, Péret, and Jindrich Heisler—appeared in 1953. From various remote outposts Leonora Carrington, Mary Low, Irène Hamoir, and Valentine Penrose were publishing books throughout the decade.

Surrealism in the late forties and fifties also brought new surrealist games: "Would You Open the Door?" and "One in the Other," and new collective enthusiasms, such as their discovery of ancient Gaulish art, the poetry of the Celtic bards, the music of Thelonious Monk, the songs of Billie Holiday, the works of Charles Fort, the animated cartoons of Tex Avery, and unpublished letters of Flora Tristan. These new passions and others are chronicled in the French group's periodicals: the newspaper *Néon* (five issues, 1948–1949), the broadsheet *Médium: Informations surréalistes* (eight issues, 1952–1953), and the journals *Médium: Communication surréaliste* (four issues, 1953–1955), *Le Surréalisme, même* [Surrealism, Itself] (five issues, 1955–1958), and *BIEF: Jonction surréaliste* (twelve issues, 1958–1960) (Bonnet and Chénieux-Gendron 1982). Group exhibitions, most notably the 1955 "Alice in Wonderland" exhibition organized by Charles Estienne and the 1959 International Surrealist Exhibition devoted to eros, were other notable achievements of surrealism in the fifties, in which women played a large role. Based on elective affinities and passional attraction, these games, exhibitions, and other manifestations of what Mimi Parent has called the movement's "potlatch" and "festival" quality—collective play, experiment, improvisation, and pursuit of objective chance—are the very heart of surrealism. More than a momentary release from the pressures of everyday misery, they are a rich source of revolutionary poetic knowledge, suggesting ways of overcoming the depressing complex of ruling ideologies that Breton denounced as *miserabilism* (Breton 1972, 347–348).

The fifties were also fruitful years in the realm of theory and criticism, though here again women's contributions have been little noticed outside the movement. A high point of surrealist intervention during the Cold War was the Paris group's collaboration on the anarchist weekly, *Le Libertaire,* in 1951–1953. Their column "Billet Surréaliste" [Surrealist Ticket] enabled the surrealists, who lacked a periodical of their own at the time, to develop new approaches to problems facing the revolutionary movement.[11] Especially notable in the series, which included contributions by Breton, Péret, and Adrien Dax as well as by many younger comrades, are two articles by Jacqueline Senard: an ironic history of reason and a forceful text blending black humor and radical ecology. A social worker, Senard also seems to have been a feminist, though whether she ever called herself one is not known. It appears that she was a principal instigator and perhaps would have been coeditor of *La Mante surréaliste* (the title plays on the words *l'amante*/lover and *la mante*/praying mantis), a proposed surrealist journal more specifically addressed to women readers than any previous group publication. This journal was announced for publication in January 1953 but never appeared.[12]

A revolutionary and indeed *surrealist* feminism, enhanced by a profound ecological awareness, informs the sparkling work of Nora Mitrani. More than any surrealist of the older generation or her own, she concerned herself with woman-related issues. Educated as a philosopher and sociologist, she felt perfectly at home in the world of scientific thought and critical theory. Mitrani wrote on a wide range of subjects, from Kierkegaard and *film noir* to the critique of bureaucracy and the dangers of nuclear power. Her contributions to the critique of misery and miserabilism are second to none. Her writings on women are of special interest, because they are an innovation in surrealism as well as in feminism.

Outside surrealism and the small revolutionary movement of that period, the writings of Senard and Mitrani attracted little notice. Today we recognize them and the work of other surrealists of those years, women and men, as writings that seem, in a very real sense, ahead of their time. They seem so, however, only because the majority opinion in their day was so pitifully behind their time. Racing ahead of a sluggish political reality, the surrealist imagination suggests bold answers to questions that most people have not even gotten around to asking.

"Surrealism is what *will be*": so closed the surrealist declaration "Inaugural Break" in 1947.[13] Beyond the ranks of the movement itself and a few of its supporters, these words provoked only derision. For those who succumbed to the Cold War mentality, surrealism was old hat and not worth the time of day. Who could imagine that, twenty-one years later, in the streets of Paris and all over France, surrealism would find a social resonance capable of shaking all Europe to its foundations? How funny the old Cold War obituaries for the movement must have sounded in May 1968, when surrealism was the very voice of youth in revolt.

Notes

1. Stalinist polemics against surrealism include Vailland 1948, and Tzara 1948.

2. Notwithstanding his membership in the Communist Party, Aimé Césaire nonetheless contributed a poem to *Le Surréalisme en 1947*, catalog of the International Surrealist Exhibition in Paris, and in numerous interviews he reiterated his basic solidarity with surrealism. The Surrealist Group in Paris welcomed his *Discourse on Colonialism* (1955) as well as his *Open Letter to Maurice Thorez* (1956), announcing his break with Stalinism.

3. Information on the early history of surrealism in Romania and on women's participation in it has been kindly provided by Antonia Rasicovici, whose letters of 25 January and 19 March 1996 have been especially helpful.

4. Cesariny 1966 remains the best documentary history of surrealism in Portugal. My principal source of information on women's participation in Portuguese surrealism has been my correspondence with Cesariny, Artur do Cruzeiro Seixas, and Isabel Meyrelles. See also Correia 1973. On Vieira da Silva, see Cesariny 1984. On Paula Rego, see McEwen 1992.

5. On the New Orleans Climax Jazz, Art and Pleasure Society and its journal *Climax,* see Garon 1989.

6. See Noël Arnaud, *"Le surréalisme-révolutionnaire,"* in Biro and Passeron, eds., *Dictionnaire général du surréalisme,* 1982, 391; Jaguer, "Le Corsage du deux soeurs," introduction to the reprint of the Belgian journal, *Les Deux soeurs* (Jaguer 1985).

7. Lambert 1983; Jaguer 1979; "The 'Phases' Movement," in Pellegrini 1966, 283–292; *Rétroviseur: Le Mouvement Phases* (1972); *Phases: L'expérience continue, 1952–1988* (Le Havre 1988); Dąbkowska-Zydroń 1994.

8. Sandler 1970 includes biographies of fifteen artists, all male. More recently, some critics have conceded a place in the history of abstract expressionism to Lee Krasner. Raspaud and Voyer 1972 list a total of seventy members of the Situationist International between 1957 and 1970, including seven women, four of whom were expelled by spring 1962 (11–14). Later, in the 1960s and 1970s, the group around the French journal *Tel Quel* [As Is] also sometimes pretended to be a kind of supersession of surrealism. However, their ultra-academicism, avant-garde pretensions, and nonactivist Maoist politics show them up rather as professional renovators of the very "literature" that surrealism rejected.

9. Excerpts from Sullivan's article are included in this volume. See also Breton 1991, and "Sybil Shearer," in Franklin Rosemont 1980.

10. André Breton 1960; an interview cited in Matthews 1969, 176, 236.

11. The "Billet surréaliste" columns in *Le Libertaire* have been reprinted in book form in Pierre, ed., 1983.

12. Published information on the ill-fated *La Mante surréaliste* project appears to be nonexistent. I have relied on correspondence with Elie-Charles Flamand, Gérard Legrand, and Michel Zimbacca, who were active in the Paris Surrealist Group at that time, and with Edouard Jaguer, who was a close friend of Jacqueline and Jean-Pierre Duprey.

13. "Rupture inaugurale" is reprinted in Pierre, *Tracts surréalistes* II, 1982, 30–36. Excerpts in English translation are included in Breton 1978, 340–343.

Thérèse Renaud

The author, at eighteen, of the first surrealist poems written and published in Canada (1945), Thérèse Renaud was the youngest of a trio of sisters (the others were Jeanne and Louise) who formed part of the Quebec-based "automatist" movement. This militant group of painters, poets, and dancers affirmed its solidarity with surrealism in a sensational manifesto, *Refus global* (1948), cosigned by Thérèse. Meanwhile, she married automatist painter Fernand Leduc and moved to Paris, where they were active for a time in the Paris Surrealist Group. Although various disagreements led to her withdrawal from collective activity after a few months, Renaud's support for the movement's fundamental aims and principles remained intact, and she continues to this day to regard herself among its partisans.

Her first collection of poems, *Les Sables du rêve* [The Sands of Dream], with drawings by fellow automatist J.-P. Mousseau, was published by Les Cahiers de la file indienne in 1946 and reissued in 1975. Her later poetic volumes include *Plaisirs immobiles* [Frozen Pleasures] (1981) and *Jardins d'éclats* [Explosive Gardens] (1990). She is also the author of an autobiography, *Une mémoire déchirée* [A Torn Memory] (1978). Thérèse Renaud lives in Paris.

Originally issued separately in 1945, the following poem was included in *Les Sables du rêve.*

I LAY MY HEAD

I lay my head in an oyster shell. The grass turned ankle and I went to meet three travelers.

They said: "Come with us. The road is long and hard, but at the end there is a clearing where flowers laugh in the sun and a stream shines in the night." One traveler had a gloved hand. This glove represented the wail of the wind.

On the way I broke my thumb. When a bear came to lick it, I took up some pebbles and threw them behind me.

The second night I brushed against the fire cast away by the hastening stars and felt the burning caress of the moon.

Once at the clearing I picked up my sick feet and threw them into the stream.

I set my body down in the graves and shut the oyster shell. . . .

Translated from the French by Rikki Ducornet

Françoise Sullivan

Born in Montréal, Québec, where she still lives, Françoise Sullivan was initially a painter but, with her friend Jeanne Renaud, turned to dance and choreography while still in her teens. Sullivan studied dance with Franziska Boas while Renaud took classes with Hanya Holm, and together they saw Martha Graham dance in New York in 1946. In the light of surrealism, however, as members of the Montréal "automatist" group, they soon worked out their own radically different conception of dance. Sullivan and Renaud organized the April 1948 Automatist Festival, one of the group's major manifestations, which featured Sullivan's dances, including one inspired by a poem by Jeanne Renaud's sister, Thérèse. That same year Sullivan performed her celebrated outdoor improvisation, "Dance in the Snow." In the realm of surrealist dance, as Edouard Jaguer has noted, Sullivan is the "unique intermediary link between Hélène Vanel and Alice Farley."

Sullivan not only cosigned the inaugural automatist manifesto, *Global Refusal* (1948), she added a substantial text of her own to it: her lecture on dance (originally titled "La Danse et l'espoir" [Dance and Hope]), delivered on 16 February 1948, excerpts of which appear here in translation.

During the 1960s Sullivan devoted herself largely to sculpture. She became interested in the activity of the Situationist International, and looked up some of its members in Paris. In 1980 she returned to painting and since then has had many solo exhibitions in many countries.

DANCE AND AUTOMATISM

Dance is above all a reflex, a spontaneous expression of vividly experienced emotions. In dance humankind has found a means of satisfying its desire for tangency with the universe.

• • •

We must reject as a profound error the static idea of a dance that is always the same.

Academic dance, still with us at this late date, offers the viewer an exclusively visual pleasure by means of an exceptional virtuosity of the limbs, opposed to the rest of the body. It tends to derive solely from the law of gravity.

Confined by such obsolete methods, the dancer becomes a mechanical instrument executing meaningless movements. In a language withered and weak, choreography repeats what has already been said. Thus we get "pure dance," "art for art's sake": expressions of decadence, crystallization, and death.

And thus dance loses its human character, which consists in translating the intensity of life in all its sentiments and aspirations, individual as well as social. Reduced to acts that are contrary to life, dance loses its poetic place in reality and drags mankind downward. Academism is a vicious circle.

• • •

In dance today we see a return to the magic of movement, to natural and subtle human forces. Dance today aspires to exalt, to charm, to hypnotize—to wholly engage the sensibility.

It is a matter of restoring to our movements the expressive surplus enclosed in the human body, this marvelous instrument. In line with current needs, we must rediscover the truths already known to the ancients, to primitive peoples, and to Oriental civilization, as concretized in the dances of the African fetishist, the whirling dervish and the Tibetan rope-dancer. . . . Dance attains its reason for being when it knows how to enchant its onlookers and to revive them by means of the organism. . . . For that to happen, we must be unafraid to go as far as necessary in exploring our whole person. . . .

• • •

Today we are striving to reconstruct the world. Our lifesaver in this task is instinct. Part of our effort now consists in uncovering our instincts, which have been imprisoned for so long.

Happily, there are vital needs, irresistible forces. There is hope and, besides, there is knowledge which must not be isolated but rather must preside, as in olden times, over our adoration and our magic. Everything must be organized for liberation, for the rediscovery of vertigo and love.

• • •

Let us penetrate to the human depths, to the domain of the unconscious. Its elements are tendencies, desires, appetites, and repulsions. The true treasure to be found there is *energy*—a fragment of cosmic energy: master of internal forces, motive of our actions. This we have learned from the study of antiquity.

The dancer must liberate the energies of the body by means of spontaneous gestures dictated in the course of the dance. One does this by putting oneself in a state of receptivity, like a medium. Through the violence of the intervening force, one will reach the state of trance, the magic points.

Energy creates a necessity which, in turn, dictates movements. Because the propulsive phenomenon and the concept are inseparable, they contain all their value and great efficacy. That is the way to reach the knowledge of the seat of emotions in the body and to understand how the unique tension, totally expressive of a feeling, is born.

Automatism allows the dancer to rediscover the body's localizations: depending on one's own individual strength and dynamism, one's personal work becomes general. The affective side governs everything: not only is it localized on specific points of the human body, but it also drives the dancer through time, space, and gravity. It unifies the groupings and modifies the whole body's inflection.

Therefore, the dancer's main effort must be to attain the perfect coordination of all the elements, for what matters most is that the emotions creating rhythms (and the style that gives them shapes) must be found again in their plastic representation, so that they are animated by the shiver of life.

• • •

If dancers obey an oneiric rhythm in regard to matter, how will they join others in a communicating expansion? Through the play of forces and feelings vividly expressed. In order to group themselves affectively, dancers must be liberated and disciplined in the same manner, in agreement with the potentialities of their art. They must also be imbued with a shared conception, often related to the social needs of the period. I mean the heartfelt needs recorded in the sensibility, not abstractly defined; by being linked to that sensibility, dance situates itself within cosmic rhythms. A powerful emotional shock will also reach those rhythms; the sensitive and emotional unity will set each individual toward the same goal; the group will be a living unit where all become the same body.

Human energy is the common denominator and the source of such a life. Going from an inner rhythm to another which is imposed from outside, dancers participate in the creation of a world and in its evolution.

Such a reality, materialized by dancers pursuing their dreams and letting loose the forces of their own nature, will produce intense reactions on other dancers, through its sheer variety. Conflicts will appear, a drama—thanks to the mysterious symbiosis of meaning and form.

A universe is created; a whole world breathes. Viewers witness the efflorescence of life. . . . The performance must act upon them and transform them. In that transformation lies the efficacy and magic of dance.

Translated from the French by Guy Ducornet

Irène Hamoir

After a successful career as a circus performer in her teens, Irène Hamoir found her way to the Surrealist Movement in the early 1930s. For the rest of her life she remained one of the great personalities of Belgian surrealism, not only as the companion of poet Louis Scutenaire, but as an important poet and author in her own right.

Hamoir collaborated on the principal periodicals and other collective publications of the Belgian surrealists, including *Documents 34* (1934), *Le Ciel bleu* [The Blue Sky] (1945), *Les Deux soeurs* [The Two Sisters] (1946–1947), and *Savoir vivre* [Knowing How to Live] (1946). Her many pamphlets of poems—some published simply under the name Irine—were collected in 1949 in one volume, *Oeuvre poétique 1930–1945*, and, more recently, as well as more comprehensively, in *Corne de brune* (1976). She also wrote a humorous novel with a circus setting, *Boulevard Jacqmain* (1953), in which Magritte, Mesens, Nougé, and other Belgian surrealists appear as characters.

PEARL

To have white bouquets
She died young
White wreaths and white regrets

To have a white tumulus
She died in December
A large white garden and white weeping willows

To have white hair
She would have had to wait
Dragging through gray days living white wakeful nights

Translated from the French by Myrna Bell Rochester

ARIA

The sailor fishes for herring
Will he soon return to port?
The girl stays home
And patches her skirts
How many herring, how many pearls in the basket?

Flowers, festivals, whites above, and whites below

Love!
She waits
The boat is at sea
The boat is in port
With the herring
They are gleaming, fresh and fat

Because they swallowed
The sailor's belly
Now, my girl, you ate the herring

And you died
All the same
Long live the bride!

Translated from the French by Myrna Bell Rochester

THE PROCESSION

Wide and long, a roadway ascends. I am at the top of this empty, terribly empty roadway, its tall bleak buildings with their windows close-set, like teeth.

From the foot of the roadway, silent men move forward, carrying aloft flags and banners in the still, tin-colored air.

The demonstrators, tight-lipped, dressed in black, march in orderly pairs down the middle of the road, keeping far from the jaws of the sidewalks. Do they see me? They pass by. Then a second group, and a third. They march on, serious and resolute, to enter another street with a bend so sharp that I can see only the entrance. They disappear into the mouth of that street.

Next to me appears a tall, well-dressed gentleman—probably emerging from the next building where a door has been slammed with a noise of broken bones.

He raises his arm: "Stop! I am the King's Procurator! You are all rebels! In the name of order, I forbid this demonstration!" And then, politely, to me: "Madam, I'm so sorry to deprive you of such an exciting spectacle!"

I reply angrily, "Just looking at my clothes, you think I am some nosy bourgeoise? But I am as much a rebel as they are, sir! Let them go through!"

The Procurator steps aside and the group marches on.

Another group arrives, trumpets raised. At a signal they start playing a slow processional.

Behind the musicians, three legless cripples drag themselves along, three lovely girls, nicely dressed, a poke-bonnet around their faces, singing a plaintive ballad. Their eyes are at the tears at the back of their eyes. But for me they smile knowingly, showing ravishing teeth!

Then, on a bicycle, comes an old, a very old lady with brown skin and well combed white hair, wearing a wide black gathered skirt and a black jacket.

She rides by majestically, sitting very straight on the pedals of her tall machine. Her eyes are those of a very intelligent soul; her look, serenity itself. Her voice is incredibly calm as she speaks, and her teeth shine between worn lips:

"I am Rosa Smith. I am all the Rosa Smiths in the world. I carry all the joys and all the sorrows, the vices and virtues of the Rosa Smiths of this entire world. I shall never die because, as I said, I am all those who were, who are and who will come. I am *the* Rosa Smith."

The procession moves on.

Translated from the French by Guy Ducornet

Emmy Bridgwater, Ithell Colquhoun, Irène Hamoir, and Edith Rimmington

SURREALIST INQUIRY: WHAT DO YOU HATE MOST?

> *Editor's note: This inquiry appeared in the one-shot Belgian surrealist journal* Savoir vivre, *edited by René Magritte (1946).*

1) *What do you hate most?*

2) *What do you love most?*

3) *What do you want most?*

4) *What do you fear most?*

Emmy Bridgwater

1) I hate being brushed by the black vestments of a nun.
2) I love looking through windows—outside as well as inside. Wrinkles on water and on a face. Old faces, new faces, new hats. Surprises in poems, men, and images. Cats, French food, peaches and cream. Rays of sunshine, lightning, and all the red roses in the world.
3) I hope for a new personality that doesn't want the moon.
4) I fear hubbub, tiny insects creeping slowly on the ceiling, stupid people, and the next war.

Ithell Colquhoun

1) London traffic, radio, fog.
2) The sea, finding birds' nests, erotic pleasure.
3) To live peacefully in a marvelous place.
4) The folly of science (entirely different from the folly of poetry).

Irène Hamoir

What I hate, love, want, or fear most depends on the moment, my humor, the hour of the day, the landscape, the weather. Right now, what I hate most is the expression of stupidity. What I love most is to travel, anywhere and everywhere. What I want most is "sunshine tonight." What I fear most: phantoms at sundown in the country.

Edith Rimmington

1) Crocodile tears and snakes in the grass.
2) Everything that excites my curiosity, from the sun to the life created by a rotten apple.
3) All that helps me to protect my spirits and to protect my madness in a sane world.
4) All that constrains my freedom to be curious.

Translated from the French by Penelope Rosemont

Lise Deharme

I DIDN'T KNOW GERTRUDE STEIN

Me, I didn't know Gertrude Stein. I met her one day in a great English house, or perhaps at the home of an Englishwoman from a great house. I didn't have time to think about her from an historical angle (she died a few days later), but I had time to speak to her dog.

It was a big white poodle, with a lion-like, dandified clip. An old, very blasé dandy who only lacked a pearl-studded tie, a monocle, bone shoes, and a hat. But to me the dog seemed sadder than his mistress. Perhaps he knew she was going to die, perhaps she didn't know it. Dogs, even dogs from good families, have a hidden instinct for heart-rending things, and of course, they love, they love till heartbreak, till suicide till eternal despair. They don't forget, for even if they're gluttonous, they're not frivolous.

The dandy with white curls slowly climbed the staircase, step by step, taking the same steps as she. His deep look was telling her to temper that useless, vain, tiring trip in an ungrateful, squalling world: "Don't climb the stairs anymore, Gertrude, it's bad for you; don't get winded speaking the language of eternal childhood to those people; they don't understand. Come with me to the country, in an old one-story house, with a garden and the setting sun. We'll stay there together, waiting for the peace of the night. With my ear on your heart I'll count out the end of your life, so I may leave with you. I love you."

Gertrude Stein's old hand rested on the dog's head.

I didn't know Gertrude Stein. But she loved her dog as he loved her, and that's why I'm writing this, me who didn't know her.

(From the "La Femme Surréaliste" issue of *Obliques,* 1977)
Translated from the French by Myrna Bell Rochester

Maria Martins

One of the most amazing modern sculptors, Maria Martins—generally known simply as Maria—was born in Campanha, Brazil, in 1900. After studying in Paris and Rio de Janeiro, she lived briefly in Ecuador, Holland, and Denmark. She became a Brazilian diplomat in 1934 and studied philosophy with D. T. Suzuki at the University of Kyoto. In New

York in 1943 she met André Breton and other surrealists in exile, collaborated on the journal *VVV*, and worked at Stanley William Hayter's Atelier 17. In 1947 Breton celebrated her sculpture in his preface to a catalog of her solo show at the Julien Levy Gallery in New York, asserting that "Maria owes nothing to the sculpture of the past or the present—she is far too sure, for that, of the *original* rhythm which is increasingly lacking in modern sculpture; she is prodigal with what the Amazon has given her—the overwhelming abundance of life" (the complete text is included in his *Surrealism and Painting* [1965]). She took part in International Surrealist Exhibitions in Paris (1947 and 1959–1960), New York (1960–1961), and São Paulo (1967). She died in Rio de Janeiro in 1973.

Published here are excerpts from a poem she wrote in New York in 1946 for her show at the Valentine Gallery, and an abridged version of an untitled message (written by Martins on behalf of a group of artists), which Congressman Jacob Javits of New York read into the U.S. *Congressional Record* on 18 June 1947 (Vol. 93, Part 12, Appendix, A2943).

I AM THE TROPICAL NIGHT'S HIGH NOON

I am the tropical night's high noon
All is calm and splendor, not a leaf stirs
No fault line breaks the day's eternity
Agonizing and mute
thick with bird colors and flower aromas
languor weaves the same dream
Jaguar himself slouches sweetly surrendered to the drunkenness of sleep
Only a cicada's rapid trance
pierces the tepid density of mellow silence

Suddenly space grows heavy
All atremble and wild-eyed the forest awakens
in a shiver of expectation and a surge of joy
A breath of madness rises here
Wind soars to a proud frenzy
wind singing and rattling
the great song of energy and desire
Howling growling overflowing desperate wind
in a breathless uproar
cries its monstrous love

Translated from the French by Rachel Blackwell

ART, LIBERATION, AND PEACE

My message is a confession of faith in a world of freedom in which the manifold differences of race, nationalities, religions, social conditions, and opinions have full expression on the basis of free interchange. Such a world of diversified aspects, which play their adequate part without restrictions of preconceptions, privileges, or hatreds is a world of rich creative activity, not of destructive conflicts. It is our world—the world of art—for which and in which every being is good and therefore beautiful.

First of all, contrary to common belief, art is not an appeal to delicate sentiments only; it does not request from man the best in man only; but it is an appeal to all the emotions, deep and superficial, delicate and strong, measured and unruled; it is a mobilization of all in man.

As such an absorption of everything in man—his spirit and his body, his virtues and his passions, his patience and his violence, his diligence and his intuitions—as such a universal demand upon man, it is the best program and guaranty of peace, because art is directed to creation, not to destruction; to achievement, not to domination; to expression, not to elimination; to construction and integration, not to dissociation and oppression. . . .

In the second place, art is a liberation, not only for the artist, but for the admirer of art, the simple observer of artistic realizations.

To a certain extent, the contemplation of a work of art is a second creation; the sculpture, the oil painting, the song as they are touched or seen or heard impress the individual soul according to each individual nature, each individual sentiment, each individual transient mood.

Each one, educated or not to art, recreates art and by so doing grows to a higher level of human life, the level of creation. . . .

Now liberation is synonymous with peace, not a stagnant peace, not a transitory peace, but a dynamic peace. It is a wrong belief, too frequently shared, to think that only war is dynamic. There is a dynamic peace, a creative peace, the peace through art.

It was by destruction of works of art, the so-called *Auto-da-fé,* the bonfires of German-Jewish literary works as of those of a Heine, that Hitler began his nihilistic drive of conquest, domination, and destruction. Art is liberation and construction; it is by art that we must rebuild this shattered world.

What I mean is not art in the narrow sense; such narrow sense of art is a convenient example, a magnificent point of reference, a superior result of art.

What I mean is art in its universal sense, the artistic spirit, the education to art, the aesthetic contemplation, the natural inclination to regard everything in its peculiar aspect to beauty. . . .

After all, beauty is not only in everything but belongs to the essence of everything; beauty is transcendental.

In the third place, art is immortal, it is in a continuous process of renewal. I wish to emphasize that political regimes die, statesmen's combinations disintegrate, social theories shift from one extreme of individualism to the other extreme of totalitarianism.

Art is eternal not in its styles, not in its schools, not in its technique, not in its conceptions, nor in its subjects, but in its ideal, in its definition, in its aims, in its consequences. Art is the most solid basis of peace.

Helen Phillips

Born in Fresno, California in 1913, sculptor Helen Elizabeth Phillips was a graduate of the California School of Fine Arts, where she later taught. In 1939 she married Stanley William Hayter in Paris, and lived and worked with him for extended periods in Paris, London, San Francisco, New York, Philadelphia, and Chicago. She was one of eight artists—the others were Arshile Gorky, Gerome Kamrowski, David Hare, Wifredo Lam, Matta, Isamu Noguchi, and Jeanne Reynal—who took part in the last collective manifestation of the surrealist exiles' group in New York during World War II: the "Bloodflames 1947" exhibition organized by Nicolas Calas. Her work was also included in the "Abstract and Surrealist American Art" exhibition at the Art Institute of Chicago (1947–1948). Long recognized as one of the foremost sculptors of her time, Helen Phillips died in New York in 1995.

The statement reprinted here appeared in a symposium, "14 Sculptors Speak," in *The Tiger's Eye* no. 4 in June 1948. (*The Tiger's Eye* was an eclectic review of art and literature published in Westport, Connecticut; work by many surrealists—including Arp, Gorky, Tanguy, Matta, Toyen, Kamrowski, Lamantia, Ernst, Sage, and Masson—appeared in its pages.)

THE IMAGE: RECOGNITION OF A MOMENT

In the face of opposition, in the midst of insecurity, among conflicting directions and ideas, one grasps an image.

And although it is denied even by oneself, it remains.

Ignored, it asserts itself. Rejected, it camouflages itself and returns. Condemned, it becomes an obsession.

It is the recognition of a moment, a moment that recurs again and many times with different faces.

The image is my stability. The moment there is the evidence of touch and sight that the image exists, it becomes another planet in an unshakable solar system and the world can safely revolve on its axis.

Vera Hérold

One of the "live wires" of surrealism in the immediate post–World War II years, France Binard married Romanian painter Jacques Hérold, who had been active in surrealism since the mid-1930s. As Vera Hérold she coedited the Paris group's first postwar periodical—the newspaper-format journal, *Néon* (1948)—in the third issue of which her poem, "The Big L," was published (May 1948). Later that year she left the group in the wake of a complex dispute that resulted in the expulsion of Victor Brauner and several young poets who were close to him. Curiously, one of the accusations against this faction, with which Vera Hérold was identified, was its alleged apolitical dandyism. In 1960, however, Vera Hérold—who had resumed the name France Binard—turned out to be an important figure in the "Jeanson Ring": activist partisans of the Algerian National Liberation Front in France. For her services in this revolutionary cause, France Binard served several years in prison. After her release she moved to Algeria and became a citizen of that country. I have not succeeded in locating any information regarding her later life.

THE BIG L

The axis around which the many-centered spiral unwinds is only the projection of a point L situated at the heart of the Earth's nucleus; its virtual image is the North Star.

All the centers move in a perpetual vortex.

And when they collide, the universe will expand. The curve will snap, cities will collapse and a new star will appear in the north as the Earth's crust explodes under pressure from the Big L.

Then we shall see Woman, liberated by this upheaval, lift all inhibitions.

Love *will be.*

And in one spasm, all tongues will be untied.

Translated from the French by Guy Ducornet

Gisèle Prassinos

PEPPERMINT TOWER IN PRAISE OF GREEDY LITTLE GIRLS

Homage to Hans Bellmer

I know that my sister smells of banana. Her long hair rubbed against my nose, exudes an ordinary smell, like wasted dessert: but when she looks over to me and her mouth half opens in a smile, this new scent feels so good that I want to bite her lips and her tongue.

Underneath, there is something that crackles and carries one away.

My sister is about to fall asleep: I grab her pointed arms and I fold them over her eyes so that the lost light shuts them tight. But she keeps smiling triumphantly, and the scent rises, and it is so strong that I suddenly feel like killing her in order to steal it.

I have thrust my knife through her pretty shirt; her hands are white and cold under the sheets. Mine are too much alive; they have no strength. But in her palm I see a tiny fruit, studded with pink shiny fragments which I melt between my fingers.

(From *Hans Bellmer, 1934–1950*, Paris, 1950)
Translated from the French by Guy Ducornet

Ithell Colquhoun

THE MANTIC STAIN: SURREALISM AND AUTOMATISM

The principle used in many processes of surrealist painting is to make a stain—by chance, or automatically, as we say, and then to look into it and see what forms it suggests to our imagination; and finally to develop these forms into a completed work of art. The method is at least as old as Leonardo da Vinci—we all know the story of his gazing at the stains of damp in an ancient wall and seeing the suggestion of the mountains, ravines, and fantastic foliage of a dream landscape. And it seems too that in distant China there are sculptors who cut and polish stone in a special way so as to show to best advantage its natural veining, and at times to interpret this pattern in forms carved according to hints it gives to the artist's vision. The homely "pictures in the fire," or the cloud-images of childhood's visionary stare belong to the same faculty in embryo.

Here and today, the development of the initial stain may proceed along the line of a complete abstraction—that is to say, the resulting shapes may not recall directly anything seen in external nature; or, on the other hand, they may suggest natural objects which can be organized and intensified into a design; or again they may bring up from a world of dreams—that fantastic life of which so many of us are hardly aware in our waking consciousness—a treasury of symbolic scenes or "mind-pictures." In this way, an almost inexhaustible flow of inspiration can be tapped, and a few simple blobs of color, or patches of light and dark, can point the way to the finished picture.

Perhaps the most interesting and significant thing about all these processes is the fact that in spite of the many vagaries of hazard, each tends to produce its own characteristic forms and suggests its own peculiar themes. For example, *decalcomania* tends toward landscapes, with foliage, marine morphology, feathers, and reptilian scales; *fumage* to semihuman figures or "personages," larvae or "astral" forms; and *parsemage* often combines the two.

All these automatic processes we will describe shortly, but for the moment let us note that all are closely dependent on the unconscious mood of the operator; for, if a number of experiments in a single process are undertaken on one day, a great similarity of form will be noticeable throughout; while the same operator experimenting with the same process on another day will produce a quite different series of forms, though these latter will be linked to one another by a "family likeness" of their own. It is for this reason that I feel these stains to have a "mantic" or divinatory quality, which may in some sort be compared with the practices of clairvoyants, who use ink-splashes, sand, pins flung together by chance, and the irregular patterns left by tea leaves and coffee grounds to release the contents of the unconscious. The famous crystal globe or "scrying-glass" has approximately the same function. And all have an august ancestry in that they are traceably allied to the "great work" of alchemy. In many fascinating psychological studies Jung has shown how the alchemist would release the contents of his own subliminal fantasy by intently watching the contents of the alembic.

An Open Entrance to the Closed Palace of the King, by Eirenaeus Philalethes, a seventeenth-century alchemist says: "The Reign of the Moon lasts just three weeks, but before it closes, the substance exhibits a great variety of forms: it will become liquid and again coagulate a hundred times a day; sometimes it will present the appearance of fish eyes and then again of tiny silver trees, with twigs and leaves. Whenever you look at it you will have cause for astonishment, particularly when you see it all divided into beautiful but very minute grains of silver, like the rays of the sun."

This is nothing less than "projection," a term frequently used in alchemical literature, and one which might be adopted to describe the imaginative interpretation of a "mantic stain." Indeed, I wonder whether we may not take this analogy from our medieval inheritance still further and seek a correspondence between the four elements of earth, air, fire, and water, and some of our automatisms. "Fire" can easily be related to *fumage* with the candle flame as its chief agent; "water" to those processes which employ this element, mainly *écrémage* and its derivatives; "earth" to *decalcomania* with its basis of thick and solid impasto; and air to certain techniques by which light dusty or powdered material is blown or fanned and allowed to settle by hazard on a smooth surface. We can go even further than this and relate the varieties of *shut-eye* drawings to "darkness," while we assign Man Ray's *rayograms* and other automatisms connected with photography, to "light."

To return to our own day, affinities may also be noticed with the Rorschach method, a means of diagnosis recently evolved by the Swiss psychologist. It consists in a series of sheets marked with irregular particles of color, at which the patient is asked to look and then say what each suggests to him. Many practitioners are finding that the individual answers provide a useful preliminary guide to each "case."

There is no doubt that automatism can be used with stimulating effect in the teaching of art, both for children and adults. The "play" aspect of it appeals to children, as I know from my own experience in schools. And it is easy to see that, to a beginner of whatever age, the fact that he is faced not with a blank white rectangle which he must somehow cover effectively but with a suggestive chiaroscuro, or color combination with potentialities, will itself tend to give him confidence. And that self-confidence is the first step toward revealing the mind's profounder imaginative riches.

In recent years it is chiefly to the adherents of the Surrealist Movement that we owe the discovery of automatic processes. One of these automatisms, that called *decalcomania*, was invented by the painter Oscar Dominguez; though the name was modish in early Victorian times, and occurs in an old family chronicle describing the decoration of furniture by "transfer" patterns. *Décalquer* is, of course, "to trace," and refers to the double image which is "traced" by pressure.

I cannot do better than quote the directions given by André Breton on the modern procedure. He calls these directions: "How a window may be opened at will on the loveliest landscape of this and other worlds":

> With a thick brush, spread black gouache on a sheet of shiny paper, diluting the paint here and there with water. Cover it at once with a similar sheet and press them together fairly hard with the hand. Then, by the upper edge, slowly lift this second sheet . . . ready to reapply it and lift it again; repeat until it is almost dry. What you have before you is perhaps only the old paranoiac wall of da Vinci, but it is this wall *carried to its own perfection.* In fact, if you then entitle the image thus obtained according to what you discover in it after looking at it from a little distance, you may be certain that you have expressed yourself in the most personal and valuable way.

Breton here does not deal with any possible *development* of the automatic image beyond conveying the possibility of this by an imaginative title. Several well-known painters, however, in particular Max Ernst, have carried the process beyond the automatic stage, using it as an inspirational basis. Again, Breton suggests using as a medium black gouache; but oil color in black, black and white, or several colors, or else black and colored inks, may be used in the same way with equally striking effects.

In the case of oil color, the pigment may be laid on prepared canvas or board, and must be diluted here and there with some appropriate medium. Inks, of course, cannot be diluted unless they are of the nonwaterproof kind, and so a variety of textures, which is the most characteristic beauty of *decalcomania,* must be obtained merely by varying the *quantity* of the ink used in different areas.

Another painter who worked with the Surrealist Movement, Wolfgang Paalen, was the inventor of a similar process (*Fumage*) which gives very lovely results. By this, the paper or board is held horizontally just above the flame of the candle, and passed more or less rapidly to and fro without conscious direction. The resultant smoky trace is then sprayed with fixative like a charcoal drawing to prevent smudging, while the operator gazes into it to see what themes will emerge. The chosen forms are then stressed, either in ink, watercolor or oil, and the irrelevant patches painted over with a background, or otherwise erased.

Frottage is simply "rubbing" that is, the placing of canvas or paper over an uneven surface—stone, wood-graining, the thick weave of a carpet, for instance—and passing over charcoal, chalk, carbon pencil, or paint, on the principle of taking a brass rubbing. The resultant marking is, of course, looked into in the usual way. Max Ernst has, besides working on *decalcomania,* made great use of *frottage* in his pictures, having first become aware of its possibilities while staring at the rough boards in the floor of his bedroom at a small country inn.

Écrémage is "skimming"; the method is to take a bowl of water and cover the water surface with some oily substance—oil paint, or an ink with an oily base—and to pass a board or stiff piece of paper just below the surface. This is then lifted out of the water, skimming off the oil while the water drains away. ("Marbling" for end-papers is produced in a very similar manner). A variant of this method, developed by myself and named *parsemage,* that is "scattering," is to sprinkle powdered charcoal or dust of colored chalk on the water surface; this, of course, yields a very different type of stain from that left by the trace of oil.

Recently a number of experiments have been made by members of a surrealist group in Bucharest, and some interesting booklets have reached me from them. One of their automatisms is to search out and mark with a tiny dot any slight spot, irregularity, or change of color in the surface of a blank piece of paper. The dots are then connected by lines, and the resulting forms may be interpreted by the induced "vision," as before described. Our Romanian friends, however, seem to have a certain distrust of interpreting the stain and prefer to leave the automatism in its pristine state, simply entitling it as Breton recommends.

(From *Enquiry,* London: October–November, 1949)

Dorothea Tanning

Born of Swedish parents in Galesburg, Illinois, in 1912, Dorothea Tanning attended art school in Chicago before moving to New York in the 1930s. The 1936 "Fantastic Art, Dada and Surrealism" show at the Museum of Modern Art sparked her interest in surrealism. Not until 1942, however, as an exhibitor in Peggy Guggenheim's "31 Women" show, did she actually meet participants in the Surrealist Movement—among them Max Ernst, whom she married four years later. As writer as well as painter she collaborated on *VVV,* and she also took part in the International Surrealist Exhibition in Paris in 1947. Her first solo show was in New York in 1944. She and Ernst lived in Arizona for several years and moved to France in 1955. Best known as a painter, Tanning is also the author of two books: *The Abyss,* written in 1947 but unpublished until she brought it out herself in 1977, and an autobiography, *Birthday* (1986). She lives in New York.

"Legend" first appeared in Max Ernst's *At Eye Level and Paramyths,* the catalog of the "Max Ernst: 30 Years of His Work" exhibition in Beverly Hills in 1949.

LEGEND

A young sinner grew weary of Olympus. He went to the head of the stairs where the three graces sat knitting sweaters for their earthly sons. (Winter was at hand.) Each of them smiled secretly at the young sinner, each believing she was the only one whom he had provided with pleasant memories. But they wouldn't let him pass.

"It's a cruel place," said one. "How will you nourish yourself?"

"On destinies," he answered promptly. "Take the laughter of seven maidens, stir in several of the moonbeams that fall across their beds. Add the head of a procession, a few umbrella ribs and a tale of hilarious crime. Season it madly and serve on collection plates."

"But," said another, barring the way, "Where will you go?"

"To picnics," said he, making a perfect triple pirouette.

The third grace laid her knitting in her lap where it formed a pretty, medium-sized figleaf. She turned her eyes up to him and said softly, "What will you do?"

She looked so charming that for a moment the young sinner hesitated. Perhaps he wouldn't go after all. But he recovered himself and said:

"Please be advised that I will vaccinate the world with a desire for violent and perpetual astonishment. Disguised in my own presence, I will conduct a horde through the five aqueducts of knowledge, after which their guardians will ask the authorities for replacements. I will provoke prodigies. When I have built the torpid town, certain words will fall into disuse: eminent prominent peerless noble honorable lordly stately august princely majestic sacred and sublime. I will make rhapsodies from grains of sleep. I'll wrap up a manmaking hat and drop it in the mailbox. I'll hold a revolver up to nature. When professional critics lose themselves in the swamp I'll arrange a delegation of chimeras with their own language and their own secrets. As for the night, I will discover all its phases. And I will fall in love."

The three graces had been looking rather sleepy; but at the last words they opened their mouths in horror, then picked up their knitting and fled.

With his glittering blue eyes the young sinner sent lightning strokes after them—a parting gift. Then he ran down the steps, two at a time.

Nora Mitrani

Born in 1921 in Sofia, Bulgaria, of Spanish-Jewish and Italian parents, Nora Mitrani moved to Paris in her teens. A philosophy student at the Sorbonne, she completed a thesis on Malebranche and Maine de Biran. A Trotskyist during the war, she later frequented the anarchist milieu. For many years she worked at the Paris Center for Sociological Studies (directed by Georges Gurvitch).

She joined the Surrealist Group in 1947 and remained one of its most active militants and spokespersons until her death of cancer in 1961, shortly before her fortieth birthday. She collaborated on all of the group's periodicals in those years—*Néon, Médium, Le Surréalisme, même,* and *BIEF*—as well as several other collective publications, and she co-signed virtually every surrealist tract during those years.

In 1950 she contributed an important text, "Rose au coeur violet" [Violet-Hearted Rose], to the volume *Hans Bellmer, 1934–1950;* it included a series of anagrams (based on Mitrani's title) coauthored with Bellmer. She traveled to Portugal the same year, where she encountered Portuguese surrealist poet Alexandre O'Neill and the work of the great presurrealist, Fernando Pessoa, which she was among the first to introduce to France.

Mitrani's writings are not voluminous, but they cover a wide range: the Marquis de Sade, popular culture, Kierkegaard, film noir, and critical studies of technocracy, bureaucracy, and nuclear energy. Most of her contributions to surrealist publications were collected in 1988 under the title *Rose au coeur violet* (Paris: Terrain Vague), prefaced by Julien Gracq.

"Scandal With a Secret Face" appeared in the *Almanach Surréaliste du démi-siècle* (1950); "Blacker Than Black," in *Médium: Informations surréalistes* no. 4 (February 1953); "About Cats and Magnolias," in *Le Surréalisme, même* no. 1 (October 1956); "Poetry: Freedom of Being," introducing a letter of Fernando Pessoa's and several of his poems, in *Le Surréalisme, même* no. 2 (1957); "On Slaves, Suffragettes and the Whip," in *Le Surréalisme, même* no. 3 (1957); and the "Definitions" from the *Succinct Lexicon of Eroticism* included in the catalog of the International Surrealist Exhibition in Paris (1959).

SCANDAL WITH A SECRET FACE

If Truth burst forth absolutely naked, she would be beautiful without being terrifying; but, firstborn of the flame, a veil of smoke obscures her long, admirable body. For allowing itself to remain in shadow, the form of the body is even better divined; for Truth, the ambiguous veil is fatal shamelessness; its name, *scandal*.

When the thousandth night of love is still the first, the powers of destruction that each night veil the eyes of assassins and abused children clutch at the foundations of society to threaten and destroy them. But love, replacing outdated currency, will not have put back into circulation the one designed for uniquely passional ends. No, we must, above all, make love; and the house is not yet rebuilt: the same life goes on. The monsters of an unfinished thrust are resuscitated, ever more derisive, to chastise those who flouted them.

We told you so . . . Condemned to listen a thousand and one times to the hideous sentence are those who, however, loved one another courageously. Love dies for not having known, in place of a world masked in contradictory currents, how to construct its own totality, ruled by uniform laws of passion.

But bodies go on seeking one another and making love, as if the burning night were ignorant of morning despair. Every couple, with all its strength and for its own sake, plays the game of "as if" in its multiple forms, the "as if" of enchanted modesty, the "as if" of ignorance, the "as if" of commitment, and, leading all the others, the "as if" as salvation from cynicism. We try to circumscribe love within the infinitely narrow zone limited by fear, legality, sunrises.

Equivocal inscriptions on so many walls. Sincere? Yes. Full of modesty? Yes. But how sad the solitude, the separation sickness that guided them. Or then, lucid, already liberating, eroticism appears. Every man and every woman knows or desires, whether or not he or she wants to, erotic dazzlement and its cortege of bitter ecstasies and disavowed impossibilities. But very quickly the instant arrives in which the fatally despised, poor body appears touching and absurd, its dreams and childhood equally absurd. It would perhaps agree, to save me from loneliness, to re-enter, with me, the hermeticism of the same womb.

But if, beyond the occasional clasp of bodies, there were granted for each lover the autonomy of an independent, private life, not concerned by love, eroticism would be enriched by every one of the demands refused elsewhere. To survive, love would strive toward the destruction of a hostile, societal context, eroticism would rediscover the same elementary laws and the same lines of force, but their point of application would no longer be simply corporal. Eroticism would thus present itself as it really is: the transposition, upon the plane of the loving mechanics of bodies, of those gestures of revolt that from

Spain to China make children's faces look bad; eroticism swollen with black sun, laden with unrequited loves and nervous twitching.

Injustice, totalitarian exploitation, and debaucheries for adults, abominable.

Kicks and blows are not forgotten, however. Sexual crime becomes the triumphant and bitter revenge of that death instinct which, not capable of being carried out through legitimate channels, for the greatest good of freedom, recreates itself as Eros to attack the very origins of a life without freedom.

Since man carries evil in his heart, long live the magnificent evil that can destroy him, the passion of love, and the innumerable crimes it has generated.

(The Marquis de Sade, moreover, desired even more: "When the crime of love is no longer to the measure of our intensity, we could perhaps attack the sun, rob the universe of it, or use it ourselves to ignite the world—now, those would be true crimes." [*120 Days*])

Thus Sade handled wonderfully the most murderous weapon of his era. But, at the same time, he managed to not turn it into an antique weapon: it's the arrow sharpened this very night on gleams of hate and the desire to love the impossible love, arrow of poisonous light stubbornly aimed at a stubbornly maintained penumbra. Sexual life, whore of unutterable evil spells; there she is, illuminated as never before by a light whose icy whiteness is made up of the 120 colors of the human passions.

This new synthesis fits well enough, if we are to believe all the rehabilitative and dialectic Christianizing prefaces that have afflicted Sade's writings. His work has, for all that, lost none of its initial quality: it remains scandalous.

Scandalous for two concurrent reasons: the merciless revelation of amorous obsessions will certainly not stop troubling people of good conscience. But there's a second, still more merciless disclosure: Sade's universe is sadist for the same reason as man is, or further, human sadism evolves only as a function of nature's. Recall the final episode of *Justine or the Misfortunes of Virtue.* The pure Justine, rescued and coddled by her sister Juliette, will be struck down just as it seems her misfortunes are over, killed by a will whose mathematical perfidiousness has no common measure with man. The same type of frenetic current thus roams the world at every level and human nature becomes dehumanized to acquire attributes of invulnerability, mechanical steadiness, while the forces of nature take on human intentionality. Man is perhaps better than nature, in any case, nature is not better than he. That's a restful truth Sade would on occasion enjoy proving, and it's the most scandalous truth of all: it is decentralization. Any revealing of the still irradiated totality of the blackheads of revolt has earned the death penalty for whomever dared to undertake it. Every time a mind tried to destroy any type of centrism in the name of that totality, it's been accused, beaten, humiliated. This was the case with the iconoclasts of geocentrism, theocentrism, and anthropocentrism. We saw it when formal logic and its old identity principle were overcome, their dualism of values superseded by Einsteinian space and the polyvalent logic by which possibilities were installed within the very heart of the real, like a perpetual threat and source of magical charms.

We may formulate a law about scandal's very genesis. Scandal occurs every time a different principle, forever esteemed base and accursed, replaces the identity principle of logicians: that other principle is *analogy.*

Every science called accursed is based on the principle of analogy; witches and heretics were burned simply because they knew its secrets.

Nearer to us, if Hegel, Sade, or Marx seem, for various reasons, accursed thinkers, it's because, desacralized as it is, deprived of its passional coloration, the same occult principle underlies their work. Inscribed in the web of the real, no worldly force has yet succeeded in stifling it. For its content is too extraordinarily childlike: the same processes go on by analogy in the part as in the whole, in consciousness as in the object, in the human body as in the solar system.

But reason clings to the identity principle insofar as it is the basis of any sure discernment of risk-free exploration. Thus it plays a permanent role as safety barrier. Only, would it know how to struggle with the no less constant duplicity of the living being that never stops substituting for it its principle of false identity or analogy? There is in fact a constant conflict between the exterior object and a certain image—lived, already sensed, adored—of this same object. No identity is offered, it will need to be discovered by the analogy that would suddenly have materialized that precise joy of adequacy of the object to its image, of reality to its myth.

And the greater the conflict, the more audacious the analogies to be discovered, free and measureless. Some might judge them delirious, while, through them, others would be able to glimpse a certain equation so esoteric in its verbal essence as it is common in its lived expression, like vertigo, simultaneously fascinating and detestable, humiliated and princely:

Poetry = Science of Relationships

But there exist very few or no ready-made analogies. Consciousness is reduced to having to rediscover continually, in the night and fear of its dark burrow, the means of identification or transfer that could become an acceptable means of existence. The principle is always the same: to create for oneself, analogically, virtual centers by which one can augment or diminish the intensity of the real centers.

At the source of the most intensely black and scandalous works, we believe there exists this sort of passage from passion to action, a secret need for equilibrium, the urge to create an imaginary evil from which we may take pleasure within the excesses of intellectual passion, in order to cure ourselves of the real evil we're suffering.

Only when love can no longer tolerate itself, when love's desire has become exasperated and a grief to endure, does eroticism come into play. Then—since each action is hard for its object—then, the roads to cruelty open before it.

And, in the same way that the scandal-for-the-other always ends up becoming a scandal-for-the-self, love, always a scandal for the world, through eroticism, meets up with the convulsive and vertiginous face of scandal itself.

Translated from the French by Myrna Bell Rochester

"BLACKER THAN BLACK . . ."

Behold the smile of Koho, a young Toma chief from French Guinea, who is now back among his own people. He has abandoned his Western disguise to take part in an initiation ceremony, at the threshold of the Sacred Forest. During this rite, great powers will be conferred upon him. Who could decipher this smile?

At Koho's side, young girls with hard breasts, circumcised girls, contemplate the dance of the bird-men, the Ounilawogui, and the lunar procession of the little forest boys. Plastered with kaolin, only the heads of these marchers emerge from their yokes of lianas.

The Bakoulouni, or Guardian of the Forest, has promised the explorers Gaisseau and Fichter that they will be allowed, *next time,* to penetrate to the very heart of the shadows' mysteries. After them, perhaps we shall see what no white person has ever seen before. But just as they are, the three films they brought us, *Naloutai, Bassari* and *Forêt Sacrée,* have already shown us the innocent and frantic face—the solemn face—of Black Africa.

Translated from the French by Franklin Rosemont

ABOUT CATS AND MAGNOLIAS

Women dote on sugar and Chantilly lace, on the perfume of Bulgarian roses, and on candied chestnuts lavished upon them by all the reporters of all the fashion magazines in the world. They let themselves be cradled by holiday mists, nauseatingly sweet, out of which the Shetland and brocaded satin professionals create, just for them, an insulated, padded, vegetable and animal (but from those plants, from those timid animals from which perfumes are extracted) world, a world foreign to a soul devastated by the pain of being. "He no longer looks deep into your eyes when he loves you, he watches you pronounce 'magnolia,' and, then, something wonderful happens . . . Since the expression of the mouth is more important than that of the eyes, since the mouth has become the mirror of the soul . . .". Those are the words today's prince of fashion[1] uses to orchestrate the advertising for his new line of lipstick. It's clever, it flatters a woman, it settles and affirms her, she who is offered simultaneously as prey and trap, in the silky universe where her body undulates, joyful to be only a body giving pleasure. She is the advertising echo, the strategy, and the tactic born of these lines by Jean Paulhan: " . . . in them [women] everything is sex, up to and including the mind. Ceaselessly, they must be nourished, bathed, made up, and ceaselessly beaten."[2]

These women are the Marilyns and other sumptuous creatures of Technicolor movies, who dance sheathed in red velvet, their mouths and eyelids half open, wild, in the raw world of men. From all directions, waves of laughter and catcalls rise up, only to break on Marilyn's haunches. This unfurled laughter cannot create a protective mask, nor can it suppress the heart palpitations and the hateful excitement inspired by those for whom everything is sex. . . .

But excitement is preferable to gender confusion . . . That men of all eras reproach women for exuding that violent pink sexuality, as Paulhan does, seems almost entirely false. So that the excitement may remain contained and thoughts noble, unoccupied, for the serious life—the boys' life—they would prefer all women to slip into Marilyn's fascinating mold. To the proudest, to the most hard-bitten among women, they hold out the prospect of access to the masculine world, on the condition that they "behave like real women," with moist, swollen lips made up with that brilliant, sonorous rouge testifying to the male appetite for the female, the easy woman; her intense mouth is already half open . . . The glittering wild animal with sugar-candy nails has a soul: it can be inhaled, like perfume hidden in the warm hollow of a bodice.

Most often, women try to submit to this melting-erotic image of themselves. A great many convergent suggestions and desires urge them to do so. But they also know how to fend it off. In their own fashion. For women know well that the mouth cannot be the mirror of the soul, and that such images are invented by men who don't want women to become their sisters. And so they fight on, using weapons that remain feminine: from the makeup arsenal they choose kohl and bistre for their eyes, disdaining the provocation of lipstick. They make themselves evanescent, with immense eyes and pale lips, just like last summer's look ordained by today's cosmetics empress[3], just like—way before it was fashionable—the little existentialist girls at the Café Mabillon spontaneously made themselves up, finally, just the way that German boy, mad about Bach and Hegel, wanted his beloved to look.

They also knew very well, at least a few women knew, that, even more troubling than Marilyn, deep within man there lies coiled the age-old image of a noble, veiled woman, small-breasted, with narrow thighs. Proud but entirely devoted to love, inspiring the most brilliant adoration, her name is Queen Guinevere of the Knights of the Round Table; she is Dante's Beatrice and the Woman with the Unicorn in the Cluny tapestries; the art of the Primitives celebrates her, as does that of Jean Clouet and the painters of the Fontainebleau School. She dwells in the forests and sits beside springs; the reeds impart their secrets to her.

In winter 1954 fashion briefly attempted to resuscitate the Lady, adorning her with all the artifice of silks from the Orient and wild mink. Women, docile as ever, adopted the H line: with a double row of buttons, from mid-calf to the base of the neck, the head emerging alone like a precious corolla, they hid from watchful gazes and transformed themselves into haughty princesses.[4] It was once again their entirely feminine way of protecting themselves against the Marilyn inflation and of showing that there can be another way.

But since feminine beauty is in league with animal nature, even when we're in another realm, deep eyes, eyes of violated ardor, are, in women's language, called doe's eyes, cat's eyes, or gazelle's eyes . . . even though we've in fact suddenly traveled to another plane. As if woman wished to pierce through the cocoon in which they're trying to encase her and suddenly undertake a dialogue with the world. The woman-poet conceived by Rimbaud sometimes raises her eyelids, even if she isn't conscious of it, believing she's merely following the dictates of fashion.

For the surrealists, the loved one is, ambiguously and by turns, the cozy cocoon dweller and the one who lives in the space outside where the strident soul is crazed by its own lucidity; at times a creature too carnal, poisonous, a common rose, at others, Nadja, eyes rimmed in black, a magician, a sibyl, medium for the invisible.

Isn't it possible, though, that she will know, that she already knows, how to assume both roles at once? (In that case, the masculine categories will no longer be worth much, and men will get scared.)

The ambiguity of the female-woman is transferred to love, whose object—or whose accomplice—she remains.

Notes

1. Christian Dior

2. Jean Paulhan, preface to *The Story of O*

3. Elizabeth Arden

4. Once more, we are referring to Christian Dior, promoter of the H line, who on occasion knows how to capture and (luxuriously) translate women's dreams.

Translated from the French by Myrna Bell Rochester

POETRY, FREEDOM OF BEING

In Fernando Pessoa, the Portuguese poet, we recognize the pride of Hegel and the philosophers of nature, the exemplary attitude of the idealist thinker who knows that nothing is impossible for the human spirit, not even the fight of life. In this man, possessed but miraculously free (for he plays with those who possess him), the poetic act becomes verifiable in its genesis at the heart of the being who, willingly, breaks adrift in order to seek the fabulous adventure, always recommenced—to tear the Others from themselves, to dress them in living flesh and, projecting them into space, give them their chances. Thus the poet will be saved (or lost) as Rimbaud or Lautréamont were, when they ferociously unleashed the monsters that haunted them—and as Antonin Artaud failed to be when, wishing to tame them, he was their prisoner instead.

In a letter to his friend Adolfo Casais Monteiro, Fernando Pessoa explained the mental genesis of the characters who haunted him—his "heteronyms," as he called them. As it can be judged, each of them assumes his own poetic creation at his own risks.

Is it necessary to add to this presentation a last word which will not surprise those who burn frontiers in the domain of reality: Fernando Pessoa knew the sources and the snares of occult knowledge: in his work, the Rosicrucian symbol appears in filigree. In the same letter to Casais Monteiro, he agrees to offer a few clarifications, but, faithful to esoteric teachings, he asks his friend not to divulge in writing that last paragraph.

Translated from the French by Guy Ducornet

ON SLAVES, SUFFRAGETTES, AND THE WHIP

"Woman is a human being." I read that profound thought when I was in Royaumont, in a book called *The Phenomenology of Woman,* whose author I can't name, for my memory—for most obvious reasons—refused to record his name. Such a peremptory declaration should make no one smile, and women even less than others. After all, it's worth reflecting on, and perhaps since the first day of the world, it's remained to be proven that woman isn't a gazelle, or a poor little cat, or a birdbrain, or a beautiful plant, or a gate to Hell, or a fairy, or a perdition. "And above all, don't try to prove anything!" a few women will perhaps cry. "Don't betray us that way! What if we enjoy being called cats or fairies? We are never in a better position as when man, that human being, treats us like charming little animals that need to be dressed, caressed, and perfumed. If he suspected that we both belonged to the same species, then, in less time than it takes to say it, oof!—We'd be strapped into uniforms that hurt our breasts, we'd be booted, armed, marching across the gloomy deserts of Israel, in the China deserts, in the deserts of the U.S.S.R., yelling, uglified by patriotism and filth. Would you really like that? No, better not bother trying to prove it then. . . ."

We wouldn't have it any other way. Except that there exists a race of intelligent women who, every day, with their theses in philosophy, their brilliant actions and their juridical triumphs, work to demonstrate that they possess a brain and nerves built like men's. They sit up straight, they are self-affirming, they have hard muscles and lofty words, they are the founders of American charitable organizations and administrators of metallurgical enterprises,* they become engineers, expert logicians, judges, representatives, ministers of state, and above all, presidents of whatever can be presided over. They aren't necessarily ugly (to claim that this is so already proves the fundamental misogyny, not only of men, but also of pretty, slightly backward, women who defend themselves as they can against women who have qualities besides prettiness); however, they do display a certain offhandedness with regard to physical beauty alone. If one of these female presidents knows, in addition, the art of choosing a lip color that harmonizes with the color of her very beautiful eyes, she'd provoke endless stupor, and lizards would come to threaten those old, easily manipulated generalizations: in women the dissociation of beauty and

* Here is an outline of the career of Mme. Foinant, president of the Association of Women in Management: "Ironmaster, vice-president of the National Union of Hand Tooling, first woman elected to the Paris Chamber of Commerce, officer of the Légion d'Honneur . . . this electric individual works 18 hours a day, hops into her Dyna, hops out of it in a whirlwind to preside over banquets, her tongue well hung [*sic*] and her fork lively, where she reduces to silence three or four floored but smiling ministers of state, in front of hundreds and hundreds of women candymakers, notions merchants, directors of driving schools, and transportation entrepreneurs. . . ."

mental autonomy, with the explanation that the latter would serve only to compensate for the grief felt by a woman whose face lacks grace.

What? You'll allow yourself to be pretty too? But of course, look at that mouth, those flamenco dancer's ankles . . . The president and the ideologue may prove that they are human beings and thus work toward "destroying the infinite servitude of woman" and arrange it so that the all-knowing, abominable laughter of men freezes on their lips, but only on one condition: that they wear their beauty as a challenge and a scandal, like a knight with his sword, that they endlessly fascinate hearts and senses at the same time as they charm the mind.

But alas! In woman, the combination of extreme beauty and intellectual audacity still remains rather exceptional, for on the one hand, the clever man sees to it that the pretty woman cannot become liberated (let her thrive as his luxury slave, his beauty queen, his cover girl), and on the other, that the liberated woman cannot claim to be beautiful. The result, since the dawn of time, has been the infinite misfortune of being female, and today it is more so than ever to the extent that the poor things imagine liberation to be within reach, for their hands now hold ballots and checkbooks. They haven't understood or have badly interpreted Rimbaud's great hope; he desired them human but different, poets in a manner still unknown on earth: "Will her worlds of ideas differ from ours? She will discover strange, unfathomable things . . ." In reality, the most intelligent among them have found nothing that indicates a different night or a distant planet . . . They restrict themselves to adopting men's logic, their works and their fears, and they do not seem satisfied unless their writings make the reader forget their sex. Mlle. Suzanne Bachelard, asked why she had chosen such an arduous topic for her thesis defense ("Formal Logic and Transcendental Logic in the Thought of Husserl"), gave this strange answer: "For love of abstraction." I know nothing more pathetic than those words, to the extent that I may feel analogous desires, without, moreover, being able to surrender to them, since I do not share Mlle. Bachelard's mathematical genius.

Women still possess a way of proving to themselves that they have ceased to be slaves: that is, in the context of love, the concrete, symbolic, and literary use of the whip. Simone de Beauvoir claims for woman a position in lovemaking that no longer humiliates, no longer prone, at the mercy, but upright, in the man's way, dominating. Thanks to Simone de Beauvoir, the pleasure of a few women must surely have been soured, but she has without a doubt made some others smile.

For it perhaps would be better not to reveal that Madame d'O, in spite of her degradation, perhaps because of it, without it seeming necessary to venture so far however, is a happy, fulfilled woman; finally she owns her revenge, she throws her scandalous way of life back into men's faces. The woman as object, up to that point consenting, because it is her pleasure, horsewhipped, but this represents a way of aggression with respect to men: they no longer recognize one another.

One last important thing: in that position, the woman must not forget to remain fundamentally unsubmissive, fiercely protective of what she has not yet obtained: freedom of the mind.

Translated from the French by Myrna Bell Rochester

CONCUPISCENCE AND SCANDAL: DEFINITIONS FROM THE *SUCCINCT LEXICON OF EROTICISM*

Concupiscence: The root of a natural inclination which makes us crave the pleasure of sensory experience, above all, carnal pleasure. To fondle and possess a body conjures the burning provoked by its image. The church forbids both the fire and the cure.

Scandal: The sudden provocative unveiling of what conventional morality tolerates camouflaged: the so-called "private" parts, the exploitation of man by man, the fact of torture but also the unbearable shine of someone out of sync with his environment.

Translated from the French by Rikki Ducornet

Valentine Penrose

I DREAM

I dream. Youth is beyond the rain she arrives.
But walking the long-drawn embankments
Made to fly a hundred times in love on skimming water you shall speak
to me.
Put back the dream you wake me only you.

Under the eaves swallows glitter

(From *Dons des Feminines,* 1951)
Translated from the French by Roy Edwards

Valentine Penrose, collage, 1951. From *Dons des Feminines*.
Courtesy of M. G. Devise.

BEAUTIFUL OR UGLY IT DOESN'T MATTER

Beautiful or ugly it doesn't matter.
In their nightgowns of comforting sweat
Forearms over eyes if travail has left even that strength
That thousandfold elegance. Most delicate hand
And eyes made naked by their precious inheritance of weasels' blood.

(From *Dons des Feminines,* 1951)
Translated from the French by Roy Edwards

Jacqueline Johnson

TAKING A SIGHT 1951

The innocent and beautiful creatures of air and earth and water seem to us, in their slow changes, to have their principle of growth within their substance, and without division live, while we, who are humans, have to seek out the form of our being, that we must imagine, without being able to conceive the whole, or put terms to it. We strain toward it in various images. We are hot, we are cold, we have an intuition. We are not able to *see* what we know and that yet surpasses us, anywhere in the world until we have made the image of it. And then vision can grow. Yet in this way possessing only what is past and already realized. For there is in back of our heads, in back of our eyes, the great form. Beyond the edge of the known, beyond the corner where the mirror stops, there is the *openness.* And this openness invites us always toward a new unity of being, toward the unknown beginning to be known, out of which action finds again and again its proportion and its justness.

This openness invites us, at its simplest, as the objects of nature invite us (the crane leans forward gray on the water; its breast feathers touch the water; the displaced center for longing joins me to it), objects whose magic is in the extent to which, beyond any use, they can offer pleasure its disponibility, its perspectives of invention, its water that can run uphill; to the extent that they offer the direction of the unknown wish, can offer on the other side, a base for the sudden arches of imagination discovering what we fear, or want, or know, discovering the forms of its freedom.

It is as though vision, acting for the other senses and presenting to us what is distant, what we cannot touch or taste or reach, has given us a pattern of a different fulfillment. As though the sight of distant objects, of a whole horizon stretching around and far from us, has in it mystery which we have an idea of surprising, by what is present to the inner eye. And in doing so, of becoming some quite different thing, like coming out of the cave into the light. Always we have the intention of metamorphosis. And to the extent that the world is beyond our grasp forever, it is poetry. Out of it from the beginning men have made new things, acts, truths. As we will do forever. *For more life.*

For the image, in the largest sense, has given us a vocabulary of thought and feeling. We have grown by living its form that is inner and outer at once, of the mind and of the senses, displacing in itself some part of the living center of being that goes into its form and is revealed for the first time. The greatest images, of consciousness and of conscience, have stretched us as a deer swallowed whole stretches the snake. They have become our substance, they have created us.

The election of images is the election of love, by which we find outside ourselves some part of the innermost myth whose elaboration has been the secret web of being and of all our acts in what they had of fierce participation, of purity, of claiming what was our own; that myth of memory, desire, and dream that gives us all our value, by which we surpass ourselves. Myth which is yet not clearly a man's own, nor clearly bounded by his knowing or his life, having a further boundary in lives around us, and past and to come; like the sculptures of New Hebrides in which reside for a time, indefinitely mingled, the power of the mythological ancestor, of the grandfather, and of the man himself who made it, becoming his own child. We are not separate, we create each other. And it is here the responsibility begins that is rooted in what gives value to life.

• • •

When I say images, I mean too those seminal forms by which all the factors that play upon groups of men are brought into syntheses by mind; seminal forms that in objects and creative of objects, speak of relations between man and what eternally is, speak of meanings. All that we know of cultures and of civilizations tells us they depend on such seminal forms, that coming out of a way of life, mark that way of life, and are seen pervasively, in the eyes, in the gestures, in the walk, in all the objects of use and adornment; marking from the center the variations and inventions of a people as of a person, so that each one, unique, is what it is and not other than it is. This perhaps is the real history.

When the symbol of a magic act becomes meaningful for us, apart from its purpose, which may be unknown, such a symbol is a record of an enduring relation between mind and nature; in it magic is part of the greatest magic we know: communication of experience.

• • •

In 1924 the *Manifesto of Surrealism* crystallized what had been in the air since the end of the First World War and touched the main current of sensibility of our time with what it carries from the poetic discoveries of the past. The manifesto turned around the method of automatism, defined as "pure psychic automatism, thought's dictation without conscious, aesthetic, or moral control." The whole effort was to provoke the inner murmur, and Breton stands like a signal man at night, signaling the passage of a great lighted train, the passive life of the intelligence.

After all the shock and the controversy we can see now the admirable relevance this theory and this method had to the problem of painting. When Picasso started the adventure of cubism, there was immediate recognition of the new direction, but it bogged down. It bogged down because the imagination was held not only by habits of visual organization but by conventions as to conception, as to the extent and limits of experience that could be brought into the field of consciousness for use. The open sea was uncharted.

• • •

Something should be said of the wider aspects of the growth in sensibility for which we take the discoveries of Rimbaud and of cubism as signposts. Why was it that certain men, just before the First World War and just after it, widely separated, whose interest lay in making discoveries which would be for contemporary consciousness crystallization points, were led into the investigation of what Dada called instinct and chance?

What widening desire of the mind brings at this time—each one so precious, so indispensable an answer to still undefined need, and all so doubtfully united under the sign of the aesthetic—works as different as those of Picasso, Picabia, Rousseau, Chirico, Duchamp, Ernst, Arp?

The quite imaginary point at which their work intersects is on the borderlines, no longer as clear as they had been, of those questions which radiate out morally and aesthetically from a central problem of orientation in a reality which physics, biochemistry, and psychology were revolutionizing conceptually, which war, technology, and capitalist decay were altering economically and socially—at a moment when social theory had begun to lay its hand on future and past, when philosophy was standing as well as it could with one foot in the objective and the other in the subjective. The question was, indeed, *that of reality itself.*

The rift in reality which cubism had made, widened by futurism, began to show streaks of a sky unknown before, an unimagined freedom. Dropping torn papers like Arp, signing ready-mades like Duchamp, pasting together incongruous images like Ernst, painting visions like Chirico, the next steps were taken; they discovered the extensibility of the interpretative powers of the mind, the synthesizing leap which can, on occasion, lift into new realms, just as Jack climbed the beanstalk from the known into the unknown. They were engaged in making traps, or making molds wherein the newly discovered current of the imagination might flow and come to know itself. Everything was permitted except what had been seen before.

• • •

The whole modern era is marked, in painting as in poetry, by a shift of interest from sentiment, from the self as actor to the self as theater of action; and the real message is a transformation of reality by a transformation of our awareness. . . .

The integrity of that which appears before the inner eye, in the moment of creation, at what one must regard as supreme moments, marked unmistakably by wonder, has ordained its own autonomous state. The straining to express personal emotion or opinion, as such, by the conscious imposition of interpretation and reference, themselves belonging to a doubtful analytical order, is to import meanings into art that are relevant to propaganda or protest or private document, but not to poetry, at this time our purest need, the gauge of our best freedom in an uncertain future. This means that art is not the proper field for the exposition, in a restrictive sense, of certain immediate problems, and these of the most crucial. It does not take the place of action, although it is an action.

Subjectivity, since Baudelaire described the emergence of a pure art which was to create a subjective magic containing at once the object and the subject, has evolved consistently in a direction which was to be foreseen even in the beginning. As the subject has become more internal, subjectivity has become more impersonal. Our life draws through us the thread of the world and of the dream inextricably mingled; and the insight which can illumine all that our senses perceive and our minds reflect on, the atmosphere in which, at our best, we live and breathe, is a selfless passion. That is to say that at a certain moment what unfolds within us seems no more our own than what constantly unfolds before our open eyes.

New imaginative constructions in the language of paint are now possible. Poetic vision has freed itself as well as the eyes, again the visual terms of the painter's medium may unite with the visionary, and the conscious forming powers open to an inwardness unlimited in invention.

Modern art turns toward those meanings by which we are *another dimension of the Earth*. It is the hidden door which has been there always. It has nothing to do with optimism, it has nothing to do with pessimism. The place on which it opens, the planet that swims into view, will never be completely discovered, never fully explored, never exploited.

(From *Dynaton 1951*)

Alice Rahon

PAINTER AND MAGICIAN

In earliest times painting was magical; it was the key to the invisible. In those days the value of a work lay in its powers of conjuration, a power that talent alone could not achieve. Like the shaman, the sibyl, and the wizard, the painter had to make himself humble, so that he could share in the manifestation of spirits and forms. The rhythm of our life today denies the primordial principle of painting: conceived in contemplation, the emotional content of of the picture cannot be perceived without contemplation.

The invisible speaks to us, and the world it paints takes the form of apparitions; it awakens in each of us that yearning for the marvelous and shows us the way back to it—the way that is the great conquest of childhood, and which is lost to us with the rational concepts of education.

Perhaps we have seen the Emerald City in some faraway dream that belongs to the common emotional fund of man. Entering by the gate of the Seven Colors, we travel along the Rainbow.

(From the catalog, *Alice Rahon*, Willard Gallery, New York, 1951)

Jacqueline Senard

Young, brilliant, vigorous, and incidentally a good piano-player, Jacqueline Senard joined the Surrealist Group in Paris around 1949 and for several years was one of its quickening forces. Old-timers recall that she arrived at Surrealist Group meetings on her motor scooter.

A social worker and, according to some reports, openly feminist, Senard was instrumental in arranging the regular surrealist collaboration on the anarchist paper, *Le Libertaire,* in 1951–1952. For a time she hosted a radio show on which she related surrealism to problems of daily life. Moreover, as her "Cat = Clover" indicates, Senard's surrealism had a strong ecological dimension. As José Pierre emphasized in his introduction to *Surréalisme et anarchie,* this article is surely "one of the major results of the surrealists' collaboration on *Le Libertaire.*"

Senard was a longtime companion of the surrealist poet and sculptor Jean-Pierre Duprey, whose suicide in 1959 was a shattering experience for her from which she never recovered. She died in the 1960s.

Both articles published here are from the "Surrealist Ticket" columns in *Le Libertaire* in 1952: the first from the issue of 18 January, and the second from the issue of 25 May. The poem, "Polar," appeared in the catalog of a Jean-Pierre Duprey exhibition.

REASON AND SAFETY FACTORS*

The event that has most marked the development of society in modern times is, without a doubt, the birth of what is commonly known as Cartesianism.

As faith's heaven became ever darker, Cartesianism reawakened the divine spark that had for centuries gleamed peacefully behind the human brow. Like the celestial spirit, it blew in its own right, suddenly relighting the spark, inciting the creature to rise up against its creator, urging it to seek its own path alone, beyond the divine.

---

* A figure, usually between 5 and 10, by which the result of abstract calculations must be multiplied when one begins to use a certain material. For example: When calculating the building of a floor, one determines the section of the supporting planks by supposing that the floor will need to support a load 8 or 10 times greater than the planned upper load limit. Thus, 8 or 10 are the safety factors.

And yet, for a while longer, man tempered his new faith with the humanism that had been revived during the Renaissance; but soon, claiming the absolute, starving for truth, he became so enthralled with his own reason that he recreated the divine in it and made of it his new heaven.

Later, the Scientists, larded with systems, began to proliferate and undertook to put the globe—nay, the entire Universe—into equations. As long as they applied mathematics to material points gravitating in space, they did all right for themselves. It was a mere matter of abstraction and movement, and the initial results could only confirm the notion they had invented concerning the preeminence of intelligence. So easily did it penetrate the secrets of the cosmic world that they had no doubt that it would one day guide man upon the path to the One and Only. But as soon as they obliged mathematics to come down from heaven to earth and tried to mingle it with the material objects they thought they knew well since they worked with them every day, nothing of the absolute, no certainty remained. For all that, they did not stop tracing their diagrams. They continued doing their calculations with equal precision. They were, however, forced to introduce the safety factor, that awkward artifice that robbed their work of its indisputable character of logical certainty where intelligence finds delight and where it can admire its own glory.

The Greeks had not let themselves be taken in. For them, Mathematics was a type of game, a showy intellectual exercise whose rigid absoluteness confounded them. They noticed early on that the meeting between mathematics and matter completely destroyed the exactitude of the former. As long as that exact science went round and round in their brains, it remained exact; but as soon as it ventured several steps out, it turned into an exiled goddess floundering around among earthly realities.

After practicing Cartesianism for some time, the "intellectual elite" quickly came to the same conclusion and convinced itself that reasoning only attains perfection when the objects to which it applies itself have dissipated in the thin smoke of abstraction; in other words, when it has been emptied of all content. It becomes obvious that mathematical science, in particular, could not be considered an exact science unless there existed, somewhere, a world without dimension nor weight, that is, a world where even the idea of such a science would be simply unthinkable.

But, while the intellectual elite was conducting this experiment, Cartesian faith, thanks to popularization, had gained disciples within the deep strata where neither dilettantism nor skepticism is appropriate. Anxious to fill the void left in their souls by the fall of the divine, thirsting for belief, these individuals took the thing very seriously. Technicians were transformed into technocrats and spread themselves throughout the world. With the unconsidered zeal of neophytes, they undertook to turn the universe upside-down. (Some began to think that they were succeeding all too well.) If god had created a praiseworthy piece of work when he made the celestial bodies revolve in space, it appeared, when one studied the earth carefully, that, in the details, his creations were no longer marked with the divine seal of intelligence; rather, they more resembled the crude work of some bungler. Order needed to be reestablished.

It was then that Sufficiency, Stupidity, Presumption, and Inconsequence began, for their part, to forge systems and took the globe as their first experimental field. They noticed that each man could be counted as an individual unit and remain so in the calculations. Moreover, since, according to numerous philosophers, he is not only made of matter but also of intelligence, it was noticed that, as far as he was concerned, one could largely reduce the safety factor, if only he would expend some energy in trying to understand what was expected of him.

Thus, the abstractors set to work with great enthusiasm. To obliterate from human nature anything that could distort the calculations, they resorted to a very old object—the Procrustean bed—and, at the same time and once again, they recognized that judicious use of the stake helped greatly to reduce those annoying coefficients.

Since they were building a perfect construction, it was important to plan everything ahead, to provide for all contingencies. According to many philosophers, the creator, in his designs, had determined to reserve for humankind a certain area where he forbade himself to interfere: freedom. That was indisputably a mistake: man makes such bad use of this freedom that he is in continual danger of damnation. What is more, determinism, son of pure reason, and, consequently, son of heaven, excludes freedom. Thus it was absurd, on god's part, to reserve free will for man. Therefore, there is no room for freedom in a rational organization of Society.

Since everything was thus prepared and put into place, one could, from that point, proceed without any interference with the construction of a political and social system that was to bring to humanity, with the same absolute certainty as one plus one makes two, Liberation, and, above all, Safety and Happiness.

Translated from the French by Myrna Bell Rochester

CAT = CLOVER

If, on a March night, some tyrant, prevented from sleeping by the yowling of cats, had decreed their execution, the result would have been a less abundant harvest of clover; and it isn't likely that there would have been a Darwin then to explain to the tyrant with what subtle strand, in this case, the effect was linked to the cause.

It was indeed Darwin who noticed that the presence of cats affected the abundance of clover, and this is how: In the absence of cats, field mice proliferated; now, field mice love to eat bumblebees; and bumblebees fertilize pistils when they carry pollen from flower to flower. Therefore, no cats = no bumblebees = no clover.

The use of vaccines, prophylactic measures, and powerful medications has considerably reduced the death rate, and now it can be seen that the spread of polio is probably due to the fact that, protected from numerous relatively benign illnesses, the organism, unused to struggle and stripped of certain microbes, is unable to resist the one whose germs it carries in their latent form.

Thus it is that if we consider the constructions that mark the road to knowledge, and that—falsely—appear to grow in size as they approach us, we may ask ourselves what they have brought to humankind after all, and if we ought not fear that some force of unknown origin might not burst forth to destroy its barely finished edifices. We see this in certain species of fish, which, having proliferated unusually, are suddenly decimated, as though by a decree of the occult powers.

This also occurs in the human species when, in certain regions, famine and epidemics tend to reestablish the biological balance that was threatened.

In another realm, we observe that the descendants of revolutionaries have, for their own benefit, reinstituted the titles abolished by their ancestors, and that there is not a single administrator or office manager who, imitating the "Sire" of yesteryear, doesn't demand that everyone call him "Sir." Castes have a persistent tendency to recreate themselves, and, in order to stand out above the rest, adopt a specialized or initiates' language. Every branch of learning has its own jargon, and, seduced by Latin or Greek, stultifies a language that popular usage had already rendered sensitive, suggestive, and lively. Our own *grandes écoles* reflect these tendencies when they adopt a private lingua franca where passwords flourish and where even certain quirks of language and types of cap become features of a class attitude.

The human individual is a being that recognizes himself as existing in three dimensions; the universe might admit of an infinite number. Generally speaking, human intelligence projects a grid that is more or less perforated, depending on the individual, in the direction of the code the universe has constructed. All that passes through is intelligible; that which does not pass is not only unintelligible but remains completely unknown to him. Nevertheless, that which does not penetrate does not, for all that, stop existing, dwelling, or acting within the very nature of man. Thereupon follows an unknown that no Darwin could illuminate.

Thus we may well be worried about a world where so many blind relationships are established and what it has reserved for us. For example, between a person and an object not really desired, selected, or worked on there intervenes the mechanism that halts emotion. Newly anonymous forms are projected by an automatic gesture which, excluding all interference, disinfects the atmosphere till it becomes an absolute void.

Elsewhere contacts are cut off: the mystery is hunted down to the very heart of the forest swept clean of paths where those enamored with the "average" stupidly buzz about, forests cleared for stingy ends, stripped of their souls—the deer and the wolves—by the automaton-like stupidity of hunters. This present-day world where the sorcerer's apprentices, puffed up with pride in their fragment of knowledge, make edicts, promulgate for the good of a model individual and, so doing, remain arrogantly ignorant of the unpredictable consequences of the reactions provoked by their decrees, and so certain, moreover, that they are always up to the task of bringing order to Warsaw.

They say that the human is still too close to the Stone Age, his ancestral impulses still ever-present coiled springs; and that many modes of activity are just a suspicion, a simulacrum of the activities of another time. Profit-making is the present-day form of prey and the hunger for power. Combats are mimed in stadiums and rings that serve as outlets for a fascinated audience.

But is it impossible not to submit to this connection and to push back the limits of memory, imagining that it is arbitrary to stop in the Stone Age rather than in any other moment of the limitless past and, that finally, Pithecanthropus is perhaps only a cousin?

There is little doubt that by reconsidering our ancestry, which—we must not forget—identifies itself with the infinite and, consequently, contains all possibilities there may be found incandescent sites where lay the switching points that we must discover.

Translated from the French by Myrna Bell Rochester

POLAR

Hold your hand in your ear
And don't open
Out onto the south pole
There where the chirring star is,
In its chirp cone
That you must
Knock, knock to hear it.
The compasses' glass has frozen.
The tingling index finger pointed to the north.
Once and for all.

Translated from the French by Myrna Bell Rochester

Elisa Breton

"The most remarkable woman in the group . . . a profound and marvelous person . . . a great presence . . . a very strong, very interior, deep woman, who contributed enormously to the evolution of surrealism": That is the opinion expressed by Marie Wilson, an American artist active in the Paris Surrealist Group from 1953 to 1960, on Elisa Breton.

Chilean-born Elisa Bindhoff was a young divorcee who had just lost her daughter when she met André Breton in New York in 1943; they married a year and a half later. With André, she traveled to the Gaspésie peninsula in Canada (see *Arcanum 17*), to Chicago, and to the land of the Pueblo, the Hopi, and the Zuni in the American Southwest, and in 1946 to Paris.

Although she was a mainstay of the Paris Surrealist Group until the big split of 1969, Elisa Breton did not like to put herself forward. As an artist she is best known for her objects and collages, but she rarely exhibited them, and her paintings are hardly known at all. Similarly, her published writings are few. Her 1949 conversation with Breton and Péret on the painter Riopelle is included in Breton's *Surrealism and Painting*, and she contributed some comments on handwriting to *Le Surréalisme, même* no. 5 (1959). Published here are her responses to a newly invented surrealist game, published in *Médium: Communication surréaliste* no. 2 (February 1954).

Elisa Breton, *Object,* 1950s. Photograph by Francine Cany. Courtesy of the artist.

Following the break-up of the Paris group, Elisa Breton maintained her distance from the competing factions that multiplied over the next decade, but never ceased to communicate her enthusiastic support to authentic surrealist efforts in France and abroad. She lives today in a nursing home outside Paris.

The texts here are examples of the surrealist game, "One in the Other," invented by André Breton and Benjamin Péret that year. Based on the idea, in Breton's words, that "any object is . . . 'contained' in any other object," the game stimulates the creative collision of analogy, metaphor, and image. Three or more players are required. As one of them leaves the room to select an object that she/he will "be" in the game, the others also select an object, which they then reveal to the first player. The first player must now describe her/his object in terms of the specific qualities of the other object, until the rest of the players guess what it is.

ONE IN THE OTHER

I am a green BUTTERFLY, slender and flexible. Of my three antennas, one points to the ground. I am hunted in the woods in springtime. I provide humankind with an indispensable life-giving element. Although I have been replaced by mechanical butterflies lately, I continue to be wanted by those who have the gift of awakening my powers.

Dowser's Wand

I am a flat SUGARED ALMOND, the color of the tiny spherical ones often present in boxes with others. I often take the shape of ordinary sugared almonds, but larger. Rather than for children, I am for adolescents and adults who may find me sweet or bitter. I am supposed to inspire suspicion among savages. Very ancient peoples credited me with magic powers.

Mirror

I am a CHRISTMAS TREE several days after the festivities. My upper part is a triangle like all Christmas trees. And like them, I am full of surprises for children. I also continue to touch a certain category of grown-ups, because I participate in past and present life.

Attic

Translated from the French by Guy Ducornet

Elisa Breton, Anne Seghers, and Toyen

SURREALIST INQUIRY: WOULD YOU OPEN THE DOOR?

> *Editor's note: This playful inquiry ("Ouvrez-vous?" in French) was featured on the first page of the first issue of* Médium: Communication surréaliste *(1953), prefaced by André Breton.*

EB = Elisa Breton; AS = Anne Seghers; T = Toyen.

Would you open the door for

Baudelaire? Yes, overwhelmed (EB). Yes, completely amazed (AS). Yes, with affection (T).

Bettina? No, too cunning for me (EB). Yes, she's a curiosity (AS).

Cézanne? No, he's too involved with his calculations (EB). No, because I love apples (AS). No, enough still-lifes (T).

Chateaubriand? Yes, with admiration (EB). No, with many excuses (AS). No, devoid of interest (T).

Juliette Drouet? Yes, with sympathy (EB). Yes, because of the sweetness of her face (AS).

Fourier? Yes, joyfully (EB). Yes, as one welcomes spring (AS). Yes, with the greatest interest (T).

Freud? Yes (a great miner) (EB). Yes, but not very sure of myself (AS). Yes, to make him psychoanalyze me (T).

Gauguin? Yes, in his aura of light and refusal (EB). No, out of fear of being disappointed (AS). Yes, in friendship (T).

Goya? Yes (the magic eye) (EB). Yes, saluting him with reverence (AS). Yes, with joy (T).

Caroline von Gunderode? Yes, deeply moved (EB). Yes, she's a good friend (AS).

Hegel? Yes (the atmosphere of high peaks) (EB). Yes, but with some confusion (AS). Yes, with respect (T).

Huysmans? Yes, trying to win him over (EB). Yes, hoping he would stay a long time (AS). Yes, out of curiosity (T).

Lenin? Yes (a human breach) (EB). Yes, respectfully (AS). Yes, I would be very pleased to see him (T).

Mallarmé? Yes, but distantly (EB). No, too glacial (AS). No, I'm not ready to go to sleep (T).

Marx? Yes, but silently (EB). No, we would be bored together (AS). Yes, in the friendliest way (T).

Nerval? Yes, but slowly (EB). Yes, after some hesitation (AS). Yes, I hope to be able to stroll through Paris with him (T).

Novalis? Yes, as in a dream (EB). Yes (night's great Emperor Moth) (AS). Yes, to enter into his strange light (T).

DeQuincey? Yes, from elective affinities (EB). Yes, with my heart beating (AS). Yes, to dream with him (T).

Henri Rousseau? Yes, with love (EB). Yes, an intimate friend (AS). Yes, with admiration (T).

Seurat? Yes (rigor and charm) (EB). Yes, as with a bird tapping at the window (AS).

Van Gogh? Yes, bounding toward the fire (EB). Yes (the sun) (AS). Yes, but with a fear of fatigue (T).

Verlaine? No (too Jesuitical) (EB). No, too weepy (AS). No, he's had too much to drink (T).

Translated from the French by Franklin Rosemont

Joyce Mansour

Born in Bowden, England, of Egyptian parents, Joyce Mansour was educated in Switzerland and moved to Paris in 1953. A high-jump champion and track star, she became one of the outstanding poets of our time. Her first collection, *Cris* [Shrieks] (1953), was greeted enthusiastically in the surrealist journal *Médium: Communication surréaliste,* and she joined the Surrealist Group the following year. In his *Vingt ans du surréalisme, 1939–1959* [Twenty Years of Surrealism] (1961) Jean-Louis Bédouin emphasized that Mansour "brought to the life of the group a unique, irreplaceable element." Her poems and tales—such as *Les Gisants satisfaits* [The Satisfied Bodies] (1958), which André Breton hailed as "this century's *Garden of Earthly Delights*" and a masterpiece of black humor—sounded a new and wildly rebellious note in women's writing. Compared to Mansour, as Alain Bosquet put it, "*The Story of O* is mere rosewater and Henry Miller a choirboy." Breton considered her one of the three most important French-language surrealist poets to have appeared since World War II.

After the break-up of the Paris group in 1969, Mansour took part in the regroupment around the *Bulletin de liaison surréaliste* and collaborated on *Arsenal/Surrealist Subversion.* Her bibliography includes nearly a dozen books of poems and stories, with illustrations by such artists as Jean Benoît, Pierre Alechinsky, Enrico Baj, Hans Bellmer, and Matta. Several of her works have appeared in English translation, including *Flying Piranha* with Ted Joans (1978), *Flash Card* (1978), and *Floating Islands* (1992). Joyce Mansour died in Paris in 1986.

The two poems published here are from *Cris.* "Practical Advice" (slightly abridged here) appeared in *BIEF: Jonction Surréaliste* no. 12 (April 1960); and "To Come, Possession, Prick Tease" is from the *Succinct Lexicon of Eroticism.*

INTO THE RED VELVET

Into the red velvet of your belly
Into the blackness of your secret cries
I have ventured
And the earth spins round humming
The red earth of your poison-gnawed innards
A demon's blood flows blind river of your nights
Eats at your soft spots the inflammation of your derisions
Into the dark corridor of your eyes
Into the red satin of your death
I have ventured
And the earth spins round humming
And my head unbolts with joy

Translated from the French by Peter Wood and Guy Flandre

LOVELY MONSTER

The disease with floating moustaches
Lies in wait for me
Each time my eyes meet under the table
Its long musical hand
Rummages between my breasts
And strangles my abscess

In the egg
My nose runs like a sewer
My hair falls sadly down
And the stench of voluntary humiliations
Torments me
My legs fly high even higher
Open shells glossy furs
Inviting tender mouths
Scissors sea-horses with greedy claws
To share their delights
Their smiles their adornments
And the suppurating pimples
Of their teens

(From *Cris*)
Translated from the French by Peter Wood and Guy Flandre

PRACTICAL ADVICE FOR WAITING

The constant retouching of your face paint, the care of an ever-ready body, all the errands necessary for dressing well, all this confers feminine dignity upon you, but to be a woman, it's not enough to be beautiful, you must also know how to wait.

To know how to wait under a sunshade, nervously, jealously, unruffled by fatigue, for the arrival of an old Turk, a messenger from another world, for the sword thrust of a gullible man or the jeers of a passerby. Enslaved by circumstances, to wait, without vanity, uncalculatingly and available, for the whim of the marketplace; to wait, without pleasure, for routine or for chance.

Learn how to wait while staying pretty, relaxed, spotless . . . despite the draining away of hours more elastic than your corset (wear it all the time: it keeps anxiety from settling between your ribs and your sympathetic nerve, thus speeding up the disappearance of your true face). You must learn to deceive your boredom. Wait without looking like you're waiting and watch out for signs of aging! Waiting will wear out your nerves all the more if the curtain lets the sunset's rays pass through.

Wait in a train station if you're attracted by foreign men, but learn to predict and check for mechanical breakdowns; become an experienced conductor, a clever knitting machine, a switching technician (and all that in six sessions thanks to the new practical training program "Introduction to Locoemotivity") before crossing swords with chance. If your stockings aren't best quality, sleep anywhere else but on the tracks; everyone knows about the force of mimesis (statistics prove it: beautiful features lead to exclamation points, pen-pushers, rotten tomatoes, etc.). Despite all that, don't lie down on the tracks; the train can stop without your help, it already knows how to; you don't.

Be bright, colored with sincere happiness (choose your colors with the same skill you use to choose your hebdromadary personality), always have a cup of coffee within reach; don't forget, for men it's always coffee time.

If you wait in a restaurant: This is a rendezvous you should dispense with. Be elsewhere. A starving man is better shielded than a blockhouse.

If you need to wait at City Hall? At home? Are you over twenty-one? Suitable for marriage? Maid for marriage? If not, wait until you are before considering marriage.

Don't wait in the street: Actual little hooligans will drag you off far from today and then where will the beautiful finery of your defects end up?

Wait for him at the heart of the struggle among the scorched leaves and the caramel-colored vapors of your discriminations. Hide your voracity under a semilunar smile (can be obtained in the following sizes: 42, 43, 44) and above all, sport a chilly bosom; you must prevent your partner from being unsatisfied, this state commingles values and embitters the character. Be certain of its cause. Adopt an attitude radically different from the one you usually take in bed. Be as glossy as a widow with rigid morals. Isolated and sulky. And console yourself if you don't know how to begin waiting; women who don't know how to be faithful can be practical, but in this case you'd better hurry; tickets are scarce and behind the broom, implacable death is taking shape.

Translated from the French by Myrna Bell Rochester

TO COME, POSSESSION, PRICK TEASE: DEFINITIONS FROM THE *SUCCINCT LEXICON OF EROTICISM*

Jouir/To Come: To feel a stunning spasm of joy and deliverance which beginning as a tingling in the head, agitates the body from the mouth to the sex and culminates in a sneeze of intense delight. This spasm is often followed—at least for men—by an agreeable stupefaction. In order not to lose their vital force, certain yogis come internally without a splash and without effect—except for the one produced in the head.

Possession: The state of a person inhabited—with complacency or not—by a demon. Prolonged possession by a superior may end in one of two ways:

(1) Total annihilation (madness, suicide, vampirism, marriage) of the possessed and to the possessor's advantage. (2) The exorcism of the possessed by himself in which he acquires in totality or in part the expelled demonic force. All other exorcisement (priests, healers, sorcerers) may place the practitioner at risk and prove fatal. To be possessed one must want to be, and the terrain of the unconscious must be favorable to the void.

Prick Tease: A generally noncombustible person who takes it upon herself to ignite as many hearts as she can without thought of financial profit.

Translated from the French by Rikki Ducornet

Meret Oppenheim

AUTOMATISM AT A CROSSROADS

That there are lines, spots, or a bouquet of flowers on a painting is unimportant; but one absolutely must have the impression that "something is looking at you"—a meaning that isn't described in the painting, but rather emanates from it, floats around it. . . .

Works engendered by the automatic method (there is, of course, another automatism that refers only to the pictorial craft, and, in this sense, all "good painting" is automatic) will always be alive and revolutionary, in the only efficient way possible, because they are in an organic relationship with nature.

The form in which inspiration appears is subject to unpredictable influences. For example, I imagine waves moving unceasingly in the universe and that, touching us, they continually influence the spiritual direction of humanity. And across diverse individuals, every new situation will uncover a different expression. For that reason, all criticism is in vain that attacks the new or unfamiliar appearance of a work. And any artistic production that presents itself in a traditional form or in a "fashionable" form (which, after all, is the same thing) makes us doubt its own authenticity (in the sense of the research I'm referring to).

(From *Medium: Communication surréaliste* no. 4, 1955)
Translated from the French by Myrna Bell Rochester

I HAVE TO WRITE DOWN THE BLACK WORDS

I have to write down the black words of the swans. The golden coach at the end of the avenue splits, topples over, and melts on the rain-dampened road. A cloud of colorful butterflies takes wing and fills the sky with its sound.

Oh, red meat and blue clover, they go hand in hand.

1957
Translated from the German by Catherine Schelbert

Judit Reigl

Born in Kapuvar, Hungary, in 1923, Judit Reigl moved to Paris in 1950 and was active in the Surrealist Group in the years 1953–1955. In a catalog preface later reprinted in his *Surrealism and Painting*, Breton saluted her as the first painter to translate the lyrical violence of Lautréamont into the "language of the eyes." The very titles of her paintings—"Glimmers of Fever," "Torches of Chemical Weddings," and "They Have an Undying Thirst for the Infinite"—have a Maldororian ring.

In 1957 Reigl and her husband, painter Simon Hantai (also from Hungary), suddenly abandoned surrealism and joined abstractionist Georges Mathieu (promoter of a monarchist "mysticism" strongly influenced by the later antisurrealist Dalí) with whom they staged a reactionary manifestation commemorating the Inquisition, openly identified with the extreme right-wing elements in France. This manifestation was denounced in a surrealist tract, *Coup de semonce* [Warning Shot]. Reigl appears to be the only woman to desert surrealism for the Far Right.

These reflections on the future of surrealism in painting appeared as responses to an inquiry on the situation of painting in *Médium: Communication surréaliste* no. 4 in 1955.

POINTS OF DEPARTURE FOR A NEW REVOLT

What are, for you, the founding principles of pictorial activity? In what direction(s) do you think surrealist painting, considering its past, can extend today? Are these new possibilities subject to certain overdeterminations? In painting, how do you see, for example, woman, bird, the sea, nature, and its elements?

The essential foundation of any creative act is the desperate desire to destroy the contradictions and the limits of human and universal existence, and to extend itself by means of permanent revolt.

• • •

If we reexamine surrealist theory, we notice that the possibilities it offers to the quest for new dimensions have been only partially developed. Realization of the theory necessitates a new revolt today on the pictorial level. This revolt can take, as points of departure and as means, the three most revolutionary discoveries of the surrealist past:

1. Automatism;
2. The conception of functioning machines (Duchamp, Jarry);
3. The organic disintegration of all external signs, objects, and symbols (as in Matta's work).

Taken separately, each of these discoveries is still full of secret promises; together they may become the magic key to a vast new space, hidden from sight till now.

Such an effort may take the shape of a "machine-instrument" animated by the dynamic and absolute automatism (both physical and psychological) of its creator, who can change the point of total disintegration into a point of transmutation, transforming texture, color, and rhythm into an energy from which one can, with such an instrument, isolate space-time forces as one processes each phase of their birth, of their metamorphoses—from the electron to the Great Transparent One.

It is therefore extremely important that the machine-instrument, slowly experienced by the exploring intellect, becomes neither an obstacle nor a limit, but rather a subtle analogue to our multidimensional aspirations. And so it will be concave and convex, straight and curved at the same time. And in compliance with our movement, it will revolve mechanically, always on one of its surface-facets, and it will trace linear and plastic space-forms, solid or transparent, all of which will interpenetrate.

• • •

Representation of woman will be the dynamic-magical representation of what is unique and universal in her. Matter will be transformed into the very *logos* of woman, revealing its specific substance as a force of attraction, as a magnetic field, a plenitude, a spell, a nostalgia, an inspiration, a perfume—beyond objective nature.

Translated from the French by Guy Ducornet

Isabel Meyrelles

Born in 1929 in Matosinhos, Portugal, Isabel Meyrelles met surrealists Artur do Cruzeiro Seixas and Mario Cesariny in 1949, and has remained their lifelong comrade. After studying sculpture with Américo Gomes and Antonio Duarte in Lisbon, she moved to Paris where she pursued her education at the Sorbonne and the School of Fine Arts, and where she has made her home ever since.

As a sculptor she has taken part in several surrealist group shows, including the International Exhibition of Surrealism and Fantastic Art (1984) and the "Premeiro exposiçao o de surrealismo ou nao" [First Exhibition of Surrealism or Not] in 1994, both in Lisbon, and has had numerous solo shows in Paris. Her first book of poems, *Em voz baixa* [In a Low Voice], came out in 1951, and since then she has published three other collections. She writes in French as well as Portuguese. Her *Anthologie de poésie portugaise* (1971) is the standard collection and features many presurrealist and surrealist poets, including Fernando Pessoa, Cesariny, Natalia Correia, and Luiza Neto Jorge. Meyrelles is represented in Cesariny's anthology, *Poets of Surrealism in Portugal* (1981). More recently she has translated Cesariny's *Labyrinthe du chant* (1994) and edited her own bilingual (Portuguese/French) *Antologia de poesia surrealista* (forthcoming).

These three poems are from her *Palavras Nocturnas* [Night Words] (1954).

NIGHT WORDS

Appointments you did not make
on streets you do not know
I shall wait
until the nights glide

over me and
I am transformed
into a tree

• • •

Once again
time is shattered
in my hands
once again
you will be the silence
around me

• • •

To forget
the pine tree sound
of your hair
and your eyes
black stones
To forget these petrified days
far from you

I shall be water
green water
motionless
opaque
stagnant
I shall be water
where only you
can be reflected
nothing else

Translated from the Portuguese by Jean R. Longland

Anneliese Hager

Born in Dresden in 1904, Anneliese Hager participated as a photographer in the diverse currents of modern art in 1920s Germany until the reign of Nazism forced her into a reclusive, semiunderground existence. At war's end with her companion, painter Karl-Otto Gotz, she took part in the renewed artistic ferment, most notably in the Cobra movement (1948–1951). In 1954 she collaborated on Max Holzer's *Surrealistische Publikationem.* As an "old master" of the photogram, Hager's late 1920s splash-and-drip automatism prefigures surrealism's 1939 "return to automatism" in painting, not to mention the still later current known as "abstract expressionism."

A collection of Hager's poems, *Die rote Uhr und andere Dichtungen* [The Red Clock and Other Poems], edited and introduced by Rita Bischof and Elisabeth Lenk, was published in Zurich in 1991. It is from this collection that the poems published here were selected.

Anneliese Hager lives in Dusseldorf.

OF THE POISON OF DREAMS

I offer you the fog of ideas in the poison cup of dreams. Veil the false stars (of those who know) and immerse your body down to the ground. You will seek in vain the last sip, for the cup sinks, like you, with every stroke of the hour, deeper and deeper into the torn mouth of time. Despairingly, you hang your eyes like lights on a walls of fog, where blossoms of the instant they speak glittering prayers.

Yet your glance dissolves in the shadow of their rays. In vain they seek the bronze arteries in the astral body of windblown shapes and their last light fractures, in chorus, from the hollow sound of longlegged parables. Why should I cry? Never will the poison cup be empty, and when you look at it properly, its sinking ground will also lead you into the hanging palanquins of the Pharaohs.

You are the breath of my dreams, you look back from the hands of a long-buried future, and glue your splintered face onto the fluttering world graves. You mirror your plumage in the mirror of nights and bend your uprooted head heavily over time's velvet morass. Your eyes are empty, yet birds of paradise come and they are filled with pearly song.

I drink the fragrance of your dragging garment that has cleared thoughts from dust, and I call with the fervor of repressed forces your Hallelujah—hallelujah—again and again through the roaring grid of fading orgies, until their bloated smile will hang itself in your radiant sounds.

Translated from the German by Miriam Hansen

Anneliese Hager, *Mystery of Nature,* 1948. Photograph courtesy of Galerie 1900–2000, Paris.

THE BLUE SPELL

Out of the stony jungle grows a cold order—blossoms and decays. Its blue ashes blanket the streets. I stand and wait—the city rolls by—but the blue lies immobile and stares at me. Does it speak to me? I listen in vain but hesitate simply to climb across it.

Moist breath of the stones—they breathe clouds of soil and blow fat bodies against the nocturnal wall. I forget the blue spell and listen to the talk of the cloudbodies. I catch their voices and throw them back and see them as red spots flashing up in the monotonous night. I take off my dress and the shoes heavy with day and cover myself with this blazing coat, which bombards my eyes with its jumble of voices. I slowly move on, the nocturnal garment trailing behind me.

The blue spell stands mute—a deserted wall—grows pale and finally dies in the gold of the sprouting day.

Translated from the German by Miriam Hansen

AUTOMATIC DREAM

Blade of light, gray with drizzling rain, drips and you don't hear the rattling dance? Ah—this was long ago—today the morass reaches the window's cross and smothers all musical violets.

Why don't you turn the handle one more time—the lightning drowns out the entire picture—now it's all right. How neatly the crochet ribbon twitters—I love the sound of the charms close to my ear. No—not like this—higher, much higher—there is so much sand on the throne . . .

Away from the corner—the din of the false ring—are you coming along? Ah, the old woodstaff always breaks up the musical riffraff and the red moon is much too proud. In the meantime, I will sit on the railing—what are you waiting for?

When I have pleasure the swamp beast howls—howls and howls through all the cracks in the shed. Bend it still further back!—that's it—but tomorrow the ramrider yawns, and I still don't know the machine—why should the domestic fuel not go on. All the bricks are stacked.

Do come with me—so alone my travelcoat trembles marble pale. I will find the way—let's go along here—soon we'll be there. Do you hear me when I loudly—very loudly—look through here? Ah, you are—I know you are—just quietly lay your hands in the large vortex—and it will contract all right. But there, in the corner, the hammer . . . ah, yes, up and away . . . But the lid keeps rattling and the brown tower has a wise smile. I love to go there. Yes—Yes—it rains . . .

Translated from the German by Miriam Hansen

Drahomira Vandas

Like Martiniquan poet Simone Yoyotte and Egyptian photographer Hassia, Drahomira Vandas is one of surrealism's women of mystery. Poet, playwright, and Doctor of Laws, she was born in 1919 of Czech origin, but nothing seems to be known regarding her birthplace, family background, or early life. She settled in Paris around 1951 and soon joined the Surrealist Group, in which she remained active until 1953. After the death of her companion, Czech surrealist poet Jindrich Heisler (1914–1953), Vandas moved to Venezuela and became a citizen of that country. In the early 1960s she returned to Paris and wrote plays, a novel, and a collection of poems, *Je m'élance parmi les lumières* [I Soar Among the Lights] (1962), most of which remains unpublished. The selections here are from that collection, kindly made available by Edouard Jaguer.

LIGHT THROWS SHADOWS

The light throws shadows
Behind my closed eyelids
My eyes know it's daytime
Darkness spurts with lightbeams
When sparks
Swirl up in the shade
It is nighttime
To stare at immobility
To drive the nail's glance
Between two solidified wings
Of motionlessness
And then my eyes know
That night has come
Enough! Enough! Enough!
I soar amidst the lights
Sparks or stars
Angrily I rip the vacuum
This void which only appears to be full.

Translated from the French by Guy Ducornet

AN EGG HATCHES OUT A FLAME

Ceremoniously an egg
hatches out a flame
Bulls and white wolves pull their chains
In step
The cavern's mouth throws two brambles
which go up and down
In step.
On them the ebony bird sings its silence
Solemnly, I bow to it

And later I enter
Into the blackness
In step.

Translated from the French by Guy Ducornet

RAIN MAN

Water bubbles! Water bubbles!
Over here! Water bubbles! Who wants round water?
Round water? Circles of water?
Water bubbles?
Bubbles! Hollows falling from way up high!
Bubbles for those who love to go down!
Who wants to ride hollow waters?
What a joyous way to spend the time
Before crashing!

Translated from the French by Guy Ducornet

Olga Orozco

Surrealism as an organized movement in Argentina began in 1926, when poet/critic Aldo Pellegrini formed the first Surrealist Group outside of France in Buenos Aires. Although this "Pellegrini group" dispersed and regrouped several times—its last incarnation flourished in the early and mid-1950s—a basic continuity of surrealism in Argentina is nonetheless evident. Among the transitional figures between the earlier and current Argentine surrealist generations, Olga Orozco stands in the forefront.

Born in 1920 in Toay (La Pampa), Olga Orozco moved to Buenos Aires in 1936. Loosely associated with Pellegrini and his comrades in the early 1940s, she took an active part in the more sporadic surrealist ferment in the postwar years as a collaborator on the surrealist journal *A Partir de cero* [Starting From Zero], edited by Pellegrini and Enrique Molina in the 1950s.

Long recognized as a major Argentine poet and an influential figure of the "Generation of 1940," Orozco is the author of more than a dozen books. *Desde lejos* [From Afar] (1946), *Las muertes* [Deaths] (1951), and *Los juegos peligrosos* [The Dangerous Games] (1965)—in which the poem published here originally appeared—contain her most important contributions to surrealism, although she is also the author of tales that are often compared to those of Leonora Carrington.

Olga Orozco lives today in Buenos Aires.

TWILIGHT (BETWEEN DOG AND WOLF)

They fold me up into myself
They divide me in two
Every day they create me in patience
and a black organism that roars like the sea.
Afterward, they cut me again with nightmare scissors
and I fall into this world half my blood flowing on either side:
a face carved from the bottom up
by the fangs of fury itself,
and another that dissolves in the mists of the great wolfpacks.
I can't decide who is master here.
Under my skin I change from dog to wolf.
I decree the plague and flanks aflame
I straddle the plains of past and future;
I lean forward to nibble at the little bones of so many dead dreams between
    celestial pastures.
My kingdom is in my shadow and goes with me wherever I go,
or crashes over in ruins, doors open to enemy invasion.
Each night I rip to shreds all the knots lashed to my heart,
and each dawn I find myself on a hill within my cage of obedience.
If I devour my god I wear his face under my mask,
and nonetheless, I drink only from the people's trough
velvety poison of piety that stings the guts.
I worked the tournament into the warp and woof of the tapestry:
Exposed to the elements, I have won my fool's scepter,
and I also awarded banners of gentleness as prizes.
But who conquers me?
Who defeats my remote outpost in the desert, the sheet of sleep?
And who gnaws at my lips slowly, in the dark, from between my own teeth?

Translated from the Spanish by Natalie Kenvin

Blanca Varela

Although Blanca Varela (born 1926) has long been renowned as one of the foremost poets of her native Peru—and indeed, of Spanish-speaking America—it is not widely known that in her youth this outstanding writer took part in the Surrealist Movement. In the mid-1950s she allied herself with surrealist poets Aldo Pellegrini and Enrique Molina, and collaborated on their journal, *A Partir de cero*; the text published here appeared in its fourth (and last) issue in 1956.

Varela's poetry, seething with rebellion, was highly praised by Octavio Paz in the 1960s. By and large she has remained true to her original poetic fury. In recent years she has contributed to such surrealist-oriented periodicals as *Punto Seguido* [Straight Point] from Colombia and *Resto del Mundo* [The Rest of the World], published in Brazil.

DANCE CARD

I'm just a primate, nothing more, climbing this gigantic red flower. Each one of my dark bristles is a wing, a being overcome by desire and happiness.

I have twenty nimble black fingers; they all respond to my will. Perhaps I'm the only survivor, the only one to coil and uncoil on the mud, and the just-hatched snake. The spinning top, the human sunflower, hairy and smooth; the solitary singer, the anchorite, the plague itself. I am undoubtedly the one you can hear breathing, *weaving* to capture the act, the prickly evidence of eyes and tongues still trembling, still holding memories.

What makes us moan and fall to our knees? Courage! There is plenty of time; let the feast continue. Honored guests, you with filthy scarabs tied to your memories, display your airy skulls. Must I tell you, if only to see you frightened and pale, that you'll have to *catapult* yourselves through the air, and, rejected by more powerful hands, leap into the blackness without echo or opposite, beginning or end?

I love this flower which has no innocence.

The torment begins with light. Up above, a deaf lantern illuminates everything.

To reveal the body, the asshole has the face of a saint. The elephant and justice begin the dance. Who will win?

Translated from the Spanish by Natalie Kenvin

Marianne van Hirtum

Born in 1935 in Namur, Belgium, Marianne van Hirtum moved to Paris in 1952, met André Breton in 1956, and joined the Surrealist Group in 1959. Noted for her exquisite colored ink drawings as well as for her poetry and tales, she collaborated on *BIEF: Jonction surréaliste, La Brèche: Action surréaliste, L'Archibras, Bulletin de liaison surréaliste* (all published in Paris), *Brumes Blondes* (journal of the Bureau of Surrealist Research in Amsterdam), and *Arsenal: Surrealist Subversion.* In addition to her many solo shows, she took part in the International Surrealist Exhibition in Paris in 1959, the World Surrealist Exhibition in Chicago in 1976, and the surrealist collage exhibition in Paris in 1978. Her Paris apartment, overflowing with her drawings and curious objects as well as cats, snakes, and lizards, was a "port of call" for visiting surrealists from all over the world.

Van Hirtum's first book, *Poèmes pour les petits pauvres,* appeared in 1953 and was followed by two others during her lifetime, as well as several posthumous collections. *John the Pelican,* a volume of English translations by Peter Wood and Guy Flandre, was published by Hourglass in 1990.

A thoroughgoing nonconformist, ecology-minded by nature, a revolutionary not only in politics but above all in daily life, she remains a profound influence on the younger generation of surrealists today. Unlike the many artists whose commitment to revolutionary thought changed with the political temperature, Marianne van Hirtum for nearly thirty years exemplified *absolute surrealism.* She died in 1988.

"In Those Rooms" is from *Les Insolites* [The Unusual] (1956), and "Abandon, Meeting, Orgasm, Seduce, Vice" from the *Succinct Lexicon of Eroticism.*

IN THOSE ROOMS . . .

In those rooms
the morning honey shall not enter
as those rooms are the mind's.
And yet the propeller-like sweetness
of your fair hair appears to me
under the opaque windowpane
I can dance snowfalls:
and at once discover myself
ready to tell everything
What if the ragman's youth comes along

Marianne van Hirtum,
ink drawing, 1983.
Courtesy of Jean-Luc Majouret.

Will you hold me responsible then?
—no yellow spells and little hope:
I can hear gondolas playing
with wind briny strings.
I dream up a mammoth's life for me
as leaves harder
than the three stones of our love.
if you have nothing else to say
come and share my cylindrical solitude
where as little girls we still dance in a ring
I can close my hands on your woman's body.

Your triangle head will be the most loved
lying between the breasts.
This morning I am the beast who can do
anything.

Translated from the French by Peter Wood and Guy Flandre

ABANDON, MEETING, ORGASM, SEDUCE, VICE: DEFINITIONS FROM THE *SUCCINCT LEXICON OF EROTICISM*

Abandon: The instant when, succumbing to the vertigo of passion, one consents to an irresistible resolve—which is not one's own—to fuse with another being in order to create the unique and solemn place of delight's efflorescence.

Meeting: The harmonious shock produced between two beings previously unknown to one another. If the bow is unerring, the arrow does not always inflict a wound. The shaft is represented by chance and the point by necessity. A magic operation which may bring about the metamorphosis of two distinct bodies into one body with two heads. Act that affirms the total freedom of the unconscious: any machine finds itself all at once capable of taking its commands into its own hands. In the middle of the clearing, the trying on of a spasm sewn of pious, sympathetic thread, of which the cords of wax abruptly receive too much sun.

Orgasm: Tidal culmination of the totality of sensations both physical and supraphysical, fused in a unique function which like the ocean tide is each time on the verge of returning to the other side of the beach—the sea itself—but which, because of the equilibrium postulated by the continuity of *movement,* cannot. The sea, here represented by *LIFE,* at the border between *BIRTH* and *DEATH.*

Seduce: To bring into play—knowingly or not—the sum of the attractions, charms, and grace in one's possession in order to attract the passionate interest of another being. Highly idiosyncratic, this vital, silent function—whether impelled by the libido or veiled by modesty—animates the pursuit of a complementary being in view of amorous union. Capitulation of the king before royalty itself.

Vice: Aggregation of particularities peculiar to each individual, embodying the modality of the amorous mechanism: Carnal act accomplished by an individuality with an asexual sex, disembodied and gigantic. Commonly: anarchy of the senses manifesting themselves by an abnormal comportment essential to the functioning of the erotic machine. Discordancy of sensation, decomposition of erotic sentiment. "Voluptuousness in vice: one is three and one is alone" (Malcolm de Chazal, *Sens Plastique* [Plastic Sense]). Letter sent in the usual manner to the wrong address, arriving at destination and entailing a response.

Translated from the French by Rikki Ducornet

Leonora Carrington

COMMENTS ON *THE TEMPTATION OF ST. ANTHONY*

Editor's note: In 1947 filmmaker Albert Parsons Lewin, a surrealist sympathizer and friend of Man Ray, sponsored a competition among artists to paint a picture based on the legend of St. Anthony, to be used in his film version of Maupassant's 1885 novel of bourgeois corruption, Bel Ami. *Eleven artists took part, including Leonora Carrington, Dorothea Tanning, Horace Pippin, Salvador Dalí, and Max Ernst (who won the prize).*

This text—a delicious surrealist commentary on a surrealist work—appeared in the catalog of the traveling exhibition of all eleven paintings in the competition.

The picture seems pretty clear to me, being a more or less literal rendering of St. Anthony, complete with pig, desert, and temptation. Naturally one could ask why the venerable holy man has three heads—to which one could always reply, why not?

You will notice the veteran's suit to be whitish and of an umbrellaoid form which would lead one to believe that the original color had been washed or bleached out by the vagaries of the weather or that the monkish apparel had been cleverly constructed out of used mummy wrappings in umbrella or sunshade form as a protection from sandstorms and sun, practical for someone leading an open-air life and given to contemplation (as Egyptologists apparently didn't exist in those days, mummy wrappings were no doubt to be gathered like blackberries and therefore to one of an economical and modest turn of mind they would provide durable and apt clothing for the desert).

The saint's traditional pet pig who lies across the nether half of the picture and reviews the observer out of its kindly blue eye is adequately accounted for in the myth of St. Anthony, and likewise the continually flowing water and the ravine.

The bald-headed girl in the red dress combines female charm and the delights of the table—you will notice that she is engaged in making an unctuous broth of (let us say) lobsters, mushrooms, fat turtle, spring chicken, ripe tomatoes, gorgonzola cheese, milk chocolate, onions, and tinned peaches. The mixture of these ingredients has overflowed and taken on a greenish and sickly hue to the fevered vision of St. Anthony, whose daily meal consists of withered grass and tepid water with an occasional locust by way of an orgy.

On the right, the Queen of Sheba and her attendants emerge in ever-decreasing circles out of a subterranean landscape toward the hermit. Their intention is ambiguous, their progress spiral.

And last to the ram with the earthenware jar one could only quote the words of Friar Bacon's brazen head: Time was—Time is—Time is past. I was always pleased with the simple idiocy of these words.

ON MAGIC ART: A CONVERSATION, 1996*

Why do you want to change the statements that appeared in the inquiry?

My answers were too pragmatic and too reductive. Now I feel the subject has much wider frontiers, which I am unable to define.

---

* Editor's note: André Breton's last major work, *L'Art magique* [Magic Art] (1957), concludes with seventy-six responses to an inquiry on magic and art addressed to surrealists and others who shared their interests, including ethnologists, historians, and philosophers. What was called for were reflections on the notion of *magic* applied to works of art past and present. Among the respondents was Leonora Carrington, who wrote in part:

> At the very beginning of the Surrealist Movement, the artist began to feel the age-old nostalgia for magical powers. Wandering unprepared and ignorant in the depths whence at times strange "fish" emerge, he himself is astonished at what his being contains, and he is too dizzied to stop to learn what he is actually doing. The true obligation of the artist is to know what he is doing and to transmit his knowledge precisely. He must always lift the skirts of Venus or of her twin sister Medusa: if he cannot do this, he should change jobs.
>
> Truth consists of the strange, the Marvelous. What we take for "Reality" is the petty coagulated nightmare in the mind of the man who rules over our species: "the man of good position," the man of power. That is to say, the man turned to stone inside his daily nightmare, like flies in those fake ice cubes that they buy in America to scare cocktail party guests. Now, we may wonder: "How can one escape from the ice cube?" . . .

Probably [in 1957] I got into Breton's word game—he was an ideal verbal playmate, but the whole nonverbal part of magic was excluded.

If magic is the transformation of matter, then what would correspond to the transformation of images in painting?

Alchemy is a form of magic, so the transformation of images, or bodies, in art acts on dream/psychic substance.

In alchemy there is the Athanor (oven) and the Stone. Which would be the Athanor and Stone in painting?

The Athanor is my Body-Psyche and the Stone is finding the right place.

Feeling and sensing something could be part of the enigma, how do you relate to this?

It is being aware of Presence without definition.

Why was it so easy for you to define what magic was?

One is mutable—as a younger woman I tried to express opinions, and now my opinions are becoming difficult to define.

Until the artist has become once more a magician, that is, ruling over the magical art, that begins with himself, we may only say that destinies in art are as obscure and dangerous as weapons in the hands of modern politicians and heads of state. Luckily, man is generally much too insensitive to feel the influences spat out by his brother artists. Ignorance also protects. Like a piece of meat, more or less dead, man has nothing to fear. The "sensitive" man suffers from this, without knowing why, at times he dies of it. Let's then look for a way to possess the subtle organs that will let us spread beneficent magic, or receive it, while at the same time creating protections against the multifarious venoms of the invisible world. It's only in the strange magic ocean that a being may find salvation for himself and for his sick planet. . . . To be clear in questions of magic is first to be chaotic; for the two, at the beginning, were only one. (Translated from the French by Myrna Bell Rochester)

In 1996, in the course of preparing this anthology, I asked Carrington about this text. She replied that her 1957 response no longer seemed valid to her, but that she still regarded magic art as a question of great importance. The issue, in her view, was to assess "what would magic art be in the present time."

This text, published here for the first time anywhere, is the result of a conversation between Carrington and her son, Gabriel Weisz.

You addressed one part of the question, but what about magic itself?

There are so many different Magics—we would have to choose more specifically.

In painting there are different substances, different places, different feelings. How do these affect the painter?

It's how you ride an image into that place.

Kay Sage

Katherine Linn Sage was born into a wealthy family in Albany, New York, in 1898. Her mother was a morphine addict, her father a New York senator. Kay, as she liked to be called, studied art in the U.S. as well as in Milan, Italy. She became a princess by marrying Prince Ranieri di Faustino in Rome in 1925, but divorced her husband ten years later and devoted herself to painting. In 1937 she moved to Paris where she met the surrealists. Initially an abstractionist, her encounter with surrealism completely transformed her outlook. Her paintings at the Salon des Independents in 1938 attracted the attention of André Breton, who commented on her work in his 1942 "Genesis and Perspective of Surrealism in the Plastic Arts" (Breton, 1965).

Sage met Yves Tanguy in France and married him in New York in 1940. They settled in Woodbury, Connecticut, where their home became a vacation spot for surrealist exiles in New York. Sage took part in the International Surrealist Exhibitions in New York in 1942 and Paris in 1947 and had many solo shows.

Although her work as an artist is routinely ignored in academic studies of surrealist painting, Sage is much better known as a painter than as a poet. Her first volume of poems, *Piove in Giardino,* was a book for children published in Italy, in Italian. It was followed by a series of volumes of poetic nonsense for adults, including *The More I Wonder* (in English, 1957). She also prepared and prefaced the *catalogue raisonée* of her husband's art, *Yves Tanguy: A Summary of His Work* (1963). Seriously ill, depressed by her husband's death in 1955, and further troubled by failing eyesight, Kay Sage shot herself in 1963.

The statement "Painter and Writer" appeared without title on the flyleaf of *The More I Wonder;* "An Observation," "The Window," and "Chinoiserie" are from the same book. "Fragrance" is from the catalog, *Kay Sage: 1898–1963* (1977).

PAINTER AND WRITER

I am, primarily, a painter. I paint serious pictures. When I am not quite so serious, or in a different mood, I write down certain impressions, observations, and sudden, apparently imperative thoughts which come to me. There is absolutely no conflict between these two forms of expression, nor do they have any connection. They simply replace each other. I have always painted and I have always written but never at the same time.

AN OBSERVATION

The more I wonder,
the longer I live,
how so much water
can stay in a sieve.

THE WINDOW

My room has two doors
and one window.
One door is red and the other is gray.
I cannot open the red door;
the gray door does not interest me.
Having no choice,
I shall lock them both
and look out of the window.

CHINOISERIE

English, French, Italian,
I can write in all of these,
but, at best, they are translations.
I think in Chinese.

FRAGRANCE

I feel unexpectedly
delicious fragrance

a perfume full of memories
of youth, of spring
which seems to follow my smile
the motion of my hands.
I look in vain
I cannot find it
what can it be?
And then
in a flash, I've got it
I know
that's it
that fragrance
is the memory
of me.

Mimi Parent

One of the major forces for surrealism in painting since World War II, Mimi Parent developed her own unique genre-transgressing medium, the object-tableau: paintings incorporating diverse elements so as to present intimate glimpses of heretofore unseen worlds. Born in Montreal, Quebec, in 1924, she studied with Alfred Pellan at the School of Fine Arts, where she met Jean Benoît; they remained lifelong companions. Expelled from school for indiscipline, she went to Paris with Benoît in 1948, and the couple have made their home there ever since.

Although she and Benoît identified with surrealism even in Montreal, where they had some association with the automatists, shyness prevented them from joining the Paris Surrealist Group until 1959, when they played a major role in the International Surrealist Exhibition devoted to Eros. Organizer of the hall devoted to fetishism, Parent also designed the lavish exhibition catalog (in which the definitions below originally appeared). A collaborator on *BIEF: Jonction surréaliste, La Brèche: Action surréaliste,* and *L'Archibras* (all published in Paris), as well as *A Phala* and *Analogon* and other surrealist journals, she has taken part in International Surrealist Exhibitions in Paris (1965), São Paulo (1967), Prague (1968), Chicago (1976), as well as "Surrealism Unlimited" in London (1978), "Permanence of the Surrealist Gaze" in Lyon (1981), and numerous other collective shows. She has illustrated books by Guy

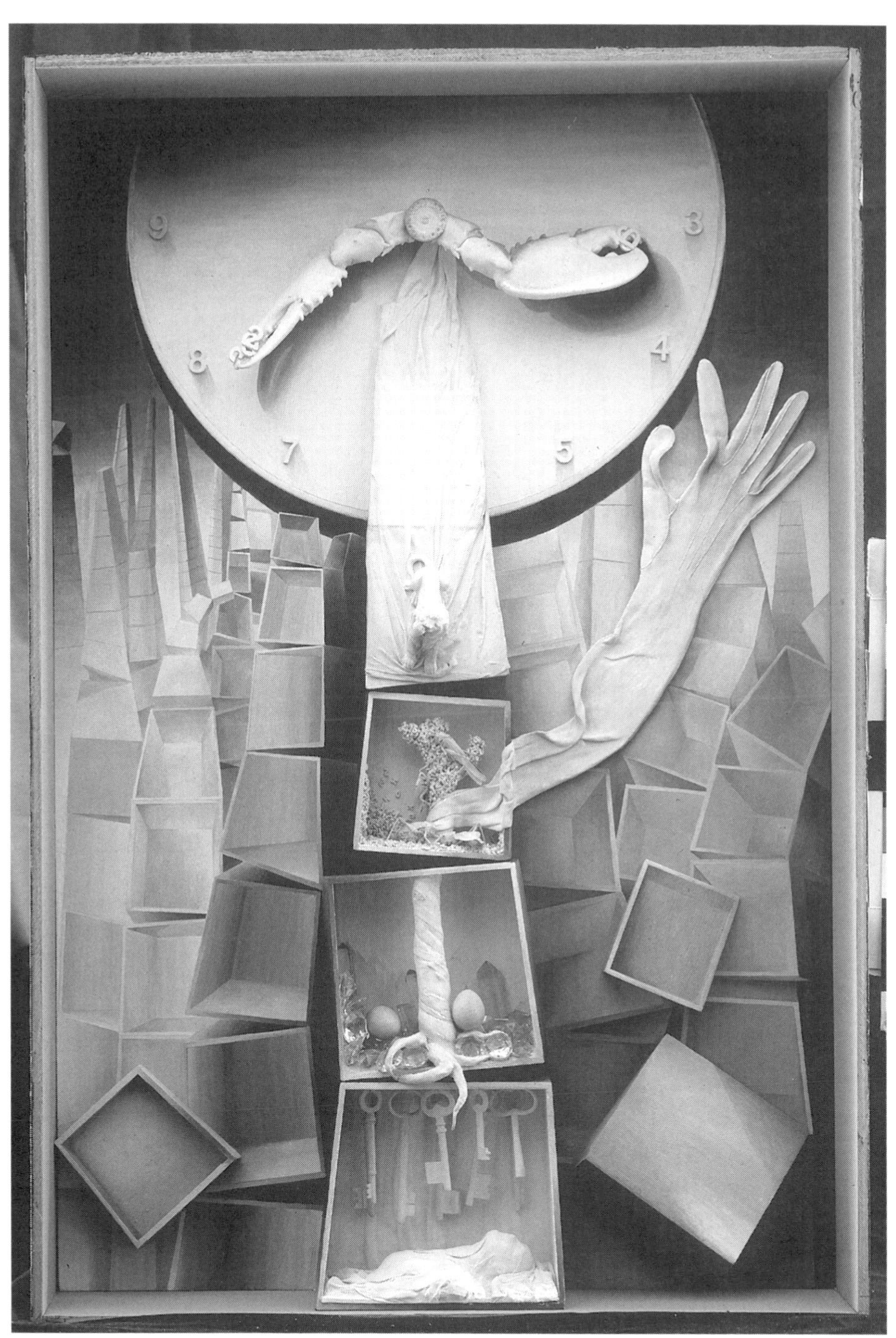

Mimi Parent, *Eve Dreams*, 1973. Courtesy of the artist.

Cabanel and José Pierre. André Breton's preface to one of her solo shows was reprinted in his *Surrealism and Painting* (1965).

Though still not widely known in the U.S., Mimi Parent's gardens of earthly and other assorted delights and terrors are among the most splendorous paintings of our time, or any time. Her surrealism, moreover, as a statement included in the next section demonstrates, has always been incorrigibly wild and absolute.

DEPRAVED PERSON, LICENSE, MASTURBATION, VOYEUR: DEFINITIONS FROM THE *SUCCINCT LEXICON OF EROTICISM*

Depraved person: One who descends the ascending staircase of pleasures.

License: Beyond the barriers of what is imposed as moral. "All license except against love" (Maurice Barrès).

Masturbation: The hand in the service of the imagination.

Voyeur: One who, from his own point of view, shares the life of others.

Translated from the French by Franklin Rosemont

Sonia Sekula

NOTES FROM A JOURNAL: THE OCCURRENCE OF MEETING A FACE CONTRA A FACE

Supposing you are a woman facing another man? What happens? You talk and you see. You walk toward him and feel quite natural about it. Yet there is no reason to take the other man for a natural phenomenon. He is a stranger to himself and to you. The sound that you hear, while you look at his lips is not concerned with either you or himself. It is addressed to an internal conception of what might be or should be.

The man smiles. You watch his eyes and you don't understand what they say. You don't know what happens behind the man's back, behind his eyes or what happens under his feet. You don't know what he does with his hands while you watch his mouth.

You don't know what goes on or goes not on in his body. The man walks along with you. Do you hear his steps? And what about your own steps? Be silent and listen to the eventual secret they might convey to you. Explain it.

You and the man stop. There is no more sound. Yet you feel his breath. You see his breath coming out into the air like smoke. A winter morning.

How do you associate yourself with his breath and your own breath?

The man sings. Where does the song come from? What depth lies under the song and by what surface is it covered? Answer me, who is the stranger you talk, walk, step, and sing with?

You say he is your lover. You say that he and you lie together at night. How do you know what the night does to him. How do you know that his eyes see in the darkness. Have you any conception of his body?

You say that you love him.

Where and when and why and what is it in him that you love?

Then you awake. The man awakes too.

Do you know whether he has a hard time to open his eyes or not?

What happens to him when he enters the morning? Are you concerned with the happiness he received from you—or the joy he gave to you? And if so, why?

And afterwards, when he brushes his teeth and looks into the mirror, do you know what goes on in him then? Does he know why the mirror face is so unlike himself?

Let us all laugh together . . .

But believe me, you shall never come nearer to that man than he comes near to his own shadow.

And he shall never unfold your shadow though he feels your kisses on his burning hand.

You are both strangers to each other and to yourselves and yet you told me that you are lovers.

May I then congratulate you my dear and wish you much luck for the future?

Remedios Varo

Born Remei Lissaraga Varo in Anglès, Catalonia, in Spain in 1913, Remedios Varo studied at the San Fernando Institute in Madrid before moving to Barcelona in 1935, where she exhibited with the surrealist-influenced "logicophobist" group and became a close friend of painter

Esteban Francès. The following year, in the midst of revolution, she met French surrealist poet Benjamin Péret, who was also a Trotskyist volunteer in the anarchist militia, and with whom she moved to Paris. Varo was active in the Paris Surrealist Group from 1937 to 1942, when the Nazi occupation forced her and Péret to emigrate to Mexico. In the New World she and her husband were key figures in the informal surrealist community that also included Leonora Carrington, Wolfgang Paalen, Alice Rahon, Luis Buñuel, Frida Kahlo, Kati Horna, and the young Octavio Paz. Varo's paintings were included in the International Surrealist Exhibitions in Paris and Amsterdam (1938), Mexico (1940), and Paris (1947).

Péret returned to Paris in 1947, but Varo stayed in Mexico, where she later married Walter Gruen. Having painted intermittently for years, in 1953 she took it up with passion in the course of a close friendship with Leonora Carrington.

Although not a published author in her lifetime, Varo left an extraordinary manuscript, *De Homo Rodans:* an elaborate chronicle of imaginary discoveries written in a quasiscientific style with an abundance of quotations in a humorous invented Latin, posthumously published in 1970. Included in the book is the recipe published here, a delightful example of surrealist black humor and *détournement* of a subliterary genre often stereotyped as "quintessentially feminine."

A RECIPE: HOW TO PRODUCE EROTIC DREAMS

Ingredients: One kilo black radishes; three white hens; one head of garlic; four kilos honey; one mirror; two calf's livers; one brick; two clothespins; one whalebone corset; two false moustaches; two hats of your choice.

Pluck the hens, carefully setting aside the feathers. Boil in two quarts of unsalted distilled water or rainwater, along with the peeled, crushed garlic. Simmer on a low fire. While simmering, position the bed northwest to southeast and let it rest by an open window. After half an hour, close the window and place the red brick under the left leg at the head of the bed, which must face northwest, and let it rest.

While the bed rests, grate the black radishes directly over the consommé, taking special care to allow your hands to absorb the steam. Mix well and simmer. With a spatula, spread the four kilos of honey on the bedsheets, sprinkle the chicken-feathers on the honey-smeared sheets. Now, make the bed carefully.

The feathers do not all have to be white—they can be any color, but make

Remedios Varo, *Solar Music,* oil on masonite, 1955. Courtesy of Walter Gruen.

sure you avoid Guinea hen feathers, which sometimes provoke a state of prolonged nymphomania, or dangerous cases of priapism.

Put on corset, tighten well, and sit in front of the mirror. To relax your nerves, smile and try on the moustaches and hats, whichever you prefer (three-cornered Napoleonic, cardinal's hat, lace cap, Basque beret, etc.).

Put the two clothespins on a saucer and set it near the bed. Warm the calf's livers in a waterbath, but be careful not to boil. Use the warm livers in place of a pillow (in cases of masochism) or on both sides of the bed, within reach (in cases of sadism).

From this moment on, everything must be done very quickly, to keep the livers from getting cold. Run and pour the broth (which should have a certain consistency) into a cup. As quickly as possible, return with it to the mirror, smile, take a sip of broth, try on one of the mustaches, take another sip, try on a hat, drink, try on everything, taking sips in between. Do all this as rapidly as you possibly can.

When you have consumed all the broth, run to the bed and jump between the prepared sheets, quickly take the clothespins and put one on each big toe. These clothespins must be worn all night, firmly pressed to the nails, at a 45° angle from the toes.

This simple recipe guarantees good results, and normal people can proceed pleasantly from a kiss to strangulation, from rape to incest, etc., etc.

Recipes for more complicated cases, such as necrophilia, autophagia, tauromachia, alpinism, and others, can be found in a special volume in our collection of *Discreetly Healthy Advice*.

Translated from the Spanish by Walter Gruen

5. The Making of "May '68" and Its Sequels

MARVELOUS FREEDOM VIGILANCE OF DESIRE

CATALOG OF THE

WORLD SURREALIST EXHIBITION

(with the participation of the Phases movement)

Chicago 1976

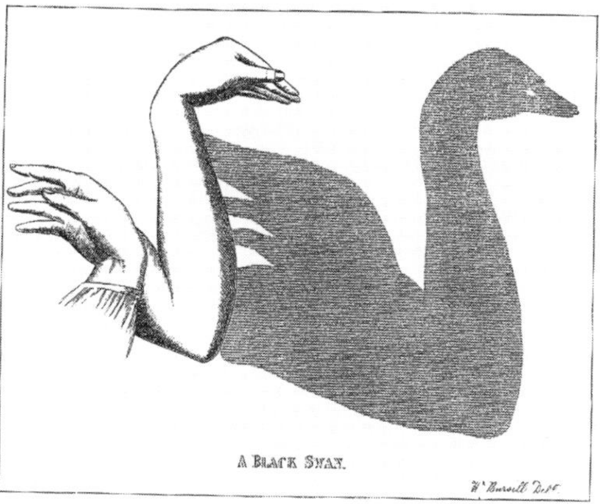

GALLERY BLACK SWAN

500 North LaSalle Street
(Entrance at 148 Illinois)
Chicago, Illinois 60601

On the cover—E.F. GRANELL: The Lovers are Walking with their Mirror

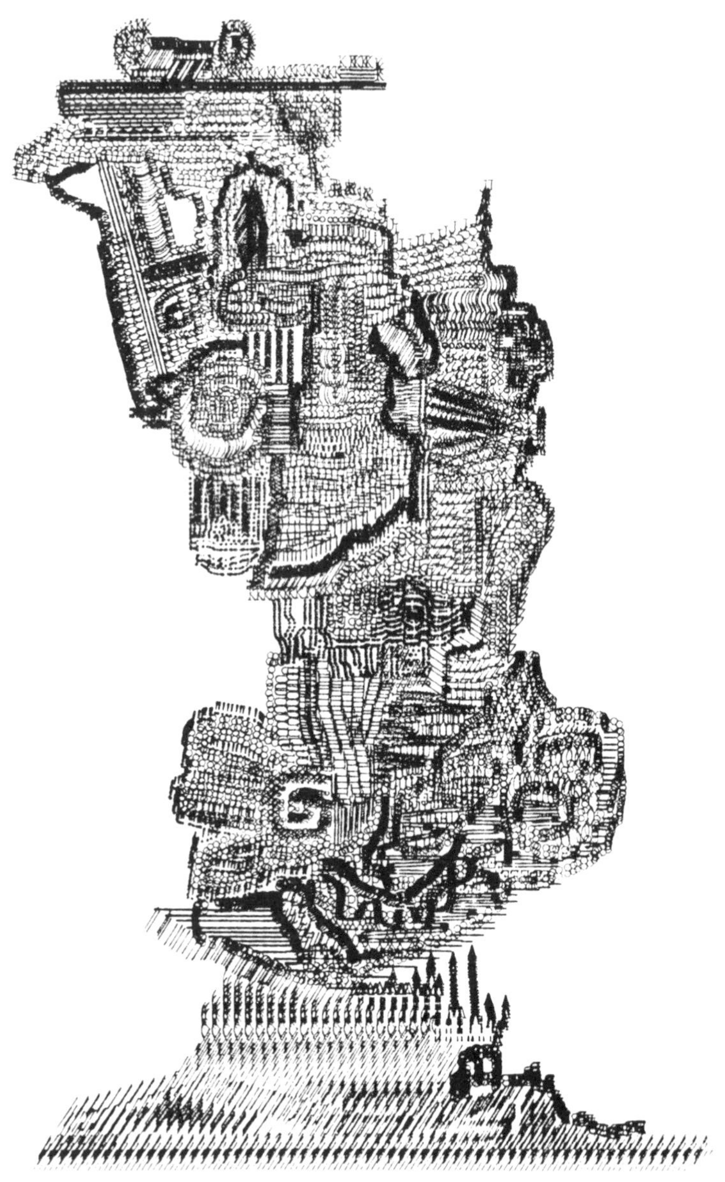

Giovanna, drawing made on a typewriter, 1967. Courtesy of the artist.

INTRODUCTION

Women in the Surrealist Resurgence of the 1960s and 1970s

It is hard to say what is impossible.

—Clara Reeve

As Herbert Marcuse was one of the first to point out, the French worker-student uprising in May 1968 vindicated surrealism with a vengeance (Marcuse 1968). This should not be misconstrued to mean simply that certain dreams dating back to the 1920s were finally realized in the streets forty years later. To view the relationship so superficially would be to forget that human activity is the essential factor in social life. "Poetry," as Isidore Ducasse wrote in 1870, "must have practical truth for its goal" (Lautréamont 1978). And the fact is, no group in France during the 1950s and early 1960s did more to prepare the way for the near-revolution known as "May '68" than the poets who made up the Surrealist Group.

As the fifties wore on, the Surrealist Group persisted as part of the small minority that said no to both antirevolutionary superpowers. Although surrealists in France were able to publish openly and to show their works—mostly in noncommercial galleries such as Sophie Babet's L'Etoile scellée [The Sealed Star]—their activity was usually ignored in the media, which continued to maintain the pretense that surrealism was a thing of the past. In the academic world the movement was in the lowest depths of disfavor. Like anarchism, bebop, and the Beat Generation, surrealism during the early years of the Cold War was basically a "subterranean" phenomenon. Ironically, this fear and loathing on the part of the establishment helped the Surrealist Movement win the respect of growing numbers of dissenting young people. Few surrealist books and periodicals were available at mainstream bookstores, but they could always be had at the smaller, more rundown "hip" stores frequented by young rebels, where one could also find jazz and film journals, anarchist papers, science fiction, and comic books.

By 1960 surrealism's against-the-current tenacity was in evidence everywhere. After long years of political reaction and therefore of intellectual timidity, a new radicalism suddenly entered the picture. The short-lived but dramatic revolution in Hungary in 1956—warmly championed in a Surrealist Group tract—had done a lot to discredit the U.S.S.R.'s brutal brand of "socialism" and thus helped liberate large sectors of the working class and the intelligentsia from the paralyzing grip of Stalinism; resignations from the Communist Party in France, as in many other countries, reached a new high.[1] Revolution in Cuba on New Year's Day 1959, the ongoing struggle for independence in Africa, and the civil rights movement in the U.S.—all welcomed by surrealists—also stimulated the rise of a youthful radical resurgence that owed little to the existing parties and sects. Many young dissidents were so eager to distinguish their ends and means from the corrupt social-democratic and Stalinist traditions that they began to call themselves a *new* Left.

Indicative of the Surrealist Group's key role in this emerging movement was the lively political journal *Quatorze juillet* [Fourteenth of July], which rallied opposition to the De Gaulle "regime." Only three issues of this publication, initiated and edited by surrealists, appeared in 1958, but the desire for uncompromising inquiry that it inspired bore fruit as years went by.

"In Defense of Surrealism," a February 1960 BBC radio program, offered a foretaste of the sixties' surrealist resurgence. For obvious reasons the movement rarely had access to the airwaves and perhaps had never before had an opportunity to reach so large an audience. Spokespersons for the movement on this live-discussion broadcast were Joyce Mansour (who was born in London of Egyptian parents), Bulgarian-born Nora Mitrani (of Spanish-Jewish ancestry), Moroccan-born Robert Benayoun, and Mexican Octavio Paz. Thus a movement that most critics pretended was all-male and exclusively French was officially represented by a quartet of whom half were women and none of French nationality![2]

More sensational in its impact was the celebrated "Manifesto of the 121" issued in September 1960, a key document in the development of an international New Left.[3] In flagrant violation of French law, this tract, *On the Right of Insubordination in the Algerian War*—to cite its full title—urged total noncomplicity in France's war in North Africa, including desertion from the French army. Among its signers were such well-known figures as Simone de Beauvoir, Jean-Paul Sartre, Marguerite Duras, and Daniel Guèrin, as well as Breton and other surrealists, but it was the Surrealist Group that proposed the statement and prepared the first draft.

Sixties radicalism is a broad category that includes the New Left and counterculture as well as such movements as Black nationalism and women's liberation. Remarkably, in view of its simultaneous and autonomous eruption in many countries and on all continents except Antarctica, this many-sided current remained relatively homogeneous as a world movement, at least until the mid-1970s. Until recently, however, only a few historians have noted something even more remarkable: that the essential features of this new radicalism—the qualities that distinguish it from pre–World War II versions of Marxism and anarchism—were largely anticipated by surrealism.

In the basic defining elements of New Left theory and practice, surrealism's prefigurative influence is pervasive. The New Left's first move was to reject everything that the surrealists disliked about the old: Stalinism and all other dogmatism and authoritarianism; myopic "workerism," which denies revolutionary potential to any sector other than the industrial working class; "economism," the naive belief that economic change is all that counts. The surrealists' open-ended approach to revolutionary strategies, their recognition that there are many ways of being revolutionary, their nonsectarianism, and their search for signs of revolution outside the narrowly "political" all became distinctive features of the New Left.

Surrealists did not need the *Quotations from Chairman Mao* to recognize the critical role of the Third World, for these peoples and their struggles had always figured prominently in surrealist publications. Unlike Maoists, moreover, surrealists insisted on the intrinsic value of Third World cultures and of the "Fourth World" as well: the tribal societies of Africa, Oceania, and the Americas. While most of those who called themselves Marxists relegated these so-called "primitives" to damnation as irrelevant to modern class struggle, surrealists always have recognized them as inspirations and models for alternative ways of living and have supported their struggles against capital, church, and state.

Yet another aspect of surrealism—its passionate attention to everyday life, to the way people actually live their lives—became the keystone of the counterculture, which emphasized the need for experimental lifestyles. Here too the impact of forty years of surrealism was suddenly visible everywhere. The surrealists' penchant for scandalous direct action, their emphasis on the importance of play, their critique of work, their hatred of militarism, their research into alternate states of consciousness (via alchemy, Zen, drugs), their interest in utopias, and, not least, their *humor*: All are hallmarks of the sixties' underground press. From the Hegel revival to women's liberation, from sexual freedom to deep ecology, from antipsychiatry to animal rights, there is hardly a facet of sixties (or post-sixties) radicalism that surrealism did not anticipate.

Just as surrealism helped shape a New Left, so too the new radicalism of the sixties gave surrealism new strength and greater social impact. As the youth of all countries united in struggle, interest in surrealism spread like wildfire—and so did the international Surrealist Movement. The Bureau of Surrealist Research in Amsterdam, which Her de Vries had opened in 1959, kept up a whirlwind of exhibitions, pamphlets, and tracts, and issued a periodical, *Brumes Blondes* [Blond Mists]. New surrealist groups, with the encouragement of Breton and the Paris group, were formed in Chicago and São Paulo, and the Prague group, underground since 1948, was at last able to renew contact with the international movement. International Surrealist Exhibitions were held in Paris (1959–1960), New York (1960–1961), Milan (1961), Paris again (1965–1966), São Paulo (1967), Prague (1968), and Chicago (1976). The standard reference on the subject cites the last as "an unprecedented panorama of *living* surrealism," featuring nearly 600 works by nearly 150 surrealists from 31 countries (Biro and Passeron 1982, 368). Other important manifestations took place in Athens, Havana, Copenhagen, Geneva, Lisbon, Caracas, London, Milwaukee, Buenos Aires, and Warsaw. Surrealist publications sprouted in many languages.

In Paris Surrealist Group activity multiplied geometrically and smaller groups formed in Lyons, Nantes, Strasbourg, Marseilles, and Caen. In addition to the major international exhibitions noted above, numerous smaller group shows and solo exhibits took place in Paris and the provinces. In the 1960s eight titles were brought out under the Editions Surréalistes imprint in France (four of them written or illustrated by women), and nearly fifty tracts and other collective declarations were issued. *BIEF: Jonction surréaliste* (twelve issues, 1958–1960) was succeeded by eight issues of a more substantial journal, *La Brèche: Action surréaliste* (1961–1965), in turn followed by seven issues of *L'Archibras: Le surréalisme* (1967–1969) (Bonnet and Chénieux-Gendron, 1982).

Although Breton and the other old-timers had turned over the group's direction to younger members years before, Breton's death in September 1966 was a tragic setback, not only for the French but for surrealists throughout the world, whose widely scattered groups were just beginning to coalesce. Breton expected and desired the Surrealist Movement to continue after him, and in Paris and all other places where the movement was active the decision to continue the surrealist adventure was unanimous. The journal *L'Archibras,* which first appeared in April 1967, was one of the handsomest and most exuberant surrealist publications ever, bursting with the spirit of "May '68" a year in advance.

When the student rebellion broke out, followed by the workers' general strike, the Surrealist Group was one of the very few radical organizations that was even close to being ready for it. "We never left the streets," as one of them put it.[4] Surrealists formed part of that revolutionary minority denounced by

De Gaulle and the Communist Party as "enragés." Essential documents here are the group's 5 May tract of solidarity with the revolutionary youth (drafted by Annie Le Brun) and the special "May '68" issue of *L'Archibras,* headlined "Long Live Adventurism!" and condemned by the authorities for its "offense to the President of the Republic" as well as its "apology for crime" and "defamation of the police."[5]

After the May days, however, as often happens in the aftermath of revolutionary upsurges, the Paris group lapsed into a severe internal crisis. Tensions mounted during the summer as throngs of newcomers (youthful "veterans" of May) flocked to Surrealist Group meetings to join up. Unfortunately, the group proved unable to accommodate this sudden groundswell or to contend with the admittedly formidable dilemmas confronting the Surrealist Movement after the defeat of a popular uprising that everyone recognized as fundamentally surrealist. Collective activity came to an impasse, and the group began to fall apart. In March 1969, after forty-five years of uninterrupted agitation in Paris and in exile, the world's first Surrealist Group splintered, and many of its members went their separate ways.[6] A handful of well-known members publicly declared the Surrealist Group disbanded. A majority of the group, however, including Mimi Parent, Joyce Mansour, Micheline Bounoure, and Marianne van Hirtum, resolved to continue surrealist activity and in 1970 issued the first *Bulletin de liaison surréaliste*.

The attempt to formally disband the Paris group was not endorsed by any of the surrealist groups in other countries. At least one of these—the Prague group—had an unbroken history dating back to 1934 and, despite the obstacles imposed by Stalinism, remained the largest and most dynamic surrealist group outside Paris. The Czechs might well have rallied the surrealists of all countries, but the brief "Prague Spring" was ended by Russian invasion. Once again surrealists in Prague were driven underground. Military dictatorship also put an end to the public activity of the next largest group, in São Paulo, Brazil.

Even as the revolutionary wave receded, however, surrealist groups continued to develop, particularly in countries where the movement had not previously shown much activity. Just as the spirit of the sixties existed in some places before 1960, so too it flourished in other places well into the seventies. Nineteen seventy-three was Year One for the Arab Surrealist Movement in Exile, a Paris-based group with members from Iraq, Algeria, Lebanon, and Syria (Biro and Passeron, eds. 1982, 140).[7] Surrealism in the Arab world has roots going back to the mid-1930s, when Georges Henein, soon joined by Ikbal El Alailly, Ida Kar, and others, started an agitation in Cairo. Most of the Cairo group's publications, however, were in French, whereas the Arab surrealists of the seventies published voluminously in their own language. Mimeographed at first and later printed, their sometimes bilingual (Arabic-French) journal *Le Désir libertaire* [Libertarian Desire] was—as they proudly proclaimed—"Banned in All Arab Countries." Haifa Zangana, an important figure in the group—as collagist, painter, poet, social critic, and theorist—has since participated in surrealist publications and exhibitions in many countries.

Africa and the world of the African diaspora had many encounters with surrealism in the seventies. The involvement of Blacks in the movement had started in 1932 with the *Légitime Défense* group of Martiniquan students in Paris (among them, Simone Yoyotte) and expanded in later years with the arrival of Wifredo Lam and, shortly afterward, the *Tropiques* group in Fort-de-France. Many Black artists and writers—including Malangatana Valente (Mozambique), Hervé Télémaque (Haiti), Inacio Matsinhe (Angola), Cheikh Tidiane Sylla (Senegal), and U.S.-born globetrotter Ted Joans—developed close ties to organized surrealism in the sixties and seventies.[8] In the mid-1970s the Surrealist Movement and African American poet Jayne Cortez found each other. Author of ten books of poems and eight recordings, Cortez is one of the most resoundingly shamanic and revolutionary voices of our time.

Surrealism in Japan started early (in 1925) and produced many outstanding figures through the years, but only in the seventies did the first Japanese woman surrealist appear: the painter and graphic artist Yoshiko (Biro and Passeron, eds., 1982, 222–223). Other women helped organize or reorganize surrealist groups or otherwise foment surrealist activity in Argentina, Australia, Denmark, Switzerland, Ireland, England, and other countries.

Indeed, all through this world surrealist resurgence of the sixties and seventies, women were more active than ever and now increasingly had turns at the helm. When I joined the Surrealist Group in Paris in 1966 I was immediately impressed by the forceful, energetic presence at the group's daily meetings, of such women as Mimi Parent, Nicole Espagnol, Joyce Mansour, Elisa Breton, and Toyen. In every surrealist group on the globe, women assumed more dynamic roles. Some became editors of surrealist journals and anthologies; some organized group exhibitions. Joyce Mansour was part of the surrealist delegation to the Cultural Congress of Havana in 1967.[9] Between 1959 and 1979 women surrealists wrote more books and published more in periodicals than ever before. As demonstrated by Meret Oppenheim's opening manifestation at the 1959–1960 "Eros" exhibition and Mimi Parent's contributions to the plan of the 1965–1966 *L'Ecart absolu* [Absolute Divergence] show, women's involvement in the life of the movement and their international impact—not only within surrealism but outside as well—was much more evident than in earlier years.

By May 1968 painters Agar, Carrington, Toyen, Oppenheim, and Parent had won a measure of world renown, as had Maria Martins in sculpture and Joyce Mansour in poetry. The women's liberation movement, which outlived the rest of the New Left, greatly enlarged these women's sphere of influence. Thanks to this worldwide grass-roots movement against what Nelly Kaplan called the "Ladies and Gentlemen of the Patriarchy," several women with long-standing surrealist connections found themselves in the spotlight. The writings of Meret Oppenheim and Leonora Carrington enjoyed wide circulation in many languages. Carrington's *The Hearing Trumpet* (1974) appeared as a mass-market paperback (Carrington 1977). Many other women who had not been involved in collective activity for years—including Agar, Bridgwater, and Colquhoun—took part in newly organized surrealist groups.

In the visual arts, the sixties and seventies brought us Mimi Parent's exquisite object-tableaux, Giovanna's typewritten drawings, Anne Ethuin's coated collages, Irena Dedicova's mathematical moonscapes, Marianne van Hirtum's gothic totems, Leonora Carrington's *Magic World of the Mayans,* a powerful series of symbolic portraits by Alice Rahon, the last splendid works of the great Toyen, Rikki Ducornet's drawings of lusty flora and riotous comic-strip poems, Aube Elléouët's eco-collage bestiary, Miriam Bat-Yosef's kaleidoscopic enigmas, Eva Švankmajerovà's black rebuses, and Haifa Zangana's aleatory maps. The work of these artists has long since found a sizable audience and is now probably even "taught" in art history classes. Less well-known are the creations of many other artists who collaborated on surrealist journals and took part in collective exhibitions in those years: the paintings of Anne-Marie Guillon, Hilary Booth, and Jocelyn Koslofsky; the collages of Debra Taub; Mado Spiegler's papercuts; the drawings of LaDonna Smith, Halina Zalmanowicz, and Susana Wald. And finally, a curious example of simultaneous but independent surrealist invention: Monique Charbonel's ronéograms, made in Paris, and my own mimeograms, in Chicago. (In the best spirit of the sixties, these variants of *decalcomania* were made with mimeograph stencils and thick black mimeo ink.)

New games further helped to expand the horizons of surrealism's always timely and effective genre-transgressing activities. In Time-Travelers' Potlatch players describe the gifts they would present to historic or imaginary figures. In Parallel Collage each player independently uses the same elements to make a collage. The results, always startling, provoke new interpretations of the world and thus contribute to its transformation.

Other highlights of surrealism's sixties resurgence include Giovanna's ceremonial, "La Carte absolue," performed with her husband, Jean-Michel Goutier, at the opening of the *L'Ecart absolu* exhibition in 1965; Nelly Kaplan's landmark film *Néa*, released in 1976; and Alice Farley's surrealist dance at the World Surrealist Exhibition in Chicago the same year.

In the realm of theory and polemic, women's contributions were also more plentiful and had more far-reaching effects than those of women surrealists in the thirties and forties. Particularly notable are the writings of Joyce Mansour, Marianne van Hirtum, Annie Le Brun, and Micheline Bounoure in French, Elisabeth Lenk in German, Eva Švankmajerová, Alena Nádvorníková, and Vera Linhartová in Czech, Leila Ferraz in Brazilian Portuguese, Haifa Zangana in Arabic, Nancy Joyce Peters, Hilary Booth, Jayne Cortez, and Rikki Ducornet in English. Highly articulate in expressing radical criticism and new ideas, these women are also poets, as are most of the visual artists noted above. All but a few have published books of their poems. They do not let us forget that surrealism is *poetry above all!*

Most of the women in this section of the anthology are alive, active, still making trouble. Not one has turned her back on the nonconformist and emancipatory ideals of her youth. Although not all of them still think of themselves as participants in surrealism as an organized movement, each one, in different ways, continues to denounce injustice, demand revolutionary change, and defend the cause of poetry, freedom, and love.

Notes

1. The Paris Surrealist Group tract, "Hongrie: Soleil levant" [Hungary: Rising Sun] is included in Pierre, ed., *Tracts surréalistes*, II, 1982, 161–162; an English translation appears in *What Is Surrealism?* Breton 1978, 344–345. See also Caute 1964, 227–234.

2. More than half of the excerpts from this program, published in *BIEF: Jonction surréaliste* No. 12 (Paris, April 15, 1960), are by the women participants.

3. Marcelle A. Abell, in Evanier and Silverzweig 1961, 74–79; Palmier 1973, 557–558.

4. Philippe Audoin, letter to Penelope and Franklin Rosemont, 13 January 1969. An English translation appears in Rosemont et al. 1997, 252–253.

5. "Pas de pasteurs / pour cette Rage!" is reprinted in Pierre, ed., *Tracts surréalistes*, II, 1982, 276; information on the publication and repercussions of this tract and of *L'Archibras* no. 4 may be found in the notes, 429–431.

6. Mayoux 1969 is the fullest account of the crisis that led to the shattering of the Paris group. See also Bounoure, ed., 1970, a compilation of responses to an inquiry that resulted in a regroupment of more than half of the former group around a new internal publication, the *Bulletin de liaison surréaliste*. A smaller group led by Jean Schuster renounced the word "surrealist" and published seven issues of a newspaper-style journal, *Coupure*, before splintering into four hostile factions.

7. See also the entries for "Art et liberté," "*Le Désir libertaire*," "Georges Henein," and "El Janaby."

8. A sizable literature exists on the *Tropiques* group; see, for example, Kesteloot 1974. However, few studies examine that group's contributions to surrealism, and even fewer consider the activity and impact of Black surrealists in Cuba, Haiti, Europe, and the U.S.

9. At the congress Mansour gave the Stalinist David Alfaro Siqueiros (an accomplice in the assassination of Leon Trotsky) a swift kick in the pants as a statement of the Surrealist Group. See "A Memento from André Breton," *Intercontinental Press* (16 February 1968), 140.

Nora Mitrani

IN DEFENSE OF SURREALISM

Editor's note: These passages are from the radio program, "In Defense of Surrealism," broadcast on BBC, London (19 February 1960). As BBC could not locate a transcript of the show, I have relied on a translation from the excerpts published in BIEF: Jonction surréaliste *no. 12 (April 1960).*

The exploitation of man by man has kept its traditional forms: religion, respect due to parents, duties toward the state; but new forms have appeared: respect for bureaucracy, the discovery of nuclear energy with its military applications. It seems to me that the manipulation of humankind by capitalism is as grievous as sociological manipulations like "group ethics" or "the art of human relations," as psychologists call them.

The science of human relations or "human industry" was invented simultaneously in the United States and in the U.S.S.R. Its purpose is to create an "average man," well-surrounded and perfectly adapted to the group—all sorts of groups: corporations, administrations, clubs, the armed forces, etc. . . . so that he remains contentedly united to others. . . .

To all these forms of exploitation, surrealism opposes its unflinching refusal. Surrealism ignores the stale wisdom of those who pretend to know how to live. Naturally, we want individual revolt to flourish and to develop into revolution. But if it is a matter of political and social revolution as defined by the Marxists, let us say that it falls far short of what surrealism wants. This type of revolution is not enough, and it will never be enough. All the conquests of the proletariat in recent years, from a higher standard of living to leisure and vacations for all, have been won through reformism, not revolution. . . . This promotion of the masses is in fact a betrayal: class consciousness is replaced by the struggle for security and by bureaucratic types of organized irresponsibility. It is true that there are more and more workers with clean hands and white collars. But what does that change for us, for each human being? . . .

In this mass civilization, humankind has struck a miserable bargain: it has exchanged its independence and the mind's freedom for a higher standard of living and the consumption of "token appearances." . . . And even on this level, by the way, there is much more to do and to gain. But for surrealism, such a bargain is pitiful, and no bargain in the world can satisfy us. There is no other choice but solitude, or the company of the few human beings who share our spiritual values.

Translated from the French by Guy Ducornet

Nelly Kaplan

Born in Buenos Aires, Argentina, into an old Argentine family of Russian origin, Nelly Kaplan was an economics student at the University of Buenos Aires when she suddenly quit school to go to Paris, where she still lives today. In 1954 she became the assistant of the renowned filmmaker Abel Gance for ten years. A chance encounter with André Breton led to her involvement in surrealism, including collaboration on the journal *Le Surréalisme, même*. She also wrote for the surrealist-oriented film journal *Positif*.

Starting in 1961 she directed a series of films on artists: Gustave Moreau, André Masson, Picasso, and others. Later she began writing and directing full-length feature films, including *La Fiancée du pirate*, known in English as *Dirty Mary* or *A Very Curious Girl* (1967; rereleased in 1977), which Picasso described as "insolence considered as one of the fine arts"; and *Néa* (1976), which Nancy Joyce Peters hailed as the revolutionary and "transcendent prefiguration" of "the new woman, conferring the promise of a happier existence, as she speaks not only her own reality (now oppressed under Patriarchy), but a higher reality, too" (see the complete text on pages 352–356). Among her later films are *Charles et Lucie* (1979) and *Plaisir de l'Amour* [Love's Pleasure] (1991).

In 1966, under the name Belen, Kaplan published a collection of erotic tales of black humor, *Le Réservoir des sens* [The Well of the Senses], illustrated by Masson. Her later books include *Le Collier de Ptyx* (1972) and *Un Manteau de Fou-Rire ou les Mémoires d'une Liseuse de Draps* [A Coat of Hysterical Laughter or Memoirs of a Lady Sheet-Diviner] (1974), excerpted here.

"At the Women Warriors' Table" first appeared in *Positif* no. 61–63, June–August 1964. "Enough or Still More" is from *Etudes cinématographiques* no. 40–42 (1965). "All Creation Is Androgynous" is a late 1970s interview supplied by the author.

MEMOIRS OF A LADY SHEET DIVINER

After a few minutes' walk we came to a modern building that immediately reminded us both of the diminishing form of a gigantic ten-story pagoda. Lyris mentioned that the place was so famous that they'd given its name—The Obsexion—to the artificial town, exclusively devoted to pleasure, that had grown up around it. At the entrance to the pagoda, a doorman in livery came up to hand us menus showing the complete list of services offered by the house.* But as soon as he recognized Lyris he stopped short and ushered us in, adding respectfully that Mr. Amer was waiting in his office.

The foyer was painted in gold and azure, and with the clever use of *trompe-l'oeil* photos, it transported the visitor to an ocean beach, while movie projectors hidden in the walls, but still noticeable by their humming and the glimmers of light they inevitably emitted—using a foreground dolly system, like ocean waves lapping at the beach—cast upon the water this eternal, repeating caption:

> Que la vie est douce
> au bord de la mer . . . !
>
> [How sweet life is
> on the seashore . . . !]**

This pun, as obviously transparent as it was, simply delighted me. I love word play, especially when the questionable joke shocks the good bourgeois. I then understood that I was bound to like Mr. Amer.

We went up to his office at the top floor of the pagoda, from which he controlled not only the whole Obsexual Palace but, in addition, a great portion of Shanghai. He greeted Lyris affably, and, while they spoke about various problems involving the theater (which he owned, along with three quarters of the erotic village), I had plenty of time to study the walls and their owner.

Mr. Amer was a very likable, charming, knowledgeable homosexual of about fifty. His nationality? Unclear. His office was stuffed with masterworks all featuring erotic themes. An unfamiliar Gustave Moreau painting immediately attracted my attention because of its unusual subject:

> On the Last Supper table, the Christ gleams, his skin encrusted with jewels, while the Apostles fling themselves upon him, some for fellatio, some for irrumation, and some for pedication. Four of them, stuck in a

---

* Later Lyris explained the use of this card: As the customer received services, accurate punch-holes were marked in the appropriate column. One simply paid one's bill at the exit. This system of sex services proved to be quite efficient. Those caught cheating were mercilessly thrown out and forbidden to reenter for sixty-nine days, and were reduced to a laughable 0.0009 percent.

** Translator's note: In French the second line of the caption also conveys the meaning "at the bitter brothel" (the name Amer is in fact the French word for bitter).

strange position in order to carry out a very complicated arabesque of masturbatory solidarity, let their semen fall in a pearly shower upon the ecstatic eyes of the Savior. While his own seminal liquor shoots up toward the heavens to vanish in the clouds under the admiring glance of Mary Magdalen (at the bottom extreme left of the painting), she is executing with Mary herself some sweet arpeggios in the delicate cunnilingual art. At the right of the picture, above the master's signature, appeared this enigmatic phrase: ". . . and the pleasure of dying!" alongside the date, 1856.

I lingered over that painting, fascinated by the beauty of its colors, the imperturbable purity of its androgynous faces, the minuteness of every last detail, from the delicacy of the foreskin folds to the iridescence of each drop of semen! At the time, I only knew Moreau's work from a few reproductions and from a wonderful movie filmed in his museum that I'd seen several times in the Pessoas' personal screening room at Uliellea. Much later, during a long stay in Paris, I often went to the phantasmagoric Moreau Museum at 14 rue de la Rochefoucauld, where nearly all the artist's works are displayed. There, in those often deserted rooms freezing in winter, cool in summer, chance occasionally caused me to encounter various out-of-the-ordinary persons. I often wonder if some of those beings really existed, for every time I think back on my sojourn in Paris I am gripped by a powerful sense of the unreal. But I have plenty of tangible evidence: letters, photos, the magic ring I still wear on my left hand, the indelible scars I collected in my struggle with the Vampires . . .

But let us get back to Shanghai and the unknown Gustave Moreau painting. Mr. Amer, delighted by my fascination with the work, was eager to tell us about its strange origins.

This blasphemous painting, unique in Moreau's work, was executed three hours after the death of the artist's very close friend—also a painter. It's a howl of rebellion against the stupid cruelty of the God who had just robbed him of one of the main reasons for his existence. The canvas, glimpsed by Gustave's mother a few days later, caused the old woman to suffer an attack of nerves, interspersed with fainting spells. She managed to get her son to promise to destroy the sacrilegious picture.

But Gustave, above all an artist, could not bring himself to annihilate such a perfect creation. He decided to ship it secretly to an extremely rich collector in Hang-Chow who had wanted to acquire one of the master's paintings. Moreau knew for a fact that there was absolutely no likelihood that the painting would return to the West. And indeed, it was handed down from father to son, until one descendent, more greedy for yen than for aesthetic frissons, sold it very dearly to Mr. Amer. Amer quickly hung it in the place of honor where

I hope it still remains, despite the passage of years and the explosive events that have since transformed the superstructure of Asia. For I consider ". . . and the pleasure of dying!" a supreme painting in the work of Gustave Moreau and in the entire history of art.

But I ramble. I beg my reader to forgive me. Like me, he knows that memories and sensations rarely respect chronology. Let's return once more to the past: Mr. Amer, having finished his art history lesson, finally asked us the point of our visit. Lyris then explained briefly who I was and my need to find lodgings and work protected from the steelish intrigues. Amer thought for a few moments, scrutinizing me through half-closed lids, then proposed a solution that offered the double advantage of giving me a job in his establishment while ensuring my safety within his system of ultradeveloped checkpoints. The job of officer in charge of sheets happened to be available; the person who held it had just left with a Mandarin. Mr. Amer was offering it to me.

I accepted gratefully and immediately started work.

Translated from the French by Myrna Bell Rochester

AT THE WOMEN WARRIORS' TABLE

> Love is a word that must be used very carefully. In certain cases it has a sexual meaning.
>
> —*The News of the World*

A specter is haunting the world—the specter of eroticism. To subdue it the Holy Alliances are ceaselessly in action, O paradox. But nothing is harder to destroy than a specter, nothing less annihilable than this "asserting of life up to the point of death." And then the Holy Alliances begin to get anaemic.

If in this domain the cinema has already performed miracles, one facet is absent nevertheless. Is there anything as exciting as a beautiful woman knowingly caressed by the caprices of a lens? Yes, the sight of a beautiful young man captured by a heterosexual camera. "These fauns, you want to *perpetrate them*, hoofs turned uppermost . . ." Smile, but not for long, Ladies and Gentlemen of the Patriarchy.

When the endless servitude of woman is broken, wrote the Seer,* *then will she find things strange, unfathomable, repulsive, delicious,* then will she know how to offer us the

* Translator's note: The "Seer" is Rimbaud. Marx and Engels, Bataille and Mallarmé are also invoked.

song of seaman and mattress instead of the boring laments on some sad, drifting little women they vainly try to make us swallow; *she, too, will be a poet!* It isn't a matter of reversing the roles within *the same stories,* of having a King Kong, submitting to the outrages of an Amazon in rut, cry out in fear (however curious it would be to contemplate such a version), but of discovering the *unknown,* expressing that "other" eroticism still so badly, so infrequently represented on the screen. On this planet are a few seers, female ones, who armed with a lens would cause a great stir in the world of the darkened theater. That would put the admirable Matilda in *The Monk* or the Rebecca of *La Motocyclette* in a completely new light. And neither Lewis nor Mandiargues would be betrayed one bit but on the contrary would be given an extra dimension.

Since you have only your chains to lose and a whole sensory world to win, erotics of all countries, unite!

Translated from the French by Paul Hammond

ENOUGH OR STILL MORE

Painting and color, beauty and convulsion, cinema and surrealism—certain relationships are so self-evident that we end up, as in *The Purloined Letter,* no longer perceiving them. They become part of us and our landscape.

Dislocation of time and space; amalgam of dreams and what is called reality; incantation of faces where a close-up unveils *the eye in the savage state* and the hint of a quiver at the corner of the mouth. All adventures (from Latin *adventurus:* what ought to happen) made possible and, like a unique handrail, the ambiguity of a nearly smooth fragment of cloth, a fragile two-dimensional frontier between the voyeurs of the third dimension and the seers of the fourth.

To those who know that the imaginable—even the unimaginable—is only the antechamber of the real, cinema is thus made flesh and blood by our looking, so that the latter ends up in some ways conditioning the former. I often order the arabesque of a dream—or is it the dream which orders me?—in the manner of a cinematic decoupage. On my wakening, each *scene* appears with such clarity of focused image that nothing remains but to film it. I have remarked elsewhere (and I owe the fixity of my attention on this to the reading of John W. Dunne's *Experiment with Time*) that dreams often have a premonitory aspect, which a kind of snare of the memory prevents us from verifying further.

Thus a dream is also an adventure (from Latin *adventurus:* what must happen). To film our maddest dreams would be equivalent—would it not?—to throwing the dice which will abolish chance, surrendering it to the triumph of all revolts, of love without constraints, of this *truth in a soul and a body,* road of the absolute.

"The composition of images is a spirit in a body," wrote Picatrix. "As to what images are, sages call them *Thelgam* or *Tetzavi,* which is interpreted as a transgressor, because everything that makes an image makes it through violence."

The adventure of cinema (from Latin *adventurus:* what must happen) will be convulsive: surrealism. Or it will not be at all.

Translated from the French by Nancy Joyce Peters

ALL CREATION IS ANDROGYNOUS: AN INTERVIEW

You have made three feature films. One of them, A Very Curious Girl, *has been released in the U.S. How was it received?*

Universal bought the world rights for *Curious Girl* after its great reception at the Venice Film Festival in 1969. When the film came out in New York it got a good reception from the critics . . . and then was taken off after two weeks! I learned later that one of the distribution executives at Universal had decided that the subject was "distasteful." I do admit that the heroine of the film—in order to avoid being raped—defends herself by kicking her attacker in the balls. Now this may appear to some as an offensive and vulgar way of defending oneself. . . . Perhaps the guy from Universal saw this scene as a personal attack. . . . Fortunately for me, the film was invited to the New York Women's Film Festival in 1972, and there, every one of the "distasteful" scenes was cheered by an enthusiastic audience! One young woman, who was working in the 16mm department at Universal, saw the film at the festival and took it upon herself to get the film reduced to 16mm. Ever since that day—and right up to the time Universal's possession rights ran out in 1976—*A Very Curious Girl* had a successful career on the university circuits, to such an extent that the film became a sort of myth.

Why do you think Curious Girl *has this mythical reputation in the U.S.? Can you analyze it?*

I have often wondered about it. Perhaps it's not for me to reply, but on thinking it over, I suppose the film brought a gust of revolt, of nonresignation and the idea that one cannot—indeed should not—accept life as it is. This "insolence considered as an art form," albeit "distasteful" for clotted brains, nevertheless delights all those who remain capable of questioning everything . . . beginning with oneself.

You have been quoted as saying that there is no difference between women filmmakers and men. Can you explain?

If I cut off the credits from my films, people wouldn't be able to tell if they were made by a woman or by a man. Films are made by filmmakers, period. That's all there is to it. If the woman has a cinematographic eye, a film made by a woman is no different from a film made by a man.

And what about the content?

Women have been oppressed for 40,000 years; therefore, from an atavistic or cerebral point of view we see some of the problems a different way. I think all creation is androgynous. I insist that technically and formally there is no difference between men's and women's films. When people tell me they could tell my films were made by a woman (without the credit), I say it's only because my films are not misogynous. But men can make nonmisogynist films, once in a million, or twice, when they touch the androgynous state of grace required. Of course, my films are a little misandrous. We live under patriarchal oppression. We have to combat the "enemy" until he understands that it is not in his interest to put us down.

There is always a lot of humor in your films. Do you think humor has ceased to be an exclusively male domain?

Humor is an essential element of revolt. When the women's movements are dull and take themselves too seriously they offer men a pretext for criticizing them. The only thing that interests me is not to take myself too seriously. Life may be tragic, but never serious . . .

Do you think the woman's position in society has changed over the last few years?

The problems are still the same—that is: to fight against prejudice, stupidity and misogyny. As Einstein said, "A prejudice is harder to split than an atom." The day women realize they can go out to buy a pack of cigarettes and never come back, things will have changed.

And the women who resist this change?

Of course there are always "*collaborateurs*." I cannot oblige women to change if they don't want to. We were born females, we must earn the status of women. At the risk of being shot at, I'd say that when a woman is narrow-minded she is often more so than a man. The women who resist change—for differing reasons of security, atavism, and servility—are ten times harder to convince than a man.

In the past, when women filmmakers were rare, you used to call yourself an alibi for the males of the film world. Nowadays there are more women filmmakers. What do you think of this?

In the world there are as many men as women, but there are many more men filmmakers than women. In France we are how many? Twenty or thirty at most. It's a drop in the ocean. But I don't think it's all the men's fault. Women always have a guilt complex. They should make up their minds and get on with it.

Will your next script cover the same ground as Fiancée?

It is not at all the same subject, but it no doubt deals with my principal obsessions: the hatred of all forms of prejudice, the love of humor, and the love of love.

Do you like to shock people?

Baudelaire spoke of "the aristocratic pleasure of displeasing." Perhaps I am like that. Perhaps I do have a tendency to provoke. I hate everything which is dormant, so when I see sleepiness around me I feel like giving it a prod, provoking a change. This attitude has often brought me trouble. People either love me or hate me, but if I tell you the truth and nothing but the truth, that doesn't exactly displease me.

And what about the sex in your films? Is that done deliberately to shock?

No, I write my films the way I feel them. If people are shocked that is their affair. It is true that some people have gone to see my films for the wrong reasons, but that doesn't matter. In that case, the sex becomes a sort of Trojan horse which breaks through opposition. As long as people are exposed to what I have to say I don't care why they came in. It is the intention which counts. All images are incantations: you call up a spirit and that is the spirit which appears.

You give your heroines flamboyant appetites: for food and wine, for the sun and the sea, for love and pleasure. Are these your appetites?

Yes. I love good wines; I like strange dishes; I adore the sun and the sea. I have many appetites. That's all right.

Don't you think that in general women's education tends to curb these appetites?

Of course! For example, I am sure that if we did not have a sense of sin we would not put on weight. We get fat from all those repressed desires. When I am unhappy, I get fatter. But as soon as I begin to notice it, I say to myself, "you are depriving yourself of something and that is harming you." As soon as I get my serenity back, I can eat and drink without putting on an inch.

You have said in the past that you refuse to have children, is that right?

Yes. Maternity doesn't interest me in the world as it is today. And as maternity doesn't interest me, I don't see why I should have children just because somewhere a lot of silly things are written about a woman's "biological destiny"!

But isn't it because you prefer to keep yourself for your professional activities?

No. I think one can do both, but it just doesn't interest me. On the other hand, one can also examine the problem from the ecological point of view. There are many women who want to have children. Our planet is overcrowded already, so if a woman doesn't feel like it, it is infinitely preferable that she abstain. A lynx needs 400 kilometers of territory, otherwise it dies. People need space, and they haven't got enough. Have you seen the expressions of people in the street? Have you seen how uptight they are? They really frighten me, because when things are like that, anything can happen, they are in such a state of despair. They feel that life is a dead-end. I feel less despair because I am lucid. I know that life has positive aspects and that "on the other side" there is neither paradise nor hell and that it is now that one must live. My motto is: "We are not two-legged for nothing. If we walk on two legs instead of four, it is so that we are closer to the stars. But we must also be worthy of that."

Translated from the French by Nelly Kaplan

Nicole Espagnol

Born in Paris in 1937, Nicole Espagnol participated in the activities of the Paris Surrealist Group from early 1959 until the group's "dislocation" (as she calls it) ten years later. A strong, defiant presence in the group, she was part of an extreme-left current within it, along with Alain Joubert, Elisabeth Lenk, Robert Lagarde, and, for a while, Gérard Legrand. Espagnol's intransigence and vigilance were crucial in neutralizing the various retrograde elements that sometimes attempt to insinuate themselves into surrealism.

A collection of her poems, *Little Magie,* was published by Editions Bordas in 1983, illustrated by Jorge Camacho. Currently she collaborates on the surrealist-oriented journal *Le Cerceau* [The Hoop] with Alain Joubert, Véronique Leblond, François Leperlier, Anne-Marie Beeckman, Pierre Peuchmaurd, and others.

The poems published here appeared in the French group's journal, *La Brèche: Action surréaliste* no. 7 (December 1964).

FEMALE SOCKET

Funeral March in B Flat
The step is missed
The mouse is in the pâté
What fun! And his bow tie
Spins around under the fires
What a night!
The jars are broken
The egg in the milk
"Waiter a crazy alcohol!"
Half-closed eyes on the languorous taste of his smile
It gleams from his pupil
So the cherry revolves in the spirits
And inhaled the unctuous, peppered marrow
And its odor heavy with sweetness
Spread it imperceptibly
Deep into the cushions
What a morning!

Translated from the French by Myrna Bell Rochester

HEARTSTOPPING

Crossed over on the other shore
The lovers are edge to edge
The town crier has lost his voice
The path is without shadow
A stone in the gorge
Fear of the ravine
Their hands clasped in the extreme
He yells his pride
She laughs, extravagant
Our eyes are two torrents Where happiness jousts
The clock is stopped
At the inexhaustible hour

Translated from the French by Myrna Bell Rochester

THE CONCLUSION IS NOT DRAWN

Acrimony hangs at the curtain
One evening's espagnolette
Devil comes, goes
(He leaves)
When suddenly the mist streams out
The air has no voice
(Pause)
Games given the lie by telegram
The trunk stationed at the watch
(Stop)
An acrobat appears
Stretches out and sleeps
The quarrel is at the front
Recovery is
Imminent

Translated from the French by Myrna Bell Rochester

THE WIND TURNS

The rope is braided in colors of love
The keyboard has lost its star
And this is the moment she chooses
Felicia! Her braids trained on hangers
Her hand on the coat peg
Let the galley ship sail!
Unknown latitude
But this high-handedness is exposed
The shrew's uncontested victory
The tame falcon sorts the dollars
The door swings open
And the one no one expected
Makes his way through the costume ball

Translated from the French by Myrna Bell Rochester

Annie Le Brun

Born in Rennes in 1942, Annie Le Brun started taking part in surrealist activity in 1963 and remained active in the Paris group until the great split of 1969, after which she collaborated for a time on the review *Coupure*. In 1972 with Georges Goldfayn, Radovan Ivsic, and Toyen, she helped initiate a new collective activity *via* the "Editions Maintenant." Her first book, *Sur-le-champ* [Right Now] (1967), illustrated by Toyen, revealed a poet of exceptional playfulness and provocation. Much better known, however, is Le Brun's work as essayist and polemicist. Her 1966 paper "Black Humor" is still the best short treatise on the subject, and *Les Chateaux de la subversion* [Castles of Subversion] (1982), on Gothic novels and their relation to revolutionary ferment, is a landmark study. *Lâchez tout* [Drop Everything] (1977), a merciless critique of certain retrograde aspects of French neofeminism (its title taken from a pivotal 1924 text of Breton's), brought her instant notoriety.

As editor of the *Complete Works* of the Marquis de Sade, author of a major study of Sade, organizer of a massive Sade exhibition in 1986, and a vigorous critic of contemporary social and cultural trends, Le Brun has remained an outstanding figure of controversy in French intellectual life. Unquestionably the best-known woman surrealist writer of the 1960s generation in France, she has also proved to be among the most prolific, uncompromising, and individualistic, adamant in her refusal to be "recuperated" either by the apparatus of repression or its reformist pseudo-oppositions.

INTRODUCTION TO *DROP EVERYTHING!*

I have a horror of not being misunderstood.
—Oscar Wilde

At sixteen, I decided my life would not be what others intended it to be. This determination—and perhaps luck—allowed me to escape most of the misfortunes inherent in the feminine condition. Rejoicing that young women today increasingly manifest their desire to reject the models heretofore offered them, I nonetheless deplore their seeming readiness to identify with the purely formal negation of these old-fashioned models, that is, when they do not settle for simply bringing them back into fashion. At a time when everyone complacently intones that one is not born a woman but one *becomes* a woman, hardly anyone seems to trouble herself about *not* becoming one. Indeed, it's just the opposite. Contrary to the efforts of eighteenth- and nineteenth-century feminists who endeavored to eliminate the illusory difference that gave men real power over women, the neofeminists of recent years have made it their business to establish the reality of that difference in order to claim an illusory power that women are said to have been denied. So thoroughly do they work at establishing the reality of this illusive difference that in the end, the revolt against *impossibility of being* tends to vanish under the blows of militant stupidity, thus introducing the *obligation to be*. Do we forever need to remind ourselves that in matters of revolt, we need no ancestors? And definitely, *no* technical advisers eager to exchange their recipes for feminine insubordination from A to Z.

In view of the extent of the crimes more or less legally perpetrated, not only against women but also against all those who refuse the social codification of sexual roles (homosexuals in particular), this revolt can only be regarded as urgent—so urgent that I cannot refrain from disrupting the chorus of those, male or female, who claim they are abstracting it from the private obscurity where it violently takes shape, and from whence it draws its overwhelming strength. I insist: this rebellion is always directed against the collective morale, no matter upon what bases the collectivity was founded. How, then, can we fail to see that today every woman will be dispossessed of the recovery of her self if she does not notice that every one of her tirades might be redirected and used to build an ideology as contradictory in its proposals as it is totalitarian in its intentions? We even find her more or less tacitly encouraged on all sides to reveal the claims of her sex, ever since the so-called "women's cause" was presented as the image of a rebellion tamed inside the net of the negative normalization that our epoch is so proficient at casting over the most remote spaces on the horizon.

Having always disdained masters who act like slaves as well as slaves eager to slip into the skins of masters, I confess that the ordinary conflicts between men and women have been of very little concern to me. My sympathy goes rather to those who desert the roles that society assigns them. Such people never claim to be constructing a new world, and therein lies their fundamental honesty: they never impose their notion of well-being on others. With a powerful determination that can often overturn the established order, they are just happy to be the exceptions that negate the rule.

Oscar Wilde interests me more than any bourgeoise woman who agreed to marry and have children, and then, one fine day, suddenly feels that her oh so hypothetical creativity is being frustrated.

And that's how it is.

I shall not list my preferences in this regard: it would be useless to do so, and extremely discouraging for the cause of women.

The fact that I have done my best as far as possible, to avoid biological destiny's psychic, social, and intellectual hold upon me is my own business, but I shall never give in to society's attempt to make me feel guilty in the name of all women, and to force me back into the limitations of that destiny. Such sudden and inexorable promiscuity in search of each woman's identity indeed threatens women at the very heart of their freedom when the gender difference is asserted at the expense of all other specific differences. Let us just consider calmly what we have *all* had to endure in the name of God, Nature, Man, and History. It seems, however, that all of that was not enough, for it is all starting up again under the banner of Woman. Specialists in coercion make no mistake when with sudden zeal they increase the numbers of national and international organizations dealing with "la condition féminine" without actually effecting any legislative change. And they can hardly go very far astray, since the moment when Louis Aragon, that choirboy of repression for almost half a century, announced that woman is "Man's Future." I have the gravest doubts about a future that might look anything like Elsa Triolet.

In all that is said and written in the name of woman, I see the return—under the pretext of liberation—of everything that has traditionally diminished women: They denounce the family but extol motherhood as the foundation of the family. They attack the notion of woman-as-object but promote the revival of "feminine mystery." And the exposure of the relations between men and women as power relations initiates theories about the most sickening and inane conjugal squabbles. For me these are just so many more reasons to be glad that I have definitively turned my back on the *dead-ends* of so-called "feminine sensibility." Moreover, nothing could make me alter my natural aversion to majorities, especially when they are composed of part-time martyrs—largely a phenomenon of the western world.

The more deafening the noise of our time, the more I feel certain that my life is elsewhere, gliding along my love whose shapes entomb the passing of time. I look at you. We shall meet on the bridge of transparency before diving into the night of our differences. We shall swim, near one another or at a distance, tense or distracted, going against the stream of our enigma to find ourselves in the uncertain embrace of our fleeting shadows. We are not the only ones who have encountered a point of transparency before plunging into the night of our differences and who have come up not caring whether we are male or female. And if very few men find it easy to recognize themselves in Francis Picabia's avowal, "Women are the agents of my freedom," it is perhaps because that comes only with the triumph of a *Marvelous* that men and women have yet to discover. That is why I object to being enrolled in an army of women engaged in struggle simply because of a biological accident. My frantic individualism is exactly in proportion to all that strives toward the interchangeability of all beings.

This book is a call for desertion.

Translated from the French by Guy Ducornet

Giovanna

Born Anna Voggi in Reggio-Emilio, Italy, Giovanna began participating in surrealist activity in Paris in 1965. With Jean-Michel Goutier she performed the ceremonial "La Carte absolue" in November of that year, shortly before the opening of the International Surrealist Exhibition, *L'Ecart absolu.* She exhibited drawings made on a typewriter at the International Surrealist Exhibition in São Paulo in 1967 and took part in the "Poetic Furor" exhibition organized by José Pierre in Paris the same year. Her extravagantly playful work has also been featured in several other collective exhibitions, including "22 Surrealist Painters" (Paris, 1977), "Surrealism Unlimited" (London, 1978), and "Presencia viva de Wolfgang Paalen" (Mexico City, 1979). In recent years she has exhibited with the Phases movement. Her first solo show in Brussels in 1976 was the first of many in the Old World and the New. Her book-object, *L'herbe du Diable et la petite fumée,* was issued in 1978. Her other books include *William Blake* and *Deus ex machina,* both published in 1977, and most recently *Pacifique que ça!,* with Jean-Michel Goutier (1995). She lives in Paris.

Published here are Giovanna's response to an inquiry of José Pierre's from the journal *Si et No* in 1975 and three poems kindly sent by the author.

WHERE ARE WE IN RELATION TO SURREALISM?

It is as brutal as a critique pinned on a turban spinning around its axis.

Decades are not always poetic. But it is neither severely reprehensible nor justifiable to eliminate the somnolence of each atrocity by rushing into writing as into a bivouac, while hoisting one's elaborate membrane in the style of a Renaissance pylon. Before protesting, language protests; it shamelessly develops the justification of private lessons beloved by dead criteria.

"A house boy" finds the muse a bit whorish and makes up anathemas that circulate in manuscript form—salacious and protective. Tiny kit for the rhyme and reflexibility of prosody. Mental fireguard in the highest sense of the word.

Desperate colloquy of colors on the turtleneck sweaters of suntanned desires.

Inconceivable realism entices news in brief without prose having to bleed while the sweetness of sea-bathing forces the drowned men to wet the last cigarette.

At sunrise one bangs on the atlas to reconcile it with the advent of the regulating poem. More illegible than unforeseeable, actuality coils up exotically like a symbolic element on an unmade bed. To lie down on the gloss reduces the typical speed of the pulse caught in the act, under the pressure of time. The syntax resembles those feminine ornaments, so exciting as to become paralyzing. Mount Irony dominates the inert plastic sense and agrees to find a shadow of autonomy at the origin of every refusal. The earth stomps its foot when it is not concerned by the obscene gesture of the airplane created by the gracious hills.

To counter reality when it pretends to be in fine shape, some evening, when a simple profile takes on the appearance of a long discourse.

The scandal was consummated at the end of a meal when the key reappeared, supported by a door. One gets over a marble that splits.

As for myself, I imperceptibly race down the yo-yo while nibbling on the meridian.

All along the hook, exciting nights are stretching.

Translated from the French by Guy Ducornet

BAKING CHOCOLATE AND DIALECTICS

The most dialectical name: Augustus.

The most paradoxical first name: Felicity or even Celeste, though Celeste is more dialectical than paradoxical.

"Why is the bourgeois woman called Françoise and the maid called Fortunée?" asked the little prince.

"Why is the Virgin called Mary and why is Mary, in spite of her meeting with that son of a whore, always in such deep shit?" asked Annunciation.

"Because of the need for justice that moves us all," she was answered.

"Why, after forbidding the use of tobacco to ensure, it would seem, the 'future' of the carpeting, does Madam make such a great show of concern about the more or less harmonious functioning of Carmen's constitution, when both blind men and amputees can be healthy?" added little Robert.

"Carmen received that smoking prohibition head on. Was it in fact she who prevented Madam—completely deformed, however, by her watercolor work—from continuing to look good?"

Why does Madam cultivate redundancy as soon as she takes "poor" Dolores into her confidence?

For Prudence's sake Gladys called herself Eugenia.

For Clemency's sake Immaculate called herself Céline.

For Constancy's sake Constance called herself Constance.

Translated from the French by Myrna Bell Rochester

WHAT DO I KNOW . . .

What do I know
about the nested structure of the laughing cow?

What do I know
about the advantages of mild cigarettes?

What do I know
about the cunning idealism of managers?

What do I know
about Santa Claus's logic?

What do I know
about the itching line?

What do I know
about private fold-away cupboards?

What do I know
about the status of decline?

What do I know
about neuromuscular praxis?

. . . .

Baudrillard's stuff? I don't give a damn!

Translated from the French by Myrna Bell Rochester

THERAPY

I refuted it all
Cabernet from the Gatinais
The human and the wolfman
Plumb line and soldier's girl
Prospective imagination
Pestilential psalms
Faked reciprocity
Phenomena of viscosity
Lubricant in an aerosol can

Since then I shit like a Madonna

Translated from the French by Myrna Bell Rochester

Monique Charbonel

Monique Charbonel was born in Paris in 1941. As a young revolutionary militant she belonged to a small group called RUpTure, whose chief purpose—at least initially—was to reconstitute in the 1960s the pre–World War II International Federation for an Independent Revolutionary Art, or FIARI. (Inaugurated by the Breton/Trotsky *Manifesto for an Independent Revolutionary Art* in 1938, the FIARI had ceased to function by 1940.) Although RUpTure founder Pascal Colard had collaborated on the seventh issue of the Surrealist Group's journal *La Brèche* in 1964, the two groups proved unable to work together. As adherents of a Trotskyist sect, the Organisation Communiste International (OCI, also known as "Lambertistes" after their spokesperson, Pierre Lambert), the RUpTurists upheld a political rigidity alien to the Surrealist Group and, like the Communist Party–oriented "Revolutionary Surrealists" of 1947, soon proclaimed themselves more revolutionary, and more surrealist, than the surrealists! In effect, RUpTure saw itself as a kind of surrealist "Left Opposition."

Monique Charbonel, the only woman in this group, produced work of an exceptional quality. Poet, painter, collagist, and inventor of the *ronéogram*—a new kind of decalcomania using mimeograph stencils—she published poems (and an article on ronéograms) in the group's journal and took part in its 1967 exhibition, "Signes précurseurs" [Precursor Signs]. She left RUpTure in the aftermath of the revolutionary events of "May '68" and died three years later, in 1971, at the age of thirty, leaving behind a small but impressive body of work reflecting her total commitment to surrealist aims. Her husband and fellow RUpTurist, painter Jean-Claude Charbonel, later joined the Phases movement.

Monique Charbonel's poems have not been collected in book form. The poem translated here appeared in French in *RUpTure* no. 5 in 1967.

IT'S A WONDER

It's a wonder
to see you leaning over
to wander from the nape of your neck
to your hands
from your loins
to your eyelids
that darken in contact with my body
and that my finger unfolds
between two beats
between two
before sleep
after the starry path
of black stones and
white feathers
between walls
of flesh
like a train in the night

Translated from the French by Myrna Bell Rochester

Unica Zürn

Born in 1916 into a prosperous family in Berlin, Unica Zürn grew up oblivious to the horrors of Nazism and remained so until around 1943–1944, when by chance she heard an underground radio report of the concentration camps. After this shattering experience she never returned to any kind of "normal" life. Later diagnosed as schizophrenic, she was at various times hospitalized in institutions in Paris, Berlin, and La Rochelle.

Her meeting with Hans Bellmer in 1953 was a determining one, and they became one of the most extraordinary couples in the history of surrealism. Zürn frequented the Surrealist Group in Paris throughout the 1950s, exhibited at the Galerie Le Soleil dans la Tête, and took part in the 1959 International Surrealist Exhibition devoted to Eros. Celebrated for her anagrams (*Hexentexte,* 1954), she also wrote two powerful narratives: *Dark Spring* (1969) and *Jasmine Man* (1971).

Unwilling to adapt to the deteriorating vicissitudes of life, she jumped from a window to her death in 1970.

The following text is excerpted from her narrative, *Lying in Ambush.*

LYING IN AMBUSH

Rain is falling in Rashomon's forest. With slow, sorrowful steps, the rascal's lady-love crosses the street to buy some unsweetened chocolate.

Meanwhile, advancing slowly through the forest on a white horse is the white-veiled woman in her high white hat. Reverently her husband squeezes her tiny, cold hand; he has no fear of murderers. Seated beneath the temple's open roof, which is supported by four round pillars, are four priests and a woodchopper. The rain persists, and a thick fog hovers in the trees. The day is long, sad, completely white. Each of the five witnesses offers a completely different version of the murder.

Each one saw everything that happened; each one envies the others' stories. Silence reigns in the forest as Rashomon rouses himself from a deep and prolonged slumber. Down the ancient trail he strolls, and not even the snap of a twig can be heard under his bare feet. Flicking aside the white veil from her brow, the white woman looks over the scene. Not a sound can be heard.

'Tis a sleepy sort of day. Shiny with dampness, the moss has swelled up like a sponge. As the hour of death draws nigh, the samurai gazes darkly into the downpour. On his shoulders lies the responsibility for his wife, who quivers like a rich white pudding in a bowl of the best porcelain. She has no love for her husband, and were it not for the fact that he is wealthy and, indeed, an aristocrat, she would have left him long ago. She is childless and values her breasts too highly to use them for nursing small mammals. On and on they ride, but no inn comes into view. Night is approaching, full of dangers. They have neither pillows on which to rest their heads, nor blankets to shield their bodies from the cold.

With long, tapered fingers the Black Baron draws a Queen of Hearts from his billfold and cleverly makes it disappear in the moist air. Breathing down the

Queen's neck is a black King of Spades, who gallantly tips his crown. The time has come to cook the onion soup and to dry the soaking-wet wigs of the wax women's heads. The Black Baron, who goes for slim little girls, is chummy with the vice squad. Taking a drag of a marijuana cigarette which is no thicker than a matchstick, he waits until the clock in the tower strikes noon. Dark indeed are days like this, and how far away the sun is! We are so tired; the bed's a filthy mess but we might lie down in it anyway. They never clean the laundry here. As for the patriarch's bathtub, it's used once every three months at the most.

Out of the temple in the forest, the five witnesses advance toward the Palace of Justice. As the hour of death draws nigh, the samurai gazes darkly into the downpour. Being responsible for his wife is not at all to his liking. She quivers like a rich white pudding in a bowl of the best porcelain. She has no love for her husband and, indeed, would have left him long ago were it not for the fact that he is wealthy and an aristocrat. She is childless, and values her breasts too highly to use them for nursing small mammals. On and on they ride, but no inn comes into view. Night is approaching, full of dangers, but they have neither pillows on which to rest their heads nor blankets to shield their bodies from cold.

With long, tapered fingers the Black Baron draws a Queen of Hearts from his billfold, and in a flash a black King of Spades is breathing down the Queen's neck. Gallantly, the King of Spades lifts his crown.

The time has come to cook the onion soup, and to dry the soaking-wet wigs of the wax women's heads. The Black Baron, who goes for slim little girls, is chummy with the vice squad. Taking a drag of a marijuana cigarette which is no thicker than a matchstick, he waits until the clock in the tower strikes noon. Dark indeed are days like this, and how far away the sun is! We are so tired; the bed's a filthy mess but we might lie down in it anyway. They never clean the laundry here. As for the patriarch's bathtub, it's used once every three months at the most.

Out of the temple in the forest, the five witnesses advance toward the Palace of Justice. How magnificent it looks with a hundred vast windows wide open on the sun. The judges are merciless, tired of waiting, eager for a head to roll. The executioner sharpens his axe, embellishing its handle with precious gems. No buyers are here from distant lands as the clock in the tower strikes noon. As for the Black Baron's pockets, they are empty. When he turns them inside-out, flakes of tobacco spill onto the ground. Splayfooted pigeons waddle around the square like ducks as old crones toss them chunks of bread. This rain paralyzes not only our loins but our very lives. What will become of us, the rascal's lady-love asks herself. The soup has the bitterness of bile; the bread is stale. The life we lead is harsh and terrifying. How I wish I were dead and afloat on the lake like lovely, mad Ophelia, with water-lilies woven into my streaming, soaking-wet hair. . . .

• • •

The samurai released his wife's tiny hand. Foxlike, his ears go up. In Rashomon's forest, something is stirring. An eerie, subterranean world is awakening, and nobody knows what to expect during the next few hours. A dreadful catastrophe is bubbling up. Always on the verge of a fit of tears, the white lady nestles down like a friendly cat before the fire. Slowly but surely things are being readied for a duel. . . .

The forest is soaking wet like a sponge, and white clouds float in it like fish, silent and belly-up.

Translated from the German by Eloise Ryder.

Elisabeth Lenk

German-born poet and scholar Elisabeth Lenk studied philosophy for several years at the Frankfurt School before moving to Paris in 1962. She first met surrealists at a dinner honoring an Algerian war deserter who had just been released from prison. Attracted by what she calls the surrealists' "metapolitics," she joined the Paris group and in 1964 contributed important articles on Heidegger's involvement in Nazism to the journal *La Brèche: Action surréaliste* (nos. 6 and 8).

Active in the near-revolution of May 1968, Lenk returned to Germany later that year. Author of *Das springende Narzis: André Bretons poetischer Materialismus* [Narcissus Leaping: André Breton's Poetic Materialism] (1971), she has also edited, prefaced, and translated works by Breton, Aragon, Dalí, Fourier, and Bataille, and with Rita Bischof edited the collected poems of Anneliese Hager.

Formerly on the faculty of the Free University in Berlin, Elisabeth Lenk currently lives in Hannover, where she is a professor at the city university and regards herself as a militant feminist ally of surrealism.

Her statement on surrealism in Germany is from a letter included in Alquié (1940, 543–544), and the automatic text (from the cycle, *Dancing Waves*) served as a preface to a 1991 exhibition of Anne Ethuin's coated collages.

SURREALISM: A LIBERATING AND CATALYZING ELEMENT IN GERMANY TODAY

One may ask—and I have been asked in private conversations—whether the second Enlightenment which is, in today's Germany, a reaction against a most barbarian irrationalism, might not be a necessary and salutary reaction: salutary for a world that was the victim of Nazism and also for the Germans themselves, who might have found, in a rigid Reason, something capable of preventing the blind furor from surfacing again. I do not think so.

The second Enlightenment (which should be defined more precisely than I can do here) merely reproduces the deep contradictions of German culture, which must be considered in order to explain the Nazi phenomenon. Young contemporary German poets who claim kinship with either structural or engaged poetry (such as Bertolt Brecht's), share this shameful and torn consciousness, so strikingly similar to the Protestant consciousness—the Lutheran, to be more precise. Luther declared that it was better not to be too respectful of that old inflexible Adam who had to be drowned each day. Similarly, today's German poet offers the spectacle of someone who ceaselessly represses and drowns that other, internal Adam, in his or her own self, the romantic self which is suspected of being Nazism's accomplice. This tyrannical and pedantic instance which rejects, represses, and drowns—isn't it precisely the Understanding, already denounced as the mortal enemy of all creation and of all true spirit by those who protested against the first German Enlightenment? No Understanding can heal the deep inner break which occurs when the human individual is cruelly facing himself. On the contrary, the power of a disincarnated Understanding can provoke again the terrible revenge of the forces he wants to keep out of consciousness. If they are locked up and kept in the dark, those forces are most harmful when unleashed. But these same forces may reach a new quality if they are allowed to receive light. This is to my mind the surrealist message, as well as that of German romanticism.

And this is why I believe that surrealism could be a liberating and catalyzing element in Germany today. Surrealism would help us rediscover the most repressed part of German romanticism. Let us be clear: I do not mean the romanticism of decline, so often evoked in Germany, whose representatives were ready to seek refuge in Catholicism. Nor do I extend my hand to the reactionary and repressive powers. I speak of that initial romanticism, that original impulse toward reconquering what a torn humankind had lost. This would be the true *Aufarbeitung der Vergangenheit* [to assume one's past?] that one hears so much about. Perhaps a new Reason will spring from this, capable of receiving—and even expressing—the full wealth of all that it is not.

Translated from the French by Guy Ducornet

AUTOMATIC TEXT FOR ANNE ETHUIN

And I thought to go through the walls
that separate human beings from each other.

Lots of stripes
Is there still iron on the iron track?
Leaden
I am not modest, I am
unassuming, that is something else
Going on and on endlessly
My favorite occupation for years
You swap with me
Have you seen the cards?
Seen yes but not understood
"Never explain the slightest item"
was my high ambition
In the 20th century the dandies are crushed
trampled underfoot in a kind of rage
Seven ounces of common sense
And all doors open
One man in 20-fold multiplication
for whom the same door always opens magically
A young lady is reading *The Modern Female*
Cold rage of money
Uninterrupted economic aggression
For me the sky was blue, for me
alone
I give up my habits but not you
My habits are my prison
Lots of child-men
Nearly all the men I know could be called child-men
Trousers roll
frayed souls
dead trees
The trousers roll to and fro and are empty
To the extent that he was unselfish
he lacked the ability to
adapt to American conditions
The present is not against me

it comes to meet me
This lady laughs too much
Her laugh is false
The child-men exert themselves and the lady laughs
Sometimes she laughs high sometimes low
Faster and faster
A concrete ruin glides past
And a woman all in pink
A hundred leaves on a solitary tree but
some have already fallen
I have released myself from the future
between two plastic walls on splints
I have found presence
Money is more relentless than any ideology
I live in the Northern Station
From there I always head north
A laughter full of anxiety
A laughter that sounds wrong
Child-men are like clowns
They keep inventing new jokes
An unshaven dark man with a punk hairdo
remains on the track
He wants to stab money in the heart
But money has no heart
Far too many words
But I do not feel anything
Now he flies home in his European striped shirt
And I see a woman's white arm
There is no fixed sequence
With me the climax comes before the low point
The end before the beginning
Or do they all occur simultaneously?
I don't go out
Because at any moment I expect
my own arrival

Translated by Gisela Baumhauer and Greta Wenziger

Penelope Rosemont

Descended from freethinking Bohemians who came to the U.S. in the mid-1800s, Penelope Rosemont was born in Chicago in 1942 and was educated for a career as a chemist. Early inclined toward radicalism, she took part in Chicago's *Rebel Worker* group ("the left wing of the Beat Generation") and later served on the national staff of the Students for a Democratic Society. In Paris in 1966 André Breton welcomed her and her husband Franklin into the Surrealist Group. After several months' participation in the group's daily meetings at the café Promenade de Vénus, they returned and cofounded the first indigenous Surrealist Group in the U.S., in Chicago.

Rosemont took part in the U.S. surrealists' first group show (Gallery Bugs Bunny, 1968), and her paintings and alchemigrams have been included in major surrealist exhibitions in France, England, Holland, Mexico, and other countries. At the World Surrealist Exhibition in Chicago in 1976, she elaborated the Domain of Robin Hood. Her work was also featured in the "Art & Alchemy" exhibition at the 1986 Venice Biennale. More recently she has invented two new extensions of collage: the landscapade and the prehensilhouette.

Her first book of poems, *Athanor,* appeared in 1970, and her second, *Beware of the Ice* (illustrated by Enrico Baj), in 1992. *Surrealist Experiences,* a collection of her articles and essays, appeared in 1998. Coeditor of *Arsenal: Surrealist Subversion* and of *Free Spirits,* she has contributed to surrealist publications all over the world—including *L'Archibras, Phases,* and *Le Désir libertaire* in Paris, *Analogon* in Prague, *Brumes Blondes* in Amsterdam, and *Salamandra* in Spain—as well as such U.S. radical periodicals as *Radical America* and *Earth First!* She lives in Chicago.

"Passage" and "Candle" are both from *Athanor*. "Rising Asleep," written in the 1970s, first appeared in *Free Spirits* in 1982.

PASSAGE

in celebration of Benjamin Péret

the lettuce devours its leaves
the night its stars
the insect becomes hopeful
the unfortunate cow
dissolves unnoticed

while the soap eats grass
and grows fat
the avenues forget their names
and are referred to only
as Smith
mud puddles take the initiative
to spring at well-dressed men
and top hats aren't safe from snowballs
even in the midst of summer

(Paris, 1966)

CANDLE

The owl hid his eyes
  under his hands
He hid his hands
  under his feet
He hid his feet
  behind his ears
He hid his ears
  between his toes
He tucked his toes
  under his belt
And completely disappeared

RISING ASLEEP

in celebration of Toyen

The wind today is full of fish
The branches of the trees
are full of mirrors

Whirlpool woven of wilderness
your knife is an octopus
your lips are a dance
your two hands are revolving doors
you are the North Pole

Penelope Rosemont, *Euclid's Last Stand,* oil on canvas with collage, 1976. Courtesy of the artist.

Joyce Mansour

A MANGO

I feel like a mango
I have a horror of men who don't know how to eat
Without dispensing their wisdom with quick saliva
You weep
Alone wounded and cured by my friendly lip
You see a phallus eating with its fingers
I crave dust
There is no lodging large enough
No century no beach empty enough for my taste
Put to sleep the day before by Caesar's descendants
I molt without a shudder too sad to defend myself
My heart needs a mango
We must kill no one
Today they say for prudence's sake
Love's eyes are dry
Oil slicks take the place of corn on our walls
The heavy chariots of dawn
Pass endlessly
Behind the teddy bear
The drunken look of the snake
And my mother dreaming in English far far away
Far away the mango with its odor of night

(From *Carré blanc,* 1965)
Translated from the French by Mary Beach

NIGHT IN THE SHAPE OF A BISON

I think too often of funeral ceremonies
Flop little goldfish
I think too often of ravaged graves
Of oppressive wakes
I don't know how to repulse the widow nor soften her parchment
Servant of cemeteries since lost antiquity
The earth is the roof of my house

Everywhere in my dreams floats a feminine odor
Like an erotic sore with ultrafine needles
Like a ruin
How to drive away corpses carriers of contagion
Vast assembly in orange pyjamas
And antique dealers' windows
How to seal the catafalques without touching the soup
How to dust a dead man without disturbing his eyelids
Where will I go when all roads are watched

(From *Carré blanc,* 1965)
Translated from the French by Mary Beach

TEN TO ONE TO NO

Flashing wild horses of Europe
Chaos of broken limbs
Moving walls
Suns
Bloody cobblestones thrown by blind hands
Into the mayonnaise
Into the mud
Into the sewer familiarly gaping
Into all which is known and dare not reveal itself
The Arab in me shivers on each stair of passive
Flesh
Capable of waiting a long time for the sad promised masting
Hail o my friends death with its flights its fusions
For her alone there are no forbidden regions
In the brasero of passionate love
Then
Once night has come
Night night storm
I return to my youth
The frantic phosphorus
The bestial heat
The waves of permitted revenge
The sand
The yawning of fragile night
The ether

At the moment when Paris lights up
The free animal still runs in our headlights
Exquisite soul
The lovely veiled apple no longer vomits its worm
Moonlight
True I am a Jewess
Capable of learning freedom in the street
Where infamy is displayed
I cursed in me the woman who accepts
The triangular face of the padlock
Silence
I spit on those who listen
Behind their limpid eyes
Their flies stomped by too many cracked brains
Their doors filthily shut
Nomenclature of nightmares
A single drop of urine on the pavement
Every muzzle points

(From *Carré blanc,* 1965)
Translated from the French by Mary Beach

WILD GLEE FROM ELSEWHERE

for Reinhoud

Hard calloused dreams
Burst palefully
Through the seams of tasteless
Yesterday
Don't whine for help
Lie bleeding
Life is a perpetual sneeze
Listen to the screech of iron in the rocky
Vacuum
Of an eyeless
Socket
To the mouthless prayer of ambiguous men
Stretched out in anguish and surgical green
Listen

Sharpen your tongue on the soft white womb
Nestling in formaldehyde
Then all shouting done
Watch brittle sperm rain down like cheese
Collect the bubbles
Hustle sour winds up the sidewalk
Suck the fresh flesh of the ruby
Leave it screaming
No matter
Strange shallow dreams eat at random
And shriek not with age
Soundless laughter like the midnight sea
Will toil back to slumber
And there will the bodiless breaker unroll its metal
Dip thunder and vanish
In a thousand grim echoes
Far beyond the bloody swelling of a mother's breast
"Pardon me" said she dressed in small-town bereavement
And Humpty-Dumpty closed a huge savage eye

(From *Phallus et Momies,* 1969)
Translated from the French by the author

ABSOLUTE DIVERGENCE: THE INTERNATIONAL SURREALIST EXHIBITION, 1965–1966

Mnemotechnic Elements for a Future Dream

Without beginning or end, memories and their ectoplasm, photographs come to contradict themselves on the retina of actual imaginary experiences.

The conscious development of an image from a lost past depends upon the reverie angle. A thousand tiny lost notations run between the lines, a thousand imprisoned words go moldy between the cobblestones of glossy paper: like a mirage against reality. It was, it is the responsibility of the visitors as well as the practitioners of "absolute divergence" to embroider endlessly on this canvas and to trace their paths as they please. Certain places, certain times push our imagination into contortions which are normally impossible. And so, on that day, I shall be simultaneously inside the Galerie de l'Oeil, rue Séguier, last year, 1965, spins around. An immense creature comes toward me, howling, its journalistic entrails publicly churned and tossed and soaped up, with its hairless chicken skin and its hysterical halo: the Consumer.

Fleeing under sponge umbrellas and shovelsful of bread crumbs. . . .

Then, the test of the room, walled by man's inhumanity to man. The Disordainer: myth and quest and ritual, all at once: the electronic Gordian Knot of the king of rats, oval and Bonapartist like the wheel of honorific labor. I shall dip my eyes into the plate-glass night, my fingers will waltz on the instrument's panel until, finally free from the "simple and clear solution" of daily routine, I shall move on to seek the exit. An exit. Any exit. The Consumer will throw street names to the face of the Arch-of-Defeat as it awaits on its crutch the coming of its metallic death, in a well-armed armchair, just as Dante awaited his Divine.

A man will dive head first into the refrigerator-prison: the Consumer's back will tear nuptial veils, tufts of postscripts and orange blossoms, and other fibrous appendixes.

The Sardine will close its good eye. The floating bones, the motorized chest of drawers, and the ceilings of legion-of-honor meat will proudly strut about in the very back room. Maldoror's dog will tear his claws away from the bloody marsh so as to leap onto the lanes of Central Park.

Nibbled by his obscene hunger, nacreous under his tombstone necklace, silent and milky as an oyster inside its shell, the Necrophile will part his lips and show his prelunar tongue. The dreamy stone distills and dilutes itself as mercury in the vertigo of logistics. It was yesterday. Elsewhere, the Necrophile sleeps standing up under his glass bell. "Let's build a trap that will neither kill nor injure its victim, but will hold it until it wakes up. . . ." The street has become another, more ancient; the lights in the window are turned off: it's tomorrow already.

(From *L'Archibras: le surréalisme* no. 1, 1967)
Translated from the French by Guy Ducornet

Mimi Parent

ARE YOU A SURREALIST?

Are you a surrealist?

My own discovery of surrealism coincided with my growing awareness of the enemies of my freedom: Family, Fatherland, Religion. Naturally I also needed to know who my allies were, and where.

Reading the *Manifestoes* soon convinced me that surrealism held the rich revelatory vein of Life such as I had resolved to live it: love, poetry, freedom.

Mimi Parent, drawing, 1984. Courtesy of the artist.

Several years passed before I was able to meet members of the Surrealist Movement. I longed for that moment, that Festival, but at the same time I dreaded it, fearing that I would "show up empty-handed." For me the idea of Festival is inseparable from the idea of potlatch.

My enthusiastic expectations were not disappointed. I entered the group just as the 1959 International Surrealist Exhibition was getting under way. Action and ideas (these being the essential for me) joined forces in an atmosphere of play and games which gave rise to the glorious agitation of the grand preparations.

After the festival was over, day fell and brought Seriousness with it. Seriousness sat at the café table every evening from 6 to 8. And Seriousness took itself Very Seriously, with occasional outbursts of laughter—no doubt to catch its breath and to show that one could be Serious without necessarily having to be Serious all the time. For my part, I sensed that the Age of Reason was quite settled in among us, to the detriment of the Golden Age. Sometimes I yawned a lot, but mostly to myself, out of timidity and also out of respect for certain guests. I must not have been the only one, for the Surrealist Movement [in Paris] vanished in a great big yawn for the simple reason that it failed to reconcile itself to its own madness.

The recent failure of collective activity has forced several among us to become individualist *enragés*. Nonetheless, I want to believe that the Festival will resume one day—*spontaneously*. The live coals are ready and waiting; all it takes is the right day, with a strong wind.

23 February 1970
(From Vincent Bounoure, *Pour communication: réponses à l'enquète, 'Rien ou quoi?'*)
Translated from the French by Franklin Rosemont

Marianne van Hirtum

THE FUTURE OF SURREALISM: RESPONSE TO AN INQUIRY

Paris, 12 December 1969

I have opted for the confidence and generosity that it seems to me necessary to maintain, in order to protect what I consider the essential, and which is, was, and will remain essential for me, for the rest of my life: namely, that my reason for existing, and my only reason, is the *surrealist* reason. I myself could care less whether I am or seem to be an exemplary individual compared with all those who have taken it upon themselves to uphold its spirit and permanence, provided that what we are all defending is itself the exemplary object. And that, for me, is not a problem, since surrealism is to my mind exemplary or is not surrealism. (I am speaking of its essence: that is what for me is eternal!—in mere "apparent" opposition to "historical" surrealism, which is made up of various "chances along the way," but does not invalidate the essential.)

In this regard, a qualitative judgment is not required. It's simple: Do I belong or not? How could I *not* belong? How could I alter the appearance of my own face? . . .

I desire and long for only one thing: the solidarity of each and all of us in our adherence to the *essential* that formed our lives. . . .

I can only remain—and want only to remain—passionately and definitively what I am: someone for whom there exists, has existed, will exist only the *surrealist quest,* whatever it may be called in the future . . .

Moreover, I know where to situate my personal action—I know it well: It is at the point where a state of mind (with all the "possibilities" that might come of it), a mental attitude, and my own creations come together. Concerning that point, I would rather be silent forever than prove unworthy of it.

(From Vincent Bounoure, *Pour communication: réponses à l'enquète, 'Rien ou quoi?',* Paris, 1970)
Translated by Myrna Bell Rochester and Franklin Rosemont

WHILE WE SPEND OUR LIVES IRONING . . .

While we spend our lives ironing
an ancient iron with a new sock,
the Principle arrives at the end.
Dressed in a coal-dust suit that makes his eyes sparkle
like two distant stars kept at the bottom of the sea.

The Principle is followed by the crowd of his little ones.
Oh!—Aren't these little ones well behaved!
How sweet are their fingers' caresses
each one carrying in seed a grain of the incomprehensible laugh.
Marvelous family with no particular goal
far holier than the previous one.

They do not look at all like the weeping fan
They do not look at all like the anemone closing its doors
on Sundays when they nail up wool.

On Saturdays when steel is embroidered as altar covers
They do not look like those little incandescent berries
flowering at night where station signals,
wrongly called "bleeding hearts,"
which break away as pale butterflies
from lighthouses hoisted up over the sea.

I have sought in all places and even beyond
what might look like them and I found out never.

Of this "Never," I shall make my very own Principle.
Precious reserve for days to come.

Bright gloomy brother for the necessary survival
of the bald wig, under the large hat of black eternity.

(From *La Nuit mathématique,* 1976)
Translated from the French by Peter Wood and Guy Flandre

AND I SHALL BE THE MOUTH OF COPPER . . .

And I shall be the mouth of copper
which the sleeper's eyes will look at askance.

A stamp, that the pretty faces of fallen republics
will place on emerald pupils.
A breath of crystal, where the blond wind of terrifying axles
calms down in death alone, weaving its widow's cloth;
A brushwood on fire around this slate vase
where the last autumn sky shows through.

Glorious Medusa, supreme contempt for chaste abandon
in lives as beautiful as storms.
Gloomy, by eroding the volcanoes that lava has dug
out of the man-siren's head.

I am also this whole man,
whose steel belly answers the call
when the time comes for giving birth on the huge tower
to the black cormorant of fear.

Sleep comes along upright
before I took the trouble to turn my head
with greedy lips it sucks in the very base of my reason
come to rest in a foam-mill.

It is a miracle
The raving tree carries away the mourning horses
to the amber sapphire cordillera
Sole point where the lover's breathing is still possible
In this evening mixed with fiery triumphs
Which change into crenels the vanquished lovers
Now leaning on the very long chairs of violence
and constantly threatened with death

Such is the story of my impure angel's sleep
donning children's roses every morning

(From *La Nuit mathématique,* 1976)
Translated from the French by Peter Wood and Guy Flandre

THE NAKED TRUTH

The naked truth: that's not her,
dressed in a thousand dark corridors.
The green pavement of her legs
might well resemble the funereal alleyways
where Desire, in his suit of ashes
travels along on his innocent donkey
that may have lost its way going to the Asylum.
What fear it needed, to climb to the top
of three old lampposts,
habitation of the wise toad with eyes
more moving than those of young girls.
Powerful fingers arranged like colored dice
take the loving life at its word
bathing its body the size of night
in a thimble-death.
A procession of torch-headed dragonflies carrying,
in their closed arms
the wedding of my blue eye
with a diamond snail.

(From *La Nuit mathématique,* 1976)
Translated from the French by Myrna Bell Rochester

VAMPIRO NOX

Come dreadful child
I'll make your cradle in a cloud of magic
Your mother is a black bird
It's the mole with two rings
Right next to the angelus
Sounded by the cuckoo

On the wallpaper decorating
the storm kitchen
Blessed roofs colored by the bigamous fringes
which go on papering
the square of easy solitude:
not the one you find in cities
but thunder's only one
sitting on a silken saddle
spouting out the whole lot in profane damnation
Machiavellian granddaughter
with eyes as round as rubies
on the nail of the virgin owl
who only asks to hoot in fours
holding out the poisoned apple his egg
from which will hatch the cog-wheel
braced to wipe our courtrooms
with its little hooked broom
Brought to life by prehistoric breath
is the great wind laying down
the great fir of the moon
with its head between the hands of the frog
wearing a nightcap
Suddenly she jumps out of her hammock
—let the little bugger live.

(From *John the Pelican,* 1990)
Translated from the French by Peter Wood and Guy Flandre

SURREALISM: RISING SIGN

I was born into the big bear skin of surrealism. Even before my birth it was incorporated into my cells, my spine, guiding me, just as the sea iguana is guided to algae and bees to nectar. . . . And if the elephant's element is the savanna and the ocean the whale's, surrealism is my element, my vital substance. Ah! Let's speak of the whale and her song—so beautiful, so terrible! Does it cause her anxiety? Does she consider its composition, hesitating for centuries before singing in the ocean's great depths? Of course not! If this were so, she would not be singing now. And her song is an interrogation. All this to say: surrealism is a vital, a constitutional need. Those whom it recognizes spontaneously belong to the same element. Always familiar, for me surrealism is life itself. Why? Because true life has nothing to do with what has insidiously been sanctioned by the repressive powers of mortality, religion, and law. Powers—oh how fallacious—whose end is nothing less than the enslavement of the majority for the profit of a minority of impostors animated by terrorism of all kinds: churches, philosophies, ideologies, politics . . . all representing enslavement or death (which are one and the same thing). Surrealism is the conscious attempt to restore humanity's true capacity to be and to desire without moral or physical constraint through the unlimited exercise of the imagination. Those who have the luck to remain "primitive" recognize each other. . . . When I met André Breton, I was not so much astonished as amazed at the realization of something intimated, not yet experienced and longed for. All the operations of my life, and that one too—I mean that extraordinary meeting—have happened as if by magic; I mean truly magically. Because magic is the superior instance to which I have always confided my life. What is life? Owl cry, the growth of the wild palm, a summer night's rain, wind, snow, and also typhoon, maelstrom, volcanic eruption. . . . It is in these things that I recognize myself in what we choose to call automatism, automatism being a way to give "carte blanche"—a lovely expression!—to inspiration and the sources of the unconscious; *clairvoyance* in other words. I associate to the no less significant ("montrer patte blanche") wanting, before my destiny, to empty-handedly bring only what was always mine *unknown to me*. (O! Yes! Above all unknown to me!) I am an automaton, my gestures decided by the key that contains life's mystery, animated by the blind trust in everything that comprises the natural being. I can't name the ways by which I permit this instancy to function more freely. I say: *magic, the marvelous clairvoyance*. The "primitive" societies still in direct contact with living natural phenomena have more than my support. They have my love and will not cease to fascinate me. Because magic reveals our instinct's original destination, our true place. In exact contradiction with those who think that man, having invented everything, has separated himself from nature. Which he has done, but in a way he denies: by becoming a foreign body, a cancerous growth that sooner or later will destroy itself. I, however, have a lion's share of the instinct of self-preservation! I love life and I love it to the extent that I have found nothing more vivifying than SURREALISM and all that it embraces and exemplifies. Attention! Be attentive to signs. I say: *Rising Sign*.

(From *Marianne van Hirtum: Peintures, dessins, objets*, 1991)
Translated from the French by Rikki Ducornet

Anne Ethuin

Born in 1921 in Coteau in northern France, Anne Ethuin has lived in Paris since 1943. She started painting in 1949 and took part in the first Cobra show in Copenhagen that year. In 1954 she cofounded the journal *Phases* with her husband, poet Edouard Jaguer (a member of the *Main à plume* surrealist group during the Resistance), and has since taken part in all activities of the international Phases movement. Her glorious coated collages (*collages revêtus*), which she began to make in 1970, were featured at the World Surrealist Exhibition (Chicago, 1976), "Surrealism Unlimited" (London, 1978), "Surrealism in 1978: 100th Anniversary of Hysteria" (Milwaukee, 1978), "Diversité surréaliste" (Paris, 1991), and at Phases exhibitions in France, Belgium, Portugal, Canada, Mexico, Peru, etc. Many surrealist poets have written prefaces for the catalogs of her solo shows, including Jean-Louis Bédouin, Jean-Michel Goutier, Petr Kral, Gérard Legrand, Elisabeth Lenk, and Arturo Schwarz.

At the magic crossroads of objective chance, humor, and the Marvelous, Ethuin's coated collages are among the high spots of the poetic spirit in painting today. A book of them, *Regards obliques sur une histoire parallèle*, with texts by Edouard Jaguer, was published by Editions Oasis in 1977.

Written in 1964, this poem was first published in the collection *Lumière du jour* (Paris: Actual, 1989).

LEGEND

Hidden in a mother-of-pearl drawer
Lies a marvel made of lead I am after it
I was told of replicas in the Saffron Palace
Owned by the Lady of a thousand clocks
But I hate to hear the hours strike

This town has embroidered rooftops
Young women must do this work on rainy days
While playing proverbs
All the trees were saved this way
From destruction

Anne Ethuin, *The Tables of the Law,* coated collage, 1976. Courtesy of the artist.

Why?
I did not ask

But this evening—a ball
In the Egrets' Garden
In honor of the fairest
Will you be there?
Dancing in porcelain slippers only:
So as not to disturb the water in the great pond
Or the blue wizard who sleeps within it, awakening,
will change the destiny of the land
So says an ancient legend

No one can remember his name
Perhaps he was that long ago king
Drowned by his subjects in the vanished river
And whose image reappears in filigree
On certain days each year
Under the hand of the silken clockface
On the Forbidden Plaza

Is this tale real?
Little by little in time
The loveliest stories shrink
And their thread wears too thin
To bear the weight of ceaseless additions
So what?
Tomorrow will be your wedding feast
For every stranger who spends one night here
Must be married at dawn
Can you hear the doors shutting?

Translated from the French by Guy Ducornet

Isabel Meyrelles

I WILL TELL YOU DURING THE WALK . . .

I will tell you during the walk to Fomalhaut
I will tell you red on gray

I will tell you with flowers (why not?)
I will tell you here or elsewhere
I will tell you that elsewhere or here . . .
I will tell you that the key wants to go home
I will tell you that the present is easily seen through
I will tell you that we have other fish to fry
I will tell you that I hate the telephone
I will tell you that—Yeah—perfectly neat oblivion—
I will tell you I no longer want anguish after 6 P.M.
I will tell you that nobody never as much
I will tell you it's not the end of the world
I will tell you that my eagle thinks of you
I will tell you that my death is no longer so lonely
I will tell you : don't tell an ear what a hand knows
I will tell you : To tears! Citizens!
And may an impure time drench our furrows!*

(From *Le Livre du Tigre*)
Translated from the French by Guy Ducornet

TYGER, TYGER

Supple
slender
sinuous
sybaritic
sultan of the afternoon
silken
sudden
seditious
seductive
secretly
satanic

---

* The last two lines are puns on the first and last line of the *Marseillaise*: "Aux armes, citoyens!" = To arms, citizens!
"Qu'un sang impur abreuve no sillons" = May impure blood drench our furrows.

sumptuous
sorcerer
subtly
sinking my
sources
savage king
saffron-colored
striped with black, I
savor your
superb roar
sovereign
sacker
of silence, and I
submit
serenely to your rule, O
solitary
Seigneur of
somber beauty

(From *Le Livre du Tigre*)
Translated from the French by Penelope Rosemont

Luiza Neto Jorge

One of the best-known Portuguese poets of her time, Luiza Neto Jorge was born in 1939 in Lisbon, where she studied at the Faculty of Letters. She began frequenting the surrealist milieu in her teens. Her first book, *A noite vertebrata* [The Vertebrate Night], was published in 1960. Two years later she moved to Paris, where she remained for eight years. Her later books include *Quarta diminsão* [Fourth Dimension] (1963) and *O seu a seu tempo* [To Each In His/Her Own Time] (1966). A large collection of her poetry, titled *Poesia,* was published in 1993. She also translated many French works into Portuguese, including Breton's *L'Amour fou* and important works by Jarry, Artaud, Raymond Queneau, Boris Vian, and Ionesco. Her translation of Oskar Panizza's *Council of Love* was suppressed by Salazarist censorship. Luiza Neto Jorge died in 1989.

The following poems, first published in the 1970s, are from her *Poesia* (1993).

ANOTHER GENEALOGY

I

The poet is a long animal
from infancy

II

The animal would begin by being
a slow movement beneath the darkness

III

Peopled are the rooms
by nonhuman broods
gnawing creatures
importuning

IV

Come mythic animals
or mystics with their attentive saint
those who flare up in high autumn
hermaphrodites
abductors of women
procreators of children
heraldry experts
coffin lids
men by mistake
winged fliers
succubi
satans
come wild animals
inside voracious
bones

V

I don't accept zoological orders
anything that facilitates
so earthly a permanence
so aerial so aquatic
so mysterious so cosmic
a circulation
so full of natural facilities
of natural gifts of nature

of meadows of cliffs of fresh waters
of pillows

Between going to bed and getting up
I sit down I kneel I do acrobatics
I learn an infinity of gestures that
lead me to numberless denser
situations
to some impieties of the body and how many
severe toothaches
transported to the spirit that eliminates me
from the other animal kingdom

An animal (any)
if it raises a thick paw over the world
torments

Translated from the Portuguese by Jean R. Longland

"MONUMENT TO BIRDS" (MAX ERNST)

With the exact security of the hoisting crane
they rise transporting
the intense weight
of the object that rises

Atmosphere of birds
(wizards riding the
high reality)
aerial mountain transposed
by us the birds

The weight of those plump birds
the wide fact of flight of those birds
leads our emigration

Translated from the Portuguese by Jean R. Longland

FABLE

The animal understands itself:
it has hoofs makes them serve

has skin
warms
closes itself in its eyes to fall asleep
all it remembers it forgets
Spends itself.
Remains.

THE FORCE OF GRAVITY

Your gravity:
the exact weight you employ
for laughing.

SPHERICITY: FEROCITY

dangerous quality that of some
solids when lost they turn
toward us.

Translated from the Portuguese by Jean R. Longland

Alejandra Pizarnik

It appears that the only reason Argentine poet Alejandra Pizarnik (1936–1972) did not belong to a surrealist group in her homeland is that none were active there when she arrived on the scene. Unwaveringly, however, she affirmed her solidarity with the movement's basic aims and principles, and until her suicide a few years later her poetic activity helped give surrealism a powerful resonance in Argentine culture. It is no accident that the animators of surrealism in South America today—not only in her native country but also in Brazil, Colombia, and elsewhere—regard her unequivocally as one of their own.

In addition to her mighty achievements as a poet (she wrote eight volumes in her lifetime, and many collections have appeared since), Pizarnik also translated several works by French surrealist poets into Spanish, most notably *L'Immaculée conception* [The Immaculate Conception] by Breton and Eluard.

Poemas, an anthology of her work published in Medellín in 1982—from which the following poems are taken—includes appreciations of her work by two central figures of Spanish-language surrealism in the New World, Enrique Molina and Octavio Paz.

CAROLINE VON GÜNDERODE

to Enrique Molina

I wandered through the infinite as one who remembers.
—C. von G.

The hand of the wind's own lover
caresses the face of the absent one.
With "bird skin bag" she who was deceived
flies from herself with a knife in her memory.
And the one devoured by the mirror
enters a casket of ashes and soothes the beasts of oblivion.

IN A COPY OF *LES CHANTS DE MALDOROR*

Under my dress blazed a field of flowers as joyous as the children of midnight.

The breath of light in my bones comes over me when I write the word earth. Word or presence followed by perfumed animals; sad as itself, beautiful as suicide; and that flies over me like a dynasty of suns.

Translated from the Spanish by Natalie Kenvin

Leila Ferraz

Born in 1944, in São Paulo, Brazil, Leila Ferraz recognized herself as surrealist in 1965. In Paris the following year with her husband, poet/collagist Sergio Lima, she took part in the meetings of the Surrealist Group and helped plan the International Surrealist Exhibition, scheduled to open in São Paulo in 1967. Later in 1966 she cofounded the Surrealist Group in São Paulo. She exhibited drawings and surrealist objects at the 1967 international exhibition, and collaborated on the Brazilian surrealist journal, *A Phala*.

The São Paulo Surrealist Group disbanded in 1969, largely because of the repressive political situation in Brazil, but surrealism continued as an underground ferment. After the early 1970s, however, Ferraz took no further part in organized surrealist activity.

The article and poem published here in abridged form originally appeared in *A Phala* (1967).

SECRETS OF SURREALIST MAGIC ART

> Magic is in itself only a will, and this will is the great mystery of every miracle and every secret: it operates through the appetite of the being's desire.
>
> —Jacob Boehme

Magic is the cultivator of the very desire that makes it "beyond good and evil" in a sphere belonging to enchantment and violation—the feeling (or rather *sensation*) of power that transforms *what I have* into *what I am*, hurling me against everything that seems to obstruct my self-movement.

Magic: The alien and the exterior trespassing the barriers of the representation of my will in order to transform themselves precisely into that which does not appear to me alien or make me feel exterior. Or rather, it is the *introduction to my relationship with the world*: the breaking apart of the unit *reason-will*—the resacralization of Love.

In the fundamental magic attitude there is a "collapse of barriers" that suppresses the difference between individuals or, more correctly, between elements. Reencountering itself at every moment as part of a system of realities ordinarily described as domains of prohibition, or forbidden zones, this collapse of barriers creates in turn a new interconnectedness of supreme knowledge, in which my representation mingles and merges with the integrity of an entire *movement* of analogies.

In no way does this *enthusiasm for the secret* presuppose a religious attitude before it evolves toward poetry. Although in magic the *secret principle* bears a certain resemblance to that of religion—as much as it does to the "Occult"—they are opposed in essential points. This is because religion presupposes a power different from and indeed fundamentally alien to the human—a power on which humankind is supposed to depend and to which it must submit.

Essentially natural, magic belongs to what is spontaneous—to Evil, but to an Evil that does not contradict Good, and yes, to a realm in which Evil and Good constitute a single movement of the same intensity and strength, although tending toward the creation of a basic difference: an *opposing sense* (as we speak of opposing directions in space). For Heraclitus, the contrary is agreement, from discord is born the most beautiful harmony, and everything becomes struggle.

• • •

[Magic art] is a universal play process (*processus-ludicus*) in which gestures, lines, and movements aim at the same point of cosmic encounter and return endowed with desires.

It is the carrying out of *action*, as revealed to us by magic intuition, inscribed for us like sparkling characters on black stones. The insignia of the Magic Natural Alchemist establish a *legible* language whose intimate characters correspond to the process of analogy and metaphors, and whose function is to establish primary contact between people, between myself and the universe, and between my magic art and humankind.

Above all it is necessary to make thought speak orally in the domain of the Marvelous. . . .

Oral thought, materialized through the word, writing, and work of art, is the gesture of the Voice inside our mechanism of symbols. It is the visualization of the poetic image which is the created object—indeed, it is the very act of the object's creation. . . .

Translated from the Portuguese by Jean R. Longland

MY LOVE, I SPEAK TO YOU OF A LOVE

My love, I speak to you of a love
that takes the form of all the powers of time. . . .
I speak to you of a love of ancient recognitions
and of perpetual encounters,
of a beam of light poised on your forehead
in the direction of the cardinal points of your body. . . .
Your elongated pubic hairs trickle over my Evening Gypsy legs!
Our sighs mark in Space a confusion of interlaced stars of Mercury
and our zodiac sign speaks of the same formula that extends the limits of the Supernatural to the Human.
Our powers link themselves to the mysteries in the Universe of things
and transform life into an eternal fluttering,
like butterfly wings.
My love

I speak to you through the viper's tongue
through the gifts of ruined castles
and through the fires built in my heart.

Translated from the Portuguese by Jean R. Longland

Rikki Ducornet

Poet, novelist, short-story writer, artist, and essayist, Rikki Ducornet was born in New York in 1943 and attended Bard College. She lived for many years in North Africa, Canada, South America, and the Loire Valley of France. On an anti-Vietnam War demonstration in New York in 1967, she chanced to meet several members of the Chicago Surrealist Group, and she has participated in surrealist activity ever since, collaborating on *Arsenal: Surrealist Subversion* and other collective publications as well as taking part in the 1976 World Surrealist Exhibition and numerous other group shows around the world. She has also participated in the international Phases movement. Ducornet is the author of fourteen books, including six volumes of poems (starting with *From the Star Chamber,* 1974), five novels (starting with *The Stain,* 1984), two collections of short stories (*The Complete Butcher's Tales,* 1994, and *The Word "Desire,"* 1997), and two children's books. Illustrator of books by Jorge Luis Borges and Robert Coover, she has also designed a Tarot deck and, with Guy Ducornet, two surrealist board games.

All of Rikki Ducornet's works, as poet and as storyteller, are black, gothic-comic phantasmagorias, full of dark enigmas, opalescent terror, faraway laughter, and loose ends of myth, hilarious and disturbing.

She lives in Denver.

"My Special Madness" first appeared in *From the Star Chamber* (1974); "Necromancy" and "Dark Star, Black Star" in *Weird Sisters* (1976); "Machete" in *Knife Notebook* (1977); and "Clean" in *Arsenal: Surrealist Subversion* no. 3 (1976).

MY SPECIAL MADNESS

My special madness
A green window
The smell of boxwood, of the lion's den
The smell of ether, the bite of quick-silver in the lungs

The green-house overgrown, the floor a river of glass
No secrets but silence
Spores fall
The sound of moss spreading

The agony of meat caught in the lion's jaw.

Today I send my own police of rats
To do their terrible justice to my heart
Stagnating beneath the fat of a day's lies.

There is a crystal center
That spins deep within the living shell
Fed by my blood, distant
My hallucinating planet
Hungry for fresh meat, blue copper
Refracting light, teethed images
A forest and a sea—cruel and deep beyond recovery
But pulsating

My hallucinating planet, my hungry center
Where languages are muddled
Where words are clawed to death

The moon is stretched out across the sky as on a wheel and beaten.

NECROMANCY

She is a file
She is a cleaver
She is a needle
Scissors, acid, knife.
She is bitter
Green on my lips
Yellow in my throat.
She is cold
An eel sleeping beneath the ice.

Rikki Ducornet, *Black Isis*, etching, 1991. Courtesy of the artist.

DARK STAR, BLACK STAR

I want to be simple
Legs spread, hands glued to your hands
My mouth easy, my mind one color

You walk up from the road
The sky is white—there dragons hide breathing smoke
Your face a stone catching light

This is your star whole perfect rising
Your black twin your tame serpent

An atmosphere of rain—green and fragrant
Your face the sun devouring the moon
The air hides danger the forest whispers
Thorns! Roots!

My own dark star black star
My breath caught and held in your tight cage
Chosen marble cat's eye
My prize.

MACHETE

Your machete slices through my jungle.
Your body is perfect. Is a coiled sphere of gleaming copper.
Your taste is my taste.
Rust and forest.
Your fistful of hornets inhabits my cunt.
Taste of copper. Mossy mysteries and the agile tower!
We play the game of ice and thunder.
The fire game the sword game.
The rules are intricate, secret.
We play blind.

Today you are wearing *her* mask of sugar.
I lick your face . . .

CLEAN

Dogs are dirty, birds are filthy, fish are clean except for the intestines which are dirty.

People love to wash and that's why in the eyes of Jesus they are best. Dogs don't go to heaven, they turn into worms, but good Christian people stay just the same, younger and smelling good all the time. All the people get washed when they die and sit at the table of Holy Lightning with Jesus, eating all that clean food. Jesus smiles when he sees the people washing. He knows the people like cleanliness and that's why he likes them better than the animals who eat any crap dirty.

Clean people who don't smell like vinegar sit at His table, only younger, with new hair, teeth and skin, all naked but not fornicating, eating all that clean food. That's why it's important to get the old folks soaped and combed and into bed between those nice sheets boiled four times and ironed into nice even creases—twelve creases for Jesus—and their toenails pared. Our old people look good, just simple people the color of milk and veal roast. When it's time Jesus calls them. He says: "O have you pared your nails?" And they answer: "O yes, Sweet Lord, we have pared our nails and ironed our sheets twelve times." And Jesus says: "Are you *clean?*" Which is a joke because He knows they are and the old folks laugh a lot at this. And Jesus says: "Do you smell good and are you the color of veal roast?" And the old folks answer: "O yes, Lord, we smell good and we are clean and our thoughts are like white sauce and our blood is like water and we are ready, O sweet Jesus."

Then Jesus gathers them up in His arms and gives them clean teeth, the better to eat at His Holy table, and clean ears, the better to hear His Holy Music, and clean eyes, the better to see and worship Him.

Nancy Joyce Peters

Poet, essayist, painter, theorist, and editor, Nancy Joyce Peters was born in Seattle in 1936. Employed for a time as a librarian at the Library of Congress, she later traveled all over Europe, North Africa, and the Near East, where she researched Egyptian myth. She is also a serious student of Native American culture (and is of Cherokee descent herself). For eight years she lived in France and Spain, working at a variety of jobs, from community services director and tour guide to actress and theater director. Since 1971 she has been codirector of City Lights Books in San Francisco.

Peters has participated in surrealism since 1974, when she coedited the extensive "Surrealist Movement in the United States" section of the *City Lights Anthology*. Her poetry—a veritable "ecology of the Marvelous"—resounds with the secret rhythms of the inner life of all things. A collection of her poems, *It's in the Wind,* appeared in the Surrealist Research & Development Monograph Series in 1978 and has since been reprinted. Her other books include *Literary San Francisco,* with Lawrence Ferlinghetti (1980)—a volume especially notable for helping to revive interest in such writers as Charlotte Perkins Gilman, Mary Austin, Prentice Mulford, and others—and a militant anthology of responses to the U.S. Persian Gulf Massacre of 1992, *War After War* (City Lights, 1992). Her poems and other writings, and reproductions of her paintings and drawings, have appeared in *Arsenal: Surrealist Subver-*

sion, Marvelous Freedom/Vigilance of Desire, The Octopus-Typewriter, Surrealism and Its Popular Accomplices, and many other collective publications, and in 1981 she coedited *Free Spirits: Annals of the Insurgent Imagination.* Her artwork has been featured at the World Surrealist Exhibition (Chicago, 1976), the "100th Anniversary of Hysteria" show (Milwaukee, 1978), "Surrealism Unlimited" (London, 1978), and many other shows.

Peters married surrealist poet Philip Lamantia and lives in San Francisco.

The following poems are from *It's in the Wind* (1977). The article on Nelly Kaplan's *Néa* is from the "Surrealism and Its Popular Accomplices" issue of the journal *Cultural Correspondence* (1979).

TO THE DEATH OF MIRRORS

In a tedious evening of trick or treat
history got stuck
when required to deliver the goods
the ladies of glittering infamy
threw their children under the bed
and headed for a less wretched climate
under the supervision of a mad cycle
that leaps from the bridge
in a fury of spokes
the day commits new crimes
aviaries are slain
just as if wings were of no importance
the animals are disappearing
though they're under everything we think
the day is vampirized by scientific fangs
it wears the cloak of genocide
it wears the hat of an occult numbskull
it can no longer speak
still in the unarticulated foliage
of the world's great wing
we will act
we will put up the sign of human liberty
we will rent a room
in the house of transmutation and never give away the key

GENERAL STRIKE

Mesmeric hunter of the unseen
I stalk through a numbing cinema
stretching out my hands to seize
silken numbers for factoring the unknown
I look into the abyss of the sea
to find what the moon left behind
when she abandoned its embrace
the moon playing baccarat with owls
moon that invented that hand that writes
I track the sun that never
appears in dreams
the sun unloosing its will in the doldrums
sun that will marry the redwoods
profound sun of Hopi dancers
whose syllable husks confront all limits
Mesmeric hunter of the unachieved
I run out my door
like the true aim of terror
like the desire of the general strike
onto that transfigured desert
where nothing is quite certain
except the chemical thrust
of imagination
willing the metamorphic world

NELLY KAPLAN'S *NÉA*: WOMAN & EROTICISM IN FILM

> Smile, but not for long, Ladies and Gentlemen of the Patriarchy.
>
> —Nelly Kaplan

Although widely admired for its wit and elegance, a delightful eroticism, and the beauty of its lush color photography, Nelly Kaplan's film *Néa* has met with some oddly paradoxical responses: "controversial," "reactionary," "progressive," "a satire of interest to feminists only," "ultimately anti-feminist," "not for the squeamish." This is surely because *Néa* zeroes in on an explosive problematic: how female power—sexual and intellectual—is perceived, imagined, experienced, or might potentially be realized. Moreover, Kaplan takes the scandalous position of insisting on love. The film's use of image, symbol and discourse violates (at the same time that it gratifies) conventional expectations with a finesse and comic irony which in no way negate its moral rigor.

Sybil (Ann Zacharies), a rebellious sixteen-year-old virgin, escapes from the claustrophobic atmosphere of her bourgeois family by reading the world's erotic masterpieces and trying her hand at writing her own in an eccentrically decorated hideaway she shares with her cat, Villiers d'Ile de Cumes. She chafes under the stupid, repressive rules imposed by her father, a philistine Geneva industrialist; she is contemptuous of her fatuous sister and fascinated with her mother's lesbian liaison with her aunt. On her way home from school, she is caught shoplifting pornographic books in the bookstore of a handsome young publisher, Axel (Sammy Frey). She boasts to him that she could write a great erotic novel which he promises to publish if she does. Back in her lair she writes in a furious automatistic trance, but realizing she needs more than imagined sexual experience, she chooses the attractive Axel to provide "material" for her book. He reluctantly complies; they become lovers and both know great sensual happiness. He publishes the book which becomes an astounding bestseller, but to "protect" her anonymity he makes her agree not to see him until the snow melts from the chapel roof. Denied love, Sybil suffers and waits while Axel protects himself in promiscuous encounters with others, including her conventional seductive sister. When she discovers his betrayal she sets up a phony rape scene, a gem of black humor in which the bleeding Sybil, whom everybody imagines has been violated, falls down in the snow in the midst of a bourgeois wedding party coming out of the chapel. Axel eventually returns to get even, but in a surprising denouement, she confronts him with psychic and carnal truths too powerful to be denied, and the lovers are re-united, setting out together in their boat across the dark lake to Axel's castle.

Kaplan wrote in 1964, "If in this domain (eroticism) the cinema has already performed miracles, one facet is absent nevertheless. Is there anything so exciting as a beautiful woman knowingly caressed by the caprice of the lens? Yes, the sight of a beautiful young man captured by a heterosexual camera." There is more to this statement than meets the eye, for it goes beyond the reversal of convenient roles—Sybil as active protagonist, a sexual subject as well as sexual object—in a Romantic narrative. It also and more crucially opens up the revolutionary possibility of challenging the Patriarchal order because it dissects and subverts the way in which we signify and order reality. In this it courageously sets out on quite new terrain.

How woman's sexuality is contained and assimilated into Patriarchy during a period of desublimation has been a central issue in popular culture commentary for the last decade. Woman's image in the movies has always been abundantly analyzed and everybody knows that a woman in control of her erotic and intellectual destiny almost invariably gets married off, jailed, exiled, defeated or killed. Parker Tyler, an early commentator of the sad decline of the movie heroine's integrity, noted that after the 1930s the representation of a woman who was sexually assertive, intelligent, and endowed with strong personality and moral energy, virtually disappeared from the screen. Ado Kyrou (*Amour, Erotisme et Cinéma*) concurred, finding at this same historical moment that with rare exceptions American film began moving in the direction of mechanical sex, Coca-Cola eroticism, gratuitous sadism and a despicable hatred of women. On the most accessible level, films reflect subjective experiences and social realities so that many feminists tend to evaluate only whether or not what happens to the women characters is positive or negative, under the unfortunate assumption that ideology is conferred from above by some mysterious office of sexism. Such an approach to cinematic analysis, looking for role models and realistic depictions of liberated women, imposes severe limitations in the long run. Perceptual reality is illusory enough in real life; in film it is profoundly more so since cinema is located in a nexus of fluctuating ego identifications, libidinal wanderings, desire dreaming itself. Kaplan's brilliant use of types, symbolic images and mythic elements has the effect of dislocating a frozen reality. By overloading the circuits of conceptual thematics—blowing the realist fuse, so to speak—she is able to achieve allegorical resonances of great complexity in a fluid elaboration of external and internal, real and symbolic at once. In one respect *Néa* takes the guise of a perverse fairy tale: Instead of the wicked stepmother and the good father, we have a repressive patriarch and a mother emanating a benign bisexual voluptuousness. Sybil does not wait to be "exchanged" by her father; she refuses his world leaving him with the sister who is adjusted to her "inferior" woman's place. Sybil is her own fairy godmother, effecting transformations through her desire and will, rescuing the handsome prince from his sleep, *i.e.*, a neurotic attachment to the memory of his dead mother and an inability to love.

From another angle, *Néa* simultaneously explores the myth and fact of woman's sexual nature, revealing how she is imagined by both man and woman. The skillful disorientation of categories, highly self-reflected, provoke a consciousness of woman as fetish and as woman might be beyond fetish. Sybil the witch, accompanied by her charming feline familiar, works a magic, very real yet beyond the confines of the rational. For instance, the subversive power of her sexuality is wonderfully realized in a "chance happening": Unwilling to wait for the snow to melt, the chapel bursts into flames under her gaze as her desire overpowers the regular procession of the seasons. This conflagration of female sexuality has, of course, been represented by the figure of the witch both mythically and in history. The significance of witch is illuminated, yet

Sybil is never reduced to the vulgar witch, and she is decidedly no femme fatale. Her naturalness and directness allow her to carry the image of a normal, insurgent adolescent girl, and to me she is reminiscent of Stendhal's devastatingly honest *Lamiel* in her purity and innocent inevitability.

Molly Haskell (*From Reverence to Rape: The Treatment of Women in the Movies*) traces in depth the escalating hostility to love expressed in American films, pointing out how themes of love have been contemptuously relegated to a despised genre, the "woman's movie." She underscores this finding by singling out in particular the neglect of that masterpiece of mad love *Peter Ibbetson* in which the lovers, separated by prison walls, are "transfixed at the sublime moment of their love (denying yet improving on reality) by the power of the imagination, by the screen, by their permanence in our memories." Even these films, good ones at any rate, were rare, and in the present period of crisis, threats to deeply entrenched sexism being launched on all sides, love between men and women, she notes, has been dispensed with altogether. Narcissistic affective relations occur between men, a tendency Ado Kyrou remarked in *The Outlaw* where Jane Russell, reduced to breast fetish, is continuously debased and never allowed to interfere with the erotic flows circulating between man and man (or between man and horse); today the touch of hyperbolic self-parody in this film has disappeared in the process of expropriating the mode.

It is true that films are evidence of actual experience and the workings of ideology and so it comes as no surprise that many women regard love as impossible; they see only one choice—*either* emancipation *or* love. This is a grave situation and one for which there is no facile solution, given the phallocentric nature of the world, yet to relinquish love is clearly insanity; even if it appears utopian I think we must demand a future in which love triumphs and triumphs absolutely. Beverle Houston's perceptive review in *Film Quarterly* (Spring 1979) situates *Néa* as an essential recognition that "romantic love is valuable, honorable, thrilling, and not to be debased." Kaplan's powerful fable, she thinks, works with unexpected epistemological and moral sophistication in the way it demonstrates that love is not inevitable in the human condition, but a project of Sybil's. Like the "fiction" of her erotic novel, she and Axel elect to exalt imaginative activity, to create and liberate love. Reality (which includes love) is what we bring into being, at least in part, and derives from desiring, risking and acting. Kaplan's cinematic expression of this concept is a far cry from the customary wedding bells and incarceration in the nuclear family suggested when "The End" appears on the screen in the stereotype romance.

Surrealists have frequently observed that film is an intrinsically surrealist medium. It shares a close affinity with dreams in its delirious imagery, mechanisms of displacement, and dispersal of desire through a prismatic lens. Cinema is in a unique position to throw light on the fact that reality is a mass hallucination. For the viewer it offers an invitation to unravel how meaning and value are determined within that mass hallucination; on the movie screen is the display of not only what happens but the key to the operation of social and individual events. Like the inspired activity of automatism, latent content surfaces to scrutiny, making screen images available to decipherment and making "reality" available to demystification.

For the filmmaker, the irresistible opportunity presents itself to project images which transcend the present and imagine a future which escapes the bondage of petrified structures. Above all, the cinema spreads before us the spectacle of how the erotization of the world takes place. To caress the male with a woman's camera violates, in the psychoanalytic sense, the place in the unconscious of woman as the sign of castration. In that we live the way the difference of the sexes is experienced in the unconscious, Kaplan effects this shift of focus with subtlety, necessarily, insofar as the objectification of the male is a threat to psychic need. Kaplan gives us, through Sybil the seer, the first shadowing outlines of a new worldview, one originating in woman's *look*. Though she remains the object of desire, Sybil goes beyond being the object of desire, the passive catalyst of men's action and discourse which convey the film's meanings. A revolutionary in the realm of desire, Sybil is the transcendent prefiguration of *Néa,* the new woman, conferring the promise of a happier existence, as she speaks not only her own reality (now oppressed under Patriarchy), but a higher reality, too. Hers is a pioneer voice announcing a possible destiny, the realization of love, humanity as it would be.

Alice Farley

Born in New York in 1951, Alice Farley studied with dancers Bella Lewitzky and Mia Slavenska at the California Institute of the Arts in Los Angeles and later with the Martha Graham and Alvin Ailey schools in New York. Her participation in surrealism began in 1973 in San Francisco. Among her major choreographies and dances are "Fortunate Light," with a company of dancers (San Francisco, 1974); "Brides of the Prism," a solo dance concert (San Francisco, 1975); and "Surrealist Dance," at the World Surrealist Exhibition (Chicago, 1976). More recently Farley has performed stilt-dances in the street at antiwar demonstrations, served as consultant for the Cirque du Soleil of Montreal, designed magic illusions for Tokyo nightclubs, and collaborated with Henry Threadgill of the Association for the Advancement of Creative Musicians. The Alice Farley Dance Theater has toured extensively throughout the U.S., Canada, the Caribbean, and Asia. Farley lives in New York and Quintano Roo.

The following text appeared in the program booklet, *Alice Farley/Surrealist Dance,* issued on the occasion of a series of performances at the World Surrealist Exhibition.

NOTES TOWARD A SURREALIST DANCE

Wolves' eyes must reveal our dance. Ceaseless wanderings in the prisms of typhoons should fold the quarantine of gravity into packets of clear surrender.

There remains no choice but that dance in Western culture, if it is truly to exist at all, must become a theater of living transformation and revolution.

The time is long overdue to refuse our ancestry as the virtuoso entertainment of the bourgeoisie. (In the most revered of Western dance forms, the anachronism that is classical ballet, the esthetic and politics of Louis XIV still revolve slowly on the stage of 1976 as the "sublime" gymnastics of stagnation.)

Likewise, and perhaps more essentially, we must refuse the nauseating homage to boredom that has been constructed by the American modern dance "avant-garde." There the idolization of technique is exchanged for the vacuum of abstraction and "pure form." (Ah, if only there was no need to deal with that *impure* human body.)

We must realize again and again that it is not a matter of technique, but of transformation. *Trance* is not boredom. The dance of the dervish, of the Balinese kris dancer, the ritual of sanghyang dedari are not boredom. The simplest movement certainly can cast the spell of reverie. But only for an expenditure of *desire*.

The body is the most complete instrument, the erotic, the living instrument. The history of dance is the refusal to succumb to the physical laws of gravity, momentum, inertia. To dream the impossible and to demand it of oneself.

We must now carry this transformation of form to the transformation of content. The image must be used to reveal the latent content of all that man is and is becoming.

The theater exists to be put to surrealist use. For the most part, this has not been done. But if in America Charlie Chaplin, Buster Keaton, Harold Lloyd found ways not only to speak, but to reveal the unspeakable through their movement; and if, as well, certain modern dance pioneers (Isadora Duncan, Martha Graham, Alwin Nikolais) have found moments (though only moments) of lightning that traversed the abyss between conscious and unconscious thought—they stand only in the doorway of this vast and unexplored terrain and confirm the convulsive beauty that lies there.

Jayne Cortez

Jayne Cortez was born in Arizona in 1936, grew up in southern California, and lives in New York. Her first book of poems, *Pissstained Stairs and the Monkey Man's Wares,* was published in 1969 and has been followed by nine others—most recently, *Somewhere in Advance of Nowhere* (1996). Eight recordings of her poetry have also appeared, and her work has been featured in such publications as *Daughters of Africa, Women On War, Jazz & Poetry,* and *Black Scholar.* She has also lectured and read her poetry—often accompanied by the music of her band, The Firespitters—throughout the U.S., Africa, Asia, Europe, Latin America, and the Caribbean.

Cortez first came into contact with surrealism as an organized current in the mid-1970s. Since then she has regularly taken part in the activities of the Surrealist Movement in the U.S., via declarations such as *When Tourists Replace Seers* (protesting the 1992 "Columbus Quincentennial") and *For Tyree Guyton,* as coeditor of *Free Spirits: Annals of the Insurgent Imagination,* and as a collaborator on the movement's other collective publications: *Arsenal: Surrealist Subversion, Marvelous Freedom/Vigilance of Desire* (catalog of the 1976 World Surrealist Exhibition in Chicago), *Surrealism and Its Popular Accomplices,* and the bulletin, *WHAT Are You Going to Do About It?*

Benjamin Péret's famous maxim, "The poet has no choice but to be a revolutionist or cease to be a poet," is second nature to Jayne Cortez. One of the strongest surrealist voices of our time, she is a brave example of the *true poet* in a period in which so much intellectual life is dominated by cowardice, confusion, hypocrisy, and sham. As writer Walter Mosley has said, "Jayne Cortez's poems are filled with images that most of us are afraid to see. The words of her world are filled with truths that we suspect, and fear. [Her poetry] follows the footprints left by ecstatic dreamers on sands that are drenched with the vital fluids of revolution, hope and love."

"Consultation" and "Feathers" first appeared in book form in *Scarifications* (1973); "In the Line of Duty" in *Mouth on Paper* (1977); "Make Ifa" in *Poetic Magnetic* (1991); and "Say It" in *Somewhere In Advance of Nowhere* (1996).

CONSULTATION

I have lived in circles of solitude
in support of my involved laughter
emerging from words
from an atmosphere of folded hands
and the half lip stroke of burnt respect
becoming noble while pounding an old love bone
in withered consultation
and without warning
i wiggle through dead hairs of dead gods
no change in volume
i too can be pain in the face of your body
speak to me about this confinement
this deep revelation
between pauses
and the earth fonk of discharge
pearl tongue submissions
pearl tongue submission of enslaved tears
manhood womanhood childhood
the zig zag message from my teeth
heard by my lips
bold against painted spirits
of hunchback fear (as if i couldn't fly away from this road show
    of passing syringes)
No
it is the convulsions of limbs lying
in pose of a person
empty of all confidence
that will make the ritual invasion of death
spread like grease
through scalps of decorative hairdo's

FEATHERS

Excite my breasts
and patrol my vagrant heart
blood shot tongue of veins
today
stands
the wet kiss liver of passion
against charcoal gums
of my soul's teeth
Oh the fatness of love
(compared to tumors fly away my friends)
these scabs have taken eyes
and navels have taken off shades
to look experience in its nose
bartender of bars
a drink to the length of that
dog called loneliness the sparrow mouth ruby
dry feathers on my lovers step

IN THE LINE OF DUTY

In the line of duty
i had to recite into the right eye of a midget
i had to recite into the left ear of a dog
and there they were
a pair of recital boots
made of leather whips
squeaking and echoing
into armpits of my nervous wreck
at noontime on the job in the line of duty
i recited my emotions
into their lunches
i recited empty spaces between the spaces
   of their bites
and there they were
a pair of eggs
made of old gases
blowing rhythms
into thighpits of my eating sweat

at noontime on the job in the line of duty
i shoved my battle scars into their belches
i wiped my X on their blah blahs
and quilted images between their
    bow wows & tee hees and there they were
a midget made of hiccups
a dog made of sirens
backfiring into my stomach
at noontime on the job in the line of duty

MAKE IFA*

Make Ifa make Ifa make Ifa Ifa Ifa

In sanctified chalk
of my silver painted soot
In criss-crossing whelps
of my black belching smoke
In brass masking bones
of my bass droning moans
in hub cap bellow
of my hammer tap blow
In steel stance screech
of my zumbified flames
In electrified mouth
of my citified fumes
In bellified groan
of my countrified pound
In compulsivefied conga
of my soca moka jumbi
MAKE IFA MAKE IFA MAKE IFA IFA
    IFA
In eye popping punta
of my heat sucking sap
In cyclonic slobber

---

* Ifa = a system of divination developed by the Yoruba of Nigeria, based on the interpretation of cowrie shells tossed on a tray.

of my consultation pan
In snap jam combustion
of my banjoistic thumb
In sparkola flare
of my hoodoristic scream
In punched out ijuba
of my fire catching groove
In fungified funk
of my sambafied shakes
In amplified dents
of my petrified honks
In ping ponging bombs
of my scarified gongs
MAKE IFA MAKE IFA MAKE IFA IFA
    IFA

SAY IT

Say it
and peel off that gray iguana skin mask
Say it
and clean out your cockpit of intoxicated spiders
Tear the sexual leaves of grief from your heart
Pluck the feathers of nostalgia from your nipples
Push the slowmoving masochistic mudslide
    of contralto voices
from your afternoon skull of anxiety
Say it
and let the tooth chips fall from
    your hole of rebellious itches
Let the excremental mountain of bones shoot out from
    your ten farting poems in the fly season
because everything is like an ambush
everything is like an incursion
flesh smoking flesh
in hemp field of a fifty minute breakdown
time sodomizing time
in a circular tunnel of asphalt and ashes

space revolting against space
in roar of an artillery salvo fuck
Say it
and leave it splattered on mortuary of a moon
    reflective sap of dead weight
Say it
and store in your propane bucket of memory
    sporadic tremblations of fear
Shove it into saliva of a roach
    radula of teeth between ovum
Throw it from your spine of excessive heat
    fertility smoke of fumigated funk
Talk to yourself in automobile of the clitoris
    Soul of so much humanistic lip
Say it
and let pissy sheets of repression emerge from
your breasts of paregoric flamingos
Let crematorial paste
    in your solitary carcass of drums
push through vaginal acidity of your bodega
Say it
and plunge from invisibility of your own camouflage
Slide on fingernail filth
    of your larva of triteness
become honorary shithead in
    your own mouthful of erected statues
break through your own face of accumulated door
    slams bam bam bam bam
Last night
I dreamt
Buddy Bolden threw his horn
    into the Pontchartrain river
when I put my name under every eyelid
every anthill
every bird wing
every mask of reptilian skin drying in the sun
So say it forget it
and have a drop of grappa
The frog spits through the uterus in December

Haifa Zangana

Born in Baghdad, Iraq, in 1950, Haifa Zangana studied at the city's university where she took a degree in pharmacy in 1974. She left Iraq in 1975 to work with the Palestinian Red Crescent in Damascus, Syria, and moved to London the following year. From London she took part in the Paris-based Arab Surrealist Movement in Exile, and collaborated on its Arabic (and sometimes also French) journal, *Le Désir libertaire,* and other collective publications. She also has been active in efforts to reorganize a Surrealist Group in England and has contributed to several surrealist and surrealist-oriented publications, including *Melmoth* and the "Surrealist Supplement" to the anarchist paper *Freedom* (London), *The Moment* (Paris), and *Surrealism: The Octopus-Typewriter* (Chicago). She has participated in international exhibitions including "Surrealism Unlimited" (London, 1978), and "Surrealism in 1978: 100th Anniversary of Hysteria" in Milwaukee.

In 1979 she contributed collages to a book of poems by Salah Faiq, *Another Fire Befitting a City*; her own first book, *Through the Vast Halls of Memory,* written in Arabic and translated by herself and Paul Hammond, was published in 1991. More recently she has published two novels in Arabic. She lives in London.

Both of the following texts appeared in *Melmoth* no. 2 (1980).

CAN WE DISTURB THESE LIVING COFFINS?

I notice a big city in which people come and go bustling like insects. Here, as elsewhere, there are weapons at hand, but as we are going to work, we are merely the ghosts of ourselves. To work is the best policy, it is work which keeps everybody in haziness, it takes away love, dream, reflection, worry and hatred. It always sets a small goal before one's eyes and permits easy and regular satisfaction. Behind all this there is a loss of faith in values, there is a readiness to accept everything, to obey laws. Rationality is the form of such obedience, power is made to appear as eternal, religion trains men to subordinate their lives to more remote ends. The economic system makes man dependent upon the world of things—to a greater degree than previously; where formerly they worked for the sake of salvation, now they work for work's sake: profit is made for profit's sake: power is sought for power's sake. Can we disturb these living coffins?

At the moment we are on the outskirts, restricted by a vision of reality imposed upon us by a series of factors. Do we need to mention left and right wing politics and politicians?

Haifa Zangana, *Destruction of a Map*, collage, 1978. Courtesy of the artist.

The straight world can measure, calculate and observe. We can identify single works but we do not recognize them in their combinations. Response is atrophied and the reader quickly turns the page.

We can go to see big exhibitions sponsored by the tobacco, petrol or computer companies. Imagination is highly salable, enabling the artist to produce work which, if recognized soon enough by the art broker, might be had very cheaply and constitute an investment. The public buy and enjoy themselves immensely, they don't believe in the rebels' revolt at all. The dealers and the public galleries enthusiastically back them in this. Everything conspires to turn human instincts, desire and thoughts into the channels that feed the apparatus.

"Good graffiti are as difficult to invent as new proverbs. What you need is a wall, a can of spray paint and a brilliant idea. If you don't have all these don't worry. This week good graffiti will be out in book form. Complete with commentaries on their social significance. *London Graffiti* is published by W. H. Allen at £5.95."

Science develops rapidly, but its discoveries and inventions are shelved as soon as they seem to interfere with the requirements of profitable marketing. Accordingly human behavior is outfitted with the rationality of the machine process, and their rationality has a definite social content. The individual has his opportunity only in the short term, he must always be watchful and ready, always seeking to achieve some immediate practical goal.

What can this strange collection of silent creatures be?

Surprise, elevation of primitive instincts, naiveté, hysteria, and madness of vision, all have an essential place in surrealism.

Freedom is the most persistently lingering of desires. Shut your eyes and it will be the last to fade. Normality is a moral idea measured by the yardstick of manners and politics. Political, cultural, and financial tyrannies habitually and selfishly see to it that the world stays "normal" so that they themselves can continue to flout standards. . . .

Perhaps what we need, at the moment, more than anything, is a good humorist.

Is it better to leave?

A SYMBOL OF SIN AND EVIL THOUGHTS: INTRODUCTION TO IBN HAZM AL-ANDALUSI

Ibn Hazm Al-Andalusi was born in Al-Andalus in 994. His father was the Prime Minister and we know that he spent a happy childhood surrounded by many women and teachers. According to his book *The Dove's Collar,* he acquired much of his education through wide reading and travel. In spite of the political changes surrounding him, his main interests were always in the sciences, literature, religion and more surprisingly, love.

After the death of his father and brothers when he was twenty-five, he left his native city to live in Almeria where he was imprisoned. When he eventually gained his freedom, he went back to Qurtuba where he became a minister. This was to be the pattern of his life: moving from one city to another, from Ministry to Ministry, from prison to prison (in those days with a change of administration many of the members and supporters of the previous government were either imprisoned or killed) until his death in 1066.

His writings include books on religion and travel and these were to be followed by *The Dove's Collar: A Book about Love and Lovers*. He claimed that he wrote this book as a reply to the many letters he had received from one of his closest friends (although he never actually mentioned this friend's name) in which he had asked about the secrets of love, relationships and the tales he had heard from the women he had met in his life and in his travels. At that time Islam was the only recognized religion and nobody was allowed to speak in public or write about anything except religion, war and the occupation of foreign lands. Ibn Hazm was therefore considered a pornographer and this book was not published until 1916. As he found himself in such a difficult situation, he claimed that many of his letters were dreams, and that he was merely recording what he had seen during the night.

I have chosen three of his dreams which he called "a symbol of sin and evil thoughts."

Hilary Booth

Poet, painter, and theorist, Hilary Booth was born in 1956, lived in a treehouse as a child, cofounded the Surrealist Group in Australia in 1978, coauthored the group's inaugural manifesto, and coedited its journal, *The Insurrectionist's Shadow,* to which she contributed important texts on Black music (see the section on "Surrealism Today"). She has also collaborated on such U.S. periodicals as *Cultural Correspondence* and *Free Spirits: Annals of the Insurgent Imagination,* and has taken part in exhibitions of the international Phases movement. Her collection of poems, *I Am Rain,* appeared in Australia in 1984 under the Free Association imprint. A physicist and mathematician, her *Quantum Mechanics without Time* (1992) examines such problems as non-Hamiltonian dynamical systems and nonperturbative canonical gravity. More recently her article on "The Dirac-Maxwell Equations with Cylindrical Symmetry" appeared in the February 1997 issue of the U.S. *Journal of Mathematical Physics*. Hilary Booth lives in the countryside near Australia's University of New England.

This article appeared in the "Surrealism and Its Popular Accomplices" issue of the journal *Cultural Correspondence* (1979), reissued the following year in book form by City Lights.

THEIR GAMES AND OURS: A NOTE ON TIME-TRAVELERS' POTLATCH

In a letter to James F. Morton (1932), H. P. Lovecraft wrote, on the subject of games, both physical and intellectual: "They reveal no actual secrets of the universe, and help not at all in intensifying or preserving the tantalizing moods and elusive dream-vistas of the aesthetick imagination." And in a letter to Robert E. Howard, same year; "There is a basic difference between the tense drama of meeting and overcoming an *inevitable* problem or obstacle in real life, and the secondary or symbolic drama of meeting or overcoming a problem or obstacle which has merely been artificially set up."

One could say further that the games legitimated by this society tend to be merely an extension of the repression necessary during the workday; an extension into the few hours of "leisure" before we sleep; a stopgap to prevent real desires and fears from catching us "offguard." It is as well that miserabilism finds it impossible to harness the dream in any such fashion!

The *surrealist* use of games can only be of an absolutely opposing nature to those of which Lovecraft speaks. With the seriousness of black humor, we continually invent them for the purpose of exploring the dark realms of the unconscious, of chance, of the mysterious correspondences of thought that arise between us (due to both the universality of the language of the unconscious, and also, perhaps, thought-transference), of the consequences of love as a gorgeous vehicle of freedom, with sparks of light that are *extremely pleasurable* in themselves. Many of them, such as the exquisite corpse and the collective relation of automatic stories, have been practiced by children for many years, before the logical modes of thought extinguish such delights so brutally.

To the ludicrous domino-toppling buffoons, to the meanderings of absent-minded chess whizzes, to the pointless physical prowess of Olympic nationalist idiots and to the boredom of the daily cryptic crossword, we say: "The joke's on you!" Childish pleasures will reign supreme. When the imagination is set loose, all of Hell is too. And that, no doubt, is precisely where these gifts will have to be delivered, via the Underground Railroad, perhaps in the midst of an infernal jazz concert featuring Duke Ellington, Charlie Parker, John Coltrane and Fats Navarro—with Lautréamont on machine-gun . . .

"The things which interest me," as Lovecraft said, "are . . . *broad vistas* of dramatic pageantry in which cosmic laws and the linkage of cause and effect are displayed on a large scale."

Hilary Booth, Nancy Joyce Peters, Penelope Rosemont, Debra Taub

---

SURREALIST GAMES: TIME-TRAVELERS' POTLATCH

Invented in Chicago in 1974, Time-Travelers' Potlatch explores the experience, common in dreams and fantasies, of meeting historic or fictional personages. The game is simple: Each player indicates the gift *that she/he would present to various real or imaginary figures on the occasion of their meeting. By introducing concrete* objects *into an otherwise vaguely defined subjective relationship, the game—especially when the players note similarities and differences in their selections—affords a wide field for speculation and reverie.*

Hilary Booth

For Herman Melville: A white submarine in the shape of a snake.

For Ambrose Bierce: The phone number of Ambrose Small's mother.

For Charles Fort: An "inexplicable" rain of heated revolutionists from all corners of the world, to fall in the back-streets of Chicago.

For Bugs Bunny: A hot-dog stand in Alaska, a camel to ride along Miami Beach.

Nancy Joyce Peters

For Michael Wigglesworth: A Pisco Punch from the Eureka Saloon of Phantom Moll, Girl Footpad, and a recording of her singing "Tis a jolly life we outlawed sinners lead"

For Isadora Duncan: A glittering amphitheatre designed and constructed by a hundred birds of paradise who will accompany her in whatever ways they see fit

For King Kong: An executive desk at RKO studios, Carl Denham's skull for a paperweight, and a stack of scripts by Little Nemo

For Clark Ashton Smith: A rainforest suspended over the American River by a spider's thread

For Jack London: A pillowcase on which is embroidered in scarlet letters the secrets of Zuni

For Ma Rainey: A cloud chamber filled with elephant-tusk arrowheads in a configuration suggesting the permanent seizure of Harpers Ferry

For Buster Keaton: The wishbone from a giant bird risen from the waters of Lake Stymphalus

For Samuel Greenberg: The Sierra Nevada.

Penelope Rosemont

For G. W. F. Hegel: A black giraffe

For Ann Radcliffe: A two-week, all-expenses-paid tour of Galapagos, with Rosa Luxemburg

For Charles Fourier: An automobile decorated by New Guinea natives

For Bessie Smith: Cleopatra's royal barge, filled with oranges

For Victoria Woodhull: The U.S. Senate and House of Representatives in a bottle, including every senator and congressman, with whom she could do as she pleased

For Woody Woodpecker: A chance to direct the reforestation of the Chicago Loop, accompanied by a chorus of all the birds within 2000 miles

For Annie Oakley: A gold-plated, double-barreled shotgun, on which is engraved the whole of Mary Wollstonecraft's *Vindication of the Rights of Woman*

For Harriet Tubman: A flock of white-crested laughingthrushes (*garrulax leucolophus*) who would help her in whatever she does

Debra Taub

For Harpo Marx: A porcupine-quill coat that sings him to sleep.

For Ernie Kovacs: The tallest building in the world, turned upside-down.

For Mae West: A tropical forest on the back of a beetle.

For Lightnin' Hopkins: An island that can be moved anywhere.

For Daffy Duck: An airplane with an apple in its mouth.

Valentine Penrose

FROM THESE HUSKS ARE WORLDS MADE

Life herself, dumb and hidden woman, never inert even in the most confused of her aspects; Life herself; crawling, swarming, thickening essences, wastes which would appear to have abandoned the struggle. Before Adam, duly begotten after the Sixth and after all other succeeding, void days, life herself: a feminine essence named Hachaya (Lilith), dowered with a spontaneous movement she communicates to the worlds and to animal life, movement which holds the possibility of infinite reproduction, accomplishing activity but not that of primary production which had need of assistance before it could proclaim itself.* This support, this high universal substantiality, succeeding Lilith, became flesh, Adam's second wife; became Eve, "mother of the animate"; and Adam, himself spirit, was charged with the evolution of this shred from himself. With subtlety. No procreation: ray-creations without apparent residue, ideal molds for possibilities, extraordinary themes nonetheless boundaried by space. All without faults, fallibilities, irregularities; Precise. But, however perfectly dreamed, the Entirety was dredged, in spite of everything, from the waters of the abyss, from chaos, from the unnamed, immaterial mass of the eternal unconscious One. We speak here concerning the Waters of the deep containing the germ of life, of that queen of the Abyssal Waters, who always offers her looking glass from the desire of creation.

"Impossible to know"—following the words of St. Jerome at the time of the first Gnostics—*"if God created this Spirit, or whether it was evolved by the Waters, that the Waters should multiply relevantly to their Species"—"Bring fruits said the Upper Archangelic Assembly that liberating Dominion may multiply without limits."* Thus, before Adam, the liberating power of the Materia Prima was heralded, from the minerals that would melt and remold in the earth until they became animality, herding to emergence as grasses, already communal pasturage for the great flock on the

* Dr. G. Chauvet: *Esotérisme de la Genèse*

sixth day ("Behemah") to be its destined nourishment and long after, when death declared itself, returning again to inert straw. It is necessary to follow this process in order to bring into unity again the matter existing here below. It is such a track Tapiès has rediscovered, traced along the foundations of his painting, spoils abandoned in course of the descent.

Named in certain Hebrew and Gnostic texts are: "shards", husks, shells, whatever, in being shattered, has fallen degree by degree down to its actual state; whatever is useless, the detritus of heavens, in what number have these counted their own cycles. To the beat by which the yet immaterial regulated its buoyant forms into barely tangible spheres and globes, the residues grouped round in successive formations. The Gnosis speaks of such aeons in descending order; and these surging, changing waves, this debris from on high more or less created an idea of all that is matter. Thus from the glittering inter-stellar dust to the dust on the footpath and that in the granary.

From these husks are worlds made, shedding scales, projecting the first sounds into silence. Those that were already first fruits of the principles crystallized—after the sound—into letters and hieroglyphs replete with new saps: letters formed as drops trickling to a full stop, graffiti drawn as circles to protect flocks, columns, roofs, shelters: construction, the house, furniture and the authenticity of their usage.

(Excerpts from "Tapiès, the Innominate Sources," 1972)
Translated by Roy Edwards

Leonora Carrington

WHAT IS A WOMAN?

Fifty-three years ago I was born a female human animal. This, I was told, meant that I was a "Woman."

But I never knew what they meant.

Fall in love with a man and you will see. . . . I fell (several times), but saw not.

Give birth and you will see. . . . I gave birth and did not know, who am I? Am I? Who?

Am I that which I observe or that which observes me?

I am that I am, God the Father told Moses on the Mountain. This means nothing to me. *I am* may have been a dishonest invention meaning multitude.

Je pense donc je suis [I think, therefore I am], but why? Some kind of pretension of Monsieur Descartes?

If I am my thoughts, then I could be anything from chicken soup to a pair of scissors, a crocodile, a corpse, a leopard or a pint of beer.

If I am my feelings, then I am love, hate, irritation, boredom, happiness, pride, humility, pain, pleasure, and so on and so forth.

If I am my body, then I am a foetus to a middle-aged woman changing every second.

Yet, like everybody else I yearn for an identity although this yearning mystifies me always.

If there is a true individual *identity* I would like to find it, because like truth on discovery it has already gone.

So I try to reduce myself to facts. I am an aging human female, now: soon I will be old and then dead. This is all I know as far as facts are concerned.

These facts are not particularly edifying or original.

However, out of the depths of this humanoid female a nameless apprehension is constantly present of a no I, no me, no it, but Is, limitlessly mysterious, but there—no doubt at all.

Pre-form, pre-light, pre-darkness, pre-sound, Is.

Then in idle rumination I find pleasure in imagining that I am some kind of seed that must split and germinate into something so unlike what I appear to be that I could not imagine in my wildest moments, but intensely convinced that once the split is complete the absolute Other will take over in this field of doubting multitude I call myself and take a *step* further in evolution.

Perhaps I am talking of death or of those who are not yet born. Those we call women, perhaps Men.

If the planet is still alive for people to be born.

I dare not say that I believe in evolution because I am not at all sure there is such an I to affirm anything, but love of possible evolution feels sure as breath.

But will they give the chance to this seed to split and germinate?

On what does future organic life on this earth depend?

What induced the serpent to grow feathers?

A nameless force operating in the unknown psyche or pre-form of life that can perhaps perform miracles if miracles are allowed . . .

And the only one to give me absolute permission is myself.

Conscious deliberate permission to allow miracle.

Since civilization is rolling quickly toward absolute destruction for Earth, blind inane mass suicide for all living beings, the last hope is an act of will to step out of the mechanical trap and refuse. This will could produce a medium for evolution. If all the Women of the world decide to control the population, to refuse war, to refuse discrimination of Sex or Race and thus force men to allow life to survive on this planet, that would be a miracle indeed.

Technology—or otherwise the clever extensions of the human body, such as the caveman's club to a submarine or jet plane—is so hypnotically impressive of Man's Brainy Toys that we have passively allowed ourselves to be devoured by our own teddy bears. Surely it is time (if there is time enough) to become grown women and take away the teddy bears and other obnoxious toys that threaten to turn the nursery into a tomb.

It is a curious thought that the human cortex has been generally employed for make-believe, pretense, pretension. Pretending to be superior because of "x" nationality, pretending to be better because I have six television sets, a bigger house, a better car than you, pretending to be better than you a woman, I a man. Pretending that We Are Right because we have nastier and more totally destructive weapons than They Have.

Why all this deadly pretense?

Is it not possible that the cortex might have a real and positive function, such as a search for truth?

A will for survival of Life, a will for further mystery to unfold within the media of life?

The extraordinary and horrible abuse of the human brain by other human brains is very difficult to explain, but to quote Professor Genoves: "The same cunning that invented war could invent peace" (*Is Peace Inevitable?* by Santiago Genoves).

Pretension is, in fact, a blind alley that leads nowhere because it is a lie. I think we must try to look in through the smog in ourselves and ask who or what is this, and what within this we could evolve, live, grow. A maternal thought arising perhaps from maternal instinct—but instincts mothered consciousness, or so they say. If through consciousness we could unchain our own emotional power, then we would no longer be the passive herd driven by mad shepherds into the slaughterhouse.

In order to unchain our emotions we must observe all the elements that are used to keep us enslaved, all the false identities that we unconsciously embrace through propaganda, literature, and all the multiple false beliefs that we are fed since birth.

This is the only way to clear psychic territory for reality. Our emotions react mechanically to so much bunk that our own real emotions are practically impossible to decode. Some of us go to psychoanalysts in the hope of finding out; others try to find more and stronger illusions in the hope of never finding out; the rest accept what they are told and feel comfortable in order to conform, even if this conforming is slavery and destruction.

Emotional power, like electricity, can be manipulated in all kinds of devious ways: projecting Mickey Mouse on the screen, the electric chair, the subway or naturally by a thunderstorm. However sublime, silly, or tragic expressions are manifested, the power is the same emotional force that is subject to change by manipulation, circumstances and also by understanding. We know that subliminal persuasion touches off stronger reactions than reason because it operates on the emotional center which works on a stronger power system. What we ought to know as well is what we are going to allow to be fed into this mysterious center.

However corrupt our emotional system has become, there is nevertheless a nucleus in all beings which knows basically that which is true and that which is false. Psychoanalysis, which is still fumbling in the unknown, has shown us that we can find a great deal of self-knowledge through our dreams, even if this science is in an embryonic state. Lies we live are shown to us in dreams. There appears to be a Knower in the unconscious that is never fooled and can rise to the conscious mind if the emotions are prepared to accept some elements of truth.

The idea that "Our Masters" are Right and must be loved, honored and obeyed is, I think, one of the most destructive lies that have been instilled into the female psyche. It has become most horribly obvious what these Masters have done to our planet and her organic life. If women remain passive I think there is very little hope for the survival of life on this Earth.

First published in Mexico in 1970, this article is reprinted here from *Cultural Correspondence* nos. 12–14, 1981.

THE CABBAGE IS A ROSE

The Cabbage is a rose, the Blue Rose, the Alchemical Rose, the Blue Deer (Peyote), and the eating of the God is ancient knowledge, but only recently known to civilized occidental Humans who have experienced many phenomena, and have recently written many books that give accounts of the changing worlds which these people have seen when they ate these plants. Although the properties of the cabbage are somewhat different, it also screams when dragged out of the earth and plunged into boiling water or grease—forgive us, cabbage.

Writing and painting are alike in that both arts—music as well—come out of fingers and into some receptive artifact. The result, of course, is read, heard or seen through the receptive organs of those who receive the art and are supposed to "Be" what all these different persons perceive differently. Therefore it seems that any introduction to art is fairly senseless since anybody can think or experience according to who he is. Very likely the introduction will not be read anyhow.

Once a dog barked at a mask I made; that was the most honorable comment I ever received.

The Furies, who have a sanctuary buried many fathoms under education and brainwashing, have told Females they will return, return from under the fear, shame, and finally, through the crack in the prison door, Fury. I do not know of any religion that does not declare women to be feeble-minded, unclean, generally inferior creatures to males, although most Humans assume that we are the cream of all species. Women, alas; but thank God, Homo Sapiens!

Most of us, I hope, are now aware that a woman should not have to demand Rights. The Rights were there from the beginning; they must be Taken Back Again, including the Mysteries which were ours and which were violated, stolen or destroyed, leaving us with the thankless hope of pleasing a male animal, probably of one's own species.

History has a peculiarity of making gaps whenever they appear convenient. The Bible, like any other history, is full of gaps and peculiarities that only begin to make sense if understood as a covering-up for a very different kind of civilization which had been eliminated. What kind of civilization? Who was the wise Snake which had the wisdom that made human beings like angels?

Who are angels anyhow?

Who was Nobo Daddy who got so angry because Eve gave the wise apple to Adam?

Who was the Beautiful Black Lady who abandoned her Mother's Vineyard?

There are so many questions and so much Dogmaturd to clear aside before anything makes sense, and we are on the point of destroying the Earth before we know anything at all. Perhaps a great virtue, curiosity can only be satisfied if the millennia of accumulated false data are turned upside down. Which means turning oneself inside out and to begin by despising no thing, ignoring no thing—and make some interior space for digestive purposes. Our machinementation still reacts to colossal absurdities with violence, pleasure, pain—automatically.

Such as: I am, I am, I am. (Anything from an archbishop to a disregarded boot.) But is this so? Am I?

Indigestion is imminent; there is too much of it.

The Red Queen told Alice that we should walk backward slowly in order to arrive there faster and faster.

The Sacred Deer is still worshipped in the desert here in Mexico.

The cabbage is still the Alchemical Rose for any being able to see or taste.

Footprints are face to face with the firmament.

September 1975
(From *Arsenal: Surrealist Subversion* no. 4, 1989)

Meret Oppenheim

NOBODY WILL GIVE YOU FREEDOM, YOU HAVE TO TAKE IT

Acceptance Speech for the 1974 Art Award of the City of Basle, 16 January 1975

Note: In my speech of January 1975, I said that we still have no image for the male mind-set in women and we still have to camouflage it. Three years later it occurred to me that the allegorical image can simply be reversed. If the female mind-set, which is essential to the genius of the male poet or artist, must share in the evolution of a work, then in the case of women writers, artists, thinkers, it is the male mind-set within them that shares in the evolution of a work. Women are the "Muses" whom genius has kissed, just as man, the genius, has been "kissed by the Muse."

• • •

It is not easy to be a young artist. If you work in the same style as an accepted master, ancient or contemporary, success will not be long in coming, but if you speak a new language of your own that others have yet to learn, you may have to wait a very long time for a positive echo.

It was, and still is even more difficult for a woman artist.

The segregation begins with seemingly external things. Men, as artists, can live as they please without provoking censure, but people look disdainfully at a woman who claims the same privilege. This and much more is a woman's lot. I think it is the duty of a woman to lead a life that expresses her disbelief in the validity of the taboos that have been imposed upon her kind for thousands of years. Nobody will give you freedom; you have to take it.

Why are there still men, even young men, who refuse to concede women a creative spirit?

A great work of literature, art, music, philosophy is always the product of a whole person. And every person is both male and female. In ancient Greece, men were inspired by the Muses, which means that the female tendency within them shared in their creations, and this still applies today. Conversely, the male tendency is contained in the works of women.

We have neither an image nor a name for this. I venture to claim that the male tendency in women is still forced to wear camouflage. But why? As I see it, since the establishment of a patriarchy—in other words, since the devaluation of the female element—men have projected their inherent femininity as a quality of inferior ilk, on to women. For women this entails living not only their own femininity, but also that projected on to them by men. They have to be women to the second power. Now that really is too much. Yet it is what women have been for a long time, and what many still are today.

Of this strange breed Nietzsche says, "Women are still cats. . . ." (Note the "still"!) "Women are still cats and birds. Or cows, at best." And he's right. That is why women do not and cannot appreciate each other. You cannot appreciate a non-value. They project their male tendency on to men because they are forced to suppress it in themselves. "Women should not think." Is male self-esteem really so vulnerable? "Intellectual achievements by women are embarrassing." So, they have to be repressed and forgotten as quickly as possible. Ideas? Every genuinely new idea is by nature aggressive, and aggression, as a trait, is diametrically opposed to the image of femininity imprinted in the minds of men and projected on to women.

Men are an equally strange breed and, like women, a distorted version of what they could be.

For some years now, people have been saying that humanity has upset the balance of nature. Doesn't this justified thought embrace the veiled realization that it is the balance of humanity itself that has been upset? It has been upset by being split into two sexes locked in opposition, except that one of them has the undisputed upper hand.

Naturally neither men nor women are to blame for this development.

The great miracle, the "tool-making animal," evolved in different places on earth and, in obeying similar laws the world over, became the human being who *for the very first time* gave expression to an all-pervasive penetrating spirit—in rhythm, dance, picture, and myth.

Much later, this great miracle took another step and developed its intellect. I think, I fear, that all the peoples of the Earth will have to pass through the stage we are in today, with its appalling concretion, its brutality, its consuming greed for commodities—all side-effects of the fascinating finds of scientific scholarship.

To permit the development of the sharp instrument of the intellect, other traits had to be ignored. So much so that I think we are now suffering the dire consequences of having neglected these other qualities. I am talking about feelings, intuition, wisdom.

If we look at life on this planet since prehistoric times, we see nothing but steadily increasing complexity.

Since life means change, and since nature apparently tends to become more complex, there is no reason why nature shouldn't impel life in another direction again.

After all we mustn't forget that it was Eve who took the first bite of the apple from the Tree of Knowledge, or rather, the tree of conscious thought.

There were a few voices in the wilderness as early as the 18th century. Now women from all corners of the Earth are raising their voices and rebelling against their despised position, an indication perhaps that feelings, which have been suppressed for so long, are coming to the surface again to take their rightful place in our hearts—on equal footing with reason!

And who knows . . . maybe wisdom will also be released from its dungeon some day.

Translated from the German by Catherine Schelbert

6. Surrealism: A Challenge to the Twenty-First Century

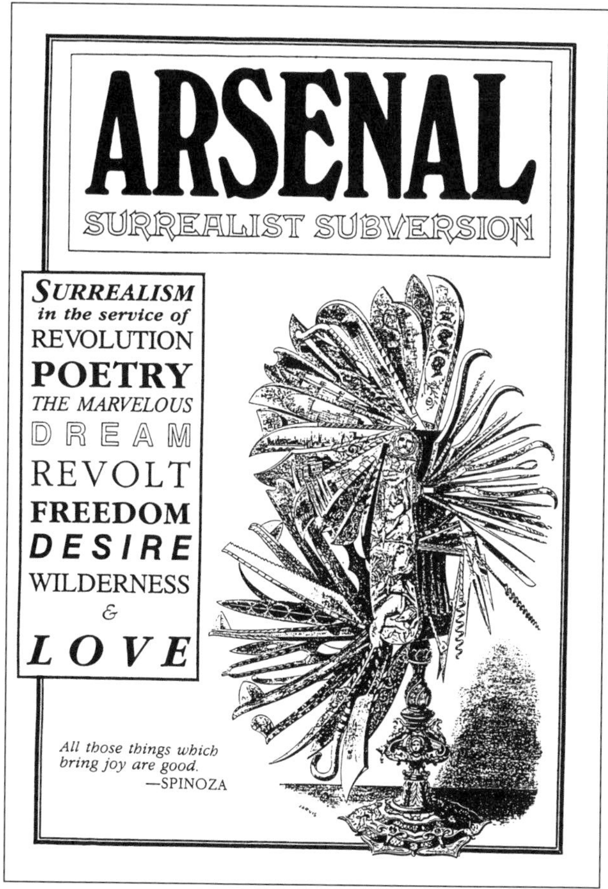

Eva Švankmajerová, *Over All,* oil, 1988. Courtesy of the artist.

Women and Surrealism Today and Tomorrow

> New beauties kindle, and new joys arise!
> —Phillis Wheatley

In a 1981 symposium on "Surrealism Today and Tomorrow," David Roediger suggested that "the maturation of major women surrealist theoreticians will vastly expand the already wide horizons of the movement" (Roediger 1981, 70). Certainly, in the world as it is today, there is plenty for surrealism's critical theorists to do! The recent writings of Haifa Zangana, Eva Švankmajerová, Alena Nádvorníková, Silvia Grénier, Hilary Booth, Nancy Joyce Peters, Rikki Ducornet, Alice Farley, Elaine Parra, Ivanir de Oliveira, and Nicole Reiss, and the poems (which double as manifestoes) by Jayne Cortez, Carmen Bruna, and Petra Mandal, are examples of bold, adventurous inquiry, rejection of dogmatism, critical interpretation as a poetic activity, absolute divergence from ruling ideologies, and a fresh start of the most desirable kind of utopian dreaming. The following selection of short texts and excerpts by these and other current participants in the movement show that in surrealism today poetry, critical theory, and revolutionary activity are perceived as one and indivisible. In their search for ways out of the social prison of the global commodity economy, such writings help fulfill Leonora Carrington's recent call for "surrealist survival kits" to enable us to get through these terrible times.[1]

Since 1968, as we have seen, surrealism has been increasingly recognized throughout the world as a forerunner and catalyst of many of the most daring and creative developments in contemporary culture and politics. However, surrealism's current viability—as a continuing current of ideas and as a living and organized movement—is a question that most critics and historians have chosen to ignore. Surrealism has been pronounced dead so many times (André Breton told an audience of U.S. college students in 1942 that its obituaries had appeared just about every month since the movement began) that few writers have bothered to look at the plentiful evidence of its present-day vitality (Breton 1978, 236).

This favoring of the past over the present is part of the *modus operandi* of the disciplines which thus far have taken surrealism as a field of study. It is no secret that art criticism, art history, and museum curatorship have generally been bastions of social conservatism. Those whose job it is to preserve and protect the traditions of the status quo prefer to look on surrealism as a dead cultural artifact. Living surrealism remains an embarrassing problem, an irritating nuisance that they prefer to ignore.

At the time the 1960s surrealist resurgence did attract considerable attention, even in the U.S. That was because the volatile cultural and political climate of those years fostered the growth of worldwide countermedia (radical and underground press, films, etc.) which in turn made it harder for establishment media to ignore the real (i.e., eye-opening, revolutionary) news of the day. In stark contrast, the great majority of recent academic literature on the subject in the U.S. pretends almost unanimously not to notice that anything has happened in surrealism since World War II.

Now and then the truth has leaked out. In *Women Artists and the Surrealist Movement*, Whitney Chadwick mentions, even if only in passing, that the 1947 International Surrealist Exhibition in Paris "heralded the arrival of a new generation of women . . . whose presence animated and helped to shape surrealism's postwar development." Although she acknowledges that "this important nucleus of younger women" has "done much to keep the surrealist banner flying," Chadwick chose not to pursue the topic ("their story, unfortunately, [is] omitted here") and has not returned to it in her subsequent writings (Chadwick 1985, 286, 10).

Most of the "new generation" of post–World War II surrealists are from Algeria, Angola, Argentina, Australia, Brazil, Bulgaria, Chile, Cuba, Colombia, Czechoslovakia, the Dominican Republic, Egypt, Haiti, Hungary, Indonesia, Iraq, Japan, Lebanon, Mexico, Morocco, Mozambique, Peru, Poland, Puerto Rico, Quebec, Romania, Senegal, Syria, Tunisia, Turkey, Venezuela, Yugoslavia, and the African diaspora: that is, from Eastern Europe and the Third World. The real evolution of the movement thus contradicts the narrow view of those who want to make us believe that surrealism can be conveniently filed away as "Western European," "French," "historically completed," "male-dominated," or "misogynist."

This concluding section of our anthology offers a tentative survey of some of those throughout the world who are convinced that the surrealist adventure is more indispensable today than ever, and that its actuality and future potential are greater than its historic achievements.[2]

Since 1980 surrealist groups have been active in São Paulo, Buenos Aires, Prague, Brno, Paris, Madrid, Stockholm, Leeds, Chicago, and Australia. Some were formed in Breton's lifetime, others are of more recent origin (surrealists have always despised genealogy, in any case). Besides these groups, smaller nuclei have agitated for surrealism—with demonstrations, publications, exhibits—in many other places, including Puerto Rico, Montreal, London, Berlin, Reykjavik, Medellín, and San Francisco, and isolated individuals have advocated the surrealist viewpoint in Angola, Belgium, Japan, Holland, Portugal, Denmark, Poland, Romania, Ireland, and Trinidad. There are also other groups which, for various reasons, no longer call themselves surrealist, but which openly derive their inspiration from surrealism and indeed think of themselves as its direct continuators.[3]

As in the past, most surrealist groups in the 1980s and 1990s have published journals. In their breadth of content and overall quality of production, several of these publications—especially the Prague group's *Analogon,* the Madrid group's *Salamandra* [Salamander], the Stockholm group's *Mannen på gatan* [Man in the Street] and *Stora Saltet* [Stirring Up the Salt], and the U.S. group's *Arsenal: Surrealist Subversion* and *Free Spirits*—are by no means inferior to the well-known surrealist periodicals of pre–World War II days. Decidedly activist, most of these groups also produce tracts on current cultural and political events (denunciations of government censorship and other repression; celebrations of rebellious, liberatory actions) and otherwise identify themselves with various currents of the Far Left. Every one of the groups mentioned, for example, has taken part in the defense of the 1994 Zapatista uprising in Chiapas, Mexico, and in the worldwide campaign to free U.S. political prisoner Mumia Abu-Jamal. Together these groups cooperate on the occasional publication of an *International Surrealist Bulletin.* The first, in English and Swedish, was jointly produced by the Chicago and Stockholm groups in 1986 and was followed shortly by an abridged Japanese translation published in Tokyo. A new series was started in 1991, published in Spanish, French, and English.

The *International Bulletin* and other collective publications offer a panorama of organized surrealism's current perspectives and activities. Surrealism's "constants"—poetry, love, freedom, dream, humor, play, eros, revolt, revolution—are highly visible in their pages, but none of these publications can be accused of simply repeating the surrealism of earlier years. In fact, one reason why contemporary surrealism seems to provoke so much consternation among critics and scholars as well as the general public is because it "fails" to copy the "classic" models of surrealism now on display in museums and therefore is not "entertaining" enough. Prisoners of frozen categories who complain, viewing a painting by Eva Švankmajerová or an object-box by Michele Finger, "*That* doesn't look like surrealism to me!" show only that they have missed the whole point. The liberation of the imagination can never be reduced to a mere style of art or a type of literary production, much less a form of amusement. In poetry, painting, collage, sculpture, photography, film, dance, games, critical theory, and politics, surrealism is always new because the subversive imagination is always *right now,* when you need it, ready or not.

What is perhaps most noticeable about surrealism today is the greatly enlarged field of its researches and applications. Entire fields that surrealists in the past either bypassed altogether or considered marginal—such as music, dance, architecture, and animated film—are now important areas of surrealist inquiry and activity. A heightened interest in Black music, for example, especially jazz and blues, has been highly visible throughout the international Surrealist Movement since the 1960s. This passional attraction has led to several important books and numerous articles as well as to an informal but fruitful collaboration and exchange of views between surrealists in several countries and the Association for the Advancement of Creative Musicians (AACM), a Chicago-based group dedicated to the propagation of "Great Black Music."[4]

The exploration of subversive currents in popular culture—comics, films, pulp fiction, radio, etc.—has been a fascinating surrealist sideline from the beginning, but in recent years has grown into one of the most luxuriant fields of surrealist research.[5] History, a discipline in which only a few surrealists intervened effectively in the past—has also emerged as a significant focus. As reinterpreters of history, surrealists such as Alena Nádvorníková, Hilary Booth, and Nancy Joyce Peters have been interested in the study of heresies, revolutionary struggles, utopias, Native American and African American culture and resistance, ecology and the relations between humankind and animals, "cranks" and other neglected figures, changes in language (especially slang), vandalism and workplace sabotage, the popular arts—and surrealism itself.

Surrealism could be considered the last of the great nonacademic intellectual movements, for like Marxism, anarchism, and psychoanalysis, it has thrived largely outside the universities. In the past couple of decades, however, notably in the Czech Republic, France, Brazil, and the U.S., several individuals who make their living as teachers—Silvia Grénier, for example, and Alena Nádvorníková—have also been active in the Surrealist Movement. Surrealist investigations in such fields as anthropology, folklore, and psychoanalysis have greatly multiplied since the sixties. A growing number of non-surrealist specialists have written sympathetically of earlier surrealist accomplishments in these areas, and to some extent, most notably in Prague, they have shown their willingness to collaborate on surrealist publications.[6] The Czech surrealists' psychological experiments—with LSD, sleep and dream research, and most recently, the imaginative implications of the sense of touch (a topic touched on by Eva Švankmajerová in this section)—have been especially productive.

Even a quick summary of surrealism's manifestations in the plastic arts since the 1976 World Surrealist Exhibition would take up many pages. The subject is well worth a book in itself. However, it is rarely chronicled in the slick, commercial art magazines. Not incidentally, surrealists today tend to situate themselves not only outside the corporate-dominated billion-dollar industry known as the "art world" but in irreconcilable opposition to it.

Among the most significant surrealist painters to appear in recent years are Turkish-born Ody Saban (active in the Paris group), Gloria Villa in Argentina, Gina Litherland and Laura Corsiglia in the U.S., Olga Billoir in Spain, and Josifa Aharony, Laila Hollo Aiach, Hilton Seawright Araujo, Lya Paes de Barros, and Heloísa Pessôa in Brazil. Though still relatively little known, these are dramatically original creators whose work, reproduced in surrealist journals and exhibition catalogs, is already an active influence on younger artists.

The disruptive art of collage, which remains one of surrealism's most consistently effective methods of discovery, has been taken up with uncompromising poetic vigor by Laila Aiach, Teresa Machado, Elaine Parra, Ivanir de Oliveira, Lya Paes de Barros, and others in Brazil, Suzel Ania in France, and Janice Hathaway and Catherine Seitz in the U.S. (My own landscapades and prehensilhouettes are also extensions of collage.) The stonework of Nicole Reiss and the object-collages of Michèle Finger—both active in the São Paulo group—are among the newest revelations of surrealism in sculpture. The graphic arts are continually enlivened by the entrancing silk screen prints of Irene Plazewska in Ireland, and the startling drawings of Katerina Piňosová and Katerina Kubiková in the Czech Republic, Lurdes Martinez and Conchi Benito in Spain, Kajsa Bergh, Aase Berg, and Petra Mandal in Sweden.

Surrealism started in poetry, and poetry remains its central nervous system. In the face of widespread retrograde trends (return to mysticism, rhyme, didacticism, the mundane, etc.), surrealists persist in celebrating poetry as the "highest language," a breath of fresh air, exaltation, the vanquishing of misery, marvelous freedom itself. All these poets—from Mary Low, who is now in her eighties, to Katerina Piňosová, who at twenty-three is the youngest writer represented in this volume—share a close community of interests rooted in subversive values and complete indifference to the usual forms of "success." These are not merely writers "influenced by" surrealism—those who borrow bits and pieces from the work of past surrealists to add glitter to their own otherwise dull verse. No, these are true poets who, through the magic light of words, embody the future of surrealism's revolution today. Carmen Bruna speaks for all of them when she points out in an interview excerpted in this section that poetry is "truly an incitement to insubordination and revolt," an expression of "total defiance." In short, these are poets who go their own way, deliberately out of step with the conventional ways and means of the literary establishment. Interestingly, however, and hopefully indicative that better times are on the way, a few of them—including Carmen Bruna, Jayne Cortez, and Rikki Ducornet, three of the foremost surrealist poets and writers of our time—also happen to be increasingly well-known to a broad public.

Politically, too, surrealism has not stood still. It is important to keep in mind that the movement's current resurgence parallels the end of Stalinism's pseudo-communist bureaucracies and the renewal of interest in anarchism and the humanistic currents of Marxism. Surrealism today is clearly polycentric, and its constituent groups are far from agreeing on the fine points of world politics. Various currents of anarchism and Marxism have individual supporters in organized surrealism today, but no existing surrealist group identifies itself with any one of these currents over all others. Surrealists in the twenties loved *The Battleship Potemkin,* Sergei Eisenstein's paean of praise to Bolshevism. While surrealists in the nineties would surely still find much to admire in that film, I think many might identify more closely with *Thelma and Louise,* with its accent on individual, affective forms of resistance.

In the absence of large-scale movements for complete social transformation in most countries, surrealists in recent years have tended to be active in more limited, often local struggles. They have taken to the streets to protest the Gulf War, the destruction of rain forests and redwoods, the extermination of wolves and whales. They have battled neo-Nazis, defended women's reproductive rights, demonstrated against apartheid, and supported sit-ins and other radical student initiatives. They have opposed nuclear power, the U.S. invasion of Grenada, the persecution of sexual minorities, the racist "war on drugs." They have helped organize and taken part in coalitions to defend striking coal-miners, mothers on welfare, immigrants, and Native Americans against state violence. In each of these struggles, moreover, they have called attention to the fragmentation inherent in "single-issue" politics and have stressed the need for a larger political vision and a larger radical movement to struggle for a new, nonrepressive society.

Support for popular revolutionary uprisings, of course, remains a "given" of surrealist politics. Thus the Chicago group issued a detailed commentary on the Los Angeles Rebellion of April–May 1992, and the Surrealist Group in Madrid published its views on the 1997 general strike in South Korea. In their analyses of these mass revolts of the dispossessed, surrealists have focused on working-class self-activity, the involvement of new sectors in struggle, the appearance of new forms of revolutionary expression, and the possibilities these revolts suggest for the development of a more effective international opposition.

Interestingly, in many ways their current approach to politics owes more to the historical experience of surrealism itself—and especially to its well-elaborated notions of imaginative activity, humor, and play—than to the terminology of Marxism that sometimes weighed down surrealist political statements in the past. This does not mean that surrealists today are anti-Marxist, but rather that they are aware that aspirations for revolutionary change must be expressed with imaginative effervescence, without limits. The surrealists' task here, as the Surrealist Group in Buenos Aires wrote in 1990, is simultaneously "to reinvent, re-elaborate and replenish the *image of revolution*" and "to preserve, replenish and revive the creative magic of language."[7]

By reinventing the image of revolution—and thus revolutionizing itself—surrealism also maintains its continuity. Inevitably, the dialectic of the historic process brings forth new priorities. In politics as in other areas, what once seemed to be only minor tendencies in surrealism have since blossomed into major emphases. Its current ecological focus is a prime example. It is no accident that surrealists in at least three widely separated countries—Australia, Sweden, and the U.S.—have taken part in Earth First!, the most radical, direct-action wing of the environmental movement. The notion of animal rights, long latent in surrealism, is also evident in movement publications today. Alice Rahon used to say that all her works were "against hunting." "If you have one of my paintings in your house," she told filmmaker and huntsman John Huston, "you will miss all the time." In those days Rahon spoke as a minority, but there are many surrealists who would echo her sentiments today.[8]

As Philip Lamantia once put it, "surrealism moves!" And its movers today, more than ever, are women. At no time in the movement's seven decades have so many women in so many countries been so involved in each and every aspect of the permanent revolution that is surrealism. I find it curious and revealing that the least acknowledged period in its history—from 1947 to the present—is exactly the period in which the participation of women and Third World peoples has been largest. Even more amazing is the fact that today, when women's involvement in the movement is greater than ever (the Surrealist Group in São Paulo, Brazil, for example, includes nearly four times as many women as men), some misguided critics persist in attacking surrealism as if it were some sort of male chauvinist plot.[9]

These antisurrealist feminists are like the feminists who call for police suppression of pornography, restrictions on free speech, and other repressive measures, thus allying themselves with neoconservatives, Christian fundamentalists, and even fascists. Perhaps unwittingly, they are examples of the sorry process by which a liberatory theory—in this case, of women's equality—can be manipulated and turned into its opposite. This is not the place for an analysis of this phenomenon, but I would like to suggest that this refusal to see things as they are conceals a genuine fear not only of surrealism but also of women's liberation on the part of those who have given up hope for worldwide radical social transformation and have trimmed their feminism down to meet the needs of a small, privileged elite of white, upper-middle-class professionals. It would seem that the last thing such people want is for women to become interested in a movement which demands and embodies *freedom now*—intellectual, erotic, social, political, economic—and defends the most revolutionary means of realizing it.

Surrealists today, female and male, are part of the international radical minority which, in the aftermath of the "death of Communism," has refused to say yes to the triumph of exploitation, militarism, white supremacy, gender bigotry, and other misery. They are fully aware that the further fruition of surrealism depends on the rise of new mass emancipatory movements seeking radical social change. In view of the prevailing unfreedom and hopelessness of these times, the fact that surrealism still exists at all is remarkable. But surrealism is never content merely to exist. In this depressingly prolonged historical moment of global reaction, unrestrained imperialist expansion, rampant racism, homelessness, ecological disaster, fundamentalist revivalism, neo-Nazism, the "men's movement," high-tech unionbusting, a burgeoning prison industry, "compassion fatigue," and rising illiteracy, surrealism—the living negation of all these horrors—not only has refused to evaporate, but is actually enjoying a promising renaissance.

A look at two recent collective declarations provides an excellent illustration of the situation of surrealism today—of its revolutionary perspectives, the role of women in the movement, and its relation to other present-day dissident currents. The 1992 international surrealist manifesto against the Columbus Quincentennial certainly marked something new in surrealism. The movement had long affirmed its solidarity with the struggles of Native Americans and other aboriginal peoples against repressive and genocidal "development," but now, for the first time, surrealist groups around the world prepared and published a joint statement; cosigned by 130 participants in surrealist groups in eight countries, plus individual signers from four other countries, it was widely reprinted and translated into many languages.[10] It is significant that this historic document was initially proposed and then drafted by Silvia Grénier, a cofounder of the Buenos Aires group and a major figure in world surrealism today.

A year later the Chicago group published "Three Days That Shook the New World Order," on the 1992 Los Angeles Rebellion. Focused on the critique of "whiteness," the police state, the hypocrisy of the media, and the ecological implications of the revolt, this well-circulated and much-translated text also discussed the crucial role of women in instigating and adding momentum to this sensational upheaval; indeed, it was almost alone in recognizing this dimension in the L.A. events. In a letter prefacing the French translation, Pierre Naville—a cofounder of surrealism and coeditor of *La Révolution surréaliste* in 1924—wrote: "I have been amazed by [this] beautiful text. . . . I would go so far as to say that [it] represents a new and exceptionally important way of showing that the world is going to experience a surrealist explosion far greater than that which burst out in Paris in 1924. . . . It is my vigorous hope that [the] Surrealist Movement will succeed in renewing what we have attempted so long ago."[11]

It remains to be seen whether Naville's prediction will be realized. In any event, revolutionary poetic thought always seems to find ways to draw on resources that most people find "unimaginable." As Walter Benjamin pointed out in 1929, surrealism discovered a "radical conception of freedom," which, he added, Europe had lacked since Bakunin (Benjamin 1978, 189). Surrealism's sense of freedom—its undeviating, irreducible, physical insistence on freedom—continues to distinguish it from all the other political and intellectual currents of our time and gives surrealist activity its special (and growing) importance in the contemporary world. Surrealism's sense of freedom is not at all abstract—it goes hand in hand with the concrete and revolutionary activity of the imagination. The São Paulo Surrealist Group said it well in a 1996 declaration: "Beyond faith in established notions, received ideas, the predictable; beyond loyal subservience to the accepted and normal; beyond alienation and the esthetic lie," surrealism is at all times "an art of disturbance" whose key methods are "provocation and refusal."[12]

Just now, as I prepare this anthology for publication, I received a book, *En Belle page* [On the Odd Page], by a relative newcomer to the surrealist milieu, Catherine Vasseur. Its opening page reveals a fragment of handwritten manuscript, beginning and ending in mid-sentence, which discusses the possibilities of discovery and self-discovery to be found in the repeated magnification of the same image. The following page is an enlargement of a part of this written fragment—and each succeeding page is an enlargement of the page preceding it. A few pages later the written words are no longer recognizable, but appear rather as calligraphic brush-strokes, or silhouettes of tree branches. A little further on, the page is almost entirely black, speckled with stars. For several pages we advance through these galaxies, in which the stars loom ever larger until the very last page—which is all white, completely blank, ready for us to renew the adventure any way we choose.

Catherine Vasseur's book is a true *invitation au voyage* that can be developed in many directions. I see it also as an example of the limitlessness of the surrealist project. It demonstrates that, no matter where one starts, the practice of poetry, followed through with imagination and rigor, automatically leads to new knowledge, radical discoveries, the Marvelous.

Or as Jayne Cortez says: "Find your own voice and use it / use your own voice and find it!" (Cortez 1996, 117). Modern as the petroglyphs in the land of the Hopi and Zuni, ancient as Mary Lou Williams' *In the Land of Oo-bla-dee,* surrealism continues. Trying to predict its future may be "like trying to unravel the future of the Future" (Peters and Lamantia 1981, 75–76), but those who are curious about surrealism's approach to the twenty-first century should find some hints in the following pages.

Notes

1. During my frequent meetings with Leonora Carrington in Chicago from 1989 to 1992, the "surrealist survival kit" was an often recurring topic of discussion.

2. For a more detailed discussion, see Bounoure 1976 and the introduction to Rosemont et al. 1997.

3. For example, the groups around the publications *Le Cerceau, Supérieure Inconnu, As, Ab irato,* and *Infosurr,* all published in Paris. The Phases movement has active participants throughout the world.

4. See Garon 1975, 1989, 1992; Franklin Rosemont 1976; and the "Surrealism & Blues" supplement in *Living Blues* no. 25, January 1976. Surrealist/AACM collaboration started in 1976 with the "Sun Song" concert (Douglas Ewart, Hamid Drake, and others) at the World Surrealist Exhibition in Chicago, and Joseph Jarman's participation in the third issue of *Arsenal: Surrealist Subversion.* It has continued down to the present, the most recent collaboration being between AACM composer Henry Threadgill and surrealist dancer Alice Farley in New York.

5. See Franklin Rosemont 1980; Buhle 1987; Roediger 1981. Surrealist studies of popular culture have been a central focus of such journals as *Arsenal: Surrealist Subversion, Cultural Correspondence,* and *Free Spirits: Annals of the Insurgent Imagination.*

6. See Ey 1945; Clifford 1988. The scope of the Czech Surrealist Group's journal *Analogon* is suggested by its subtitle: "Surrealism, Psychoanalysis, Anthropology, Crossroads of the Sciences."

7. *International Surrealist Bulletin,* New Series, 1 (1991), 18.

8. Deffebach 1991, 184. In 1971 the Chicago Surrealist Group issued a tract titled "The Anteater's Umbrella: A Contribution to the Critique of the Ideology of Zoos"; it is reprinted in Rosemont et al. 1997, 121–122. A more recent surrealist statement on animal rights, "An Unjust Dominion," by Gina Litherland and Hal Rammel, appeared in the *International Surrealist Bulletin* no. 1 (1986), 11.

9. The prize for the most far-fetched hyperbole in this regard must be awarded to Rudolf Kuenzli, director of the University of Iowa's Dada Archives, who regards surrealism as "an intensification of patriarchy's misogyny." Caws et al. 1990, 25.

10. "1492–1992: 'As Long as Tourists Replace Seers,'" in *International Surrealist Bulletin,* New Series, no. 2; also published in the Chicago Surrealist Group's bulletin, *WHAT Are You Going to Do About It?* no. 1, 1992.

11. "Three Days That Shook the New World Order" originally appeared in *WHAT Are You Going to Do About It?* no. 2, 1993; shortly afterward it was reprinted in the journal *Race Traitor* no. 2, Summer 1993, and again in the *Race Traitor* anthology (Ignatiev and Garvey, 1996). The text was translated into French as *La Révolte de Los Angeles, avril-mai 1992: Trois jours qui ébranlèrent le nouvel ordre mondial,* published by the Atelier de création libertaire in Lyons, and later into Turkish, Italian, and German. Naville's letter, published as a preface, is dated 6 April 1993. For further background on the L.A. Rebellion, see Davis 1992, and Kelley 1994.

12. "Comunicado—O Surrealismo," dated March 1992, and published in *Escrituras surrealistas* no. 1, São Paulo, 1993.

Silvia Grénier

Surrealism in Argentina has had a long, fruitful history. Its organized presence there dates from 1926 and extends, with many interruptions, to the present day. Of the several Argentine surrealist groups that have appeared over the years, the "Signo Ascendante" [Rising Sign] group, formed in 1979, which soon identified itself as the Surrealist Group of Buenos Aires, is arguably the most coherent, militant, and prolific. Silvia Grénier, a cofounder of the group, remains today among the leading animators of international surrealism.

Born in Buenos Aires in 1957, Grénier—who makes her living as a schoolteacher and librarian—is one of Argentina's outstanding poets. Her poems, slow-motion explosions of a desperate outlaw lyricism, have appeared in two collections: *Salomé o la búsqueda del cuerpo* [Salomé or the Body's Quest] (1983) and *Los banquetes errantes* [Nomadic Banquets] (1986). Grénier has also collaborated extensively, as theorist as well as poet, on the group's journal, *Signo Ascendante.*

Surrealists in Argentina, more than in most other countries, have been active in the labor movement. The history of the Buenos Aires group is largely a history of courageous struggle. They have fought against dictatorship, censorship, repressive laws, police terror, and state-sponsored genocide—it is Argentina that put the frightful expression "the disappeared" (los desparecidos) into the global political vocabulary—and have fought for workers' right to organize, freedom for political prisoners, for women's right to divorce, and abortion rights. Grénier has written lucid, impassioned articles and tracts on such issues. Particularly important are her writings in defense of native peoples. Her treatise *Tierra Adentro* [The Interior, or Back Country] provided the basis of the 1992 international surrealist declaration against the "Columbus Quincentennial."

These poems are from *Salomé o la búsqueda del cuerpo.*

SALOMÉ

In my mouth I taste sacrilege
Salome one brilliant foot over the wave's crest
Wonderfully rich in her excess
Spills the scent of her body over the thistle of the world.
Her hair envelops the full cycle of a menstrual moon
it's beautiful it's beautiful it's beautiful

beautiful as the heavy odor of incense on decapitated bodies
beautiful as the brilliant rocks that appear in dreams
On the summit encircled by the ramparts of the black hills
Inside there with my eyes closed
I can see within the walls
under a sky blacker than death
a knot of serpents around a white ankle
beautiful as those rocks or those cat eyes that appear at night
in the cornices where everything ends.
The prophets of hunger cross the desert on their knees.
The jackals with bodies shot full of holes
howl in baptismal fonts
and around the temples I have seen the women licking the stone
staircase with their tongues
Salome black silk that advances silently
prepares the decapitations and the triumphal dances
on the rock alternatively red white black
that cuts in two the forest of unbridled wind
blood runs down the stairs
night runs through the heads of hair
the thirst of the world runs through the world
your naked foot runs over the advancing water
the dagger of flame runs through the fire

Translated from the Spanish by Natalie Kenvin

SIGNS

to Carmen Bruna

You will see me in the wolf's footstep
when the hours grind down their voluptuousness at the roadside
and the cities grow like mushrooms on the beautiful plain
they're all drunk but the silence holds
unfathomable eyelashes that open the door for us
we were like stones in the river of lava
we were like fires in the stone bed
we were the few the many the one with the hidden face
we were living dead the ones with many teeth
your crazy glance prepares the way for me
we were the sleepwalkers and then life passed

like a red tornado in the middle of the sky
we were the lost souls
with our compass hands we touched the world of conquered things
there are mad dancers who crisscross the sky
from trapeze to trapeze like lit matches
there are mad dancers who cross the abyss
on the tightrope of their own suicide

Translated from the Spanish by Myrna Bell Rochester

Carmen Bruna

Born in Quilmes, Argentina (near Buenos Aires), in 1928, Carmen Bruna completed her medical studies in the early 1950s. As a traveling rural physician for thirteen years, she traversed the length and breadth of her native land, living and working in areas little known to most Argentines. Around 1955 she discovered surrealism through Aldo Pellegrini's journal *Letra y linea* [Letter and Line] and became a good friend of pioneer Argentine surrealist poet Juan José Ceselli. She was also acquainted with Enrique Molina and Alejandra Pizarnik, whose poetry she deeply admires. Later she came to know the Brazilian surrealist poet/collagist, Sergio Lima, and in 1982 she joined the "Signo Ascendante" group.

Bruna is the author of six books of poems. Two of them—*Morgana o el espejismo* [Morgana or Mirrorism] (1983) and *Lilith* (1987)—were published under the Buenos Aires Surrealist Group's own Signo Ascendante imprint, the latter volume with a "poem-preface" by Silvia Grénier.

Allergic to all forms of literary careerism, this brave surrealist poet and country doctor has always welcomed rebellious young writers and helped them in their skirmishes with the establishment. Drawing on a wide spectrum of subversive influences (she has written poems inspired by Rosa Luxemburg and Billie Holiday), she is one of the outstanding antiauthoritarians in world literature today. Her solidarity with the endless varieties of insolence and revolt—from "accursed poetry" to black anarchy through hipsterism and Black music—is evident in all her poems.

"Poetry: An Incitement to Revolt" is excerpted from an interview with Raul Henao in *Punto seguido* (Medellín, March 1993). The poems are from *Melusina o la búsqueda del amor extraviado* [Melusina or the Quest for Lost Love] (1993).

POETRY: AN INCITEMENT TO REVOLT

You see, the world of Lautréamont and Rimbaud is also my world: barbaric and hallucinatory. My poetry is the poetry of the accursed poets.

• • •

My poetry is truly an incitement to insubordination and revolt. It is the whirling and outpouring of my rebellious spirit, the fever of my blood, my total defiance.

And my contempt for academic counterfeits.

• • •

The fact that the great Latin American lyric poets are not better known in the Republic of Argentina is because of the deplorable but very real lack of interest in poetry in this country. To speak cruelly but truthfully: No yuppie would dare to say he is a poet, and the yuppies—in this hungry land where the unemployed are the great majority—never read poetry.

Poetry does not sell. Perhaps that is because true poetry is, by definition, *not for sale*.

• • •

I believe it is the indisputable right of poets to withdraw into silence whenever they desire to do so. Rimbaud silenced himself in the fullness of youth. Lautréamont died at 24. Jean-Pierre Duprey killed himself at 29. Alejandra Pizarnik also took her own life.

The gods may withdraw into silence. It is not poets who are unable to communicate—it is society that hasn't the slightest inclination to communicate with poets.

• • •

Of course I defend the myth of woman, and have made it my own. Woman: exalted, proud, and irreducible. I have also fought for women's rights—on picketlines, for example, and without foolishness. But I do not believe that women's liberation automatically leads to the most radical of revolutions. . . . Unfortunately, when women occupy positions of political authority, they mimic the mistakes of men. Power always corrupts.

And that is why my motto is that of the anarchists: *Neither God Nor Master*.

I continue to believe that women should seize their rights by any and all means at their disposal, and enjoy the fullest equality with men.

I believe in the harmony of love and sex.

Translated from the Spanish by Natalie Kenvin

"LADY FROM SHANGHAI"

Love: a plane crash with no survivors.
This is the only *truth* of love.
I'm not a realist: my domain is the world of dreams
"Lady from Shanghai" and the desperate madness
of criminal mirrors;
mirrors that repeat the murderer's image
to the Point of Infinity
hallucination of Mercury and L.S.D.
multiplication of an infinite dream of infinite death
of cruelty, love, betrayal.
Nightmares of passion in hallucinations without morality
hallucinations of ruin and drifting cadavers

Mirrors, mirrors multiplied to infinity.
Mirrors swimming in rivers of blood
and in Mozart's music
Gangsters in the fog
Revolvers of red and white smoke.
Severed vein, shocked purple blood

Cruel Lady from Shanghai—lost
victim and murderer
false as false rubies
You died in the witches' sabbath of mirrors
you died with your eyes of wild black pansy
you died with your forget-me-not eyes
The dark dilated pupils,
you died beautiful assassin without ethics or remorse
Oh "Lady from Shanghai"
sorrow of your impious and traitorous century
that stinks of stale goulash and warm beer

Translated from the Spanish by Natalie Kenvin

MOI-MÊME

I am the pure red witch
who sails at midnight every day in the month of December.
Forever the same.
The one snuggling up at the feet of the idols in the labyrinth,
The one who appears nude and with her cauldron in the presence of Saint
Anthony.
I am all your temptations and each and every one of them
I am the cat-woman and the panther woman
I am the Biblical whore and the Bearer of the Grail in the pulverized center
of the apocalypse
I am the wine of the blood of Christ
I am the heresy and the power
I am drugged sleep
I am the sweet vagina that shelters the AIDS victim in its cradle
I am the suicide of No Man's Land
I am black meat and I am Rosa Pantopon.

Open the gates of Eden for me
Like Lazarus, I have returned
from life to death.

Translated from the Spanish by Natalie Kenvin

Eva Švankmajerová

Painter, puppeteer, poet, and theorist, Eva Švankmajerová has been a dynamic and innovative presence in international surrealism for nearly three decades. Born Eva Dvoraková in Kostelec, Czechoslovakia, in 1940, she studied interior decorating in Prague in the 1950s and then switched to a course in puppet theater. It was there that she met Jan Švankmajer, puppeteer and film-animationist, whom she married and with whom she joined the Surrealist Group in Prague in 1970. Since then she and her husband have been energetic participants in—and often coorganizers of—the group's many samizdat and legal collective publications (including every issue of the journal *Analogon* from the second on), as well as its other extensive activities: surrealist researches, conferences, games, and exhibitions.

The fact that Švankmajerová is a painter definitively *outside* every "trend" in today's art market makes it all the more notable that she also happens to be one of the most widely known surrealist painters of our time. She has had numerous solo shows all over the Czech Republic and in Germany and Belgium, and has also taken part in collective surrealist exhibitions in those countries as well as in France and Holland.

Švankmajerová is also a sharp critical thinker and a poet whose dry humor *à la* Jacques Vaché is always *provoking*. She is the author of many books, all in Czech. How long must English-language readers wait for someone to translate her and other major writings by Czech surrealists?

Eva Švankmajerová lives in Sternberk.

"Emancipation Cycle" and "Tactile Lids" appeared in French in the catalog, *Eva and Jan Švankmajer* (1987). The translation of "Stunned By Freedom" (from *Chemistry*, 1976) was provided by the author. "I Don't Know Exactly" is from *Samoty a citace* [Reading Alone] (1987).

EMANCIPATION CYCLE

Since the emancipation of women is unfeasible in this civilization, at the age of twenty-six, I "established" the following paintings: "Vénisse Asleep" (1967), "The Birth of Vénisse" (1968), "Déjeuner sur l'herbe" (1968), and "The Rape of Leucipes' Sons" (1969), in which I took honorable men as my models.* Vanity of vanities! It was no joke to realize that I was supposed to spend my life doing menial physical and manual activities—so-called "women's work"—whereas any kind of intellectual human effort would be deemed remarkable for my sex, questionable for my gender. Nothing was hidden from me. When I was a child I hated the fat tractor driver with the scarf in her hair as portrayed on the posters. For twenty years I met nobody who accepted the idea that I might become a painter when I grew up. That suspicion had nothing to do with any dubious quality of mine or with my tendency to lie. Simply because of the gender indicated on my birth certificate, I had no rights; I was done for, in advance. Weird! For a while I expected some explanation for this misunderstanding. I did not particularly feel endowed with any special gifts that made the performance of certain petty, repulsive chores a suitable occupation for

---

* The works mentioned here are all based on well-known pictures of women by famous male artists; in Švankmajerová's versions, the figures were replaced by men.

me. Furthermore, I failed to observe any superior intellectual activity among the men around me—or among most men anywhere, for that matter. I have been troubled by this issue for almost twenty years now. In spite of it all, I manage to go on living.

Translated from the French by Guy Ducornet

TACTILE LIDS

Imagination is one. The means of its appearance are interchangeable. "Specialists" in painting, writing, theory, cinema, or decorative arts are nothing but "professionals of intellectual comfort." We, together with our surrealist friends, seek universality of expression, the surest way to the authenticity of creation.

The world is inundated with artistic artifacts that have become prey to the art market or are exploited by civil servants of every stripe to advertise and deify "the best and the most progressive of all political systems," whatever that may be. We despise such utilitarianism, aided and abetted by positivism as well as the scientific-technical revolution. What interests us more than the mere artifact is creativity itself, that secret boiling and bubbling of the soul. Our task is to take the lid off.

Written with Jan Švankmajer
Translated from the French by Guy Ducornet

STUNNED BY FREEDOM

To learn that:
a line can thrill you
like the flight
of fire.
Color can deprive you of your sanity
like blood
and despair.
Clay can enclose you, prison walls
a cemetery
like sperm
it soils
and when you
are finally saved
even with your thoughts.

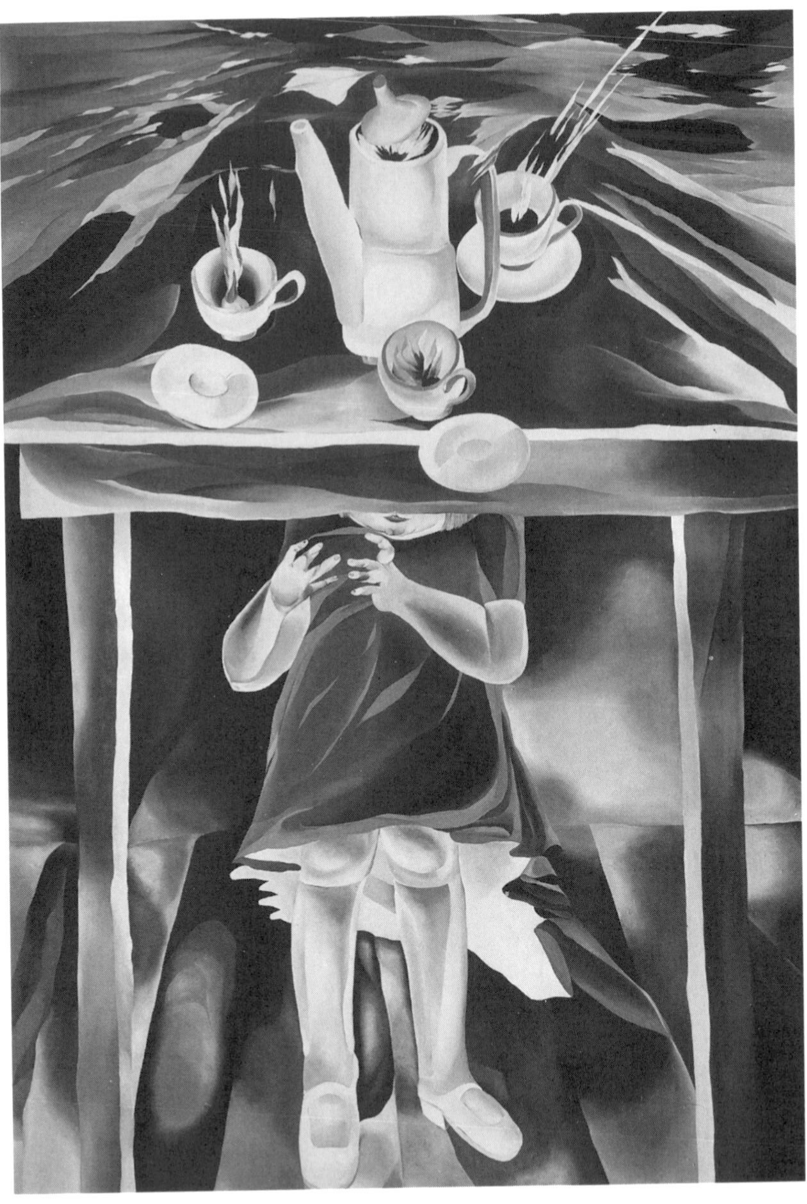

Eva Švankmajerová, *Ascendancy,* oil, 1984. Courtesy of the artist.

I DON'T KNOW EXACTLY

Your ideas of home life
are a bit distorted after all
To want my legs around your neck
all night long
and every night
I respect through eyelashes
and the hesitation to throw that gift
onto my emptiness onto life's eternal grief
onto fog onto death
and tender disappointments
onto the boredom of forced girlfriends
onto the time when it is necessary to invent
the ideal sin
Don't you need to read from my hand at this moment?
Tears of satisfied smog
moisten the imperviousness of my eye
under the roof
under that tortoise-shell coat
four hundred years old already
I loved
or I was furious too
How often I dreamed about some kind of escape
You don't know how easy it is
when a siren addresses you
Here you wave a pinion
and fly out of a dovecote
Defiance gushes from your heart
here the anger
that migraine
onto a short twinkling of life
onto phlegm
onto hurried chewing
onto a quick habit of claws
Oh you don't know how easy it is
when a siren calls you
No timidity no hurricanes
Not until we come back

I only whisper
but there was a fire

Translated from the Czech by Katerina Piňosová

Alena Nádvorníková

Born Alena Bretsnajdrová in Lipnik nad Becvu, Czechoslovakia, in 1942, Alena Nádvorníková studied art history and theory and received her Ph.D. in 1968. She joined the Surrealist Group in Prague in 1974 and—as poet, painter, graphic artist, critic, and theorist—remains one of its leading figures. A collaborator on the Czech group's *samizdat* publications and on *Analogon,* she has also contributed important articles on such pioneers of Czech surrealism as Karel Teige and Jindrich Styrsky to major exhibition catalogs. Her artwork has appeared in many Prague Surrealist Group exhibitions, as well as in several solo shows (two of which, in 1977 and 1985, were shut down by the police), and in collective surrealist exhibitions in Paris, Budapest, and Hannover. Nádvorníková has published two volumes of poems: *Praha, Parizska* (Prague, Paris Street, 1994), and *Uvnitř hlasu* [Inner Voice] (1995). Currently she teaches at Palacky University in Olomouc.

The following article on the great Czech surrealist photographer Emila Medková (1928–1986) is excerpted from a longer study; a French translation, together with English translations of the two poems, were provided by the author.

EMILA MEDKOVÁ'S PHOTOGRAPHS AND THE ANTHROPOMORPHIZATION OF DETAIL

Visible things are varied: There is not a single one to which imagination could not turn, to use as the basic material of creative interpretation. This is the guiding principle of Emila Medková's photographic activity.

It matters little whether personal interpretation occurs during the initial phase of the creative process or even at the moment when the perception of reality takes place, or if it happens only during the definitive fixing of the form as it develops into a new photographic reality. What is involved is the mind's predisposition toward a certain type of visual perception, as well as its acute

Alena Nádvorníková, *What Is Above Is also Below,* ink, 1989. Courtesy of the artist.

sensitivity to the latent polysemy of the forms of the real. These faculties mingle, evoking—in the sense in which Breton speaks of "a veritable gift for evocation"—and with a heightened richness of new imaginative contents—analogies of the individual or collective consciousness.

In the work of Emila Medková, anthropomorphization as a means of interpretation is all the more effective since its aim has nothing to do with realism. Any "veritism" in the form would only limit the free play of imagining powers

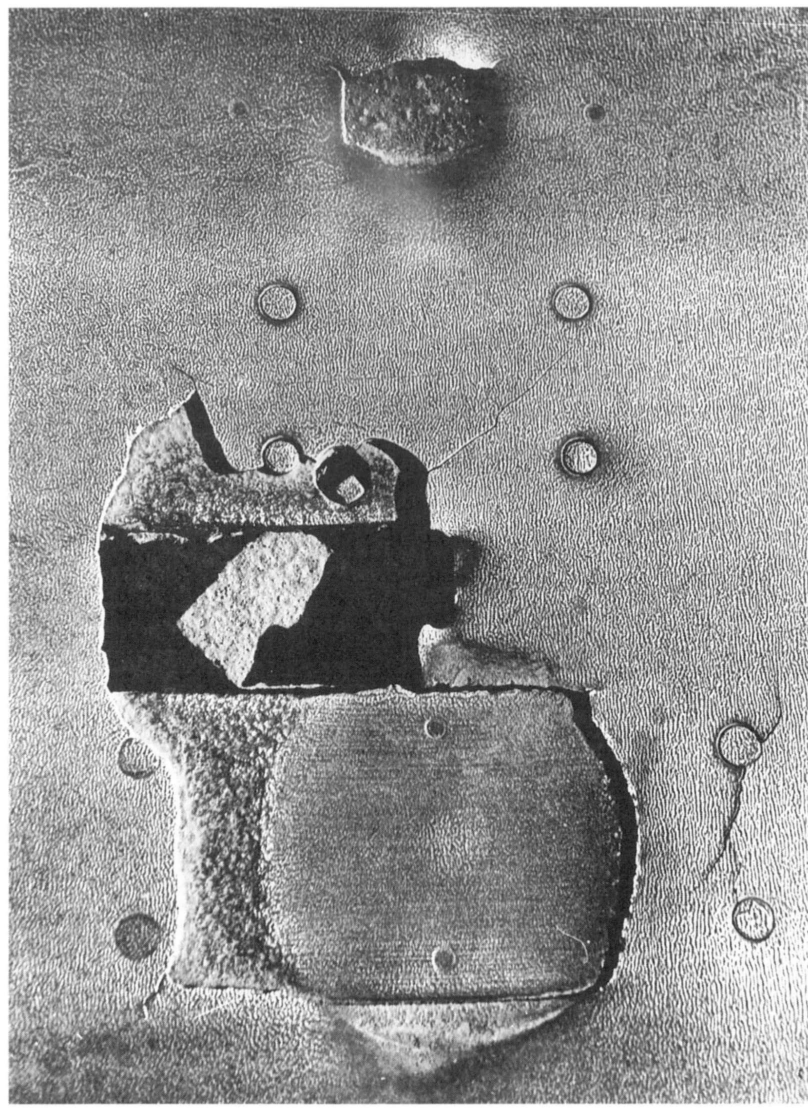

Emila Medková, *The Cut,* 1965. Photograph courtesy of Alena Nádvorníková.

and the absorption of these powers by the photographic image and would thereby only weaken the intangible unity between image and title.

The transition from the subjective to the objective mode of thought (through the projection of the subject into reality) and *vice versa* (through the objectification of unconscious representations into elements of this transformed reality) suggests the idea of a momentary but vigorous alliance between the world and the human mind. This inner unity is particularly obvious in anthropomorphic photographs. Here, differing from the "One in the Other" game, the creative act is identified with the act of interpretation. Right from the start, creation—in order to impose itself on interpretation—gradually transmutes the potential meanings of the objective world's details into subjective significations. The completed work appears precisely at their point of unity.

At that point, of course, other interpretations may arise; these, however, are not the work of the creator, but of the viewer.

Translated from the French by Guy Ducornet

DETERMINATION OF TIME

Through space, in the cold,
finally buzzes a wreath.
Steadfastly, the tree by ploy
stands up,
shooting in skipping joy.
(True salvation: with a tinge of thunder.)
How long? How often?
Take courage! On the headland.

ART HISTORY (SANDRO BOTTICELLI)

She watches him reaching for oranges,
shod in top-boots (far left).
She does not care
for the reel of plastic ideas
in transparent veils (over his shoulders),
the reel in his head
that bewitches him.

Ivana Ciglinová

One of the charms of what Greek surrealist Nicolas Calas once called the "surrealist miracle" is the movement's receptiveness to new inspirations regardless of their "ideological credentials." This is particularly evident in its spontaneous, wholehearted recognition of the contributions to surrealism sometimes made by individuals lacking in "theoretical" knowledge—"outsider artists," for example, and the so-called mentally ill, and children. As an eight-year-old schoolgirl, Ivana Ciglinová began writing unusual little stories that someone eventually brought to the attention of the surrealists in and around Brno. Impressed by her imagination and humor, the surrealists welcomed her warmly and circulated her stories in their 1980s samizdat publications.

Ciglinová later drifted off in other directions. But for a certain period during the gloomiest days of the post-1968 Stalinist reaction, this free-spirited schoolgirl was pleased to add her imaginative energies to the surrealist group, which in turn offered her intellectual stimulation and encouragement she was unlikely to have found anywhere else.

THE OLD CROW'S STORY

Once upon a time a flat-footed mouse was taking a walk through the forest. All of a sudden a raven flew down and pinched the mouse's tail with his beak.

Next day the same thing happened again. This time, however, the flat-footed mouse grew angry. It occurred to her that she could bite the raven right between the eyes in revenge.

But then, in a flash, the flat-footed mouse realized that the raven had a beak in that very place!

And with that beak the raven could tear her to pieces and eat her up!

And *that* would be the way the flat-footed mouse would die!

"Good night," said the Old Crow.

Translated from the Czech by Katerina Piňosová

Mary Low

THE COMPANION

You are my companion.

I know the ripe fruit of your rashness,
your turbulent cascades
and the hazel waters of joy.
I know the strength of your bastions,
and those walls where a breach can be made.
You have twelve Achilles' heels and a triple-edged sword.

You taste green like the freshness of morning,
or hot and acrid
like aloes in the sun.
You smell like moist moss,
young fur among the pines
or a newly honed sickle dipped in hay.

You walk like haughty Indians
and you speak like harps.
You think along an arrow-line
or down voiceless wells.
You are deep with tangible tenderness,
but hard as malachite.
Your words and your thoughts
shine like polished shields.

You are my companion.

(From *A Voice in Three Mirrors,* 1984)

Q.E.D.

Prolonged horizontal pleasures;
vertical principles
aligned like forest trees;
a hot tangent of poetry
tending toward madness.
What radius?

A mere infinity:
impulses without end
pouring off the circumference,
just as my days
overflow all margins
and come full circle.

Here I am:
point center.

(From *WHAT Are You Going to Do About It?* no. 1, October 1992)

WHERE THE WOLF SINGS

There is no wolf, of course—
merely the echo of a once-howl
scattered among the undergrowth.

Yet even now the trees seem dangerous,
forbiddingly fanged,
flinging themselves about in menace.

But the lake! Only a muddy rose of blood
where the unquiet spirits of fish
flit among drying reeds.

Where have the bright, pulsating waters gone?
And the two linked figures that used to lie
upon the conniving bank?

No one is here any more.
Only some large, idle stones
cumber the glade with white oblivion,

Then suddenly it came, from that obliterated time:
the long, the sad,
the asking, aching, unforgotten cry!

Beyond the diminished forest's utmost edge,
far off and faint, the wolf sang once again.
I heard him.

(From *Where the Wolf Sings,* 1994)

ENCOUNTER

Since first we met
I have known
the intimate joy of scissors,
sleek cats and nutmeg,
the tears of blind music at night,
and the whisper of fire among cinders.

Since first we met
all stairs and flowers
grow spurs for me;
and palm-trees whip me with their hair
in sundry mirrors.
The small hours open their wounds for me
to the sound of flutes
that shake my heart.

Since first we met
I feel like omega:
full of warm silk,
endless and groundless.

(From *Where the Wolf Sings,* 1994)

Hilary Booth

LONG HOT SUMMER: GREAT BLACK MUSIC TODAY

It has taken fifteen years for the Art Ensemble of Chicago to reach Australia in any more material form than a few scattered LPs in obscure corners of a few scattered record shops. As Lester Bowie commented, "It takes a long time for people to hear the truth." Volatile spirits, the hottest summer yet, the Art Ensemble of Chicago, and later Chico Freeman's convulsively beautiful quartet, have exploded into our lives, filling spaces that have long been left wanting, with all the warmth that grows from a dedication to love, freedom, imagination and history past and future. . . .

Black musicians are now taking steps that have never before, to such an extent, been accomplished by their ancestors. . . . They will no longer tolerate being passed off as "fads," idiotically labeled, being ignored until it is too late, the sweet fruits of their music being made sour by the imbecilic interference of critics and salesmen. With the setting up of the Association for the Advancement of Creative Musicians (AACM), they are enabling themselves to find new currents without having to put up with the new labels that *separate* one group of musicians from another, when in fact they are all creating from the same source. This source is a long tradition of imagination emancipated, inherited and innovated by each new generation of the Afrikan race. Such a *widespread* movement is without parallel in Western white culture. Once again it must be said, we owe this people an enormous respect for their achievements.

In this music, there are hopes that have never been before. The ghettoes remain, and it is easy to see that these musicians have never really left the streets in spirit. "When we [the AACM] play together, it's like playing marbles" (Joseph Jarman). And although the whims of the commercial marketeers and radio stations stand in the way of the music finding its way back to the streets (preferring to *sell* music that is as profitmaking, i.e., white-orientated as possible), the response from those who have had the chance to listen is enthusiastic, to say the least.

When the message *can* make it through the padded walls attempting to surround it, the young Black people cannot be fooled, as perhaps they were in the past (especially in the days of Charlie Parker), that it is narcotic addiction or alcoholism that inspires the musician to play with such freedom, for there is now a united voice to tell them point blank that it is no such thing. By taking upon the responsibility of their past, they also take the present into their hands. By transmitting, with all the force of their music, a determination to continue the *myth-making* of their ancestors, they may just be able to destroy the all too stark *realities* of an oppressed race in the oppressive cities. They make it clear that it is the will to survive, as a race, that drives the music—a will to live freely in music, a musical will to be free. One can only hope it is contagious.

(From *The Insurrectionist's Shadow* no. 2, 1983)

PREFACE TO *I AM RAIN*

the doors are open. we must pass through.
nothing is necessary but the bones that walk within us.
how they rattle in the bloodletting . . .
it is inevitable that at the heart of things the meat
is raw and it is blue. these poems retain blood.

life hurts us if we bother to feel, yes, work stinks,
leisure is without hope. the only way out is inward
and forward.
if we do not take it upon ourselves to struggle for
individual and social freedom our silence will damn us.
beauty pain terror hope despair
these are all the same word
it is important that we remember to feel and this is
not so obvious as it sounds.
in these poems, the I is not exactly me,
the you is not exactly you.
these growing things that strangle all life from luxury
and squeeze the almonds in a bitter embrace
the serpents take them down into the valerian underground
and the serpents feathers rake fortune into furrows.
it is an age where footholds are few and far between,
a revolutionary context is difficult to maintain,
yet we continue to seek and hold tight to the free spirit.
so follow the bones . . .

OUR SKIN IS PAPER

here, in the ear of the earth
in sharp ink
all the streets are trapped magic
within us
as day passes day
in an effort to truly see
and this is not seeing
nor believing
but growing upon oneself
the armory of innocence
the purity of lust
the incoming tides
and the turquoise

POEM FOR CENTRAL AMERICA

there is no need to personify the wound
it smells and tastes of countless minerals
it rises in a vapor from the age of stone
it unfolds mothwings from the back of a horse
it weaves a cloth of spells to throw over the mountains
it sails through canefields collecting honey
it manufactures grief to spell with swords
it shatters stained glass with a single note
it utters no cry to the alchemy
it is set alight in a mass grave
it grows into a tree that bears children

(From *I Am Rain*, 1984)

Marie-Dominique Massoni

Born in Calvi, Corsica, in 1947, Marie-Dominique Massoni realized her affinities with surrealism at the age of seventeen, but the inaccessibility of current surrealist publications made it impossible for her to communicate with the movement until much later. As a student in Lyon in the 1960s, she encountered the situationist group through its publications and took up its critique of Leninism and the "spectacle." Although she was never a member of the Situationist International, and in fact was quite critical of it—the situationists' fear of "art" having, in her estimate, led to their suppression of all poetry and creativity—she was active in what was often called the "pro-situationist" ultraleft. Only in 1978, after reading Vincent Bounoure's compilation, *La Civilisation surréaliste,* did she begin to take part in organized surrealist activity.

An animating figure of the Paris group ever since, she has published six books and collaborated on several collective publications as well as the Czech group's journal, *Analogon.* She has also written texts for the catalogs of collective surrealist exhibitions in Paris (1982 and 1985), Holland (1995), and Grenoble (1996)—where she also exhibited assemblages—as well as for solo exhibitions of Jean Terrossian, Kathleen Fox, Guy Girard, Alena Nádvorníková, and others.

A longtime activist in the women's liberation movement—a struggle which she believes is still in its earliest stages—Massoni vigorously opposes what she considers to be the "incorrect and dangerous" policy, on the part of certain feminists, to promote the separation of the sexes. She is represented here by "androgynous poems," the result of a game played with surrealist painter Guy Girard at the Café Etienne Dolet in Paris, and published in the collection, *La Diagonale du Père-Lachaise* (1995). "These are not texts of fusion," she writes, "but of *confrontation* in the crucible of complicity. So it goes in games of feminine and masculine."

Massoni is currently the editor of the Paris Group's journal, *S.U.RR—Surréalisme, Utopie, Rêve, Révolte* [Surrealism, Utopia, Dream, Revolt].

TWO SECONDS

To Michael Löwy

We're eager to look like the manufacture of chocolate
Free to wait for Don Quixote
All the way up on the ice-floe
A crossroads was losing its feathers
And we were only halfway there

Sowing fleas harvesting dragons

The essential

Translated from the French by Myrna Bell Rochester

HOW OLD IS THE OLD MOLE?

Me the youngest of the Lumière brothers
You

As one might saw a log
The voice repeats
Monsieur's Mercedes has moved forward

Carmen orders her lovers
To cover up the obscenity of the official buildings
Of all the countries of the world
With a thatched shawl

Daughter of oakum and hieroglyphics
Her job is to pass for a pelican
Reigning over the Chevreuse valley

Within living memory of a chimney-sweep
During that time of hunger
What a great occupation

The early dawn tries to be smart Alec
In the Bear Pit
Dynamite stick set down on a counter
I watch
Beyond the candid vapor
The fourth flower
Advance from the clover
And turn itself into a signature
At the bottom of a letter by Louis-Claude de Saint-Martin

A sunspot would be a beautiful target

I bleed

Translated from the French by Myrna Bell Rochester

Haifa Zangana

WHAT CHOICE?

> *Editor's note: This is an excerpt from* Through the Vast Halls of Memory, *a full-length narrative of a woman's life in Iraq (1991).*

In this darkness, in the solitude of waiting, I am seated with my eyes open, yielding to boring repetition, thinking once more of what had happened. I have tried to forget that day. Burdened by the shining sky and the bright light, which is more than just light, I begin to see things that cannot remain hidden, minute details: old family photos, dreams of a morning interrupted by the joyful voices of children playing in an alley, familiar faces, memories, the longing for friends I might meet if only I were not . . .

I have not the slightest intention of going on about a lamented childhood or of searching for a long-missed human warmth. But I will try my best to follow a friend's advice. (He is in his fifties, unremarkable in appearance, but possessing the gift of observation.) He said, "Always begin from the outside; get to the bottom of things, probe their depths, but always from the outside." His advice reminded me of a warning given years ago by my teacher: "You may, in future, go on to make a name for yourself, but, somewhere, sometime, you will be faced with a choice . . ." "What choice?," I interrupted, and without giving a response he continued, "When an individual is wholly creative, at one with her destiny, there is neither time nor space, life or death." I do not know what the link is between these two bits of advice, but, even after twenty years, I feel resentment. Why didn't I learn early on to listen?

At 2 P.M., I see the queues of taxis, broiling in the August heat. Their drivers have taken refuge in various cafés and restaurants and even under bus shelters, with their crowds of women, children in one hand, empty bottles in the other. They are off to the children's hospital nearby. The bottles, which all patients must supply, are to be filled with prescribed medicines. Was it the exceptional heat wave or my own imagination that exaggerates the picture?

I crossed the street to walk in the thin shade of the high prison walls. Despite the heat, I walked slowly to avoid being tripped by my *abaia*.* Yet I stumbled again and again, cursing the need to wear an abaia on my travels to these country towns. Maybe I will be able to remove it when I get to the cemetery. The street was empty, and I could hear the echo of my footsteps. People were napping or moving quietly behind their curtains, as they usually did at this hour. I crossed another street to walk in the shadow of another wall.

We are obsessed with building fences and walls. Our children grow up, not in fields, but behind walls; they reach their prime of life cuddling walls. There are hidden gardens, colorful lights and fountains behind walls. Whenever we moved to a new house, my mother would insist on building the fence higher to keep us protected from prying eyes. With equal persistence, my brothers would bore holes in that same fence to spy on our neighbors' daughters.

This wall, however, was different, though built of the same red brick used elsewhere. It was the wall of the cemetery. Half of the cemetery was in ruins, the other half full of palm trees. It was the breeding ground for stray dogs and cats. The afternoon we went to visit my grandfather's grave, I remember my mother explaining that the cats were so fat because they fed on the freshly buried corpses. My grandmother immediately silenced her by saying that the cats thrived on the aborted foetuses thrown to them at night by the nurses from the hospital nearby.

I remember, too, that the whole area had a peculiar smell, a mixture of orange blossom (there were orange trees on either side of the main street), roses, gardenias, and carnations placed in the Turkish martyrs' cemetery, and the phenol and antiseptic from the forensic laboratory and school of pharmacy of the old surgical and dental hospital.

I saw the cemetery guard asleep, leaning in the shade against the wall. He

---

* *Abaia*: Iraqi woman's dress.

excelled in nurturing the palm trees. Every year, he would employ one of the local peasants to prune them, and, every year, the trees produced the best-quality dates, which no one collected. Who would dare eat such fruit, thriving as it did in earth full of corpses?

Later, when I learned the rudiments of self-defense, how to kill, I wished we might all be satisfied eating such dates.

Few of the bare-footed children who ran by noticed my presence. Were they ghosts? Exhausted less by the heat than by daydreaming, I walked quickly, sweating and straining to reach the garden gate of my house. I wanted to relax in my room there, to sleep after so many days on the road, going from town to town. I hoped to enter the house quietly, without waking the inhabitants from their siesta. Opening the gate, I saw that the sitting room curtain was pulled back slightly. It twitched: the authorities were waiting for me. Why had I not rung to make sure everything was all right before returning? I threw my abaia and handbag down. Fear gripped me. The cemetery, the prison were as in a dream. I ran in fear and hope that someone might help me escape. I felt all the instincts of an animal trying to survive. I did not dare look behind me. All I wanted was to reach the main street. Suddenly, one of the pursuers grabbed my plaits. I froze, which surprised them. They were pointing their guns at me. I stood stock still, tranquil, like a statue. I had often asked myself what I would do at such a moment. Every night I had hidden behind the thin curtain of sleep, memorizing roles of characters who were not me. I was the surprise element in the play.

What happened seemed not to concern me. I told my body to adjust itself accordingly, told it to remain firm, took a grip on my shaking limbs. But my mask-like face could not help betraying emotion. (It took my face years to regain its original mien.) Although surrounded by people, I was completely alone. When I told a friend much later what had happened, she remarked, "But you talk about it as though it happened to someone else!"

I now realize how true her remark was. The road was long. Did I know the way? I had reconnoitered it beforehand. The street, the silent house, the mysterious anxiety, the fears regarding a place I had never visited, the palpitating of the heart. I wish I could lock that heart in an embrace. O heart, calm thyself. Our consolation is that young people do not age in our city, the life span here is brief. The dryness kills plants, and ordinary people kill animals as their way of venting anger.

"Why?" the man sitting next to me asked. Surely he knew! It is the challenge. We bear it, tamed by continual fear within us, and we liberate it in the moments of madness. What I did during those years was to celebrate the flames of a precious madness.

In the car I considered my luck. It appeared the driver was a very important person. The soldiers outside and inside the Qasir saluted him fervently. He stopped the car and told me to follow him. It was then I remembered my first visit to the Qasir at the age of seven. It was during the first days of the 1958 revolution. Originally built for the crown prince, El Qasir was opened to the public after the revolution. That day, I went with my mother, two aunts, grandmother and two brothers. We all went in our best clothes. I was wearing a new and uncomfortable pair of sandals and kept on complaining. Nobody took any notice because they were too busy looking, pointing and whispering. My grandmother at last took notice of my tears and said in a loud voice, "Be quiet, be quiet!" "Why should I be quiet?" Turning and scolding me, she replied, "We mustn't disturb the dead."

The Qasir had beautiful landscaped gardens. In the front yard there were stables. They were later turned into cells. In August, the hottest month of the year, I felt cold.

Translated from the Arabic by Paul Hammond and Haifa Zangana

Jayne Cortez

WHEN I LOOK AT WIFREDO LAM'S PAINTINGS

They have breasts shaped
like papayas like grapefruits like
spades & shovels & picks & mangos

They erupt
and swirl into baby tornados
They mutate and chalk into
burnt out bulbs of
decorated pus in paint

They merge and melt into other forms
Swallow themselves and gush forward

They connect their sockets
to spermatic strings
of dried centipedes
moving in half steps toward
center of the darkness of the dot
to become ancestral shadows
saturated between Damballah's tattooed toes

and Oya's fishhook fingers
between Ogun's rust colored neck
and Oshun's wine coated tongue
between Shango's red leaves matted to
tiny pyramid teeth of a barking sorcerer
and Yemaya's silver-rimmed eyelids expanding
and contracting into a cyclonic breeze of
double-headed bats

They burn up the brushes
with raffia swishing and shooting from
buttocks of vibrating nostrils
with kneecaps swelling on stilts of
bowlegged nails
with grinning horses galloping from
navels of drying fat
with purple stems of cane protruding from
green lips of machetes
with zigzagging flamingos fluctuating on
the roof tops of Matanzas

They billow and overlap in broaches of
charcoal spittle
They cross and dissolve into
a fleet of orange blotted organs
They have their bull horns
their yellow snake arrows
their triangular forest skulls
their blood vessels sprouting from daggers
their upside-down faces in pelvises rotating
and perforating in spider specked sex of the gouache

(From *Coagulations,* 1984)

BUMBLEBEE, YOU SAW BIG MAMA*

You saw Big Mama Thornton
in her cocktail dresses
& cut off boots
& in her cowboy hat & man's suit
as she drummed &

hollered out
the happy hour of her Négritude
            Bumblebee

You saw Big Mama
trance dancing her chant
into cut body of
a running rooster
scream shouting her talk
into flaming path of
a solar eclipse
cry laughing her eyes into
circumcision red sunsets
            at midnight
            Bumblebee

You saw Big Mama
bouncing straight up like a Masai
then falling back spinning her
salty bone drying kisser of music
into a Texas hop for you to
lap up her sweat
            Bumblebee

You saw Big Mama moaning between ritual saxes
& carrying the black water of Alabama blood
through burnt weeds & rainy ditches
to reach the waxy surface of your spectrum
            Bumblebee

You didn't have to wonder
why Big Mama sounded
so expressively free
so aggressively great
once you climbed
into valley roar
of her vocal spleen
& tasted sweet grapes

---

* Willie Mae "Big Mama" Thornton (1926–1984), one of the greatest blues singers.

in cool desert
of her twilight
          Bumblebee

You saw Big Mama
glowing like
a full charcoal moon
riding down
Chocolate Bayou road
& making her entrance
into rock-city-bar lounge
& swallowing that
show-me-no-love supermarket exit sign in her club ebony gut
you saw her
get tamped on by the hell hounds
& you knew when she was happy
you knew when she was agitated
you knew what would make her thirsty
you knew Big Mama
heated up the blues for Big Mama
to have the blues with you
     after you stung her
     & she chewed off your stinger
          Bumblebee
          You saw Big Mama

(From *Somewhere in Advance of Nowhere,* 1996)

SACRED TREES

Every time I think about us women
I think about the trees the trees
escaping from an epidemic of lightning
the sacred trees exploding from the
compressed matter of cuckoo spit trees
the raped trees flashing signals through the
toxic acid of sucking insects
the trees used as decoy installations trees

I have the afternoon leaves throbbing
   in my nostrils I have the struggling limbs sprouting from
   these ear lobes

I have a power stump shooting from
    out of this forehead
I have clusters of twigs popping from
    my tattooed moles
& sometimes I feel
like the tree trunk
growing numb & dead
from ritual behavior
sometimes I feel like the tree ripping
from the core of ancient grievances
    Trees
I feel like
the family tree
relocating under pressure
    Trees
I feel like the frantic tree
trying to radiate through
    scorched surfaces
sometimes I feel like
the obscure tree
babbling through the silver-plated mouth
    of a shrinking moon
& sometimes I feel like a tree
hiccuping through
the heated flint of gunpowder crevices
sometimes I feel like a tree
& every time I think about us women
I think about the trees
I think about
the subversive trees laden in blood
    but not bleeding
the rebellious trees encrusted
    but not cracking
the abused trees wounded
    but still standing
I think about the proud trees
the trees with beehive tits buzzing
the transparent trees
the trees with quinine breath hovering
the trees swaying & rubbing their

stretched marked bellies
    in the rain
the crossroad trees coming from
    the tree womb
    of tree seeds
    Trees
I think about the trees
& sometimes I feel like
a superstitious tree
smelling negative & fragile
    & full of dislocated sap
sometimes I feel like the tree stampeding from
    a cadre of earth tremors
I feel like the forgotten tree
    that can't live here no more
sometimes I feel
    like the tree that's growing wild
through the wild life left
in the petroleum pipeline
    I feel like a tree
A tree caught
in the catacomb of bones
    enslaved in
the red light districts of oppression
I feel like a barricade of trees
    I feel like a tree
& sometimes
I feel like the tree
that's lucky to be a tree
    in the time of
    missing trees
    Trees
I feel beautiful
    like an undestroyed
    rain forest of trees
I feel like a tree
    laughing in the rawness
    of the wind I feel like a tree
& every time I think about us women
    I think about the trees
    I think about the trees

(From *Somewhere in Advance of Nowhere,* 1996)

Penelope Rosemont

THE LIFE AND TIMES OF THE GOLDEN GOOSE

One of the tales collected by the brothers Grimm and published in their famous anthology in 1815, *The Golden Goose* has since been included in countless other compilations and has often been issued as a separate volume for children. Beyond the facts that it is a European tale and certainly several hundred years old, its origins and age are difficult to determine. The reason that it has survived, however, is that—like other fairy tales and nursery rhymes—it is full of many different meanings on many different levels. . . .

What can this ancient and incredibly adaptable story, with its bewildering multiplicity of possible interpretations—psychoanalytic dream-tale, hermetic allegory, revolutionary parable—mean for us today?

Now as always the forest is a symbol, a whole forest of symbols: source of the Marvelous, dwelling-place of poetic inspiration, the unconscious mind, the promise of freedom. But today, when our forests and *all* wilderness areas throughout the world are being threatened and devastated as never before by commercial/industrial exploitation, we can appreciate how securely all this symbolism rests on very real foundations. The forest symbolizes everything wild and free because it truly *is* a place of wildness and freedom, and therefore fundamentally antagonistic to everything today's born-to-shop society stands for. Religious symbolism, and even many fairy tales, reek of neurosis, sexual frustration, servility, masochism, hostility to the life instincts, fear and hatred of the entire natural world. *The Golden Goose* is different: eros-affirmative, anti-authoritarian, utopian in the best sense, subversive of the dominant paradigm. It is a tale in harmony with the Earth, a tale in which Nature and human nature are not perceived as contradictory. Looked at from this angle, the various symbolic interpretations of the tale may be seen to overlap, and their interconnections suggest new implications for today.

Significantly, the golden goose itself—in which we can recognize the Philosophers' Stone, a magical being, a surrealist object, a talisman enabling us to change life—is first of all an *animal*. This reminds us that in dreams, and in unconscious life generally, as well as in the myths and poems of all times and places, animals have symbolized the fulfillment of *desire* and a liberated sexuality (puritans have always bemoaned sex as man's "animal nature"). Psychoanalysis has shown that capitalist/christian society's repressive attitude toward animals corresponds to its attitude toward sexuality. For any truly radical alternative to today's social system, a new attitude toward animals is of the utmost importance. Human beings will not be free until they affirm their own animalness and their kinship with other species. *The Golden Goose* supports the surrealist view that individual human emancipation requires social emancipation, that both are unthinkable without sexual emancipation, and that all three are inseparable from the emancipation of Nature.

Psychoanalysis is, in a sense, one of the heirs of alchemy, and it is only natural that a Freudian reading of the tale should be confirmed by hermetic inquiry, and *vice versa.* Psychoanalytically and alchemically the golden goose, as André Breton said of the Philosophers' Stone, is that which "enables the human imagination to take a stunning revenge on all things."

The Hussite reading of the tale specifically poses the question of revolution and thus complements the others. Simpleton's sharing his food is a simple lesson that humankind must learn again in our time when inequality, exploitation, and the difference between rich and poor are greater than they have ever been in history. The tale's demonstration of the power and virtue of solidarity and mutual aid reflects the communist ideal of the most radical wing of the Hussites, which is still our best hope for a better world.

As modern technology and its side effects are fast becoming our worst enemy, Simpleton's ship that can sail on land and water (using wind power) charmingly exemplifies what has been called an "appropriate technology"—a human inventiveness that is not hostile to the natural world—the full fruition of which would be possible only in a free, communist society.

Viewed as a revolutionary fable, some aspects of *The Golden Goose* seem absolutely modern, which only shows to what extent our most advanced notions tend to be a *re*learning of primordial wisdom long ago suppressed. It is important that our hero attains the highest happiness and love not through slaying dragons or hard work or arduous, heroic journeys, but rather through innocence, naturalness, simplicity and chance. The tale is a systematic repudiation of what everyone recognizes as bourgeois values. It is utterly devoid of the "work ethic" (aside from chopping down one old tree Simpleton labors not at all), or respect for one's parents (he is so irresponsible that once he leaves home he never returns), or deference to any authority (he fulfills the king's "impossible" demands so effortlessly that the king appears ridiculous). Moreover, Simpleton not only talks to strangers but shares his food with them! There is nothing christian, capitalist, repressive, or conformist about *The Golden Goose.* The "moral" it teaches is erotic, generous, adventurous and pleasure oriented. Evangelists would find the story Satanic, and from their point of view they would be right, for it is a celebration of dream, chance, imagination and desire, which always have been enemies of God and the State.

Centuries after its author and original purpose have been forgotten, *The Golden Goose* has continued to be passed on from generation to generation, living a mysterious life of its own in the "underground" of folklore and children's literature. Exemplifying the spirit of poetry and magic that makes us affirm the Marvelous as the very center of a life worth living, the tale recalls the dream-time that is not only behind us in the past but *still with us,* if we only know where to look for it.

(From *Arsenal: Surrealist Subversion* no. 4, 1989)

THE BAD DAYS WILL END

for Jayne Cortez

In the coolness of black suns
alphabets play
forming animals
splitting stones
with their breath

Zapata's house
drifts over a curled ravine
giving bread
to flute-playing travelers

Big-eyed lions
fall asleep
beside romantic cranes

The world beneath the verb
sows its dragonseeds
by the light of the stars

(From *Beware of the Ice,* 1992)

REVOLUTION BY CHANCE

Revolutions are the great unpredictables. They loom about us everywhere, always larger than life, on a scale almost impossible to conceive. Change in the humdrum often seems as remote as a journey to Mars, yet *these things happen.* Revolutions in technology are a dime a dozen, while *social* revolution—in the U.S.A., at any rate—is made to appear so rare as to be far beyond all possibility. Yet few things are more certain than that, throughout history, rulers and ruling classes have come and gone.

Mars is nearer than ever!

But it is also certain that revolutions—*real* revolutions—are never structured and planned. They are not well-thought-out scenarios for parlor Nechaevs.

Earthquake-like, revolutions are born in the depths of turmoil and conflict, and cannot be predicted, designed, or blueprinted any more than the tremblings of the Earth. Like the seismologist, we can predict that revolutions will happen, but never exactly how or when.

Like volcanoes, revolutions follow only the litmus trails of their own imperious necessity. Beneath the apparently placid crust the interior is always seething, and in an instant—*any* instant—can release the fire of its destructive potential. Then, suddenly, the fire *leaps* and streets and buildings crumble and burn. Or, just as suddenly, people's *minds* leap, an *electrical connection* is made—Revolution!—and old ways are abandoned as the State crumbles.

It is reported that there is a 50/50 chance of a major earthquake in San Francisco in the next ten years. Chances of revolution are not reported, however, for our rulers want us to believe that none exist. But a glimpse across the borders reveals a whole world seething as never before—seething with revolution. Technology has not brought happiness to this planet, and capitalism has done little more than to enlarge and multiply (and make a profit from) the instruments of death. These conditions make reform impossible and revolution inescapable.

When revolution happens it is always by surprise, *by chance,* without preliminary ado or prior public announcement. To the extent that it *is* expected, it becomes impossible, for there are those whose sole purpose it is to impede it, to prevent it, or, if necessary, to crush it. The time-honored methods of killing revolt with the poisons of nationalism and religion are used extensively today by the rulers of jittery nations who know well that they are sitting on volcanoes of lush and splendid revolutions. Religion is a ridiculously outmoded idea, and so is the State. Ironically, the multinational capitalists are more aware of this than many radicals, for their "hands on" experience of the world economy has shown them that religion is indeed the opium *of the people* (not of the rulers), and that there are corporations that are much larger, richer and more powerful than ninety-nine percent of the world's governments. Of course capitalists also realize that, without states to do their killing for them, and without churches to assure everyone that killing is perfectly all right, their own days would be numbered and their number would be up.

Every revolution in modern times has been by chance: Russia in 1905 and 1917; Spain 1936; China 1949; Hungary 1956; Cuba 1959; Grenada 1978; the overthrow of the Shah in Iran, Somoza in Nicaragua, Marcos in the Philippines, and many others. Each and every one of them came as a surprise and a shock. Not one was expected when it happened, either by those who made the revolution, or those who tried to stop it. Most astonished of all, in every case, were the "experts" in such things—the muddling military and preposterous politicians—in spite of the fact that *billions* are spent by intelligence agencies on their own political seismographs (i.e., stoolpigeons, informers and spies) precisely to learn about such matters before it's too late.

The May '68 uprising in France was not only unanticipated, but widely held to be an *absolute impossibility*. Who would believe it—a near-revolution in a modern, civilized, full-industrialized capitalist country! Such things happen only "somewhere else," don't they?

But in truth the stability of the humdrum is *always* a veneer, and in every country of the world today, that veneer is thinner than ever.

Revolutions do happen more frequently in the Third World, where the third eye of poetry sees more clearly perhaps, and at least seems to be able to tell the living from the dead. Living as we do in the very heart of embalmed greed, we often feel cut off from the growing stalk of world revolution. But the forces that set to work the movements of decisive change in one small corner of the world map echo inexorably to all other points on the globe. Political geology has its own laws, and chance and desire, like the old mole, perform their hidden roles under the surface.

Make no mistake: The *objective* conditions for revolution exist *everywhere* today, and have existed for a long time. It is the *subjective* conditions that are not yet ripe. Our task is to develop revolutionary subjectivity as the ally of chance, and *vice versa*.

If revolution comes only by chance, *we must be ready for it at all times!* We must live expecting the unexpected, allowing the possibilities for revolution to grow, and breathing life into them whenever we can. We must *take* chances and therefore *multiply* the chances for chance to work!

How to take chances? Subvert the idols! Disobey the masters! Be implacable! Be irreconcilable! Be creative! Use your imagination! Withdraw your attachment to the slave system! Revolt against work! Assert your right to dream, to make love, to be lazy! Throw the floodgates through an open window!

Reject as much as possible of "civilization"! Look again at "primitive" social organization—the communism that allowed humans to live at peace with the Earth for eons before the advent of property, church and state. We have much to relearn from the "archaic" consciousness that adored mountains and trees and regarded wolves and ravens as brothers and sisters. Destroy in your mind the repressive myth that change is impossible!

And above all *discover your desires*, for only people who can distinguish their real desires from those that have been manufactured for them are able to make the revolution!

Once I knew a beautiful bird who lived in a cage and would not come out. One day the cage door was left open, and eventually the bird ventured out. After he had been free for a day he never could be locked up again—no matter what.

No one really knows what freedom is until one starts to *risk it*. . . .

Self-appointed leaders, small cliques of militarized conspirators: These do not make the music of revolution. Why let the forces of death ride us when with our own jug-band we can all play together in Bremen?

Chance is the secret of revolution—chance multiplied by encounters through time, chance embraced by the many for the sake of the Marvelous!

Revolution is *always* by chance: by starlight, by dreamers, by the unlikely, by the powerless!

This time the struggle is against the most powerful array of repressive forces that has ever existed. Oppression today is unprecedentedly vast and horrible because nothing *less* can hold back the surge toward revolution around the world. Time grows short. It is all or nothing—perhaps our *last* chance!

But at every moment chance awakens, unfolds itself across the horizon and stretches! At every moment chance provides us with new keys to its locked doors! And as it does so, it is chance inhaled, chance perfectible, chance luminescent—the very chanceology of chance—that guides our actions and clarifies our dreams!

(From *Arsenal: Surrealist Subversion* no. 4, 1989)

Rikki Ducornet

THE VOLATILIZED CEILING OF BARON MUNODI

The museums of Europe keep curious portraits which illustrate the assumption that the body gives the soul its shape. Da Vinci imagined a woman with a monkey's face, Rubens human lions, Della Porta a man with the profile of a ram. I myself am albino; I look like an angel and so inspire acute passions. Longing for a purifying fire men would defile me, or, taking pleasure, be absolved of sin. If I have never shared their fevers, it is because a woman has stolen my heart. Black and clairvoyant she claims that one day the world will shrivel in the sun like a plum. However, this is not the story of our love affair, but of an obsession justified by my friend's bleak vision. As my love for her, it has withstood the teeth of time.

• • •

One evening in the early seventeen-hundreds and shortly before the tragedy which was to deny the promise of Eden, the Baron Munodi described for his little son those mental mirrors made of four isosceles triangles once cherished by the Greeks. At the point where the triangles converged reigned a sacred and a potent (and potentially dangerous) conjunction: here air was transformed to fire.

Later, in lieu of a bedtime story, the Baron took his son to see the temporary workshops installed in the arcades and galleries of a new palace near Naples. Little Gustavo had heard of the workshops, everybody had, and his curiosity could be contained no longer. Over ten thousand pieces destined to be incorporated into the geodesic marquetry of the ceilings were in the process of being conceived, cut, painted, and dusted with gold. The child perceived the workshops through a refractive fog; the air was saturated with particulated gold and he was dazzled.

Baron Munodi told Gustavo that because of their beauty and the knowledge they conveyed, the paintings were deemed evil by a repugnant authority he did not choose to name, but which wielded a tragic power.

"Some believe that these images can make beasts talk," the Baron told his son, "in the manner of the serpent which tempted Eve; and that I have the power to excite tempests." If it is true that the Baron was powerful, his power, as the ceiling which blossomed in the torchlight, oscillated on the verge of an abyss.

With eager eyes Gustavo devoured green lions and gravid elephants, a submerged city of mermen shining beneath the moon, a laughing cupid, a man with the face of a camel, a girl naked as a lily. From out of a blue oval the size and color of a puffin's egg, a one-eyed sun gazed at him with such urgency that he blushed before he looked away. Then, peering around a smocked and spattered elbow, the boy saw an image which vibrated so mysteriously that he was not content to touch it, but must lick it with his tongue and putting it to his quivering nostrils, deeply inhale.

This potent picture imprinted itself not only on the child's brain, but upon the imaginations of future generations. I have awakened from startling dreams which reveal to me just what was now being revealed to Gustavo:

A mature albino ape, its heart pierced by an arrow, falls from a tropical tree. As he falls he attempts to catch the bloody ropes spouting from his breast. In truth his wound is fathomless, a mortal fracture in the body of the world. Gustavo sees that the ape's hands are very like his own.

As in the swelter of torchlight Gustavo gazed enamored of the ape, the image was gently taken from him and cipher 666 painted on the back. Then it was set down among many hundreds of others which lay scattered in the manner of the zodiacs which animate the vaults of Heaven. Soon the features of the room and the painter's faces dissolved in a vortex as red as the wings of angels: a swarm of apprentices had descended upon a freshly varnished set of pictures to dust them with gold.

That night a conflagration raged throughout the Baron's workshops. By morning all that remained of the palace was char, and of the painters a fistful of calcinated teeth. The ten thousand images were reduced to smoke; the secret of Baron Munodi's ceiling had volatilized.

Proof of the catastrophe's perfidious nature, the Baron was found assassinated, his heart pierced by a long nail with such force that his body was secured to the boards of his bed.

Awakening drenched in her beloved's blood, the Baroness—whose lucidity was legendary—was bound and carried off as one possessed to a madhouse. There she gave birth to my ancestor who, I know from one famous portrait in the Prado, I do not resemble. Gustavo died before reaching maturity; I, sole heir to the Munodi line and memory, am childless. A friend who knows such things has told me that this explains my compulsion to capture what I can in black ink on white paper.

Baron Munodi's properties and his little son Gustavo were seized by the executive officers of the Inquisition. After an exhaustive search, a pentagon was found freshly painted in an attic, and among the Baron's things a ball of feathers and a shoe studded with pins. A globe was found also, and a map of the heavens that showed the planets in orbit.

Gustavo was stripped of his silk shirt and dressed in a penitent's shift of sacking. The vivid curls of his infancy were shorn from his head, and he was forced to spend the lion's part of his days among God-fearing arsonists in prayer.

As he had neither pastimes nor companions to ease the morbid placidity of monastic life, Gustavo courted vertigo in the shape of a memory. From incessant practice he could within an instant conjure the ape and carry it perpetually before him. Image 666 was his own elementary secret, the exact center of his mind's incarnate mirror. Try as they did to discover the exact nature of the umbilicus that joined Gustavo to his past, his father's assassins had to admit to failure.

The monks explained to the Grand Inquisitor that they did not know the object of the child's worship and so could not subvert it. They knew only that it was an alien practice. The heresiarch's son was prey to an incomprehensible exultation which had nothing to do with Jesus Christ; his fervent prayers were all his own. No one knew that as the others fixed the cross, Gustavo gazed inward upon that image of the ape which was Baron Munodi's metaphor for loss, dolorous spiritual mishap and detour, and a primary element in a vast, coded message of incendiary significance. Just as the Baron's enemies feared, the ceiling was no idle inventory, but the revelation of an itinerary. Now as I write this, as the very atmosphere escapes into sidereal space and world's balloon deflates, I fear its vanished alphabets spelled out *the only itinerary.* Gustavo had seen the unassembled pages of the Book of Salvation. Envy, greed and groundless fear had destroyed it.

• • •

One rare afternoon of peace in the monastery gardens, Gustavo chanced to witness a bitter argument about the nature of the creature evoked in chapter thirteen of John's *Apocalypse* which reads: *May he who is intelligent calculate the number of the beast. The number is that of a man, and his number is six-hundred and sixty-six.*

Delirious with joy, Gustavo ran to the circle of contentious monks and cried out:

"I know! For I have seen it! And see him even now! He is an ape! Oh! A beautiful ape!"

Lifted into the air by an ear, Gustavo received such a slap that the ear was nearly torn from his head. Then he was kicked down corridors of stone and thrust into a cell, windowless but for a vertical aperture just wide enough to send an arrow into the heart of the forest.

From that time on Gustavo, in concordance with the *Instructio,* was struck each night to hammer the cruel nail of piety deep into his skull, and again at daybreak to banish whatever fancy might have slipped down his festering ear as he slept. It was said that the Baron's son could not be saved, not even by an extraordinary act of grace, that his words had divulged an unforgivable heresy:

"The child," the monks informed the Grand Inquisitor, "implies that the son of God is an ape."

What the assessors, councilors and judges of the Inquisition reviled as a crime of *lèse majesté divine,* is today, except within the most reactionary enclaves of the Middle East, North Africa and North America, common knowledge. The exemplary science of genetics has corroborated the marvel: the ape's number—give or take a chromosome or two—is the mirror of man's.

Once vigorous, a boy who delighted in pictures of the rope-dancing elephants of Rome and Pompeian acrobats, Gustavo was now but bone and nerve, subject to visions of subterranean demons. His ravaged face refused to mend and a mortal fever gnawed at his mind. He did not notice the crusted iron cross which hung suspended from a nail, threatening, at any instant, to shatter his skull. As a moon the ape had risen, and it orbited his thoughts. I who have shadowed gorillas with the hope that the quintessential nature of my ancestry be revealed to me, understand that infant's *Idée fixe*: it is my own. You see, I have inherited my purpose from a child dead over two hundred years. Some spontaneous influence, perhaps electric, has caused all the Munodis to share Gustavo's obsession: my great-grandfather spent a lifetime investigating the footprints of the *Yeti*; my father's father lived among the *Macaca speciosa* of Thailand; my great-aunt Dolorosa, when she was not tracking baboons wrote an excellent book on Rosalie Zaccharie Ferriol—the ravishing French albino (and according to a precious engraving, my Doppelganger), whose celebrated eyes burned so brightly they pierced the hearts of everyone who saw her; and an essay on *Moby Dick* in which she notes that unlike white apes, white whales are common (or, rather, *were* common; whales of any color are no longer common).

It is now time to return to Gustavo who is dying and who dreams he is once again in the Baron's workshops. In the light of resinous torches, apprentices run up and down the mazed avenues of the painter's tables, seeding the puissant images with gold. The air is so charged with gold that when Gustavo opens his eyes for the last time he sees that his dream's luminescence has flooded his cell, that he is held in the tender embrace of the beloved ape. An angel exiled from Heaven, it has fallen onto his verminous pallet of straw.

When the monks find Gustavo's body, they burn it. It is written in their erroneous books that a toad hopped from the flames and that a viper circled the pyre. These are fables. The truth is that a morbid agitation disrupted the questionable peace of that wicked place thereafter and led to its decline.

My own researches into albinism and, inevitably, melanism, have taken me to the far reaches of this our shrinking planet and evolved into a study of the coded alphabets which are visible on the backs and faces of all the beasts of the animal kingdom. Above the 40th North Parallel I have, in months of incessant night, tracked white wolves and blue foxes. In the smoky depths of forests on fire I have seen hermaphrodite snakes of ink and milk, their eyes the color of the caviar of scallops and so rare they can be counted on the fingers of one hand.

Recovering from malarial fever in France I have recorded the white spots on the backs of piebald crows (*turdus merula*), which, having beaked the tainted waters, plummet from the pollarded trees. I have spent an entire decade mapping the markings of Capricorn beetles and even the ears of tigers; their seed is crippled irretrievably. Just as the whales, the apes, and Baron Munodi's miraculous ceiling, they too shall vanish.

• • •

Recently, as I lay beside my mistress, I dreamed a disturbing dream: I had bought several pounds of fresh squid to prepare for many illustrious friends, all who had miraculously survived the gas chambers. The squid were slippery and wet, and as any inspired intuition, hard to hold. They were also perfectly white. I took each up one by one and with a very sharp knife slit them open, revealing a perfect little figure of a man, white as ivory and dressed like the princes of ancient Persia—studded turbans on their heads and scimitars in their belts. They wore neatly buttoned vests, and one had caviar—tiny white pearls of it—clinging to his loins and inner thighs.

With care I slipped each perfect man from his casing of flesh and severed the head. Then I cut the arms from the torso, and after that the legs. I feared they would waken and scream, but all slept and if one bled, his blood was pale, hardly blood at all; the blood of a fish. When I had finished I realized with a shudder that there had been one hundred and eleven manikins, and that I had sliced each one into six.

I have described this dream to a psychoanalyst, a philosopher and to my mistress.

The psychoanalyst insists that the squid is the symbol of the penis, the sleeping man I would kill rather than arouse. The philosopher suggests that these mermen are the metaphor for the soul's longing for gnosis which the mind assassinates from fear—grace more terrible to the uninformed heart than eternal darkness. I believe that my mistress's answer is by far the most satisfactory, although I know that all answers are fragments in the puzzle of True:

"The dismemberment of the body symbolizes its dissolution, the first step towards regeneration, and without which resurrection is impossible. The water that spills from the squid's body, as the blood from the heart of the wounded ape, symbolizes the amniotic fluid, and above all the primal waters from which all things descend: green algae, blue foxes, men and women both white and black."

• • •

The years pass too swiftly. Like a fantastic doctrine become ashes before it can be read, my lover and I will be reduced to dust. In one brief lifetime, I cannot undo the tragic loss of a child's life, nor begin to reconstruct an alchemical lexicon; nor can I with exactitude, chart a family tree. Even the finite combinations on the backs of common beetles elude me. Yet I am certain that should the world survive, others will be haunted in much the same way and dream similar dreams. This is my greatest hope, if Eden is to be one day reconstituted.

1991

MANIFESTO IN VOICES

> *"L'homme est descendu du signe."* [Man is descended from the sign.]
>
> —Matta

France's Uqbar, the Mas d'Azil in the Pyrénées, was once truffled with painted stones. It is supposed that these represent lunar notations. Deeper in the mountains, in the Valley of Marvels, a seemingly infinite number of drawings and engravings—maps, beasts, beings, and moons—animate the rock. These are the embryos of language: telesma, perfect things, and the potencies which once served to ignite the imaginations of our most distant ancestors. Europe and Africa, Asia, Australia and Middle America—all our fictions are seeded here, in mountains and in valleys, in such figures painted on stone—visions of the hunt, vivid reveries, barbed wands, red footprints that show the direction a narrative must take, the demons of storms, vulvas self-contained and swollen like bells.

"The word is our sign and seal," writes Octavio Paz. "By means of it we recognize each other among strangers" (*The Labyrinth of Solitude*).

What follows is about recognition, the sacred nature of the word, that "magical ambiguity" (Paz) which gives wings to the beast and meanings to the moon.

"Let us imagine something yellow," Borges invites us, "shining, changing. That thing is something in the sky, circular; at other times it has the form of an arc, other times it grows and shrinks. Someone—our common ancestor—gives to that thing the name of moon, different in different languages, and variously lovely" (*Seven Nights*).

"Now it is night," (and the voice is George Lamming's, *The Castle of Skin*); "now it is night with the moon sprinkling its light on everything. The wood is a thick shroud of leaves asleep, and the sleep, like a fog, conceals those who within the wood must keep awake."

• • •

Let us imagine that the novel is a species of variable moon and wakeful—its wilderness mapped by Alejo Carpentier, its borderlands plotted by Clarice Lispector, its body dreamed by Severo Sarduy, its atlases bound by Asturias, its circumference squared by Ray Federman, its pantries stocked by Harry Mathews, its songs sung by The Mighty Sparrow, its tigers Borgesian and which—if they can be taught to dance—refuse to carry the cumbersome baggage of orthodoxy. Let us imagine the novel as a kind of "savage beast (that springs upon us) not to rend but to rescue us from death" (W. H. Hudson, *Green Mansions*).

Not long ago the Canadian novelist Barry Callaghan was threatened by a woman (white) who expressed the intention to decock him for having written in a voice other than his own—that of a woman (black). Shortly thereafter, I, too, was aggressed for a similar offense—a character in one of my novels is an Amazonian Indian, something I am not. Next, and within the hour, I witnessed a young writer asking permission of other writers to finish her book:

"I am female, heterosexual and white," she said, "yet my novel is narrated by a male homosexual who is Chinese. Do I have the right to continue?"

In answer, I propose these words of Wilson Harris: "I view the novel as a kind of infinite canvas. By infinity I mean that one is constantly breaking down things in order to sense a vision through things. And that applies to characters as well" (*Kas Kas*).

Like the moon, the novel is a symbol and a necessary reality. Ideally it serves neither gods nor masters. Philosopher's stone, it sublimates, precipitates, and quickens. House of Keys, it opens all our darkest doors. May the Pol Pot Persons of all genders and denominations take heed: to create a fictional world with rigor and passion, to imagine a character of any sex, place, time, or color and make it palpitate and quiver, to catapult it into the deepest forests of our most luminous reveries, is to commit an act of empathy. To write a novel of the imagination is a gesture of tenderness; to enter into the body of a book is a fearless act and generous.

• • •

Mystics and physicists alike tell us that moons and tigers—all matter, inert and quickened—are made of the same reeling particles. We move through the maze of the world, and the world's maze moves through us. An intergalactic observer might judge us far less attractive than our cousins the other apes (and it is the baboons, after all, who are blessed with iridescent faces and behinds)—but ours is the species capable of acting with responsibility and an informed heart. Yet, with every volatilized jungle tree (and a species that burns its own cannot be expected to respect the lives of plants, to take the time to decode the conversations, perhaps philosophical, of elephants, creatures apparently aware, as are we, of finitude)—we prefer to pursue folly, and with an autophageous appetite.

• • •

I insist: It is not only our right, but our responsibility to follow our imaginations' enchanted paths wherever they would lead us; to heed those voices which inhabit our most secret (and sacred) spaces. . . .

It is precisely our capacity for invention which makes the world worth wanting. The capacity to dream very high dreams and to sing—as did the ancients of Dreamtime—songs potent enough to engender a universe. Those who ask us to deny our dreams would pillage our valley of marvels, would reduce our lunar notations to ashes, would flay our vivid tigers. . . .

(From *Review of Contemporary Fiction*, Normal, Illinois, 1992)

Alice Farley

PERMUTATIONS OF DESIRE

In our strange and simple-minded time where every analysis of sexual confrontation is reduced to a search for blame and identification of victim, the complexity of the real sexual dialogue is overlooked. We are not so innocent. Power and desire are not simple.

The subtle intermesh of attraction and repulsion within the sexual instinct is one of our most beautiful puzzles. In its unforgiving arbitrariness, beyond reason, love or even self-preservation, it follows no straight lines. It follows a path older than rational thought, more like that of a leaf caught in the rapids. It reveals to us a harmony, but it is a harmony of chaos.

COSTUMES: VEHICLES OF TRANSFORMATION

There is too much to be invented to waste time on imitation or competition.

I came to costuming as a dancer first, interested in the simultaneous development of costuming and movement. I approach costuming as a choreographic and visual art with the same formal criteria as apply to sculpture or painting, but animated and moving through time. Costumes are not clothing, they are masks—they are the vehicles of transformation capable of making a character's thoughts visible. Every Hopi Kachina dancer gets this, and so does every drag queen. It's only our "serious" costumers in our present and serious theater that seem so slow in catching on to this timeless and essential sensibility.

American modern dance notwithstanding, there is no such thing as a "neutral" costume. The costume, any costume, defines the visual presence of the actor/dancer. All movement emanates either honestly or dishonestly from that form. The Kabuki costume presents us a beacon of historical and emotional information; the dress of the Guatemalan Indian is a map of the stars. What modern dance has managed to communicate with its sweatsuits and unitards (those sexless, hairless sausageskin bodies) is something else entirely.

The trained dancer has the privilege of spending countless hours in the examination and analysis of design from the inside out. The ability to distinguish the 87° angle from the 90° in the line of the ballet arabesque is knowledge not just in the eye but in the muscle. Why is this unique information so seldom expanded into other forms?

Knowledge of the body among all natural forms provides us the most prescient information for design.

When André Breton said "Beauty must be convulsive or it will cease to be," or when Harry Partch spoke of the truth of the "corporeal" as opposed to the abstract in music, it is because it is the body that is the source and measure of art. The body is not fooled so often or easily as the mind. And we dancers who spend our lives trying to learn all the languages that the body speaks, should be able to do something more with that information than make imitative and self-referential dance works that only speak to ourselves.

GESTURE

The hand is so undeniably the direct link between the mind and the heart, the instrument of our survival, our expression and passion, that it has always struck me as inordinately strange that western dance would most often choose to treat it as dead wood. Yes, we can learn to dance with arms that move as tree branches, waving in the breeze, but our options should not be limited to that.

The hand in counterpoint to the posture and rhythm of the rest of the body reveals a very specific geometry of information. What is interesting here is that this information communicates, whether or not the body is human. Even in a puppet or abstract form, a gesture can be explicit. The real information is in the geometry, the rhythm and time.

We already know the gestures for hello and good-bye; perhaps it's time to look for the gesture for the color blue, or the sound of hawks dying.

(From the program booklet, *Imaginary Ancestors and Daphne of the Dunes,* Alice Farley Dance Theater, La Mama, 1994)

Irene Plazewska

Irene Plazewska was born in Chicago in 1949 of an Irish-born mother and Polish father. Active in the Students for a Democratic Society (SDS) and the antiwar movement in the 1960s, she also frequented the Chicago Surrealist Group's Gallery Bugs Bunny. In 1969 she moved to Dublin, Ireland, where she took up writing, painting, and the graphic arts, and began corresponding with surrealists in Australia, England, France, Sweden, and the U.S. She has had several one-artist shows in Ireland and has published three collections of poems: *Ironed Wood* (1985), *Plumed Tunafish* (1991), and *Purchased Moon* (1995). She has also taken part in a number of surrealist exhibitions, including "Totems Without Taboos: The Exquisite Corpse Lives!" in Chicago in 1993, and collaborated on such publications as *Arsenal* and *WHAT Are You Going to Do About It?* She lives in Dublin.

This poem is from *Plumed Tunafish.*

NEWTON'S DESCENT

Across muscles and through seizure
theft tells me it is time
Bonded neighborhood bush
rubbed bare
yellowed venetian blindmen
lockbolts crack blocks

Templars in rubber hip-boots
fish up pearled corpses
The river weighs down folds
Mist under chin
cast parts petaled
The pull makes no impression
yet sucks
On a bridge white without features
cantilevered thoughts become
pre-destined

Debra Taub

Born in Chicago in 1954, Debra Taub began her surrealist activity at the age of twenty. Initially a mosaicist, she elaborated the "Corner of Masks" at the World Surrealist Exhibition in Chicago in 1976. She has subsequently concentrated on collages which she has shown at many exhibitions, including "Surrealism in 1977" (Chicago), "Surrealism Unlimited" (London, 1978), "100th Anniversary of Hysteria: Surrealism in 1978" (Milwaukee), the International Exhibition of Surrealism and Fantastic Art organized by Mario Cesariny in Lisbon in 1984, and "Greffages 3" in Matane (France) in 1996. Her first solo exhibit was at the Platypus Gallery in Evanston, Illinois, in 1983.

Taub's poems and other texts have appeared in *Arsenal: Surrealist Subversion, Surrealism: The Octopus-Typewriter, Cultural Correspondence, The Moment, Free Spirits: Annals of the Insurgent Imagination,* and other publications. She lives in Chicago.

"A Dance in the Forest" is from *Free Spirits* (1982), and the two poems from *Arsenal: Surrealist Subversion* no. 4 (1989).

A DANCE IN THE FOREST

The Firing Squad was unarmed. When the order to fire was given, they stuck out their tongues at the ragged figure who had been their prisoner for centuries. He died, laughing.

Not far away, in a small clearing in the Great forest, a shrouded woman danced. Carefully, endlessly she kneaded the mat made of bear claws with her feet. It cracked and snapped beneath her like the heels of the Gypsies stamping out the fire of their pulse in an Andalusian cave.

She kneaded the mat in a trance until the sky filled with a great crimson cloud. Then, with a wail that was lightning and quicksilver, the cloud ripped open and filled the air with torrents of blood-red rain.

For days the crimson fog covered everything. No one could see or breathe in the silence of this terrible storm.

In despair, the Captain and his Squad followed the distant sounds of rattles and drums to the small clearing, where the ghost of a dream danced on hypnotically, in the shadows of Desire.

They made her an offering of the body of a man they had so cowardly murdered.

She only laughed a laugh of earthquakes and hurricanes that shattered them like china.

She laughed another laugh of molten iron and lava, and the dead man rose and brushed the centuries of moral grime and calculated misery from his silky hair.

She laughed the laugh of jungle birds, sweet and proud. As he passed her, he whispered his name in her ear, before vanishing into the Great Forest forever. His name was Donatien-Alphonse-François—Sade.

EXQUISITE ALCHEMY

Curtains part to reveal the equal parts
of Ivory and Ebony
again entwined in the endless
ring of the bell.
Planets spin in Victorian cellars
hidden beneath oriental carpets
woven with exquisite erotica.
Tell me again the name
of the day I am to return
to the fever of these secret streets.
Sweet water emerging
from deep forest grottoes
whispers your name.
I can hear the dangerous groaning
under the weight of my lacy dreams
but I am nowhere
to be found.

SECRET MELODIES

Long ago the ancient flutes sang
under our smoking fingers and we danced with lunar delight.
Long ago, before the warriors stole
our singing flutes (or thought they did).
Hidden in the secret lodges
where moonlight was forbidden
they could only make the sounds of war.
But we tricked them
and swallowed the secret melodies

and they took only the hollow reed shells
that resembled these flutes.
You can hear the mists of the lunar songs
trembling on the wind when we dance
and when we spread
our wings.

Gina Litherland

Born in Gary, Indiana, in 1955, Gina Litherland studied literature at Indiana University and painting and photography at the School of the Art Institute in Chicago. She discovered surrealism at nineteen through the 1929 Buñuel/Dalí film, "Un Chien anadalou" [An Andalusian Dog]. Further inspired by Maya Deren's "Meshes of the Afternoon," she went on to read Breton's *Surrealist Manifestoes* and *Nadja*, and to actively explore surrealism through painting, writing, and collective theater performance. In 1985 she became a member of the Chicago Surrealist Group. She has collaborated on such surrealist journals as *Arsenal* (Chicago), *Naknar Lappar* (Stockholm), and *Analogon* (Prague), as well as the *International Surrealist Bulletin*, and her paintings have been included in exhibitions throughout the U.S. She has also been active in Earth First! and for a time coordinated its "No Jails For Whales!" campaign in Chicago. She lives in southeastern Wisconsin.

This article is from *Arsenal: Surrealist Subversion* no. 4 (1989).

IMAGINATION AND WILDERNESS

Wilderness overflows with animals, plants, stones and trees that are dreaming of vast utopias unknown to any of us. The current of these verdant contemplations can be felt during long walks through the forest, or while sitting beneath the trees, or while quietly drifting through vapors of thought.

Soaring through the trees with owls and crows, the wind sings, dances, paints, and whispers the rare language of wilderness. The imagination is a wilderness—liberating, ecstatic, waiting to grow and fly and howl. From a brush dipped in verdigris or terre verte, wilderness waits to creep vinelike over canvases and panels, curling and flowing, collecting on the edges of forms like frost and sleeping in deep pools of viridian and ultramarine. It grows from poetic associations, unfolding its leaves to reveal shadows and phrases momentarily obscured from view.

In the proliferation of wilderness and imagination I see hope for all that has been laid to waste in the world. Civilization and technology have done much to annihilate wilderness, for what wilderness inspires is dangerous to those who seek to control and dominate. To suppress the natural world, civilization created the supreme patriarch, and by his law women were charged with the crimes of intuition, emotion, and secret knowledge; third world (really first world) peoples were charged with ignorance and heathenism; and animals were caged, vivisected, slaughtered and sacrificed to the god of scientific rationality. For centuries wolves, owls, bats and hundreds of other species have been made the scapegoats of society's fears, and exterminated for the economic convenience of the wealthy and powerful.

What remarkable species of the imagination have been wiped out with our wild and beautiful sisters and brothers? At one time humans knew animals as their teachers; they listened to the complex symphonies of the birds and the howling of the wolves, and watched the bowerbird build his delicate archway, leading his lover to a glittering bed of shells and bones. In dressing like animals and painting their images, humans hoped to gain some of the animals' cleverness, agility and power.

Many of us still feel a sense of wonder at the pure creative spirit of wildness that animals reflect. In painting animals, not as we see them retinally but as we see them psychically, we make talismans of wilderness, of howling, of flying, of leaping, of dancing, of silence. We remember that we have not always been in a world that values things only for their "usefulness," but that we once were, and still are, a part of a world that rejoices in its own being, in the rising of the moon, in the reverberating sound of its own ecstatic voice.

In painting, dancing, singing, howling, chirping, and squawking we reforest the Earth with arboreal dreams of liberation for all species of all worlds—of those we can see and hear, and of those we can wildly imagine.

Ivanir de Oliveira

Surrealism in Brazil counts a number of remarkable women forerunners, including cabaret singer and song-anthologist Elsie Houston (companion of Benjamin Péret) in the early period and writer/revolutionist Patrícia Galvão (known as Pagu) in the 1930s and 1940s. However, apart from sculptor Maria Martins, few Brazilians of either sex took part in organized surrealism until Sergio Lima and his wife Leila Ferraz formed the São Paulo Surrealist Group in 1967. The nation's repressive political regime made it impossible for this group to carry on for long, but several of its members pursued the surrealist adventure in isolation or exile.

In 1992, in the midst of extensive international discussion between surrealist groups in different countries, the São Paulo group was reorganized. It has been one of the most active groups ever since and the only one in which women are a large majority.

Ivanir Vicente de Oliveira, born in 1954, discovered surrealism in 1987 during an intensive study of collage. Recognizing what she calls her "visceral and spiritual identification" with surrealist theory and practice, she became one of the cofounders of the São Paulo group in 1992 and remains one of its key activists. As collagist and theorist she has collaborated on the group's periodical anthology, *Escrituras surrealistas* [Surrealist Writings], and participated in all its collective manifestations. She has also had several solo shows. She was the principal organizer of the Brazilian surrealists' important 1996 exhibition, "Collage: Image of Revelation," which doubled as a tribute to André Breton during the centennial of his birth. The text published here is excerpted from her preface to the catalog of that exhibition.

COLLAGE: IMAGE OF REVELATION

The difference between *papiers collés* and collage is exactly this: The *papiers collés* take elements from a given system and place them in another, whereas collage presumes a nonlinear interpretation, as well as a simultaneous and circular imagery that creates (as Sergio Lima has put it) "shocks." Collage emerges from the point at which desire and freedom hold sway. Starting from an interior model, these images do not heed established aesthetic values. The sense of beauty that is sought is that defined by the surrealists: a break with past conventions and with rational thought. It is what André Breton called "convulsive" beauty.

Seeking to represent reality—that is, the objective world—and beginning with human desire, we use objects found by chance and reimagine them in new contexts in order to create *new encounters* capable of expanding knowledge beyond the boundaries of immediate and everyday reality.

The selection of fragments and figures that compose the work derives from a relationship of amorous reciprocity with objects which are also seen as subjects. It is from the affinity of the subject-artist with the subject-object that the choice is made. There is no deliberate search; rather it happens by chance, precisely when we give in to abandon. The Chinese call this direct perception *kuan* (contemplation without concentrated attention). This method resembles that of the heron, motionless at the edge of a lake gazing at the water. Although it does not appear to be looking for a fish, when one comes along the heron plunges for it.

This is what happens when we gather an object to be integrated into a collage. When we open a drawer, circumnavigate the fleamarket, or simply wander through the streets, certain elements naturally catch our eye. Hardly majestic, these materials present us with a challenge. Like an alchemist who creates gold from base metals, we seek to extract the marvelous from these discarded objects that are marked by the attrition of time. And incidentally, it is this "ignoble" matter that the anonymous alchemist quoted by Eugene Canseliet expressed as "Light arising from itself out of the darkness."

To work with collage is to reject the smooth, familiar roadways of conventional life, and to venture into the wilderness. As the "already seen" objects and clippings that constitute our materials are liberated from their original constraints, the physical limitations of these scraps and fragments are transcended in the very act of creating new revelations that call into question the hegemony of the habitual.

Translated from the Portuguese by Nicole M. Knight

Nicole E. Reiss

Born in Bucharest, Romania, in 1947, Nicole Evelyne Reiss has lived in Brazil since 1961. After completing her architectural studies in São Paulo, she pursued postgraduate work in Paris in the 1970s. Later, back in São Paulo, she worked on an "Architecture and Urbanism" project and took up watercolor, graphic arts, and stone sculpture, which awakened her interest in surrealism. A cofounder of the Surrealist Group in São Paulo in 1992, she has participated actively in all its activities, publications and exhibitions.

"Divagations" is from *Escrituras surrealistas II* (1996), which also served as the catalog of the São Paulo Surrealist Group exhibition, "Collage: Image of Revelation." "A Delirious Voyage" is Reiss's spontaneous response to a question posed by Ivanir de Oliveira in the course of an interactive game played by the São Paulo Surrealist Group.

DIVAGATIONS

This is a fragment of a shell that I found one day on the beach: it is the fragment of a creature at one specific moment of its life. Now it is inert material, but it still carries signs of its living being. The mollusk it had been is gone. It fought for its life, coping with a gamut of situations, restrictions, and stimuli that are inconceivable to me in a qualitative sense. The environment in which it lived—at least from the point of view of my mollusk—is totally strange to me.

The sea, with its movement, its life, its density, creates an environment inadequate for the straight line. Lines are defined according to the consistency of the material and vital movements of creatures and the seas. There is nothing straight here. It is a world without straight lines. There is no reason for them. There is no Reason. The lines here express all their ingredients, contextually and existentially. Their value is immense. It is the expression of immanence itself. My capacity for perception establishes the limit of contact.

I look at my shell fragment. It is a contribution to materiality that the mollusk produced with its life, in this way transcending itself into time. The world is no longer the same after the life of my mollusk, because without it there would not be this shell that I am holding now.

It teaches me, tells me something about smoothness, where it is smooth, about roughness, where it is rough, and about the relation of curves and thicknesses, about tones and colors (because Aphrodite was born of a shell, or a pearl of its defensive gesture). Most of all it tells me something of the perception of beauty and of the marvelous harmony that it expresses.

With the passing of time, this shell fragment, together with its fellow creatures, will tend to become part of the sands of a beach, thus losing its peculiarity of being. Who knows if my trajectory has not also been changed by my perception of this fragment? How many other fragments that we find speak to us of wholes?

A DELIRIOUS VOYAGE INSIDE A CIRCLE

Initially the interior of a circle gives the impression of an inexpugnable prison, indicating to the person in a state of delirium the image of the outside of this circle. There is, however, the circle whose limits are vaguely defined and which, instead of strangling or confining, allows delirium as an interior possibility. Allow me to describe some round deliriums.

The sensations that can occur when voyaging in the vertiginous acceleration of a tornado or a whirlpool are delirious. The sensations of spinning and disorientation are caused by mind-numbing speed and connect the senses obsessively to a visceral urgency, fusing my urgency with that of the tornado itself. Both it and I struggle with the speed between the center and the limits, whirling deliriums and anxieties in a circular movement, with our survival depending on our knowledge of our circle.

Also delirious is the wet calm of the outspreading of a circle formed in water. It arises from the contact of my skin with the smooth softness of the water as I emerge from a dive into the motionless lake. This sensation stretches out further and further, extending the outline of my shape and together with it, dissolves into the water without ever leaving the circle, which merges with the sporadic movements of the lake's surface, as does my sensitive shape.

An explosion also follows a concentric trajectory. It is delirious to feel an extreme, instantaneous expansion of all the senses dissolving, spent in space. The shape of this delirium is also round.

Translated from the Portuguese by Nicole M. Knight

Elaine Parra

Elaine Parra was born in São Paulo in 1952. A collagist, painter, and sculptor as well as writer and theorist, she had already exhibited widely when she encountered other surrealists in Brazil in 1990. Two years later she became a charter member of the São Paulo group, which is today among the largest and liveliest groups in the international Surrealist Movement. A collaborator on all the group's publications and a participant in its many collective exhibitions, Parra has also had numerous solo shows.

The text published here is excerpted from a not-yet-published study of Friedrich Schiller (1759–1805), focused on his important philosophical treatise, *On the Aesthetic Education of Man* (1801), a work which was also one of the inspirations of Herbert Marcuse's *Eros and Civilization*. The translation was graciously provided by the author.

TO RADICALIZE WITH BEAUTY AND LOVE

To follow Schiller's thought is to see through a multifaceted crystal the development of an idea concerning the quest for human fulfillment through the creative process, in art as in life. . . . Schiller announces the *aesthetic man* who, through beauty, becomes free—no longer the slave of matter or of the laws of reason. Not only does he call our attention to the *play impulse* (which is antecedent to the aesthetic) he considers it precisely the vehicle by which humankind can attain that "happy balance"—the active interplay of reason and sensuousness.

Schiller was an eighteenth- and early-nineteenth-century thinker; his life spanned Weimar classicism and romanticism, and his writings are included in what is generally known as "post-Kantian philosophy." Although he was born in an era far distant from our own, Schiller and his ideas appear to us today as an authentic *restorative* that can truly heal and thus improve our reality.

As its basic reference the twentieth century upholds industry and its development, which of course are accompanied by numerous "side effects" and their consequences. Preoccupied with *having*, people today tend to relegate *being* to the second plane. Octavio Paz has said that "Man is infinite desire." But if desire is concentrated on *having*, nothing can come of it, and the result can only be a catastrophic downward movement. According to Schiller this movement should rather be directed upward, so that the individual may encounter true morality and happiness. As he teaches us, this may be attained through "aesthetic education," in which no limitation is placed on either of the two impulses—rational and sensuous—which are now, moreover, in his view, understood as being *energies* and therefore necessarily stand in a causal relation.

On the other hand, we have *poetry*, which can lead us to *poetic freedom* and can also guide humankind in an ascending movement. To be able to see what lies beyond our horizon—often so narrow and so near—we must leap over it, advance beyond it. Poetic freedom is the fruit of the poetic intuition that surrealism has redeemed for us and which is ours to use freely, not merely to help us assimilate known forms but above all to enable us to become daring creators of new forms.

In the social relationships of our daily lives as well as in our dreams and nightmares, as this century and this millennium come to an end, each day brings us new evidence of the fundamental *precariousness* of the world in which we live. Everywhere, landmarks of modernist stability are toppling before our startled eyes, as are the so-called "alternative models" set up by modernism's opponents. And it is *now*, in this very era, the historic period in which we are living, that it has grown *urgent* to permit the release—the free, untrammeled flow of the creative process—of that which comes to us spontaneously from a seed of desire germinated at the first instant of life. For although it is a romantic notion—generally considered inappropriate for our era—we maintain that human beings are, originally and in essence, *good*. . . . And today, when the decadence of "power" is staring us in the face, the time has come to radicalize with *beauty* and with *love*—love-as-life, life-as-poetry: humankind's truly inexhaustible resources.

Sarah Metcalf

Born in Corbridge, Northumberland, England, in 1963, Sarah Metcalf has lived in Leeds, Yorkshire, since 1981. She first encountered surrealism at seventeen, when she saw Luis Buñuel's *L'Age d'or* at a local movie theater. Only in 1991, however, while studying for a degree in art and film history at Newcastle Polytechnic and growing increasingly dissatisfied with what she calls the "academic misunderstanding and misrepresentation of surrealist ideas," did she actually read Breton's *Manifestoes* and other surrealist works. She began to consider herself an active surrealist in 1993 and, in March of the following year, cofounded the Leeds Surrealist Group. Later in 1994 she coorganized the film festival, "Surrealists Go to the Cinema," at the National Museum of Photography, Film and Television in Bradford, near Leeds. In April 1994 she participated in the exhibition "Curiouser and Curiouser: Surrealists and Their Friends in Great Britain Since 1967," at the Hourglass Gallery in Paris. Metcalf also collaborates on the production of the Leeds group's quarterly internal journal, *Black Lamplight*, and its occasional bulletin, *Manticore*.

Relentless experimentation and new methods of irrational research have been hallmarks of the Leeds surrealists as indicated in the pages reprinted here from the book, *A Game of Slight Disturbances* (1995).

A GAME OF SLIGHT DISTURBANCES

Note: This game was played by the Leeds Surrealist Group from April to August 1995. Using found objects symbolizing individuals in the group, each of us built a composite object—a self-portrait—which were placed around the Leeds city center to interrupt the daily routines of passersby. However, the game operated on many levels: our subjective relationships with objects and places; the intersubjective relationships between individuals in the group; the nature of the "lost" and "found," of absence and presence. From finding individual objects to the loss of my totem in the city, the game entered my deepest thoughts and dreams, "disturbing" my consciousness.

Wednesday, 16th August, 1995—Waiting

Walking to the Victoria Pub just before 6:30 P.M. I saw lots of red petals scattered on the ground near the gardens in front of the Civic Hall. I wondered where my object might be found.

Settled into my seat in the Victoria at 6:30 P.M. with my glass of water, I feel very alert. I had felt a sense of apprehension before coming in because I have never been in a pub on my own before, but I actually feel quite inconspicuous now.

Beneath each lamp on the bar a brass elephant holds up the rail in its trunk. Judy Garland is singing in the background and there is a feeling of timelessness. This is the closest bar in Leeds to the Czerny Pivovar in Prague.

I felt quite nervous and excited as we drove into Leeds. I feel no sense of loss and I might never see my object again. Although I never felt attached to it I have learned a lot from it. The final decision not to change it was right. I cannot fabricate an attachment which is not there. This detachment is the nature of my relationship with the parts of me and my experience which the object represents. I wonder where it will lead the others? Perhaps it's the heat, but I think it longs to be in or near water. It may take them to Boar Lane, a part of the city which fascinates me.

There is a sense of completion that the objects which we found, took into our possession, have become lost, or found, objects again. Although they have significance for us, perhaps they also have significance for those who found or lost them before us. These objects have their own history, and future, independent of us.

I won't know until I see my object, but I think that when I do it will be more a representation of me than it was when it just stood in a room in the house. Finding the place where it belongs (before its next adventure) also completes it. This place is a vital part of its meaning. Perhaps in my case it will provide the link which I am having such difficulty in finding.

The wobbling fan has a hypnotic effect. I recall a nightmare from last night. Someone, or something, came into our room brandishing my object. I remember sitting up in bed and shouting, then waking up. I don't know if I dreamed I sat up and shouted or if I actually did. (Kenneth might know.)

7:10 P.M.–7:25 P.M.—*Drawing*

What is this shadowy creature which haunts my dreams? A distant relative of the white rabbit? Another line of evolution? My eye catches a print near the door—it looks Pre-Raphaelite in style from here. A man in black kneels before a woman in white who is standing in a doorway—the virtuous Victorian woman. A female voice croons, "That's why the lady is a tramp." 7:35 P.M. I'm getting to the stage where I jump every time someone walks in.

Looking into the back room of the bar, it has a nautical feel, like the room in my dream where I saw my object reconstructed. The stained glass dome in the roof has a motif of red roses with green leaves. The two prints I can make out on the wall are of naked lounging ladies. They remind me of the naked women on the playing cards I found in Paris, and they contrast with the stern portraits of Queen Victoria in the room where I am sitting. Also in the room are two black feather dusters perched above the lunch bar. Maybe I should go and sit in the back room. A particularly ugly group of people have just come and sat at the table next to me.

8:00 P.M. I can't help feeling a bit impatient now! Perhaps they can't find the place. I wonder what is guiding them. Having been on three walks I can see how different each one has been. We have come to each place by a different process of exploration—different sorts of signs interpreted in different ways. A sudden rush of people at the bar. It must be the end of visiting time at the hospital. Here they come!

Searching

I knew where the object was as soon as I looked at the map and I went straight to the place. Although I expected to see it in the fountain when I looked over the side, it still gave me a fright. I sat on a bench for a while.

8:15 P.M. A couple approach. She looks into the fountain, sees the object, turns away then goes back for another look. He has a video camera and is videoing the Civic Hall. He doesn't notice the object and she doesn't mention it. Another man and then three girls also walk past and look into the fountain. In each case I can see a question cross their faces but this is seemingly dismissed almost instantly. None of them stop or take a second look.

Later I wondered why seeing the object gave me a fright. I think my initial reaction was that I was looking at something which had drowned. Perhaps it will always give me a fright to see something under water looking up at me. (I have a phobia about sunken ships.) Also, I don't think expectation can prepare you for the unexpected.

Katerina Piňosová

In addition to the flourishing Surrealist Group in Prague, which has had an unbroken history since 1934, the Czech Republic has another Surrealist Group in Moravia, whose members—eleven of them as this book goes to press—are mostly in their twenties and live in such cities as Prostějov, Brno, and Sternberk. Katerina Piňosová—poet, graphic artist, and collagist—is one of the sparkplugs of this dynamic young group. (Strictly speaking, she explains, the Moravian group is neither separate from the Prague group nor a branch of it; rather, in the Czech Republic surrealism is "one movement with two centers.")

Born in Prostějov in 1973, Piňosová joined the group in 1995 and has already taken part in several of its collective exhibitions throughout the country. She collaborates actively both on the Moravian group's journal, *Intervence* [Intervention], as well as the Prague group's *Analogon*.

As one might expect in the land of Kafka and Hasek, humor is a prime factor in Czech surrealism. Piňosová's humor has a lot of the spirit of the trickster in it. In her wonderful drawings, many of them silhouettes, whole menageries take to the streets at night to engage in the most outrageous pranks. Her poems, fairy tales that make us think of Harpo Marx's dreams, overflow with equal doses of terror, playfulness, and the secrets of alchemy.

THE PIECE OF BONE

I saw a tree
similar to the quiet bell that just struck ten to five
Like a torn skirt with a slip hidden underneath
it was made of glass
It crossed my mind to open all the little bells
before they let themselves be advised
and before the little craftswomen
grow breasts as big as towers
I have to hide myself inside the tree a while
until I can calm its old bark
that is already too weak
to resist my rubbing against it
My dress
sewn with broken pieces of craftswomen's tears
is dirty with a strange-smelling mood
like wheat in winter
and a slightly open grave
I saw my tears frozen in my lap
and I was sleeping at the time
I walked on a slide where there were frozen fish
with their eyes open
I saw a tree holding a handkerchief
and I saw myself in its belly
drawing a tower
It was ten to five

Translated from the Czech by Katerina Piňosová

Katerina Piňosová, ink drawing, 1966. Courtesy of the artist.

Lenka Valachová

Lenka Valachová, along with Katerina Piňosová and graphic artist Katerina Kubiková, is a leading activist in the newly formed Surrealist Group in Moravia. She was born in Brno in what was then called Czechoslovakia, in 1973. As a theater arts student at the University of Brno, Valachová encountered the Moravian surrealists in 1991, and has taken part in all their activities since 1995. A regular collaborator on the group's journal, *Intervence*, she has also toured the Czech Republic several times as a performer in her father's celebrated Clown Theater. She lives in Brno.

THE STERILE DISH

Above the window a gray obelisk hangs
Its chin is as big as its forehead
The division seems erotic to me—
yellow nudity in front and dark hair behind
Next to a first-floor window it hangs
This way it casts a shadow on a third of the inhabited house
If you want to force your way to the window
You must delicately kiss the young lady's ankle
Automatically she will lift her leg and put it on a stair

The level of excitement
The screen still extending
The green-colored hill overgrown with surgical artery-clips
holding flower-stalks
Their heads are made of insects
Their mandibles are strange and their eyes are formed of tiny pinheads
As you stop while making your way through the neat tufts they leave
because of your ugly complexion
You are burned all over
For the first time they let you notice
that they have opened a tin drum
On its bottom is a glove
fingers spiking out of fingers

Translated from the Czech by Katerina Piňosová

Kajsa Bergh

In surrealism today Kajsa Bergh is best known for her hauntingly magical (and at the same time stunningly humorous) paintings and drawings, but she is also the author of serious theoretical texts as well as poems of vibrant lyricism. One of the seven cofounders of the Surrealist Group in Stockholm in midsummer 1986, she has participated in all of the group's subsequent activities and collective publications, from *Naknar Läppar* [Nude Lips] (1987) through *Stora Saltet* (1996). Her work has also appeared in the *International Surrealist Bulletin* and in other surrealist journals throughout the world, including *Analogon* (Prague) and *Arsenal: Surrealist Subversion* (Chicago).

The text published here, a searching plunge into the depths of one of surrealism's—and life's!—perennial preoccupations, was published in *Arsenal* no. 4 (1989).

DESIRE

Your eyes that make the mirror look so dumb.

My thought is in your eye and I shake inside myself, outside myself. The limitless landscape spreads inside my body, and everything I touch becomes blue. Memory and the second before and the second afterward—I thought—that the lungs are too small—until the explosion of what rushes out of small membranes on my body is noticeable—my world and the shuddering of the skin before the unknown.

Do not forget that my home is a castle and that I dance when I want to. Do not forget that my home is full of seconds. To wake up each day on a new side of night. That thought alone weighs more than a thousand suns. Do not forget the red color on my cheeks, and that it is you who made it up.

So I shall not forget that your walls are adorned with rope-ladders and that the spider in the web has things to tell of a time when one still slept in beds. That my tears make lakes of wombs and that my laughs taste of almond in your carpet of fingertips.

Desire is in reality the instant when the sky wants to lower itself so deeply down to the ground that the bodies disintegrate into themselves and when the sound of dripping that is heard is the eyes falling into the surface of the sea that gets a hundred years of memory out of only one second—the sea in which we are drowning, and which gives us birth at the same moment.

Translated from the Swedish by Bruno Jacobs

Petra Mandal

Poet, painter, theorist, and graphic artist, Petra Mandal cofounded the Surrealist Group in Stockholm, Sweden, in midsummer 1986, and has since collaborated on virtually every one of its collective publications, including *Naknar Läppar, Kvicksand* [Quicksand], *Mannen på Gatan,* and *Stora Saltet,* as well as *Arsenal: Surrealist Subversion* (Chicago) and the *International Surrealist Bulletin.* A collection of Mandal's sparkling poems and drawings, *Halla i Huvut,* appeared under the "Surrealistförlaget" [Surrealist Editions] imprint in Stockholm, 1987. She has also illustrated a volume by surrealist writer Bruno Jacobs.

In its original publication in Swedish in *Mannen på Gatan* no. 1 (1991), the poem published here was made up of captions to a series of illustrations by the author. However, as with Max Ernst's celebrated collage-novel, *La Femme 100 têtes* [The 100-Headed/or Headless Woman], the captions by themselves constitute a powerful statement. The English translation was published in a photocopied bulletin, *The Man in the Street, Part 2.*

FIRST-HAND KNOWLEDGE

1. I am undivided because the world has divided me.

2. The core of creation.

3. My first dance step.
   I lifted my arms over the sea, in the air where there was a circle which I followed, which divided the sea and the air.

4. Image of clitoris.
   The lack of blue in nature, food.

5. 0 = woman I = man was child.
   Man tottering. Woman firm.

6. Two pigs have cleared the tables.
   It is always two. Opposites always separate simultaneously. Because of this one—one meets a reacting force.

7. There is no emptiness.
   Because there is always something outside. Outside the black holes, that which makes the holes.

Petra Mandal, ink drawing, 1989. Courtesy of the artist.

8. Reality the divided illusory.
   Like when I flew out of the image, out of reality.

9. To create from the (hand) spirit. [*Mens-manus* in Latin.]

10. The doctrine of correspondences.

11. How does one squeeze a woman into a four-dimensional room without kissing her first?
    1. *Take a ladder.*
    2. *Follow it until the breathing stops.*

   3. *Take to the right.*
   4. *Leave your imprint.*
   5. *Escape.*
   6. *And she's in.*

12. How does one know what is inside?
   1. *Make a circle.*
   2. *Follow its edge.*
   3. *Open the eye.*
   4. *And you're out.*

13. How does one know what a square is?
   1. *Take a lighthouse.*
   2. *Strike a whole in the sky.*
   3. *Kiss the ground.*
   4. *Close the door.*
   5. *Shut off the TV.*

   And it's yours.

Translated from the Swedish by Bruno Jacobs

Nancy Joyce Peters

WOMEN AND SURREALISM

Women and surrealism: two things strike one immediately. First, the almost obsessive appearance of Woman as image, and secondly, the disproportionately large number of women surrealists in comparison with token women artists elsewhere. It is inescapable that Woman is the dominant poetic figure in early surrealist painting and poetry. Feminists, in particular, have suggested that an apparent extension of the blessed damsels and *belles dames sans merci* inherited from late romanticism is, in surrealism, just another objectification of women. However, surrealism's allegorical Woman goes much further, as her image becomes multiple, ironic, and mythically complex. In fact, the tension between contradictory variants (e.g., Hans Bellmer's perverse doll and André Breton's cherished *femme*) destroy mythic boundaries. Connections made and broken produced massive fragmentation, until Woman began to recede as a central motif.

At the same time, when women are said to be always excluded from representation only to return within it as an object, i.e., the thing represented, it is paradoxical that surrealism should be the milieu in which numerous women have worked triumphantly as *representors*. More than a few have attained world prominence. Sculptor Meret Oppenheim, filmmaker Nelly Kaplan, poet Joyce Mansour, painters Leonora Carrington, Remedios Varo, Dorothea Tanning, and Toyen come to mind at once. In the 1976 World Surrealist Exhibition in Chicago, there were scores of works by women not only from Europe but the Americas, Africa, the Middle East and Asia.

At the beginning, just after World War I, there was scarcely a hint of the theoretical emphasis on Woman and the feminine, nor of the many women who were to take part in the adventure of surrealism. Nonetheless, the philosophical foundations of surrealism were to undermine sexual conventions expected of male artists, to advance exploration of the female principle, and to allow women to follow their independent vision. That's obviously never been easy in the fundamentally misogynist art world. In large measure, it was up to the women in surrealism to evolve powerful new conceptions of femininity, and, for that matter, of human possibility.

The first surrealists aimed to reorient thought—and that new orientation, although never feminist, has had prophetic parallels with contemporary feminist concerns. A deliberate stand against patriarchy and its institutions—the State, patriotism, militarism, control, rules, the Church, piety, domesticity—sabotages the underlying structures of women's oppression. By discrediting Judeo-Christian-Classical aesthetic and moral presumptions in favor of animism and the dazzling art and thought of non-Western peoples, women as well as third-world artists have been drawn into the surrealist orbit. European old-boy craft networks with apprenticeships and traditional art and university training became nonessential. The rancorous estate of "professional" poets with academic chairs and government grants is undermined where poetry and life are one. And where work and life are fused, women's lives have value as *human* lives.

In expression, surrealism gives precedence to intuition, receptivity, relational cognition, relatedness with "other." Because these modes have been assigned by culture to women, women are already in a position to excel in them. Methods of provoking idea and image through contact with the unconscious allow diversity and difference to appear naturally; gender is effectively neutralized. Uncovering the unknown by paths of dream and desire, and the practice of psychic automatism to arrive at truths uninhibited by convention or prejudice, puts men and women on absolutely equal footing. And so, for example, it was possible for Gisèle Prassinos, a fourteen-year-old schoolgirl published in early surrealist reviews, to enchant readers with her tales of poetic revolt.

Most significantly, as men sought the feminine in themselves, women moved into the normative masculine arena of expression: individualist objectivity, analytic thought, and vigorous self-transcending creation. Surrealism broke new ground here. It encouraged diversity and recognized difference without perpetuating oppositions. What that meant was that women had neither to sacrifice their singular feminine experience by taking on a male *persona*, nor be bound, for that matter, to a specifically "women's art."

Defined by biological complementarities, the man-woman interface is at the heart of dualism. It could be said, in fact, to be the foundation of every binary opposition. How immense is that double star of existence where Love and Death dance through the whole life of the body and mind. Myth everywhere represents the first division of the One and the Other: order and chaos, spirit and matter, above and below, sacred and profane, male and female. This dichotomy and its flowering in thought assigns attributes to the sexes in opposition, fixing the division of labor, and even the way we define ourselves from day to day. Yet how these binary voyages of the mind are mediated by pure chance is evident in the many ways gender is lived, whether in traditional societies or great urban complexes. Deep-rooted myths of feminine danger and evil have deadly repercussions when misogyny and the denial of Eros are solidified in powerful modern institutions. We see them in rape, battered women, homophobia, and indeed in sexual unhappiness of every kind.

Men's fear of women, flight from women. Women's anger, contempt for men. Male initiation rites, male pretense of competence; female intellectual passivity, self-sacrifice, mock helplessness. Men's need of ceremony, women's weak bonding. Mutual envy and guilt. These are the bad habits of the human race. Now there's no *reason* why human beings must remain in these conditions of wretchedness. To continue ontologizing mutually exclusive male and female principles not only perpetuates male supremacism, but has now brought the world to its present discontent under the looming shadow of annihilation. It's all very well for bull elephant seals to gouge one another for evolutionary benefits, but the lethal weapons of the territorial human male are deadly displays that must come to an end. Women's emancipation requires a massive transformation of erotic dynamics—and this is a psychic and social revolution scarcely yet imagined. It's an essential one if we are to survive.

However different men and women are, we are alike in everything essential: in the texture of our dreams, the voluptuous wanderings of the instincts, in intelligence, hope for our children, our vulnerability in the face of death. The present women's liberation movement has cast light on how false differences are codified, culturally reproduced and enforced for purposes of control in a world dominated by the implacable flow of Capital. Obviously there will always be differences between men and women; biology insures a unique sexual experience for each. There are two sexes; but gender is multiple. Because human sexuality is linked to a complex mental life—imaginal, emotional, reasoning—it's possible to make a thousand changes in those antagonistic relationships, deliberately cultivated and sometimes even glorified, that prevent our becoming living beings. And they preclude love too, for "true union, or love proper," as Hegel claimed, "exists only between living beings from every point of view."

To exorcise the dualist curse has always been a first priority of surrealists, who mean to recover lost powers, to *change life,* to create *another being.* Very early on, Breton had sought "a certain point in the mind by means of which life and death, real and imaginary, communicable and incommunicable, high and low, cease to be perceived in terms of contradiction." This radical intention goes well beyond a superficial change of perspective; it takes a vertiginous plunge into a non-binary universe. Among other effects, such a confrontation with the binary medusa subverts petrified notions of gender. Through poetic allegories, a kaleidoscope of mutable beings play through surrealist works, aspects of each sex attaching to the other and changing our perceptions. In the erotic embrace, Annie Le Brun observed in her brilliant polemic *Lâchez Tout,* "we encounter a point of transparency before plunging into the night of our differences and come up not caring whether we are male or female." Within this flow of masculine-feminine exchange, the seer, the rebel poet, the woman-child, the non-aggressive man, the woman-transformer, the sleep-walker, the androgyne, and the lovers move in a world *in posse,* where will and imagination have the power to transfigure.

It is redundant to say that the surrealist attitude, or that surrealist art is full of unresolved conflicts and ambivalence toward women. Precisely. Ambivalence toward women is an inescapable fact. Legends of man favor the hero, bringer of fire, tools, ritual and law. Woman belongs to the raptures of the deep. She is life, the birthgiver, the blossoming and fruitful earth, feast, wisdom, beauty. Her other face is death, the destroyer, famine, the earth that takes back. We are stunned by the sheer inhumanness of these phantoms. In the black sun of the unconscious, for all our rationality, woman leads a disquieting life—obsessing desire, eluding definition. For men, certainly, but for us too, in whom she lives at once an intimate and an alien. So she haunts the makers of images and is the perennial subject of the arts, impelling us to search out the truth of her mystery. Yet woman in image, as in life, changes in time. We know there is no eternal woman, an abstraction of qualities, nor can her image stand for unrepresentable concepts. Reality is not a transcendent truth but a historical configuration; a multidimensional social process, taking place in individuals who desire, think, act and change together.

They are not so laudatory, the centuries of sweet madonnas, benignant mothers with child, bourgeois portrait-sitters or Stalinist heroines behind whose unambivalent rationalistic icons generations of women have suffered. This kind of art can patronize, erase contradiction, mask reality. Some feminists are strenuous in opposing objectification of women; and one response to that has been a "women's art" which itself portrays Woman as object, usually an abstraction of female sexual specificity. If she no longer stands for Purity, or Seduction, or Justice, she'd now stand for Fecundity or Nurturing or some such other figure of the unrepresentable.

Perhaps this is not so strange. For each of us, in truth, Woman is an undiscovered continent. She is our first love, first pleasure. She is also the first anguish, the pain of primal separation and loss. As Dorothy Dinnerstein argues in her pioneering book *The Mermaid and the Minotaur,* the pre-Oedipal mother is the sum of all sensual, mental, polymorphous erotic life, lived in the unconscious as unmitigated power long before that power can be understood rationally. Men and women collaborate to keep Woman under control, granting overt power to the real subsidiary sex—Male. The failure of the first revolution against this overwhelming Mother is the paradigm for every failed revolution in our history. And so, if the unconscious is allowed to shine in waking vision, Woman will take many guises and some of them will disturb and perplex.

Myths, whether in the form of narrative or visual images, are fields of discourse on which are projected deep and ancient beliefs. This sometimes makes them profoundly conservative, but they can be liberative too, because they display emblems of desire, provoke thought, and shape acts. It is through myth that humanity supersedes its limitations, *goes beyond.* A nomadic force in surrealist myth, woman takes innumerable forms, explosively magical, measureless. It is through an extreme mobility and the untenable paradoxes between these figures that the clash between the fictions and facts of her power and powerlessness are made transparent. She is restored as a Being-of-Power, not an artificial power designed to obscure impotence, but a real power—though it's often forced to lead a subterranean life.

In men's paintings she is a focus of erotic desire, awe, anxiety, esteem, love. She is a spiritual mediator, and her superior clarity and coherence are qualities to be assimilated. The erotic-ideal types of the *femme-enfant,* exalted for innocence of spirit and intuition, or the *femme-fatale,* challenging and rebellious, like some revolutionary daemon, are moving tributes. They are not altogether unpredictable, however, rooted in themes traditional to male discourse. What most astonishes in retrospect is that this group of European men should have, so many decades ago, begun clearing a place for women to stand—as lovers, comrades, and equals. They deserve immense credit, too, for fully elaborating, for the first time since the heretical interlude of the troubadours, the exceptional idea of *reciprocal* love. Historically, this egalitarian notion is the most uncommon, love generally having been regarded as an unwanted affliction, a kind of disease that prevented men from getting on with their work. Even today, it's regarded with much skepticism.

Although many attempts have been made to define the "surrealist woman," she escapes confinement, even at a conceptual level. How completely distinct are Paul Eluard's lady of supreme grace, Max Ernst's bird-headed divas, Marcel Duchamp's machinic bride, Philip Lamantia's desert mermaids, Clovis Trouille's saboteurs, Ted Joans' amorous menagerie, David Gascoyne's aerial traveler, Joseph Jablonski's woman of the cave, Paul Delvaux's Terrible Mother, Max-Walter Svanberg's androgynous rulers of the celestial vault.

In painting, poetry, theater, dance, and film, woman in representation is a complex unfolding of self and other. Women invent their own beauty and dignity, express directly their own energy, sensuality and humor. Meret Oppenheim's inaugural manifestation for the International Surrealist Exhibition in Paris, 1959–60, undercut the tyranny of the conventional male-viewed mythic woman with typical verve. Laid out on her back, filling the eye with fruit and flesh, here was woman-as-feast, an effigy of perfect passivity, simultaneously homage to women's delectable attributes and a witty mockery of the Nurturer and of Woman Objectified. Woman invades the old order from below, astonishing us, overturning preconceptions of women's place and being. She refuses limits: Joyce Mansour's cannibal bacchantes, Mimi Parent's sorceress of the gate, Penelope Rosemont's ice maidens, Marianne van Hirtum's bad girls, Yahne Le Toumelin's lamplighter, Alice Rahon's twilight seer, Valentine Penrose's Bloody Countess, Leonora Carrington's insurrectionary debutantes, LaDonna Smith's manic fiddler, Marie Wilson's fearful symmetries, Dorothea Tanning's restless maternities and childhood dreams, Anne Ethuin's mineral specters, Debra Taub's gypsy convulsionaries, Elena Garro's initiatrice, Manina's neon ornithologers, Rikki Ducornet's Alexis who tells the truth.

Painter, writer, sculptor and playwright, Leonora Carrington raises the curtain of an analogic theater, on whose stages wondrous beings enact dramas that expose psychic realities behind physical ones. They have great range, some evoking a sort of gnawing domestic anxiety, and others, the terrible beauties of theophany. Not a few of her paintings are inhabited by the Tuatha de Daanan—people of the Celtic goddess Daana—or by figures from Mayan and

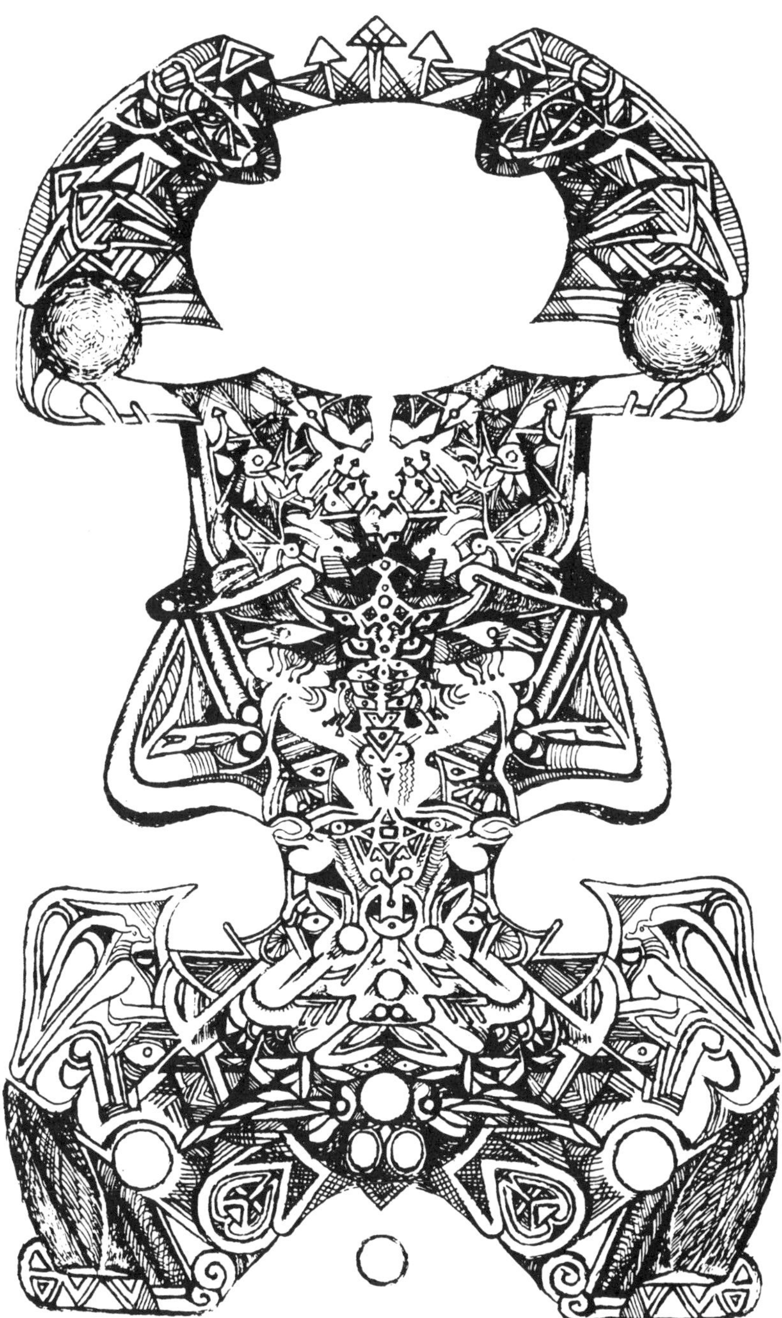

Marie Wilson, ink drawing, n.d. Courtesy of the artist.
California-born Marie Wilson took part in surrealist activity in Paris throughout the 1950s. Profoundly automatistic in origin, her haunting symmetrical drawings recall Tibetan tantras and certain Oceanic designs. She lives in Oakland; her husband is the Greek surrealist poet Nanos Valaoritis.

Aube Elléouët, *The Engulfed Cathedral,* collage, 1996. Courtesy of the artist. Aube Elléouët was born in Paris in 1937, the daughter of Jacqueline Lamba and André Breton. Active in surrealism since the 1950s, she is especially well known for her free-spirited ecology-inspired collages, which she has shown in numerous solo and collective exhibitions. She lives in the French countryside in Azay le Rideau.

other mythologies. We witness, in a pre-christian world, celebrations of mysteries, and feasts that suggest rebirth and spiritual metamorphosis. Masks which hide the face, and sometimes the entire body, imply a synesthesia of the senses; and a visionary eye gazes at realities that lie behind appearances. In a delightful novel, *The Hearing Trumpet,* Marian the 92-year-old protagonist, consigned to a nursing home by her children, awakens ancient cthonic forces to seize lost female powers. Carrington regards woman as a potential agent of change, perhaps even to lead the species toward an evolutionary leap.

Susana Wald has suggested that "one day perhaps the masculine and feminine spirit will be fused, and then women contribute to the creation of a new mode of thought that will renew us all." The androgyne, quintessential metaphor of transformation and a familiar surrealist motif, is taken in a new direction by women. They convey a greater mutability of gender, less of a gulf between clearly defined sexual qualities. With alchemical imagery, they often summon the bisexual libido and the androgynous unconscious of the *prima materia* in the work of transmutation. The "female," rather than a drop or essence needed to complete the man, is seen by women as the active principle of transformation. Woman presides, active rather than passive, over evolution or revolution—as warrior, magician, rebel, mathematician, seer, witch, lover, or alchemist. Through a subtle shifting of the usual roles of men and women, Nelly Kaplan's films give graphic examples of how the crippling polarity of the sexes might be overcome. If the image of the lovers can be argued to represent circularity, a dream of original unity with the mother, Kaplan takes that image far beyond those self-defeating limits. Always led by the woman, her lovers so integrate masculine and feminine that wholly new kinds of relationships emerge, relationships that encourage tolerance and humor, that allow love to triumph.

Surrealist men's erotic models have no corresponding ideal male figures developed by women theorists, yet eros is affirmed in other ways. It is less the matrix of romantic/orgasmic explosion, rather a sexualization of *being* expressed through the cruelties of birth and death, links between organic and inorganic, and the uses of magic and transformation. The American dancer-choreographer Alice Farley, inspired by the trance-dances of traditional cultures, uses costume, lighting and settings to bring an erotic lyricism to theater space. There is always present in her work the mediated carnality implied in Nietzsche's claim that "the demand for art and beauty is an indirect demand for the ecstasies of sexuality communicated directly to the brain." The fierce sexuality and acid humor of the Egyptian poet Joyce Mansour's tales and poems have nothing of the conventionally feminine about them. Her Gnostic intensities are always characterized by a virile liberty. Another remarkable artist, the Californian Marie Wilson, directs a kind of underground sexual energy into her symmetrical drawings and paintings which become force-fields that mirror the crossing densities of birth, growth and death. Intricate twining organic forms reel with the vitality that is present at the splitting of a simple amoeba or the explosion of a supernova.

Valentine Penrose, who is best known for her crystalline, hermetic poems, sweeps away the fraudulent perspectives of Christianity with regard to women and nature, in her explosive re-creation of the life and crimes of Erzsebet Bathory, *The Bloody Countess*. Sade would have admired this bold and dizzying book that probes, in the black forests of Bathory's cruelties, the furious chaos of desire. And in so doing reveals secrets of the world occults. Here is a primal energy that can be suppressed and perverted with disastrous consequences, or unleashed in the cause of true liberty.

Born in Catalonia and long resident in Mexico, Remedios Varo combines in her paintings the profundity of the child's question "why?" with sophisticated philosophical speculation. Why are cats made of fur and not fern? What scientific principle connects all things in the universe? An insouciant young woman, upon opening a small chest, encounters only an image of herself, but there are other unopened boxes still on a shelf. Perhaps she'll encounter something new? A serene woman leaves a psychoanalyst's office carrying the head of the Father by its beard. From a high window, a wide-eyed being watches a man made of water, as his footprints attest, greeted at the door by a woman clothed in fire. Varo's gift for mathematics is visible in her themes. Astronomers experiment with disobedient planets; geometers make very curious measurements; musicians play on strings of sunlight or charm fossilized stones into architectural marvels. As a great wheel of fog enters the window, a watchmaker disassembles a clock. Behind him are eight grandfather clocks all set exactly at 12:15; but imprisoned in each are personages dressed in the costumes of different eras. In these enchanting narratives you can meet women made of lichen or yarn, men of feathers, vegetable cathedrals, vegetarian vampires. Varo takes us to parallel worlds, antiworlds, possible worlds where animal, plant, and mineral don't stay in their places, where things are always liable to change into something else.

The Czech painter Toyen moved, after the destruction of her native Prague in the Second World War, to Paris, where she produced in powerful drawings and paintings a moving testament against war, as in her series *War, Hide Yourself!*, or paintings such as *The Dangerous Hour* and *Safe*. The 1950s and '60s saw a newly luminous erotic power in the work of this great painter. Toyen brings to a subaqueous landscape a special quality of enigma. She seems to catch that moment between shape and shadow, sign and thing, that bears the grace of poetry.

If the disparate arts of surrealist women are linked by the vigor of their ideas, by wit and imaginative power, the sense of flow, of a flying truth caught in an instant, most distinguishes them. Whether abstract or figurative painting, dance or poem, they are open, dynamic, incommensurable. Nothing is forbidden, nothing locked in. They refuse *telos.* It is curious that woman is said to represent "absence" and immanence, as compared with man's superior identification with "becoming." Yet her passages and doorways, transitions and metamorphoses are signs, not of stasis and emptiness, but of hope and transcendence.

Her dress an unclosed cone, a little girl holding a butterfly net faces a horizon on whose expanse the future is yet to be written: Toyen's *The Dreaming Girl* is a fitting emblem for this time. Such images not only inspire and give pleasure. They invite us to be seers, to be oracle and its answer. Bounteous and boundless—they free us.

(From *Arsenal: Surrealist Subversion* no. 4, 1989; slightly abridged)

Bibliography

I. BASIC SOURCES

Note: The five volumes listed here (in chronological order) are cited throughout this bibliography.

Breton, André. 1972. *Surrealism and Painting.* Translated by Simon Watson Taylor. New York: Harper and Row. Originally published in 1965 as *Le Surréalisme et la peinture* (Paris: Gallimard).

La Femme surréaliste. 1977. Special issue of *Obliques,* no. 14–15.

Dictionnaire Général du surréalisme et de ses environs. 1982. Edited by Adam Biro and René Passeron. Paris: Presses Universitaires de France.

Das surrealistische Gedicht. 1985. Edited by Heribert Becker, Edouard Jaguer, and Petr Kral. Bochum: Zweitausendeins und dem Museum Bochum.

La Femme et le surréalisme. 1987. Exhibition catalog. Lausanne: Musée cantonal es Beaux-Arts.

II. WORKS BY AND ABOUT WOMEN REPRESENTED IN THIS ANTHOLOGY

Eileen Agar

Agar, Eileen. 1988. *A Look at My Life.* London: Methuen.

Jaguer, Edouard. 1982. "Eileen Agar." In *Dictionnaire Général du surréalisme.*

Remy, Michel, and E.L.T. Mesens. 1982. "Eileen Agar." In *Les Enfants d'Alice: la peinture surréaliste en Angleterre, 1930–1960,* 19–23. Paris: Galerie 1900/2000.

"Eileen Agar." 1987. In *La Femme et le surréalisme,* 92–98.

Fanny Beznos

Breton, André. 1960. *Nadja.* Translated by Richard Howard, 52–55. New York: Grove Press. Originally published in 1928 (Paris: Gallimard).

"Fanny Beznos." 1987. In *La Femme et le surréalisme,* 498.
Pastoureau, Henri. 1992. *Ma Vie surréaliste.* Paris: Maurice Nadeau.

Hilary Booth

Booth, Hilary. 1984. *I Am Rain.* Adelaide: Free Association.

Elisa Breton

Breton, Elisa. 1959. "De qui est-ce?" *La Brèche: Action surréaliste* 5 (Spring): 46–48.
Schuster, Jean. 1959. "Elisa circule dans le plus cohèrent des mondes," *La Brèche: Action surréaliste* 5 (Spring): inside front cover.
Breton, Elisa, André Breton, and Benjamin Péret. 1972. "Aparté." In *Surrealism and Painting,* 218–219.
van Hirtum, Marianne. 1982. "Elisa Breton." In *Dictionnaire Général du surréalisme.*
"Elisa Breton." 1987. In *La Femme et le surréalisme,* 149, 500.

Emmy Bridgwater

"Emmy Bridgwater." 1982. In *Les Enfants d'Alice: la peinture surréaliste en Angleterre, 1930–1960,* 30–33. Paris: Galerie 1900/2000. Texts by Toni del Renzio, Edouard Jaguer and Michel Remy. Exhibition catalog.
Remy, Michel. 1982. "Emmy Bridgwater." In *Dictionnaire Général du surréalisme.*
"Emmy Bridgwater." 1985. In *Das surrealistische Gedicht,* 151–156.
"Emmy Bridgwater." 1987. In *La Femme et le surréalisme,* 498.
Emmy Bridgwater. 1990. Exhibition catalog. London: Blond Fine Art.

Carmen Bruna

Bruna, Carmen. 1980. *Bodas.* Buenos Aires: Ediciones El Lorraine.
———. 1983. *Morgana o el espejismo.* Buenos Aires: Signo Ascendente.
———. 1987. *Lilith.* Buenos Aires: Ediciones Signo Ascendente.
———. 1991. *La Luna Negra de Lilith.* Buenos Aires: Libros del Empedrado.
———. 1993. *Melusina o la búsqueda del amor extraviado.* Buenos Aires: Libros del extraviado.
Henao, Raul. 1994. "Carmen Bruna, La Hermana de Cain," *Punto Seguido* 35 (September): 4–7.

Claude Cahun

Cahun, Claude. 1930. *Aveux non avenus.* Paris: Editions du Carrefour.
———. 1934. *Les Paris sont ouverts.* Paris: José Corti.
———. 1992. *Ballon captif.* Brive: Myrddin.

Leperlier, François. 1992. *Claude Cahun, l'écart et la métamorphose.* Paris: Jean-Michel Place.

Leonora Carrington

Carrington, Leonora. 1964. *El Mundo Magico de los Mayas.* Mexico City: Museo Nacional de Antropologia.

———. 1972. *Down Below.* Chicago: Black Swan Press; new edition, 1983. Originally published in English in *VVV* no. 4 (New York, 1944).

———. 1975. *The Oval Lady.* Santa Barbara, CA: Capra Press.

———. 1977. *The Hearing Trumpet.* New York: Pocket Books. New edition, San Francisco: City Lights, 1985.

———. 1977. *The Stone Door.* New York: St Martin's Press.

———. 1988. *The House of Fear.* New York: Dutton.

———. 1989. *The Seventh Horse.* New York: Dutton.

Breton, André. 1966. *Anthologie de l'humour noir.* Paris: Jean-Jacques Pauvert.

———. 1972. *Surrealism and Painting,* 76.

Chénieux, Jacqueline. 1977. "Leonora Carrington et la tunique de Nessus." In *La Femme surréaliste,* 83–90.

Rouvre, Germaine. 1977. "Entretien avec Leonora Carrington." In *La Femme surréaliste,* 91–92.

Mabille, Pierre. 1981. "A propos de *En Bas* de Leonora Carrington." In *Traversées de nuit,* 33–41. Paris: Editions Plasma.

Paoli-Lafaye, Elisabeth. 1982. "Leonora Carrington." In *Dictionnaire Général du surréalisme.*

Leonora Carrington—The Mexican Years, 1943–1985. 1991. San Francisco: The Mexican Museum. Exhibit catalog.

Schlieker, Andrea, ed. 1991. *Leonora Carrington.* London: Serpentine Gallery.

Suzanne Césaire

Breton, André. 1948. "Pour Madame Suzanne Césaire." In *Martinique, charmeuse de serpents.* Texts and illustrations by André Masson, 41. Paris: Sagittaire.

Rosemont, Franklin. 1996. "Suzanne Césaire: In the Light of Surrealism." In Vèvè Clark and Marie-Agnès Sourieau, eds., *Re-Membering Lost Bodies: Negritude and Beyond. Antillean Women's Writings, 1930–1970.* Forthcoming.

Sourieau, Marie-Agnès. "Suzanne Césaire et *Tropiques:* de la poésie cannibale à une poétique créole," *French Review* 68, no. 1 (October 1994).

Monique Charbonel

Charbonel, Monique. 1967. "Du ronéogramme, de la bille de verre et de la comète au coeur de fourrure," *RUpTure* no. 6 (October): 38–41.

Ithell Colquhoun

Colquhoun, Ithell. 1955. *The Crying of the Wind*. London: Peter Owen.
———. 1957. *The Living Stones*. London: Peter Owen.
———. 1961. *The Goose of Hermogenes*. London: Peter Owen.
———. 1973. *Grimoire of the Entangled Thicket*. Stevenage: Ore.
———. 1975. *Sword of Wisdom: MacGregor Mathers and "The Golden Dawn."* New York: Putnam.
———. 1980. *Ozmazone*. Orkeljunga, Sweden: Dunganon.
Ithell Colquhoun, 1936–1976. 1976. Exhibition catalog, The Newlyn Orion Galleries, Cornwall, England. Includes reminiscences by Colquhoun.
Les Enfants d'Alice: la peinture surréaliste en Angleterre, 1930–1960. 1982. Texts by Michel Remy and Edouard Jaguer. Paris: Galerie 1900/2000.
Remy, Michel. 1982. "Ithell Colquhoun." In *Dictionnaire Général du surréalisme*.

Jayne Cortez

Cortez, Jayne. 1969. *Pissstained Stairs and the Monkey Man's Wares*. New York: Phrase Text.
———. 1971. *Festivals and Funerals*. New York: Bola Press.
———. 1973. *Scarifications*. New York: Bola Press.
———. 1977. *Mouth on Paper*. New York: Bola Press.
———. 1982. *Firespitter*. New York: Bola Press.
———. 1991. *Poetic Magnetic*. New York: Bola Press.
———. 1995. *If the Drum Is a Woman*. New York: Bola Press.
———. 1996. *Somewhere in Advance of Nowhere*. New York: High Risk Books.
Cortez, Jayne, Paul Buhle, Nancy Joyce Peters, et al., eds. 1982. *Free Spirits: Annals of the Insurgent Imagination*. San Francisco: City Lights.
———, and Ted Joans. 1982. *Merveilleux Coup de Foudre Poetry of Jayne Cortez and Ted Joans*. Paris: Handshake Editions.
———, and Mel Edwards. 1994. *Fragments*. New York: Bola Press. Photographs of sculpture by Mel Edwards and poetry by Jayne Cortez.

Nancy Cunard

Cunard, Nancy. 1925. *Parallax*. London: Hogarth Press.
———. 1931. *Black Man and White Ladyship*. Paris: Privately published.
———. 1934. *Negro: An Anthology*. London: Wishart, 1934. Reprinted in paperback, edited and abridged, with an introduction by Hugh Ford (New York: Frederick Ungar, 1970).
———, and George Padmore. 1942. *The White Man's Duty: An Analysis of the Colonial Question in the Light of the Atlantic Charter*. London: W. H. Allen.
———. 1969. *These Were the Hours: Memories of My Hours Press, Réanville and Paris, 1928–1931*. Edited with a foreword by Hugh Ford. Carbondale: Southern Illinois University Press.

Charters, James. 1965. *Hemingway's Paris*. New York: Tower Books. First published in 1938.
Ford, Hugh, ed. 1968. *Nancy Cunard: Brave Poet, Indomitable Rebel, 1896–1965*. Philadelphia: Chilton.
Garvey, Marcus. 1974. "An Apostrophe to Miss Nancy Cunard." In John Hendrik Clarke and Amy Jacque Garvey, eds., *Marcus Garvey and the Vision of Africa*, 314–316. New York: Vintage. (Garvey's text is dated 1932.)
Chisholm, Ann. 1979. *Nancy Cunard: A Biography*. New York: Knopf.

Lise Deharme

Deharme, Lise. 1933. *Cahier de curieuse personne*. Paris: Editions des Cahiers libres.
———. 1937. *Le Coeur de pic*. With photographs by Claude Cahun. Paris: José Corti.
———, André Breton, Julien Gracq, and Jean Tardieu. 1954. *Farouche a quatre feilles*. Paris: Grasset.
Lise Deharme. 1955. *Le Poids d'un Oiseau*. Paris: Le Terrain vague.
Pieyre de Mandiargues, André. 1977. "Lise Deharme." In *La Femme surréaliste*, 93–97.
Legrand, Gérard. 1982. "Lise Deharme." In *Dictionnaire Général du surréalisme*.

Rikki Ducornet

Ducornet, Rikki. 1974. *From the Star Chamber*. Frederickton, New Brunswick: Fiddlehead Poetry Books.
———. 1975. *Wild Geraniums*. Deal, Kent, U.K.: Actual Size Press.
———. 1976. *Weird Sisters*. Vancouver: Intermedia.
———. 1977. *Knife Notebook*. Vancouver: Fiddlehead Poetry Books.
———. 1979. *The Illustrated Universe*. Toronto: AYA Press.
———. 1984. *The Stain*. New York: Grove Press.
———. 1986. *Entering Fire*. London: Chatto & Windus.
———. 1989. *The Fountains of Neptune*. Toronto: McClelland & Stewart.
———. 1993. *The Jade Cabinet*. Normal, IL: Dalkey Archive.
———. 1989. *The Cult of Seizure*. Erin, Ontario: Porcupine Quill.
———. 1994. *The Complete Butcher's Tales*. Normal, IL: Dalkey Archive.
———. 1995. *Phosphor in Dreamland*. Normal, IL: Dalkey Archive.
———. 1997. *The Word "Desire."* New York: Henry Holt.
Matthews, J. H. 1989. "Rikki Ducornet's No-nonsense Almost Fairy Tales," *Symposium*, special issue on surrealism, XLI, 312–327.

Ikbal El Alailly

El Alailly, Ikbal. 1945. *Vertu de l'Allemagne*. Cairo: Editions Masses.

Nicole Espagnol

Espagnol, Nicole. 1982. *Little Magie.* Paris: Editions Bordas. Illustrated by Jorge Camacho.

Anne Ethuin

Ethuin, Anne, and Edouard Jaguer. 1977. *Regards obliques sur une histoire parallele.* Paris: Oasis.

Kral, Petr. 1982. "Anne Ethuin." In *Dictionnaire Général du surréalisme.*

"Anne Ethuin." 1985. In *Das surrealistische Gedicht,* 417–423.

Alice Farley

Farley, Alice. 1976. *Surrealist Dance.* Chicago, Gallery Black Swan. Includes texts by Paul Garon, Joseph Jablonski, Philip Lamantia, Franklin Rosemont, Laurence Weisberg and others.

———. 1977. *In(Visible Woman).* New York: Theater for the New City.

———. 1977. *Surrealist Dance.* Evanston: The Norris Center, Northwestern University.

Matthews, J. H. 1982. "Alice Farley." In *Dictionnaire Général du surréalisme.*

La Mama Etc. Presents Alice Farley Dance Theater: Imaginary Ancestors and Daphne of the Dunes. 1994. New York: Performance program.

Leila Ferraz

Ferraz, Leila. 1965. "Das Possibilidades do vampirismo." In the program for the series of "terror" films at the Cinemateca Brasileira, Rio de Janeiro.

Marcelle Ferry

Ferry, Marcelle. 1938. *L'Ile d'un jour.* Paris: Editions Surréalistes.

Renée Gauthier

Aragon, Louis. 1924. "Une vague de rêves," *Commerce* II (Autumn): 118–119.

Breton, André. 1924. *Les Pas perdus.* Paris: Gallimard.

"Renée Gauthier." 1987. In *La Femme et le surréalisme,* 501.

Giovanna

Giovanna (as Anna Voggi). 1976. *William Blake, "Innocence et Experience."* Paris: Le Soleil Noir. Illustrated by Giovanna.

———. 1977. *Deus ex machina.* Paris: Le récipiendaire.

Giovanna (as Anna Voggi) and Jean-Michel Goutier. 1995. *Pacifique que ça!* Paris: La Goutte d'Eau.

Goutier, Jean-Michel. 1967. "Le Mulhiou, ou comment Giovanna détourne la machine à écrire." In *L'Archibras: le surréalisme* 1 (April): 46–48; reprinted in *La Femme surréaliste,* 130–131.

Jaguer, Edouard. 1982. "Giovanna." In *Dictionnaire Général du surréalisme.*

"Giovanna." 1987. In *La Femme et le surréalisme,* 501.

Silvia Grénier

Grénier, Silvia. 1983. *Salomé o la búsqueda del cuerpo.* Buenos Aires: Signo Ascendente.

———. 1986. *Los banquetes errantes (diario de viajes).* Buenos Aires: Ediciones Signo Ascendante.

Anneliese Hager

Jaguer, Edouard. 1982. *Les Mystères de la chambre noire: le surréalisme et la photographie.* Paris: Flammarion.

Neusüss, Floris M. 1990. *Das Fotogramm in der Kunst des 20. Jahrhunderts.* Cologne: DuMont.

Lenk, Elisabeth, and Rita Bischof, eds. 1991. *Die rote Uhr und andere Dichtungen.* Zurich: Arche.

Irène Hamoir

Hamoir, Irène [known as Irine]. 1949. *Oeuvre poétique (1930–1945).* Saint-Generou près Saint Julien de Voventes: Maitre François, editeur.

———. 1976. *Corne de brune.* Brussels.

Jaguer, Edouard. 1982. "Irène Hamoir." In *Dictionnaire Général du surréalisme.*

Vera Hérold

"Vera Hérold." 1987. In *La Femme et le surréalisme,* 501.

Pastoureau, Henri. 1992. *Ma Vie surréaliste.* Paris: Maurice Nadeau.

Théolleyre, Jean-Marc. 1995. "Le procès du 'réseau Jeanson.'" *Le Monde,* 11 September.

Laurence Iché

Iché, Laurence. 1942. *Au fil du vent.* Paris: Les Editions de la Main à Plume. Illustrated by Oscar Dominguez.

———. 1943. *Etagère en flamme.* Paris: Les Pages Libres de la Main à Plume. Illustrated by Picasso.

Faure, Michel. 1982. *Histoire du surréalisme sous l'Occupation.* Paris: La Table Ronde.

Jacqueline Johnson

Dynaton Before and Beyond. 1992. Exhibition catalog. Malibu: Frederick R. Weisman Museum of Art, Pepperdine University.

Luiza Neto Jorge

Jorge, Luiza Neto. 1993. *Poesia.* Introduction by Fernando Cabral Martins. Lisbon: Assirio & Alvim.

Frida Kahlo

Kahlo, Frida. 1995. *The Diary of Frida Kahlo: An Intimate Self-Portrait.* Introduction by Carlos Fuentes. Essay and commentaries by Sarah M. Lowe. New York: Abrams.

Breton, André. 1972. *Surrealism and Painting,* 141–144.

Tiberghien, Gilles A. 1982. "Frida Kahlo." In *Dictionnaire Général du surréalisme.*

Herrera, Hayden. 1983. *Frida: A Biography.* New York: Harper & Row.

"Frida Kahlo." 1987. In *La Femme et le surréalisme,* 234–241.

Images of Frida Kahlo. 1989. Box of postcard reproductions, with booklet introduction by Angela Carter. London: Redstone Press.

Simone Kahn

Pastoureau, Henri. 1992. *Ma Vie surréaliste.* Paris: Maurice Nadeau.

Nelly Kaplan

Kaplan, Nelly (as Belen). 1960. *La Reine des Sabbats.* Illustrations by Le Maréchal. Paris: Losfeld.

——— (as Belen). 1966. *Le Réservoir des sens.* Preface by Philippe Soupault. Illustrations by André Masson. Paris: La Jeune Parque.

———. 1971. *Le Collier de Ptyx.* Paris: Pauvert.

——— (as Belen). 1973. *Memoires d'une liseuse de draps.* Paris: Pauvert.

Soupault, Philippe. 1977. "Qui est Belen?" In *La Femme surréaliste,* 67–68.

Sebbag, Georges. 1997. *Le Point Sublime: Breton, Rimbaud, Kaplan.* Paris: Jean-Michel Place.

Ida Kar

Kar, Ida. 1962. "Ida Kar: An Interview." *British Journal of Photography*, 16 March.

Williams, Val. 1989. *Ida Kar, Photographer: 1908–1974*. London: Virago Press.

Greta Knutson

Chénieux-Gendron, Jacqueline. 1977. "Greta Knutson retour amont." In *La Femme surréaliste*, 157–164.

Carassou, Michel. "Greta Knutson." 1982. In *Dictionnaire Général du surréalisme*.

"Greta Knutson." 1987. In *La Femme et le surréalisme*, 503.

Jacqueline Lamba

Lamba, Jacqueline. 1975. "La rencontre Trotsky-Breton." *Les Lettres Nouvelles* 4/75 (September/October): 99–111.

Jaguer, Edouard. 1982. "Jacqueline Lamba." In *Dictionnaire Général du surréalisme*.

"Jacqueline Lamba." 1987. In *La Femme et le surréalisme*, 503.

Annie Le Brun

Le Brun, Annie. 1967. *Sur-le-champ*. Illustrations by Toyen. Paris: Editions Surréalistes.

———. 1970. *Les Mots font l'amour (Citations surréalistes)*. Paris: Eric Losfeld.

———. 1972. *Les pâles et fiévreux après-midi des villes*. Paris: Editions Maintenant.

———. 1972. *Tout près, les nomades*. Illustrations by Toyen. Paris: Editions Maintenant.

———. 1974. *Les Ecureuils de l'orange*. Paris: Editions Maintenant.

———. 1977. *Annulaire de lune*. Illustrations by Toyen. Paris: Editions Maintenant.

———. 1977. *Lâchez tout*. Paris: Editions Le Sagittaire.

———. 1982. *Les Châteaux de la subversion*. Paris: Pauvert.

———. 1984. *A Distance*. Paris: Pauvert.

———. 1988. *Appel d'air*. Paris: Plon.

———, ed. 1989. *Petits et grands théâtres du marquis de Sade*. Paris: Paris Art Center.

———. 1990. *Vagit-prop, Lâchez tout et autre textes*. Paris: Pauvert.

———. 1991. *Qui vive: Considérations actuelles sur l'inactualité du surréalisme*. Paris: Pauvert.

———. 1991. *Sade: A Sudden Abyss*. Translated by Camille Naish. San Francisco: City Lights. Originally published in 1986 as *Soudain un bloc d'abime, Sade*, the introductory volume to Sade's *Oeuvres complètes* (Paris: Jean-Jacques Pauvert).

———. 1996. *Jean Benoit*. Paris: Galérie 1900–2000.

Hubert, Renée Riese. 1977. "Annie Le Brun et Toyen." In *La Femme surréaliste*, 174.

Legrand, Gérard. 1982. "Annie Le Brun." In *Dictionnaire Général du surréalisme*.

"Annie Le Brun." 1985. In *Das surrealistische Gedicht,* 691–699.
"Annie Le Brun." 1987. In *La Femme et le surréalisme,* 503.

Sheila Legge

Remy, Michel. 1982. "Sheila Legge." In *Dictionnaire Général du surréalisme.*

Elisabeth Lenk

Lenk, Elisabeth. 1965. "Suite à l'affaire Heidegger." In *La Brèche: Action surréaliste* no. 8 (November): 44–51.
———. 1971. *Der springende Narziss: André Bretons poetischer Materialismus.* Munich: Rogner & Bernhard.
———, and Rita Bischof, eds. 1991. *Die rote Uhr und andere Dichtungen.* Zurich: Arche.

Denise Lévy

Lévy, Denise (as Denise Naville), Pierre Naville, and Jean van Heijenoort, eds. 1989. *Leon Trotsky: Correspondence, 1929–1939.* Paris: L'Harmattan.
Bonnet, Marguerite. 1975. *André Breton: Naissance de l'aventure surréaliste.* Paris: José Corti.
Naville, Pierre. 1977. "Les traductions de Denise Naville." In *Le temps du surréel,* 479–481. Paris: Editions Galilée.

Gina Litherland

Litherland, Gina. 1989. "The Politics of Looking" (Review of *Caught Looking: Feminism, Pornography and Censorship*). In *Arsenal: Surrealist Subversion* no. 4:70. Chicago: Black Swan Press.

Mary Low

Low, Mary, and Juan Breá. 1937. *Red Spanish Notebook: The First Six Months of the Revolution and the Civil War.* London: Secker and Warburg, Introduction by C. L. R. James. New edition, San Francisco: City Lights, 1979, Introduction by E. F. Granell.
Mary Low. 1939. *La Saison des flutes.* Paris: Editions Surréalistes; reissued in Paris by Arabie-sur-Seine, 1991, with a preface by Edouard Jaguer.
———. 1943. *La Verdad contemporanea.* Havana. Preface by Benjamin Péret. Introduction by Roberto Pérez Santiesteban.
———. 1957. *Tres Voces, Three Voices, Trois Voix.* Preface by Augustin Tamargo. Cover by J. M. Mijares. Havana: Editorial Sanchez.

——— (as Mary Machado). 1975. *In Caesar's Shadow.* Elizabeth, NJ: American Press.
——— (as Mary Machado). 1981. *El Triunfo de la vida/Alive In Spite Of.* Preface by Cristobal A. Zamora. Miami: Ediciones del Tauro.
———. 1983. *Dossier Surrealismo.* In *Guangara Libertaria* (Miami), IV: 16, October, 7–11.
———. 1984. *A Voice in Three Mirrors.* Collages by the Author. Cover by J. M. Mijares. Chicago: Black Swan Press.
———. 1986. *Alquimia del recuerdo.* Preface by A. Baeza Flores. Drawings by Wifredo Lam. Madrid: Editorial Playor; first published in Cuba, 1946.
———, ed. 1991. *Poèmes d'alor.* Poems by Juan Breá. Paris: Collection Phases/Arabie-sur-Seine. Introduction by Mary Low. Frontispiece by Perahim. Illustrations by Dominique Lambert.
———. 1994. *Where the Wolf Sings.* Chicago: Black Swan Press. Afterword by Franklin Rosemont. Collages by the author.
——— (as Mary Machado). 1996. *On Caesar's Trail.* Miami: *Classics Chronicle.*
Jaguer, Edouard. "Mary Low." 1982. In *Dictionnaire Général du surréalisme.*
———. 1984. "La Saison des flutes," *Ellebore* 8, Paris, 37–38.

Maruja Mallo

Aranda, Francisco. 1981. *El Surrealismo Español.* Barcelona: Editorial Lumen.
Jaguer, Edouard. 1982. "Maruja Mallo." In *Dictionnaire Général du surréalisme.*
Maruja Mallo, 1992. Madrid: Guillermo de Osma Galeria.

Petra Mandal

Mandal, Petra. 1987. *Halla I Huvut.* Stockholm: Surrealistförlaget.

Joyce Mansour

Mansour, Joyce. 1958. *Les Gisants Satisfaits.* Paris: Pauvert.
———. 1960. *Rapaces.* Paris: Seghers.
———. 1968. *Le Bleu de Fonds.* Paris: Le Soleil Noir.
———. 1969. *Phallus et Momies.* La Louvière, Belgium: Daily-Bul.
———. 1970. *Ça.* Paris: Le Soleil Noir.
———. 1978. *Flash Card.* Translated by Mary Beach. Cherry Valley, NY: Cherry Valley Editions. Originally published in 1965 as *Carré Blanc* (Paris: Le Soleil Noir).
———, and Ted Joans. 1978. *Flying Piranha.* New York: Bola Press. Cover by Cogollo.
Joyce Mansour. 1991. *Julius Caesar.* Translated by Peter Wood. Paris: Hourglass. Originally published in 1958 as *Jules César* (Paris: Seghers).

———. 1992. *Floating Islands.* Translation of the second tale by Guy Flandre and Peter Wood. Paris: Hourglass. Originally published in 1973 as *Histories nocives: Jules César, Iles flottantes* (Paris: Gallimard).
———. 1993. *Shrieks.* Translated by Peter Wood and Guy Flandre. Paris: Hourglass. Originally published in 1954 as *Cris* (Paris: Seghers).
Hubert, Renée Riese. 1958. "Three Women Poets," *Yale French Studies* 21 (Spring–Summer): 40–48.
Matthews, J. H. 1969. *Surrealist Poetry in France.* Syracuse: Syracuse University Press.
Lambert, Jean-Clarence. 1982. "Joyce Mansour." In *Dictionnaire Général du surréalisme.*
"Joyce Mansour." 1985. In *Das surrealistische Gedicht,* 782–791.

Maria Martins

Breton, André. 1972. *Surrealism and Painting,* 318–321.
Jaguer, Edouard. 1982. "Maria." In *Dictionnaire Général du surréalisme.*

Marie-Dominique Massoni

Massoni, Marie-Dominique. 1995. *Toujours à retardement.* Lyon: Atelier de creation libertaire.
———, and Guy Girard. 1995. *La Diagonale du Père Lachaise.* Paris: Le Chemin de la cave.

Jeanne Megnen

Megnen, Jeanne. 1938. *O rouge! O delivrée!* Paris: G.L.M.

Isabel Meyrelles

Meyrelles, Isabel. 1951. *Em vox baixa.* Lisbon: Privately published.
———. 1954. *Palavras Nocturnas.* Lisbon: Privately published.
———. 1966. *O Rost Deserto.* Lisbon: Privately published.
———, ed. 1971. *Anthologie de poésie portugaise en langue française.* Paris: Gallimard.
———. 1976. *Le Livre du Tigre.* Paris: Privately published.
Cesariny, Mario. 1981. *Poets of Surrealism in Portugal.* Honolulu: Mele.
Jaguer, Edouard. 1982. "Portugal." In *Dictionnaire Général du surréalisme.*

Nora Mitrani

Mitrani, Nora. 1988. *Rose au coeur violet.* Edited by Dominique Rabourdin. Preface by Julien Gracq. Paris: Le terrain vague.

Suzanne Muzard

Rabourdin, Dominique. 1992. "Suzanne Muzard, 1900–1992," *Docsur* no. 21 (March).

Nadja

Breton, André. 1960. *Nadja.* Translated by Richard Howard. New York: Grove Press. Originally published in 1928 (Paris: Gallimard).

Lambert, Jean-Clarence. 1982. "Nadja." In *Dictionnaire Général du surréalisme.*

Alena Nádvorníková

Nádvorníková, Alena. 1990. *Les Miroirs des Fantomes: Discours sur la photographie.* Paris: Hourglass.

———. 1994. *Praha, Pařížská.* Prague: Votobia.

———. 1995. *Uvnitř hlasů.* Prague: Cesky Spisovatel.

Alena Nádvorníková. 1994. Exhibition catalog. Olomouc: Olomouc Art Museum.

Meret Oppenheim

Oppenheim, Meret. 1981. *Sansibar.* Basle: Fanal.

Orenstein, Gloria. 1977. "Meret Oppenheim." In *La Femme surréaliste,* 198.

Pieyre de Mandiargues, André. 1977. "Meret Oppenheim." In *La Femme surréaliste,* 195–197.

Jaguer, Edouard. 1982. "Meret Oppenheim." In *Dictionnaire Général du surréalisme.*

"Meret Oppenheim." 1987. In *La Femme et le surréalisme,* 298–309.

Curiger, Bice. 1989. *Meret Oppenheim, Defiance in the Face of Freedom.* Translated by Catherine Schelbert. Cambridge: MIT Press.

Burckhardt, Jacqueline, and Bice Curiger, eds. 1996. *Meret Oppenheim: Beyond the Teacup.* New York: Independent Curators.

Olga Orozco

Orozco, Olga. 1984. *Paginas de Olga Orozco, seleccionadas por la autora.* Buenos Aires: Editorial Celtia.

Grace W. Pailthorpe

Pailthorpe, Grace W. 1932. *Studies in the Psychology of Delinquency.* London: His Majesty's Stationery Office.

———. 1932. *What We Put in Prison and in Preventive Reserve Homes.* London: Williams and Norgate.

Les Enfants d'Alice: la peinture surréaliste en Angleterre, 1930–1960. 1982. Paris: Galerie 1900–2000, 76–78. Texts by Edouard Jaguer and Michel Remy.
Remy, Michel. 1982. "Grace Pailthorpe." In *Dictionnaire Général du surréalisme.*
Gunston, Rose. Ca. 1985. *Surrealism and Beyond: A Symbiosis of Psychology and Art in the Work of Grace Pailthorpe.* Research paper provided by the Murry Feely/John Bonham Fine Art Gallery in London.
"Grace Pailthorpe." 1987. In *La Femme et le surréalisme,* 311.

Gertrude Pape

Pape, Gertrude (as Evelyn Palmer). 1944. *Verses of a Female Robinson Crusoe.* Privately printed.
———. 1981. *Die Schone Zakdoek.* Amsterdam: Meulenhoff.
de Vries, Her, and Laurens Vancrevel, eds. 1988. *Surrealistische Ontmoetingen.* Amsterdam: Meulenhoff.
———, and Laurens Vancrevel, eds. 1989. *De automatische verbeelding.* Amsterdam: Meulenhoff.
Pape Gertrude. 1995. "Gertrude Pape," unpublished biographical sketch.

Mimi Parent

Breton, André. 1972. *Surrealism and Painting,* 391.
Pierre, José. 1977. "Mimi Parent." In *La Femme surréaliste,* 201.
Kral, Petr. 1982. "Mimi Parent." In *Dictionnaire Général du surréalisme.*
Mimi Parent. 1984. Exhibition catalog. Bochum: Museum Bochum. Texts by Peter Spielman, José Pierre, Pierre Cadare, Milan Napravnik, Annie Le Brun, Radovan Ivsic, and Heribert Becker.
"Mimi Parent." 1987. In *La Femme et le surréalisme,* 314–317, 506.

Valentine Penrose

Penrose, Valentine. 1935. *Herbe à la lune.* Paris: G.L.M.
———. 1936. *Le Nouveau Candide.* Paris: G.L.M.
———. 1937. *Poèmes.* Paris: G.L.M.
———. 1937. *Sorts de la Lueur.* Paris: G.L.M.
———. 1945. *Martha's Opera.* Paris: Fontaine.
———. 1951. *Dons de feminines.* Paris: Librairie "Les pas perdus."
———. 1970. *The Bloody Countess.* Translated by Alexander Trocchi. London: Calder & Boyars. Originally published in 1957 as *Erzsébet Bathory, la Comtesse Sanglante* (Paris: Mercure de France).
———. 1972. *Les Magies.* Paris: Les main libres. Illustrations by Miro.
———. 1977. *Poems & Narrations.* Translated by Roy Edwards. Manchester: Carcanet Press.

Jaguer, Edouard. 1982. "Valentine Penrose." In *Dictionnaire Général du surréalisme.*
Penrose, Roland. 1983. *80 Ans du surréalisme.* Paris: Cercle d'Art.
"Valentine Penrose." 1985. In *Das surrealistische Gedicht,* 1005–1011.
Peuchmaurd, Pierre. 1995. "Valentine Penrose." In *Le Cerceau* no. 5 (Spring): 6–7.

Nancy Joyce Peters

Peters, Nancy Joyce. 1978. *It's In the Wind.* Chicago: Black Swan Press, Surrealist Research & Development Monograph Series, no. 10. With papercuts by Mado Spiegler.
———, and Lawrence Ferlinghetti, eds. 1980. *Literary San Francisco.* San Francisco: Harper & Row.
———, Paul Buhle, Jayne Cortez, et al., eds. 1982. *Free Spirits: Annals of the Insurgent Imagination.* San Francisco: City Lights.
Peters, Nancy Joyce, ed. 1992. *War After War,* special issue of *City Lights Review* on the Persian Gulf War. San Francisco: City Lights.
"Nancy Joyce Peters." 1985. In *Das surrealistische Gedicht,* 1042–1045.

Helen Phillips

Calas, Nicolas. 1947. *Bloodflames 1947,* exhibition catalog. New York: Hugo Gallery.

Katerina Piňosová

Solarik, Bruno. 1996. "Katerina Piňosová." In *Obratnik: poetická revue.* Prague, II:13.

Alejandra Pizarnik

Pizarnik, Alejandra. 1982. *Poemas.* Medellín: Editorial Endymion.

Irene Plazewska

Plazewska, Irene. 1985. *Ironed Wood.* Dublin: self-published.
———. 1989. *Plumed Tunafish.* Dublin: self-published.
———. 1996. *Purchased Moon.* Dublin: self-published.

Gisèle Prassinos

Prassinos, Gisèle. 1935. *Le feu maniaque.* Paris: Collection Sagesse.
———. 1935. *La sauterelle arthritique.* Paris: G.L.M.
———. 1935. *Une demande en mariage.* Paris: G.L.M.
———. 1936. *Quand le bruit travaille.* Paris: G.L.M.
———. 1937. *Facilité crépusculaire.* Paris: Editions René Debresse.

———. 1938. *La lutte double.* Paris: G.L.M.
———. 1938. *Une belle famille.* Paris: G.L.M.
———. 1939. *La revanche.* Paris: G.L.M.
———. 1939. *Le feu maniaque,* expanded edition. Paris: R. J. Godet.
———. 1939. *Sondue.* Paris: G.L.M.
———. 1947. *La rêve.* Paris: Editions Fontaine.
Breton, André. 1966. *Anthologie de l'humour noir.* Paris: Jean-Jacques Pauvert.
Chénieux, Jacqueline. 1977. "Gisèle Prassinos disqualifiée disqualifiante." In *La Femme surréaliste,* 207–215.
van Hirtum, Marianne. 1982. "Gisèle Prassinos." In *Dictionnaire Général du surréalisme.*
"Gisèle Prassinos." 1985. In *Das surrealistische Gedicht,* 1083–1091.
"Gisèle Prassinos." 1987. In *La Femme et le surréalisme,* 329–331.

Alice Rahon

Rahon, Alice (as Alice Paalen). 1936. *A même la terre.* Paris: Editions Surréalistes.
——— (as Alice Paalen). 1938. *Sablier Couché.* Paris: Editions Sagesse.
——— (as Alice Paalen). 1941. *Animal noir.* Mexico City: Editions Dolores La Rue.
"Alice Rahon." 1985. In *Das surrealistische Gedicht.*
Alice Rahon: Exposicion Antologica. 1986. Exhibition catalog. Mexico City: Museo del Palacio de Bellas Artes. Texts by César Moro, Lourdes Andrade, and others.
"Alice Rahon." 1987. In *La Femme et le surréalisme,* 336–341, 506.
Deffebach, Nancy. 1991. "Alice Rahon: Poems of Light and Shadow, Painting in Free Verse," *On the Bus,* double issue 8–9, III:2 and IV:1:173–196.
Hubert, Renée Riese. 1994. *Magnifying Mirrors: Women, Surrealism and Partnership.* Lincoln: University of Nebraska Press.

Regine Raufast

Dotremont, Christian. 1946. "Regine Raufast, la reine des murs, est morte." In *Suractuel* (July); reprinted in facsimile in Mariën 1979 (see Other Works Consulted, below).
Faure, Michel. 1982. *Histoire du surréalisme sous l'Occupation.* Paris: La Table Ronde.

Judit Reigl

Breton, André. 1972. *Surrealism and Painting.*
Passeron, René. 1982. "Judit Reigl." In *Dictionnaire Général du surréalisme.*

Thérèse Renaud

Renaud, Thérèse. 1946. *Les Sables du Rêve.* Montréal: Les Cahiers de la file indienne.
———. 1978. *Une mémoire déchirée.*
———. 1981. *Plaisirs immobiles.*

———. 1988. *Le choc d'un murmure.*
———. 1988. *Subterfuges e Sortilèges.*
———. 1990. *Jardins d'éclats.*
Jaguer, Edouard. 1982. "Thérèse Renaud." In *Dictionnaire Général du surréalisme.*

Edith Rimmington

Remy, Michel, and Edouard Jaguer. 1982. "Edith Rimmington." In *Les Enfants d'Alice: la peinture surréaliste en Angleterre, 1930–1960,* 89. Paris: Galerie 1900–2000.
"Edith Rimmington." 1985. In *Das surrealistische Gedicht,* 1132–1135.
"Edith Rimmington." 1987. In *La Femme et le surréalisme,* 362, 506.

Penelope Rosemont

Rosemont, Penelope, and Franklin Rosemont. 1967. "Situation du surrealisme en états-unis," *L'Archibras: le surréalisme* no. 2 (October): 73–75.
Rosemont, Penelope. 1970. *Athanor.* Chicago: Surrealist Editions.
———, Paul Buhle, Jayne Cortez, et al., eds. 1982. *Free Spirits: Annals of the Insurgent Imagination.* San Francisco: City Lights.
Rosemont, Penelope. 1992. *Beware of the Ice and Other Poems.* Chicago: Surrealist Editions. Drawings by Enrico Baj.
———, ed. 1997. Introduction to Mary MacLane, *The Story of Mary MacLane and Other Writings.* Chicago: Charles H. Kerr.
———. 1998. *Surrealist Experiences: 1001 Dawns and 221 Midnights.* Chicago: Black Swan Press. Foreword by Rikki Ducornet.
———, Franklin Rosemont, and Paul Garon, eds. 1997. *The Forecast Is Hot! Tracts and Other Collective Declarations of the Surrealist Movement in the United States, 1966–1976.* Chicago: Black Swan Press.
Mansour, Joyce. 1970. "A comme *Athanor.*" *Bulletin de liaison surréaliste* 1 (November): 12.
Jaguer, Edouard. 1982. "Penelope Rosemont." In *Dictionnaire Général du surréalisme.*
———. 1982. *Les Mystères de la chambre noire: le surréalisme et la photographie.* Paris: Flammarion.
———. 1983. Preface to *Penelope Rosemont: Surrealism Now & Forever!* Catalog of an exhibition at Platypus Gallery, Evanston, IL.
———. 1989. "Penelope Rosemont." In *Arsenal: Surrealist Subversion,* no. 4, 92–93. Chicago: Black Swan Press.
"Penelope Rosemont." 1985. In *Das surrealistische Gedicht,* 1160–1164.
Schwarz, Arturo. 1986. *Arte e alchimia.* Venice: Venice Biennale.
"Penelope Rosemont." 1987. In *La Femme et le surréalisme,* 506.
Neusüss, Floris M. 1990. *Das Fotogramm in der Kunst des 20. Jahrhunderts.* Cologne: DuMont.

Kay Sage

Sage, Kay. 1957. *Demain, Monsieur Silber.* Paris: Seghers.

———. 1957. *The More I Wonder.* New York: Bookman Associates.

———. 1959. *Faut dire c'qui est.* Paris: Debresse-Poésie.

———. 1962. *Mordicus.* Paris: privately printed.

———, ed. 1963. *Yves Tanguy, A Summary of His Works.* New York: Pierre Matisse.

———. 1997. *China Eggs/Les Oeufs de porcelaine.* Edited by Judith Suther. Bilingual; French translation by Elisabeth Manuel. Charlotte/Seattle: Starbooks/Editions de L'Etoile.

Kay Sage: Retrospective Exhibition. 1960. Exhibition catalog. New York: Catherine Viviano Gallery.

Breton, André. 1972. *Surrealism and Painting,* 82.

Kay Sage. 1977. Exhibition catalog. Ithaca: Herbert F. Johnson Museum of Art. Introduction by Régine Tessler Krieger.

Matthews, J. H. 1982. "Kay Sage." In *Dictionnaire Général du surréalisme.*

"Kay Sage." 1987. In *La Femme et le surréalisme,* 363–367, 507.

Sonia Sekula

Sekula, Sonia. 1996. *Sonja Sekula, Im Zeichen der Frage, im Zeichen der Antwort.* Basel: Lenos Verlag. Edited and introduced by Roger Perret.

Duits, Charles. 1969. *André Breton a-t-il dit passe.* Paris: Les Lettres Nouvelles.

Schwartz, Dieter. 1996. *Sonja Sekula.* Exhibition catalog. New York: The Swiss Institute.

Jacqueline Senard

Pierre, José, ed. 1983. *Surréalisme et anarchie.* Paris: Plasma.

"Jacqueline Duprey." 1987. In *La Femme et le surréalisme,* 500. Exhibition catalog. Lausanne: Musée cantonal es Beaux-Arts.

Françoise Sullivan

Sullivan, Françoise. 1978. *Dance in the Snow: A Portfolio.* Montréal: privately printed.

Françoise Sullivan: Retrospective. 1981. Exhibition catalog. Montréal: Musée de'art contemporain. Texts by Martine Bousquet-Mongeau, Claude Gosselin and David Moore.

Jaguer, Edouard. 1982. "Françoise Sullivan." In *Dictionnaire Général du surréalisme.*

Récital de danse de Françoise Sullivan et Jeanne Renaud: 1948–1988. 1988. Performance program. Montréal: Musée d'art contemporain.

Françoise Sullivan. 1993. Exhibition catalog. Montréal: Musée de Québec. Texts by Louise Déry and Jean Dumont.

Eva Sulzer

"Eva Sulzer." 1987. In *La Femme et le surréalisme*, 507.

Eva Švankmajerová

Švankmajerová, Eva. *Jeskyně Baradla*. 1981. Geneva: Coopérative d'Impressions Nouvelles.
———. 1982. *Desátý Dům*. Prague: Privately published.
———. 1987. *Samoty a citace*. Geneva: Coopérative d'impressions Nouvelles.
———. 1991. *Cisařský Řez*. Prague: Gallery Vaclava Spaly.
———. 1995. *Jeskyně Baradla*. Prague: Edice Analogonu.
Césarienne. 1978. Exhibition catalog. Paris: Le Triskèle. Preface by Vratislav Effenberger.
Kral, Petr. 1982. "Eva Švankmajerová." In *Dictionnaire Général du surréalisme*.
Eva et Jan Švankmajer. Bouillonnements cachés: tableaux, dessins, gravures, collages, ceramiques, objets et films. 1987. Brabant, Belgium: Editions Confédération Parascolaire. Texts by Vratislav Effenberger, Alena Nádvorníková, Martin Stejskal and others.

Dorothea Tanning

Tanning, Dorothea. 1977. *The Abyss*. New York: Standard Editions.
———. 1986. *Birthday*. San Francisco: Lapis.
Plazy, Gilles. 1976. *Dorothea Tanning*. New York: Filipacchi.
Matthews, J. H. 1982. "Dorothea Tanning." In *Dictionnaire Général du surréalisme*.
Bailly, Jean-Christophe. 1985. *Dorothea Tanning*. Translated from the French by Richard Howard. New York: Braziller.
"Dorothea Tanning." 1987. In *La Femme et le surréalisme*, 382–386.

Debra Taub

Taub, Debra. 1980. "Dance and the Transformation of the World," in *Surrealism and Its Popular Accomplices*. Edited by Franklin Rosemont, 87–90. San Francisco: City Lights Books.
Debra Taub. 1983. Exhibition catalog, Platypus Gallery, Evanston, IL.

Lucie Thésée

Damas, Léon-Gontran. 1947. *Poètes d'expression française, 1900–1945*. Paris: Editions du Seuil.

Toyen

Toyen. 1945. *Tir*. Twelve drawings, with a text by Karel Teige and a poem by Jindrich Heisler. Prague: Borovy.

———. 1947. *Cache-toi guerre!* Nine drawings, with a poem by Jindrich Heisler. Prague: Borovy.

———. 1967. *Débris de rêves,* twelve drawings, with *Le Puits dans la tour,* poems by Radovan Ivsic. Paris: Editions Surréalistes.

———. 1973. *Vis-à-vis*. Twelve collages. Paris: Editions Maintenant.

———. 1974. *Specters of the Desert.* Surrealist Research & Development Monograph Series. Chicago: Black Swan Press. Originally published in 1939 as *Les Spectres du désert* (Paris: Albert Skira). Twelve drawings, with a poem by Jindrich Heisler.

Breton, André, Jindrich Heisler, and Benjamin Péret. 1953. *Toyen*. Paris: Editions Sokolova.

Toyen. 1958. Exhibition catalog. Paris: Galérie Furstenberg. Texts by Robert Benayoun, André Breton, Yves Elléouët, Georges Goldfayn, E. L. T. Mesens, Benjamin Péret, Jean-Claude Silbermann.

Breton, André. 1972. *Surrealism and Painting,* 207–215.

Ivsic, Radovan. 1974. *Toyen*. Paris: Filipacchi.

Smejkal, Frantisek. 1982. "Toyen." In *Dictionnaire Général du surréalisme.*

von Holten, Ragnar. 1984. *Toyen*. Koping: Lindfors Forlag.

"Toyen." 1987. In *La Femme et le surréalisme,* 388–391.

Hélène Vanel

Hugnet, Georges. 1972. *Pleins et deliés: témoignages et souvenirs, 1926–1972*. Paris: Guy Authier.

"Hélène Vanel." 1987. In *La Femme et le surréalisme,* 508.

Rosemont, Franklin. 1989. "The Iris of Mists." In *Arsenal: Surrealist Subversion* no. 4, 99. Chicago: Black Swan Press.

Marianne van Hirtum

van Hirtum, Marianne. 1953. *Poèmes pour les Petit Pauvres.* Paris: Seghers.

———. 1956. *Les Insolites.* Paris: Gallimard.

———. 1976. *La Nuit Mathématique.* Paris: Rougerie.

———. 1990. *John the Pelican.* Translated from the French by Peter Wood and Guy Flandre. Paris: Hourglass Editions.

———. 1991. *Proteus Volens.* Paris: Hourglass.

Marianne van Hirtum. 1970. Exhibition catalog. Paris: Le Ranelagh. Preface by Vincent Bounoure.

Hirtum. 1972. Exhibition catalog. Paris: L'Envers du miroir. Texts by Jean-Louis Bédouin, Vincent Bounoure, Michel Zimbacca, Jorge Camacho, Roger Renaud, and Dominique Lambert.

Camus, Michel. 1977. "La Sorcière." In *La Femme surréaliste,* 143.
Caroutch, Yvonne. 1977. "Une magicienne en marge de notre temps." In *La Femme surréaliste,* 142.
Carassou, Michel. 1982. "Marianne van Hirtum." In *Dictionnaire Général du surréalisme.*
"Marianne van Hirtum." 1987. In *La Femme et le surréalisme,* 508.
Marianne van Hirtum: Peintures, dessins, objets. 1991. Exhibition catalog. Hourglass Gallery, Paris.

Blanca Varela

Varela, Blanca. 1986. *Canto villano: poesia reunida, 1949–1983.* Mexico City: Fondo de cultura economica.

Remedios Varo

Varo, Remedios (as Remedios). 1970. *De Homo Rodans.* Mexico City: Calli-Nova.
Breton, André. 1964. "Remedios Varo," *La Brèche: Action surréaliste* no. 7 (December): inside front cover.
Paz, Octavio & Roger Caillois. 1966. *Remedios Varo.* Mexico D.F.: Ediciones Era.
Jaguer, Edouard. 1981. *Remedios Varo.* Paris: Filipacchi.
———. 1982. "Remedios Varo." In *Dictionnaire Général du surréalisme.*
"Remedios Varo." 1987. In *La Femme et le surréalisme,* 396–401.
Kaplan, Janet. 1988. *Unexpected Journeys, The Art and Life of Remedios Varo.* New York: Abbeville Press.

Simone Yoyotte

"Simone Monnerot." 1987. In *La Femme et le surréalisme,* 505.
Rosemont, Franklin. Forthcoming. "Simone Yoyotte: Poet of *Légitime Défense.*" In Vèvè Clark and Marie-Agnès Sourieau, eds., *Re-Membering Lost Bodies: Negritude and Beyond. Antillean Women's Writings, 1930–1970.*

Haifa Zangana

Zangana, Haifa. 1991. *Through the Vast Halls of Memory.* Paris: Hourglass.

Unica Zürn

Zürn, Unica. 1954. *Hexentexte.* Berlin: Springer.
———. 1971. *Sombre printemps.* Translated from the German by Ruth Henry and Robert Valançay. Paris: Belfond.
———. 1994. *The Man of Jasmine.* Translated by Malcolm Green. London: Atlas. Published in 1971 as *L'Homme-Jasmin* (Paris: Gallimard).

Henry, Ruth. 1977. "Le printemps noir d'Unica Zürn." In *La Femme surréaliste,* 255–260.
Carassou, Michel. 1982. "Unica Zürn." In *Dictionnaire Général du surréalisme.*
"Unica Zürn." 1985. In *Das surrealistische Gedicht,* 1382–1386.
"Unica Zürn." 1987. In *La Femme et le surréalisme,* 410–414.

III. JOURNALS AND OTHER PERIODICALS (IN CHRONOLOGICAL ORDER)

A. Surrealist Publications

Littérature (Paris, 1919–1924)
La Révolution surréaliste (Paris, 1924–1929)
Que (Buenos Aires, 1926–1930)
Distances (Brussels, 1928)
Le Surréalisme au Service de la révolution (Paris, 1930–1933)
Nadrealizam danas i ovde (Belgrade, 1931–1932)
Légitime Défense (Paris, 1932)
Minotaure (Paris, 1933–1939)
Linien (Copenhagen, 1934)
Mauvais Temps (La Louvière, 1935)
Konkretion (Copenhagen, 1935–1936)
Bulletin International du Surréalisme (Prague, Canary Islands, Brussels, London, 1935–1936)
Surrealismus (Prague, 1936)
Mandragora (Santiago de Chile, 1938–1943)
El Uso de la Palabra (Lima, 1938)
London Bulletin (London, 1938–1940)
L'Invention Collective (Brussels, 1940)
Tropiques (Fort-de-France, 1941–1945)
La Main à Plume (Paris, 1941–1945)
Arson (London, 1942)
Leitmotiv (Santiago de Chile, 1942–1943)
Dyn (Mexico City, 1942–1944)
VVV (New York, 1942–1944)
Boletin Surrealista (Santiago de Chile, 1943)
Message from Nowhere (London, 1944)
La Terre n'est pas une Vallée de Larmes (Brussels, 1945)
Le Ciel Bleu (Brussels, 1945)
Troisième Convoi (Paris, 1945–1951)
La Clair de Terre (Paris, 1945)
Savoir vivre (Brussels, 1946)
Free Unions (London, 1946)
La Révolution la Nuit (Paris, 1946–1947)

Les deux soeurs (Brussels, 1946–1947)
Le Part du Sable (Cairo, 1947)
Le Surréalisme revolutionnaire (Paris, 1948)
Ciclo (Buenos Aires, 1948)
NEON (Paris, 1948–1949)
Cahiers surréalistes (Lisbon, 1948–1950)
Surrealistische Publikationem (Klagenfurt, 1950–1954)
L'Age du cinéma (Paris, 1951–1953)
A Partir de Cero (Buenos Aires, 1952–1956)
Médium: Informations surréalistes (Paris, 1952–1953)
Médium: Communication surréaliste (Paris, 1953–1955)
Les Lèvres nues (Brussels, 1954–1960)
Le Surréalisme, même (Paris, 1956–1959)
BIEF: Jonction surréaliste (Paris, 1958–1960)
Front unique (Milan, 1959–1960)
La Brèche: Action surréaliste (Paris, 1961–1965)
Rhétorique (Brussels, 1961–1966)
Brumes Blondes (Amsterdam, first series 1964–1967; new series 1968–1976)
RUpTure (Paris, 1965–1975)
L'Archibras: le surréalisme (Paris, 1967–1969)
A Phala (São Paulo, 1967)
Fulgur (Marseilles, 1968)
Surrealist Insurrection (Chicago, 1968–1972)
Analogon (Prague, 1969; resumed publication 1990)
Antinarcissus: Surrealist Conquest (San Francisco, 1969–1970)
Bulletin de liaison surréaliste (Paris, 1970–1976)
Arsenal: Surrealist Subversion (Chicago, 1970–1989)
Envoi surréaliste (Caen, 1971)
Bulletin of Surrealist Information (Chicago, 1973)
Le Désir libertaire (Paris, 1973–1982)
Surréalisme (Paris, 1977)
Surrealism: The Octopus-Typewriter (Chicago, 1978)
Le La (Geneva, 1978–1981)
Surrealist Challenge (London, 1979)
Surrealism (London, 1979)
Luz Negra: Comunicacion Surrealista (Madrid, 1979)
Melmoth (London, 1979–1980)
The Insurrectionist's Shadow (Adelaide, 1979–1980)
Hinn surrealiski uppskurdur (Reykjavik, 1980)
Signo Ascendante (Buenos Aires, 1980)
Wyk (São Paulo, 1980)
Free Spirits: Annals of the Insurgent Imagination (San Francisco, 1982)
Dies und Das (Berlin, 1984)

The Revenge of the Shadows (Adelaide, 1985)
International Surrealist Bulletin (Chicago/Stockholm, 1986; abridged Japanese edition Tokyo, 1986)
Nakna Läppar (Stockholm, 1987–1988)
Salamandra: Comunicacion surrealista (Madrid, 1987–)
Surrealist Enlightenment (Harrisburg, then Stockholm, 1988–1989)
Gambra (Prague, 1989)
Kula: Comunicacion Surrealista (Gijon, Spain, 1990)
Mannen på Gatan (Stockholm, 1991–1994)
International Surrealist Bulletin (new series, Paris, Stockholm, Madrid, 1991–)
WHAT Are You Going to Do About It? (Chicago, 1992–)
Lagarto Verde: El Surrealismo en Puerto Rico (Aguadilla, 1993–1994)
Escrituras Surrealistas (São Paulo, 1993–)
¿Que Hay de Nuevo? (Madrid, 1993–)
Intervence (Brno, 1995–1996)
Black Lamplight (Leeds, 1995–)
Stora Saltet (Stockholm, 1995–)
S.U.RR.: Surréalisme, Utopie, Rêve, Révolte (Paris, 1996–)
Manticore (Leeds, 1997–)

B. Publications Related to Surrealism

Gaceta de arte (Santa Cruz de Tenerife, 1932–1936)
Clé (Paris, 1939)
La Poesia Sorprendida (Ciudad Trujillo, 1943–1945)
Le Surréalisme-révolutionnaire (Paris, 1948)
Cobra (Brussels, 1948)
Phases (Paris, 1954–)
Climax (New Orleans, 1955–1956)
Quatorze juillet (Paris, 1958)
Boa (Buenos Aires, 1958–1960)
Documento-Sud (Naples, 1958–1962)
Edda (Brussels, 1958–1965)
The Rebel Worker (Chicago, 1964–1967)
Coupure (Paris, 1969–1971)
Flagrant Délit (Nancy, 1978–1979)
Ellebore (Paris, 1979–1984)
The Moment (Paris, 1979–1980)
Signes (Champs des activités surréalistes) (Paris, 1984–1993)
Docsur: Documents sur le surréalisme (Paris 1986–1992)
Pleine Marge (Paris, 1986–)
Le Cerceau (Paris, 1994–)
Supérieure Inconnu (Paris, 1995–)

Le Tortue-Lièvre (Montreal, 1995–)
Infosurr: Le Surréalisme et ses alentours (Paris, 1996)

C. Special Surrealist-Edited Issues of Other Publications

Variétés (Brussels, 1929)
This Quarter (Paris, September 1932)
Documents 34 (Brussels, June 1934)
Contemporary Poetry and Prose (London, June 1936)
Cahiers GLM: "Rêve" (Paris, March 1938)
View 7–8 (New York, October–November 1941)
La Nef 63–64, *Almanach surréaliste du démi-siècle* (Paris, March–April 1950).
La Rue 5–6 (Paris, June 1952)
Radical America, "Surrealism in the Service of Revolution" (Madison, January 1970).
City Lights Anthology. 1974. San Francisco: City Lights Books. "The Surrealist Movement in the United States," 199–251.
Living Blues, "Surrealism & Blues" (Chicago, January–February 1976).
Freedom: Anarchist Fortnightly, "Surrealism: The Hinge of History" (London, March 1978).
Cultural Correspondence 12–14, "Symposium: Surrealism Today & Tomorrow" (Providence, Summer 1981), 60–100.

D. Other Periodicals Consulted

The Little Review (Chicago, New York, Paris, 1914–1929)
Transition (Paris, 1927–1938)
Vu (Paris, VI:286, 6 September 1933)
The Tiger's Eye (Westport, 1947–1949)
Trafik, special issue on "Der libertäre Esprit in der surrealistischen Revolution" (Mulheim, 1989).
Opus International: André Breton et le surréalisme internationale, 123–124, (Paris, April–May 1991).

IV. EXHIBITION CATALOGS (IN CHRONOLOGICAL ORDER)

A. Catalogs of International Surrealist Exhibitions

International Surrealist Exhibition (London, New Burlington Galleries, 1936)
Dictionnaire abrégé du surréalisme (Paris, Galerie des Beaux-Arts, 1938)
Exposicion internacional del surrealismo (Mexico, Galeria de Arte Mexicano, 1940)
First Papers of Surrealism (New York, Coordinating Council of French Relief Societies, 1942)
Le Surréalisme en 1947 (Paris, Galerie Maeght, 1947)

Exposition inteRnatiOnale du Surréalisme (Paris, Galerie Daniel Cordier, 1959)
Surrealist Intrusion in the Enchanters' Domain (New York, D'Arcy Galleries, 1960–1961)
Mostra internazionale del surrealismo (Milan, Galleria Schwarz, 1961)
L'Ecart absolu (Paris, Galerie de l'oeil, 1965–1966)
Marvelous Freedom, Vigilance of Desire (Chicago, Gallery Black Swan, 1976)

B. Catalogs of Other Surrealist Exhibitions

Exhibition of the Surrealist Group in Czechoslovakia (Prague, 1935)
Surrealist Objects and Poems (London, London Gallery, 1936)
Surrealistisk Manifestation (Stockholm, Expo Aleby, 1949)
Surrealistischen Ontmoetingen (Leyden, Academiegbouw, 1961)
Bestendigheid van het surréalisme (Arnheim, Gelderskunstcentrum Epok, 1967)
Surrealist Exhibition (Chicago, Gallery Bugs Bunny, 1968)
Surrealism in 1978: 100th Anniversary of Hysteria (Milwaukee, Ozaukee Art Center, 1978)
Surrealism Unlimited: 1968–1978 (London, Camden Arts Center, 1978)
Le Collage Surréaliste en 1978 (Paris, Galerie Le Triskèle, 1978)
Permanence du regard surréaliste (Lyons, ELAC, 1981)
Exposicion Surrealista (Madrid, Estudio Ancora, 1992)
Terre intérieure (Paris, Galerie Hourglass, 1993)
Totems without Taboos: The Exquisite Corpse Lives! (Chicago, Heartland Gallery, 1993)
Ensanchamiento del Mundo (Madrid, Galeria del Progreso, 1994)
Primeira Exposiçao do Surrealismo ou Nao (Lisbon, Galeria S. Mamede, 1994)
Collage: A Imagem da Revelaçao (São Paulo, Espaço Expositivo Maria Antonia, 1996)

C. Catalogs of Retrospective and Documentary Exhibitions

Fantastic Art, Dada, Surrealism (New York, 1936)
Abstract and Surrealist American Art (Chicago, 1948)
Surrealismo en la Argentina (Buenos Aires, 1967)
Britain's Contribution to Surrealism (London, 1971)
Rétroviseur: Le Mouvement Phases (Nice, 1972)
Le Cadavre exquis, son exaltation (Milan, 1975)
Imagination (Bochum, 1978)
Dada and Surrealism Reviewed (London, 1978)
Presencia viva de Wolfgang Paalen (Mexico City, 1979)
Les Enfants d'Alice: la peinture surréaliste en Angleterre, 1930–1960 (Paris, 1982)
La Femme et le surréalisme (Lausanne, 1987)
Surrealismo en Catalunya, 1924–1936 (Madrid, 1988)
Phases: L'expérience continue, 1952–1988 (Le Havre, 1988)
I Surrealisti (Milan, 1989)
El Collage Surrealista en España (Teruel, 1989)
Czech Modernism, 1900–1945 (Houston, 1989)

El Surrealismo Entre Viejo y Nuevo Mundo (Las Palmas, Canary Islands, 1989)
André Breton: La beauté convulsive (Paris, 1991)
"The Foundations of Behavior": Women Artists of the Surrealist Movement (London, 1992)
Lateinamerika und der Surrealismus (Bochum, 1993)
Ismos: Arte de vanguardia (1910–1936) en España (Madrid, 1993)
Phases: 87 images 71 artistes 23 pays de la planisphere (Ploeuc/Lié, 1994)
Le rêve d'une ville: Nantes et le surréalisme (Nantes, 1994)
El Poeta Como Artista (Las Palmas, Canary Islands, 1995)

V. OTHER WORKS CONSULTED

Abell, Marcelle A. 1961. "Revolt of the French Intellectuals." In *The Nonconformists: Articles of Dissent*, edited by David Evanier and Stanley Silverzweig. New York: Ballantine.

[Alcoforado, Marianna.] Ca. 1930s. *Love Letters of a Portuguese Nun.* Girard, Kansas: Haldeman-Julius, Little Blue Book 84, n.d.

Alexandre, Maxime. 1968. *Mémoires d'un surréaliste.* Paris: La Jeune Parque.

Alexandrian, Sarane. 1974. *Le surréalisme et le rêve.* Paris: Gallimard.

———. 1977. *Les Libérateurs de l'amour.* Paris: Editions du Seuil.

Anderson, Bonnie S., and Judith P. Zinsser. 1989. *A History of Their Own: Women in Europe from Prehistory to the Present.* New York: Harper and Row.

Apollinaire, Guillaume. 1909. Introduction to *L'Oeuvre du Marquis de Sade.* Paris: Bibliothèque des curieux.

Aragon, Louis, and Dominique Arban. 1968. *Aragon Parle.* Paris: Seghers.

Aranda, Francisco. 1981. *El Surrealismo Español.* Barcelona: Editorial Lumen.

Baron, Jacques. 1969. *L'An 1 du surréalisme.* Paris: Denoël.

Bataille, Georges. 1973. *Literature and Evil.* New York: Urizen.

———. 1994. *The Absence of Myth: Writings on Surrealism.* Edited, translated, and introduced by Michael Richardson. London: Verso.

Bédouin, Jean-Louis. 1961. *Vingt ans de surréalisme, 1939–59.* Paris: Denoël.

Béhar, Henri. 1990. *André Breton: Le grand indésirable.* Paris: Calmann-Lévy.

Benayoun, Robert. 1965. *Erotique du surréalisme.* Paris: Jean-Jacques Pauvert.

———. 1988. *Le Rire des surréalistes.* Paris: Le Bougie du Sapeur.

Benedikt, Michael, ed. 1974. *The Poetry of Surrealism.* Boston: Little, Brown.

Benjamin, Walter. 1978. "Surrealism." In *Reflections: Essays, Aphorisms, Autobiographical Writings*, 177–192. New York: Harcourt Brace Jovanovich.

Berneri, Marie-Louise. 1982. *Journey Through Utopia.* London: Freedom Press.

Bonnet, Marguerite. 1975. *André Breton: Naissance de l'aventure surréaliste.* Paris: José Corti.

———, ed. 1988. *Vers l'action politique: juillet 1925–avril 1926.* Paris: Gallimard.

———. 1992. *Adhérer au Parti communiste?: Septembre-décembre 1926.* Paris: Gallimard.

Bonnet, Marguerite, and Jacqueline Chénieux-Gendron. 1982. *Revues surréalistes françaises autour d'André Breton.* Millwood, New York: Kraus International.

Bounoure, Vincent. 1969. *Rien ou quoi?* Paris: Privately published.

———. 1970. *Pour communication: reponses à l'enquête, "Rien ou quoi?"* Paris: Privately published.

———, ed. 1976. *La Civilisation surréaliste.* Paris: Payot.

Bourassa, André-G. 1977. *Surréalisme et Littérature québéçoise.* Montreal: Edition's l'Etincelle.

Breton, André. 1934. *Point du jour.* Paris: Gallimard.

———. 1935. *Position politique du surréalisme.* Paris: Gallimard.

———. 1937. "Convulsionnaires." Foreword to Man Ray, *La Photographie n'est pas l'art.* Paris: G.L.M.

———. 1948. *Martinique, charmeuse de serpents.* Texts and illustrations by André Masson. Paris: Sagittaire.

———. 1960. Interview by Jacqueline Piatier. *Le Monde,* 13 January.

———. 1967. *Manifestoes of Surrealism.* Translated by Richard Seaver and Helen R. Lane. Ann Arbor: University of Michigan Press. Originally published in 1962 as *Le Manifestes du Surréalisme* (Paris: Jean-Jacques Pauvert).

———. 1969. *Entretiens (1913–1952).* Paris: NRF.

———. 1970. *Perspective cavalière.* Paris: Gallimard.

———. 1978. *What Is Surrealism? Selected Writings of André Breton,* edited and introduced by Franklin Rosemont. New York: Monad Press, 1978; London: Pluto Press, 1978. Reprinted New York: Pathfinder Press, 1996.

———. 1987. *Mad Love.* Translated by Mary Ann Caws. Lincoln: University of Nebraska Press. Originally published in 1937 as *L'Amour fou* (Paris: Gallimard).

———. 1988. *Oeuvres complètes,* Volume I. Paris: Gallimard, Bibliothèque de la Pléiade.

———. 1990. *The Communicating Vessels.* Translated by Mary Ann Caws. Lincoln: University of Nebraska Press. Originally published in 1932 as *Les Vases communicants* (Paris: Cahiers libres).

———. 1991. *Katherine Dunham.* Paris: Editions de l'Ebrasement.

———. 1994. *Arcanum 17.* Translated by Zack Rogow. Los Angeles: Sun & Moon Press. Originally published in 1947 as *Arcane 17* (Paris: Seghers).

———. 1995. *Free Rein.* Translated by Michel Parmentier and Jacqueline D'Amboise. Lincoln: University of Nebraska Press. Originally published in 1967 as *La Clé des champs* (Paris: Jean-Jacques Pauvert).

Breton, André, and Gérard Legrand. 1991. *L'Art magique.* Paris: Phebus; first published in 1957.

Buhle, Paul, and Ed Sullivan, eds. 1997. *Images of American Radicalism.* Hanover: Christopher.

Buhle, Mari Jo, with Paul Buhle and Dan Georgakas, eds. 1990. *Encyclopedia of the American Left.* New York: Garland Publishing.

Buñuel, Luis. 1983. *My Last Sigh.* New York: Alfred Knopf.

Calas, Nicolas. 1940. "Surrealist Pocket Dictionary." In *New Directions 1940.* Norfolk: New Directions.

———. 1942. *Confound the Wise.* New York: Arrow Editions.

Carmody, Francis J., and Carlyle MacIntyre. 1953. *Surrealist Poetry in France.* Berkeley: California Book Co.

Carter, Angela. 1978. *The Sadean Woman and the Ideology of Pornography.* New York: Pantheon.

Caute, David. 1964. *Communism and the French Intellectuals, 1914–1960.* New York: Macmillan.

Caws, Mary Ann, with Rudolf Kuenzli and Gwen Raaberg, eds. 1991. *Surrealism and Women.* Cambridge: MIT Press. Originally published as issue 18 of the journal *Dada/Surrealism.*

Celly, Jean-Jacques, ed. 1997. "Brève Anthologie du surréalisme américaine." In *Le Cri d'os.* Paris: La Lucarne Ovale.

Césaire, Aimé. 1972. *Discourse on Colonialism.* Translated by Joan Pinkham. New York: Monthly Review Press. Originally published in 1955 as *Discours sur le colonialisme* (Paris: Présence Africaine).

Cesariny, Mario. 1966. *A Intervençao Surrealista.* Lisbon: Editora Ulisseia.

———. 1977. *Textos de Afirmaçao e de Combate do Movimento Surrealista Mundial.* Lisbon: Perspectivas & realidades.

———. 1984. *Vieira da Silva, Arpad Szenes, ou o castelo surrealista.* Lisbon: Assirio e Alvim.

Chadwick, Whitney. 1985. *Women Artists and the Surrealist Movement.* Boston: Little, Brown.

Clifford, James. 1988. *The Predicament of Culture: Twentieth-Century Ethnography, Literature and Art.* Cambridge: Harvard University Press.

Cone, Michèle C. 1992. *Artists Under Vichy: A Case of Prejudice and Persecution.* Princeton: Princeton University Press.

Correia, Natalia. 1973. *O surrealismo na poesia portuguesa.* Mem Martins: Europa-America.

Crastre, Victor. 1963. *Le Drame du surréalisme.* Paris: Les editions du temps.

Crevel, René. 1925. "*Les Mystères de l'amour* par Roger Vitrac." *Les feuilles libres* no. 40 (May–June): 282–283.

———. 1930. *Les Soeurs Brontë, filles du vent.* Paris: Editions de Quatre Chemins.

———. 1932. *Le Clavecin de Diderot.* Paris: Editions Surréalistes.

Dąbkowska-Zydroń, Jolanta. 1994. *Surrealizm po surrealizmie: Międzynarodowy Ruch "Phases."* Warsaw: Institut Kultury.

Dalí, Salvador. 1942. *The Secret Life of Salvador Dalí.* New York: Dial Press.

Davis, Mike. 1992. "In L.A., Burning All Illusions," *Nation* 254, no. 21 (1 June): 743–746.

Debord, Guy. 1967. *La Société de spectacle.* Paris: Buchet/Chastel.

Debout, Simone. 1978. *L'utopie de Charles Fourier.* Paris: Payot.

del Renzio, Toni, ed. 1943. "Surrealist Section." *New Road 1943.* Billericay, Essex, U.K.: Grey Walls Press.

de Sade, Donatien-Alphonse-François. 1954. *Selected Writings of de Sade.* Edited by Leonard de Saint-Yves. New York: British Book Centre.

Desanti, Dominique. 1976. *A Woman in Revolt: A Biography of Flora Tristan.* New York: Crown; published in French in 1972.

Desnos, Youki. 1957. *Les Confidences de Youki.* Paris: Librairie Arthème Fayard.

Deveney, John Patrick. 1996. *Paschal Beverly Randolph: A Nineteenth-Century Black American Spiritualist, Rosicrucian and Sex Magician.* Albany: State University of New York Press.

de Vries, Her, and Laurens Vancrevel. 1988. *Surrealistische Ontmoetingen.* Amsterdam: Meulenhoff.

Duchamp, Marcel. 1930. "Formule de l'opposition hétérodoxe dans le domaines principaux," *Le Surréalism ASDLR* 2 (October): 18–19.

———. 1956. "The Mary Reynolds Collection." Preface to Edwards, Hugh, *Surrealism and Its Affinities.*

Ducornet, Guy, ed. 1975. "Le Surréalisme actuel aux U.S.A.," *Phases,* Nouvelle Serie 5 (October): 66–74.

———. 1992. *Le Punching-Ball et la Vache à lait: La critique universitaire nord-américaine face au surréalisme.* Paris: Deleatur.

Duhamel, Marcel. 1972. *Raconte pas ta vie.* Paris: Mercure de France.

Duits, Charles. 1969. *André Breton a-t-il dit passe.* Paris: Les Lettres Nouvelles.

Edwards, Hugh. 1956. *Surrealism and Its Affinities: The Mary Reynolds Collection. A Bibliography.* Chicago: The Art Institute. Revised edition, 1973.

Eluard, Paul, and Benjamin Péret. 1933. "Revue de la Presse." *La Révolution surréaliste* no. 5 (15 May): 27–28.

Ey, Henri. 1945. *Le Psychiatre devant le surréalisme.* Paris: Centre d'Editions psychiatriques.

Faure, Michel. 1982. *Histoire du surréalisme sous l'Occupation.* Paris: La Table Ronde.

Flanner, Janet. 1972. "Murder Among the Lovebirds." In *Paris Was Yesterday: 1925–1939.* New York: Popular Library.

Flournoy, Theodore. 1963. *From India to The Planet Mars: A Study of a Case of Somnambulism with Glossolalia.* New Hyde Park: University Books.

Ford, Charles Henri, ed. 1945. *A Night with Jupiter and Other Fantastic Stories.* New York: View Editions.

Fourier, Charles. 1966. *Théorie des quatre mouvements.* Paris: Editions Anthropos.

Garon, Paul. 1989. "The Midnight Revolution: Surrealism and Jazz in New Orleans in the 1950s." In *Arsenal: Surrealist Subversion,* no. 4, 145–146. Chicago: Black Swan Press.

———. 1993. "The Chicago Surrealist Group and Black Swan Press/Surrealist Editions: A Checklist," *Progressive Librarian* 8 (Fall), 36–65.

———. 1996. *Blues and the Poetic Spirit.* San Francisco: City Lights.

———, and Beth Garon. 1992. *Woman with Guitar: Memphis Minnie's Blues.* New York: DaCapo.

Gascoyne, David. 1982. *A Short Survey of Surrealism.* San Francisco: City Lights; first published in London, 1935.

———. 1991. *Collected Journals: 1936–1942.* London: Skoob Books.

Gauthier, Xavière. 1971. *Surréalisme et sexualité.* Paris: Gallimard.

Godlewski, Susan Glover. 1996. "Warm Ashes: The Life and Career of Mary Reynolds," in *Museum Studies*, Vol. 22, No. 2. The Art Institute of Chicago.

Graham, Angus C. 1985. *Reason and Spontaneity.* London: Curzon Press.

Guggenheim, Peggy. 1979. *Out of This Century: Confessions of an Art Addict.* New York: Universe Books.

Hause, Steven C. 1987. *Hubertine Auclert: The French Suffragette.* New Haven: Yale University Press.

Heine, Maurice. 1934. "Promenade à travers le Roman noir," *Minotaure* 5 (May): 1–4.

———. 1950. *Le Marquis de Sade.* Paris: Gallimard.

Hill, Vicki Lynn, et al. 1974. *Female Artists Past and Present.* Berkeley: Women's History Research Center. With 1975 Supplement.

Hubert, Renée Riese. 1988. *Surrealism and the Book.* Berkeley: University of California Press.

———. 1994. *Magnifying Mirrors: Women, Surrealism and Partnership.* Lincoln: University of Nebraska Press.

Hugnet, Georges. 1972. *Pleins et deliés: témoignages et souvenirs, 1926–1972.* Paris: Guy Authier.

Ignatiev, Noel, and John Garvey, eds. 1996. *Race Traitor.* New York and London: Routledge.

Jablonski, Joseph. 1982. "Millennial Soundings: Chiliasts, Cathari, and Mystical Feminism in the American Grain." In *Free Spirits: Annals of the Insurgent Imagination,* no. 1, 9–26. San Francisco: City Lights.

———. 1989. "The War Against Leisure," introduction to *The Right To Be Lazy,* by Paul Lafargue. Chicago: Charles H. Kerr Company.

Jaguer, Edouard. 1979. "The Cobra Moment and Surrealism," *The Moment* 2: 34–50.

———. 1982. *Les Mystères de la chambre noire: le surréalisme et la photographie.* Paris: Flammarion.

———. 1985. "Le Corsage du deux soeurs," introduction to the reprint of the 1946–47 Belgian journal, *Les Deux soeurs.* Paris: Editions Jean-Michel Place.

Jean, Marcel, ed. 1980. *The Autobiography of Surrealism.* New York: Viking.

———, and Arpad Mezei. 1960. *The History of Surrealist Painting.* New York: Grove Press.

Joans, Ted. 1968. "Black Flower," *L'Archibras: le surréalisme* 3 (March): 10–11.

———. 1991. "I, Black Surrealist," *Opus International: André Breton et le surréalisme internationale,* 123–124 (April–May): 74–75.

Kelley, Robin D. G. 1994. *Race Rebels: Culture, Politics, and the Black Working Class.* New York: The Free Press, Macmillan.

Klüver, Billy, and Julie Martin. 1989. *Kiki's Paris: Artists and Lovers, 1900–1930.* New York: Abrams.

Krauss, Rosalind, and Jane Livingston. 1985. *L'Amour fou: Photography and Surrealism.* Washington: Corcoran Gallery of Art.

Lacan, Jacques. 1933. "Motifs du crime paranoiaque," *Minotaure* 3–4 (December): 25–28.

Lamantia, Philip. 1976. "Poetic Matters." In *Arsenal: Surrealist Subversion*, no. 3, 6–10. Chicago: Black Swan Press.

Lambert, Jean-Clarence. *Cobra*. New York: Abbeville, 1983.

Lautréamont, Comte de [Isidore Ducasse]. 1978. *Maldoror and Poems*. Translated by Paul Knight. New York and London: Penguin.

Lecoin, Louis. 1965. *Le Cours d'une vie*. Paris: The Author.

Levy, Julien. 1936. *Surrealism*. New York: Black Sun Press.

Lewis, Helena. 1988. *The Politics of Surrealism*. New York: Paragon House.

Lima, Sergio. 1995. *A Aventura surrealista*, Vol. I. Rio de Janeiro: Editora Vozes.

Lippard, Lucy. 1970. *Surrealists on Art*. Englewood Cliffs: Prentice-Hall.

Loeb, Harold. 1959. *The Way It Was*. New York: Criterion Books.

Löwy, Michael. 1993. *On Changing the World: Essays in Political Philosophy, From Karl Marx to Walter Benjamin*. Atlantic Highlands, NJ: Humanities Press.

Mabille, Pierre. 1981. *Traversées de nuit*. Paris: Editions Plasma.

Marcuse, Herbert. 1962. *Eros and Civilization: A Philosophical Inquiry into Freud*. New York: Vintage Books.

———. 1968. Interview. *New York Times*, 27 October.

———. 1989. "Letters to Chicago Surrealists." In *Arsenal: Surrealist Subversion*, no. 4, 39–47. Chicago: Black Swan Press.

Margerie, Anne de. 1983. *Valentine Hugo, 1887–1968*. Paris: Jacques Damase.

Mariën, Marcel, ed. 1979. *L'Activité surréaliste en Belgique*. Brussels: Editions Lebeer-Hossmann.

Matthews, J. H., ed. 1975. *The Custom-House of Desire: A Half-Century of Surrealist Stories*. Berkeley: University of California Press.

Maturin, Charles Robert. 1819. "On the Necessity of Female Education." In *Sermons*. London: Constable.

Mayoux, Jehan, ed. 1969. *Dossier relatif à l'éclatement du groupe surréaliste*. Ussel: Privately published.

———. 1979. *La liberté une et divisible: textes critiques et politiques*. Ussel: Editions Peralta.

McEwen, John. 1993. *Paula Rego*. London: Phaidon Press.

Mitchell, Juliet. 1975. *Psychoanalysis and Feminism*. New York: Vintage.

Moulin, Jeanine, ed. 1955. *Marceline Desbordes-Valmore*. Paris: Seghers.

Nadeau, Maurice. 1965. *The History of Surrealism*. Translated by Richard Howard. New York: Macmillan. Originally published in 1945 as *Histoire du Surréalisme* (Paris: Editions du Seuil).

Nash, Paul. 1988. *Outline*. London: Columbus Books; originally published in 1949.

Naum, Gellu. 1995. *Zenobia*. Translated from the Romanian by James Brook and Sasha Vlad. Evanston: Northwestern University Press.

Naville, Pierre. 1977. *Le temps du surréel*. Paris: Editions Galilée.

Nezval, Viteslav, ed. 1936. *Surrealismus*. Prague: Edice surrealismu.

Orenstein, Gloria. 1973. "Women of Surrealism," *Feminist Art Journal*, 2:2 (Spring): 1, 15–21.

Palmier, Jean-Michel. 1973. *Herbert Marcuse et la nouvelle gauche.* Paris: Belfond.

Paz, Octavio. 1973. *The Bow and the Lyre.* Austin: University of Texas Press.

Pellegrini, Aldo. 1966. *New Tendencies in Art.* New York: Crown.

Penrose, Antony. 1985. *The Lives of Lee Miller.* London: Thames and Hudson.

Penrose, Roland. 1983. *80 Ans du surréalisme.* Paris: Cercle d'Art.

Péret, Benjamin. 1956. *Anthologie de l'amour sublime.* Paris: Albin Michel.

———. 1969. *Le Grand jeu.* Paris: Gallimard. First published 1928.

Pierre, José. 1979. *An Illustrated Dictionary of Surrealism.* Translated from the French by W. J. Strachan. Woodbury, NY: Barron's.

———, ed. 1980; 1982. *Tracts surréalistes et declarations collectives.* Paris: Eric Losfeld/ Le terrain vague; I, 1980; II, 1982.

———. 1983. *Surréalisme et anarchie.* Paris: Plasma.

———. 1992. *Investigating Sex.* Translated by Malcolm Imrie. New York and London: Verso. Afterword by Dawn Ades. Originally published in 1990 as *Recherches sur la sexualité* (Paris: Gallimard).

Raspaud, Jean-Jacques, and Jean-Pierre Voyer. 1972. *L'Internationale situationniste: protagonistes, chronologie, bibliographie.* Paris: Editions Champ libre.

Read, Herbert. 1936. *Surrealism.* New York: Harper.

Richardson, Michael, ed. 1993. *The Dedalus Book of Surrealism: The Identity of Things.* Cambs, U.K.: Dedalus.

———. 1994. *The Myth of the World: Surrealism 2.* Cambs, U.K.: Dedalus.

———. 1996. *Refusal of the Shadow: Surrealism and the Caribbean.* New York and London: Verso.

Rimbaud, Arthur. 1957. *Illuminations and Other Prose Poems.* Translated by Louise Varèse. New York: New Directions.

Rochester, Myrna Bell. 1978. *René Crevel: Le Pays de miroirs absolus.* Saratoga, CA: Anma Libri.

Roediger, David R. 1981. "Symposium on Surrealism," *Cultural Correspondence* 12–14 (Summer): 69–70.

———. 1990. "Surrealism." In *Encyclopedia of the American Left.* Edited by Mari Jo Buhle, Paul Buhle, and Dan Georgakas. New York: Garland.

———. 1994. *Towards the Abolition of Whiteness: Essays on Race, Politics and Working Class History.* New York and London: Verso.

Rosemont, Franklin. 1976. "Black Music and Surrealist Revolution." In *Arsenal: Surrealist Subversion,* no. 3, 17–27. Chicago: Black Swan Press.

———, ed. 1978. *What Is Surrealism? Selected Writings of André Breton.* New York: Monad Press, 1978; London: Pluto Press. Reprinted New York: Pathfinder Press, 1996.

———. 1980. *Surrealism and Its Popular Accomplices.* San Francisco: City Lights Books.

———. 1989. "Marcel Duchamp and New forms of Heterodox Opposition." In *Arsenal: Surrealist Subversion,* no. 4, 163–167. Chicago: Black Swan Press.

———. 1990. "Dada." In *Encyclopedia of the American Left.* Edited by Mari Jo Buhle, Paul Buhle, and Dan Georgakai, 177–178. New York: Garland.

———. 1991. "Revolution in the Service of the Marvelous: Notes on Surrealism in the U.S., 1966–1991." In *Artpaper* 10:8 (April): 14–15. Minneapolis: Visual Arts Information Service.

———. 1997. "The Voice of Surrealism in America," introduction to reprint of *VVV*. Paris: Editions Jean-Michel Place.

Rosenthal, Gérard. 1975. *Avocat de Trotsky*. Paris: Robert Laffont.

Rubin, William S. 1968. *Dada and Surrealist Art*. New York: Abrams.

Sandler, Irving. 1970. *The Triumph of American Painting: A History of Abstract Expressionism*. New York: Harper and Row.

Saporta, Marc, ed. 1988. *André Breton ou le surréalisme, même*. Paris: L'Age d'homme.

Schwarz, Arturo. 1977. *André Breton, Trotsky et l'anarchie*. Paris: 10/18.

Sebbag, Georges. 1993. *Les Editions Surréalistes, 1926–1968*. Paris: Institut Mémoires de l'edition contemporaine.

Short, Robert S. 1980. *Dada and Surrealism*. New York: Octopus.

Soupault, Philippe. 1981. *Mémoires de l'Oubli*. Paris: Lachenal and Ritter.

Suleiman, Susan Robin. 1990. *Subversive Intent: Gender, Politics, and the Avant-Garde*. Cambridge: Harvard University Press.

Thévenin, Paule, ed. 1988. *Bureau de recherches surréalistes: Cahier de permanence*. Paris: Gallimard.

Thirion, André. 1975. *Revolutionaries without Revolution*. Translated by Joachim Neugroschel. New York: Macmillan. Originally published in 1972 as *Révolutionnaires sans révolution* (Paris: Robert Laffont).

Tzara, Tristan. 1948. *Le surréalisme et l'après-guerre*. Paris: Editions Nagel.

Vaché, Jacques. 1970. *Lettres de guerre*. With four essays by André Breton. Paris: Eric Losfeld. First published in 1919.

Vailland, Roger. 1948. *Le surréalisme contre la révolution*. Paris: Editions sociales.

Vasseur, Catherine. 1996. *En Belle page*. Montreuil: Brocéliande.

Violette Nozières. 1933. Brussels: Editions Nicolas Flamel. Reissued in facsimile, Paris, Terrain vague, 1991, with supplements and a preface by José Pierre.

Weber, Eugen. 1994. *The Hollow Years: France in the 1930s*. New York: Norton.

Young-Bruehl, Elisabeth, and Laura Wexler. 1992. "On 'Psychoanalysis and Feminism,'" *Social Research* 59:2 (Summer): 453–483.

Index

Page numbers set in boldface type indicate biographical sketches; page numbers followed by *il* indicate illustrations; and page numbers followed by *n* or *nn* indicate notes.